Psychodynamic Psychiatry in Clinical Practice

Third Edition

Psychodynamic Psychiatry in Clinical Practice

Third Edition

Glen O. Gabbard, M.D.

Washington, DC
London, England

Copyright © 2000 American Psychiatric Press, Inc.
ALL RIGHTS RESERVED
Manufactured in the United States of America on acid-free paper
03 02 01   4 3
Third Edition

American Psychiatric Press, Inc.
1400 K Street, N.W., Washington, DC   20005

Library of Congress Cataloging-in-Publication Data
Gabbard, Glen O.
    Psychodynamic psychiatry in clinical practice / Glen O. Gabbard. —   3rd ed.
      p. ; cm.
    Includes bibliographical references and index.
    ISBN 1-58562-002-5 (alk. paper)
    1. Psychodynamic psychotherapy. I. Title.
    [DNLM: 1. Mental Disorders—therapy. 2. Biological Psychiatry.
    3. Psychoanalytic Therapy.   WM 400 G112p 2000]
    RC489.P72 G33   2000
    616.89′1—dc20
    DNLM/DLC   99-054484
    for Library of Congress   CIP

British Library Cataloguing in Publication Data
A CIP record is available from the British Library.

To My Teachers, My Patients, and My Students

About the Author

Glen O. Gabbard, M.D., is Professor of Psychiatry at Baylor College of Medicine, and Training and Supervising Analyst at The Houston-Galveston Psychoanalytic Institute, Houston, Texas.

Contents

SECTION I

Basic Principles and Treatment Approaches in Dynamic Psychiatry

SECTION II

Dynamic Approaches to Axis I Disorders

SECTION III

Dynamic Approaches to Axis II Disorders

Source Acknowledgments

The author gratefully acknowledges permission to reprint portions of the following material:

American Psychiatric Association: Diagnostic and Statistical Manual of Mental Disorders, 4th Edition. Washington, DC, American Psychiatric Association, 1994. Portions reprinted with permission.

Gabbard GO: The exit line: heightened transference-countertransference manifestations at the end of the hour. J Am Psychoanal Assoc 30:579–598, 1982. Portions reprinted with permission.

Gabbard GO. The role of compulsiveness in the normal physician. JAMA 254:2926–2929, 1985. Copyright 1985, American Medical Association. Portions reprinted with permission.

Gabbard GO: The treatment of the "special" patient in a psychoanalytic hospital. International Review of Psychoanalysis 13:333–347, 1986. Portions reprinted with permission.

Gabbard GO: A contemporary perspective on psychoanalytically informed hospital treatment. Hospital and Community Psychiatry 39:1291–1295, 1988. Portions reprinted with permission.

Gabbard GO: Patients who hate. Psychiatry 52:96–106, 1989. Portions reprinted with permission.

Gabbard GO: Splitting in hospital treatment. Am J Psychiatry 146:444–451, 1989. Copyright 1989, American Psychiatric Association. Portions reprinted with permission.

Gabbard GO: Two subtypes of narcissistic personality disorder. Bull Menninger Clin 53:527–532, 1989. Portions reprinted with permission.

Gabbard GO: Psychodynamic psychiatry in the "decade of the brain." Am J Psychiatry 149:991–998, 1992. Copyright 1992, American Psychiatric Association. Portions reprinted with permission.

Preface to the Third Edition

When the second edition of this book was
published in 1994, it bore the subtitle "The DSM-IV Edition." Our assumption at
that time was that the next update would appear around the time that DSM-V was
ready for publication. However, the DSM-IV edition of the text became outdated
sooner than expected. Hence, this third edition was rewritten not in response to a
nomenclature change but rather to reflect changes in the science and art of psychodynamic psychiatry.

Investigations in the field of neuroscience have led to impressive advances in
our understanding of gene-environment interaction and brain function. As a result, psychodynamic psychiatry has increasingly become a truly integrative psychiatry that synthesizes the psychosocial and the biological. Accordingly, this edition
has much greater integration of neuroscience and psychodynamics throughout
each chapter. In addition, Chapter 1 now contains an expanded section on the
mind-brain interface.

There have also been rather substantial shifts in the use of theory within psychoanalysis that have been incorporated in this rewrite. Although both the first
and the second editions strongly emphasized theoretical pluralism, the field has
moved even further in the direction of embracing multiple models of the mind.
Postmodern trends, including constructivism, relational theory, and intersubjectivity, have been particularly influential over the last 5–10 years. Moreover,
attachment theory, while always in the background of psychoanalytic discourse,
has now shifted to the foreground as a broad consensus has been reached that development can best be understood by supplementing the dual drives of sexuality

and aggression with the need for attachment and relatedness. Chapter 2 highlights these newer theoretical trends, and the implications of these theoretical developments for clinical practice are touched on in many of the subsequent chapters.

Another trend in both psychiatry and psychoanalysis is an increasing emphasis on empirical demonstrations of treatment effectiveness. Hence, many of the chapters in this edition of the text now contain relevant research findings to bolster the case for a psychodynamic approach.

New information from more recent literature has been added to every single chapter within the text. These revisions have been more extensive (and more time consuming) than I had originally expected; however, this painstaking effort to be comprehensive and integrative has never been more important. In an era of "quick fix" managed care approaches and reductionistic models of mental illness, an integrative psychodynamic strategy for teaching and for clinical diagnosis and treatment is essential. The basic principle of understanding and treating the person with the illness in addition to the illness itself must not be lost because of economic priorities established by profit-driven third and fourth parties. Although psychoanalytic and psychodynamic thinking continues to be under attack in some quarters, our need to understand our fellow human beings is as compelling as ever. In an unusual development in publishing, the second edition of this text actually sold more copies than the first, an occurrence that reflects its wide adoption as a text throughout the world. Psychodynamic thinking in the delivery of mental health services and in the classrooms where mental health professionals are trained appears to be alive and well.

I would like to express my appreciation to colleagues who have read portions of this manuscript and helped me to improve it. These colleagues include Drs. Jon Allen, Joyce Davidson Gabbard, Philip Ringstrom, Drew Westen, and Martin Willick. I would also like to thank Carol Nadelson, Claire Reinburg, Pam Harley, and Stacy Jobb at American Psychiatric Press for their steadfast support and encouragement. Finally, a special thanks goes to Faye Schoenfeld for her careful attention to typing, editing, and reference checking.

Glen O. Gabbard, M.D.

SECTION

I

Basic Principles and Treatment Approaches in Dynamic Psychiatry

C H A P T E R

1

Basic Principles of Dynamic Psychiatry

It would be far easier if we could avoid the patient as we explore the realm of psychopathology; it would be far simpler if we could limit ourselves to examining the chemistry and physiology of his brain, and to treating mental events as objects alien to our immediate experience, or as mere variables in impersonal statistical formulae. Important as these approaches are for the understanding of human behavior, they cannot alone uncover or explain all the relevant facts. To see into the mind of another, we must repeatedly immerse ourselves in the flood of his associations and feelings; we must be ourselves the instrument that sounds him.

John Nemiah

Psychodynamic psychiatry (used interchangeably with dynamic psychiatry in this volume) is now beginning its second century. Ellenberger (1970) traced the first usage of the term to the period between 1880 and 1900. Leibniz originally used *dynamic* to emphasize the contrast with *static*. Herbart applied this distinction to states of consciousness. Fechner appropriated the term to refer to mental energy and probably influenced Freud in this regard. *Dynamic* then came to be used by the French physiologists to connote *functional* as opposed to *organic*. Eventually, the eminent neurologist Hughlings Jackson borrowed the term to mean physiological as opposed to anatomic, functional as opposed to organic, and regressive as opposed to the status quo. In fact, Jackson's notion of mental energy very likely caught Freud's eye.

Dynamic psychiatry owes its greatest debt to Freud. Whatever else it may be, this approach is steeped in psychoanalytic theory and knowledge. (Although some would argue that dynamic psychiatry subsumes a broader purview than that of psychoanalytic psychiatry, the predominant contemporary usage is to equate *psychodynamic* with *psychoanalytic*.) Modern dynamic psychiatry has often been viewed as a branch of psychiatry that explains mental phenomena as the outgrowth of *conflict*. This conflict derives from powerful unconscious forces that seek expression and require constant monitoring from opposing forces to prevent their expression. These interacting forces may be conceptualized (with some overlap) as 1) a wish and a defense against the wish, 2) different intrapsychic agencies or "parts" with different aims and priorities, or 3) an impulse in opposition to an internalized awareness of the demands of external reality.

In the last couple of decades, psychodynamic psychiatry has come to connote more than the conflict model of illness. Today's dynamic psychiatrist must also understand what is commonly referred to as the "deficit model" of illness. This model is applied to patients who, for whatever developmental reasons, suffer from weakened or absent psychic structures. This compromised state prevents them from feeling whole and secure about themselves, and as a result, they require inordinate responses from persons in the environment to maintain psychological homeostasis. Also contained within the purview of psychodynamic psychiatry is the unconscious internal world of relationships. All patients carry within them a host of different mental representations of aspects of themselves and others, many of which may create characteristic patterns of interpersonal difficulties. These representations of self and others reside in the patient's unconscious, where they form the world of internal object relations.

Above all, psychodynamic psychiatry is a *way of thinking*—not only about one's patients but also about oneself in the interpersonal field between patient and treater. In fact, to characterize the essence of dynamic psychiatry, one might well use the following definition: *Psychodynamic psychiatry is an approach to diagnosis and treatment characterized by a way of thinking about both patient and clinician that includes unconscious conflict, deficits and distortions of intrapsychic structures, and internal object relations and that integrates these elements with contemporary findings from the neurosciences.*

Although dynamic psychotherapy is one of the foremost tools in the dynamic psychiatrist's therapeutic armamentarium, dynamic psychotherapy is not synonymous with dynamic psychiatry. The dynamic psychiatrist uses a wide range of treatment interventions that depend on a dynamic assessment of the patient's needs. Dynamic psychiatry simply provides a coherent conceptual framework within which all treatments are prescribed. Regardless of whether the treatment is dynamic psychotherapy or pharmacotherapy, it is *dynamically informed*. Indeed, a crucial component of the dynamic psychiatrist's expertise is knowing when to avoid exploratory psychotherapy in favor of treatments that do not threaten the patient's psychic equilibrium.

Psychiatry has grown beyond the era when typical practitioners passed their days in the privacy of their consulting rooms, seeing one neurotic patient after another in long-term, insight-oriented psychotherapy. Just as psychiatry as a field has changed, so has dynamic psychiatry. Today's dynamic psychiatrist must practice in the context of impressive advances in the neurosciences, integrating psychoanalytic insight with biological understanding of illness. Nevertheless, the dynamic psychiatrist is still guided by a handful of time-honored principles derived from psychoanalytic theory and technique that provide psychodynamic psychiatry with its unique character.

The Unique Value of Subjective Experience

Dynamic psychiatry is further defined by contrasting it with descriptive psychiatry. Practitioners of the latter approach categorize patients according to common behavioral and phenomenological features. They develop symptom checklists that allow them to classify patients according to similar clusters of symptoms. The patient's subjective experience, except as used to report items in the checklist, is less important. Descriptive psychiatrists with a behavioral orientation would argue that the patient's subjective experience is peripheral to the essence of psychiatric diagnosis and treatment, which must be based on observable behavior. The most extreme behavioral view is that behavior and mental life are synonymous (Watson 1924/1930). Moreover, the descriptive psychiatrist is primarily interested in how a patient is *similar to* rather than *different from* other patients with congruent features.

In contrast, dynamic psychiatrists approach their patients by trying to determine what is unique about each one—how a particular patient *differs* from other patients as a result of a life story like no other. Symptoms and behaviors are viewed only as the final common pathways of highly personalized subjective experiences that filter the biological and environmental determinants of illness. Furthermore, dynamic psychiatrists place paramount value on the patient's internal world—fantasies, dreams, fears, hopes, impulses, wishes, self-images, perceptions of others, and psychological reactions to symptoms.

Descriptive psychiatrists approaching an occluded cave nestled in the side of a mountain might well describe in detail the characteristics of the massive rock obstructing the cave's opening, while dismissing the interior of the cave beyond the rock as inaccessible and therefore unknowable. In contrast, dynamic psychiatrists would be curious about the dark recesses of the cave beyond the boulder. Like the descriptive psychiatrists, they would note the markings of the opening, but they would regard them differently. They would want to know how the cave's exterior reflected the inner contents. They might be curious about why it was necessary to protect the interior with a boulder at the opening.

The Unconscious

Continuing with our cave metaphor, the dynamic psychiatrist would figure out a way to remove the boulder, enter the dark recesses of the cave, and perhaps with a flashlight, illuminate the interior. Artifacts on the floor or markings on the wall would be of special interest to the explorer because they would shed light on the history of this particular cave. A steady gurgling of water coming up through the floor might suggest an underground spring applying pressure from below. The dynamic psychiatrist would be particularly interested in exploring the depths of the cave. How far into the mountainside does it extend? Is the back wall the true limit that defines the inner space, or is it a "false wall" that gives way to even greater depths?

As the cave metaphor suggests, a second defining principle of dynamic psychiatry is a conceptual model of the mind that includes the unconscious. Freud (1915/1963) recognized two different kinds of unconscious mental content: 1) the preconscious (i.e., mental contents that can easily be brought into conscious awareness by merely shifting one's attention) and 2) the unconscious proper (i.e., mental contents that are censored because they are unacceptable and therefore are repressed and not easily brought into conscious awareness).

Together, the unconscious, the preconscious, and the conscious systems of the mind compose what Freud (1900/1953) termed the *topographic model*. He became convinced of the unconscious because of two major pieces of clinical evidence: dreams and parapraxes. Analysis of dreams revealed that an unconscious childhood wish was usually the motivating force of dreams (1900/1953). The dreamwork disguised the wish, so analysis of the dream was necessary to discern the true nature of the wish.

Parapraxes consist of such phenomena as slips of the tongue, "accidental" actions, and forgetting or substituting names or words. A typist, for example, repeatedly typed "murder" when she intended to type "mother." The notion of the "Freudian slip" is now a thoroughly entrenched part of our culture that connotes the unwitting revelation of a person's unconscious wishes or feelings. Freud (1901/1960) used these embarrassing incidents to illustrate the breakthrough of repressed wishes and to demonstrate the parallels between the mental processes of everyday life and those of neurotic symptom formation.

The dynamic psychiatrist views symptoms and behaviors as reflections of unconscious processes that defend against repressed wishes and feelings, just as the boulder protects the contents of the cave from exposure. Moreover, dreams and parapraxes are like the artwork on the walls of the cave—communications, symbolic or otherwise, in the present that deliver messages from the forgotten past. The dynamic psychiatrist must develop sufficient comfort with this dark realm to explore it without stumbling.

Another primary way that the unconscious manifests itself in the clinical setting is in the patient's nonverbal behavior toward the clinician. Certain characteristic patterns of relatedness to others set in childhood become internalized and are enacted automatically and unconsciously as part of the patient's character. Hence, certain patients may consistently act deferentially toward the clinician, whereas others will behave in a highly rebellious way. These forms of relatedness are closely linked to Squire's (1987) notion of procedural memory, which occurs outside the realm of conscious, verbal, narrative memory.

Studies of memory systems have greatly expanded our knowledge of behavior in the clinical setting. A widely used distinction that is relevant to psychodynamic thinking is the differentiation of memory into explicit (conscious) and implicit (unconscious) types (Figure 1–1).

Explicit memory can be either *generic,* involving knowledge of facts or ideas, or *episodic,* involving memories of specific autobiographical incidents. Implicit memory involves observable behavior of which the subject is not consciously aware. One type of implicit memory is *procedural* memory, which involves knowledge of skills, such as playing the piano and the "how to" of social relatedness to others.

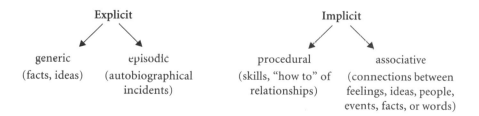

FIGURE 1–1.   Two memory systems.

The unconscious schemas referred to as internal object relations are to some extent procedural memories that are repeated again and again in a variety of interpersonal situations. Another type of implicit memory is *associative* in nature and involves connections between and among words, feelings, ideas, people, events, or facts. For example, one may hear a particular song and feel inexplicably sad because that song was playing on the radio when news of a family member's death arrived.

An integration of current memory research (which emerged from the laboratory) and psychoanalytic thinking (which emerged from clinical observation) cuts the memory pie somewhat differently (Westen 1999a). According to this view, the implicit/explicit distinction is not quite the same thing as the declarative/procedural one (Figure 1–2). The dichotomy between declarative and procedural memory centers on the type of knowledge each form involves. Declarative involves facts, whereas procedural involves skills. The explicit versus implicit memory distinction relates to whether knowledge is expressed and/or retrieved with or without conscious awareness.

When an individual remembers a triumphant sporting event that occurred at the age of 8, the type of knowledge is declarative and the mode of retrieval is explicit (conscious). When that same individual starts to feel anxious on entering his boss's office because it unconsciously reminds him of earlier experiences with his father—but he *does not consciously connect* the anxiety with the earlier experiences—the type of knowledge is declarative, but the mode of retrieval is implicit (without conscious awareness). Procedural knowledge may also be explicit or implicit. The use of defense mechanisms, which are procedures, illustrates this distinction. If the same individual, on entering his boss's office, behaves in a deferential and overly polite manner through the defensive use of reaction formation, the type of knowledge is procedural, while the mode of expression is implicit (without conscious awareness). In the former instance, when the presence of his boss triggered memories of interactions with his father, the association evoked a feeling of anxiety linked to an *episode* in the past. When the defense mechanism automatically kicked in, a *procedure,* or a way of acting, was evoked. Declarative is

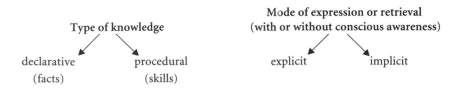

FIGURE 1–2. Type of knowledge versus mode of expression.

knowledge "of"; procedural is knowledge "how." Defense mechanisms may also be conscious, or explicit, as when one suppresses unpleasant feelings by deliberately driving them out of one's awareness.

The notion that much of mental life is unconscious is often challenged by psychoanalytic critics but has been extensively validated by literature from experimental psychology (Westen 1999b). Research subjects who have bilateral lesions to the hippocampus have great difficulty learning that two discrete events are connected, but their emotional responses suggest that they have made an unconscious connection between the two events (Bechara et al. 1995). Subliminal presentation of stimuli that have emotional or psychodynamic meanings to research subjects have been shown to influence a wide range of behavior, even though the subjects have no conscious awareness of the stimuli (Weinberger and Hardaway 1990). Studies of brain event-related potentials demonstrate that emotional words evoke different electroencephalogram (EEG) alpha waves than do neutral words, even before they are consciously recognized. In one study, a team of clinicians assessed which conflicts were relevant to identified patient symptoms. Words reflecting those conflicts were then selected and presented both subliminally and supraliminally to the patients (Shevrin et al. 1996). Different patterns of response were documented for those words consciously related to the patient's symptoms and those hypothesized to be unconsciously related.

Psychic Determinism

To assert that symptoms and behavior are external manifestations of unconscious processes is to touch on a third principle of dynamic psychiatry—psychic determinism. The psychodynamic approach asserts that we are consciously confused and unconsciously controlled. We go through our daily lives as though we have freedom of choice, but we are actually far more restricted than we think. In actuality, we are but characters living out a script written by the unconscious. Our choices of marital partners, our vocational interests, even our leisure-time pursuits are not randomly selected; they are shaped by unconscious forces in dynamic relationship with one another.

By way of example, one young woman learned in the course of her psychotherapy that her choice of medicine as a career was profoundly shaped by events in her childhood and her reactions to them. When she was 8 years old, her mother had succumbed to cancer. The little girl witnessing this tragedy felt helpless and powerless at the time, and her decision to be a physician was partly determined by an unconscious wish to gain mastery and control over disease and death. At an unconscious level, being a physician was an attempt to actively master a passively experienced trauma. On a conscious level, she simply experienced medicine as a fascinating and compelling field.

When human behavior becomes markedly symptomatic, the limits of free will become more obvious. A man who can only reach orgasm during masturbation by imagining humiliation at the hands of a muscle-bound sadist has lost the freedom to choose his sexual fantasies. The dynamic psychiatrist approaches these symptoms with the understanding that they represent adaptations to the demands of an unconscious script forged by a mixture of drives, defenses, object relations, and disturbances in the self. In short, behavior has meaning.

The meaning is rarely as simple and straightforward as the foregoing example involving the physician. More commonly, a single behavior or symptom serves several functions and solves many problems—a notion that Waelder (1930) referred to as the principle of multiple function. He developed the principle out of dissatisfaction with Freud's more restrictive concept of overdetermination, which implied that several intrapsychic factors must operate together to create sufficient cause for a specific effect (a behavior or symptom). As Sherwood (1969) pointed out, "Freud clearly held that the causes of behavior were *both* complex (overdetermined) and multiple (in the sense of their being alternate sets of sufficient conditions)" (p. 181). In other words, certain behaviors or symptoms are at times caused by a specific intrapsychic constellation of factors, but in other instances they are produced by a multitude of other etiological forces. Suffice it to say that the psychodynamic view of human behavior defines it as the end result of many different conflicting forces that serve a variety of different functions corresponding both to the demands of reality and to the needs of the unconscious.

The principle of psychic determinism, although certainly a bedrock notion, calls for two caveats. First, unconscious factors do not determine all behaviors or symptoms. When a patient with Alzheimer's disease forgets the name of his spouse, it probably is not a parapraxis. When a patient with partial complex seizures ritualistically buttons and unbuttons his shirt during the aura of his seizure, the symptom can likely be attributed to an irritable focus of the temporal lobe. The dynamic psychiatrist's task is to sort out which symptoms and behaviors can or cannot be explained by dynamic factors.

The second caveat derives from experience with patients who make no effort to change their behavior because they claim to be passive victims of unconscious forces. Within the concept of psychic determinism, there is room for choice. Although it may be more restricted than we like to think, conscious intention to change can be an influential factor in recovery from symptoms (S. A. Appelbaum 1981). The dynamic psychiatrist must be wary of the patient who justifies remaining ill by invoking psychic determinism.

Past Is Prologue

A fourth basic principle of dynamic psychiatry is that the experiences of infancy and childhood are crucial determinants of the adult personality. In the succinct words of William Wordsworth, "The child is father of the man." The dynamic psychiatrist listens intently when a patient speaks of childhood memories, knowing that these experiences may play a critical role in the current presenting problems. Indeed, etiology and pathogenesis are often linked to childhood events in the dynamic view. In some cases, overt trauma, such as incest or physical abuse, leads to disturbances in the adult personality. More often, the chronic, repetitive patterns of interaction within a family are of greater etiological significance.

The dynamic point of view also takes into consideration the fact that infants and children perceive their environment through highly subjective filters that may distort the real qualities of the figures around them. Similarly, certain children are constitutionally difficult to raise no matter how effective their parents may be. Research has revealed several discrete constitutional temperaments in newborn infants (Thomas and Chess 1984). The etiology of some psychiatric illness may be related to how good the "fit" is between the temperament of the child and the temperament of the parenting figure. The hyperirritable child who does reasonably well with a calm and low-key mother may do poorly with a high-strung mother. This model of "goodness of fit" avoids blaming either parents or children for the latter's psychiatric problems.

The psychodynamic tradition has sometimes been regarded as overemphasizing environmental influences on psychiatric illness and neglecting constitutional factors. However, from the beginning of psychoanalysis, Freud always recognized the convergence of nature and nurture:

> Psychoanalysis has talked a lot about the accidental factors in aetiology and little about the constitutional ones; but that is only because it was able to contribute something fresh to the former, while, to begin with, it knew no more than was commonly known about the latter. We refuse to posit any contrast in principle between the two sets of aetiological factors; on the contrary, we assume that the two sets regularly act jointly in bringing about the observed result. (1912/1958, p. 99)

The process of development is an ongoing interplay between the inherited traits and the environmental factors that shape those traits. Indeed, twin studies (Bouchard et al. 1990) suggest that, in part, identical twins are so similar because they tend to elicit and seek out highly similar environments. Infants who are born with similar temperaments are likely to elicit similar parenting responses. Erik

Erikson (1963) observed: "Babies control and bring up their families as much as they are controlled by them; in fact, we may say that the family brings up a baby by being brought up by him" (p. 69).

Theories of childhood development have always been central to dynamic psychiatry. Freud postulated that a child passes through three principal psychosexual stages on the road to maturity. Each of these—the oral, the anal, and the genital—is associated with a particular bodily zone where Freud believed that the libido, or sexual energy, of the child was concentrated. As a result of environmental trauma, constitutional factors, or both, a child may become developmentally arrested at the oral or anal phase, resulting in a fixation that is retained into adult life. Under stress, the adult may regress to this more primitive phase of development and manifest the mental organization of the instinctual gratification associated with that phase. Although Freud reconstructed childhood development retrospectively based on the reports of adult patients in psychoanalysis, subsequent psychoanalytic investigators have studied development prospectively through direct infant and child observation. These studies have led to more elaborate developmental theories of normal and abnormal personality and to a greater emphasis on the nature of the child's relatedness to others as opposed to the vicissitudes of instinctual energies. These theories will be discussed in more detail in Chapter 2.

Transference

The persistence of childhood patterns of mental organization in adult life implies that the past is repeating itself in the present. Perhaps the most compelling example of this is the core psychodynamic concept of transference, in which the patient experiences the doctor as a significant figure from the patient's past. Qualities of that past figure will be attributed to the doctor, and feelings associated with that figure will be experienced in the same way with the doctor. The patient unconsciously *reenacts* the past relationship, instead of remembering it, and in so doing introduces to the treatment a wealth of information about past relationships.

Although the concept of transference is generally associated with psychoanalysis or psychotherapy, the therapeutic relationship is merely one example of a more general phenomenon. As Brenner (1982) put it: "*Every* object relation is a new addition of the first, definitive attachments of childhood. . . . Transference is ubiquitous, it develops in every psychoanalytic situation because it develops in every situation where another person is important in one's life" (pp. 194–195). More recent contributions to the understanding of transference acknowledge that the clinician's *real* characteristics always contribute to the nature of the transference (Hoffman 1998; Renik 1993). In other words, if a therapist is silent and detached from the patient, a transference may develop to that therapist as cold, remote, and disengaged. While the transference may stem in part from early attachments of childhood, it is also influenced by the therapist's actual behavior. Hence, every relationship in the clinical setting is a mixture of a real relationship and transference phenomena.

Some psychoanalysts argue that there are two dimensions of transference: 1) a repetitive dimension, in which the patient fears and expects the analyst to behave like the parents did, and 2) a selfobject dimension, in which the patient longs for a healing or corrective experience that was missing in childhood (Stolorow 1995). These aspects of transference oscillate between the foreground and the background of the patient's experience.

The dynamic psychiatrist recognizes the pervasiveness of transference phenomena and realizes that the relationship problems about which the patient complains will often manifest themselves in the patient's relationship with the treater. What is unique about the doctor-patient relationship in dynamic psychiatry is *not* the presence of transference, but the fact that it represents therapeutic material to be understood. When subjected to hateful invective from their patients, dynamic psychiatrists do not angrily reject them as most other people in their lives would. Instead, they attempt to determine what past relationship of the patient is being repeated in the present and what contribution their real characteristics may be making to the situation. In this sense, dynamic psychiatrists are defined as much by what they do *not* do as by what they do.

Countertransference

An overarching principle embraced by those of us who practice dynamic psychiatry is that we are basically more similar to our patients than we are different from them. The psychological mechanisms in pathological states are merely extensions of principles involved in normal developmental functioning. Doctor and patient are both human beings. Just as patients have transference, treaters have countertransference. Since every current relationship is a new addition of old relationships, it follows logically that countertransference in the psychiatrist and transference in the patient are essentially identical processes—each unconsciously experiences the other as someone from the past. The difference lies in how the feelings are handled in the therapeutic encounter (Brenner 1982). While transference is discussed and analyzed as part of the therapeutic process, countertransference is monitored by the constant internal vigilance of the psychiatrist.

The concept of countertransference has undergone considerable evolution since its inception (Hamilton 1988; Kernberg 1965). Freud's (1912/1958) narrow definition referred to the analyst's transference to the patient or the analyst's response to the patient's transference. Implicit in this conceptualization is the emergence of unresolved conflicts from the analyst's unconscious. Winnicott (1949), however, in working with psychotic patients and those with severe personality disorders, noted a different form of countertransference. He termed the feeling *objective hate,* because it was not a reaction stemming from unresolved unconscious conflicts in the treater, but rather was a natural reaction to the patient's outrageous behavior. It is objective in the sense that virtually everyone would react similarly to the patient's provocative behavior.

As Kernberg (1965) predicted, this broader definition of countertransference as the therapist's conscious and appropriate total emotional reaction to the patient is gaining greater acceptance, particularly because it helps characterize the work with patients with severe personality disorders, which are an increasingly common segment of the dynamic psychiatrist's practice. This definition serves to attenuate the pejorative connotation of countertransference—unresolved problems in the treater that require more analysis—and to replace it with a conceptualization that views countertransference as a major diagnostic and therapeutic tool that tells the treater a good deal about the patient's internal world. In this volume I will attempt to clarify whether the narrower or broader sense of countertransference is being used in a given instance.

As the definition has continued to evolve, countertransference is now generally regarded as involving *both* the narrow and the totalistic, or broad, characteristics. Most theoretical perspectives view countertransference as entailing a jointly created reaction in the clinician that stems in part from contributions of the clinician's past and in part from feelings *induced* by the patient's behavior (Gabbard 1995). In some cases the emphasis may be more on the contributions of the clinician than on those of the patient; in other cases the reverse may be true. Countertransference is both a source of valuable information about the patient's internal world and an interference with the treatment.

Resistance

The last major principle of dynamic psychiatry involves the patient's wish to preserve the status quo, to oppose the treater's efforts to produce insight and change. In his early papers on technique, Freud (1912/1958) had already noted these powerful oppositional forces: "The resistance accompanies the treatment step by step. Every single association, every act of the person under treatment must reckon with the resistance and represents a compromise between the forces that are striving towards recovery and the opposing ones" (p. 103). Resistances to treatment are as ubiquitous as transference phenomena and may take many forms, including being late to appointments, refusing to take medications, forgetting the psychiatrist's advice or interpretations, being silent in therapy sessions, focusing on unimportant material during the sessions, or forgetting to pay the therapy bill, to name only a few. Resistance may be conscious, preconscious, or unconscious. All resistance has in common an attempt to avoid unpleasant feelings, whether anger, guilt, hate, love (if directed toward a forbidden object such as the therapist), envy, shame, grief, anxiety, or some combination of these.

Resistance defends the patient's illness. The patient's characteristic defense mechanisms designed to safeguard against unpleasant affects come to the fore during dynamic treatment. In fact, resistance may be defined as the patient's defenses as they manifest themselves in psychodynamic treatment (Greenson 1967). The difference between resistances and defense mechanisms is simply that the former can be observed, whereas the latter must be inferred (Thomä and Kächele 1987). The strength of the defense or resistance is necessarily proportional to the strength of the underlying impulse. As Ralph Waldo Emerson once observed, "The louder he talked of his honor, the faster we counted our spoons."

The dynamic psychiatrist expects to encounter resistance to treatment and is prepared to address this phenomenon as part and parcel of the treatment process. Whereas other treaters may get angry when their patients do not comply with prescribed treatments, dynamic psychiatrists are curious to know what this resistance is protecting and what past situation is being reenacted. Despite the connotation of resistance as an obstacle that must be removed to conduct the treatment, to a large extent, understanding the resistance *is* the treatment. Freud tended to use resistance to mean two different phenomena: 1) a stoppage of the patient's free associations and 2) a revelation of a highly significant internal object relationship from the patient's past transported into the present moment with the treater (Friedman 1991). The manner in which the patient resists is likely to be a re-creation of a past relationship that influences a variety of present-day relationships. For example, patients who spent their childhoods rebelling against their parents may unconsciously find themselves rebelling against their doctor as well as other authority figures. The dynamic clinician helps the patient understand these patterns so that they become fully conscious.

Mind and Brain in Psychiatry

One of the most unfortunate developments in contemporary psychiatry is the polarization between biologically oriented and dynamically oriented psychiatrists. At the root of this conflict lies the age-old mind-body problem. Is the etiology of mental illness in the brain or in the mind? Should the treatment of mental illness be somatic or psychotherapeutic? The main problem with the debate between these polarized factions is the questions posed. It is not a situation of "either/or," but "both/and." The dynamic psychiatrist who neglects the biological dimension of experience and the biologically oriented psychiatrist who neglects the psychological realm are both guilty of narrow-minded reductionism.

Related to this unfortunate tendency toward dichotomization is a widely held but poorly supported view of treatment: namely, that psychotherapy is a treatment for "psychologically based" disorders, while "biologically based" disorders should be treated with medication (Gabbard, in press). This conceptualization is related to a Cartesian dualism that fragments the patient into a mind and a brain. Although these two domains have their own languages and can be separated for purposes of discussion, they are always integrated. What we call "mind" can be understood as the activity of the brain (Andreasen 1997), although the complexity of a person's unique subjectivity is not reducible to chemistry and physiology (Searle 1992). Mental phenomena arise from the brain, but subjective experience also affects the brain.

There is irony in the polarization of psychiatry into a biological and a psychodynamic approach because we now stand on the threshold of embracing a sophisticated understanding of the interaction between the brain and the environment that can lead to truly integrative treatment strategies. The growing awareness that the brain is among the most plastic organs in the body allows us to begin to conceptualize a neurobiologically informed model of psychotherapy that reflects the dynamic nature of gene-environment interaction.

Intensive study of the genetic contributions to psychiatric disorders has led investigators to the conclusion that neatly predictable Mendelian patterns of inheritance do not apply to mental illness. Variable expressivity and incomplete penetrance are typical of the major disorders, suggesting that environmental and developmental factors must interact with genes to produce psychiatric illness. Indeed, the study of brain plasticity has shown that once genes are activated by cellular developmental processes, the rate at which those genes are expressed is highly regulated by environmental signals throughout life (Hyman 1999).

Experimental animal models have been of considerable heuristic value in understanding the mechanisms involved in gene-environment interaction. In a series of innovative experiments with the marine snail *Aplysia*, Kandel demonstrated how synaptic connections can be permanently altered and strengthened through the regulation of gene expression connected with learning from the environment (Kandel 1979, 1983, 1998). In this organism, the number of synapses double or triple as a result of learning. Kandel postulated that psychotherapy may bring about similar changes in brain synapses. In the same way that the psychotherapist conceptualizes representations of self and objects as malleable through psychotherapeutic intervention, Kandel noted that the brain itself is a plastic and dynamic structure. If psychotherapy is regarded as a form of learning, then the learning process that occurs in psychotherapy may produce alterations of gene expression and thereby alter the strength of synaptic connections. The sequence of a gene—the template function—cannot be affected by environmental experience, but the transcriptional function of the gene—the ability of a gene to direct the manufacture of specific proteins—is certainly responsive to environmental factors and regulated by those influences.

Studies with mammalian species have also demonstrated the plasticity of the brain in response to environmental input. Rats raised in a social environment that requires complex learning to survive have significantly greater numbers of synapses per neurons compared with rats raised in isolation (Greenough et al. 1987).

The impact of environmental factors on gene expression explains why there are phenotypic differences between identical twins and discordance for many illnesses. Two children in the same household may experience a profoundly different environment. Studies of etiology and pathogenesis have repeatedly noted that the *nonshared family environment* may be a crucial factor in determining which child in a family becomes ill (Reiss et al. 1995). One dimension of this construct relates to how children in the same family are treated differently by the parents, resulting in different outcomes in the children's psychological health. Moreover, the individual's genetic endowment influences the type of parenting he or she receives, and this developmental input from parents and other figures in the environment may, in turn, influence the further readout of the genome. The brain is obviously not a blank screen, and the impact of environmental factors is constrained by the basic genetic endowment of the individual. Nevertheless, environmentally derived activity appears to drive the development of dendrites so that they conform to cognitive schemes for the construction of mental representations.

Neural connections between the cortex, limbic system, and autonomic nervous system become linked into circuits in accordance with specific experiences of the developing organism. Hence, emotion and memory circuits are linked together because of consistent patterns of connection resulting from stimuli in the environment. This developmental pattern may be summarized as follows: Neurons that "fire together wire together" (Schatz 1992, p. 64).

There is preliminary evidence from lower species that social cues available in the environment may affect how a specific neurotransmitter affects the organism. Investigators have identified a neuron in crayfish whose response to the neurotransmitter serotonin differs dramatically depending on the animal's social status (Yeh et al. 1996). This particular neuron controls the tail-flip reflex in crayfish, which is relevant to the fight/flight response. In a dominant animal, serotonin makes the neuron more likely to fire. However, the same neurotransmitter suppresses firing in subordinate animals. The response to serotonin is not permanently encoded. If the animal's social status changes, the effect of serotonin on the neuron also changes. For example, when two previously subordinate crayfish were placed together, one would eventually become dominant. When that animal was tested, its response to serotonin was consistent with that of dominant animals (i.e., serotonin stimulated the tail-flip reflex rather than suppressing it). These findings suggest that the perception of one's place in a relationship may influence the activity of neurotransmitters and their effect on the brain.

Alterations in relationships have also been shown to produce lasting biochemical changes in rhesus monkeys. Suomi (1991) found that infant rhesus monkeys separated from their mothers developed behavioral abnormalities that suggest a variant of social anxiety. These infants could overcome their behavioral difficulties when exposed to peers who were raised by their own mothers. However, the behavioral abnormalities returned when stressful or novel situations were encountered. In Suomi's research, the infants reared by peers still had higher levels of cortisol and adrenocorticotropic hormone (ACTH) in response to separation and lower cerebrospinal fluid levels of norepinephrine. They also had higher levels of 3-methoxy-4-hydroxyphenylglycol (MHPG).

An even stronger demonstration of how interactions with nurturing figures in the environment can influence genetic vulnerability emerged from a related investigation in Suomi's laboratory. About 20% of the infants in the monkey colony who were reared by their mothers nevertheless reacted to brief separations with increased cortisol and ACTH levels, depressive reactions, and exaggerated norepinephrine turnover. This vulnerability appeared to be genetic. However, when unusually nurturant mothers within the monkey colony were placed with these infants, the inborn vulnerability to separation anxiety disappeared. These monkeys ultimately rose to the top of the social hierarchy in the monkey colony, suggesting that the "supermothers" helped the young monkeys develop their innate sensitivity in an adaptive direction that allowed them to be more attuned to social cues and to respond to those cues in a way that was advantageous to them.

Mild trauma has also been studied in primates and appears to produce specific biochemical and behavioral changes. Rosenblum and Andrews (1994) randomly assigned infant monkeys either to normal mothers or to mothers temporarily made anxious by an unpredictable feeding schedule. Those placed with anxious mothers showed diminished capacity for normal social interaction and were socially subordinate. However, the changes did not manifest themselves until adolescence, confirming the psychoanalytic notion that disturbances in early phases of development can produce psychopathological changes in later developmental periods. These behavioral changes were also associated with serotonergic and noradrenergic alterations. Because genetic influences were controlled by random assignment, the findings suggest that distraction and anxiety in the mother were central to the identified changes.

Research data of this nature suggest that there are windows in time during which a gene is dependent on a certain type of environmental influence to determine its expression. Investigators have found similar windows in human development for periods of major structural change in brain formation (Ornitz 1991; D. B. Perry et al. 1995; Pynoos et al. 1997). Bremner et al. (1997), for example, have shown that adults with posttraumatic stress disorder who had experienced childhood physical and sexual abuse had dramatically reduced left hippocampal volumes compared with matched control subjects. It may well be that traumatic experiences during unstable periods of brain development can produce a form of regression to an earlier stage of neural function and structure (Pynoos et al. 1997).

The implications of this research enable us to broaden our understanding of psychiatric interventions by regarding all of them as biopsychosocial. In other words, medications have a "psychological" effect in addition to their impact on the brain, and psychotherapeutic interventions affect the brain in addition to their "psychological" impact.

Researchers in Finland showed that psychodynamic therapy may have a significant impact on serotonin metabolism (Viinamäki et al. 1998). At the beginning of a 1-year psychotherapy process, single photon emission computed tomography (SPECT) imaging was undertaken with a 25-year-old man suffering from borderline personality disorder and depression. Another man with similar problems also underwent imaging but did not receive psychotherapy or any other treatment. Initial SPECT imaging showed that both patients had markedly reduced serotonin uptake in the medial prefrontal area and the thalamus compared with 10 healthy control subjects. After 1 year of psychodynamic therapy, repeat SPECT imaging showed that the patient who received psychotherapy had normal serotonin uptake, whereas the control patient who did not receive psychotherapy continued to have markedly reduced serotonin uptake. Because the patient who received psychotherapy did not take medication in conjunction with the therapy, this finding suggests that the dynamic therapy itself may have normalized the serotonin metabolism.

A corollary of this view is that just as mental experience can affect biology, so, too, can biology have an influence on psychology. As Roose and Pardes (1989) have suggested, the well-known "mellowing" phenomenon of middle age, associated with the shift to more mature defenses (Vaillant 1976), may well be linked to the dramatic drop-off in norepinephrine levels in the locus coeruleus that occurs between ages 40 and 60 years.

Intrinsic to this model of the mind-brain relationship is the notion that we must differentiate causation from meaning. Psychiatry that loses the domain of meaning is mindless. The presence of biologically generated symptoms in no way diminishes the importance of meaning. Preexisting psychodynamic conflicts may attach themselves to biologically driven symptoms, with the result that the symptoms then function as a vehicle for the expression of the conflicts (Gabbard 1992). Consider an analogy: when a magnet is placed under a sheet of paper containing iron filings, the filings line up in formation and follow the movement of the magnet along the surface of the paper. Similarly, psychodynamic issues frequently appropriate the magnet-like biological forces for their own purposes. Auditory hallucinations are generated by alterations in neurotransmitters in persons with schizophrenia, but the content of hallucinations often has specific meanings based on the patient's psychodynamic conflicts.

Another area in which a psychodynamic approach works synergistically with pharmacotherapy is the realm of noncompliance. Failure to comply with pharmacotherapeutic regimens often can be understood along conventional lines of transference, countertransference, and resistance issues. A considerable literature has accrued on the practice of dynamic pharmacotherapy (P. S. Appelbaum and Gutheil 1980; Book 1987; Docherty and Fiester 1985; Docherty et al. 1977; Gutheil 1977, 1982; Karasu 1982; Ostow 1983; Thompson and Brodie 1981; Wylie and Wylie 1987), and there has been a broad consensus that psychodynamic meanings of medications may pose formidable obstacles to compliance with medication regimens. In Chapter 5 I will consider dynamic approaches to pharmacotherapy in some detail.

The Role of the Dynamic Psychiatrist in Contemporary Psychiatry

In an age when impressive advances in the neurosciences occur almost weekly, dynamic psychiatry has lost some of its luster. Only a generation ago, psychoanalysts and dynamic psychiatrists enjoyed unparalleled prestige. They have since been upstaged by biologically oriented researchers, whose contribution to the field is beyond question. However, above the din of optimistic proclamations about the genetic-biochemical basis of all mental illness, another cry can be heard, one that is growing in intensity. Groups of psychiatric residents in biologically oriented programs complain that they know all about neurotransmitters but do not know how to talk to their patients. Freshly trained private practitioners ask analysts for consultation and supervision when their patients fail to respond to medications. Even patients are beginning to demand that they be listened to rather than simply medicated.

Advances in any scientific field conform to a predictable pattern—an initial flurry of excitement is followed by sobering disillusionment. Our own field of psychiatry is no exception in this regard. The post–World War II enthusiasm for psychoanalysis as a panacea for a host of social problems led to a bitter disenchantment in the decade of the 1960s. American psychiatrists today are encountering the limitations inherent in the tools of biological psychiatry. Indeed, the advances in neuroscience have made it eminently clear to clinical investigators that the psychosocial dimension must be taken into account to fully understand pathogenesis and treatment.

Training in dynamic psychiatry significantly broadens the scope of the clinician's expertise. One real advantage of the dynamic approach is its attention to the role of personality factors in illness. In fact, personality and its influence on the patient is a principal area of expertise for dynamic psychiatrists (Michels 1988). As S. Perry et al. (1987) persuasively argued, since every treatment involves therapeutic management and modification of the patient's personality, a psychodynamic evaluation is applicable to all patients, not simply those referred for long-term psychoanalytic psychotherapy. Characterological resistances to treatment frequently torpedo the medication program designed to maintain the patient in remission. Symptoms are embedded in character structure, and the dynamic psychiatrist recognizes that in many cases one cannot treat the symptoms without first addressing the character structure.

A dynamic therapeutic approach is certainly not necessary for every psychiatric patient. Those who respond well to medications, electroconvulsive therapy, or behavioral desensitization may not require the services of a dynamic psychiatrist. As with all other schools of psychiatry, the dynamic psychotherapeutic approach cannot effectively treat all psychiatric illnesses or patients.

A strictly dynamic therapeutic approach should probably be reserved for patients who most need it and who will not respond to any other interventions. However, a *dynamically informed* approach to most—if not all—patients will enrich the psychiatrist's practice and enhance the clinician's sense of mastery over the mysteries of the human psyche. It will also help the dynamic psychiatrist identify and understand the daily countertransference problems that interfere with effective diagnosis and treatment. In a survey of private psychiatric practitioners and academic psychiatrists, Langsley and Yager (1988) found that the second most highly regarded skill was the ability to "recognize countertransference problems and personal idiosyncrasies as they influence interactions with patients and be able to deal with them constructively" (p. 471). The dynamic approach is the only one that systematically addresses the psychiatrist's conscious and unconscious contributions to the process of treatment and evaluation.

References

Andreasen NC: Linking mind and brain in the study of mental illness: a project for a scientific psychopathology. Science 275:1586–1593, 1997

Appelbaum PS, Gutheil TG: Drug refusal: a study of psychiatric inpatients. Am J Psychiatry 137:340–346, 1980

Appelbaum SA: Effecting Change in Psychotherapy. New York, Jason Aronson, 1981

Bechara A, Tranel D, Damasio H, et al: Double association of conditioning and declarative knowledge relative to the amygdala and hippocampus in humans. Science 269:1115–1118, 1995

Book HE: Some psychodynamics of non-compliance. Can J Psychiatry 32:115–117, 1987

Bouchard TJ, Lykken DT, McGue M, et al: Sources of human psychological differences: the Minnesota study of twins reared apart. Science 250:223–228, 1990

Bowers JS, Schachter DL: Implicit memory and test awareness. J Exp Psychol Learn Mem Cogn 16:404–416, 1990

Bremner JD, Randall P, Vermetten E, et al: Magnetic resonance-imaging based measurement of hippocampal volume in posttraumatic stress disorder related to childhood physical and sexual abuse: a preliminary report. Biol Psychiatry 41:23–32, 1997

Brenner C: The Mind in Conflict. New York, International Universities Press, 1982

Docherty JP, Fiester SJ: The therapeutic alliance and compliance with psychopharmacology, in Psychiatry Update: American Psychiatric Association Annual Review, Vol 4. Edited by Hales RE, Frances AJ. Washington, DC, American Psychiatric Press, 1985, pp 607–632

Docherty JP, Marder SR, Van Kammen DP, et al: Psychotherapy and pharmacotherapy: conceptual issues. Am J Psychiatry 134:529–533, 1977

Ellenberger HF: The Discovery of the Unconscious: The History and Evolution of Dynamic Psychiatry. New York, Basic Books, 1970

Erikson EH: Childhood and Society, 2nd Edition. New York, WW Norton, 1963

Freud S: The interpretation of dreams (1900), in The Standard Edition of the Complete Psychological Works of Sigmund Freud, Vols 4, 5. Translated and edited by Strachey J. London, Hogarth Press, 1953, pp 1–627

Freud S: The psychopathology of everyday life (1901), in The Standard Edition of the Complete Psychological Works of Sigmund Freud, Vol 6. Translated and edited by Strachey J. London, Hogarth Press, 1960, pp 1–279

Freud S: The dynamics of transference (1912), in The Standard Edition of the Complete Psychological Works of Sigmund Freud, Vol 12. Translated and edited by Strachey J. London, Hogarth Press, 1958, pp 97–108

Freud S: The unconscious (1915), in The Standard Edition of the Complete Psychological Works of Sigmund Freud, Vol 14. Translated and edited by Strachey J. London, Hogarth Press, 1963, pp 159–215

Friedman L: A reading of Freud's papers on technique. Psychoanal Q 60:564–595, 1991

Gabbard GO: Psychodynamic psychiatry in the "decade of the brain." Am J Psychiatry 149:991–998, 1992

Gabbard GO: Countertransference: the emerging common ground. Int J Psychoanal 76:475–485, 1995

Gabbard GO: A neurobiologically informed perspective on psychotherapy. Br J Psychiatry (in press)

Greenough WT, Black JE, Wallace CS: Experience and brain development. Child Dev 58:539–559, 1987

Greenson RR: The Technique and Practice of Psychoanalysis. New York, International Universities Press, 1967

Gutheil TG: Psychodynamics in drug prescribing. Drug Therapy 2:35–40, 1977

Gutheil TG: The psychology of psychopharmacology. Bull Menninger Clin 46:321–330, 1982

Hamilton NG: Self and Others: Object Relations Theory in Practice. Northvale, NJ, Jason Aronson, 1988

Hoffman IZ: Ritual and Spontaneity in the Psychoanalytic Process: A Dialectical-Constructivist View. Hillsdale, NJ, Analytic Press, 1998

Hyman SE: Looking to the future: the role of genetics and molecular biology in research on mental illness, in Psychiatry in the New Millennium. Edited by Weissman S, Sabshin M, Eist H. Washington, DC, American Psychiatric Press, 1999, pp 101–122

Kandel ER: Psychotherapy and the single synapse: the impact of psychiatric thought on neurobiologic research. N Engl J Med 301:1028–1037, 1979

Kandel ER: From metapsychology to molecular biology: explorations into the nature of anxiety. Am J Psychiatry 140:1277–1293, 1983

Kandel ER: A new intellectual framework for psychiatry. Am J Psychiatry 155:457–469, 1998

Karasu TB: Psychotherapy and pharmacotherapy: toward an integrative model. Am J Psychiatry 139:1102–1113, 1982

Kernberg OF: Notes on countertransference. J Am Psychoanal Assoc 13:38–56, 1965

Langsley DG, Yager J: The definition of a psychiatrist: eight years later. Am J Psychiatry 145:469–475, 1988

Michels R: The future of psychoanalysis. Psychoanal Q 57:167–185, 1988

Nemiah JC: Foundations of Psychopathology. New York, Oxford University Press, 1961, p 4

Ornitz EM: Developmental aspects of neurophysiology, in Child and Adolescent Psychiatry: A Comprehensive Textbook, 2nd Edition. Edited by Lewis E. Baltimore, MD, Williams & Wilkins, 1991, pp 39–51

Ostow M: Interactions of psychotherapy and pharmacotherapy (letter). Am J Psychiatry 140:370–371, 1983

Perry DB, Pollard RA, Blakeley TL, et al: Childhood trauma, the neurobiology of adaptation and "use-dependent" development of the brain: how "states" become "traits." Infant Mental Health Journal 16:271–291, 1995

Perry S, Cooper AM, Michels R: The psychodynamic formulation: its purpose, structure, and clinical application. Am J Psychiatry 144:543–550, 1987

Pynoos RA, Steinberg AM, Ornitz EM, et al: Issues in the developmental neurobiology of traumatic stress, in Psychobiology of Posttraumatic Stress Disorder. Edited by Yehuda R, McFarlane AC. New York, New York Academy of Sciences, 1997, pp 176–193

Reiss D, Hetherington EM, Plomin R, et al: Genetic questions for environmental studies: differential parenting and psychopathology in adolescence. Arch Gen Psychiatry 52:925–936, 1995

Renik O: Analytic interaction: conceptualizing technique in light of the analyst's irreducible subjectivity. Psychoanal Q 62:553–571, 1993

Roose SP, Pardes H: Biological considerations in the middle years, in The Middle Years: New Psychoanalytic Perspectives. Edited by Oldham JM, Leibert RS. New Haven, CT, Yale University Press, 1989, pp 179–190

Rosenblum LA, Andrews MW: Influences of environmental demand on maternal behavior and infant development. Acta Paediatr Suppl 397:57–63, 1994

Schatz CJ: The developing brain. Sci Am 267:60–67, 1992

Searle JR: The Rediscovery of the Mind. Cambridge, MA, MIT Press, 1992

Sherwood M: The Logic of Explanation in Psychoanalysis. New York, Academic Press, 1969

Shevrin H, Bond J, Brakel LA, et al: Conscious and Unconscious Processes: Psychodynamic, Cognitive, and Neurophysiological Convergences. New York, Guilford, 1996

Squire LR: Memory and Brain. New York, Oxford University Press, 1987

Stolorow RD: An intersubjective view of self psychology. Psychoanalytic Dialogues 5:393–399, 1995

Suomi SJ: Early stress and adult emotional reactivity in rhesus monkeys, in Childhood Environment and Adult Disease (CIBA Foundation Symposium No. 156). Edited by Bock GR and CIBA Foundation Symposium Staff. Chichester, England, Wiley, 1991, pp 171–188

Thomä H, Kächele H: Psychoanalytic Practice, Vol 1: Principles. Translated by Wilson M, Roseveare D. New York, Springer-Verlag, 1987

Thomas A, Chess S: Genesis and evolution of behavioral disorders: from infancy to early adult life. Am J Psychiatry 141:1–9, 1984

Thompson EM, Brodie HKH: The psychodynamics of drug therapy. Current Psychiatric Therapies 20:239–251, 1981

Vaillant GE: Natural history of male psychological health, V: the relation of choice of ego mechanisms of defense to adult adjustment. Arch Gen Psychiatry 33:535–545, 1976

Viinamäki H, Kuikka J, Tiihonen J, et al: Change in monoamine transporter density related to clinical recovery: a case-control study. Nordic Journal of Psychiatry 52:39–44, 1998

Waelder R: The principle of multiple function: observations on overdetermination, in Psychoanalysis: Observation, Theory, Application. Edited by Gutman SA. New York, International Universities Press, 1930, pp 68–83

Watson JB: Behaviorism (1924). New York, WW Norton, 1930

Weinberger J, Hardaway R: Separating science from myth in subliminal psychodynamic activation. Clin Psychol Rev 10:727–756, 1990

Westen D: Mind, Brain, and Culture, 2nd Edition. New York, Wiley, 1999a

Westen D: The scientific status of unconscious processes: is Freud really dead? J Am Psychoanal Assoc 47:1061–1106, 1999b

Winnicott DW: Hate in the counter-transference. Int J Psychoanal 30:69–74, 1949

Wylie HW Jr, Wylie ML: An effect of pharmacotherapy on the psychoanalytic process: case report of a modified analysis. Am J Psychiatry 144:489–492, 1987

Yeh SR, Fricke RA, Edwards DH: The effect of social experience on serotonergic modulation of the escape circuit of crayfish. Science 271:366–369, 1996

C H A P T E R
2

The Theoretical Basis of Dynamic Psychiatry

Nothing is as practical as a good theory.

Kurt Lewin

Like a sailor without a sextant, a psychiatrist who sets out to navigate the dark waters of the unconscious without a theory will soon be lost at sea. Psychoanalytic theory is the foundation of dynamic psychiatry. It brings order to the seemingly chaotic inner world of the patient. It allows the psychiatrist to supplement and transcend the descriptive level of cataloging symptoms and applying diagnostic labels. It provides a means of entering and understanding the cavernous interior of the mind. Theory not only guides clinicians toward diagnostic understanding, it also informs the choice of treatment for each patient. Theoretical understanding helps the dynamic psychiatrist decide what to say, when to say it, how to say it, and what is better left unsaid.

Contemporary dynamic psychiatry subsumes at least four broad psychoanalytic theoretical frameworks: 1) ego psychology, derived from the classic psychoanalytic theory of Freud; 2) object relations theory, derived from the work of Melanie Klein and members of the "British School," including Fairbairn, Winnicott, and Balint; 3) self psychology, originated by Heinz Kohut and elaborated by many subsequent contributors; and 4) postmodern views, a group of loosely related theories, including constructivism, intersubjectivity, interpersonal theories, and the relational-conflict model.

27

Although volumes have been written on each of these schools of thought, here we will merely examine the salient features of the four theoretical frameworks. In subsequent chapters the theories will be "fleshed out" to illustrate their application to clinical situations.

Ego Psychology

Freud's early years as a psychoanalytic investigator were heavily influenced by his topographic model (described in Chapter 1). Hysterical symptoms were seen as the result of repressed memories of events or ideas. Freud hypothesized that psychotherapeutic intervention could lift repression, leading to the recall of memories. In turn, a detailed verbal description of the remembered pathogenic idea or event, accompanied by intense affect, would lead to the symptom's disappearance. For example, a young man's paralyzed arm might be the result of a repressed wish to hit his father. According to this model, the young man might regain the use of his arm by retrieving the wish from his unconscious, verbalizing it, and expressing the anger toward his father. This cathartic method, also known as abreaction, makes conscious the unconscious pathogenic memory.

But the topographic model soon began to fail Freud. He repeatedly encountered resistances in his patients to his therapeutic maneuvers. Some memories could not be brought back into consciousness. The defense mechanisms responsible for this resistance were themselves unconscious and therefore inaccessible. These observations led Freud to conclude that the ego has both conscious and unconscious components.

With the publication of "The Ego and the Id," Freud (1923/1961) introduced his tripartite structural theory of ego, id, and superego. In the structural model, which superseded the topographic model, the ego was viewed as distinct from the instinctual drives. The conscious aspect of the ego was the executive organ of the psyche, responsible for decision making and integration of perceptual data. The unconscious aspect of the ego contained defense mechanisms, such as repression, which were necessary to counteract the powerful instinctual drives harbored in the id—specifically, sexuality (libido) and aggression.

The id is a completely unconscious intrapsychic agency that is only interested in discharging tension. The id is controlled both by the unconscious aspects of the ego and by the third agency of the structural model—the superego. For the most part, the superego is unconscious, but aspects of it are certainly conscious. This agency incorporates the moral conscience and the ego ideal. The former *proscribes* (i.e., dictates what one should *not* do based on the internalization of parental and societal values), while the latter *prescribes* (i.e., dictates what one ought to do or be). The superego tends to be more sensitive to the strivings of the id and is therefore more immersed in the unconscious than is the ego (Figure 2–1).

Ego psychology conceptualizes the intrapsychic world as one of interagency conflict. The superego, the ego, and the id battle among themselves as sexuality and aggression strive for expression and discharge. Conflict between the agencies produces anxiety. This signal anxiety (Freud 1926/1959) alerts the ego that a defense mechanism is required. The mechanism of neurotic symptom formation may be understood in this manner. Conflict produces anxiety, which results in defense, which leads to a compromise between the id and the ego. A symptom, then, is a compromise formation that both defends against the wish arising from the id and gratifies the wish in disguised form.

An accountant with an obsessive-compulsive personality disorder was always concerned that his boss might be angry with him. He secretly resented his boss, and his anxiety about his boss's anger was a projection of his own wish to explode at his boss and tell him what he thought of him. As an unconscious defense, he was obsequious and ingratiating toward his boss to make sure that he could not possibly be accused of being angry with him. The boss found this behavior irritating, and as a result there was an ever-present tension between the two of them. In other words, the accountant's obsequious style defended against the eruption of his own anger, but it also contained an attenuated expression of his aggressive wishes because of the reaction it produced in his boss.

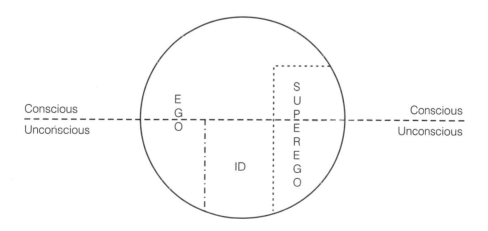

FIGURE 2–1.   The structural model.
Note.   The preconscious has been deleted for the sake of simplicity.

Such compromise formations are a normal mental process (Brenner 1982). Neurotic symptoms represent only the pathological variety. Character traits themselves can be compromise formations and may represent adaptive and creative solutions to intrapsychic conflict.

Defense Mechanisms

Freud acknowledged the existence of other defense mechanisms, but he devoted most of his attention to repression. Freud's daughter Anna, in her landmark work, *The Ego and the Mechanisms of Defense* (1936/1966), expanded his work by describing in detail nine individual defense mechanisms: regression, reaction formation, undoing, introjection, identification, projection, turning against the self, reversal, and sublimation. Even more important, she acknowledged the implications that this increased scrutiny of the defensive operation of the ego had for treatment. No longer could the psychoanalyst simply attend to the uncovering of unacceptable wishes from the id. Equal attention would need to be paid to the vicissitudes of defensive efforts put forth by the ego, which would manifest themselves as resistances in treatment.

In shifting the emphasis of psychoanalysis from drives to ego defenses, Anna Freud anticipated the movement of psychoanalysis and dynamic psychiatry away from neurotic symptom formation and toward character pathology. We now partially define many forms of personality disorder according to their typical defensive operations. Hence, the dynamic psychiatrist must be thoroughly familiar with a broad range of defense mechanisms because of their usefulness in understanding both neurotic problems and personality disorders.

All defenses have in common the protection of the ego against instinctual demands from the id (Freud 1926/1959). Some of the principal neurotic defense mechanisms are repression, displacement, reaction formation, isolation of affect, undoing, somatization, and conversion.

1. *Repression.* Freud viewed this mechanism as the queen of all defenses. It operates unconsciously by expelling unacceptable wishes, feelings, or fantasies from conscious awareness. Although repression is used by virtually all neurotics, it is a hallmark of the higher-level hysterical personality (see Chapter 18).
2. *Displacement.* This defense is an unconscious process by which feelings attached to one source are redirected toward another. Transference is an obvious example of displacement, since feelings for a person in the past are transferred to a figure in the present. Phobias are the classic example of this defense, because the anxiety associated with an unconscious source is redirected to a con-

scious substitute, often harmless in and of itself. Displacement is also one of the chief mechanisms of disguise in dreams, where anxiety is reduced and sleep is preserved by substituting a neutral figure for a more emotionally charged one.

3. *Reaction formation.* This common defense is characterized by warding off an unacceptable wish or impulse by adopting a character trait that is diametrically opposed to it. Reaction formation is commonly found in obsessive-compulsive personality disorder.

4. *Isolation of affect.* This mechanism, also commonly found in obsessive-compulsive patients, divorces affect from ideation. A traumatic memory, for example, may be easily retrieved but will be stripped of any concomitant intense feelings. Isolation often operates hand in hand with intellectualization, which performs a similar function of avoiding affect.

5. *Undoing.* Sometimes referred to as doing and undoing, this mechanism is also characteristic of obsessive-compulsive patients. It involves magical thinking, with a symbolic action performed to reverse or cancel out a completed and unacceptable thought or action. One patient took literally the superstition, "Step on a crack, break your mother's back." Whenever he inadvertently stepped on a crack in the sidewalk, he would return to retrace his steps so he could repeat them without hitting the crack.

6. *Somatization.* This defense, typical of hypochondriacal patients, involves the transfer of painful feelings to body parts. Psychotherapy with somatizing patients is often frustrating because feelings are unacceptable, and their emotional concerns can be communicated only through physical complaints.

7. *Conversion.* Most commonly, though not exclusively, associated with hysteria, this mechanism is characterized by the symbolic representation of an intrapsychic conflict in physical terms. As in the case of the young man with hysterical paralysis of his arm (referred to at the beginning of this chapter), the motor or sensory symbolization frequently involves a defense against an unacceptable wish.

Defense mechanisms have been classified according to a hierarchy from the most immature or pathological to the most mature or healthy (Vaillant 1977). The primarily neurotic defenses enumerated above are only a partial list. Some of the more primitive or immature defense mechanisms, including splitting, projective identification, introjection, and denial, are discussed later in this chapter. None of us is without defense mechanisms, once again illustrating the dynamic principle that psychological health and illness are on a continuum. In fact, a profile of your typical defense mechanisms is a good barometer of your psychological health. Vaillant (1977) emphasized four mature defenses in particular: 1) *suppression*—the *conscious* (as distinct from repression, which is unconscious) banishing of unacceptable thoughts or feelings from your mind; 2) *altruism*—the subordination of your own needs and interests to those of others; 3) *sublimation*—an unconscious process by which consciously unacceptable drives or wishes are channeled into socially acceptable alternatives (e.g., a wish to stab a sibling rival is converted into a surgical career); 4) *humor*—the ability to playfully poke fun at yourself and the situation you're in—an invaluable part of mental health.

Adaptive Aspects of the Ego

The ego's importance to the psyche is not limited to its defensive operations. Heinz Hartmann established himself as one of the foremost contributors to contemporary ego psychology by focusing on the nondefensive aspects of the ego. He turned the ego away from the id and refocused it on the outside world. Hartmann (1939/1958) insisted that there was a "conflict-free sphere of the ego" that develops independently of id forces and conflicts. Given an "average expectable environment," certain autonomous ego functions present at birth are allowed to flourish without being impeded by conflict. These include thinking, learning, perception, motor control, and language, to name a few. Hartmann's *adaptive* point of view, then, is an outgrowth of his concept of the existence of an autonomous, conflict-free area of the ego. Through neutralization of sexual and aggressive energies, Hartmann believed, even certain defenses could lose their connection with the instinctual forces of the id and become secondarily autonomous or adaptive.

David Rapaport (1951) and Edith Jacobson (1964) picked up where Hartmann left off and further refined his seminal contributions to ego psychology. It is commonplace today for clinicians to consider ego functions, ego strengths, and ego weaknesses as part of their routine psychodynamic evaluation of a patient. Bellak et al. (1973) systematized ego functions into scales used both for research and for clinical evaluation. The most important of these ego functions include reality testing, impulse control, thought processes, judgment, synthetic-integrative functioning, mastery-competence, and primary and secondary autonomy (after Hartmann).

Object Relations Theory

The view of ego psychology is that drives (i.e., sexuality and aggression) are primary, while object relations are secondary. (It is a well-established, though perhaps unfortunate, tradition in psychoanalytic writing to use the term *object* to mean *person*. Despite the somewhat pejorative connotations of *object*, I will retain the usage here for the sake of consistency and clarity.) In other words, the infant's most compelling agenda is tension discharge under the pressure of drives. Object relations theory, on the other hand, holds that drives emerge in the context of a relationship (e.g., the infant-mother dyad) and therefore can never be divorced from one another. Some object relations theorists (Fairbairn 1952) would even suggest that the drives are primarily geared to object seeking rather than tension reduction.

Stated in its simplest terms, object relations theory encompasses the transformation of interpersonal relationships into internalized representations of relationships. As children develop, they do not simply internalize an object or person; rather, they internalize an entire *relationship* (Fairbairn 1940/1952, 1944/1952). A prototype of loving, positive experience is formed during periods when the infant is nursing (Freud 1905/1953). This prototype includes a positive experience of the self (the nursing infant), a positive experience of the object (the attentive, caretaking mother), and a positive affective experience (pleasure, satiation). When hunger returns and the infant's mother is not immediately available, a prototype of negative experience occurs, including a negative experience of the self (the frustrated, demanding infant), an inattentive, frustrating object (the unavailable mother), and a negative affective experience of anger and perhaps terror. Ultimately, these two experiences are internalized as two opposing sets of object relationships consisting of a self-representation, an object representation, and an affect linking the two (Ogden 1983).

The internalization of the infant's mother, usually referred to as introjection (Schafer 1968), begins with the physical sensations associated with the presence of the mother during nursing but does not become meaningful until a boundary between inner and outer has developed. Around the 16th month of life, isolated images of the mother gradually coalesce into an enduring mental representation (Sandler and Rosenblatt 1962). At the same time an enduring self-representation forms, first as a body representation and later as a compilation of sensations and experiences perceived as belonging to the infant.

The positively colored or "good" object representation begins as a hallucinatory wish fulfillment growing out of the hungry infant's longing for its mother (Schafer 1968) and is later transformed into an internal presence as the infant's cognitive/perceptual apparatus develops. A major motivating force in the introjection of the positive, loving aspects of the mother seems to be the infant's fear of losing the mother (Schafer 1968). The reasons for the introjection or "taking in" of the negative, "bad" aspects of the mother are more complex. Possible motivating factors include the fantasy of controlling the object by containing it within oneself (Segal 1964), gaining a sense of mastery through repeated traumatic experiences with the object (Schafer 1968), and a preference for a "bad" object over no object at all (Schafer 1968). Clinical experience suggests that intense attachment to an internalized hostile object may also be connected with the yearning for a more positive relationship with the object (Meissner 1981). Furthermore, the object that has been introjected does not necessarily correlate with the real external object. For example, a mother who is unavailable to feed her infant on demand may simply be occupied with an older sibling, but is *experienced* and *introjected* by the infant as hostile, rejecting, and unavailable. Object relations theory acknowledges that there is *not* a one-to-one correlation between the real object and the internalized object representation.

Object relations theory also views conflict differently than it is viewed by ego psychology. Unconscious conflict is not merely the struggle between an impulse and a defense; it is also a clash between opposing pairs of internal object relations units (Kernberg 1983; Ogden 1983; Rinsley 1977). In other words, at any one time different constellations of self-representations, object representations, and affects vie with one another for center stage in the intrapsychic theater of internal object relations.

Internalization of object relations always involves a splitting of the ego into unconscious suborganizations (Ogden 1983). These fall into two groups:

(1) self-suborganizations of ego, i.e., aspects of the ego in which the person more fully experiences his ideas and feelings as his own, and (2) object suborganizations of ego through which meanings are generated in a mode based upon an identification of an aspect of the ego with the object. This identification with the object is so thorough that one's original sense of self is almost entirely lost. (Ogden 1983, p. 227)

This model clearly shows the influence of Freud's notion of the superego, which is commonly experienced as though it is a "foreign body" (i.e., an object-suborganization of the ego that monitors what a self-suborganization of the ego is doing). Ogden's model also provides a pathway back from the intrapsychic to the interpersonal. In this framework, transference can be viewed as taking one of two forms—either the role of the self-subdivision of the ego or that of the object-subdivision of the ego may be externalized onto the treater, a process that will be discussed in detail later in this chapter.

A Historical Perspective

Originating in the United Kingdom, object relations theory has flourished there and in South America. Only recently has it taken hold in the United States. Melanie Klein is usually seen as the founder of the object relations movement. She emigrated from Budapest, and later from Berlin, to England in 1926, where her theory of early infantile development became highly controversial. She was influenced by

Freud, but also broke new ground in her focus on internal objects. Through psychoanalytic work with children, she evolved a theory that relied heavily on unconscious intrapsychic fantasy and that compressed the developmental timetable of classical theory into the first year of life. The Oedipus complex, for example, was viewed by Klein as coinciding approximately with weaning in the latter half of the first year.

In the first few months of life, according to Klein, the infant experiences a primal terror of annihilation connected with Freud's death instinct. As a way of defending against this terror, the ego undergoes splitting, in which all "badness" or aggression deriving from the death instinct is disavowed and projected onto the mother. The infant then lives in fear of the mother's persecution—which may be concretized as a fear that the mother will get inside the infant and destroy any goodness (deriving from libido) that has also been split off and is protected inside the infant. This latter fear is the primary anxiety of what Klein (1946/1975) termed the *paranoid-schizoid position*. This early mode of organizing experience gains its name from the prominent defense mechanisms of splitting of the ego ("schizoid") and projection ("paranoid"). Indeed, projection and introjection are crucial to understanding the paranoid-schizoid position. These mechanisms are used to separate "good" and "bad" as much as possible (Segal 1964). After persecuting, or bad, objects have been projected onto the mother to separate them from good, or idealized objects, they may be reintrojected (i.e., taken back inside) to gain control and mastery over them. Concomitantly, the good objects may be projected to keep them safe from the "bad," which is now inside.

These oscillating cycles of projection and introjection continue until the infant begins to realize that the "bad" mother and the "good" mother are not in fact different, but are rather the same person. As children integrate the two part-objects into one whole object, they become disturbed that their sadistic, destructive fantasies toward the mother may have destroyed her. This newfound concern for the mother as a whole object is termed *depressive anxiety* by Klein and heralds the arrival of the *depressive position*. This mode of experience involves concern that one may harm others, in contrast to the paranoid-schizoid position, where the concern is that one will be harmed by others. Guilt becomes a prominent part of the affective life of the infant, who attempts to resolve it through *reparation*. This process may involve acts toward the mother that are designed to repair the "damage" inflicted on her in actuality or in fantasy. Klein recast the Oedipus complex as an effort to resolve depressive anxieties and guilt through reparation.

Klein's formulations have been criticized for relying exclusively on fantasy and thereby minimizing the influence of real persons in the environment, for overemphasizing the death instinct—a concept that is largely discounted by contemporary psychoanalytic theorists—and for attributing sophisticated adult forms of

cognition to infants in their first year of life. Nevertheless, her brilliant development of the paranoid-schizoid and depressive positions is of extraordinary clinical
value, especially if we view these positions as two modes of generating experience
that are lifelong and that create a dialectical interplay in the mind rather than viewing them as developmental phases that are passed through or outgrown (Ogden
1986). This conceptualization of lifelong modes of experience decreases the significance of Klein's developmental timetable.

For Klein, the drives were really complex psychological phenomena intimately
tied to specific object relations. Rather than originating in the body, drives were
seen as merely using the body as a vehicle for expression (Greenberg and Mitchell
1983). Similarly, the drives were not viewed as simply seeking tension reduction
but as being directed toward specific objects for specific reasons. During the 1940s,
this perspective and others held by Klein led to acrimonious debate in the British
Psychoanalytic Society. Anna Freud was Klein's principal nemesis, and when a
schism finally ruptured the society, one segment, known as the B Group, followed
Anna Freud's leadership, while the A Group remained loyal to Klein. A third segment, the Middle Group, refused to take sides. Although these groups still exist today, their borders are much more permeable, and considerable cross-fertilization
has occurred over the last half-century. The Middle Group, to some degree influenced by Klein's thinking, created the theory of object relations as we know it today (Kohon 1986). The individuals associated with this third segment did not
officially designate themselves a group until 1962, when they became known as the
"Independents." Among the key figures in the Independents, sometimes referred
to as the British School of object relations (Sutherland 1980) were D. W. Winnicott, Michael Balint, W. R. D. Fairbairn, Paula Heimann, Margaret Little, and
Harry Guntrip. This group dominated the British society in terms of numbers after
the Controversial Discussions of 1943 and 1944 (see King and Steiner 1992), even
though there was no central figurehead who had published a coherent theory
(Tuckett 1996). Although there were in fact significant differences in the writings
of these thinkers, their work shared common themes. All were concerned about
early development prior to the Oedipus complex, and all focused on the vicissitudes of internal object relations rather than on drive theory. Moreover, like Klein
and unlike the B Group, they tended to treat sicker patients with psychoanalytic
methods, perhaps thereby obtaining a more intimate glimpse of primitive mental
states.

The Independents served to counterbalance Klein's overemphasis on fantasy by
stressing the influence of the infant's early environment. Winnicott (1965), for example, coined the term *good-enough mother* to characterize the minimum environmental requirements needed by the infant in order to proceed with normal
development. Balint (1979) described the feeling in many patients that something

was missing, which he termed the *basic fault*. He viewed this lack as caused by the mother's failure to respond to the child's basic needs. Fairbairn (1963), perhaps the most divorced from drive theory, saw the etiology of his schizoid patients' difficulties not in drive frustration but in their mothers' failure to provide experiences that reassured them they were truly loved for themselves. He believed that the instincts or drives were not pleasure seeking but rather object seeking.

These thinkers were all impressed with the fact that a theory of *deficit*, as well as a theory of conflict, was necessary for a complete psychoanalytic understanding of the human being. Analysts have another task in addition to the analysis of conflict. They also serve as a new object to be internalized by their patients so as to bolster deficient intrapsychic structures. This point is critical for a clinical theory of object relations—the patient's internal object relations are not etched in granite; they are open to modification through new experiences. This point of view is even acknowledged to some extent by proponents of classical ego psychology, such as Blum, who credited Stone (1967) in noting: "Even in adult analysis the role of the analyst as a real new object rather than the object of transference must be considered along with identification with the analyst and analytic attitudes" (Blum 1971, p. 51).

Another key concept emerging from the British School is that an infant has an inborn tendency to grow toward self-realization (Summers 1999). Winnicott, in particular, felt that there was a *true self* whose growth could be facilitated or impeded by the responses of the mother and other figures in the environment. Bollas (1989) expanded on this view by arguing that the primary motivator within the child is the need to become him- or herself, which is facilitated by the mother's capacity to let the child express his or her true self in interaction with her. The mother who cannot serve in this facilitating capacity may contribute to the child's development of a *false self* in the service of accommodating the mother's needs and wishes.

Self and Ego

Whereas ego psychologists tend to minimize the significance of the self in their pursuit of a thorough understanding of the ego, the object relations theorists, because of their focus on the self as it relates to objects, have sought to clarify further the place of the self in the psychic apparatus. Certain American theorists, including Kernberg, Mahler, and Edith Jacobson, have worked to integrate object relations theory with ego psychology, considering the relationship of the ego and the self.

Few concepts in modern psychoanalytic discourse are more controversial than the self. The controversy has its historical roots in Freud's ambiguous usage of *Ich*.

Literally translated from the German as "I," the term was used by Freud with two different connotations. At times *Ich* referred to an impersonal intrapsychic structure, while at other times it clearly connoted the individual's personal self-experience (Kernberg 1982; Meissner 1986). Strachey's subsequent translation of *Ich* as "ego" in the Standard Edition of Freud's works profoundly influenced this controversy. Ego became definitively associated with the tripartite structural theory as one of three impersonal intrapsychic agencies. Freud's other use of the term to mean self-experience became lost in the standardization of the impersonal meaning.

Hartmann (1950/1964) further divorced the two meanings of *Ich* by differentiating ego and self according to their interactional contexts. In this view, the ego interacted with the other intrapsychic agencies, the id and superego, while the self interacted with objects. Although critics believe that this historical development blurs the distinction between psychoanalytic and sociological concepts (Kernberg 1982), other theorists find that this clarification establishes a framework for development of the theory of object relations. In other words, the self evolves as the result of interactions with significant objects in the environment and with corresponding internal objects (Meissner 1986).

Another major controversy surrounding the self is whether it refers to an intrapsychic representation of the individual or a source of action and agency in its own right. The tendency among ego psychological thinkers has been to view the self as representational rather than as a source of subjective autonomous activity (Meissner 1986). However, numerous authors (Guntrip 1968, 1971; Meissner 1986; Schafer 1976; Sutherland 1983) have expressed concern that the structural theory and the model of the self as an intrapsychic representation provide little basis for a concept of the self that includes subjective experience or personal agency. Structural theory, by its nature, is oriented to specific functions that are impersonal in nature. Sutherland (1983), for example, asserted that a basic feature of the self is its active initiating role with the environment—striving toward relatedness and unity.

There is room for both the self-as-representation and the self-as-agency. In fact, the self may be viewed as embedded in the ego and may be defined as the end product of the integration of the many self-representations (Kernberg 1982). This integrated end product, however, should not be regarded as a continuous, unvarying entity (Bollas 1987; Mitchell 1991; Ogden 1989; Schafer 1989). Although we often wish to maintain an illusion of a continuous self, the reality is that we all are composed of multiple discontinuous selves that are constantly being shaped and defined by real and fantasized relationships with others. Schafer (1989) has understood this phenomenon as a set of narrative selves or story lines that we develop to provide an emotionally coherent account of our lives. Mitchell (1991) has observed that a paradox of psychoanalytic work is that as patients learn to tolerate these multiple facets of themselves, they begin to experience themselves as more durable and more coherent.

Defense Mechanisms

In the preceding section on ego psychology, we considered several neurotic defense mechanisms. In keeping with the historical trend associating object relations theory with more profoundly disturbed patients, in this section we will discuss a number of more primitive defenses characteristic of personality disorders and psychoses: splitting, projective identification, introjection, and denial.

Splitting. This mechanism is an unconscious process that actively separates contradictory feelings, self-representations, or object representations from one another. Although Freud (1927/1961, 1940/1964) made scattered references to splitting, it was Klein (1946/1975) who exalted it to the position of the cornerstone of emotional survival during the first few months of life. Splitting allows the infant to separate good from bad, pleasure from unpleasure, love from hate so as to preserve positively colored experiences, affects, self-representations, and object representations in safely isolated mental compartments, free from contamination by negative counterparts. Splitting may be viewed as a basic biological mode of ordering experience, by which the endangering is separated from the endangered; it is secondarily elaborated into a psychological defense (Ogden 1986). It is also a fundamental cause of ego weakness (Kernberg 1967, 1975). The integration of libidinal and aggressive drive derivatives associated with "good" and "bad" introjects serves to neutralize aggression. Splitting prevents this neutralization and thus deprives the ego of an essential source of energy for growth.

In Kernberg's view, splitting is characterized by certain clinical manifestations: 1) alternating expression of contradictory behaviors and attitudes, which the patient regards with lack of concern and bland denial; 2) selective lack of impulse control; 3) the compartmentalization of everyone in the environment into "all good" and "all bad" camps, which is often referred to as idealization and devaluation; and 4) the coexistence of contradictory self-representations that alternate with one another. Although Kernberg viewed splitting as the key defensive operation in patients with borderline personality disorder, splitting may be observed in all patients at times (Rangell 1982), and it does not clearly differentiate borderline patients from those with other personality disorders (Allen et al. 1988). Kernberg distinguished between neurotic and borderline characters partly on the basis of the latter's preference for splitting over repression, but empirical research suggests that these two defenses operate independently and may coexist in the same individual (Perry and Cooper 1986).

Projective identification. A second defense mechanism, projective identification, is an unconscious three-step process by which aspects of oneself are disavowed and attributed to someone else (see Figures 2–2, 2–3, and 2–4). The three steps (Ogden 1979) are as follows:

1. The patient projects a self- or object representation onto the treater.
2. The treater unconsciously identifies with what is projected and begins to feel or behave like the projected self- or object representation in response to interpersonal pressure exerted by the patient (this aspect of the phenomenon is sometimes referred to as *projective counteridentification* [Grinberg 1979]).
3. The projected material is "psychologically processed" and modified by the treater, who returns it to the patient via reintrojection. The modification of the projected material, in turn, modifies the corresponding self- or object representation and the pattern of interpersonal relatedness.

These three steps are presented in an artificially linear manner for the sake of clarity. However, Ogden (1992) stressed that these aspects are not truly linear, but actually should be conceptualized as creating a dialectic in which the patient and analyst enter into a relationship in which they are simultaneously separate but also "at one" with each other. A unique subjectivity is created through the dialectic of an interpenetration of subjectivities. Nevertheless, transference and countertransference can be correlated with steps 1 and 2, respectively. In this regard, projective identification has an interpersonal dimension in addition to its role as an intrapsychic defense mechanism. Splitting and projective identification are highly interrelated mechanisms that work together to keep "good" and "bad" separated (Grotstein 1981). The interpersonal element inherent in Ogden's definition of projective identification derives from Bion's (1962) conceptualization of the therapist as a container for the projections of the patient, much as the mother contains the projections of her infant.

Contemporary Kleinian analysts in London view projective identification somewhat differently. They are more inclined to conceptualize the defense as involving not the projection of a part of the patient, but rather a fantasy of an object relationship (Feldman 1997). In this regard, the transformation of the target of the projection is not absolutely necessary. Nevertheless, a growing consensus is emerging from the Kleinians that the analyst or therapist is always influenced to some degree by what the patient is projecting and that some degree of responsiveness to "nudges" by the patient to act in accord with the patient's projections may help the analyst become consciously aware of what is being projected (Joseph 1989; Spillius 1992).

Analysts of a more classical orientation (Chused 1991; Jacobs 1986; McLaughlin

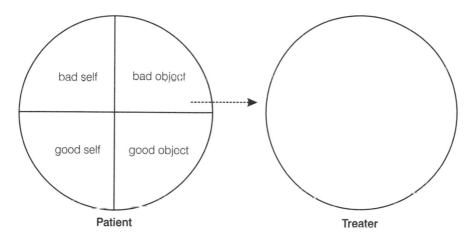

FIGURE 2–2. Projective identification—Step 1. Patient disavows and projects bad internal object onto treater.

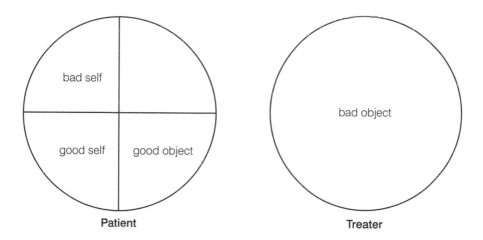

FIGURE 2–3. Projective identification—Step 2. Treater unconsciously begins to feel and/or behave like the projected bad object in response to interpersonal pressure exerted by the patient (projective counteridentification).

1991) have recognized that countertransference *enactments* are inevitable. They have also acknowledged that enactments are often evoked by the patient's efforts to transform the analyst into the transference object or objects. This view is remarkably similar to projective identification. Chused (1991), for example, noted: "En-

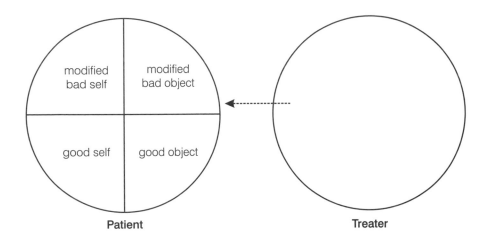

FIGURE 2–4.   Projective identification—Step 3. Treater contains and modifies the projected bad object, which is then reintrojected by the patient and assimilated (introjective identification).

actments occur when an attempt to actualize a transference fantasy elicits a countertransference reaction" (p. 629). Indeed, both Kleinians and ego psychologists are converging around the view that countertransference is a joint creation involving contributions from both patient and clinician (Gabbard 1995). The patient evokes certain responses in the therapist, but it is the therapist's own conflicts and internal self- and object representations that determine the final shape of the countertransference response. In other words, the process requires a "hook" in the recipient of the projection to make it stick. Some projections constitute a better fit with the recipient than do others (Gabbard 1995).

To confine the concept of projective identification to a defense mechanism is unduly limiting. Because of the interpersonal component, it may also be regarded as 1) a means of communication, in which patients coerce the treater into experiencing a set of feelings similar to their own; 2) a mode of object relatedness; and 3) a pathway for psychological change, in the sense that the reintrojection of the projected contents after they have been modified by the treater results in a modification of the patient. Although this model of projective identification emphasizes what takes place in a clinical setting, projective identification regularly occurs in nontherapeutic situations as well. In these nonclinical settings, the projections may be returned in completely distorted forms, or "crammed back down the patient's throat," instead of being modified or contained.

The distinction between projection and projective identification is also somewhat controversial. Grotstein (1981) conceptualized all projection as projective identification because an empathic identification with the projected material is always retained within the projector. The projection outward of something within the self would be meaningless unless the individual maintained some connection with that which is projected, in Grotstein's view. By Ogden's definition, however, all projection is not projective identification. Paranoid individuals may project malevolent intentions onto many figures in their environment with whom they never come in contact. They simply avoid those individuals and keep to themselves. Projection becomes projective identification when the target of a projection begins to be transformed by the projection. When paranoid individuals begin to have direct contact with the objects of their projections and begin to accuse those persons of malevolent motives, the targets of the projections are likely to identify unconsciously with the "bad object" projections and begin to become defensive and angry about the unfair accusations. A third view is suggested by Kernberg (1987b), who disagreed with the traditional view of projection as a primitive mechanism. He saw projection as typical of higher-level neurotic patients. He described it as involving no empathy with the material projected, no evocation in the treater of behavior typical of the projected aspects of the patient, and no process of reintrojection. Projective identification is a more primitive process, in Kernberg's view, because it involves more permeable self-other boundaries in the sense that the material returns to the patient more easily than it does in projection, where the self-other boundary is firm.

Introjection. This third defense is an unconscious process by which an external object is symbolically taken in and assimilated as part of oneself. This mechanism may exist as a part of projective identification, where what is taken in was originally projected, or it may exist independently as the converse of projection. Classically, Freud (1917/1963) formulated depression as a result of the introjection of an ambivalently viewed object. Anger focused on this introject within the depressed patient resulted in self-depreciation and other symptoms of depression. In contemporary object relations parlance, introjection is distinguished from identification as one of the two principal modes of internalization. If a parent, for example, is *introjected,* then the parent is internalized as part of the object subdivision of the ego and is experienced as an internal presence that does not substantially alter the self-representation. On the other hand, in identification, the parent is internalized as part of the self-subdivision of the ego and materially modifies the self-representation (Sandler 1990).

Denial. The fourth defense mechanism, denial, is a direct disavowal of traumatic sensory data. Whereas repression is generally used as a defense against *inter-*

nal wishes or impulses, denial is ordinarily a defense against the external world of reality when that reality is overwhelmingly disturbing. Although associated primarily with psychoses and severe personality disorders, this mechanism may also be used by healthy people, especially in the face of catastrophic events.

Self Psychology

Kohut

While object relations theory emphasizes the *internalized* relationships between *representations* of self and object, self psychology stresses how *external* relationships help maintain self-esteem and self-cohesion. Derived from the seminal writings of Heinz Kohut (1971, 1977, 1984), this theoretical approach views the patient as in desperate need of certain responses from other persons to maintain a sense of well-being.

Self psychology evolved from Kohut's study of narcissistically disturbed outpatients he was treating in psychoanalysis. He noted that they seemed different from the classic neurotic patients who presented for treatment with hysterical or obsessive-compulsive symptoms. Instead, they complained of nondescript feelings of depression or dissatisfaction in relationships (Kohut 1971). They were also characterized by a vulnerable self-esteem that was highly sensitive to slights from friends, family, lovers, colleagues, and others. Kohut observed that the structural model of ego psychology did not seem adequate to explain the pathogenesis and cure of these patients' problems.

Kohut noted that these patients formed two kinds of transferences: the mirror transference and the idealizing transference. In the mirror transference the patient looks to the analyst for a confirming, validating response that Kohut linked to the "gleam in the mother's eye" in response to phase-appropriate displays of exhibitionism on the part of her small child, what Kohut called the *grandiose-exhibitionistic self.* These approving responses, according to Kohut, are essential for normal development in that they provide the child with a sense of self-worth. When a mother fails to empathize with her child's need for such a mirroring response, the child has great difficulty in maintaining a sense of wholeness and self-regard. In response to this failure of empathy, the child's sense of self fragments, and the child desperately attempts to be perfect and to "perform" for the parent to gain the hungered-for approbation. This form of "showing off" is another manifestation of the grandiose-exhibitionistic self (Baker and Baker 1987). The same phenomena constitute the mirror transference in adults who seek treatment. The adult patient who "performs" for his or her therapist in a desperate attempt to gain approval and admiration may be developing a mirror transference.

The idealizing transference, as implied in the name, refers to a situation in which the patient perceives the therapist as an all-powerful parent whose presence soothes and heals. The wish to bask in the reflected glory of the idealized therapist is a manifestation of this transference. Just as the child may be traumatized by the empathic failures of a mother who does not provide mirroring responses to her child's grandiose-exhibitionistic self, so can that same child be traumatized by a mother who does not empathize with the child's need to idealize her or who does not provide a model worthy of idealization.

In either case, the adult patient who suffers from such early disturbances of parenting and who presents these kinds of transference dispositions is struggling with a defective or deficient self—one that is developmentally frozen at a point where it is highly prone to fragmentation. Kohut's view was that the structural model of conflict associated with ego psychology is not sufficient to explain these narcissistic needs for mirroring and idealization. Moreover, he noted a moralizing, pejorative tone in the attitudes of analysts who approached narcissism from a classical point of view. He believed that much harm was done by following Freud's (1914/1963) model, which proposed a transition from a state of primary narcissism to object love as part of the normal maturational process. The offshoot of Freud's thinking was that one should "outgrow" narcissistic strivings and be more concerned about the needs of others.

Kohut thought that this point of view was hypocritical. He asserted that narcissistic needs persist throughout life and that they parallel development in the realm of object love. He postulated a *double-axis* theory (see Figure 2–5) that allowed for ongoing development in *both* narcissistic and object love realms (Ornstein 1974). As infants mature, they attempt to capture the lost perfection of the early maternal-infant bond by resorting to one of two strategies—the grandiose self, where the perfection is captured within, and the idealized parent imago, where it is assigned to the parent. These two poles constitute the *bipolar self.* In his last book (1984, posthumously published), Kohut expanded this conceptualization to a *tripolar* self by adding a third pole of selfobject needs, the twinship or alter ego. This aspect of the self appears in the transference as a need to be just like the therapist. It has its developmental origins in a wish for merger that is gradually transformed into imitative behavior. For example, a young boy might play at lawn mowing while his father cuts the grass. This third pole of the self has limited clinical usefulness compared with the other two and is often excluded from discussions of selfobject transferences. If failures of empathy were typical of the parental responses to these strategies, a developmental arrest occurs. With adequate parenting, on the other hand, the grandiose self is transformed into healthy ambitions, and the idealized parent imago becomes internalized as ideals and values (Kohut 1971). Hence, therapists could empathize with the narcissistic needs of their patients as developmentally normal rather than regarding them with contempt for being self-centered and immature. Whereas classical ego psychological theory conceptualizes the patient as having infantile wishes that need to be renounced, Kohut regarded patients as having *needs* that must be understood and partially met in the treatment (Eagle 1990). Kohut's first book proposed this theoretical formulation as applicable primarily to narcissistic character pathology. By the time his last (1984) book appeared, he had greatly expanded the scope of self psychology:

> Self psychology is now attempting to demonstrate . . . that all forms of psychopathology are based either on defects in the structure of the self, on distortions of the self, or on weakness of the self. It is trying to show, furthermore, that all these flaws in the self are due to disturbances of self-selfobject relationships in childhood. (Kohut 1984, p. 53)

The term *selfobject* came to be a generic term to describe the role that other persons perform for the self in regard to mirroring, idealizing, and twinship needs. From the standpoint of the growth and development of the self, others are not re-

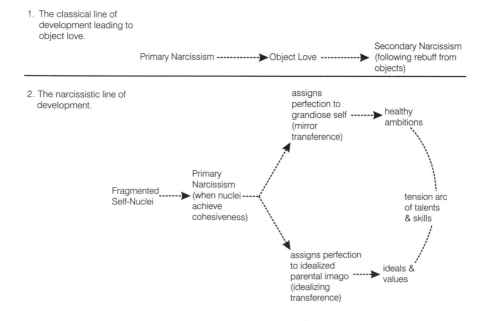

FIGURE 2–5.　Kohut's double-axis theory (1971).

garded as separate persons but as objects to gratify these needs of the self. In a sense, then, selfobjects may be viewed more as functions (e.g., soothing, validating) than as people. The need for selfobjects is never outgrown, according to Kohut, but rather persists throughout life—we need selfobjects in our environment for emotional survival much as we need oxygen in the atmosphere for physical survival (Kohut 1984).

One implication of Kohut's final theoretical statement is that separation is a myth. His view differs dramatically from Mahler's object relations view, which pivots around intrapsychic separation, in that self psychology views the separation of the self from the selfobject as impossible. We all need affirming, empathic responses from others throughout life to maintain our self-esteem. Maturation and growth move away from a need for archaic selfobjects toward an ability to use more mature and appropriate selfobjects. In the clinical setting, the goal of treatment is to strengthen the weakened self so it can tolerate less than optimal selfobject experiences without a significant loss of self-cohesion (Wolf 1988).

Kohut always resisted a simple definition of the self, which he believed was such an overarching structure that it defied crisp definition. However, by the time of his death in 1981, his view of the self had clearly gone from that of a self-representation to that of a "supraordinate self as the primary psychic constellation, the center of experience and initiative and the main motivating agency" (Curtis 1985, p. 343). Further implications include a pervasive deemphasis on the ego and the vicissitudes of drives and defenses, a greater focus on conscious subjective experience, and the conceptualization of aggression as secondary to failures of selfobjects (e.g., narcissistic rage) rather than as a primary or innate drive. Defenses and resistances in this framework, or "defense-resistances," as Kohut (1984) came to refer to them, are viewed entirely differently: "My personal preference is to speak of the 'defensiveness' of patients—and to think of their defensive attitudes as adaptive and psychologically valuable—and not of their 'resistances' " (p. 114). Clearly, they are valuable and adaptive because they preserve the integrity of the self.

In contrast to the ego psychologists, Kohut viewed the Oedipus complex as of secondary importance. The oedipal conflicts involving sexuality and aggression are mere "breakdown products" of developmentally earlier failures in the self-selfobject matrix. If a mother adequately fulfills the selfobject needs of her child, the Oedipus complex can be weathered without the child's becoming symptomatic. The fundamental anxiety, according to self psychology, is "disintegration anxiety," which involves the fear that one's self will fragment in response to inadequate selfobject responses, resulting in an experiencing of a nonhuman state of psychological death (Baker and Baker 1987). From the standpoint of self psychology, most forms of symptomatic behavior (e.g., drug abuse, sexual promiscuity, perversions, self-mutilation, binge eating, and purging) do *not* grow out of neurotic conflict related to castration anxiety. Rather, they reflect "an emergency attempt to maintain and/or restore internal cohesion and harmony to a vulnerable, unhealthy self" (Baker and Baker 1987, p. 5). These fragmentations of the self occur along a continuum that ranges from mild worry or anxiety to severe panic over the perception that one is completely falling apart (Wolf 1988).

The emphasis of self psychology on the failures of parenting figures and the resulting deficiencies of the self resonate with the British object relations theories. Echoes of Winnicott's good-enough mothering and Balint's basic fault can be heard in the themes of self psychological writings. Although Kohut does not acknowledge the contributions of these theorists, their influence is unmistakable. However, the object relations theorists did not develop the notion of the self to the extent that Kohut did, perhaps because of their adherence to a model of maturation that retains the moralizing potential eschewed by Kohut (Bacal 1987). Kohut also has made a significant contribution in recognizing the significance of self-esteem in the pathogenesis of psychiatric disturbances.

Post-Kohut Contributions

After Kohut's death, a new generation of self psychologists elaborated and expanded aspects of his theory. Wolf (1988) identified two other selfobject transferences. The *adversarial selfobject transference* is one in which the patient experiences the analyst as a benignly opposing individual who nevertheless maintains some degree of supportiveness. The analyst is also perceived as encouraging a measure of autonomy for the patient's self by accepting the patient's need to be adversarial. The second selfobject transference observed by Wolf is related to the mirror transference, but because of its relationship to an intrinsic motivation to achieve mastery, it is sufficiently different to warrant a unique title. Known as the *efficacy selfobject transference,* it involves a perception by the patient that the analyst is allowing the patient to effectively produce necessary selfobject behavior in the analyst.

Other analysts influenced by self psychology believe that information outside the empathic-introspective mode of perception must be integrated into the analyst's knowledge base. Lichtenberg (1998; Lichtenberg and Hadley 1989) regards knowledge of "model scenes" prototypical of childhood and infant experiences as highly relevant to reconstructing and understanding the patient's early experience. He argues that five discrete motivational systems must be taken into account to fully understand the forces at work in the patient. Each of these systems is based on innate needs and associated patterns of response. One system develops in response to the need for attachment and affiliation. The second system involves responses to the need for psychic regulation and physiological requirements. The third system evolves in response to the need for assertion and exploration. The fourth system is responsive to the need to react to aversive experiences through withdrawal and/or antagonism. The fifth system involves responses to the need for sensual enjoyment and, ultimately, sexual excitement. These systems are in dialectical tension with one another and undergo continuous hierarchical rearrangement. Each of the five systems can develop only in the presence of a reciprocal response from caregivers. Lichtenberg had reservations about Kohut's theory because of its tendency to relegate sexual and nonsexual pleasure to a relatively peripheral position.

Bacal and Newman (1990) have sought to integrate self psychology with object relations theory. They argue that self psychology can be understood as a variant of object relations theory and that Kohut failed to acknowledge the influence of the British School of object relations on his ideas. Bacal and Newman point out that the self in connection with its object, rather than in isolation, is the true basic unit of self psychology.

Other revisionists have questioned the mode of therapeutic action endorsed by Kohut, which involves optimal frustration of the patient's needs in the context of empathic understanding. Although Kohut repeatedly emphasized that his technique was essentially interpretive, some observers (e.g., Siegel 1996) have stressed that his approach was quite different from the type of frustration proposed by Freud. In his last book, Kohut acknowledged the role of corrective emotional experience. Nevertheless, Bacal (1985) was critical of Kohut's notion of optimal frustration and suggested that "optimal responsiveness" was just as important to the analytic process. Lindon (1994) had similar concerns and proposed the term *optimal provision* to address the problem of too much abstinence on the part of the analyst. However, he did not view this type of provision as curative. Rather, Lindon's conception of provision involved creation of an atmosphere to facilitate exploration of the patient's unconscious, not necessarily to repair developmental defects. He stipulated that provisions should be in the service of furthering analytic work rather than subversions of the analytic process.

Postmodern Views

Freud and the ego psychological version of analysis that derived from Freudian ideas are often regarded by contemporary thinkers as representing *modernity*—that is, a positivist search for an objective truth contained in the patient that is dispassionately observed by the analyst. A variety of contemporary theoretical perspectives in psychoanalysis have challenged this traditional view. Among these views are intersubjectivity, constructivism, relational theory, and interpersonal psychoanalysis, all of which regard absolute objectivity as a myth (Aron 1996; Gill 1994; Greenberg 1991; Hoffman 1992, 1998; Levine 1994; Mitchell 1993, 1997; Natterson 1991; Renik 1993, 1998; Stolorow et al. 1987). A common theme in this literature is that the clinician's perceptions of the patient are inevitably colored by the clinician's subjectivity.

These theoretical departures from classical theory are often described as *postmodern* views. A skepticism about any fundamental truth whatsoever is inherent in postmodern thinking. In this regard, the concept of *essentialism*—that things are as they are, independent of the observer's subjectivity—is often a foil for the postmodernist. Reality itself is viewed as growing out of social and linguistic constructions. Postmodernists frankly doubt that any theories or ideas represent an accurate reflection of an objective reality "out there" (Aron 1996; Holland 1983; Leary 1994).

These postmodern schools are often referred to collectively as "two-person theories" or "two-person psychologies." Although they are often unfairly accused of not endorsing any objective reality at all, they actually approach the clinical situation with a combination of realism and perspectivism that acknowledges the presence of an external reality but emphasizes that each participant in the analytic dyad brings his or her own perspective to bear on that reality (Gabbard 1997).

Among the most influential of these two-person theories is Mitchell's relational-conflict model (1993, 1997). Mitchell views conflicts as relational configurations rather than as tension between intrapsychic agencies, as in the structural model. Conflict is inherent in relationships, and these conflictual relationships are internalized early in life and reexperienced in adulthood. Mitchell frankly acknowledges his debt to theorists from the British School of object relations, such as Fairbairn and Winnicott, and to interpersonalists, such as Sullivan. Like the British Independent Group, most of the postmodern theories have in common the perception that object seeking is more fundamental in the realm of human motivation than the pursuit of instinctual pleasure.

Because the notion of objectivity is challenged by the postmodernists, the term *intersubjectivity* is frequently applied to some of the theories subsumed by postmodernism. This trend has created confusion in the literature, because the core meaning of intersubjectivity—namely, that the two persons in the room mutually influence one another—is not confined to any particular theoretical perspective in psychoanalysis (Aron 1996; Dunn 1995; Gabbard 1997; Levine 1996). Natterson (1991) has argued for a radical intersubjectivity characterized by a coequal and mutual role of analyst and analysand in the analytic process. Aron (1996), on the other hand, differentiates mutuality and symmetry. In this view, although both members of the dyad are experiencing strong feelings toward one another, offering unique and valid perspectives on the interaction, and mutually influencing one another, the relationship is asymmetrical in that one pays the other a fee for a service, one has a set of ethical standards to which he or she adheres, and the primary focus is on understanding the *patient's* experience in the service of improving the patient's life.

Benjamin (1990) regards intersubjectivity as a developmental achievement involving a full recognition of the other party's separateness and autonomy. A goal of analysis is for the patient to learn to treat the analyst and others as separate subjects rather than as objects to be used by the patient for the gratification of the patient's needs. Benjamin states it succinctly: "Where objects were, subjects must be" (1990, p. 34). Another version of intersubjectivity proposed by Stolorow and Atwood (1992) does not require such recognition of separateness. The mere presence of the two members of the analytic dyad in the same consulting room constitutes an intersubjective situation. Stolorow and Atwood regard the isolated mind as a myth. Influenced by Kohut and self psychology, they have endorsed an interactional contextualism that Kohut wished to eschew. The notion of the intersubjective field differs from the concept of the self-selfobject relationship (Stolorow 1995). In Stolorow and Atwood's view, the patient turns to the analyst for selfobject experiences, as Kohut describes, but the analyst also turns to the patient for such experiences, so that the intersubjective field is a system of reciprocal mutual influence (Beebe and Lachmann 1988).

Renik (1993, 1998), in his version of intersubjectivity, stresses the irreducible and unavoidable subjectivity of the analyst in analytic listening and in formulating all interventions. The analyst can never transcend his or her unconscious personal motivations in attempting to understand or help the patient.

Rather than emphasizing the shift from the drive model to the relational model, constructivism (Gill 1994; Hoffman 1983, 1991) focuses on the replacement of the positivist orientation with a constructivist view in which the analyst's personal involvement is seen as having a continuous effect on what the analyst understands about the patient and the interaction. This paradigm also radically alters basic transference theory in the analytic situation. In other words, as noted in Chapter 1, transference is not simply the repetition of an intrapsychic stereotyped template based on past relationships. It is also influenced by the *real behavior* of the analyst. Rather than regarding transference as purely distortion, Hoffman considers it to be a plausible construct, with the implication that the patient may accurately recognize unconscious aspects of the analyst's behavior. Finally, meanings within the dyad are also jointly constructed through active negotiation and dialogue about the two distinct perspectives. While this variant of postmodern thinking was originally known as social constructivism, Hoffman (1998) later referred to it as the *dialectical-constructivist* view, reflecting a dialectical mode of therapeutic action that oscillates between following a set of prescribed conventions of psychoanalytic technique and "throwing away the book" in spontaneous enactments.

Developmental Considerations

To some extent, all psychoanalytic theories are based on developmental thinking. Just as psychoanalytic theory has evolved from an emphasis on drives, defenses, and intrapsychic conflict between agencies into concerns with self, object, and relationships, so has developmental research moved in that direction. The early theories of development associated with ego psychology focused on libidinal zones and were largely reconstructions of early development based on psychoanalytic work with adults. Erikson (1959), following the lead of Hartmann, made an effort to weave interagency conflict into the broader fabric of ego psychology. He focused on psychosocial issues from the environment, which allowed him to evolve an epigenetic developmental scheme characterized by a psychosocial crisis at each phase. For example, during the oral phase of development, the infant must struggle with basic trust versus basic mistrust. The crisis of the anal phase involves autonomy versus shame and doubt. During the phallic-oedipal phase, the child grapples with initiative versus guilt.

The oedipal phase of development begins around age 3 years and is associated with a more intense focus on the genitals as the source of pleasure. Accompanying this interest is an intensified longing to be the exclusive love object of the parent of the opposite sex. However, at the same time, the child's dyadic or mother-child frame of reference changes to a triadic one, with the child becoming aware of a rival for the affections of the parent of the opposite sex.

In the case of the male child, the first love object is the mother, which does not require a shift of affection. He desires to sleep with her, caress her, and be the center of her world. Since the father interferes with these plans, the child develops murderous wishes toward his rival. These wishes result in guilt, fear of retaliation by the father, and a sense of anxiety about that impending retaliation. Freud repeatedly observed that the leading source of the male child's anxiety during this phase of development is that the father's retaliation will come in the form of castration. To avoid this punishment, the boy renounces his sexual strivings for his mother and identifies with his father. This identification with the aggressor carries with it the decision to look for a woman *like* the mother so that the boy can be *like* his father. As part of this oedipal resolution, the retaliatory father is internalized around the end of the fifth or sixth year, forming the superego, which Freud viewed as heir to the Oedipus complex. Contemporary thinking about the oedipal phase of development has clarified that there is also a libidinal longing for the *same*-sex parent associated with a wish to be rid of the *opposite*-sex parent. This view is often referred to as the *negative Oedipus complex.*

Freud had more difficulty explaining the little girl's oedipal development. In a series of papers (1925/1961, 1931/1961, 1933/1964), he frankly acknowledged his bewilderment by female psychology, yet struggled to chart female development. One way he dealt with this difficulty was to assume that females' development was basically analogous to that of males. As Freud saw it, whereas in boys the Oedipus complex is resolved by the castration complex, in girls it is *promulgated* by an awareness of "castration." In the preoedipal phases of development, in Freud's view, the little girl feels essentially like a little boy until she discovers the existence of the penis. At that point, she begins to feel inferior and falls victim to penis envy. She tends to blame her mother for her inferiority, so she turns to her father as her love object, and the wish for a child from her father replaces her wish for a penis. Freud believed that one of three paths was available to the female child after discovery of her "genital inferiority": 1) cessation of all sexuality, that is, neurosis; 2) a defiant hypermasculinity; or 3) definitive femininity, which entailed renunciation of clitoral sexuality. In the normal oedipal resolution, loss of the mother's love, rather than fear of castration by the father, was postulated as the key factor.

More contemporary psychoanalytic authors have raised serious questions about Freud's formulation of female development. Stoller (1976) disagreed with Freud about the evolution of femininity as a product of sexual differentiation, penis envy, and unconscious conflict. He felt that femininity was an inborn potential and that a confluence of sex assignment at birth, parental attitudes, neurophysiological fetal brain organization, early interactions between the infant and the parents, and learning from the environment formed a complex nucleus around which a mature sense of femininity would ultimately become organized. He termed this first step *primary femininity* because it was not viewed as a product of conflict. Tyson (1996) has stressed that mature femininity begins with primary femininity but that conflict resolution, as well as identifications made with both parents, will ultimately determine the final form.

Stoller shared the view of other authors, such as Lerner (1980) and Torok (1970), that penis envy is only one aspect of the development of femaleness, not the origin of it. Contemporary feminist psychoanalytic theory has stressed the adverse therapeutic implications of viewing penis envy as a "bedrock" phenomenon (Freud 1937/1964) that defies further analysis and understanding. One hazard of the "bedrock" view is that it may lead to a misguided attempt on the part of therapists to help female patients accept a view of themselves as an inferior form of male. Frenkel (1996) has stressed that female patients do not generally feel that their genitalia or genital arousal are inadequate, in contrast to Freud's thinking, and that the clitoris, far from being viewed as an inferior organ, is a locus for the initiation of intense pleasure and occasional orgasm as early as ages 4–6 years. Vaginal awareness also is present at that age. Current thinking about the construction of gender emphasizes the influence of culture, object relations, and identifications with parents rather than narrowly tying it to anatomic differences (Benjamin 1990; Chodorow 1996).

Development does not cease with the resolution of the Oedipus complex. Defensive constellations change with each succeeding phase—latency, adolescence, young adulthood, and old age. In fact, Vaillant (1976) has documented an orderly shift during adult life from immature defenses to more mature defenses such as altruism and sublimation, suggesting that personality is truly dynamic and malleable over the entire life cycle.

Mahler

Over the last 25 years, a much more empirically based developmental theory has emerged in psychoanalysis. The infant observation studies of Margaret Mahler and her colleagues (1975) were among the earliest such studies and are often viewed as providing a bridge between ego psychology and object relations theory. Through observation of normal and abnormal mother-infant pairs, Mahler et al. were able to identify three broad phases of the development of object relations.

In the first 2 months of life, an *autistic* phase occurs in which the infant appears self-absorbed and concerned with survival rather than relatedness. The period between 2 and 6 months, denoted as *symbiosis,* begins with the smile response of the infant and the visual ability to follow the mother's face. Although the infant is vaguely aware of the mother as a separate object, the infant's primary experience of the mother-infant dyad is one of a dual unity rather than of two separate people.

The third phase, *separation-individuation,* is characterized by four subphases. Between 6 and 10 months, in the first subphase of *differentiation,* the child becomes aware that the mother is a separate person. This awareness may lead to the child's need for a transitional object (Winnicott 1953/1971), such as a blanket or pacifier, to help deal with the fact that the mother is not always available. *Practicing* is the next subphase; it occurs between 10 and 16 months. With the newfound locomotor skills of this age, toddlers love to explore the world on their own, although they frequently return to their mothers for "refueling." The third subphase, *rapprochement,* is characterized by a sharper awareness of the separateness of the mother and occurs between 16 and 24 months of age. This awareness brings with it a heightened sense of vulnerability to separations from the mother.

The fourth and final subphase of separation-individuation is marked by the consolidation of individuality and the beginnings of object constancy. The achievement of this period, which roughly corresponds to the third year of life, is the integration of split views of the mother into a unified whole object that can be internalized as an emotionally soothing inner presence that sustains the child during the mother's absence. This achievement corresponds with Klein's depressive position and sets the stage for the child to enter the oedipal phase.

Stern

As noted earlier, however, Kohut's perspective challenged Mahler's emphasis on separation-individuation by suggesting that some form of selfobject response from others in the environment was essential throughout life. In addition, the infant observation research of Daniel Stern (1985, 1989) called into question the idea that infants emerge from the womb in a state of autistic self-absorption. Stern's work demonstrated that the infant seems to be aware of the mother or caretaker from the first days of life. In keeping with Kohut's ideas, Stern observed that affirming and validating responses from the mothering figure are crucial to the developing infant's evolving sense of self. He stressed that the infant develops a sense of self-with-other in response to the caretaker's attunement. Stern differed with Klein in that he regarded fantasy as having only minimal significance. By contrast, he viewed the infant as primarily experiencing reality. He concluded that infants are adept observers of reality and that it is only as older toddlers that they begin to make significant use of fantasy and distortion in an effort to alter their perceptions.

Stern described five discrete senses of self. Rather than viewing these as phases that are superseded by subsequent and more mature developmental periods, he regarded them as different domains of self-experience (emergent or "body" self, core self, subjective self, verbal or categorical self, and narrative self), each of which remains for the entire life span and operates in concert with the other coexisting senses of self. From birth to 2 months of age, an emergent self appears that is predominantly a physiologically based body self. From 2 to 6 months, a core sense of self emerges that is linked with greater interpersonal relatedness. A sense of subjective self appears between 7 and 9 months and is a major event because it involves the matching of intrapsychic states between infant and mother. Between 15 and 18 months of age, coinciding with the ability to think symbolically and to communicate verbally, the verbal or categorical sense of self emerges. The narrative sense of self arrives between 3 and 5 years of age. This historical view of self is what Stern believed is encountered when patients tell their life stories in the analytic setting.

Stern delineated four essential features of a sense of self: coherence, affectivity, agency, and continuity (or historicity). He believed that attachment, trust, and security are not phase specific but continue to be vital issues throughout the entire life span. One of Stern's central tenets is that the infant develops as a result of sensitive affective attunement by the mother or caretaker. Kohut and subsequent self psychologists have argued that a similar form of empathic resonance is necessary in the analytic situation to strengthen the patient's self.

The concept that development proceeds in a self-other format has been extensively validated in further developmental research (Beebe et al. 1997; Fogel 1992). In accord with Kohut's and Winnicott's theoretical views, what is emerging is a dyadic systems view of communication between mother and infant that results in the internalization of a self-in-relation-to-object. In other words, as Fairbairn stressed, it is not an object but an object *relationship* that is internalized in development. What is represented by the infant is an interactive process, complete with a patterned sequence of movements, the rules for regulating these movements, and the self-regulatory consequences to the infant (Beebe et al. 1997). In keeping with postmodernist views, developmental research is suggesting that all face-to-face interaction is jointly constructed or bidirectionally regulated (Fogel 1992).

Attachment Theory

The significance of early parenting is further supported by the empirical research associated with attachment theory. Although John Bowlby's seminal works on the subject (1969, 1973, 1980) have been around for a long time, only recently has attachment theory enjoyed a wide psychoanalytic audience. Attachment is a biologically based bond between the child and the caregiver that is designed to ensure the safety and survival of the child. In this model, the child seeks proximity to the caregiver to elicit a helpful and soothing response. Internal working models of relationships are developed and stored as mental schemas based on integration of past experiences regarding expectations of the behavior of others toward the self.

Attachment strategies, which are largely independent of genetic influences, are adopted in infancy and remain relatively stable. Ainsworth et al. (1978) studied these strategies in a laboratory scenario known as the Strange Situation. This situation, involving a toddler's separation from the caregiver, tended to elicit one of four behavioral strategies. Secure infants simply sought proximity with the caregiver upon her return and then felt comforted and returned to play. Avoidant behavior was seen in infants who appeared less anxious during the separation and snubbed the caregiver on her return. These infants showed no preference for the mother or caregiver over a stranger. In a third category, termed *anxious-ambivalent* or *resistant,* infants showed great distress at separation and manifested angry, tense, and clinging behavior when the caregiver returned. A fourth group, termed *disorganized-disoriented,* had no coherent strategy whatsoever to deal with the experience of separation. There is growing evidence that these attachment patterns have continuity into adulthood, and these categories of attachment style can be measured with sophisticated interviews (George et al. 1996). The four responses to the Strange Situation correspond respectively to adult categories of attachment as follows: 1) secure/autonomous individuals who value attachment relationships; 2) insecure/dismissing individuals who deny, denigrate, devalue, or idealize past and current attachments; 3) preoccupied individuals who are confused or overwhelmed by both past and current attachment relationships; and 4) unresolved or disorganized individuals who often have suffered neglect or trauma.

All of these attachment categories are supported by empirical research, and there are also data indicating that expectant parents' mental models of attachment predict subsequent patterns of attachment between infant and mother and between infant and father. The caregiver's capacity to observe the infant's intentional state and internal world appears to influence the development of secure attachment in the child. A key concept in attachment theory is *mentalization,* which refers to the capacity to understand that one's own and others' thinking is representational in nature and that one's own and others' behavior is motivated by internal states, such as thoughts and feelings (Fonagy 1998). Parents or caregivers who themselves have the capacity to mentalize tune in to the infant's subjective mental state, and the infant ultimately finds itself in the caregiver's mind and internalizes the caregiver's representation to form a core psychological self. In this manner, the child's secure attachment to the caregiver engenders the child's capacity to mentalize. In other words, through the interaction with the caregiver, the child learns that behavior can best be understood by assuming that ideas and feelings determine a person's actions.

The Role of Theory in Clinical Practice

Faced with a bewildering array of psychoanalytic theories, one may choose to deny the value of theory altogether. Who needs it? Why not just begin de novo with each patient and stick to the clinical material? To advocate this approach is simply to advocate the formation of new theories. As Kernberg (1987a) noted, "All observations of clinical phenomena depend upon theories, and when we think that we are forgetting about theory, it only means that we have a theory of which we are not aware" (pp. 181–182).

A more sensible solution is to become familiar with the phenomena described by all the major theories and to focus on each perspective as it is clinically appropriate with a given patient. Psychoanalysis and psychodynamic psychiatry are tragically beset with needless polarities—is it oedipal or preoedipal, conflict or deficit, classical theory or self psychology, tension reduction or object seeking? Such questions tend to be cast in terms of right or wrong. But is it possible that all models are valid in certain clinical situations? Is it not possible for both oedipal and preoedipal, conflict and deficit, to be relevant in the understanding of an individual patient? Of course it is. Wallerstein (1983) made this point eloquently in a critique of self psychology:

> For in the flow and flux of analytic clinical material we are always in the world of "both/and." We deal constantly, and in turn, both with the oedipal, where there is a coherent self, and the preoedipal, where there may not yet be; with defensive regressions and with developmental arrests; with defensive transferences and defensive resistances and with re-creations of earlier traumatic and traumatized states. (p. 31)

Wallerstein reminds us of the fundamental psychoanalytic principles of overdetermination and multiple function.

Some aspects of all four theoretical perspectives examined in this chapter will most likely prove useful in the treatment of the majority of patients. From a developmental perspective, certain aspects of early childhood experience are better explained by one theory than another, and with certain patients, the emphasis will be more in one direction than another, depending on the clinical data (Pine 1988). In most patients, however, we will find both deficit and conflict. As Eagle (1984) noted in his appraisal of the role of theory in psychoanalysis: "We are most conflicted in the areas in which we are deprived. . . . It is precisely the person deprived of love who is most conflicted about giving and receiving love" (p. 130). In practice, clinicians find themselves serving both as selfobjects and as real, separate objects for their patients.

For some clinicians, however, shifting from one theoretical perspective to another, depending on the patient's needs, is too cumbersome and unwieldy. Wallerstein (1988) has pointed out that it is possible for clinicians to pay attention to the *clinical phenomena* described by each theoretical perspective without embracing the entire metapsychological model. For example, one can address self- and object representations, mirror and idealizing transferences, and impulse-defense configurations as they appear in the clinical setting without having to resort to invoking the entire theoretical edifice on which such observations are based. Others advocate greater theoretical flexibility (Gabbard 1996; Pine 1990; Pulver 1992), suggesting that different patients and different types of psychopathology require different theoretical approaches.

Each of these approaches to the theoretical pluralism of modern dynamic psychiatry is workable for some clinicians. Regardless of which approach is found more suitable, all clinicians should be wary of rigidly imposing theory onto clinical material. The patient must be allowed to lead the clinician into whatever theoretical realm is the best match for the clinical material. Although familiarity with all three theoretical models of dynamic psychiatry requires greater breadth of knowledge, it allows for a richer understanding of patients and their psychopathology. Finding the theoretical framework that best fits a particular patient entails a good deal of exploratory trial and error, but as we stumble through the cave, we may eventually find the path and may be far better off than other travelers with a map of an altogether different cave.

References

Ainsworth MS, Blehar MC, Waters E, et al: Patterns of Attachment: A Psychological Study of the Strange Situation. Hillsdale, NJ, Lawrence Erlbaum, 1978

Allen JG, Deering CD, Buskirk JR, et al: Assessment of therapeutic alliances in the psychiatric hospital milieu. Psychiatry 51:291–299, 1988

Aron L: A Meeting of Minds: Mutuality and Psychoanalysis. Hillsdale, NJ, Analytic Press, 1996

Bacal HA: Optimal responsiveness and the therapeutic process, in Progress in Self Psychology, Vol 1. Edited by Goldberg A. New York, Guilford, 1985, pp 202–227

Bacal HA: British object-relations theorists and self psychology: some critical reflections. Int J Psychoanal 68:81–98, 1987

Bacal HA, Newman KM: Theories of Object Relations: Bridges to Self Psychology. New York, Columbia University Press, 1990

Baker HS, Baker MN: Heinz Kohut's self psychology: an overview. Am J Psychiatry 144:1–9, 1987

Balint M: The Basic Fault. Therapeutic Aspects of Regression. New York, Brunner/Mazel, 1979

Beebe B, Lachmann F: The contribution of mother-infant mutual influence to the origins of self- and object representations. Psychoanalytic Psychology 5:305–337, 1988

Beebe B, Lachmann F, Jaffe J: Mother-infant interaction structures and presymbolic self- and object representations. Psychoanalytic Dialogues 7:133–182, 1997

Bellak L, Hurvich M, Gedimen HK: Ego Functions in Schizophrenics, Neurotics, and Normals: A Systematic Study of Conceptual, Diagnostic, and Therapeutic Aspects. New York, Wiley, 1973

Benjamin J: An outline of intersubjectivity: the development of recognition. Psychoanalytic Psychology 7 (suppl):33–46, 1990

Bion WR: Learning From Experience. New York, Basic Books, 1962

Blum HP: On the conception and development of the transference neurosis. J Am Psychoanal Assoc 19:41–53, 1971

Bollas C: The Shadow of the Object: Psychoanalysis of the Unthought Known. New York, Columbia University Press, 1987

Bollas C: Forces of Destiny: Psychoanalysis and Human Idiom. Northvale, NJ, Jason Aronson, 1989

Bowlby J: Attachment and Loss, Vol 1: Attachment. London, Hogarth Press and the Institute of Psycho-Analysis, 1969

Bowlby J: Attachment and Loss, Vol 2: Separation: Anxiety and Anger. London, Hogarth Press and the Institute of Psycho-Analysis, 1973

Bowlby J: Attachment and Loss, Vol 3: Loss: Sadness and Depression. London, Hogarth Press and the Institute of Psycho-Analysis, 1980

Brenner C: The Mind in Conflict. New York, International Universities Press, 1982

Chodorow NJ: Theoretical gender and clinical gender: epistemological reflections on the psychology of women. J Am Psychoanal Assoc 44 (suppl):215–238, 1996

Chused JF: The evocative power of enactments. J Am Psychoanal Assoc 39:615–639, 1991

Curtis HC: Clinical perspectives on self psychology. Psychoanal Q 54:339–378, 1985

Dunn J: Intersubjectivity in psychoanalysis: a critical review. Int J Psychoanal 76:723–738, 1995

Eagle MN: Recent Developments in Psychoanalysis: A Critical Evaluation. New York, McGraw-Hill, 1984

Eagle M: The concepts of need and wish in self psychology. Psychoanalytic Psychology 7 (suppl):71–88, 1990

Erikson EH: Identity and the life cycle: selected papers. Psychol Issues 1:1–171, 1959

Fairbairn WRD: Schizoid factors in the personality (1940), in Psychoanalytic Studies of the Personality. London, Routledge & Kegan Paul, 1952, pp 3–27

Fairbairn WRD: Endopsychic structure considered in terms of object-relationships (1944), in Psychoanalytic Studies of the Personality. London, Routledge & Kegan Paul, 1952, pp 82–136

Fairbairn WRD: Psychoanalytic Studies of the Personality. London, Routledge & Kegan Paul, 1952

Fairbairn WRD: Synopsis of an object-relations theory of the personality. Int J Psychoanal 44:224–225, 1963

Feldman M: Projective identification: the analyst's involvement. Int J Psychoanal 78: 227–241, 1997

Fogel A: Movement and communication in human infancy: the social dynamics of development. Human Movement Science 11:387–423, 1992

Fonagy P: An attachment theory approach to treatment of the difficult patient. Bull Menninger Clin 62:147–169, 1998

Frenkel RS: A reconsideration of object choice in women: phallus or fallacy. J Am Psychoanal Assoc 44 (suppl):133–156, 1996

Freud A: The ego and the mechanisms of defense (1936), in The Writings of Anna Freud, Vol 2 (Revised Edition). New York, International Universities Press, 1966

Freud S: Three essays on the theory of sexuality (1905), in The Standard Edition of the Complete Psychological Works of Sigmund Freud, Vol 7. Translated and edited by Strachey J. London, Hogarth Press, 1953, pp 123–245

Freud S: On narcissism: an introduction (1914), in The Standard Edition of the Complete Psychological Works of Sigmund Freud, Vol 14. Translated and edited by Strachey J. London, Hogarth Press, 1963, pp 67–102

Freud S: Mourning and melancholia (1917), in The Standard Edition of the Complete Psychological Works of Sigmund Freud, Vol 14. Translated and edited by Strachey J. London, Hogarth Press, 1963, pp 237–260

Freud S: The ego and the id (1923), in The Standard Edition of the Complete Psychological Works of Sigmund Freud, Vol 19. Translated and edited by Strachey J. London, Hogarth Press, 1961, pp 1–66

Freud S: Some psychical consequences of the anatomical distinction between the sexes (1925), in The Standard Edition of the Complete Psychological Works of Sigmund Freud, Vol 19. Translated and edited by Strachey J. London, Hogarth Press, 1961, pp 241–258

Freud S: Inhibitions, symptoms and anxiety (1926), in The Standard Edition of the Complete Psychological Works of Sigmund Freud, Vol 20. Translated and edited by Strachey J. London, Hogarth Press, 1959, pp 75–175

Freud S: Fetishism (1927), in The Standard Edition of the Complete Psychological Works of Sigmund Freud, Vol 21. Translated and edited by Strachey J. London, Hogarth Press, 1961, pp 147–157

Freud S: Female sexuality (1931), in The Standard Edition of the Complete Psychological Works of Sigmund Freud, Vol 21. Translated and edited by Strachey J. London, Hogarth Press, 1961, pp 223–243

Freud S: Femininity (1933), in The Standard Edition of the Complete Psychological Works of Sigmund Freud, Vol 22. Translated and edited by Strachey J. London, Hogarth Press, 1964, pp 112–135

Freud S: Analysis terminable and interminable (1937), in The Standard Edition of the Complete Psychological Works of Sigmund Freud, Vol 23. Translated and edited by Strachey J. London, Hogarth Press, 1964, pp 209–253

Freud S: Splitting of the ego in the process of defence (1940), in The Standard Edition of the Complete Psychological Works of Sigmund Freud, Vol 23. Translated and edited by Strachey J. London, Hogarth Press, 1964, pp 271–278

Gabbard GO: Countertransference: the emerging common ground. Int J Psychoanal 76:475–485, 1995

Gabbard GO: Love and Hate in the Analytic Setting. New York, Jason Aronson, 1996

Gabbard GO: A reconsideration of objectivity in the analyst. Int J Psychoanal 78:15–26, 1997

George C, Kaplan N, Main M: The Adult Attachment Interview. Department of Psychology, University of California–Berkeley, 1996

Gill MM: Psychoanalysis in Transition: A Personal View. Hillsdale, NJ, Analytic Press, 1994

Greenberg J: Oedipus and Beyond: A Clinical Theory. Cambridge, MA, Harvard University Press, 1991

Greenberg J, Mitchell SA: Object Relations in Psychoanalytic Theory. Cambridge, MA, Harvard University Press, 1983

Grinberg L: Countertransference and projective counteridentification, in Countertransference. Edited by Epstein L, Feiner A. New York, Jason Aronson, 1979, pp 169–191

Grotstein JS: Splitting and Projective Identification. New York, Jason Aronson, 1981

Guntrip H: Schizoid Phenomena, Object-Relations, and the Self. New York, International Universities Press, 1968

Guntrip H: Psychoanalytic Theory, Therapy, and the Self. New York, Basic Books, 1971

Hartmann H: Ego Psychology and the Problem of Adaptation (1939). Translated by Rapaport D. New York, International Universities Press, 1958

Hartmann H: Comments on the psychoanalytic theory of the ego (1950), in Essays on Ego Psychology: Selected Problems in Psychoanalytic Theory. New York, International Universities Press, 1964, pp 113–141

Hoffman IZ: The patient as interpreter of the analyst's experience. Contemporary Psychoanalysis 19:389–422, 1983

Hoffman IZ: Discussion: toward a social-constructivist view of the psychoanalytic situation. Psychoanalytic Dialogues 1:74–105, 1991

Hoffman IZ: Some practical implications of a social constructivist view of the psychoanalytic situation. Psychoanalytic Dialogues 2:287–304, 1992

Hoffman IZ: Ritual and Spontaneity in the Psychoanalytic Process: A Dialectical-Constructivist View. Hillsdale, NJ, Analytic Press, 1998

Holland NN: Post-modern psychoanalysis, in Innovation/Renovation: New Perspectives on the Humanities. Edited by Hassan I, Hassan S. Madison, WI, University of Wisconsin Press, 1983, pp 291–309

Jacobs TJ: On countertransference enactments. J Am Psychoanal Assoc 34:289–307, 1986

Jacobson E: The Self and the Object World. New York, International Universities Press, 1964

Joseph B: Psychic Equilibrium and Psychic Change: Selected Papers of Betty Joseph. Edited by Feldman M, Spillius EB. London, Routledge, 1989

Kernberg OF: Borderline personality organization. J Am Psychoanal Assoc 15:641–685, 1967

Kernberg OF: Borderline Conditions and Pathological Narcissism. New York, Jason Aronson, 1975

Kernberg OF: Self, ego, affects, and drives. J Am Psychoanal Assoc 30:893–917, 1982

Kernberg OF: Object relations theory and character analysis. J Am Psychoanal Assoc 31 (suppl):247–272, 1983

Kernberg OF: Concluding discussion, in Projection, Identification, Projective Identification. Edited by Sandler J. Madison, CT, International Universities Press, 1987a, pp 179–196

Kernberg OF: Projection and projective identification: developmental and clinical aspects, in Projection, Identification, Projective Identification. Edited by Sandler J. Madison, CT, International Universities Press, 1987b, pp 93–115

King P, Steiner R: The Freud-Klein Controversies 1941–45. London, Routledge, 1992

Klein M: Notes on some schizoid mechanisms (1946), in Envy and Gratitude and Other Works, 1946–1963. New York, Free Press, 1975, pp 1–24

Kohon G: The British School of Psychoanalysis: The Independent Tradition. New Haven, CT, Yale University Press, 1986

Kohut H: The Analysis of the Self: A Systematic Approach to the Psychoanalytic Treatment of Narcissistic Personality Disorders. New York, International Universities Press, 1971

Kohut H: The Restoration of the Self. New York, International Universities Press, 1977

Kohut H: How Does Analysis Cure? Edited by Goldberg A. Chicago, IL, University of Chicago Press, 1984

Leary K: Psychoanalytic "problems" and postmodern "solutions." Psychoanal Q 63:433–465, 1994

Lerner HE: Penis envy: alternatives in conceptualization. Bull Menninger Clin 44:39–48, 1980

Levine HB: The analyst's participation in the analytic process. Int J Psychoanal 75:665–676, 1994

Levine HB: The analyst's infatuation: reflections on an instance of countertransference love. Paper presented at the annual meeting of the American Psychoanalytic Association, New York, NY, December 1996

Lichtenberg JD: Experience as a guide to psychoanalytic theory and practice. J Am Psychoanal Assoc 46:17–36, 1998

Lichtenberg JD, Hadley JL: Psychoanalysis and Motivation. Hillsdale, NJ, Analytic Press, 1989

Lindon JA: Gratification and provision in psychoanalysis: Should we get rid of the "rule of abstinence?" Psychoanalytic Dialogues 4:549–582, 1994

Mahler MS, Pine F, Bergman A: The Psychological Birth of the Human Infant: Symbiosis and Individuation. New York, Basic Books, 1975

McLaughlin JT: Clinical and theoretical aspects of enactment. J Am Psychoanal Assoc 39:595–614, 1991

Meissner WW: Internalization in Psychoanalysis. New York, International Universities Press, 1981

Meissner WW: Can psychoanalysis find its self? J Am Psychoanal Assoc 34:379–400, 1986

Mitchell SA: Contemporary perspectives on self: toward an integration. Psychoanalytic Dialogues 1:121–147, 1991

Mitchell SA: Hope and Dread in Psychoanalysis. New York, Basic Books, 1993

Mitchell SA: Influence and Autonomy in Psychoanalysis. Hillsdale, NJ, Analytic Press, 1997

Natterson JM: Beyond Countertransference: The Therapist's Subjectivity in the Therapeutic Process. Northvale, NJ, Jason Aronson, 1991

Ogden TH: On projective identification. Int J Psychoanal 60:357–373, 1979

Ogden TH: The concept of internal object relations. Int J Psychoanal 64:227–241, 1983

Ogden TH: The Matrix of the Mind: Object Relations and the Psychoanalytic Dialogue. Northvale, NJ, Jason Aronson, 1986

Ogden TH: The Primitive Edge of Experience. Northvale, NJ, Jason Aronson, 1989

Ogden TH: The dialectically constituted/decentred subject of psychoanalysis, II: the contributions of Klein and Winnicott. Int J Psychoanal 73:613–626, 1992

Ornstein PH: On narcissism: beyond the introduction, highlights of Heinz Kohut's contributions to the psychoanalytic treatment of narcissistic personality disorders. Annual of Psychoanalysis 2:127–149, 1974

Perry JC, Cooper SH: A preliminary report on defenses and conflicts associated with borderline personality disorder. J Am Psychoanal Assoc 34:863–893, 1986

Pine F: The four psychologies of psychoanalysis and their place in clinical work. J Am Psychoanal Assoc 36:571–596, 1988

Pine F: Drive, Ego, Object, and Self: A Synthesis for Clinical Work. New York, Basic Books, 1990

Pulver SE: Psychic change: insight or relationship? Int J Psychoanal 73:199–208, 1992

Rangell L: The self in psychoanalytic theory. J Am Psychoanal Assoc 30:863–891, 1982

Rapaport D: Organization and Pathology of Thought: Selected Sources. New York, Columbia University Press, 1951

Renik O: Analytic interaction: conceptualizing technique in light of the analyst's irreducible subjectivity. Psychoanal Q 62:553–571, 1993

Renik O: The analyst's subjectivity and the analyst's objectivity. Int J Psychoanal 79:487–497, 1998

Rinsley DB: An object relations view of borderline personality, in Borderline Personality Disorders. Edited by Hartocollis P. New York, International Universities Press, 1977, pp 47–70

Sandler J: On internal object relations. J Am Psychoanal Assoc 38:859–880, 1990

Sandler J, Rosenblatt B: The concept of the representational world. Psychoanal Study Child 17:128–145, 1962

Schafer R: Aspects of Internalization. New York, International Universities Press, 1968

Schafer R: A New Language for Psychoanalysis. New Haven, CT, Yale University Press, 1976

Schafer R: Narratives of the self, in Psychoanalysis: Toward the Second Century. Edited by Cooper AM, Kernberg OF, Person ES. New Haven, CT, Yale University Press, 1989, pp 153–167

Segal H: An Introduction to the Work of Melanie Klein. New York, Basic Books, 1964

Siegel A: Heinz Kohut and the Psychology of Self. London, Routledge, 1996

Spillius EB: Clinical experiences of projective identification, in Clinical Lectures on Klein and Bion. Edited by Anderson R. London, Tavistock/Routledge, 1992, pp 59–73

Stern DN: The Interpersonal World of the Infant: A View from Psychoanalysis and Developmental Psychology. New York, Basic Books, 1985

Stern DN: Developmental prerequisites for the sense of a narrated self, in Psychoanalysis: Toward the Second Century. Edited by Cooper AM, Kernberg OF, Person ES. New Haven, CT, Yale University Press, 1989, pp 168–178

Stoller RJ: Primary femininity. J Am Psychoanal Assoc 24 (suppl):59–78, 1976

Stolorow RD: An intersubjective view of self psychology. Psychoanalytic Dialogues 5:393–399, 1995

Stolorow RD, Atwood GE: Contexts of Being: The Intersubjective Foundations of Psychological Life. Hillsdale, NJ, Analytic Press, 1992

Stolorow RD, Brandchaft B, Atwood GE: Psychoanalytic Treatment: An Intersubjective Approach. Hillsdale, NJ, Analytic Press, 1987

Stone L: The psychoanalytic situation and transference. J Am Psychoanal Assoc 15:3–58, 1967

Summers FL: Transcending the Self: An Object Relations Model of Psychoanalytic Therapy. Hillsdale, NJ, Analytic Press, 1999

Sutherland JD: The British object relations theorists: Balint, Winnicott, Fairbairn, Guntrip. J Am Psychoanal Assoc 28:829 860, 1980

Sutherland JD: The self and object relations: a challenge to psychoanalysis. Bull Menninger Clin 47:525–541, 1983

Torok M: The significance of penis envy in women, in Female Sexuality: New Psychoanalytic Views. Edited by Chasseguet-Smirgel J. Ann Arbor, MI, University of Michigan Press, 1970, pp 135–170

Tuckett D: Editorial introduction to "My Experience of Analysis With Fairbairn and Winnicott" by Guntrip H. Int J Psychoanal 77:739–740, 1996

Tyson P: Female psychology: an introduction. J Am Psychoanal Assoc 44 (suppl):11–20, 1996

Vaillant GE: Natural history of male psychological health, V: the relation of choice of ego mechanisms of defense to adult adjustment. Arch Gen Psychiatry 33:535–545, 1976

Vaillant GE: Adaptation to Life. Boston, MA, Little, Brown, 1977

Wallerstein RS: Self psychology and "classical" psychoanalytic psychology: the nature of their relationship (1983), in The Future of Psychoanalysis: Essays in Honor of Heinz Kohut. Edited by Goldberg A. New York, International Universities Press, 1983, pp 19–63

Wallerstein RS: One psychoanalysis or many? Int J Psychoanal 69:5–21, 1988

Winnicott DW: Transitional objects and transitional phenomena: a study of the first not-me possession (1953), in Playing and Reality. New York, Basic Books, 1971, pp 1–25

Winnicott DW: The Maturational Processes and the Facilitating Environment: Studies in the Theory of Emotional Development. London, Hogarth Press, 1965

Wolf E: Treating the Self: Elements of Clinical Self Psychology. New York, Guilford, 1988

CHAPTER
3

Psychodynamic Assessment
of the Patient

Whenever two people meet there are really six people present. There is each man as he sees himself, each man as the other person sees him, and each man as he really is.

William James

The psychodynamic assessment of a patient does not stand apart from the thorough evaluation of history, signs, and symptoms growing out of the medical-psychiatric tradition. Dynamic psychiatrists value such information as a crucial component of the diagnostic assessment. However, their approach to gathering that information differs from the purely descriptive approach to diagnosis. Moreover, other information is of interest to the dynamic psychiatrist, so the psychodynamic assessment may be viewed as a significant extension of the descriptive medical-psychiatric evaluation.

The Clinical Interview

Any description of the psychodynamic approach to clinical interviewing must begin with the fundamental importance of the doctor-patient relationship. When psychiatrist and patient meet for the first time, two strangers are coming into contact, each with a variety of expectations concerning the other. Establishing rapport and a shared understanding must always be the first agenda in a psychodynamic interview (MacKinnon and Michels 1971; Menninger et al. 1962; Thomä and Kächele 1987). The first task of the interviewer, then, is to convey that the patient is accepted, valued, and validated as a unique person with unique problems.

Interviewers who attempt to immerse themselves empathically in their patients' experience will promote a bond between them based on the interviewer's obvious attempt to understand the patient's point of view. Such an approach does not require reassuring comments such as, "Don't worry, everything will be all right." Rather than allaying the patient's anxiety, these hollow reassurances are usually doomed to failure because they resemble similar past comments of friends and family members. They will only lead the patient to believe that the interviewer does not appreciate true suffering. Interviewers may instead build better rapport with comments such as, "I can understand how you feel, considering what you've been through." Challenging a patient's statements early in the interview will simply confirm any preexisting fears that psychiatrists are judgmental parental figures.

Differences Between Psychodynamic and Medical Interviewing

In medical interviewing, physicians pursue a direct course from the chief complaint to its etiology and pathogenesis. Patients generally cooperate with this process because they are eager to eliminate the pain or symptoms associated with their illness. Psychiatrists who attempt to steer a similarly linear course in the clinical interview will encounter potholes and detours at every turn. Moreover, psychiatrists often find that patients rarely are capable of coming quickly to the point because of their inability to pinpoint what is really bothering them (Menninger et al. 1962). They may also be highly ambivalent about giving up their symptoms because psychiatric illness is somehow always a workable adaptation. Finally, psychiatric patients are often embarrassed about their symptoms and may conceal information to make a good impression (MacKinnon and Michels 1971).

Another major difference between medical history taking and psychodynamic interviewing is the interrelationship of diagnosis and treatment. A physician evaluating a patient for appendicitis approaches the interview with a clear mind-set—diagnosis precedes treatment. In the psychodynamic interview, however, any distinction between diagnosis and treatment would be artificial (MacKinnon and Michels 1971). The dynamic psychiatrist approaches the interview with the understanding that the manner in which the history is taken may in and of itself be therapeutic. The dynamic view, which intimately links diagnosis and treatment, is empathic in the sense that it takes into account the patient's perspective. As Menninger et al. (1962) noted: "The patient comes to be *treated* and everything that is done for him, so far as he is concerned, is treatment, whatever the doctor may call it. In a sense, therefore, treatment always *precedes* diagnosis" (p. 3).

A third distinction between medical and psychodynamic interviewing lies in the dimensions of activity and passivity. To a large extent patients are passive participants in the medical diagnostic process. The patient complies with the physician's evaluation by cooperatively answering questions. The physician, however, must fit together the pieces of the diagnostic puzzle to arrive at a definitive diagnosis. The dynamic psychiatrist tries to avoid this division of roles. Instead, the dynamic approach involves actively engaging the patient as a *collaborator* in an exploratory process (Shevrin and Shectman 1973). The patient is viewed as someone with a great deal to contribute to the ultimate diagnostic understanding. If a patient begins an interview with anxiety, the psychiatrist does not try to eliminate it to facilitate the interview. On the contrary, the psychiatrist might attempt to engage the patient in a collaborative search for the origins of the anxiety with such questions as: "What concerns about this interview might cause you to be anxious right now?"; "Does this situation remind you of any similar anxiety-provoking situations in the past?"; or "Have you heard anything about me or about psychiatrists in general that might contribute to your anxiety?"

In a productive dynamic interview, the psychiatrist will elicit information regarding symptoms and history that allows for a descriptive diagnosis. To promote more openness on the part of the patient, however, psychiatrists must guard against an overemphasis on diagnostic labeling that precludes the unfolding of the complex relationship between doctor and patient. MacKinnon and Michels (1971) warned that "the interview that is oriented only toward establishing a diagnosis gives the patient the feeling that he is a specimen of pathology being examined, and therefore actually inhibits him from revealing his problems" (pp. 6–7).

A fourth difference between the medical and the dynamic orientation in clinical interviewing revolves around the selection of relevant data. Reiser (1988) expressed alarm at the tendency of contemporary psychiatric residents to stop the data collection after eliciting a symptom inventory that satisfies a descriptive diagnostic category and that allows for pharmacotherapeutic prescription. He warned that a DSM diagnosis is only one aspect of the diagnostic process and that the residents' lack of interest in understanding the patient as a person forms an obstacle to establishing a therapeutic relationship. For dynamic psychiatrists, the intrapsychic life of the patient is a crucial part of the data pool.

Another unique aspect of the psychodynamic interview is the emphasis on the doctor's feelings during the process. The surgeon or internist who notes feelings of anger, envy, lust, sadness, hatred, or admiration views these feelings as annoyances that interfere with evaluating the illness. The typical physician suppresses these feelings in the service of maintaining objectivity and proceeding with the examination. For the dynamic psychiatrist, such feelings constitute crucial diagnostic information. They tell the clinician something about what reactions the patient elicits in others. These considerations lead us directly to two of the most important aspects of the psychodynamic assessment—transference and countertransference.

Transference and Countertransference

Given the fact that transference is active in every significant relationship, you can be certain that transference elements exist from the first encounter between doctor and patient. Indeed, transference may even develop before the initial contact (Thomä and Kächele 1987). After making the first appointment, the soon-to-be patient may begin attributing qualities to the psychiatrist based on bits of factual information, previous experiences with psychiatrists, media portrayals of psychiatrists, positive or negative experiences with other physicians in the past, or general attitudes toward authority figures. One young man who first met his psychiatrist in the waiting room exclaimed, "Why, you're not at all like I expected you to be!" When the psychiatrist asked the patient to elaborate, the young man explained that the psychiatrist's name evoked images of a distinguished elderly man, and he was shocked at the youth of the actual psychiatrist.

Transference is a critical dimension of the evaluation because it profoundly affects the patient's cooperation with the doctor. Patients who view doctors as stern, disapproving parents, for example, will be much less forthcoming with embarrassing aspects of their history. Likewise, patients who view psychiatrists as intrusive busybodies may stubbornly withhold information and refuse to cooperate in the interview. Psychiatrists who address the transference distortions early in the interview may remove obstacles to effective history taking.

During the first few minutes of a consultation with a psychiatrist, one patient was struggling to overcome his inhibitions about talking. The psychiatrist asked if any of his actions or comments made it difficult for the patient to talk. The patient confided that he had harbored the notion that psychiatrists were like mind readers and that he needed to be wary of what he did or said in their presence. The psychiatrist replied humorously, "I'm afraid we're not that good." Both laughed, and the patient found it much easier to open up during the rest of the interview.

By definition, transference is a repetition. The feelings associated with a figure from the past are being repeated with the psychiatrist in the present situation. This premise implies that transference patterns in a clinical interview provide glimpses of significant relationships from the patient's past. The patient's view of the examiner and the patient's feelings toward the examiner are somehow repetitions. Furthermore, these repetitions also reveal a good deal about the patient's current significant relationships. Since transference is ubiquitous, the same patterns from the past are repeated again and again in all the patient's relationships. For example, a woman patient came to a psychiatrist, complaining that men seemed uninterested in her. In response to her psychiatrist's inquiries, she was able to link this feeling of being neglected with her childhood perception that her father ignored her. When the psychiatrist looked at his clock late in the interview, she accused him of not paying attention to her—just like all other men.

To keep from labeling all the patient's reactions to the doctor as transference, psychiatrists must keep in mind that the patient-doctor relationship is always a mixture of transference and a real relationship. The psychiatrist who glanced at his clock provided a kernel of reality to the patient's transference fear that yet another man was losing interest in her. Psychodynamic assessment requires continuous self-monitoring throughout the diagnostic process. The psychiatrist accused of being inattentive must question whether he really is feeling boredom (and conveying it to the patient) or whether the patient is distorting the situation. If boredom is the problem, then the psychiatrist needs to determine whether his interest is waning because of interference from his own issues, or because the patient is doing something to evoke inattentiveness, or both.

These considerations are, of course, countertransference concerns. The conceptual framework of the dynamic interview is that it involves two persons (dare I say two patients?). Each brings a personal past into the present and projects aspects of internal self- and object representations onto the other (Langs 1976). It is commonplace for dynamic psychiatrists to find themselves relating to a patient as though the patient were someone else. The psychiatrist might note a striking physical resemblance between a patient and someone from the past. As a result, the psychiatrist then attributes qualities of the past figure to the patient.

An ongoing task for dynamic psychiatrists is to monitor their own countertransference enactments and feelings as they emerge in the interview with the patient. How much of the countertransference is the clinician's own contribution? How much is *induced* by the patient's behavior toward the clinician? As I noted in Chapter 2, ordinarily countertransference is a joint creation that involves contributions from both members of the dyad. Making the distinction between the induced variety of countertransference and that brought to the situation by the clinician's own unconscious conflicts is often a challenging task. Because the ability to make this distinction depends greatly on familiarity with one's own internal world, most dynamic psychiatrists find a personal treatment experience (either psychoanalysis or psychotherapy) of enormous value in monitoring and understanding countertransference.

Familiarity with one's own typical responses is helpful in sorting out the relative contributions. One child psychiatrist, for example, observed that she could tell when she was dealing with a victim of child abuse because she would develop an irrational feeling of anger, accompanied by an impulse to abuse the child. In other words, an internal abusing object in the child was projected onto the psychiatrist, who in turn became provoked by the child's obnoxious and provocative behavior to the point where she identified with what had been projected onto her. Awareness of those feelings helped her to understand the nature of the patient's internal object world and the typical problems in the patient's interpersonal relationships.

Approaches to History Taking

The history-taking aspect of the interview should involve two simultaneous goals: a descriptive diagnosis and a dynamic diagnosis. To accomplish these goals, the psychiatrist must maintain a flexible interviewing style that shifts from a structured pursuit of specific facts (e.g., about symptoms, family history, stressors, duration of illness) to an unstructured posture of listening to the natural ebb and flow of the patient's thought processes. Throughout both structured and unstructured portions of the history taking, the examiner makes a fine-tuned assessment of the patient-doctor interaction. Kernberg (1984) characterized one form of the dynamic interview—the structural interview—as a systematic movement from a symptom inventory to an active focus on defensive operations in the here-and-now relationship with the interviewer.

Initially the interviewer must simply create an atmosphere in which the patient feels free to talk. Beginning psychiatric residents commonly err in aggressively interrogating patients only to elicit history and symptoms. Another common error is the assumption of a pseudoanalytic attitude of abstinence, virtual silence, and passivity. Residents who may be warm and personable individuals suddenly become stiff, overly formal, and cold when they interview a patient. The interviewer will get much further by becoming an active participant in the relationship—by warmly and empathically seeking to understand the patient's point of view. This posture, while dynamically informed, departs from the classical view of the analyst as a nongratifying, neutral observer (Viederman 1984). A dynamic interview is not a psychoanalytic therapy session.

The psychiatrist can learn a great deal by allowing the patient to ramble freely for a while. Initial comments should be designed to facilitate this rambling (e.g., "tell me more," "please go on," "I can understand your feeling that way," or "that must have been upsetting"). Besides eliciting essential historical and mental status data, interviewers can discern patterns of association that may reveal significant unconscious connections. The order in which events, memories, concerns, and other psychological issues are verbalized is seldom random. Mathematicians have long known that it is impossible for any individual to generate prolonged sequences of random numbers. Within a short time, the numbers will fall into meaningful patterns. The mind prefers order to chaos. So it is with the verbalizations of the patient. Deutsch and Murphy (1955) based their approach to interviewing—known as "associative anamnesis"—on this principle:

> The method . . . consists in recording not only what the patient said, but also how he gave the information. It is of consequence not only that the patient tells his complaints, but also in what phase of the interview, and in which connection he introduces his ideas, complaints, and recollections of his somatic and emotional disturbances. (p. 19)

Although patients may be consciously baffled by their symptoms, the ordering of their associations may provide clues to unconscious connections. For example, a 31-year-old man who came with his parents for a psychiatric evaluation began the morning with a psychiatrist while his parents met privately with a social worker in a different building. The young man began by explaining that he had been unable to keep a job. He suddenly became overwhelmed with anxiety because he was uncertain of his parents' whereabouts. The psychiatrist clarified that they were with the social worker in the office building next door. The patient asked if he could use the psychiatrist's phone to call them. The psychiatrist silently noted that the patient's anxiety about his parents' location followed immediately on the heels of his complaint of not being able to hold a job. He asked the patient if the two concerns were connected. After a moment's reflection, the patient acknowledged that when he was away from his parents at work, he worried that something would happen to them. This interchange led to a productive discussion about the patient's concerns that his growing up and becoming independent would be destructive to his parents.

Because of the central role of developmental theory in dynamic psychiatry, a developmental history must be part of a thorough dynamic assessment. Was the patient a product of an unwanted pregnancy? Did the patient's birth occur after an older sibling had died? Did the patient achieve developmental milestones such as talking, walking, and sitting up at the appropriate ages? Were there traumatic separations or losses during the formative years? Obtaining such invaluable information often necessitates interviews of parents and other family members—either by the psychiatrist or by a social worker associated with the psychiatrist. Obviously, patients will be unable to recall some significant events of childhood and will distort others.

Despite their imperfect memories for historical events, patients should nevertheless be engaged in a review of childhood and adolescent development. A fundamental principle of the dynamic interview is that the past is repeating itself in the present. To enlist the patient as a collaborator in the diagnostic process, the interviewer can encourage the patient's curiosity about links between historical events and present-day feelings. A variety of open-ended questions serve to establish this collaborative partnership: "Does the anxiety you're experiencing today remind you of feelings you've had at any time in your past?" "Were there any events in your childhood that may have contributed to your feeling as an adult that women cannot be trusted?" "Do your current marital problems have any similarities with problems you've had in other relationships in the past?" As the patient begins to collaborate in the search for links between past and present, the examiner should note particular historical events and periods that seem important to the patient. Similarly, conspicuous omissions from the developmental history are also noteworthy. Does the patient, for example, focus exclusively on one parent as the cause of all current problems while omitting any reference to the other parent? What about the patient's cultural and religious background? How do these factors affect family relationships and the acceptability of emotional problems?

After several minutes of open-ended questions designed to facilitate a free-flowing history of the present illness and family and developmental issues, the psychiatrist can then fill in the gaps with more specific, direct questions. These may be geared to the descriptive diagnosis (e.g., specific symptoms necessary for the DSM-IV [American Psychiatric Association 1994] diagnosis, information about the duration of the illness, exclusions of other illnesses) or may be directed toward a more complete dynamic diagnosis (e.g., specific developmental traumas, relationship patterns, or recurrent fantasies and daydreams). As the patient fills in the gaps, the dynamic psychiatrist can begin to formulate hypotheses that link the patient's past relationships with current relationships and with emerging transference paradigms (Menninger 1958). In other words, how are repetitions of past relationship patterns creating problems in the present?

Axis IV of DSM-IV mandates that stressors be considered during the diagnostic appraisal of the patient. Events that precipitate an episode of illness are vital to both the descriptive and the dynamic diagnosis. However, careful history taking is essential when evaluating Axis IV because patients may distort their memory of a stressor's timing in an effort to retrospectively explain their illness or problems as directly attributable to an external event (Andrews and Tennant 1978). Also, dynamic psychiatrists must always be attentive to the idiosyncratic meanings given to stressful life events by patients. A seemingly minor stressor may have extraordinary significance to a particular patient, causing a major impact on the patient's capacity to function.

Patients can nevertheless provide important dynamic information about their perception of the connections between events and symptoms. Again the examiner should think in terms of how issues from the past are evoked by stressors in the present. One female executive developed extraordinary anxiety after receiving a promotion. She identified the promotion as the stressor, but could not determine why it provoked anxiety, because she had sought the new job for several years. In the course of the interview, she frequently referred to her younger sister, who was divorced and supporting two children through a menial job. Further exploration of intense sibling rivalry that had existed between the sisters during childhood revealed that the executive's anxiety was related to guilt feelings. She was convinced that her promotion had been destructive to her sister. These feelings resonated with her childhood wish to triumph over her sister and be the only child in the eyes of their parents.

Holmes and Rahe (1967) developed a scale that ranks the severity of stress in a number of different life events. Although such scales can help provide consensual estimates of the effects that accompany particular life events, the dynamic psychiatrist must approach each patient as a unique individual and not assume a priori that a certain life event has only one specific meaning. For example, one young man reacted to his father's death with a liberated sense that he was finally free to pursue his career without incessant criticism. Hence, the stressor resulted in improved school performance and enhanced overall functioning.

In addition, the examiner should keep in mind that some stressors may operate at an unconscious level, preventing the patient from identifying any precipitating event when asked to do so. One function of the interview may be to work together to determine whether any stressors have been overlooked. Anniversary reactions, for example, are common stressors the patient may neglect. One chronically depressed patient became acutely suicidal on the anniversary of her brother's suicide. In another instance, when a happily married physician began having marital problems for no apparent reason, he called on a psychiatric colleague for advice. During the course of their phone conversation, the doctor suddenly realized that he was calling on the tenth anniversary of his divorce from his previous wife. This insight revealed that his current anger at his present wife was partially linked to his stormy relationship with his first wife.

The Mental Status Examination

Like descriptive psychiatrists, dynamic psychiatrists are interested in mental status data, but they approach the information somewhat differently. First, to the extent that it is reasonable and possible, they prefer to weave mental status questions into the fabric of the interview rather than to add them at the end in a list of formal mental status questions (MacKinnon and Michels 1971). Although some specific mental status questions should obviously be appended to the interview if they are not elicited during it, there is an advantage in minimizing the formal mental status examination. When these questions are brought into the body of the interview, the patient views distortions of perception, thought, and affect in a meaningful context. Moreover, in determining connections between such distortions and the illness, the patient becomes more involved as a collaborator rather than as merely a passive responder to questions.

Orientation and perception.   A patient's orientation to time, place, and person is often clear in the course of history taking. To ask specific orientation questions of someone who is obviously well oriented is likely to disturb the rapport of the doctor-patient relationship. Hyperalertness is a mental status finding that will also reveal itself without direct questioning. Significant perceptual symptoms such as auditory or visual hallucinations will often be evident at the beginning of the interview when the patient is asked to explain why psychiatric treatment is being sought. But the dynamic psychiatrist is interested in more than the presence or absence of hallucinations. If a patient hears voices, the psychiatrist wants to know what the voices say, under what circumstances they speak, whose voices they sound like, and what the voices mean to the patient. One male paranoid schizophrenic patient always heard his father telling him that he would never amount to anything. His hallucinations correlated with his childhood experiences of never being able to do enough to please his father.

Cognition.   The presence of a formal thought disorder will usually be clear from the history-taking portion of the interview. As alluded to earlier, even loose associations are connected idiosyncratically in the patient's mind. The examiner's task is to understand the nature of such connections. Delusions are also more likely to be elicited by open-ended historical questions than by specific questions about "false beliefs." The presence or absence of delusions is only part of the psychodynamic assessment; their meanings and functions are equally relevant. The grandiose delusions of the paranoid patient may serve to compensate for devastating feelings of low self-esteem.

Because cognition affects language and communication, the psychiatrist must also listen for parapraxes, or slips of the tongue, that reveal glimpses of the unconscious at work. A pregnant woman whose obstetrician referred her for a psychiatric consultation was resentful about seeing a psychiatrist, and at one point she exclaimed, "I don't want to be a psychiatric parent—I mean patient!" The examining psychiatrist could conclude from this parapraxis that the patient was highly ambivalent about becoming a mother.

The patient's manner of answering questions may reveal a good deal about his or her unconscious character style. The obsessive-compulsive patient may respond to questions with an overinclusive attention to detail, frequently asking the examiner to elaborate on specifically requested information. By contrast, the hysterical patient may be so completely uninterested in detail as to provide vague responses that frustrate the interviewer. The passive-aggressive patient may produce anger in the interviewer by asking for questions to be repeated and by generally thwarting attempts to elicit historical data. The paranoid patient may constantly read hidden meanings into the questions, thus placing the examiner on the defensive.

Determining the presence or absence of suicidal ideation is essential to any psychiatric evaluation. Suicidal patients should be asked outright if they have a suicide plan and if they have a support system of people they can talk to before acting impulsively. The psychodynamic assessment should discern the meaning of the contemplated suicide. Is there a reunion fantasy with a deceased loved one? Is suicide a vengeful act designed to devastate someone else just as that person once devastated the patient? Is suicide really designed to kill an internal object representation that is hated and feared? Of the many possible solutions to a patient's problems, why is suicide so compelling?

Affect. Observations about the patient's emotional states provide a gold mine of information about defense mechanisms. After all, the management of affect is one of the most important functions of defenses. Patients who describe extraordinarily painful events in their lives without being moved in the least may be employing isolation of affect. Hypomanic patients who assert that they always are in a good mood and are unusually jocular with the examiner may be using denial to defend against feelings such as grief and anger. Borderline patients who express contempt and hostility toward the key figures in their lives may be employing splitting to ward off any integration of good and bad feelings toward others. Mood, a subcategory of affect involving a sustained, internal feeling tone, should also be assessed. Exploration of moods with a patient often reveals that they are linked with significant self- and object representations.

Action. A wealth of information is communicated through nonverbal behavior in the clinical interview. What particularly sensitive subjects result in the patient's fidgeting? What topics evoke silence? What issues cause the patient to break off eye contact with the examiner? Despite the fact that patients attempt to conceal essential data from the examining psychiatrist, their nonverbal behaviors will consistently betray them. Freud made the following observation in 1905:

> When I set myself the task of bringing to light what human beings keep hidden within them, not by the compelling power of hypnosis, but by observing what they say and what they show, I thought the task was a harder one than it really is. He that has eyes to see and ears to hear may convince himself that no mortal can keep a secret. If his lips are silent, he chatters with his finger-tips; betrayal oozes out of him at every pore. And thus the task of making conscious the most hidden recesses of the mind is one which it is quite possible to accomplish. (Freud 1905/1953, pp. 77–78)

As Freud implied, one of the "royal roads" to the observation of the unconscious is nonverbal behavior. Early attachment relationships are internalized and encoded as implicit memory (Amini et al. 1996; Gabbard 1997). What unfolds in the relationship to the therapist is the patient's habitual mode of object relatedness shaped by those early attachment relationships, and much of that mode of relatedness is nonverbal. Patients who, for example, are shy about making eye contact, deferential in their manner, restrictive in their uses of gesture, and hesitant in their speech patterns are telling the clinician a great deal about their unconscious, internalized object relations and the way they relate to others outside of the clinical interview.

Psychological Testing

Projective psychological tests, principally the Rorschach and the Thematic Apperception Test (TAT), may be extraordinarily useful adjuncts to the psychodynamic assessment. The Rorschach consists of 10 symmetrical inkblots that present ambiguous stimuli to the patient. In the face of this ambiguity, patients will reveal a great deal about themselves through their interpretations of the amorphous shapes within the inkblots. Highly sophisticated guides to Rorschach interpretations have systematized the responses according to a psychodynamic diagnostic understanding of the patient (Kwawer et al. 1980; Rapaport et al. 1968; Schafer 1954).

The TAT operates on a similar principle. A series of drawings or woodcuts, portraying persons and situations of varying degrees of ambiguity, allow patients a good deal of latitude in interpretation. Patients are asked to invent a story to describe each picture. In making up these stories, patients project their own fantasies, wishes, and conflicts onto the pictures. Projective testing is especially useful for patients who are guarded and laconic in the psychiatric interview and therefore do not share their inner life freely with the psychiatrist. Many patients, however, will reveal so much about themselves in the course of the clinical interview that psychological testing is not necessary as an adjunct.

The Physical and Neurological Examination

For obvious reasons, the patient's physical and neurological status is as important to the dynamic psychiatrist as it is to the descriptive psychiatrist. "The head bone is connected to the neck bone," so whatever goes wrong in the body will affect the brain—and vice versa. If the assessment is taking place in a hospital setting, dynamic psychiatrists may or may not perform their own physical and neurological examinations. If the assessment is of an outpatient in a private office, most dynamic psychiatrists prefer that an internist do the physical. Regardless of who does it, exploring the meaning of the physical is usually beneficial—both in terms of transference issues and in terms of patients' fantasies about their body. In any case, neither a descriptive nor a dynamic assessment can be complete without these data.

The Psychodynamic Diagnosis

At the completion of the psychodynamic assessment, the clinician should arrive at a descriptive diagnosis (based on DSM-IV criteria) and a psychodynamic diagnosis (based on an understanding of the patient and the illness). Although both diagnoses inform the treatment planning, the descriptive diagnosis is geared to the assignment of the correct label, while the psychodynamic diagnosis is viewed as a summary of understanding that goes beyond the label. Menninger et al. (1963) elegantly described the dynamic approach to diagnosis:

> This means diagnosis in a new sense, not the mere application of a label. It is not a search for a proper name by which one can refer to this affliction in this and other patients. It is diagnosis in the sense of understanding just how the patient is ill and how ill the patient is, how he became ill and how his illness serves him. From this knowledge one may draw logical conclusions regarding how changes might be brought about in or around the patient which would affect his illness. (pp. 6–7)

The descriptive diagnosis may assist clinicians in planning appropriate pharmacological interventions. The dynamic diagnosis may facilitate the clinician's understanding of what the medication prescription means to the patient and whether compliance with the medication is likely to be a problem.

In this context, I want to emphasize that the usefulness of a dynamic diagnosis is not limited to patients whose prescribed treatment is dynamic psychotherapy. The therapeutic management of the patient's personality is an integral part of all psychiatric treatment that must always be considered in treatment planning (Perry et al. 1987).

Part of the dynamic diagnosis involves understanding how the five axes of DSM-IV interact with and influence one another. Because all illness grows out of a preexisting personality, consideration must be given to how the personality diagnosis on Axis II contributes to the Axis I syndrome. Obsessive-compulsive individuals, for example, often decompensate into a major depressive episode. Clinicians might therefore evaluate how the rigid and demanding superego of the obsessive-compulsive personality structure contributed to the self-loathing characteristic of the depression. This aspect of the diagnosis would not replace the contributions of biochemical and genetic factors to the depression but rather would work synergistically to provide a more complete understanding of the patient and the illness. Similarly, an Axis III diagnosis of carcinoma of the pancreas might contribute to an Axis I major depressive episode on a biological basis, but the patient's psychological reaction to the diagnosis of a malignancy might be another determinant of the depression. The patient who is diagnosed with narcissistic personality disorder on Axis II and panic disorder on Axis I might be unwilling to take medication for the panic disorder because the notion of having a major psychiatric disorder is too narcissistically injurious to tolerate.

As previously described in this chapter, Axis IV stressors, both obvious, conscious precipitants and hidden, unconscious ones, must also be evaluated in the dynamic diagnosis. Finally, it is helpful to assess how all the findings on the other four axes affect the Axis V level of functioning. Does the Axis I diagnosis account for the severity of the patient's functional impairment, or do characterological features on Axis II contribute to a lower level of functioning than is warranted by the Axis I diagnosis? A complete psychodynamic diagnosis also involves assessing the patient from one or more of the four major theoretical perspectives discussed in Chapter 2: ego psychology, object relations theory, self psychology, and postmodern views.

Characteristics of the Ego

A great deal can be learned about patients' overall ego strength from their work histories and their relationship patterns. Those who have been able to hold jobs and establish committed relationships for reasonably long periods are likely to have more resilient egos than those who have not.

The assessment of certain key ego functions (Bellak et al. 1973) can help psychiatrists understand a patient's strengths and weaknesses and thus enable them to prescribe the treatment program. How is the patient's reality testing? Is there an ability to distinguish what is internal from what is external, or is there a persistent pattern of delusional misperception? Is the patient's reality testing intact in structured situations but impaired in unstructured situations? What about the patient's impulse control? Is there sufficient ego to delay the discharge of impulses, or is the patient virtually driven by impulses to the point where there is danger to others or self? Judgment is another ego function that must be assessed. Can the patient adequately anticipate the consequences of actions?

In planning for the appropriate form of psychotherapy, psychiatrists should also determine the psychological mindedness of the patient. Does the patient see problems as having an internal origin, or are all difficulties externalized and blamed on others in the environment? Can the patient synthesize and integrate various bits of data and reflect on their connections to develop meaningful explanations for symptoms and interpersonal difficulties? Does the patient think in metaphors and analogies that allow for connections between various levels of abstraction? All these considerations aid in assessing the extent of psychological mindedness.

A major portion of ego assessment focuses on the defensive functioning of the ego. In the psychoanalytic setting, Waelder (1960) developed a series of questions that addresses the defensive operations of the patient. These same questions could be adapted to the dynamic assessment: "*What are the patient's desires?* What does the patient (unconsciously) want? And *of what is he afraid? . . . And when he is afraid, what does he do?*" (pp. 182–183). Pine (1990) added additional questions to assess the relationship between drives and the ego's responses to the drives:

> What wish is being expressed? what is the relation of the wish to consciousness? what is the fantasy? and how does it reflect a compromise among wish and defense and reality? how was the wish being defended against? and how effective/adaptive is the defense? can the particular anxiety seen be traced to this or that wish, ineffectively defended against? and can the particular guilt seen be understood in terms of the operation of conscience in relation to this or that wish? (pp. 44–45)

Pine also suggested that one should assess character in a similar manner by looking at the patient's characteristic defensive styles that are expressed as ego-syntonic modes of function. One can also assess the defense mechanisms on the continuum of immaturity to maturity described in Chapter 2. The patient who is able to use suppression and humor in the midst of a difficult situation is showing much greater ego strength than the patient who resorts to splitting and projective identification in the same situation.

Determining the ego's relationship to the superego is another vital part of an ego psychological assessment. Is the superego a rigid and ruthless overseer of the ego, or is there a flexibility and harmony in the relationship of superego to ego? Does the patient espouse realistic ideals, or is the patient driven by unreachable and fantastic goals? Are there antisocial tendencies in the patient characterized by an absent or underdeveloped superego? The answers to these questions also provide clues about the patient's childhood experiences with parental figures, since the superego is an internalized representation of those figures.

Object Relations

As an end result of the psychodynamic assessment, the clinician has information about the patient's interpersonal relationships in three contexts: childhood relationships, the real and transferential aspects of the relationship between the patient and the examining clinician, and current relationships outside the doctor-patient relationship. The nature of these relationships provides the psychiatrist with a good deal of information about the patient's position in family and social systems. Still needed, though, is an assessment of how the patient's family relationships influence the development of the clinical picture that brings the patient to the psychiatrist. Does an adolescent patient's symptomatic picture reflect the parents' marital problems? In other words, is the patient serving as a "carrier" of illness for the entire family?

Information about the patient's interpersonal relationships also tells a great deal about the nature of the patient's internal object relations. Interviews of family members and significant others can help sort out the extent of distortion inherent in the patient's view of other relationships. Certain easily discernible patterns seem to cut across all relationships. For example, does the patient always seem to end up as a masochistic partner in a sadomasochistic bond? Is the patient always taking care of others who are less functional and more in need of caretaking? Pine (1990) developed a series of questions specifically targeted at object relations that can be mulled over by the clinician during the course of an interview:

> What old object relationship is being repeated? and which of the roles in the object relationship is the subject (the patient) enacting—his own or that of the other? or both? Is the patient behaving like the person he was? he wished to be in the parents' eyes? they wanted him to be? they were? he wished they were? And what early passive experiences are being repeated actively? (p. 47)

Determining the level of maturity of object relations is an integral part of this assessment. Does the patient experience others ambivalently as whole objects having both good and bad qualities? Alternatively, does the patient view others as either idealized (all good) or devalued (all bad)? Does the patient see others as need-gratifying part-objects who serve only one function for the patient rather than as separate persons with needs and concerns of their own? Finally, what about object constancy? Can the patient tolerate being apart from significant others by summoning up a soothing internal image of the person who is missed?

The Self

A thorough dynamic assessment must evaluate several aspects of the patient's self. In the broad framework of self psychology, psychiatrists should examine the durability and cohesiveness of the self. Is it prone to fragmentation in response to the smallest slight from a friend or colleague? Does the patient need to be in the spotlight continually to receive affirming responses from selfobjects?

The maturity of the patient's selfobjects should also be assessed. Are the patient's selfobject needs satisfied by a mutually gratifying relationship in the context of a long-term commitment?

In addition to self-esteem, the psychiatrist should also assess the patient's self-continuity. Is the patient much the same over time, regardless of external circumstances, or is there a generalized identity diffusion? As Horowitz (1997) has stressed, without a sense of self-coherence and continuity, an individual is more likely to develop symptoms and explosive shifts in his or her state of mind. Horowitz also points out that self-coherence is more than interpersonal style—it includes integrity and virtues within one's character. Evidence for identity diffusion would indicate that different self-representations, split off from one another, are constantly jockeying for dominance over the total personality. Different self-representations would obviously arise in connection with different object representations that are highly influenced by the interpersonal context at a given moment. The boundaries of the self are also of interest. Can the patient clearly differentiate his or her own mental contents from those of others, or is there a general blurring of self–object boundaries? A related aspect would be the patient's body perception. Are the patient's body boundaries intact, or does the patient have to engage periodically in self-mutilation to define the skin boundary? Are mind and body viewed as connected over time, or are there episodes of depersonalization or out-of-body experience where the mind seems independent of the body?

Postmodern Considerations

Because dynamic psychiatrists recognize the two-person nature of diagnostic assessments, they are always exploring how their own subjectivity may affect what they are observing in the patient. Is the patient reacting to a subtle aspect of the clinician that might skew the interviewer's evaluation in a particular direction? Similarly, are the interviewer's conclusions biased in any way by certain preconceived notions about gender, culture, or religion? Dynamic psychiatrists must always take into account their own subjectivity, including beliefs and prejudices, so that those aspects of the clinician's "lens" are considered when assessing the nature of the patient's difficulties. Certain religious beliefs, for example, may be viewed as bizarre to the point of being delusional by some clinicians, whereas other clinicians might accept those same beliefs as ordinary within the patient's culture.

Explanatory Formulation

The different elements of the psychodynamic diagnosis enumerated above are the basis of an explanatory formulation. This tentative hypothesis or working model illustrates how the elements interact to create the clinical picture presented by the patient. This summary statement, sometimes referred to as a psychodynamic formulation (Perry et al. 1987), may also include comments on the biological aspects of the illness and on treatment implications. Although the formulation is intended to explain the patient's condition, it does not have to explain everything. It should succinctly highlight the major issues, especially their relevance to treatment planning.

With some patients, one theoretical model will appear to have more explanatory value than the other two. With other patients, however, more than one theoretical perspective may seem useful in conceptualizing various aspects of the patient's psychopathology. As suggested in Chapter 1, clinicians should be open-minded to all the major theoretical frameworks and should embrace a "both/and" rather than an "either/or" attitude. The formulation should also be approached with the understanding that it undergoes continual modification as treatment proceeds. In dynamic psychiatry, diagnosis and treatment are always evolving together. A sample case history illustrates these points:

> Ms. A, a 33-year-old single woman employed as a librarian, came to the hospital in the midst of a psychotic episode with paranoid features. She had become convinced that her mother was plotting to kill her, and she had barricaded herself in the apartment she shared with her brother.
>
> When Ms. A reorganized after a few doses of an antipsychotic, she presented herself as a cheerful, Pollyannaish person, commenting, "I have no anger in me." She said she felt fine and wanted to go home. Her mother was glad to see her "back to normal," but expressed concern because Ms. A's brother was still at the apartment. He had apparently exploited his sister by moving in, eating her food, and living rent-free for the past several weeks.
>
> According to her mother, Ms. A lived an isolated existence and had few interpersonal contacts outside several superficial relationships at work. Moreover, the

patient's mother revealed that Ms. A had had one previous psychotic episode 18 months earlier when her brother had moved in with her under the same exploitative circumstances. Ms. A's mother also reported a family history of bipolar affective disorder.

The following explanatory formulation was developed:

> Ms. A inherited a diathesis toward bipolar affective disorder. Her cyclic psychotic episodes, which appeared schizophreniform, were possibly a variant of bipolar illness. After stabilizing the psychosis, the psychiatrist could consider prophylaxis with lithium or another mood stabilizer.
>
> When Ms. A is nonpsychotic, her adjustment comes at the expense of massive denial of all negative feelings, especially anger, and results in a schizoid existence. The stressor of having her brother living parasitically in her apartment provoked so much anger in Ms. A that she could not maintain her usual defensive posture. Under pressure of this intense affect, she regressed to the paranoid-schizoid position, where an unacceptable self-representation harboring angry, murderous feelings was split off and projected onto her mother. After remission of Ms. A's psychosis with medication, she reintrojected the self-representation, which once again became buried under her denial.
>
> The patient lacks the psychological mindedness to see any problems to work on in an exploratory therapy process. Casework or family therapy is therefore needed to remove the stressor (i.e., the brother) and to allow Ms. A to resume her previous adjustment with a follow-up regimen of medication and supportive psychotherapy to maintain her defenses and identify other potential stressors.

While dynamic in its conceptualization, this formulation is in keeping with the biopsychosocial model of psychiatry championed by Engel (1977), Fink (1988), and others in that it takes into account genetic predisposition, social-familial influences, and intrapsychic factors.

Conclusion

Table 3–1 summarizes the steps involved in a thorough psychodynamic assessment. In the final analysis, the purpose of the assessment is to inform and guide the overall treatment planning. The case of Ms. A illustrates how a psychodynamic diagnosis, and particularly an explanatory formulation, can be useful even when dynamic psychotherapy is contraindicated. The treatment is nevertheless dynamically informed. The dynamic assessment assists all aspects of treatment planning. An evaluation of ego functions can contribute to a decision regarding whether an

TABLE 3–1. The psychodynamic assessment

Historical data
- Present illness with attention to associative linkages and Axis IV stressors
- Past history with emphasis on how the past is repeating itself in the present
  - Developmental history
  - Family history
  - Cultural/religious background

Mental status examination
- Orientation and perception
- Cognition
- Affect
- Action

Projective psychological testing (if necessary)

Physical and neurological examination

The psychodynamic diagnosis
- Descriptive DSM-IV diagnosis
- Interactions among Axes I–V
- Characteristics of the ego
  - Strengths and weaknesses
  - Defense mechanisms and conflicts
  - Relationship to superego
- Quality of object relations
  - Family relationships
  - Transference-countertransference patterns
  - Inferences about internal object relations
- Characteristics of the self
  - Self-esteem and self-cohesiveness
  - Self-continuity
  - Self-boundaries
  - Mind-body relationship
- Postmodern considerations
- Explanatory formulation using above data

individual should be an inpatient or an outpatient. For example, the extent of impulse control may be a crucial variable in deciding whether a patient should be admitted in the first place and, if so, when the patient can be discharged. A dynamic understanding of their patients can help clinicians decide whether their patients would accept a recommendation for sex therapy, behavior modification, family therapy, or group therapy. Finally, each patient's compliance with any medication regimen will be affected by that particular patient's characterological substrate. The cases discussed in subsequent chapters will illustrate how other theoretical models can be used in developing a formulation and how the dynamic assessment of the patient guides the treatment planning.

References

American Psychiatric Association: Diagnostic and Statistical Manual of Mental Disorders, 4th Edition. Washington, DC, American Psychiatric Association, 1994

Amini F, Lewis T, Lannon R, et al: Affect, attachment, memory: contributions toward psychobiologic integration. Psychiatry 59:213–239, 1996

Andrews G, Tennant C: Editorial: life event stress and illness. Psychol Med 8:545–549, 1978

Bellak L, Hurvich M, Gedimen HK: Ego Functions in Schizophrenics, Neurotics, and Normals: A Systematic Study of Conceptual, Diagnostic, and Therapeutic Aspects. New York, Wiley, 1973

Deutsch F, Murphy WF: The Clinical Interview, Vol 1: Diagnosis: A Method of Teaching Associative Exploration. New York, International Universities Press, 1955

Engel GL: The need for a new medical model: a challenge for biomedicine. Science 196: 129–136, 1977

Fink PJ: Response to the presidential address: is "biopsychosocial" the psychiatric shibboleth? Am J Psychiatry 145:1061–1067, 1988

Freud S. Fragment of an analysis of a case of hysteria (1905), in The Standard Edition of the Complete Psychological Works of Sigmund Freud, Vol 7. Translated and edited by Strachey J. London, Hogarth Press, 1953, pp 1–122

Gabbard GO: Challenges in the analysis of adult patients with histories of childhood sexual abuse. Canadian Journal of Psychoanalysis 5:1–25, 1997

Holmes TH, Rahe RH: Social Readjustment Rating Scale. J Psychosom Res 11:213–281, 1967

Horowitz MJ: Formulation as a Basis for Planning Psychotherapy Treatment. Washington, DC, American Psychiatric Press, 1997

Kernberg OF: Severe Personality Disorders: Psychotherapeutic Strategies. New Haven, CT, Yale University Press, 1984

Kwawer JS, Lerner HD, Lerner PM, et al (eds): Borderline Phenomena and the Rorschach Test. New York, International Universities Press, 1980

Langs RJ: The Bipersonal Field. New York, Jason Aronson, 1976

MacKinnon RA, Michels R: The Psychiatric Interview in Clinical Practice. Philadelphia, PA, WB Saunders, 1971

Menninger KA: Theory of Psychoanalytic Technique. New York, Basic Books, 1958

Menninger KA, Mayman M, Pruyser PW: A Manual for Psychiatric Case Study, 2nd Edition. New York, Grune & Stratton, 1962

Menninger KA, Mayman M, Pruyser PW: The Vital Balance: The Life Process in Mental Health and Illness. New York, Viking Press, 1963

Perry S, Cooper AM, Michels R: The psychodynamic formulation: its purpose, structure, and clinical application. Am J Psychiatry 144:543–550, 1987

Pine F: Drive, Ego, Object, and Self: A Synthesis for Clinical Work. New York, Basic Books, 1990

Rapaport D, Gill MM, Schafer R: Diagnostic Psychological Testing, Revised Edition. Edited by Holt RR. New York, International Universities Press, 1968

Reiser MF: Are psychiatric educators "losing the mind?" Am J Psychiatry 145:148–153, 1988

Schafer R: Psychoanalytic Interpretation in Rorschach Testing: Theory and Application. New York, Grune & Stratton, 1954

Shevrin H, Shectman F: The diagnostic process in psychiatric evaluations. Bull Menninger Clin 37:451–494, 1973

Thomä H, Kächele H: Psychoanalytic Practice, Vol 1: Principles. Translated by Wilson M, Roseveare D. New York, Springer-Verlag, 1987

Viederman M: The active dynamic interview and the supportive relationship. Compr Psychiatry 25:147–157, 1984

Waelder R: Basic Theory of Psychoanalysis. New York, International Universities Press, 1960

C H A P T E R

4

Treatments in
Dynamic Psychiatry

Individual Psychotherapy

Proficiency at individual psychotherapy is perhaps the hallmark of the dynamic psychiatrist. Evolving as it does from psychoanalysis, dynamic psychiatry understandably emphasizes the nuances of the healing relationship between psychotherapist and patient. Space considerations here limit us to a brief overview of the general principles derived from the vast literature on individual psychotherapy. Specific applications of those principles will be demonstrated and explicated in Sections II and III. Readers who are interested in a more comprehensive discussion of individual psychotherapy should consult any of several outstanding texts (E. Adler and Bachant 1998; Basch 1980; Busch 1995; Chessick 1974; Dewald 1964, 1971; Fromm-Reichmann 1950; Luborsky 1984; Ogden 1982; Roth 1987).

The Expressive-Supportive Continuum

Psychotherapy modeled on the technical principles of formal psychoanalysis has been designated by a number of different names: expressive, dynamic, psychoanalytically oriented, insight oriented, exploratory, uncovering, and intensive, to name a few. This form of treatment, geared to analyzing defenses and exploring the transference, has traditionally been viewed as wholly different from another entity known as supportive psychotherapy. The latter, which is more oriented to suppressing unconscious conflict and bolstering defenses, has been widely regarded as inferior to expressive therapy. This tendency is reflected in the clinical maxim that has guided psychotherapists for years: "Be as expressive as you can be, and as supportive as you have to be" (Wallerstein 1986, p. 688).

A number of authors have expressed concern about this traditional dichotomy (Horwitz et al. 1996; Pine 1976, 1986; Wallerstein 1986; Werman 1984). One problem with the distinction is the implication that supportive psychotherapy is not psychoanalytically oriented. In practice, supportive psychotherapy is guided by psychoanalytic understanding every step of the way. Moreover, the dichotomy portrays expressive psychotherapy and supportive psychotherapy as highly discrete entities when, in fact, they rarely occur in pure form anywhere (Wallerstein 1986; Werman 1984). Finally, the value distinction associated with the greater prestige of expressive psychotherapy or psychoanalysis has always carried with it the assumption that change achieved as a result of insight or intrapsychic conflict resolution is somehow superior to that achieved through supportive techniques. No hard data support this assumption; the changes achieved by expressive psychotherapy have not been proven in any way superior to or more durable than those achieved by supportive psychotherapy (Wallerstein 1986).

At the conclusion of a monumental study of 42 patients treated in the Menninger Foundation Psychotherapy Research Project, Wallerstein (1986) determined that all forms of psychotherapy contain a mixture of expressive and supportive elements and that changes achieved by the supportive elements are in no way inferior to those achieved by the expressive elements. Rather than regarding expressive psychotherapy and supportive psychotherapy as two distinct modalities of treatment then, we should view psychotherapy as taking place on an expressive-supportive continuum, which is in closer keeping with the reality of clinical practice and with empirical research. With certain patients and at certain points in the therapy, the therapy will be weighted more heavily toward expressive elements, whereas with other patients and at other times, the therapy will require more attention to supportive elements. As Wallerstein (1986) noted, "All proper therapy is always both expressive and supportive (in different ways), and the question at issue at all points in every therapy should be that of expressing *how* and *when,* and supporting *how* and *when*" (p. 689).

Individual psychotherapy geared to this continuum might best be termed *expressive-supportive* or *supportive-expressive.* Even psychoanalysis, situated at the most extreme point on the expressive end of the continuum, contains supportive elements associated with the treatment structure itself and the collaboration of analyst and patient to achieve certain goals (Luborsky 1984); meanwhile, most supportive psychotherapies at the opposite end of the continuum do provide insight and understanding from time to time. Hence, the effective dynamic therapist will shift flexibly back and forth along the expressive-supportive continuum, depending on the needs of the patient at a given moment in the psychotherapy process.

The concept of the expressive-supportive continuum provides a framework for considering the goals, characteristics, and indications for individual psychotherapy. Each of these elements changes accordingly as we move back and forth along the continuum.

Goals of Expressive-Supportive Psychotherapy

Historically, insight and understanding were always considered the ultimate goals of psychoanalysis and of psychotherapy derived from psychoanalytic principles. In the last 40 years, however, there has been considerable acceptance of the notion that the therapeutic relationship itself is healing independently of its role in delivering insight. Loewald (1957/1980) noted that the process of change is "set in motion not simply by the technical skill of the analyst, but by the fact that the analyst makes himself available for the development of a new 'object relationship' between the patient and the analyst" (p. 224).

While most psychoanalytic therapists endorse goals involving insight and the therapeutic relationship, there is variation in which dimension is given the most emphasis. Some focus more on conflict resolution through interpretation, while others stress the importance of developing authenticity or "the true self" (Winnicott 1962/1976). Some therapists are more ambitious regarding therapeutic outcomes; others conceptualize the psychotherapeutic process as a search for truth about oneself (Grinberg 1980). Still others believe that the capacity for reflectiveness about one's internal world should be the goal (Aron 1998). Kleinians would view the goal as the reintegration of aspects of the self that were previously lost through projective identification (Steiner 1989).

From an object relations standpoint, an improvement in the quality of one's relationships is a goal of psychotherapy, regardless of whether it is weighted toward the supportive or the expressive end of the continuum. As internal object relations change in the course of psychotherapy, one is able to perceive and relate to external persons differently. In contemporary practice, patients are much more likely to seek therapy because of dissatisfaction with the quality of their relationships than because of discrete symptoms, as they did in Freud's day. Hence, the importance of this goal cannot be overstated. One empirical study of analysis (Kantrowitz et al. 1987) demonstrated through projective psychological testing before and after treatment that analysis produces statistically significant improvement in the level and quality of object relations.

In self psychologically oriented psychotherapy, the goals involve strengthening the cohesiveness of the self and helping the patient choose more mature self-objects, as alluded to in Chapter 2. In Kohut's (1984) words, "The essence of the psychoanalytic cure resides in a patient's newly acquired ability to identify and seek out appropriate selfobjects as they present themselves in his realistic sur-roundings and to be sustained by them" (p. 77).

The goal of psychotherapy at the supportive end of the continuum is primarily to help the patient adapt to stresses while avoiding insight into unconscious wishes and defenses (Roskin 1982). The therapist hopes to strengthen defenses to facili-tate the patient's adaptive capacity to handle the stresses of daily living. This goal often involves restoring a patient to a previous level of functioning that has been compromised by a crisis. Furthermore, since supportive techniques are often used in treating patients with serious ego weaknesses, ego building is a crucial aspect of supportive psychotherapies. For example, the therapist may serve as an auxiliary ego, helping patients to test reality more accurately or to anticipate consequences of their actions and thereby improve their judgment.

Duration of Expressive-Supportive Psychotherapy

The length of expressive-supportive psychotherapy is essentially independent of the expressive-supportive continuum. Therapies that are highly supportive or highly expressive can be either brief or long. In some cases, psychoanalysis may last well over 5 years, and some supportive processes may go on even longer. On the other hand, there are instances where just one supportive or expressive therapy session (or consultation) has been highly therapeutic.

The most useful distinction is not between expressive and supportive psycho-therapies but rather between open-ended psychotherapy and brief or time-limited psychotherapy. For purposes of discussion, the open-ended variety will be consid-ered in this section and brief psychotherapy will be considered later in this chapter in recognition of its separate evolution as a special form of therapy.

Frequency of Sessions

In contrast to the duration of therapy, the frequency of sessions tends to be highly correlated with the expressive-supportive continuum. As a general rule, a greater number of weekly sessions characterizes the expressive end of the continuum. Psy-choanalysis, an extremely expressive treatment, is characterized by four or five ses-sions a week and is usually conducted with the patient lying on a couch while the analyst sits behind the couch. Toward the middle of the continuum, however, highly expressive forms of psychotherapy usually involve one to three sessions a week with the patient sitting in an upright position. In contrast, psychotherapy with primarily supportive goals rarely takes place more than twice a week and ordinarily occurs once a week or less often. It is not uncommon for supportive processes to have a frequency of once a month.

The issue of frequency is connected with the role of transference in the psychotherapeutic process (to be discussed later in this chapter). Clinical experience has shown that transference intensifies as the frequency of sessions increases. Since the more expressive treatments focus on the transference, these therapists usually prefer to see their patients more than once a week. In contrast, supportive processes work with transference to a lesser extent and thus do not require more than one session a week. Also, whereas highly expressive treatments are almost invariably administered in 45- or 50-minute sessions, supportive processes tend to use time more flexibly. Certain patients who require more frequent supportive contacts with the therapist do better with two 25-minute sessions in a week than with one 50-minute session.

The reality of psychiatric practice is that practical matters may outweigh theoretical considerations in determining the frequency of sessions. Some patients may be able to afford only one session a week even though they might do better with three. Other patients, because of inconvenient work schedules or transportation problems, may be able to get to their therapist's office only once a week. Before accepting such limitations, however, the therapist should keep in mind that resistance often finds convenient hiding places. An investigation of these practical limitations may reveal that the patient has greater flexibility in regard to time and money than can be readily acknowledged.

Free Association

Free association is often regarded as the major mode by which the patient communicates to the analyst. This requires patients to relax their usual control over their thought processes in an effort to say whatever comes to mind without censoring their words or thoughts. In actual practice, resistances inevitably intervene when patients try to free-associate. It is often asserted, only half-jokingly, that when a patient is able to free-associate without interference from resistance, that patient may be ready for termination. Patients may also use free association itself as a resistance to focusing on a particular issue in their current life situation (Greenson 1967).

Free association is also useful in highly expressive therapies, although more selectively than in analysis. The therapist, for example, may ask the patient to associate to various elements of a dream to help both patient and therapist understand unconscious connections that make interpretation of the dream possible.

Free association is far less useful further along the continuum toward the more supportively based treatments. As Greenson (1967) pointed out, the process itself requires a mature and healthy ego to maintain a split between an observing ego and an experiencing ego. Ego-deficient patients who are prone to psychosis may become increasingly regressed if allowed to free-associate in a supportive process. Moreover, such patients often lack the ego capacity to reflect on their associations and to integrate them into a meaningful and coherent understanding of unconscious issues.

Neutrality, Anonymity, and Abstinence

Between 1912 and 1915, Freud published a series of prescriptions for technique that have formed the basis of what is often referred to as the "classical" model of treatment. Principles such as neutrality, anonymity, and abstinence evolved from those papers. In recent years, however, these concepts have become highly controversial as it has become increasingly clear that the way Freud actually practiced differed considerably from some of his recommendations in his papers on technique (Lipton 1977; Lohser and Newton 1996). Whereas Freud at times admonished analysts to proceed with emotional detachment, to show nothing of themselves, and to put aside all of their own feelings, written accounts from his own patients demonstrate that he was transparent regarding his mood; frequently gossiped; offered his own opinions about other people, works of art, and current political issues; and was enthusiastically engaged as a "real person." His own subjectivity was very much in evidence. His written prescriptions for technique evidently were based on his concerns about the potential for countertransference acting out in his colleagues rather than what he felt was best to advance the analytic process.

Freud actually was not as austere in his writings on technique as he is sometimes portrayed. In his advice on technique, he tended to oscillate between endorsing flexibility and tact, on the one hand, and more authoritarian directives, on the other. His translator, James Strachey, and his disciples downplayed the former and overemphasized the latter.

Neutrality is perhaps the most misunderstood aspect of psychoanalytic and psychotherapeutic technique. Freud did not even use the word in his writings. James Strachey translated the German word *Indifferenz* as "neutrality," even though the German word actually implies an undercurrent of emotional participation in the analyst rather than detachment. It is frequently misinterpreted to mean coldness or aloofness (Chessick 1981). Even in the most expressive treatments, emotional warmth is a necessary part of the therapeutic relationship. Similarly, concern for the patient's unique situation is essential to establish rapport. Green-son (1967) stressed that the patient in analysis deserves explanations of new or strange procedures, such as the therapist's declining to answer direct questions. This humaneness and empathy are part of any effective doctor-patient relationship.

Therapists who remove themselves from the interpersonal field of the therapy by assuming an aloof, nonparticipatory attitude diminish their effectiveness by closing themselves off to the experience of the patient's internal object world (Hoffman and Gill 1988). There is a broad consensus that the therapist is a participant in the therapeutic process in a spontaneous yet transitory, disciplined, and partial way (Gabbard 1995; Hoffman and Gill 1988; Mitchell 1997; Racker 1968; Renik 1993; Sandler 1976). As Freud's own practice demonstrated, there is an irreducible subjectivity (Renik 1993) that cannot be eliminated with a mask of anonymity. Moreover, therapists who can allow themselves to respond to the patient's unconscious attempts to transform them into transference objects will gain a much greater appreciation of the patient's internal world. Therapists may become aware of countertransference feelings only *after* they have responded like one of the patient's projected internal objects or self-representations (Gabbard 1995; Sandler 1976). As noted in Chapter 1, the countertransference jointly created by the therapist's subjectivity and the patient's projected internal representations is a source of valuable information in the treatment process.

The most widely accepted contemporary meaning of neutrality is the assumption of a nonjudgmental stance regarding the patient's behaviors, thoughts, wishes, and feelings. Anna Freud (1936/1966), who did not use the term, suggested that the analyst should remain equidistant from the id, the ego, the superego, and the demands of external reality. This stance, however, is more of an *ideal* than a realistic position. Therapists are frequently making private judgments about what patients say or do, and a spontaneous, engaged therapist will sometimes reveal those judgments nonverbally if not in overt comments to the patient. Greenberg (1986) redefined neutrality as taking a position equidistant between an old object from the patient's past and the new object of the therapist in the present. This conceptual model may more accurately reflect the therapist's internal process. The therapist is drawn into a role evoked by the patient's internal world and then attempts to become disentangled from that role so as to reflect what is taking place between patient and therapist.

Anonymity has similarly been redefined in contemporary practice. Freud (1912/1958) wrote that the analyst should strive for the opacity of a mirror, but analysts and analytic therapists today recognize that anonymity is a mythical construct. Photographs, books, and other articles of personal interest are all over the therapist's office. When the therapist chooses to speak, what he or she says and how he or she responds to the patient's material are all highly revealing of the therapist's subjectivity. Hence, one is self-disclosing all the time in nonverbal as well as verbal modes. Most analysts and analytic therapists, however, still recognize that there is value in restraint. Revealing highly personal details about the therapist's family or the therapist's personal problems are rarely useful and may burden the patient in a manner that creates a role reversal in which the patient thinks he or she must take care of the therapist. Similarly, making harsh judgments about the patient's thoughts, feelings, or actions may be destructive by compounding the patient's self-criticism. On the other hand, such judgments may be necessary if the patient is about to act self-destructively.

Abstinence is a third term that has been widely misconstrued by some practitioners. Freud suggested that the analyst needed to withhold gratification of transference wishes so that those wishes could be analyzed rather than satisfied. Today there is wide recognition that partial transference gratifications occur throughout the treatment. The therapist's laughter in response to a joke, the empathic listening intrinsic to psychotherapy, and the warmth and understanding provided by the therapist all provide gratifications for the patient. The concept of therapeutic or analytic boundaries establish limits on the physical relationship so that psychological and emotional boundaries can be crossed through the process of empathy, projective identification, and introjection (Gabbard and Lester 1995). Good professional boundaries should not be construed as promoting rigidity or coldness (Gutheil and Gabbard 1998).

Interventions

The interventions made by the therapist can be placed into seven categories along an expressive-supportive continuum: 1) interpretation, 2) confrontation, 3) clarification, 4) encouragement to elaborate, 5) empathic validation, 6) advice and praise, and 7) affirmation (Figure 4–1). (This expressive-supportive continuum of interventions is derived from the work of the Menninger Clinic Treatment Interventions Project [Horwitz et al. 1996].)

FIGURE 4–1. An expressive-supportive continuum of interventions.

1. *Interpretation.*   In the most expressive forms of treatment, interpretation is regarded as the therapist's ultimate decisive instrument (Greenson 1967). In its simplest form, interpretation involves making something conscious that was previously unconscious. An interpretation is an explanatory statement that links a feeling, thought, behavior, or symptom to its unconscious meaning or origin. For example, the therapist might say to a patient who is late, "Perhaps the reason you are late is that you were afraid I would react to the success you are now having the way your father reacted." Depending on the point in therapy and the patient's readiness to listen, interpretations may focus on the transference (as in this example), on extratransference issues, on the patient's past or present situation, or on the patient's resistances or fantasies. As a general principle, the therapist does not address unconscious content via interpretation until the material is almost conscious and therefore relatively accessible to the patient's awareness.

2. *Confrontation.*   The next most expressive intervention is confrontation, which addresses something the patient does not want to accept or identifies the patient's avoidance or minimization. A confrontation may be geared to clarifying how the patient's behavior affects others or to reflecting back to the patient a denied or suppressed feeling. Confrontation, which is often gentle, carries the unfortunate connotation in common parlance of being aggressive or blunt. The following example illustrates that confrontation is not necessarily forceful or hostile. In the last session of a long-term therapy process, one patient talked at great length about car problems he encountered on the way to the session. The therapist commented, "I think you'd rather talk about your car than face the sadness you're feeling about our last session."

3. *Clarification.*   Farther along the continuum from expressive to supportive interventions, clarification involves a reformulation or pulling together of the patient's verbalizations to convey a more coherent view of what is being communicated. Clarification differs from confrontation because it lacks the element of denial or minimization. A clarification is aimed at helping the patient articulate something that is difficult to put into words.

4. *Encouragement to elaborate.*   Closer to the middle of the continuum come interventions that are neither supportive nor expressive in and of themselves. Encouragement to elaborate may be broadly defined as a request for information about a topic brought up by the patient. It may be an open-ended question such as "What comes to mind about that?" or a more specific request as in "Tell me more about your father." Such interventions are commonly used in both the most expressive and the most supportive treatments.

5. *Empathic validation.*   This intervention is a demonstration of the therapist's empathic attunement with the patient's internal state. A typically validating

comment is "I can understand why you feel depressed about that" or "It hurts when you're treated that way." In the view of the self psychologists, empathic immersion in the patient's internal experience is essential, regardless of the location of the therapy on the expressive-supportive continuum (Kohut 1984; Ornstein 1986). When patients feel that the therapist understands their subjective experiences, they are more likely to accept interpretations.

6. *Advice and praise.* This category really includes two interventions that are linked by the fact that they both prescribe and reinforce certain activities. Advice involves direct suggestions to the patient regarding how to behave, while praise reinforces certain patient behaviors by expressing overt approval of them. An example of the former is "I think you should stop going out with that man immediately." An example of the latter is "I'm very pleased that you were able to tell him that you would not see him anymore." These comments are on the opposite end of the continuum from traditional psychoanalytic interventions because they are departures from neutrality and to some extent compromise the patient's autonomy in making decisions.

7. *Affirmation.* This simple intervention involves succinct comments in support of the patient's comments or behaviors, such as "Uh-huh" or "Yes, I see what you mean."

The vast majority of psychotherapeutic processes contain all these interventions at some time during the course of treatment. However, a therapy is classified as primarily expressive or primarily supportive based on which interventions predominate. These associations of interventions with the continuum are not ironclad, however.

Pine (1986) and Horwitz et al. (1996) advocated supportive techniques to "cushion the blow" of interpretations in the supportive therapy of fragile patients. Werman (1984, p. 83) proposed making "upward interpretations" of transference behavior or feelings to relate them to current situations rather than to early experiences, thereby preventing regression in patients with serious ego weakness. These interventions are the inverse of classical interpretations in that they provide conscious, rather than unconscious, explanations of the patient's behavior or feelings.

Transference

Freud was fond of saying that what made a therapy process psychoanalytic was a focus on transference and resistance. Certainly all forms of dynamically oriented psychotherapy pay careful attention to the state of the transference. However, the specific manner in which the transference is addressed (or left unaddressed) varies considerably, depending on the expressive-supportive dimension. In formal psychoanalysis, the highlighting and resolution of the transference is of paramount importance. Cooper (1987) noted: "Despite the diversity of analytic views that abound today, analysts seem to agree on the centrality of the transference and its interpretation in analytic process and cure, differing only in whether transference is everything or almost everything" (p. 78). In the classical model of psychoanalysis, the patient's infantile neurosis would manifest itself as an all-consuming transference neurosis that would then be resolved through interpretation. In contemporary psychoanalytic practice, many analysts and therapists prefer to think of a set of transferences rather than one specific transference neurosis.

Both psychoanalysis and expressive psychotherapy employ extratransference interpretation as well as transference interpretation. Psychotherapy may be somewhat more limited than psychoanalysis in that it focuses on the transference dispositions most closely related to the presenting problems (Roskin 1982). In actual practice, though, the distinctions between psychoanalysis and expressive psychotherapy are blurred and difficult to delineate.

As noted in Chapter 1, transference is often viewed today as having a bidimensional quality involving a repetition of past experience with old objects, on the one hand, and a quest for a new object or selfobject experience that will be reparative and corrective for the patient, on the other. E. Adler and Bachant (1998) have divided transference into an archaic dimension, involving unintegrated longings and needs, and an adaptive dimension, involving the organizing activity of the evolving self, relational configurations, and higher levels of ego integration. In addition, the notion of transference as distortion has become more complex. The therapist must avoid a "blaming" approach to transference interpretation, because the patient may be legitimately responding to real behaviors or attitudes of the therapist. The therapist must always engage in ongoing self-scrutiny to sort out the repetitive, "template" aspect of transference stemming from the patient's intrapsychic world and the real contributions of the therapist to the interaction (Gabbard 1996; Hoffman 1998; Mitchell 1997).

In therapies designed primarily to be supportive, the therapist is involved in the same process of monitoring transference developments and countertransference responses. The transference is noted inwardly but is usually not addressed or interpreted to the patient. The treatment goal in refraining from interpretation is to evoke a positive dependent transference without analyzing it (Wallerstein 1986). This transference attachment is the mechanism of the "transference cure," whereby the patient gets better to please the therapist. Although changes derived from this model have traditionally been disparaged as inferior to those stemming from conflict resolution, research (Horwitz 1974; Wallerstein 1986) suggests that they may be stable and lasting.

Psychotherapists must keep in mind that transferences are multiple in any given patient. The tradition of thinking in terms of a transference neurosis has led some clinicians to speak of "*the* transference." In the therapeutic setting, however, one is likely to see sibling transferences (which may vary from one sibling to another), mother transferences, father transferences, and others.

Resistance

As noted in Chapter 1, resistance involves the emergence of the patient's character-ological defenses within the therapeutic situation. In the more expressive thera-pies, analyzing and understanding resistance is part of the daily bread-and-butter work of the therapist. If, for example, the patient is consistently late to sessions or consistently silent during them, therapists may regard these resistances with inter-est and curiosity rather than devalue them as defiant and willful behavior. Resistances are not met with proscriptions or censure. Instead, the therapist enlists the patient's help in understanding the origins of the resistance and then addresses the resistance with interpretation.

Resistance related to transference issues is referred to as transference resistance. This involves interferences with the therapeutic work deriving from transference perceptions. For example, a patient may feel unable to talk about masturbatory fantasies because he is convinced that his therapist disapproves of masturbation. To prevent receiving a negative judgment from the therapist, the patient therefore chooses to remain silent. In the parlance of object relations theory, a transference resistance may be understood as the patient's unconscious tendency to cling tena-ciously to a particular internal object relationship. This may manifest itself as a therapeutic stalemate in which the therapist is repeatedly related to as someone else.

Students of psychoanalysis and psychoanalytic psychotherapy often raise the question, "Resistance to what?" Friedman (1991) noted that the true significance of resistance is that the feelings associated with it may compel the patient into non-reflective action instead of reflective observation. He pointed out that what is re-sisted is a particular mental attitude that he describes as "a simultaneous conscious activation of repressed wishes and a cool contemplation of their significance, so that they are experienced both as wishes and as objective features of the conflicted self" (p. 590). Moreover, the current emphasis on intersubjectivity would also sug-gest that the resistance of the patient may be paralleled by a counterresistance in the therapist that may collude with the patient's difficulties in achieving the reflec-tive space necessary for psychoanalytic treatment.

In Chapter 2, I noted the different perspective on resistance that is held by self psychologists. They regard resistances as healthy psychic activities that safeguard the growth of the self (Kohut 1984). Rather than interpret them, they empathize with the patient's need for them. This view is in keeping with their concern that the classical approach of pursuing the content beneath resistance has moralistic overtones. However, this empathic approach has led some analysts to regard the self psychological technique as fundamentally supportive. It should also be noted that classical analytic technique does not include insensitive "attacks" on resistance; rather, it involves patiently examining and attempting to understand the resistance.

As implied by the previous comments about self psychology, resistance is viewed as essential and adaptive in the context of predominantly supportive psychotherapy. Resistances are often manifestations of defensive structures that need to be bolstered as part of therapy. The therapist might even encourage resistance by pointing out to the patient that certain matters are too upsetting to discuss and should be postponed until a more auspicious moment. Similarly, delay mechanisms may be reinforced in the interest of supporting a weakened ego beset by impulses. When a patient's actions usurp verbalization of painful feelings, as in acting-out, the therapist may be forced to set limits on self-destructive behavior rather than to interpret the resistance to talking, as in expressive treatment. This limit setting may involve hospitalization or insistence that the patient turn over illegal drugs to the therapist.

Working Through

Interpretations rarely result in "Aha!" responses and dramatic cures. Typically, they are warded off by the forces of resistance and require frequent repetition by the therapist in different contexts. This repetitive interpretation of transference and resistance until the insight has become fully integrated into the patient's conscious awareness is known as "working through." Although the therapist's efforts are necessary, the patient does part of the work of accepting and integrating the therapist's insights between the actual therapy sessions (Karasu 1977). The triangle of insight (Menninger 1958) is a useful conceptual model for the process of working through (see Figure 4–2). Over the course of therapy, the therapist notes certain patterns 1) in the patient's outside relationships and then links them to 2) transference patterns and to 3) antecedent relationships with family members. Eventually, the patient makes these unconscious linkages conscious. This model is related to what Luborsky (1984) referred to as the core conflictual relationship theme. This theme usually involves a wish or a need (e.g., "I want to be spontaneous with others") that is in conflict with the control function of the ego or superego (e.g., "If I try, though, I may lose control, and therefore it's better to not even try"). This theme can be tracked throughout the course of therapy as it relates to

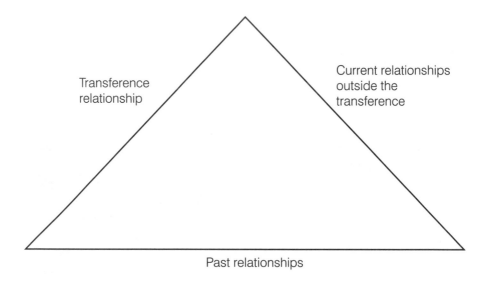

Transference
relationship

Current relationships
outside the
transference

Past relationships

FIGURE 4–2.   Triangle of insight (modeled after Menninger 1958).

the three sides of the triangle, and it can be pointed out to the patient each time it appears. As the patient sees the pattern come up again and again in new contexts, it becomes less alien, and the patient gains greater ego mastery over it.

This same model can be restated in terms of object relations theory. Recurrent self-object-affect constellations appear in the transference, in current extratransference relationships, and in memories of past relationships. In self psychological terms, the pattern may be the expectation of mirroring or the need to idealize others. Regardless of which theoretical model is employed, however, all schools of thought view the reexperiencing of these central relationship patterns in the transference as critically important to a positive outcome. This working-through process is applied almost exclusively to treatments with a significant expressive component—it is rarely used to characterize primarily supportive processes.

Use of Dreams

In psychoanalysis and highly expressive forms of therapy, the interpretation of dreams is valued as "the royal road" to an understanding of the unconscious (Freud 1900/1953, p. 608). The patient's associations to the dream elements are used to understand the latent or hidden content of the dream that lies behind the manifest or overt content. The symbols of the dream can then be interpreted to help the patient further understand the unconscious issues in the dream.

In psychotherapies on the supportive end of the continuum, the therapist listens carefully to the patient's dream and thinks about it in the same way as would an expressive therapist. However, the therapist limits interpretive efforts to upward interpretations (Werman 1984, p. 83) that help the patient associate the dream with conscious feelings and attitudes toward the therapist as a real person and to other reality situations in waking life. Free association to the dream is not encouraged because it might lead to further regression.

In between the supportive and expressive ends of the continuum, there is room for selective dream interpretation in which the therapist relates the dream to conscious or unconscious issues in a limited sector of the patient's psychological life. The focus is more on the psychological surface than on the depths of the unconscious and is geared to the specific goals of the psychotherapy (Werman 1978).

Therapeutic Alliance

Freud (1913/1958) was aware that patients were unlikely to be able to use interpretive understanding unless a proper rapport had first been established. This relatively nonconflictual and rational rapport that the patient has with the analyst was termed the *working alliance* by Greenson (1965/1978). It involves the patient's capacity to collaborate productively with the therapist because the therapist is perceived as a helping professional with good intentions.

Major research efforts on the therapeutic alliance have confirmed its influence on the process and outcome of psychotherapy (Frieswyk et al. 1986; Hartley and Strupp 1983; Horwitz 1974; Horwitz et al. 1996; Luborsky et al. 1980; Marziali et al. 1981). Much of this research points to the strength of the therapeutic alliance as a dominant factor in the outcome of a broad range of therapies (Bordin 1979; Hartley and Strupp 1983; Luborsky et al. 1980). These studies also suggest that the nature of the therapeutic alliance in the opening phase of psychotherapy is perhaps the best predictor of the outcome of that therapy.

One application of this extensive research is that in all psychotherapies, regardless of their point on the expressive-supportive continuum, therapists must attend early on to the establishment and maintenance of the therapeutic alliance. This focus does not require the formation of a positive transference that will not allow the expression of negative feelings. Rather, therapists must help their patients quickly identify their treatment goals and then must ally themselves with the healthy aspects of their patients' egos that are striving to reach those goals. Patients will then experience their therapists as collaborators who are working *with* them rather than *against* them. When working more supportively with patients with fragile egos, therapists find that the alliance is more difficult to develop and maintain (Horwitz et al. 1996). The borderline patient's chaotic transference reactions, for example, interfere with the formation of an alliance, and it is a major therapeutic accomplishment for the patient to eventually be able to perceive the therapist as a helpful person collaborating on common goals (G. Adler 1979).

Mechanisms of Change

The mechanism of change in the more expressive forms of psychotherapy is one of the most controversial issues in the field. The mode of therapeutic action depends in part on the goals of the treatment. Hence, views of change mechanisms often vary according to these treatment goals. Insight and healing relational experiences, while once thought to be mutually exclusive, are now regarded as compatible processes that work synergistically for therapeutic change (Cooper 1992; Jacobs 1990; Pine 1998; Pulver 1992). In other words, a therapeutic relationship probably will not be sustained unless there is insight into what is going on in the relationship. Conversely, the relationship itself may provide an interpretive understanding of the patient's dynamics.

There is also greater acknowledgment of multiple modes of therapeutic action that vary according to the patient. Blatt (1992) identified two types of patients who change in different ways. *Introjective* patients are ideational and preoccupied with establishing and maintaining a viable self-concept rather than with establishing intimacy in the interpersonal realm. They appear to be more responsive to insight through interpretive interventions. On the other hand, *anaclitic* patients are more concerned with issues of relatedness than self-development and gain greater therapeutic value from the quality of the therapeutic relationship than from interpretation. Blatt based his research, in part, on a reanalysis of the data from the Menninger Foundation Psychotherapy Research Project. In Wallerstein's (1986) own analysis of these data, he found that changes produced by predominantly supportive measures involved a variety of mechanisms.

The transference cure connected with the unanalyzed positive dependent transference has already been mentioned. One variant is the "therapeutic lifer" (Wallerstein 1986, pp. 690–691) who loses the gains if termination is attempted but who can be sustained at a high level of functioning as long as contact with the therapist continues indefinitely. Many patients are able to reduce the contacts to once a month or less but are prone to decompensate if there is any talk of termination. Another supportive mechanism of cure is "transfer of the transference" (p. 692), in which the positive dependency in the therapeutic relationship is transferred to another person, usually a spouse. Yet another mechanism is termed "the antitransference cure" (p. 693) and involves change through defiance and acting-out against the therapist. Still other patients in Wallerstein's sample changed via a narrowly defined variant of the corrective emotional experience in which the patient's transference behavior was met by the therapist with steady concern and neutrality. This mechanism, of course, is related to the re-parenting model or the internalization of the relationship model. Finally, some patients appear to benefit from a supportive treatment geared to giving direct nonjudgmental advice. Wallerstein termed this process "reality testing and re-education" (p. 694).

Many models of therapeutic action stress the making of meanings or a thrust toward symbolization. The patient's internal object relations are encoded in implicit memories based on early attachment experiences. A mode of relatedness observed in the transference is brought into the patient's awareness by the therapist in such a way that the patient ultimately gains a sense of mastery and understanding of what is being repeated in one relationship after another. This process is characterized by Fonagy and Target (1996a) as expanding psychic reality by *mentalizing* or developing *reflective function*. In developmental terms, a principal mode of therapeutic action is perceiving oneself in the therapist's mind while simultaneously developing a greater sense of the separate subjectivity of the therapist. This model links the interpersonal with the intrapsychic and is intimately related to Benjamin's (1995) notion that intersubjectivity is a developmental achievement in which objects are ultimately replaced by subjects regarded as having a separate internal world from oneself (Gabbard 1997).

However, the conscious mastery of the implicit and repetitive modes of relatedness is accompanied by nonconscious affective and interactive connections that have been referred to by Lyons-Ruth et al. (1998) as *implicit relational knowing*. This knowing may occur in moments of meeting between analyst and patient that are not symbolically represented or dynamically unconscious in the ordinary sense. In other words, some changes in treatment occur in the realm of procedural knowledge involving how to act, feel, and think in a particular relational context. Specific moments of mutual recognition—a look, a shared bit of humor, a feeling of intense involvement—may be remembered long after specific interpretations are forgotten. Psychotherapy can be viewed as a new attachment relationship that restructures attachment-related implicit memory. Stored prototypes are modified by new interactions with an affectively engaged therapist (Amini et al. 1996). At the same time, explicit memory involving a conscious narrative is altered by interpretive understanding.

Another implication of this model of therapeutic action is that the expressive-supportive continuum of interventions depicted in Figure 4–1 does not account for all therapeutic change. Many moments of meeting between therapist and patient occur outside the realm of "technique" (Stern et al. 1998). Spontaneous human responses by the therapist may have a powerful therapeutic impact.

Termination

Psychotherapists must resign themselves to living a professional life of continued loss. Patients come into their lives, share their most intimate thoughts and feelings, and then may never be heard from again. Because loss is an unpleasant experience for all of us, the ending of a psychotherapy process brings with it the vulnerability to transference and countertransference acting-out. Although an orderly, mutually agreed upon termination is the ideal, half or more of outpatients discontinue treatment prematurely (Baekeland and Lundwall 1975), and less than 20% of patients in community mental health center populations undergo a mutually negotiated termination process (Beck et al. 1987).

Termination may occur for a variety of reasons. It may be forced by external circumstances in the life of the therapist or the patient. Insurance companies or managed care firms may dictate the ending. The patient's own financial resources may run out. The patient may abruptly leave and refuse to return because of dissatisfaction with the therapist or anxiety over highly charged subject matter. The therapist may feel that maximum benefit has been reached and recommend termination, or the therapist and the patient may mutually agree upon a termination date.

Indications for termination are not absolute, but a good rule of thumb is that the patient is ready to stop when the goals of psychotherapy are reached. Presenting symptoms may have been eliminated or improved, the superego may have been modified, the patient's interpersonal relationships may have changed, and the patient may feel a new sense of independence. Another useful indicator is that patients are able to recognize and examine conflicts on their own and thus carry out a continuing self-analytic process without the therapist (Busch 1995; Dewald 1971). In cases of predominantly supportive psychotherapy, indications include a stability in the patient's functioning, a reversal of any regressive processes, and an overall quiescence of symptoms. Clinicians must always recognize, however, that a certain subset of highly disturbed patients may require ongoing, infrequent therapy indefinitely (Gabbard and Wilkinson 1994; Wallerstein 1986).

Once the therapist and patient have mutually agreed upon a date for termination, a number of transference manifestations may emerge. Some of the original symptoms may reappear (Dewald 1971; Roth 1987). Negative transference may surface for the first time when the patient realizes that the therapist will not be there forever. Therapists may need to assist their patients in mourning the fantasy of ultimate gratification in the transference. In supportive treatments, the therapist must stress continuing positive rapport and avoid the mobilization of unmanageable negative transferences (Dewald 1971). Because of the formidable challenges faced by the therapist during the termination process, many therapists prefer to continue the same frequency of sessions right up to the end. Others "wean" the patient by gradually decreasing the frequency of sessions.

When a patient terminates therapy unilaterally, therapists must deal with the feeling that they have somehow failed the patient. In such situations, therapists might remind themselves that the patient always has the privilege of ending the treatment and that such terminations may ultimately result in good outcomes. On the other hand, therapists can only help those patients who wish to be helped and who wish to collaborate in a process. Each therapist will have failures, and the limits of the craft must be recognized and accepted.

In instances when the termination is the therapist's unilateral decision, a different set of problems arise. When the termination is forced because of training requirements to rotate to a new clinical assignment, the therapist-in-training may wish to avoid discussing the termination process because of guilt feelings. Some therapists will even avoid letting their patients know of their departure until the last minute. In general, whenever external constraints are placed on the duration of the process, patients should be informed as early as possible so that their reactions can be accommodated as part of the treatment. When a therapist must leave the treatment for external reasons, patients often feel that the arbitrary nature of certain parental relationships has been re-created (Dewald 1971). Whatever the impact may be on the patient, the essential point is that the patient's reactions must be thoroughly explored even though the therapist may find it disconcerting to hear about the patient's anger and resentment.

Indications for Expressive or Supportive Emphasis in Psychotherapy

Before considering the indications for weighting a psychotherapy process toward the expressive or supportive end of the continuum, therapists must understand that predicting who will respond to what form of psychotherapy is an uncertain business at best. There is some indication in the literature that healthier patients tend to do better in psychotherapy than more severely ill patients (i.e., the rich get richer [Luborsky et al. 1980]). A study of who will benefit from psychotherapy (Luborsky et al. 1988) concluded that both a positive relationship at the outset and a congruence between the core conflictual relationship theme and the content of interpretations were predictors of good outcome. The strength of the therapeutic or helping alliance in the first session or two may be the best predictor of eventual outcome, according to empirical research on the subject (Morgan et al. 1982). However, this variable is greatly affected by the nature of the patient-therapist match, which is almost impossible to quantify. Kantrowitz (1987), in a study of 22 patients in analysis, concluded that even with sophisticated psychological testing, one cannot reliably predict suitability for psychoanalysis.

Despite these caveats, it is nevertheless possible to outline patient characteristics that can help clinicians decide whether a predominantly expressive or predominantly supportive focus is indicated (Table 4–1). Indications for a highly expressive modality, such as psychoanalysis, include 1) a strong motivation to understand oneself, 2) suffering that interferes with life to such an extent that it becomes an incentive for the patient to endure the rigors of treatment, 3) the ability not only to regress and give up control of feelings and thoughts but also to quickly regain control and reflect on that regression (regression in the service of the ego) (Greenson 1967), 4) tolerance for frustration, 5) a capacity for insight or psychological mindedness, 6) intact reality testing, 7) meaningful and enduring object relations, 8) reasonably good impulse control, and 9) ability to sustain a job (Bachrach and Leaff 1978). The ability to think in terms of metaphor and analogy, where one set of circumstances can be grasped as parallel to another, also augurs well for expressive treatment. Finally, reflective responses to trial interpretations during the evaluation period may suggest a suitability for expressive therapy.

Two general indications for supportive psychotherapy are chronic ego weaknesses or defects and regression in a healthy person who is undergoing a severe life crisis (Wallerstein 1986; Werman 1984). The former might include problems such as impaired reality testing, poor impulse control, and poor anxiety tolerance. Organically based cognitive dysfunction and lack of psychological mindedness are other indications for weighting the psychotherapy in a supportive direction. Pa-

TABLE 4–1. Indications for expressive or supportive emphasis in psychotherapy

Expressive	Supportive
Strong motivation to understand	Significant ego defects of a chronic nature
Significant suffering	Severe life crisis
Ability to regress in the service of the ego	Low anxiety tolerance
Tolerance for frustration	Poor frustration tolerance
Capacity for insight (psychological mindedness)	Lack of psychological mindedness
Intact reality testing	Poor reality testing
Meaningful object relations	Severely impaired object relations
Good impulse control	Poor impulse control
Ability to sustain a job	Low intelligence
Capacity to think in terms of analogy and metaphor	Little capacity for self-observation
Reflective responses to trial interpretations	Organically based cognitive dysfunction
	Tenuous ability to form a therapeutic alliance

tients with severe personality disorders who are prone to a great deal of acting out may also require supportive measures (G. Adler 1979; Luborsky 1984). Other patients who frequently do better with a predominantly supportive approach are those with seriously impaired object relations and a tenuous ability to form a therapeutic alliance. Individuals who are in the midst of a serious life crisis, such as divorce or death of a spouse or child, or who are affected by a catastrophe such as a flood or tornado, are rarely suitable for expressive or exploratory approaches because their ego may be overwhelmed by the recent trauma. After beginning a supportive process, however, these patients will sometimes shift in an expressive direction.

Although these indications are focused on the two ends of the expressive-supportive continuum, most patients will present with a mixture of indications, some pointing in the expressive direction and others pointing toward the supportive end. The therapist must continually assess how—and when—to be supportive or expressive as the process proceeds.

Brief Psychotherapy

In the past 20 years, there has been a burgeoning interest and literature on forms of brief psychotherapy derived from psychoanalytic principles. Methodologically sophisticated comparisons with other treatment modalities have demonstrated that brief dynamic psychotherapy is just as helpful as other psychotherapies (Crits-Christoph 1992). A number of superb texts outline detailed guidelines for clinicians (Book 1998; Budman 1981; Davanloo 1980; Garfield 1998; Gustafson 1986; Horowitz et al. 1984a; Malan 1976, 1980; Mann 1973; Sifneos 1972). Also available are several comprehensive review articles that compare and contrast the approaches and attempt to integrate them (Gustafson 1984; MacKenzie 1988; Ursano and Hales 1986; Winston and Muran 1996). Despite the variations and approaches, there are striking areas of consensus regarding the practice of brief psychotherapy. This brief discussion will emphasize those points of agreement.

Indications and Contraindications

In many ways, the indications for brief dynamic psychotherapy of an expressive nature parallel those associated with open-ended expressive psychotherapy. Important selection criteria include 1) the capacity for insight or psychological mindedness, 2) high levels of ego functioning, 3) strong motivation to understand oneself beyond mere symptom relief, 4) the capacity to form in-depth relationships (particularly an initial alliance with the therapist), and 5) the ability to tolerate anxiety. An additional point is central to selecting patients for brief psychotherapy—namely, the issue of focus. By virtue of its brevity, time-limited psychotherapy must be focal in nature in contrast to the pervasive breadth of psychoanalysis and highly expressive open-ended psychotherapy. Therefore, to proceed with brief therapy, the therapist and patient must identify the dynamic focus for the problem within the first or second evaluation session. Finally, brief therapy may be particularly helpful for relatively healthy individuals going through a developmental transition, such as moving from home, changing jobs, or having a first child.

Contraindications include the same factors that contraindicate open-ended psychotherapy of an expressive nature, but also encompass other features that might not contraindicate longer-term treatment. If a patient cannot circumscribe the problem to a focal dynamic issue, brief psychotherapy is contraindicated. Personality disorders that are amenable to longer-term expressive approaches cannot be expected to respond to short-term therapy, unless the patient presents with a situational complaint, such as grief, and unless the goals are limited to this temporary complaint (Horowitz et al. 1984a). Although some authors exclude chronically phobic or obsessional patients, Davanloo (1980) viewed patients with such symptoms as highly amenable to his style of brief psychotherapy.

Empirical research has confirmed that good outcomes in brief dynamic psychotherapy depend on careful selection of patients. Piper et al. (1990) have shown that the quality of object relations is one of the best predictors of outcome. Simply put, those with a capacity for more mature object relatedness tend to do better in treatment. Another study (Vaslamatzis et al. 1989) demonstrated higher dropout rates in patients who were not truly suitable for brief psychotherapy. A third project determined that bereaved patients who were highly motivated and better organized were more suitable for expressive brief therapy, whereas those with less motivation and lower organizations of the self-concept did better with supportive approaches (Horowitz et al. 1984b).

Number of Sessions

Different authors recommend different ways of handling the actual time limit of brief therapy. Mann (1973), who saw an acceptance of limits and a renunciation of magical expectations as central to the therapy process, insisted on a limit of 12 sessions. Davanloo (1980), on the other hand, averaged 15–25 sessions and did not set a specific termination at the beginning of treatment. Although Sifneos (1972) also refused to stipulate a specific number of sessions, his treatments tended to last only 12–16 sessions. As a general rule, then, brief therapy lasts as little as 2–3 months or as long as 5–6 months, and involves a range of 10–20 sessions.

Process of Therapy

Although the techniques associated with open-ended therapy are by and large applicable to brief treatments, their most striking difference is that they are markedly accelerated. Therapists must formulate their central hypothesis more quickly and must proceed to interpret resistances to insight earlier and more aggressively. Authors differ in terms of their degree of confrontation in dealing with resistances, but all acknowledge that the intensity of the process stirs up anxiety. Gustafson (1984) stressed that confronting resistances requires an *empathic* frame of reference or else the patient will feel attacked. There is also considerable consensus among authors about the critical role played by transference interpretations in producing change. Malan (1976), appropriating Karl Menninger's triangle of insight, suggested that the therapist's primary task is to link the focused complaint to patterns in past relationships, in present relationships, and in the transference. A brief example will illustrate this process.

> Mr. B, a 35-year-old military man, came to therapy with a chief complaint of "I'm too domineering." He had been married for 8 months to his second wife, who he said was already complaining about this character trait as his first wife had. In the second session Mr. B came in and began talking about the softball game he had just left. He disagreed with the umpire's decision to call him out at home plate, but noted, "You don't argue with the umpire. What he says goes. You're asking for trouble if you do," Later in the session he spoke of his father, who was a lieutenant colonel in the army. He described his father as an arbitrary man with whom you could not negotiate. The patient had always believed that his own opinions were not valued by his father. Still later in the session, Mr. B said, "I don't think 12 sessions are enough. But I guess we have to limit it to that. You said so."
>
> At this point the therapist made an intervention that joined together the three sides of the triangle: "It sounds like your experiences with the umpire, your father, and me are all similar—you feel we make arbitrary decisions in which you have no say." The therapist was then able to formulate an interpretation regarding the way the patient treated both his first and second wife. He was turning the passively experienced trauma of being completely dominated by his father into an experience of active mastery with his wife. He dominated her the way his father had dominated him.

Book (1998) has adapted Luborsky's core conflictual relationship theme to the process of brief dynamic psychotherapy. He stresses that therapists should identify three components in the patient as quickly as possible during the assessment phase: a wish, a response from the other, and a response from the self. The patient will tell stories describing relationship episodes in which these three components will soon become evident. The goal of psychodynamic brief therapy within this formulation is to help the patient actualize his or her wish by mastering the fear of how others will respond. This mastery is aided by conceptualizing that feared response as a form of a transference distortion.

Brief Supportive Psychotherapy

There is much less literature on brief psychotherapies of a supportive nature. The primary indication for brief supportive psychotherapy is a relatively healthy person who is undergoing a specific life crisis. The techniques involved are similar to those of long-term supportive psychotherapy, namely, ego building, facilitating the development of a positive transference without interpreting it, and restoring previously adaptive defenses, as illustrated in this example:

> Ms. C, a 52-year-old woman, came for consultation complaining about feelings of guilt and anxiety related to her 23-year-old daughter's out-of-wedlock pregnancy. The psychiatrist listened and empathized with the patient about the difficulty parents have seeing their children turn out differently than expected. The patient explained that she was so distracted by her guilt and anxiety over the situation that she was unable to function as usual at work or at home. The consultant attempted to restore Ms. C's usual obsessive-compulsive defenses by suggesting that she establish a structured routine at home so that she could accomplish all her usual household duties. He pointed out that staying busy would help Ms. C take her mind off her daughter. Ms. C complied with this suggestion and seemed somewhat improved at the next session. During this meeting the psychiatrist pointed out that Ms. C talked as though her daughter's pregnancy was her own responsibility. The patient responded, "You mean I didn't spread her legs?" The doctor affirmed, "That's right. You didn't spread her legs." The patient experienced a flood of relief with the doctor's words and thanked him for relieving her guilt. She called the following week and said that she need not return since she felt "100% better."

In this example the psychiatrist first helped the patient restore adaptive defenses by encouraging a return to her usual schedule. He then utilized the patient's positive transference to absolve her of guilt. This absolution from an authority figure whom she regarded with respect, if not idealization, had much greater impact on her than it would have if she had merely told herself the same message.

Determining whether to prescribe open-ended or brief psychotherapy is a complex decision. Clearly, the presence or absence of a focal issue is of considerable relevance (Ursano and Dressler 1974). If the patient's complaint is sufficiently circumscribed, a recommendation for brief psychotherapy can result in less expense and less inconvenience for the patient. Also, in one study of dropout rate in a public mental health clinic, the assignment of a specified length of therapy at the outset of treatment resulted in one-half the dropout rate compared with patients without such a clear end point (Sledge et al. 1990). However, complicated characterological problems may interfere with a patient's effective implementation of any "quick-fix" approach. In an era in which length of therapy is often determined by third- or fourth-party payers based on cost considerations, therapists must be mindful that less is not necessarily better. In a rigorous analysis of the dose-effect relationship with psychotherapy, there was clearly a positive relationship between the amount of treatment and the amount of patient benefit (Howard et al. 1986).

Finally, there is always a danger of therapists prescribing what they think the patient needs rather than what the patient wants. Is the patient asking for a fundamental examination and restructuring of personality, or is the request limited to assistance with one specific problem or complaint? The patient must clearly be a collaborator in determining the kind of treatment. We would be well advised to remember the dictum—attributed to Freud—that in some way, the patient is always right.

The Efficacy of Psychotherapy

The efficacy of individual psychotherapy is no longer in question. There is now overwhelming evidence that psychotherapy is an effective treatment (Luborsky et al. 1975; Smith et al. 1980). In fact, research shows that the magnitude of change brought about by psychotherapy is at a level that would justify the interruption of a clinical trial on the grounds that it would be unethical to withhold such a highly effective treatment from patients (Ursano and Silberman 1994). A meta-analysis of the efficacy of brief dynamic psychotherapy (Crits-Christoph 1992) found that the average brief dynamic therapy patient was better off than 86% of waiting-list control patients when target symptoms were examined. In another meta-analysis, Anderson and Lambert (1995) found that brief dynamic treatments "outperformed alternative treatments at follow-up assessment when measures of personality were used or when assessment took place 6 or more months posttreatment" (p. 512). Moreover, three significant studies have shown that accurate interpretations consonant with the patient's core issues are predictive of treatment outcome within a session (Silberschatz et al. 1986) as well as in both short-term (Crits-Christoph et al. 1988) and long-term (Joyce and Piper 1993) therapies. One study of brief supportive therapy looked at the subjects randomized to that treatment and found that 6 of 10 subjects with complete 6-month follow-up data showed significant improvement in interpersonal problems after 40 weeks of therapy (Rosenthal et al. 1999).

The evidence for the efficacy of long-term psychoanalytic psychotherapy or psychoanalysis is much more limited. If the standard randomized controlled trial were applied to extended psychoanalytic psychotherapy, the research would be extraordinarily expensive. Finding a suitable control group willing to wait around in a nontreatment condition for many years to find out if their problems remitted with the passage of time would also be next to impossible. Finally, in a long-term prospective study, the dropout rate could be prohibitive. In a brief therapy study, a 10% dropout rate over 16 weeks does not inordinately affect the statistical analysis. If that dropout rate occurred every 16 weeks over several years, it would be devastating to a long-term study. Intervening life events, medication shifts, and Axis I conditions would also create difficulties in interpreting data (Gunderson and Gabbard 1999).

Although randomized controlled studies have not yet been reported for psychoanalysis or extended psychoanalytic therapy, Bachrach et al. (1991) reviewed six systematic studies, totaling 550 patients in psychoanalysis, and found that improvement rates typically range from 60% to 90%. There are also data accumulating that suggest that longer therapy may be necessary for certain patients to make substantial improvements (Doidge 1997), especially those with personality disorders (Høglend 1993; Howard et al. 1986). Some patients appear to do better with more frequent or more intensive psychotherapy as well. Fonagy and Target (1996b) studied 763 cases of children and adolescents treated at the Anna Freud Centre in either four- to-five-times-per-week analysis or one- to-three-times-per-week dynamic psychotherapy. More frequent sessions led to greater improvements in children ages 6–12 years but not in adolescents (Fonagy and Target 1996b).

Although long-term dynamic therapy and psychoanalysis are often considered prohibitively expensive, with some conditions they may reduce hospitalization, medical visits, and disability in such a way that they are cost-effective in the long run (Dossmann et al. 1997; Gabbard et al. 1997).

Psychoanalysts and psychodynamic therapists were complacent for many years and have only recently taken the need for systematic research seriously. Further research is sorely needed to identify clear indications and contraindications for extended psychoanalytic therapy and psychoanalysis, to define the features that distinguish a psychodynamic approach from other methods, and to test in randomized controlled trials which types of patients will ultimately benefit from intensive treatment (Gunderson and Gabbard 1999).

References

Adler E, Bachant JL: Working in Depth: A Clinician's Guide to Framework and Flexibility in the Analytic Relationship. Northvale, NJ, Jason Aronson, 1998

Adler G: The myth of the alliance with borderline patients. Am J Psychiatry 47:642–645, 1979

Amini F, Lewis T, Lannon R, et al: Affect, attachment, memory: contributions toward psychobiologic integration. Psychiatry 59:213–239, 1996

Anderson EM, Lambert MJ: Short-term dynamically oriented psychotherapy: a review and meta-analysis. Clin Psychol Rev 15:503–514, 1995

Aron L: Self-reflexivity and the therapeutic action of psychoanalysis. Paper presented at the annual meeting of the American Psychoanalytic Association, Toronto, Ontario, May 29, 1998

Bachrach HM, Leaff LA: "Analyzability": a systematic review of the clinical and quantitative literature. J Am Psychoanal Assoc 26:881–920, 1978

Bachrach HM, Galatzer-Levy R, Skolnikoff A, et al: On the efficacy of psychoanalysis. J Am Psychoanal Assoc 39:871–916, 1991

Baekeland F, Lundwall L: Dropping out of treatment: a critical review. Psychol Bull 82:738–783, 1975

Basch MF: Doing Psychotherapy. New York, Basic Books, 1980

Beck NC, Lambert J, Gamachei M, et al: Situational factors and behavioral self-predictions in the identification of clients at high risk to drop out of psychotherapy. J Clin Psychol 43:511–520, 1987

Benjamin J: Like Subjects, Love Objects: Essays on Recognition and Sexual Difference. New Haven, CT, Yale University Press, 1995

Blatt SJ: The differential effect of psychotherapy and psychoanalysis with anaclitic and introjective patients: the Menninger Psychotherapy Research Project revisited. J Am Psychoanal Assoc 40:691–724, 1992

Book HE: How to Practice Brief Psychodynamic Psychotherapy: The Core Conflictual Relationship Theme Method. Washington, DC, American Psychological Association, 1998

Bordin ES: The generalizability of the psychoanalytic concept of the working alliance. Psychotherapy: Theory, Research, and Practice 16:252–260, 1979

Budman SH (ed): Forms of Brief Therapy. New York, Guilford, 1981

Busch F: The Ego at the Center of Clinical Technique (Critical Issues in Psychoanalysis 1). Northvale, NJ, Jason Aronson, 1995

Chessick RD: The Technique and Practice of Intensive Psychotherapy. New York, Jason Aronson, 1974

Chessick RD: What is intensive psychotherapy? Am J Psychother 35:489–501, 1981

Cooper AM: Changes in psychoanalytic ideas: transference interpretation. J Am Psychoanal Assoc 35:77–98, 1987

Cooper AM: Psychic change: development in the theory of psychoanalytic techniques. Int J Psychoanal 73:245–250, 1992

Crits-Christoph P: The efficacy of brief dynamic psychotherapy: a meta-analysis. Am J Psychiatry 149:151–158, 1992

Crits-Christoph P, Cooper A, Luborsky L: The accuracy of therapists' interpretations and the outcome of dynamic psychotherapy. J Consult Clin Psychol 56:490–495, 1988

Davanloo H (ed): Short-Term Dynamic Psychotherapy. New York, Jason Aronson, 1980

Dewald PA: Psychotherapy: A Dynamic Approach. New York, Basic Books, 1964

Dewald PA: Psychotherapy: A Dynamic Approach, 2nd Edition. New York, Basic Books, 1971

Doidge N: Empirical evidence for the efficacy of psychoanalytic psychotherapies and psychoanalysis: an overview. Psychoanalytic Inquiry 17 (suppl):102–150, 1997

Dossmann R, Kutter P, Heinzel R, et al: The long-term benefits of intensive psychotherapy: a view from Germany. Psychoanalytic Inquiry 17 (suppl):74–86, 1997

Fonagy P, Target M: Playing with reality, I: theory of mind and the normal development of psychic reality. Int J Psychoanal 77:217–233, 1996a

Fonagy P, Target M: Predictors of outcome in child psychoanalysis: a retrospective study of 763 cases at the Anna Freud Centre. J Am Psychoanal Assoc 44:27–77, 1996b

Freud A: The ego and the mechanisms of defense (1936), in The Writings of Anna Freud, Vol 2 (Revised Edition). New York, International Universities Press, 1966

Freud S: The interpretation of dreams (1900), in The Standard Edition of the Complete Psychological Works of Sigmund Freud, Vols 4, 5. Translated and edited by Strachey J. London, Hogarth Press, 1953, pp 1–627

Freud S: Recommendations to physicians practising psycho-analysis (1912), in The Standard Edition of the Complete Psychological Works of Sigmund Freud, Vol 12. Translated and edited by Strachey J. London, Hogarth Press, 1958, pp 109–120

Freud S: On beginning the treatment (1913), in The Standard Edition of the Complete Psychological Works of Sigmund Freud, Vol 12. Translated and edited by Strachey J. London, Hogarth Press, 1958, pp 121–144

Friedman L: A reading of Freud's papers on technique. Psychoanal Q 60:564–595, 1991

Frieswyk SH, Allen JG, Colson DB, et al: Therapeutic alliance: its place as a process and outcome variable in dynamic psychotherapy research. J Consult Clin Psychol 54:32–38, 1986

Fromm-Reichmann F: Principles of Intensive Psychotherapy. Chicago, IL, University of Chicago Press, 1950

Gabbard GO: Countertransference: the emerging common ground. Int J Psychoanal 76:475–485, 1995

Gabbard GO: Love and Hate in the Analytic Setting. Northvale, NJ, Jason Aronson, 1996

Gabbard GO: A reconsideration of objectivity in the analyst. Int J Psychoanal 78:15–26, 1997

Gabbard GO, Lester EP: Boundaries and Boundary Violations in Psychoanalysis. New York, Basic Books, 1995

Gabbard GO, Wilkinson SM: Management of Countertransference With Borderline Patients. Washington, DC, American Psychiatric Press, 1994

Gabbard GO, Lazar SG, Hornberger J, et al: The economic impact of psychotherapy: a review. Am J Psychiatry 154:147–155, 1997

Garfield SL: The Practice of Brief Psychotherapy. New York, Wiley, 1998

Greenberg JR: Theoretical models and the analyst's neutrality. Contemporary Psychoanalysis 22:87–106, 1986

Greenson RR: The working alliance and the transference neurosis (1965), in Explorations in Psychoanalysis. New York, International Universities Press, 1978, pp 119–224

Greenson RR: The Technique and Practice of Psychoanalysis. New York, International Universities Press, 1967

Grinberg L: The closing phase of the psychoanalytic treatment of adults and the goals of psychoanalysis: "the search for truth about one's self." Int J Psychoanal 61:25–37, 1980

Gunderson JG, Gabbard GO: Making the case for psychoanalytic therapies in the current psychiatric environment. J Am Psychoanal Assoc 47:679–703, 1999

Gustafson JP: An integration of brief dynamic psychotherapy. Am J Psychiatry 141: 935–944, 1984

Gustafson JP: The Complex Secret of Brief Psychotherapy. New York, WW Norton, 1986

Gutheil T, Gabbard GO: Misuses and misunderstandings of boundary theory in clinical and regulatory settings. Am J Psychiatry 155:409–414,1998

Hartley DE, Strupp HH: The therapeutic alliance: its relationship to outcome in brief psychotherapy, in Empirical Studies of Psychoanalytic Theories, Vol 1. Edited by Masling J. Hillsdale, NJ, Analytic Press, 1983, pp 1–37

Hoffman IZ: Ritual and Spontaneity in the Psychoanalytic Process: A Dialectical-Constructivist View. Hillsdale, NJ, Analytic Press, 1998

Hoffman IZ, Gill MM: Critical reflections on a coding scheme. Int J Psychoanal 69:55–64, 1988

Høglend P: Personality disorders and long-term outcome after brief dynamic psychotherapy. J Personal Disord 7:168–181, 1993

Horowitz MJ, Marmar C, Krupnick J, et al: Personality Styles and Brief Psychotherapy. New York, Basic Books, 1984a

Horowitz MJ, Marmar C, Weiss DS, et al: Brief psychotherapy of bereavement reactions: the relationship of process to outcome. Arch Gen Psychiatry 41:438–448, 1984b

Horwitz L: Clinical Prediction in Psychotherapy. New York, Jason Aronson, 1974

Horwitz L, Gabbard GO, Allen JG, et al: Borderline Personality Disorder: Tailoring the Psychotherapy to the Patient. Washington, DC, American Psychiatric Press, 1996

Howard KI, Kopta SM, Krause MS, et al: The dose-effect relationship in psychotherapy. Am Psychol 41:159–164, 1986

Jacobs TJ: The corrective emotional experience—its place in current technique. Psychoanalytic Inquiry 10:433–454, 1990

Joyce AS, Piper WE: The immediate impact of transference in short-term individual psychotherapy. Am J Psychother 47:508–526, 1993

Kantrowitz JL: Suitability for psychoanalysis. Yearbook of Psychoanalysis and Psychotherapy 2:403–415, 1987

Kantrowitz JL, Katz AL, Paolitto F, et al: Changes in the level and quality of object relations in psychoanalysis: follow-up of a longitudinal, prospective study. J Am Psychoanal Assoc 35:23–46, 1987

Karasu TB: Psychotherapies: an overview. Am J Psychiatry 134:851–863, 1977

Kohut H: How Does Analysis Cure? Edited by Goldberg A. Chicago, IL, University of Chicago Press, 1984

Lipton SD: The advantages of Freud's technique as shown in his analysis of the Rat Man. Int J Psychoanal 58:255–273, 1977

Loewald HW: On the therapeutic action of psychoanalysis (1957), in Papers on Psychoanalysis. New Haven, CT, Yale University Press, 1980, pp 221–256

Lohser B, Newton PM: Unorthodox Freud: The View From the Couch. New York, Guilford, 1996

Luborsky L: Principles of Psychoanalytic Psychotherapy: A Manual for Supportive-Expressive Treatment. New York, Basic Books, 1984

Luborsky L, Singer B, Luborsky L: Comparative studies of psychotherapies: is it true that "everyone has won and all must have prizes?" Arch Gen Psychiatry 32:995–1008, 1975

Luborsky L, Mintz J, Auerbach A, et al: Predicting the outcome of psychotherapy: findings of the Penn Psychotherapy Project. Arch Gen Psychiatry 37:471–481, 1980

Luborsky L, Crits-Christoph P, Mitz J, et al: Who Will Benefit From Psychotherapy? Predicting Therapeutic Outcomes. New York, Basic Books, 1988

Lyons-Ruth K, Members of the Change Process Study Group: Implicit relational knowing: its role in development and psychoanalytic treatment. Infant Mental Health Journal 19:282–289, 1998

MacKenzie KR: Recent developments in brief psychotherapy. Hospital and Community Psychiatry 39:742–752, 1988

Malan DH: The Frontier of Brief Psychotherapy: An Example of the Convergence of Research and Clinical Practice. New York, Plenum, 1976

Malan DH: Toward the Validation of Dynamic Psychotherapy: A Replication. New York, Plenum, 1980

Mann J: Time-Limited Psychotherapy. Cambridge, MA, Harvard University Press, 1973

Marziali E, Marmar C, Krupnick J: Therapeutic alliance scales: development and relationship to psychotherapy outcome. Am J Psychiatry 138:361–364, 1981

Menninger KA: Theory of Psychoanalytic Technique. New York, Basic Books, 1958

Mitchell SA: Influence and Autonomy in Psychoanalysis. Hillsdale, NJ, Analytic Press, 1997

Morgan R, Luborsky L, Crits-Christoph P, et al: Predicting the outcomes of psychotherapy by the Penn Helping Alliance Rating Method. Arch Gen Psychiatry 39:397–402, 1982

Ogden TH: Projective Identification and Psychotherapeutic Technique. New York, Jason Aronson, 1982

Ornstein A: "Supportive" psychotherapy: a contemporary view. Clinical Social Work Journal 14:14–30, 1986

Pine F: On therapeutic change: perspectives from a parent-child model. Psychoanalysis and Contemporary Science 5:537–569, 1976

Pine F: Supportive psychotherapy: a psychoanalytic perspective. Psychiatric Annals 16:526–529, 1986

Pine F: Diversity and Direction in Psychoanalytic Technique. New Haven, CT, Yale University Press, 1998

Piper WE, Azim HFA, McCallum M, et al: Patient suitability and outcome in short-term individual psychotherapy. J Consult Clin Psychol 58:475–481, 1990

Pulver SE: Psychic change: insight or relationship? Int J Psychoanal 73:199–208, 1992

Racker H: Transference and Counter-transference. New York, International Universities Press, 1968

Renik O: Analytic interaction: conceptualizing technique in light of the analyst's irreducible subjectivity. Psychoanal Q 62:553–571, 1993

Rosenthal RN, Muran JC, Pinsker H, et al: Interpersonal change in brief supportive therapy. J Psychother Pract Res 8:55–63, 1999

Roskin G: Changing modes of psychotherapy. Journal of Psychiatric Treatment and Evaluation 4:483–487, 1982

Roth S: Psychotherapy: The Art of Wooing Nature. Northvale, NJ, Jason Aronson, 1987

Sandler J: Countertransference and role-responsiveness. International Review of Psychoanalysis 3:43–47, 1976

Sifneos PE: Short-Term Psychotherapy and Emotional Crisis. Cambridge, MA, Harvard University Press, 1972

Silberschatz G, Fretter PB, Curtis JT: How do interpretations influence the process of psychotherapy? J Consult Clin Psychol 54:646–652, 1986

Sledge WH, Moras K, Hartley D, et al: Effect of time-limited psychotherapy on patient dropout rates. Am J Psychiatry 147:1341–1347, 1990

Smith ML, Glass GV, Miller TI: The Benefits of Psychotherapy. Baltimore, MD, Johns Hopkins University Press, 1980

Steiner J: The aim of psychoanalysis. Psychoanalytic Psychotherapy 4:109–120, 1989

Stern DN, Sander LW, Nahum JP, et al: Non-interpretive mechanisms in psychoanalytic therapy: the "something more" than interpretation. Int J Psychoanal 79:903–921, 1998

Ursano RJ, Dressler DM: Brief versus long-term psychotherapy: a treatment decision. J Nerv Ment Dis 159:164–171, 1974

Ursano RJ, Hales RE: A review of brief individual psychotherapies. Am J Psychiatry 143:1507–1517, 1986

Ursano RJ, Silberman EK: Psychoanalysis, psychoanalytic psychotherapy, and supportive psychotherapy, in The American Psychiatric Press Textbook of Psychiatry, 2nd Edition. Edited by Hales E, Yudofsky SC, Talbott J. Washington, DC, American Psychiatric Press, 1994, pp 1035–1060

Vaslamatzis G, Markidis M, Katsouyanni K: Study of the patients' difficulties in ending brief psychoanalytic psychotherapy. Psychother Psychosom 52:173–178, 1989

Wallerstein RS: Forty-Two Lives in Treatment: A Study of Psychoanalysis and Psychotherapy. New York, Guilford, 1986

Werman DS: The use of dreams in psychotherapy: practical guidelines. Canadian Psychiatric Association Journal 23:153–158, 1978

Werman DS: The Practice of Supportive Psychotherapy. New York, Brunner/Mazel, 1984

Winnicott DW: The aims of psychoanalytic treatment (1962), in The Maturational Processes and the Facilitating Environment. London, Hogarth Press, 1976, pp 166–170

Winston A, Muran C: Common factors in the time-limited therapies, in American Psychiatric Press Review of Psychiatry, Vol 15. Edited by Dickstein LJ, Riba MB, Oldham JM. Washington, DC, American Psychiatric Press, 1996, pp 43–68

Treatments in Dynamic Psychiatry

Group Therapy, Family/Marital Therapy, and Pharmacotherapy

Dynamic Group Psychotherapy

We all live and work in the context of groups. Group psychotherapy provides patients an opportunity to learn how they function in groups—the roles they play, the expectations and unconscious fantasies they harbor about groups, and the obstacles they encounter in getting along with others at work and at home. Unique dimensions of group experience can be only partially explored in individual psychotherapy.

Unique Aspects of Group Experience

Much of our knowledge of the forces operating in groups is derived from the work of Wilfred Bion (1961). After World War I, Bion began conducting small group experiences at the Tavistock Clinic. His understanding of groups revolved around his observation that two groups are present in every group: 1) the "work group" and 2) the "basic assumption group." The former is involved with the actual work task of a group and is geared toward completion of the task. Few groups, however, work rationally toward attaining their goals without interference from basic assumptions (Rioch 1970).

Basic assumptions refer to the unconscious fantasies that lead groups to behave in an "as-if manner" (Rioch 1970). In other words, the group members begin to act on an assumption about the group that is different from the reality of the task at hand. Basic assumptions fall into three categories: dependency, fight/flight, and pairing. These discrete emotional states are unconscious in origin but are easily deducible from the behavior of the group. These assumptions derail the work group and prevent completion of its task. In a psychotherapy group, the task of understanding one another's problems may be steered off course by the development of basic assumptions. However, just as Freud discovered that transference in psychoanalysis is more of a therapeutic tool than an obstacle, Bion discovered that the basic assumptions themselves can be of enormous value in helping individual members of groups understand themselves in the context of the group.

Bion's initial observations of basic assumptions were at a descriptive level, but as he gained more and more experience with group dynamics, he realized that the basic assumptions were clusters of defenses against psychotic anxieties present in everyone. Groups are powerfully regressive, and they provide patients with a window into their most primitive fears. Bion realized that the mechanisms associated with the paranoid-schizoid and depressive positions identified by Melanie Klein (see Chapter 2) were also present in the basic assumptions.

The dependency basic assumption, for example, can be viewed as a cluster of defenses against depressive anxieties (Ganzarain 1980). In this basic assumption, patients behave as though they are weak, ignorant, and incapable of helping each other and as if they are totally dependent on the therapist, whom they view as god-like. The underlying fear is that their greed (i.e., their oral neediness) will engulf the therapist and result in their being abandoned. To defend against the anxiety and guilt connected with their potential destruction of the therapist (i.e., their mother at an unconscious level), the patients believe that the therapist is an inexhaustible, omniscient, and omnipotent figure who will always be there for them and who will always have the answers.

In the fight/flight basic assumption, the group has regressed to a frank paranoid-schizoid position. All "badness" is split off and projected. The wish to fight or take flight is a cluster of defenses against paranoid anxiety. To avoid an externally perceived persecutor who will destroy them, the group can either fight or run from the persecutor. The group becomes nonreflective and views action as the only solution to the perceived threat.

The pairing basic assumption is a cluster of defenses against depressive anxieties. The assumption in this instance frequently revolves around two group members who will reproduce and bring forth a messiah to rescue the group (Rioch 1970). There is a pervasive atmosphere of optimism and hopefulness, a belief that love will prevail. This Pollyannaish attitude may be viewed as a manic defense against the group's concern that destructiveness, hate, and hostility also exist within the group. Hence, in this view pairing can be viewed as a manic reparative effort (Ganzarain 1980).

Group psychotherapists must be continually vigilant for the development of basic assumptions in their groups, so that they can interpret and examine them before they become too destructive to the task of the group. Unexamined transference may lead an individual to quit psychotherapy; unexamined basic assumptions may lead to the dissolution of group therapy.

Beyond the basic assumptions, there are other unique forces operating in groups. One of the most powerful is the phenomenon of "role suction" (Redl 1963). A common observation is that an individual's behavior in a one-to-one situation may change dramatically upon entry to a group. We frequently hear, for example, about a "good boy" who "got in with the wrong crowd." Individuals who find themselves behaving differently in groups often describe themselves as being drawn or "sucked" into playing a role that seemed outside their control. An individual patient in group psychotherapy, for example, may serve as a spokesperson for the entire group, while everyone else remains silent. Another individual may serve in the role of scapegoat, behaving in such a way as to become the target for everyone's anger. Both the spokesperson and the scapegoat phenomena can be understood as group versions of projective identification (Horwitz 1983; Ogden 1982). In scapegoating, for example, the unacceptable parts of all the group members are projected onto one individual who then feels coerced into responding like the projected parts of the other patients. If the therapist supports the scapegoat and interprets the group process, the projected parts may be reintrojected.

Characteristics of Psychotherapeutic Groups

Most group therapists meet with their groups once a week (Sadock 1983), although some who model group psychotherapy after classical psychoanalysis (Wolf 1983) may conduct as many as five group sessions a week. The sessions, which adhere to a strict time limit as in individual psychotherapy, usually last from $1\frac{1}{4}$ to $1\frac{1}{2}$ hours. Although groups vary in size, the average dynamic psychotherapy group contains 8–10 members (Sadock 1983). Smaller groups may be quite useful, provided that the members actively participate and are reasonably verbal.

The composition of a dynamic therapy group may vary considerably, although heterogeneous groups are thought to have advantages over homogeneous groups (Yalom 1985). The consensus of clinicians is that groups in which everyone is similar rarely get beyond superficial levels of interaction. On the other hand, if a group is too heterogeneous, it may be dysfunctional because of the lack of common ground among the patients. Moreover, certain individuals may feel isolated if they believe that they are vastly different from everyone else in the group by virtue of their age, cultural background, or socioeconomic status. Finally, if members of the group have highly variable levels of ego strength, the group may not gel because of the difficulty in exploring psychological issues.

The consensus of the literature is that dynamic therapy groups should be heterogeneous in terms of the conflicts of the members but homogeneous in terms of a reasonably similar level of ego strength (Whitaker and Lieberman 1964; Yalom 1985). Most of the dynamic group psychotherapy literature is weighted toward the expressive end of the expressive-supportive continuum. Groups that are more supportive in nature may be more homogeneous as well. Dynamic therapy groups are typically open-ended, and new members may be added as old members terminate. However, some homogeneous groups with a focal issue to discuss, such as victims of therapist-patient sexual abuse (Sonne 1989), may meet for a time-limited therapy process.

In recent years, with the pressures of managed care and accountability in the health care environment, briefer versions of group psychotherapy have become more prevalent, even for heterogeneous groups. MacKenzie (1997) has developed a concept of time-managed group psychotherapy in which he delineates three models of group psychotherapy based on patient need and awareness of limitations on resources available for treatment: 1) crisis intervention (1–8 sessions), 2) time-limited therapy (8–26 sessions), and 3) longer-term therapy (more than 26 sessions). Empirical research has begun to support the efficacy of briefer forms of dynamic group therapy. In one study of 12-week expressive therapy groups for outpatients who had not adapted well to loss (Piper et al. 1992), treated patients showed greater improvement than waiting-list control patients, and their improvements were maintained or even increased at 6-month follow-up.

Dynamic group psychotherapists vary in the extent to which they use a group-centered versus an individual-centered approach. In the individual-centered form of group therapy (Wolf 1983), the process is conceptualized as similar to individual psychoanalysis in a group setting. The group process itself is relatively less important than interpretation of the individual's difficulties in dealing with the other group members and with the therapist. The more extreme advocates of the group-centered approach (Ezriel 1950) have viewed the interpretation of group forces as much more important than the interpretation of the individual's conflicts. In fact, Ezriel (1950) suggested that the therapist should refrain from interpretation until a common group tension or theme has developed. A less extreme approach was advocated by Horwitz (1977), who proposed that individual interpretations may be used in the service of building up the group's awareness of a common group issue, which is then also interpreted. There are common group experiences that everyone shares and that deserve interpretation, such as not having all one's needs met by the leader, competition for support, and anxiety about being ignored. However, if there is no focus on individual issues as well, patients may feel that their individual reasons for seeking treatment have been overlooked by the therapist. Most group therapists subscribe to a combined model involving both individual- and group-centered interventions (Slipp 1988).

Transference, Countertransference, and Resistance

Transference, countertransference, and resistance are cornerstones of dynamic group psychotherapy, just as they are in individual work. However, the group modality itself significantly alters the transference. First, the intensity of the patients' transferences may be diluted by their redirection to fellow patients. This displacement of the transference from therapist to peer may be beneficial, however, as it allows a "practice ground" for working through a parental transference prior to its development in the relationship with the therapist (Wolf 1983). Group psychotherapy also allows for the formation of multiple simultaneous transferences. The therapist then is provided with a laboratory where the patients' internal object relations are displayed for all to see through externalization in relationships with individual group members. Although different transferences develop in individual therapy as well, they tend to appear over a longer period. The group setting may allow the therapist to gain a greater familiarity with the patients' internal object relations in a much shorter time.

Although transference may be diluted in group therapy, the converse is also true. Transference may be intensified when the entire group is swept up with powerful feelings of either positive or negative valence. Therapists who serve as containers for all the bad object projections in the group members rapidly realize that countertransference may also be intensified in a group setting. The countertransferential demands on the group therapist may be formidable. Fortunately, there is built-in protection against untoward countertransference acting-out because group patients will readily spot inappropriate behavior or misperceptions on the part of the therapist and insist on an explanation (Wolf 1983). To diffuse transference and countertransference, some therapists prefer to work with a co-therapist in group psychotherapy. Having a partner helps the therapist to process the intense feelings stirred up by the group.

Sibling rivalry and a transference wish to be the therapist's only or favorite child is a common development in all dynamic therapies. However, these issues may have a more compelling quality in group therapy, and the therapist must diligently avoid showing any favoritism for specific group members (Yalom 1985).

In addition to the patients' transference to the therapist and to other group members, there is a third form of transference that is truly unique to groups— transference to the group as a whole. This form of transference affords patients an opportunity to examine their expectations of other groups with which they live and work. The group as a total entity is often viewed as an idealized, completely gratifying "mother" that will satisfy the patient's yearning for a reunion with an unconditionally loving figure. In recognition of this tendency, Scheidlinger (1974) dubbed this phenomenon the "mother-group." When this form of transference is in full flower, the therapist may be viewed as a terrifying maternal figure in contrast to the all-giving benevolence of the group as a whole. Other authors (Gibbard and Hartman 1973) have viewed the idealized transference to the group as a whole as a defensive posture that avoids seeing the group (mother) as sadistic.

The working through of transference and resistance constitutes the bulk of the dynamic therapist's task, much as it does in individual psychotherapy. Indeed, Ganzarain (1983) suggested that working through is the key characteristic that distinguishes psychoanalytic group therapy from other forms of group treatment. He particularly emphasized the working through of primitive psychotic-like anxieties and their associated defense mechanisms. The regressive forces activated by group experience bring the patient in touch with anxiety stemming from the paranoid-schizoid and depressive positions much more rapidly and more profoundly than in individual treatment. The working through of transference is also facilitated by the input of other group members. An individual patient may attempt to validate a personal impression of the therapist by "checking it out" with other group patients. When peers confront the distortions inherent in the transference perception, the patient may be much more willing to listen and accept feedback than when it is provided by the therapist.

Indications and Contraindications

A number of indications for dynamic group psychotherapy are the same as those for expressive-supportive individual therapy. These include 1) strong motivation, 2) psychological mindedness, 3) a reasonably high level of ego strength, 4) sufficient discomfort that the patient is willing to endure the frustrations inherent in the process, and 5) problems in interpersonal relationships (Yalom 1985). However, the question that the clinician must address is: What specific criteria suggest that a patient is particularly suited for group psychotherapy rather than individual psychotherapy?

There has been an unfortunate tradition in the field to view group psychotherapy as a second-class treatment modality. Review articles comparing individual and group psychotherapy do not support this bias (Lambert and Bergin 1994; MacKenzie 1996). Most of these comparison studies find no difference in outcome. Dynamic group therapy is probably an underutilized modality despite its attractiveness in terms of cost-effectiveness.

There are several kinds of problems that may be dealt with more effectively in a group setting than in individual treatment (Sadock 1983). The patient who is extraordinarily anxious around authority figures may find it easier to talk and relate in the company of peers. A patient whose primary problem seems to have originated in sibling conflicts may find that a group setting reactivates the problem in a way that makes it easier to examine and resolve. Conversely, sometimes an only child who missed out on a sibling experience and who has difficulty learning to share in adult life may find that a group is the best place to address those issues. Nonpsychotic patients who rely heavily on projection may benefit from the confrontations of other group members, who repeatedly dispute the distortions brought to the group. Borderline patients who form an intensely negative transference in individual therapy may benefit from the dilution of transference inherent in group work. However, these patients almost always require individual therapy as well (see Chapter 15). When the two modalities are combined, there are additive and magnifying effects for both the individual and the group treatment (Porter 1993; Sperry et al. 1996). The additive effects of individual therapy include deep intrapsychic exploration and one-to-one corrective emotional experience. The additive effects of group therapy are the exploration of multiple transferences and the provision of a setting in which the patient can risk new behaviors. One of the magnifying effects of individual therapy is that it may provide an opportunity to explore material developing from the group sessions and thus may prevent premature dropout from the group. A possible magnifying effect of the group therapy is an additional chance to analyze transference resistances from the individual sessions.

Group therapy is generally effective for patients with higher-level personality disorders, including hysterical, obsessive-compulsive, some narcissistic, passive-aggressive, and dependent types, because a group setting may be the only place in which these patients receive feedback about how their character patterns affect others. Much of the psychopathology found in patients with personality disorders involves ego-syntonic character traits (i.e., behaviors that distress others but not the patient). The feedback from peers in group therapy often helps these patients reflect on their behavior patterns so that these traits eventually become ego-dystonic (i.e., uncomfortable to the patients themselves), which is the first step toward gaining sufficient motivation to change. The effect of group psychotherapy on particular personality disorders and the indications for combined individual and group therapy will be further addressed in Section III of this volume.

One obvious difference between individual and group psychotherapy in assessing indications is that the group therapist must constantly evaluate the fit between a prospective patient and the group as it is currently composed. One borderline patient may be quite tolerable in a group of patients with a high level of ego strength, but two may overwhelm the group with disproportionate demands for attention and disruptive acting-out. Similarly, issues such as age and gender must be balanced when deciding on indications for a particular group.

Certain clinical symptomatology is consensually viewed as contraindicating dynamic group psychotherapy. These features include 1) low motivation, 2) psychotic disorganization, 3) addiction to substances, 4) antisocial personality disorder, 5) severe somatization, 6) organically based cognitive dysfunction, and 7) serious suicide risk (Yalom 1985). Addicts and patients with antisocial features may, however, be effectively treated in homogeneous groups of a confrontational nature (see Chapters 12 and 17). As is the case with indications, some patients may be contraindicated for a particular group because of the composition of that group, but might instead be suitable for a different group.

Family and Marital Therapy

Although many family and marital therapists practicing today are not dynamically oriented, the field had its origins in the work of a number of early psychoanalytically oriented clinicians, including Theodore Lidz, Lyman Wynne, Nathan Ackerman, Murray Bowen, and Virginia Satir. The focus of these early family therapists on the psychology of the individual was dramatically altered in the decades of the 1950s and 1960s by a group of Palo Alto researchers, including Gregory Bateson, Don Jackson, and Jay Haley (1956). Systemic family therapy grew out of the work of this group, and with it the emphasis shifted from the individual to the family system. Individual psychopathology and personal history both became secondary to the family as a whole, which was viewed as a system with a life of its own. Until recently, this systemic approach to family therapy, along with its subsequent elaborations by Minuchin (1974) and Selvini Palazzoli et al. (1978), has largely dominated the field of family therapy.

Bowen family therapy has grown increasingly popular in recent years. This approach is rooted in psychoanalytic theory, but the technique that has evolved from the ideas of Bowen (1978) is largely nondynamic. In this form of treatment, one individual family member meets with the therapist on an infrequent basis (often once a month) to carefully study the intergenerational patterns in the patient's family. The patient is helped to understand how the current patterns in family relationships are repetitions of patterns from past generations. The approach is strictly cognitive, and the patient is not encouraged to express feelings. Transference issues are not viewed as important and are not interpreted. On the contrary, once patients have gained an intellectual understanding of their family patterns, they are encouraged to address the unresolved issues directly with the appropriate family members.

In the last decade or so, object relations family therapy has also grown in popularity and now stands as the most prominent present-day example of psychodynamic family therapy. Since the discussion in this chapter is restricted to dynamic approaches, we will examine object relations family therapy in some detail while omitting consideration of the nondynamic schools of family therapy.

Theoretical Understanding

Working with married couples at the Tavistock Clinic in the 1950s and 1960s, Henry Dicks (1963) began to notice that relatively healthy couples—who appeared to have satisfying marriages—were often working out primitive object relationships in their marriages. He observed that each spouse tended to perceive the other as though he or she were someone else. Typically, the husband would perceive the wife as though she were an internal object representation from his own psyche, often his own mother. Similarly, the wife would relate to the husband as though he were simply a projection from her internal world. Dicks concluded that a major source of marital discord was the failure of each partner to confirm the other's true nature or identity. Instead, the partners tended to coerce each other into behaving in highly stereotyped and constricting ways. Couples tended to deteriorate into polarized units, such as sadistic-masochistic, domineering-submissive, healthy-sick, and independent-dependent. Dicks recognized that each of these polarized halves formed a whole personality in the marital dyad, but that each individual alone was incomplete. Just as his colleague Bion was noting that groups exert a regressive force on individuals, Dicks was discovering that marriage has a similar regressive effect. Even in people with considerable ego strength, marriage seemed to regress them rapidly into parent-child relationships.

What Dicks observed, of course, was a form of transference. The marital partners were reenacting a past relationship in the present. In the language of object relations theory, the spouses were using splitting and projective identification to make an *internal* conflict an *external*, or marital, conflict, with an internal object representation, usually a parent, split off and projected onto the spouse. The projector then behaved in such a way as to coerce the spouse into behaving like the projected internal object. A husband, for example, who is used to being babied by his mother may unconsciously re-create the situation with his mother in his marriage by acting childish and evoking a motherly response from his wife. Alternatively, the marital partner may project a self-representation onto the spouse and coerce the spouse into behaving like that self-representation while the projector behaves like a complementary object representation. The case of Mr. B in Chapter 4 was such a situation. He projected a victimized, submissive self-representation onto both his first and his second wife while behaving like his domineering, aggressive father.

Marital conflict may be viewed as the re-creation of conflicts with one's parents, via splitting and projective identification. The selection of a mate is obviously much influenced by such processes. Dicks (1963) believed that such selections are "largely based on unconscious signals or cues by which the partners recognize in a more-or-less central ego-syntonic person the other's 'fitness' for joint working-through or repeating of still unresolved splits or conflicts inside each other's personalities, while at the same time, paradoxically, also sensing a guarantee that with that person they will not be worked-through" (p. 128). Hence, couples are thrown together by conflicting desires to work through unresolved object relations, on the one hand, and to simply repeat them, on the other.

Several authors have expanded this object relations understanding of marital conflict to the entire family (Scharff and Scharff 1987; Shapiro et al. 1975; Slipp 1984, 1988; Stewart et al. 1975; Zinner and Shapiro 1972, 1974). These authors noted that the identified patient in a family is frequently a carrier or container of the split-off, unacceptable parts of other family members. In that sense, the family equilibrium is maintained by this arrangement of splitting and projective identification. An adolescent boy, for example, may act on antisocial impulses that represent aspects of an unacceptable self-representation of his father that has been projectively disavowed by the father and contained by the son. A child may be idealized in the same way via projective identification of positive aspects of self- or object representations. Object relations theory lends itself well to family therapy because its constructs (e.g., splitting and projective identification) provide a bridge from the intrapsychic to the interpersonal and from the individual to the family (Slipp 1984; Zinner 1976).

Technique

The technique of object relations therapy for couples and families grows out of the theoretical understanding. The overall goal is to help members of the family or couple reinternalize the conflicts that have been externalized via projective identification (Scharff and Scharff 1991; Zinner 1976). The focus, then, must be on helping each individual to reown projected parts (Stewart et al. 1975). To accomplish this goal, the object relations family therapist will typically meet with the family for a 50-minute session every week or every other week (Slipp 1988).

The therapy process begins with a careful diagnosis of how internal self- and object representations have been distributed throughout the family via splitting and projective identification. When this pattern becomes apparent, the therapist attempts to explain how an unconscious, collusive system is formed among family members to perpetuate pathological behavior in the identified patient. The stability of the family depends on the ability of one or more individual members to contain various projected parts of other family members. As with other forms of dynamic psychotherapy, these explanatory interpretations are usually met with resistance early on. This antitherapeutic force may take the form of attempting to get the therapist "sucked into" the family system. In other words, family members unconsciously repeat the family's pathological patterns instead of verbalizing and exploring them. In marital therapy, for example, a husband may use projective identification with the therapist in the same way he does with his spouse.

Because of these powerful resistances, object relations family therapists must be especially attuned to their countertransference reactions in the broad or objective sense. In other words, it is critically important that therapists allow themselves to be containers for the projected parts of the family members so that they can more adequately diagnose and interpret what happens within the family (Slipp 1988). Therapists are then in a position to point out the pathological collusive patterns in the here and now of the therapy process and to connect them with what goes on outside that process.

The most common form of resistance at the beginning of marital therapy is for both partners to expect the therapist to "fix" their spouse (Jones and Gabbard 1988). Because the externalization of the conflict onto the partner is so well established, both spouses are more interested in persuading the therapist that they are "right" than they are in repairing the marriage (Berkowitz 1984). Therapists must consistently avoid taking sides in such conflicts. Instead, they must help couples expand their perspective to encompass an appreciation of their own contributions to the conflict in the marriage.

The transition from seeing the problem as a marital conflict to perceiving it as an internal conflict that is played out within the couple is a difficult task for each partner. Projective identification in the marital dyad requires a continued state of conflict—the polarization inherent in the splitting process maintains the stable balance (Zinner 1976). Any effort to destabilize this arrangement is likely to be highly threatening to both marital partners. The need for the spouse to be the "bad object" may be so compelling that all therapeutic efforts are for naught (Dicks 1963). Despite their understanding of the pathological interactions between them, some couples will choose to live in a state of turmoil rather than face the anxiety associated with change.

In the final analysis, of course, change in marital therapy is not the therapist's responsibility—only the marital partners themselves can decide if they wish to change their marriage. When therapists find themselves highly invested in a particular outcome, they are frequently involved in a collusive interaction in which they have become identified with projected parts of the family members. Moreover, the more the therapist pushes for change, the more the couple is likely to resist. When the therapy becomes stalemated because of such resistance, it is sometimes useful for the therapist to lay out various options to the couple and to convey to them that they are free to choose how to proceed with their lives. Divorce or no change at all must be among those options and must be considered acceptable outcomes by the therapist. Only then will the couple realize that it is ultimately up to them how they choose to live their lives.

Brief Marital Therapy

Greenspan and Mannino (1974) have developed a model for brief marital therapy based on projective identification. This model is designed for couples with considerable ego strength and with no signs of any severe pathology. The goal of this form of treatment is limited: to confront each partner with those aspects of the spouse's personality that are not being perceived because of projective identification. After listening to the wife's version of the conflict, the therapist might ask the husband to repeat the essence of his wife's concern. If he omits a particular aspect of her feelings, the therapist will point out the omission.

The therapeutic process in this model of brief intervention helps both partners listen better and develop a fuller empathic appreciation for their spouse's internal experience. As marital partners come to acknowledge that they are distorting their perceptions of one another, they begin to realize that they do not know the person they married very well. When this approach is successful, it sets in motion a process of "checking out" each other's feelings rather than assuming that the partner feels a certain way.

Intersubjective and Self Psychological Marital Therapy

In recent years the concepts of self psychology have also been applied to marital conflict. Kohut himself, in a footnote from his last book (1984), noted that "a good marriage is one in which one or the other partner rises to the challenge of providing the selfobject functions that the other's temporarily impaired self needs at a particular moment" (p. 220). He also noted that when selfobject needs are not supplied by a spouse, the result may be divorce and unending bitterness—a form of all-too-common chronic narcissistic rage.

The conflicts arising from the need for selfobject responses by one's spouse can form the basis of a strategy for marital therapy (Ringstrom 1994, 1998; Shaddock 1998). Ringstrom points out the importance of the bidimensional nature of transference in therapy with couples (see Chapter 1). Having been frustrated in their attempts to get their selfobject needs met from each other, the couple may be "locked in to reciprocally antagonistic, repetitive dimension transferences toward one another while each spouse is experiencing the yearned-for selfobject in the transference toward the therapist" (Ringstrom 1994, p. 161). Although this development may be problematic in some ways, the therapist's attunement to it may restore hope to the couple. Ringstrom has outlined a six-step model based on intersubjectivity theory and self psychology. In the first two steps, the therapist provides attunement to the subjectivity of each spouse and stresses that neither of the partners has a truer or more correct version of reality than the other. In steps 3 and 4, the therapist traces the developmental history of frustrated selfobject yearnings and demonstrates how each partner is reenacting his or her conflictual past in an effort to maintain self-cohesion. Step 5 involves the enhancement of introspective capacity so that each partner can take ownership for part of the relational difficulty. The final step centers on each spouse's capacity to support the other spouse's personal growth and introspection while attuning to his or her perspective.

Ringstrom (1998) also stresses a particular variant of countertransference difficulty in which both members of the couple are competing to extract selfobject functions from the therapist. The therapist's own needs for selfobject responses may lead him or her to be drawn into collusions with one member of the couple versus the other. The therapist must try to reestablish a special variant of a neutral stance in which he or she hears, understands, and accepts each partner's subjective perception of the other as intrinsically valid.

Indications and Contraindications

The "consumer" model is a commonsense approach clinicians can use in deciding whether a patient needs individual or family/marital therapy. What is the patient asking for? Does one "patient" come to the office or do two? Does the discussion focus on "my problem" or "our problem"? Is the problem viewed as having an internal origin or an external one? If parents come with their adolescent child, the problem of determining the therapy of choice may be more complex. Frequently, the adolescent is not convinced of the need for treatment and may remain silent throughout most of the first appointment. Meanwhile, the parents may go on and on about their son's or daughter's problems. The evaluating clinician needs to make a rapid determination regarding the next appointment. Will seeing only one "patient" be a collusion with the splitting and projective identification processes in the family (Stewart et al. 1975)? When in doubt, of course, the clinician may simply continue an exploratory evaluation process until the dynamics of the family are clearer. At times when one member of a couple or certain family members simply refuse to attend a therapy process, the therapist may be forced to work with only one family member or to do no treatment at all.

Slipp (1988) stressed the identified patient's level of differentiation from the family as a good rule of thumb in determining the therapy of choice. Individual psychotherapy is probably the treatment of choice with late adolescents or young adults who have managed to separate, psychologically and geographically, from their families and to live their own lives with reasonably mature defensive operations. But family therapy or a combination of family and individual therapy is likely to be most helpful with individuals in the same age group who are still living at home, or who are living separately but still find themselves emotionally involved with their families in an intense and conflictual manner.

A frequent problem that arises in individual psychotherapy is the patient's request to bring the spouse to an appointment to work on marital issues. If the individual process is well established, trying to convert it into a marital therapy process as well is rarely successful. The spouse who is brought in usually feels that the therapist's primary loyalty is to the other partner and is rarely able to form an alliance with the therapist. A better solution is to refer the couple to a marital therapist while continuing the original individual process.

Dynamic Pharmacotherapy

Several decades ago the phrase "dynamic pharmacotherapy" would have been considered a contradiction in terms. The legacy of mind/body dualism polarized dynamic and pharmacological approaches to psychiatric disorders for many years. Fortunately, recent integrative trends have brought contemporary psychiatry to the point where combined use of medication and psychotherapy is now almost universal practice for both nonpsychotic and psychotic conditions (Gabbard 1999; Thompson and Brodie 1981).

In situations where formal psychotherapy is not part of the treatment, psychodynamic thinking may be extraordinarily useful in improving compliance with psychotropic regimens. About one-third of patients actually comply adequately with medication as prescribed, one-third more or less comply, and one-third are noncompliant, suggesting that compliance rates generally hover around 50% (Wright 1993). Outpatient compliance with antidepressant medication is only about 40% after 12 weeks (Myers and Branthwaite 1992). Among patients with schizophrenia, 74% of outpatients become noncompliant with their neuroleptic regimens within 2 years of discharge from the hospital (Weiden et al. 1995). Although a switch to depot medication temporarily improves compliance, by 6 months postdischarge there is no difference in compliance rates between patients receiving depot medication and those taking the medication orally.

As discussed in Chapter 8, bipolar patients are also notoriously noncompliant with medication regimens. A further complication in treating noncompliance is that patients tend to seriously underreport the extent to which they are not cooperating with prescribed treatments. A number of studies have used a microprocessor-based method for continuous monitoring of compliance. In this method, a microelectronic circuit records the date and time of each opening and closing of the medication container. One study that used this technology showed that whereas self-reported noncompliance was 7% when assessed by interview, it was 53% when assessed by the microprocessor-based method for continuous monitoring (Dunbar-Jacob 1993).

The phenomenon of noncompliance can usually be understood with the aid of psychodynamic concepts such as transference, countertransference, resistance, and therapeutic alliance.

Transference

The psychiatrist prescribing medication is no less a transference figure than the psychotherapist. For patients, the decision to comply or not to comply with the doctor's recommendations activates unconscious issues of parental expectations. When patients refuse to take medication as prescribed, psychiatrists often react by becoming more authoritarian, insisting that their orders be followed without question. This approach usually backfires because it merely exacerbates the transference disposition to see the doctor as a demanding parental figure. A far more productive approach is to enlist patients' collaboration in exploring their concerns. A series of questions such as the following may be helpful: "Do you have any concerns about taking medications other than side effects?" "Do you remember problems with taking medication in the past?" "Have you heard anything on television or read anything in the newspaper about this medication?" "Does your family have any special feelings about taking medications?" "What do you think has caused your illness?" "Does this medication have any particular meaning to you?"

"What feelings do you have toward the prescribing doctor?"

One patient experienced the prescription of an antidepressant as an empathic failure on the part of the psychiatrist. When the patient's noncompliance was explored with him, he told his doctor, "I was looking for someone to validate my feelings. Instead, you tried to medicate them away." When the psychiatrist encouraged him to elaborate further, the patient was able to connect this feeling with earlier experiences with his father, whom he experienced as inattentive and uncaring about his concerns.

Other patients, especially those who have characterological tendencies to be controlling or dominating, will see medication as a threat to their counterdependent stance. Taking a pill means submitting to the domination of a powerful parental figure. These patients must be given some control over whether to take the medication (Thompson and Brodie 1981). With overly submissive patients, one often encounters the opposite situation. Pills make these patients feel "fed" and taken care of to such an extent that they may decide that they no longer need to take responsibility for any aspect of their illness.

Transference struggles may be particularly intense with whining, "manipulative help-rejecters" (Groves 1978). These patients systematically defeat every treatment intervention, pharmacological or otherwise. They frequently have gone through a lengthy list of psychotropic agents without feeling any benefit. Exploring the transference dynamics may lead to the uncovering of a great deal of resentment and bitterness toward parental figures who the patient believes did not give enough nurturance. By rejecting help offered to them, these patients may be unconsciously seeking revenge against their parents (Gabbard 1988). When such patients sense that they are making their doctor miserable, they often feel a secret triumph.

A unique aspect of transference in dynamic pharmacotherapy is transference to the medication itself (Gutheil 1982). Placebo responses to medications often have this same transference quality. A manic patient, for example, became markedly subdued after one 300-mg dose of lithium carbonate, a response that could not be explained pharmacologically. Placebo side effects are also common. Another manifestation of transference to medications is the response to changing the drug rituals of chronic patients (Appelbaum and Gutheil 1980). Such patients may decompensate into psychosis with the slightest alteration of their usual medication regimen.

The transference relationship to a medication may be most obvious in situations where the pill takes the place of the absent doctor. Pills may function as transitional objects for some patients, allowing them to maintain some sense of connectedness with their psychiatrists even when seeing them quite infrequently (Book 1987). Touching or looking at the pill may have a soothing effect on the patient. In training programs, where residents rotate through services on an annual basis, patients may deal with the loss of their doctor by becoming intensely attached to the medication prescribed by the departing doctor (Gutheil 1977).

Transferences of this type are powerful and may lead to another form of noncompliance—refusal to discontinue medications because of the unconscious meaning of the medication to the patient. Transference issues must always be taken into account when prescribing psychotropic agents to paranoid patients. In more subtle cases, the patient may discontinue a medication for the ostensible reason of unpleasant side effects, when in actuality the patient is afraid of being poisoned. Insistence on compliance will greatly increase the paranoia, while empathic exploration of the nature of the fears may help the patient to realize that they are unfounded and to view the therapist as less threatening (Book 1987).

Countertransference

The prescribing of medication is just as likely as any other treatment intervention to be contaminated by countertransference. One common manifestation of countertransference is overprescription. It is not uncommon for a patient to arrive at a hospital or an emergency room with a brown paper bag full of psychoactive agents. One such patient was taking three antipsychotics, two antidepressants, lithium carbonate, and two benzodiazepines. After a few days in the hospital, it was apparent that this patient evoked intense feelings of impotence and anger in treaters. The excessive amounts of medication reflected the countertransference despair of the attending psychiatrist.

Narcissistic injury may also be a factor in countertransference. Some psychotherapists may fail to prescribe a much-needed medication because they believe that doing so would be tantamount to conceding that their psychotherapeutic skills have been ineffective. Others may induce guilt feelings in noncompliers so that they will feel obligated to comply with the medication regimen out of a wish not to hurt their doctor.

Some psychiatrists become anxious about intense feelings of any kind in the transference. Medication may be viewed as a way to deal with this countertransference anxiety. The discussion of side effects may also be influenced by this anxiety. For example, a psychiatrist may avoid bringing up the sexual side effects of selective serotonin reuptake inhibitors (SSRIs) because of his or her own discomfort with overt sexual discussion. As a result, patients who experience these effects may simply discontinue their medication without informing the physician.

Countertransference anger, which is a common response to noncompliance in patients, may take many forms. Some psychiatrists may collude with the noncompliance to demonstrate how ill their patients will get if they do not follow the "doctor's orders" (Book 1987). Others may bully patients into taking their medications or threaten to discharge them from treatment if they do not comply. Those psychiatrists who have difficulty controlling their anger may refuse to set limits on patients who demand increasing amounts of medication. In these cases the psychiatrist hopes that gratifying the demands of the patient will keep aggression and hostility out of the therapeutic relationship. Unfortunately, the patient's demandingness and anger usually escalate.

Resistance

Resistance to treatment is as powerful a force in pharmacotherapy as it is in psychotherapy. Illness may be preferable to health for numerous reasons. It is well known, for example, that patients with bipolar affective disorder may enjoy their manic episodes so much that they will stop taking their lithium. In one study of schizophrenic patients (Van Putten et al. 1976), a similar cause of resistance was uncovered. In this investigation, side effects and secondary gain had little to do with noncompliance. An ego-syntonic grandiose psychosis was the most powerful discriminating factor that distinguished schizophrenic patients who did not comply from those who did. Clearly, the noncompliers preferred their experience of psychotic grandiosity.

Denial of illness is also a prominent cause of resistance to pharmacotherapy. For some patients, any psychotropic agent carries with it the stigma of mental illness. When an acute psychotic episode goes into remission, a patient may stop the antipsychotic medication responsible for the remission because maintenance treatment connotes a chronic mental illness. Nonpsychotic patients who are quite willing to submit to psychotherapeutic treatment will balk at the suggestion of medication because they are convinced it means that they are more seriously disturbed than they like to think. Likewise, patients who have had a relative in psychopharmacological treatment may unconsciously identify with that relative when offered the same medication (Book 1987). This identification may serve as a resistance to accepting treatment, particularly if the relative had an especially unfavorable outcome, such as suicide.

Finally, another form of resistance not related to compliance with the prescribed medication represents the flip side of the wish to deny illness. It is not at all uncommon for some patients who willingly take their medication to nevertheless resist the therapeutic effects of pharmacological agents. These patients are so powerfully invested in their illness that they tenaciously cling to their symptoms even when these are challenged by potent psychotropic agents. For such patients, a psychotherapeutic approach is the treatment of choice.

Therapeutic Alliance

The foregoing discussion about noncompliance should make it clear that the therapeutic alliance plays a crucial role in dynamic pharmacotherapy. Numerous authors have stressed that attending to the therapeutic alliance is part of the prescribing process (Docherty and Fiester 1985; Elkin et al. 1988; Gutheil 1982; Howard et al. 1970). Although much contemporary psychopharmacological research does not quantify the doctor-patient relationship, many investigators have noted its influence on compliance. One study (Howard et al. 1970) discovered that subtle aspects of the therapist's behavior, including vocal enthusiasm, body language, and use of the patient's name, differentiated psychiatrists with low dropout rates from those with high attrition rates. This study also indicated that attention to the therapeutic alliance in the first session prevented noncompliance with drug treatment.

Research on depressed patients has indicated that the therapeutic alliance may be a key factor regardless of the type of treatment. Even if a patient is being treated primarily with antidepressant medication, the psychodynamic construct of the therapeutic alliance is just as important as it is when a patient is receiving only psychotherapy. A team of researchers (Krupnick et al. 1996) examined a sample of 225 depressed patients in the National Institute of Mental Health (NIMH) Treatment of Depression Collaborative Research Program. Clinical raters scored videotaped transcripts of treatment sessions in all four cells: 16 weeks of cognitive therapy, 16 weeks of interpersonal therapy, 16 weeks of imipramine plus clinical management, and 16 weeks of placebo plus clinical management. When outcomes were assessed for these patients, the therapeutic alliance was found to have a significant effect on clinical outcome for all four cells. In fact, patient contribution to the therapeutic alliance accounted for 21% of the outcome variance on standardized outcome measures, with more of the variance in outcome attributed to the total alliance than to the treatment method itself! Among the four cells, none showed significant group differences in terms of the relationship between therapeutic alliance and clinical outcome. This was the first empirical study to show that the therapeutic alliance had the same effect on outcome regardless of whether the treatment was psychotherapy or pharmacotherapy.

Studies of the dropout rate in both psychotherapeutic and psychopharmacological treatment settings have emphasized that patient expectations can influence attrition (Freedman et al. 1958; Overall and Aronson 1963). Different patients come to a psychiatrist with different expectations of the kind of treatments available. At some point in the first interview, psychiatrists should explore their patients' expectations so that the treatment prescribed is in some way consistent with them. If the treatment of choice is counter to a patient's preconceived notions, an educational effort may be necessary to convince the patient of its usefulness.

In Chapter 4, the concept of collaboration was emphasized in the discussion of the therapeutic alliance in psychotherapy. An analogous concept of "participant prescribing" (Gutheil 1982) is relevant for pharmacotherapy. The unconscious tendency of some psychiatrists to switch to a more authoritarian mode when prescribing medications is liable to backfire in the form of noncompliance. Even in the practice of internal medicine, sensitive internists are aware that they will evoke better compliance if they discuss with their patients the reasons for antibiotics, thus enlisting the patients' cooperation in the process of treatment. The variable of patient education positively influences the development of a therapeutic alliance in pharmacotherapy. All patients should be thoroughly informed about the therapeutic and side effects of any pharmacological agent they receive. With acutely psychotic patients, however, this discussion sometimes must wait until the acute episode is under pharmacological control.

Special types of compliance problems are often encountered when medication is added to an ongoing psychotherapy process, as in the following example:

Ms. D, a 39-year-old married professional woman, came to psychiatric treatment because of feelings of depression, low energy, lack of satisfaction in her job, difficulty sleeping, and decreased sex drive. She seemed extremely grateful for the opportunity to have someone listen to her. After a few weeks and several sessions of psychotherapy, Ms. D began to feel a great deal of trust in her therapist. She poured out her heart in a poignant and moving manner during the sessions. With a great many tears, she told of the extraordinary difficulties in her life and the problems she encountered at home and at work.

After about 6 weeks of these sessions, her therapist told her that her symptoms were of sufficient severity that he was going to prescribe an antidepressant for her. The therapist wrote out the prescription, explained the side effects she might encounter, and sent her on her way with instructions to begin taking the medication immediately.

The following week Ms. D came for her appointment and began talking once again about her problems but made no mention of the medication. When her therapist asked her how she was doing with the agent he had prescribed, she said that she had not had time to go to the pharmacy to fill the prescription but that she would do so in the next few days. The therapist again emphasized the importance of starting on the medication as soon as possible. Ms. D minimized her failure to fill the prescription and reassured her therapist that she would do so before the next appointment.

A week passed and Ms. D returned for her therapy session. Once again she reported that she had failed to go to the pharmacy. Knowing that this lack of compliance was reflecting some dynamic that was not readily apparent, her therapist explored with her what reasons she might have for not wanting to take the medication. With some reluctance Ms. D admitted that she was very much afraid that she was receiving medication because her therapist did not want to hear all the complaints she brought to each session. Ms. D experienced the prescription as though she was being told to "shut up." Her therapist asked her if she had had any similar experiences in her life. She went on to say that her father was not a verbal person and that he had chastised her throughout her childhood and adolescence for complaining all the time. Ms. D also noted that her husband was much the same way and had urged her to go to a psychiatrist so he wouldn't have to listen to her complaints. She feared that her therapist would no longer see her for psychotherapy if she responded well to the medication.

The therapist told her that medication and psychotherapy were not mutually exclusive and that he would continue to work psychotherapeutically with her while she was taking medication. Ms. D seemed relieved to have that reassurance, and she complied with the prescription on a regular basis after that session.

Combined Treatment

Despite the history of polarization between psychotherapists and pharmacotherapists, the combination of psychotherapy and medication is a time-honored clinical practice in psychiatry. In three different analytic cases involving severe depression, Anna Freud enlisted a colleague to prescribe medication—with highly beneficial results (Lipton 1983). She was convinced that the addition of pharmacological agents was crucial in allowing the analysis to continue. Luborsky et al. (1975) surveyed 26 research studies evaluating combined treatment and found that in 69% of the comparisons, the combined approach was more effective than either psychotherapy or pharmacotherapy alone. Few analytically oriented clinicians still harbor concerns that medication will interfere with the psychotherapeutic process. In a survey of American Academy of Psychoanalysis therapists, 90% of respondents reported that they prescribed medications (Normand and Bluestone 1986). A Columbia University study (Roose and Stern 1995) reported that pharmacotherapy was used in conjunction with psychoanalysis in 29% of the psychoanalytic institute's supervised training cases, suggesting that medication is no longer seen as a contaminating factor that might interfere with the certification of newly graduated analysts.

Today, the question is no longer *whether* the combination of psychotherapy and medication is beneficial; rather, it is *how* the combination is beneficial (Gabbard and Bartlett 1998). There are unlimited variations in how the two may interact in any particular treatment. Likewise, there are many variations in how patients respond when medication is added to their psychotherapy. Some patients will feel that the treatment is being turned over to medication and that the therapist is giving up on them (Roose and Stern 1995). Other patients will feel that the medication helps them get more out of the therapy. Often, the patient's and the therapist's perceptions of the relative contributions of medication and therapy are directly opposed. In a case of a patient to whose analysis an SSRI was added (Solomon 1995), the patient was convinced that his analyst viewed the positive effects of the medication as primarily psychological. By contrast, the patient thought that 90% of the effect of the medication was pharmacological.

Recent findings that SSRIs may have powerful effects on so-called characterological traits (Coccaro and Kavoussi 1997; Markovitz 1995; Salzman et al. 1995) make the distinction between Axis I and Axis II disorders less clear and the interface between medication and psychotherapy more complex. Many patients experience fundamental identity questions when medication alters their sense of who they are. They may find themselves perplexed by the fine line that exists between the impact of dysfunctional neurotransmitters and a psychological indecisiveness and inability to act (Gabbard and Bartlett 1998). If traits we have traditionally regarded as characterological are influenced by medication, how does that affect the patient's sense of responsibility for feelings, thoughts, and behaviors? Svrakic et al. (1993) suggest that personality can be divided into two essential components: temperament, a genetically based biological construct, and character, an environmentally based psychological dimension. They suggest that medications may affect temperament, while psychotherapy addresses character.

Clinicians may find themselves at a loss to determine whether psychotherapy or pharmacotherapy is the best approach for treating a patient's particular symptoms. What *is* required of clinicians who combine the approaches, however, is an awareness of the "bimodal relatedness" inherent in the dual role (Docherty et al. 1977). The patient must be viewed simultaneously as a disturbed person and as a diseased central nervous system. The former view requires an empathic, subjective approach, while the latter demands an objective, medical model approach. The clinician must be able to shift between these two modes gracefully while remaining attuned to the impact of the shift on the patient.

Extensive case reports in the literature provide examples of the value of combined treatment. Wylie and Wylie (1987) reported the case of a female analytic patient who could not work within the transference in the analysis until monoamine oxidase inhibitors were prescribed for her depression. The medication reduced her affective vulnerability sufficiently to enable her to risk dealing with transference feelings. Loeb and Loeb (1987) treated seven manic patients who were taking lithium carbonate while in either psychoanalysis or psychoanalytic psychotherapy. Through analysis or therapy, these patients became aware of a marked increase in their unconscious sexual impulses and their defenses against them. The patients were then able to learn that these impulses heralded the onset of a manic episode. By making these impulses conscious, they were able to prevent future manic episodes by increasing their lithium dosage.

The fundamental compatibility of biology and psychodynamics was emphasized in Chapter 1. One instance of this marriage is the increasing practice of combining pharmacotherapy and psychotherapy. Because conceptual bridges are still being built between the two approaches, much of the practice remains empirical at this point. As in all psychiatry, the guiding principle must be to help the patient rather than to remain true to one's theoretical biases.

References

Appelbaum PS, Gutheil TG: Drug refusal: a study of psychiatric inpatients. Am J Psychiatry 137:340–346, 1980

Bateson G, Jackson DD, Haley J, et al: Toward a theory of schizophrenia. Behavioral Science 1:251–264, 1956

Berkowitz DA: An overview of the psychodynamics of couples: bridging concepts, in Marriage and Divorce: A Contemporary Perspective. Edited by Nadelson CC, Polonsky DC. New York, Guilford, 1984, pp 117–126

Bion WR: Experiences in Groups and Other Papers. New York, Basic Books, 1961

Book HE: Some psychodynamics of non-compliance. Can J Psychiatry 32:115–117, 1987

Bowen M: Family Therapy in Clinical Practice. New York, Jason Aronson, 1978

Coccaro EF, Kavoussi RJ: Fluoxetine and impulsive aggressive behavior in personality-disordered subjects. Arch Gen Psychiatry 54:1081–1088, 1997

Dicks HV: Object relations theory and marital studies. Br J Med Psychol 36:125–129, 1963

Docherty JP, Fiester SJ: The therapeutic alliance and compliance with psychopharmacology, in Psychiatry Update: American Psychiatric Association Annual Review, Vol 4. Edited by Hales RE, Frances AJ. Washington, DC, American Psychiatric Press, 1985, pp 607–632

Docherty JP, Marder SR, Van Kammen DP, et al: Psychotherapy and pharmacotherapy: conceptual issues. Am J Psychiatry 134:529–533, 1977

Dunbar-Jacob J: Contributions to patient adherence: is it time to share the blame? Health Psychol 12:91–92, 1993

Elkin I, Pilkonis PA, Docherty JP, et al: Conceptual and methodological issues in comparative studies of psychotherapy and pharmacotherapy, I: active ingredients and mechanisms of change. Am J Psychiatry 145:909–917, 1988

Ezriel H: A psycho-analytic approach to group treatment. Br J Med Psychol 23:59–74, 1950

Freedman N, Engelhardt DM, Hankoff LD, et al: Drop-out from outpatient psychiatric treatment. Archives of Neurology and Psychiatry 80:657–666, 1958

Gabbard GO: A contemporary perspective on psychoanalytically informed hospital treatment. Hospital and Community Psychiatry 39:1291–1295, 1988

Gabbard GO: Combined pharmacotherapy and psychotherapy, in Comprehensive Textbook of Psychiatry VII, Vol 2. Edited by Kaplan HI, Sadock BJ. Baltimore, MD, Williams & Wilkins, 1999, pp 2225–2234

Gabbard GO, Bartlett AB: Selective serotonin reuptake inhibitors in the context of an ongoing analysis. Psychoanalytic Inquiry 18:657–672, 1998

Ganzarain RC: Psychotic-like anxieties and primitive defenses in group analytic psychotherapy. Issues in Ego Psychology 3:42–48, 1980

Ganzarain RC: Working through in analytic group psychotherapy. Int J Group Psychother 33:281–296, 1983

Gibbard GR, Hartman JJ: The significance of utopian fantasies in small groups. Int J Group Psychother 23:125–147, 1973

Greenspan SI, Mannino FV: A model for brief intervention with couples based on projective identification. Am J Psychiatry 131:1103–1106, 1974

Groves J: Taking care of the hateful patient. N Engl J Med 298:883–887, 1978

Gutheil TG: Psychodynamics in drug prescribing. Drug Therapy 2:35–40, 1977

Gutheil TG: The psychology of psychopharmacology. Bull Menninger Clin 46:321–330, 1982

Horwitz L: A group-centered approach to group psychotherapy. Int J Group Psychother 27:423–439, 1977

Horwitz L: Projective identification in dyads and groups. Int J Group Psychother 33:259–279, 1983

Howard K, Rickels K, Mock JE, et al: Therapeutic style and attrition rate from psychiatric drug treatment. J Nerv Ment Dis 150:102–110, 1970

Jones SA, Gabbard GO: Marital therapy of physician couples, in Medical Marriages. Edited by Gabbard GO, Menninger RW. Washington, DC, American Psychiatric Press, 1988, pp 137–151

Kohut H: How Does Analysis Cure? Edited by Goldberg A. Chicago, IL, University of Chicago Press, 1984

Krupnick JL, Sotsky SM, Simmens S, et al: The role of therapeutic alliance in psychotherapy and pharmacotherapy outcome: findings in the National Institute of Mental Health Treatment of Depression Collaborative Research Program. J Consult Clin Psychol 64:532–539, 1996

Lambert MJ, Bergin AE: The effectiveness of psychotherapy, in Handbook of Psychotherapy and Behavior Change, 4th Edition. Edited by Bergin AE, Garfield SL. New York, Wiley, 1994, pp 143–189

Lipton MA: A letter from Anna Freud. Am J Psychiatry 140:1583–1584, 1983

Loeb FF, Loeb LR: Psychoanalytic observations on the effect of lithium on manic attacks. J Am Psychoanal Assoc 35:877–902, 1987

Luborsky L, Singer B, Luborsky L: Comparative studies of psychotherapies: is it true that "everyone has won and all must have prizes?" Arch Gen Psychiatry 32:995–1008, 1975

MacKenzie KR: The time-limited psychotherapies: an overview, in American Psychiatric Press Review of Psychiatry, Vol 15. Edited by Dickstein LJ, Riba MB, Oldham JM. Washington, DC, American Psychiatric Press, 1996, pp 11–21

MacKenzie KR: Time-Managed Group Psychotherapy: Effective Clinical Applications. Washington, DC, American Psychiatric Press, 1997

Markovitz P: Pharmacotherapy of impulsivity, aggression, and related disorders, in Impulsivity and Aggression. Edited by Hollander E, Stein DJ, Zohar J. New York, Wiley, 1995, pp 263–287

Minuchin S: Families and Family Therapy. Cambridge, MA, Harvard University Press, 1974

Myers ED, Branthwaite A: Out-patient compliance with antidepressant medication. Br J Psychiatry 160:83–86, 1992

Normand WC, Bluestone H: The use of pharmacotherapy in psychoanalytic treatment. Contemporary Psychoanalysis 22:218–234, 1986

Ogden TH: Projective Identification and Psychotherapeutic Technique. New York, Jason Aronson, 1982

Overall B, Aronson H: Expectations of psychotherapy in patients of lower socioeconomic class. Am J Orthopsychiatry 33:421–430, 1963

Piper WE, McCallum M, Azim HFA: Adaptation to Loss Through Short-Term Group Psychotherapy. New York, Guilford, 1992

Porter K: Combined individual and group psychotherapy, in Comprehensive Group Psychotherapy, 3rd Edition. Edited by Kaplan H, Sadock B. Baltimore, MD, Williams & Wilkins, 1993, pp 314–324

Redl F: Psychoanalysis and group therapy: a developmental point of view. Am J Orthopsychiatry 33:135–147, 1963

Ringstrom PA: An intersubjective approach to conjoint therapy, in Progress in Self Psychology, Vol 10. Edited by Goldberg A. Hillsdale, NJ, Analytic Press, 1994, pp 159–182

Ringstrom PA: Competing selfobject functions: the bane of the conjoint therapist. Bull Menninger Clin 62:314–323, 1998

Rioch MJ: The work of Wilfred Bion on groups. Psychiatry 33:56–66, 1970

Roose SP, Stern RH: Medication use in training cases: a survey. J Am Psychoanal Assoc 43:163–170, 1995

Sadock BJ: Preparation, selection of patients, and organization of the group, in Comprehensive Group Psychotherapy, 2nd Edition. Edited by Kaplan HI, Sadock BJ. Baltimore, MD, Williams & Wilkins, 1983, pp 23–32

Salzman C, Wolfson AN, Schatzberg A, et al: Effect of fluoxetine on anger in symptomatic volunteers with borderline personality disorder. J Clin Psychopharmacol 15:23–29, 1995

Scharff DE, Scharff JS: Object Relations Family Therapy. Northvale, NJ, Jason Aronson, 1987

Scharff DE, Scharff JS: Object Relations Couple Therapy. Northvale, NJ, Jason Aronson, 1991

Scheidlinger S: On the concept of the "mother-group." Int J Group Psychother 24:417–428, 1974

Selvini Palazzoli M, Boscolo L, Cecchin G, et al: Paradox and Counterparadox: A New Model in the Therapy of the Family in Schizophrenic Transaction. New York, Jason Aronson, 1978

Shaddock D: From Impasse to Intimacy: How Understanding Unconscious Needs Can Transform Relationships. Northvale, NJ, Jason Aronson, 1998

Shapiro ER, Zinner J, Shapiro RL, et al: The influence of family experience on borderline personality development. International Review of Psychoanalysis 2:399–411, 1975

Slipp S: Object Relations: A Dynamic Bridge Between Individual and Family Treatment. New York, Jason Aronson, 1984

Slipp S: The Technique and Practice of Object Relations Family Therapy. Northvale, NJ, Jason Aronson, 1988

Solomon JL: A clinical study of the effect of the introduction of antidepressant medication on the psychoanalytic process in an analysis of long duration. Journal of Clinical Psychoanalysis 4:169–184, 1995

Sonne JL: An example of group therapy for victims of therapist-client sexual intimacy, in Sexual Exploitation in Professional Relationships. Edited by Gabbard GO. Washington, DC, American Psychiatric Press, 1989, pp 101–113

Sperry L, Brill PL, Howard KI, et al: Treatment Outcomes in Psychotherapy and Psychiatric Interventions. New York, Brunner/Mazel, 1996

Stewart RH, Peters TC, Marsh S, et al: An object-relations approach to psychotherapy with marital couples, families, and children. Fam Process 14:161–178, 1975

Svrakic DM, Whitehead C, Pryzbeck TR, et al: Differential diagnosis of personality disorders by the seven-factor model of temperament and character. Arch Gen Psychiatry 50:991–999, 1993

Thompson EM, Brodie HKH: The psychodynamics of drug therapy. Current Psychiatric Therapies 20:239–251, 1981

Van Putten T, Crumpton E, Yale C: Drug refusal in schizophrenia and the wish to be crazy. Arch Gen Psychiatry 33:1443–1446, 1976

Weiden P, Rapkin B, Zymunt A, et al: Postdischarge medication compliance of inpatient converted from an oral to a depot neuroleptic regimen. Psychiatr Serv 46:1049–1054, 1995

Whitaker DS, Lieberman MA: Psychotherapy Through the Group Process. New York, Atherton Press, 1964

Wolf A: Psychoanalysis in groups, in Comprehensive Group Psychotherapy, 2nd Edition. Edited by Kaplan HI, Sadock BJ. Baltimore, MD, Williams & Wilkins, 1983, pp 113–131

Wright EC: Noncompliance—or how many ants has Matilda? Lancet 342:909–913, 1993

Wylie HW Jr, Wylie ML: An effect of pharmacotherapy on the psychoanalytic process: case report of a modified analysis. Am J Psychiatry 144:489–492, 1987

Yalom ID: The Theory and Practice of Group Psychotherapy, 3rd Edition. New York, Basic Books, 1985

Zinner J: The implications of projective identification for marital interaction, in Contemporary Marriage: Structure, Dynamics, and Therapy. Edited by Grunebaum H, Christ J. Boston, MA, Little, Brown, 1976, pp 293–308

Zinner J, Shapiro R: Projective identification as a mode of perception and behavior in families of adolescents. Int J Psychoanal 53:523–530, 1972

Zinner J, Shapiro R: The family as a single psychic entity: implications for acting out in adolescence. International Review of Psychoanalysis 1:179–186, 1974

Treatments in Dynamic Psychiatry

Dynamically Informed Hospital and Partial Hospital Treatment

Because psychodynamic principles evolved largely from the practice of psychoanalysis, these precepts are sometimes narrowly construed to be relevant only to outpatient treatment. One psychiatric resident asked his supervisor for help in understanding a hospitalized patient, only to be told, "Dynamics apply only to outpatients, not inpatients." Nothing could be further from the truth, of course. However, the supervisor's comment reflects an unfortunate trend in modern hospital psychiatry to use the psychiatric unit as a mere holding tank where patients wait for their medication to take effect. The treatment of many patients is greatly enhanced by approaching hospital treatment with a dynamic perspective.

In the waning years of the 20th century, psychiatric hospitals witnessed a dramatic decline in length of stay related to aggressive utilization review by insurance companies and managed care firms (Gabbard 1992a, 1994). As a result, much of the valuable information gleaned from extended hospital treatment of seriously disturbed patients was adapted for use in other settings, such as partial or day hospitals. Even in hospital settings, however, psychodynamically informed strategies have continued to be of considerable usefulness in modified form. In other words, just as the principles of psychoanalysis were once adapted to brief psychodynamic therapy, so have the principles of extended dynamically informed hospital treatment been modified to a more circumscribed focus in the acute care setting (Gabbard 1997). Whether the treatment is carried out during a brief hospital stay or a more extended treatment in a partial hospital service, there are certain advantages and challenges associated with a multiple-treater setting. In this chapter I examine how psychodynamic thinking can be usefully applied to such settings. The models discussed should be considered to be equally useful in hospital treatment, day hospitals, and intensive outpatient settings involving multiple treaters.

A Historical Review

The practitioner can draw on a long tradition of the application of psychoanalytic principles to hospital treatment. The history of the notion of the psychoanalytic hospital began with Simmel's work at Schloss Tegel (1929), where he noted that certain patients could not be analyzed outside a hospital because of various symptomatic behaviors, such as alcoholism or phobias. He had the idea that a hospital could extend the patient's hour on the couch by training hospital staff members to conduct quasi-analytic treatment in the milieu as issues of transference and resistance arose. In his creative and brilliant *Guide to the Order Sheet,* Will Menninger (1939/1982) deemphasized the model of individual psychoanalysis and attempted to apply the principles of psychoanalysis directly within the hospital by manipulation of the milieu. Working from the assumption that all symptoms and disturbed behaviors derive from disturbances in the proper fusion and expression of the two major instinctual drives—libido and aggression—he evolved a system of milieu treatment based largely on sublimation and not requiring insight. Rather than frustrating or interpreting unconscious wishes and conflicts, this approach focused on rechanneling energies into less harmful paths. For example, Menninger encouraged the direct expression of hostilities toward substitute objects; prescriptions for a patient might range from demolishing a building to punching a punching bag. Unfortunately, this second model could not take into account those patients with ego weaknesses involving impulse control problems who required a treatment designed to help them gain more control over drive expression rather than to redirect it. Moreover, this conceptualization was limited by confining itself to the dual instinct theory of the times, which tended to neglect the object relations context in which disturbed drives occur, nor did it allow for systematic examination of transference and countertransference in the milieu.

The third model grew out of an awareness that patients were re-creating with various staff members in the hospital setting their conflicts with their own family members (Hilles 1968). Interpretation of maladaptive behavior patterns in terms of their roots in the past was common within this model, which relied less and less on providing substitute outlets for unconscious needs. The milieu was not seen as a therapeutic community in which real, constructive experiences with peers are stressed, but rather as a screen upon which archaic patterns are projected and then examined. Schlesinger and Holzman (1970), in describing the therapeutic aspects of the milieu of a psychiatric hospital, noted that the milieu could supplement the therapist-patient relationship by providing opportunities for patients to work out in a real context what had been talked about in therapy. It also served as a kind of training ground or laboratory where patients could practice trying to change in various ways as they progressed in psychotherapy. Schlesinger and Holzman asserted that prescribing milieu therapy for hospital patients was a complex process requiring a sensitivity to the multiple functions of a patient's involvement in the hospital milieu. They proposed a schema based on the five points of view of psychoanalytic metapsychology: the structural, the economic, the dynamic, the adaptive, and the genetic.

A number of authors (Gabbard 1986, 1988, 1989c, 1992a; Harty 1979; Stamm 1985b; Wesselius 1968; Zee 1977) have pinpointed countertransference as an integral part of the treatment process. They offer the caveat that treatment effectiveness is impaired when staff members respond in a countertransferential manner as though they are one of the patient's parents. These countertransference influences occur regularly, rather than occasionally, and the systematic examination of the countertransference should be part of the routine work of the treatment team. A recurring theme throughout the various formulations of psychoanalytically informed hospital treatment is that patients re-create in the milieu environment their own internal object relations. This point of view is reflected in Kernberg's (1973) integrative attempt to synthesize psychoanalytic object relations theory, systems theory, and the use of group process in an overall approach to hospital treatment. One basic tenet of his approach is that there exists in all of us a potential for both higher-level object relationships—typical of the transference neurosis in individual psychoanalytic treatment—and more primitive levels of object relationships, leading to psychotic regression in group situations. He theorized that whereas the higher level of object relationship is activated in individual therapeutic relationships, the more primitive version is much more likely to be activated in group treatment modalities. A combination of individual and group treatment in hospitalization provides for intervention at both levels. Kernberg (1973) insisted that such a two-pronged treatment approach requires "a 'neutral' hospital milieu, that is, an attitude of staff basically equidistant from the different intrapsychic and external agencies involved in the patient's conflicts, and reflected in an overall friendly and generally tolerant, an interested and intellectually alert hospital atmosphere" (p. 372). In the context of this neutral atmosphere, Kernberg saw the therapeutic community and individual hospital therapy operating simultaneously to examine internal object relationships as well as to perform the ego or control function. He formulated hospital treatment "as the simultaneous diagnosis and treatment of the patient's control function and his internal world of object-relationships" (Kernberg 1973, p. 379).

In summary, the application of psychoanalytic/psychodynamic principles to hospital treatment has undergone a gradual shift during the past 70 years. The notion of containment of patients undergoing psychoanalysis gradually gave way to a second model involving prescribed interactions with milieu staff. The third and current model, because it shifts the emphasis to the systematic examination of transference and countertransference, views patients as re-creating their internal object relations in the milieu.

Dynamic Principles in Contemporary Hospital Treatment

A dynamic approach provides for a diagnostic understanding that pays careful attention to patients' ego weaknesses and strengths, their intrapsychic object relations as manifested in family and social relationships, their capacity for psychological work, and the childhood origins of their current problems. A psychodynamic assessment may lead a clinician to conclude that interpretive interventions and uncovering of unconscious material are ill-advised. With patients who have significant ego weakness and/or organically based cognitive impairment, ego-supportive approaches and those geared to building self-esteem may be recommended.

Psychoanalytic theories of development are useful in designing inpatient treatment plans. A psychoanalytically informed hospital team realizes that the majority of its patients are developmentally arrested. Knowledge of psychoanalytic theory allows the team to respond at an appropriate developmental level, accepting the notion that the patient is a child in an adult's body. This perspective helps the staff avoid the perils of depersonification (Rinsley 1982), whereby the patient is expected to behave as a mature and polite adult in spite of severe psychopathology. Such depersonification has often been the life story of the severely disturbed patient in terms of interactions with family members.

Psychoanalytic theory provides models of interventions geared to the patient's phase-appropriate developmental needs, such as empathic mirroring (Kohut 1971) and the provision of a holding environment (Stamm 1985a; Winnicott 1965). Within this context, the limits associated with hospital structure are viewed not as punishments for immature and irritating behavior but rather as external substitutes for missing intrapsychic structures. In a similar vein, staff members must perform auxiliary ego functions, such as reality testing, impulse control, anticipation of consequences (judgment), and sharpening of self–object differentiation. From an attachment theory perspective, milieu staff provide a secure base for patients. Intense affects are contained for patients until they can be modulated by the patients themselves. Staff members foster attachment by listening to patients' personal narratives and attempting to understand their perspectives (Adshead 1998).

Patients who enter an inpatient unit or a day hospital tend to repeat their family situations in the milieu. To be more precise, they externalize their internal object relations. The recapitulation of the patient's internal object relations in the interpersonal field of the milieu can best be understood by an examination of the defense mechanisms of splitting and projective identification. Although these mechanisms are operative in some neurotic patients, they are most prevalent in patients with borderline and psychotic levels of ego organization, features that also happen to characterize the group of patients most commonly found in inpatient settings. Moreover, these mechanisms are undoubtedly activated in part by the group dynamics inherent in inpatient or day hospital teamwork. Splitting and projective identification work in tandem to disavow and externalize self- or object representations often associated with specific affective states. This projective disavowal is also a means of coercing persons in the environment to participate in an externalized version of an internal object relationship.

Projective identification operates unconsciously, automatically, and with compelling force. Clinicians feel "bullied" or coerced into complying with the role that has been projectively attributed to them. A basic axiom of psychodynamically informed treatment acknowledges that staff members are more similar to patients than different from them. The feelings, fantasies, identifications, and introjects within patients have their counterparts in treaters. Because those counterparts may be more strongly repressed in staff, when they are activated by a patient, they often are experienced as alien forces sweeping over the treater. Symington (1990) characterized this projective identification process as a bully/victim paradigm in which one is deprived of the freedom to think one's own thoughts. Indeed, clinicians who are the targets of the projected material often feel that they are in a form of bondage to the patient in that they cannot think, feel, or function in their usual therapeutic role.

Defining projective identification in this manner suggests that much of the intense countertransference experienced by staff members can be understood as stemming from unconscious identifications with projected aspects of the patient's internal world. However, it would be naive and oversimplistic to assume that all the emotional reactions arising in treaters can be attributed to the patient's behavior. Clinicians will also manifest emotional reactions in keeping with the classical, or narrow, form of countertransference, in which treaters react to patients as though they are people from the treaters' past. One of the advantages of working in the context of a treatment team is that staff members can help one another distinguish characteristic countertransference patterns based on the staff members' own psychological issues from those that are coerced identifications with aspects of the patient's projected internal world. It would be ideal if each staff member could make such distinctions individually, but such expectations are not realistic in multiple-treater settings.

To describe the mechanisms of splitting and projective identification provides only a partial explanation of the tendency for patients to externalize their internal object relations within the milieu relationships. To point out that this repetition occurs unconsciously, automatically, and with a coercive force does not adequately account for the unconscious motivational forces behind the repetition. At least four different forces can be identified that contribute to the repetition of internal object relations (Gabbard 1992b).

Active mastery of passively experienced trauma. In re-creating internalized patterns of relating in the inpatient or day hospital setting, patients may be attempting to actively master passively experienced trauma (Pine 1990). By reactivating problematic relationships, patients may gain a feeling of mastery and control over past traumatic relationships because this time they are in charge.

Maintenance of attachments. Object relations units are also reestablished with treaters because the new relationship serves as a way of maintaining attachments to key persons from childhood, most notably parents. Even if childhood relationships with parents are abusive and conflictual, the child will nevertheless view them as a source of pleasure (Pine 1990). A sadomasochistic relationship is better than no relationship at all (Gabbard 1989b). Moreover, even "bad" or tormenting relationships may be soothing in the sense that they are predictable and reliable and provide the patient with a sense of continuity and meaning (Gabbard 1998). The alternative is a profound sense of abandonment and the associated separation anxiety.

A cry for help. To view projective identification only as a mechanism of defense is reductionistic (see Chapter 2). As the targeted person of the projected material powerfully experiences, it is also a form of communication (Casement 1990; Gabbard 1989a; Ogden 1982). Primitive anxieties operate in a way that make patients feel extraordinary pressure to get rid of unmanageable affects, including the self- and object representations associated with those affects. Some relief is provided when a treater is forced to experience projected material that is overwhelming to a patient. The patient may be unconsciously communicating to the clinician, "I cannot articulate my internal experience, but by creating similar feelings in you, maybe you can empathize with my inner struggles and somehow help me." Hence, while projective identification may be designed to rid oneself of overwhelming feelings and externalize them in an interpersonal context, it is also a means of seeking help with those feelings through a rudimentary form of empathy (Casement 1990).

A wish for transformation.   Abusive internal object relations may also be externalized in the hope that they can be transformed. Sandler and Sandler (1978) have observed that patients internalize a wished-for interaction, a fantasy of themselves relating to a parent who is responding to them in a manner that is wish fulfilling. In this sense, one can infer that old relationships are repeated with the unconscious hope that this time they will be different (i.e., both the object and the self will be transformed into the fantasy relationship for which the patient longs).

A day hospital or an inpatient unit can provide a new and different form of interpersonal relatedness that facilitates the internalization of less pathological object relatedness. In the optimal milieu, the goal of staff members is to relate to patients so as to avoid being provoked into responding as their internal object representations would. By not behaving like everyone else in the patient's world, they can offer new objects and new models of relatedness for the patient.

Initial responses to a patient may be similar to those of others in the patient's environment, but as staff members familiarize themselves with the internal object world of the patient, they strive to contain the projections rather than identify with them. In so doing, a vicious cycle is broken. The patient is confronted with a group of persons who respond differently from everyone else. These people attempt to understand the interpersonal process instead of automatically joining the "dance."

Weiss et al. (1986), who have studied audiotaped transcripts of analyses with neurotics, have concluded that one curative factor of analysis is the analyst's failure to respond as the analysand expects. According to these investigators, a patient develops pathological beliefs based on early interactions with parental figures and then seeks unconsciously to disconfirm these beliefs in analysis so that development can proceed. Their research is very much applicable to the hospital setting, where patients continually but unconsciously test staff members to see whether they will be different from previous figures in the prehospital environment. This situation requires a caveat, however. Staff members who simply "act nice" to the patient will prevent the patient from reexperiencing and working through old patterns of relatedness. Hence, there is always an optimal balance between serving as a new object and serving as an old object in any treatment setting (Gabbard and Wilkinson 1994). Over time, the "old object" patterns of relatedness are gradually replaced by new modes of relatedness based on new experiences with treatment staff and a newfound understanding on the part of the patient of his or her unconscious need to re-create past relationships.

Within this formulation of internal object relations, the therapeutic task is to diagnose carefully the patient's self- and object representations and to maintain a diligent vigilance regarding the nature of the projected internal selves and objects at any given time. Implied in this task is the assumption that treaters have sufficient familiarity with their own internal self- and object-configurations so that they can sort out the two varieties of countertransference.

In this transference-countertransference–based model of treatment, the treatment staff must maintain an openness to the powerful feelings engendered by these patients. Examining the countertransference must be an integral part of the treatment process. The staff should freely allow themselves to serve as containers for the patient's self- and object projections and for the affects connected with the object relations. On an individual basis, this approach means avoiding the "dedicated physician" stance described by Searles (1967/1979), in which the treater attempts to be loving at all times as a defense against vulnerability to directing sadism and hatred toward the patient. If the treater is overcontrolled or overdefended against emotional reactions to the patient, the diagnostic process of delineating these internal object relations will be flawed. Even more importantly, the treatment process will be a charade; the patient will be unable to view the treater as a genuine person involved in a fleshed-out whole-object relationship.

Openness to countertransference reactions must similarly exist at the group level. The persons in leadership positions on the unit must foster a noncritical, accepting attitude toward the various emotional reactions of staff members to patients. If the leaders communicate that the staff is expected to keep a lid on personal feelings in the service of delivering good treatment to patients, such exhortations will resonate with the already hypertrophied superego structures of most mental health workers and further activate their internal defenses geared to repressing, suppressing, or splitting off unacceptable feelings and identifications.

Despite increasing pressure in recent years to use staff meetings for documentation of behaviorally oriented treatment plans, the staff members' emotional reactions to patients must be discussed openly and with understanding. If staff meetings become merely task-oriented administrative sessions without time for processing transference-countertransference paradigms, subsequent staff dysfunction will cause the clinical work to suffer. Furthermore, the team will no longer be involved in dynamically informed treatment, but simply in "case management."

The attitude of the unit or team leader is crucial in setting the tone for countertransference-based discussions. The leader must model for the other staff members by openly examining his or her own feelings and relating them to the internal object relations of the patient. The leader must also value and accept the expressions of feelings on the part of other staff members and avoid interpreting them as a manifestation of unresolved and unanalyzed conflicts within the individual staff member. When a staff member shares a disturbing feeling involved in treating a patient, the leader needs to ask questions, such as "Why does the patient need to evoke that reaction in you? What is he repeating? What figure in the patient's past are you identifying with? How can we use the feelings the patient evokes in you to understand how his spouse or friends must react to him?" The leader of the treatment team should also become familiar with each staff member's usual style of relating to patients. This awareness must include a knowledge of typical countertransference reactions to certain kinds of patients as well as functioning that is more adaptive and conflict-free. This familiarity will help the team leader pinpoint deviations from the characteristic patterns of relationships with patients. Obviously, in some instances the leader of a treatment team may need to approach individual staff members privately about their need for personal treatment or a change in career.

Members of the nursing staff as well as other members of the treatment team should be given the expectation that they will experience powerful feelings toward the patient that can be used as a diagnostic and therapeutic tool. A distinction can be made between having feelings and acting on them. Obviously, staff should be advised to note and discuss with other staff but to not act on feelings of a destructive or erotic nature. They should be encouraged to process their feelings in staff meetings and to use those feelings to diagnose and understand the internal object relations of the patient. As the treatment progresses, the staff members will be armed with a greater understanding of the patient's internal object relations so that they are much less prone to countertransference identification and can instead clarify patients' distortions and the nature of their internal object worlds. Hence, if the staff members are given permission to experience powerful countertransference feelings and to discuss them early in the treatment of a given patient, they will be able to approach the patient more objectively as the treatment progresses.

If treaters are inclined to deny their countertransference hatred, anger, and contempt out of guilt, they will nevertheless communicate their intense negative feelings nonverbally (Poggi and Ganzarain 1983). Patients are extraordinarily adept at detecting these communications and may, as a result, become increasingly paranoid. As staff members acknowledge their own ambivalence and deal with it more openly, patients will be able to acknowledge their ambivalence and to be less afraid of their hatred. But as long as staff members deny their hatred, they only confirm the patient's fear that such feelings are unspeakable and must be avoided at all cost.

The model of staff-patient interaction suggested here is directly analogous to the one advocated for the psychotherapist in Chapter 4. Hospital staff members must avoid aloofness and must participate in the patient's interpersonal field in a spontaneous but controlled manner. This capacity to allow oneself to be "sucked in," but only partially, is an extraordinary asset that enables treaters to gain an empathic understanding of the patient's relationship problems (Hoffman and Gill 1988).

Splitting in the Multiple-Treater Setting

One advantage of a multiple-treater setting over individual therapy is that the patient's self- and object representations are externalized onto various staff members all at once rather than onto the psychotherapist alone gradually over time. The setting, then, serves as a superb diagnostic and therapeutic tool for understanding the process of splitting (see Chapter 2).

Splitting in hospital treatment has been well described in a number of papers on the intense countertransference evoked by treatment-resistant borderline patients (Burnham 1966; Gabbard 1986, 1989c, 1992b, 1994, 1997; Main 1957). Empirical research suggests that splitting is not unique to borderline patients, however, but rather is characteristic of a wide variety of personality disorders (Allen et al. 1988; Perry and Cooper 1986). Staff members find themselves assuming and defending highly polarized positions against one another with a vehemence out of proportion to the importance of the issue. The patient has presented one self-representation to one group of treaters and another self-representation to another group of treaters (Burnham 1966; Cohen 1957; Gabbard 1986, 1989c, 1992b, 1994, 1997; Searles 1965). Via projective identification, each self-representation evokes a corresponding reaction in the treater that can be understood as an unconscious identification with the projected internal object of the patient. The transference-counter-transference paradigm produced by one self–object constellation may differ dramatically from that produced by another. This discrepancy may first manifest itself in a staff meeting where the patient is being discussed. Staff members may become puzzled by the disparate descriptions being voiced and may ask each other, "Are we talking about the same patient?"

Full-blown splitting of this variety boldly illustrates the time-honored notion that patients recapitulate their internal object world in the hospital milieu (Gabbard 1989c). Various treaters become unconsciously identified with the patient's internal objects and play out roles in a script that is written by the patient's unconscious. Moreover, because of the element of control inherent in projective identification, there is often an obligatory quality to the treaters' responses. They feel compelled to behave "like someone else." If projective identification were not involved, the purely intrapsychic splitting that would result would cause little disturbance in the staff group. Nor would the staff group view the process as an instance of splitting, since they would probably not feel polarized and angry toward one another.

The splitting that occurs in hospital treatment represents a special instance where both intrapsychic and interpersonal splitting develop simultaneously (Hamilton 1988). The interpersonal aspects of splitting that occur in staff groups clearly parallel the intrapsychic splitting in the patient. Projective identification is the vehicle that converts intrapsychic splitting into interpersonal splitting.

Staff members who are singled out as recipients of projected internal objects of the patient are not randomly selected. More often than not, borderline patients have an uncanny ability to detect preexisting latent conflict among various staff members, and their projections may be guided accordingly. A vignette from an actual case (Gabbard 1989c) illustrates this pattern.

> Ms. E, a 26-year-old borderline patient, was admitted to the hospital in a suicidal crisis by her psychotherapist, Dr. F. Ten days after her admission, while she was still voicing suicidal ideation, Dr. F approached Mr. G, the head nurse of the unit, and said he would like to drive Ms. E to the local college campus so she could register for the semester. Mr. G replied that, according to hospital policy, patients who are on suicide precautions may not leave the unit. He suggested that Dr. F might wish to attend a unit staff meeting to further discuss the management of the patient. When Mr. G explained to Ms. E that she could not leave the unit to register, she was enraged with Mr. G and accused him of being a "tyrant" who had no regard for the individual needs of patients. She contrasted him with Dr. F, whom she idealized by saying that among all the staff members associated with her treatment, he was "the only one who understands me." At the ensuing staff meeting, a heated argument developed between Dr. F and Mr. G, who acted as a spokesperson for the unit staff. In the midst of this clash, Mr. G told Dr. F that the latter was well known for his contempt toward hospital policies and for his propensity to treat patients as "special." As a rebuttal to that accusation, Dr. F informed Mr. G that of all the nurses in the hospital, he was known as the most rigid and punitive.

This example demonstrates how splitting and projective identification do not occur in a vacuum. Ms. E clearly selected individuals who conveniently fit the internal object-relationship paradigms assigned to them. As several authors (Adler 1985; Burnham 1966; Shapiro et al. 1977) have noted, there is often a kernel of reality in the assignment of internal object projections to staff members. This vignette also reflects an observation by Burnham (1966), namely, that the cleavage is usually between those treaters who emphasize the administrative frame of reference (i.e., what is good for the group) and those who emphasize an individualistic frame of reference based on what is good for an individual patient. Finally, while all treaters are at risk for involvement in splits, the pattern described in this vignette is perhaps most common in the treatment of borderline patients: the psychotherapist is viewed as an idealized figure, while the unit staff are devalued as insensitive and punitive. Another typical feature of this arrangement is that, in psychotherapy sessions, the patient may omit information deriving from day-to-day unit activities and instead focus exclusively on childhood memories and transference material (Adler 1985; Kernberg 1984). The psychotherapist then has no awareness of the problematic interactions on the unit and is caught by surprise when nursing staff focus attention on them.

As a result of this form of splitting, Adler (1985) noted that the treatment staff may actually exclude the psychotherapist from the process of treatment planning. In this manner the unit staff members may consolidate their alliance by projecting "badness" and incompetence outside the unit group onto the psychotherapist. If this process continues unchecked, it becomes impossible for the unit staff and the psychotherapist to reconcile their differences and meet halfway. Just like the patient's internal objects, they cannot be integrated. The regressive power of groups is well known and may result in the use of splitting and projective identification in otherwise well-integrated professionals (Bion 1961; Kernberg 1984; Oldham and Russakoff 1987).

The intensive utilization review process associated with managed care also serves as a convenient nidus for splitting. Treatment staff may attempt to cement an alliance with the patient by externalizing all potential anger and aggression. The managed care reviewer is a natural and convenient repository for all negative feelings that may be felt between treaters and the patient. Hence, the insurance reviewer may be cast in the role of the "bad object" by both the patient and treaters, who can commiserate about their victimization by the reviewer while avoiding any direct discussion of transference-countertransference anger and aggression (Gabbard et al. 1991).

When a staff group reaches this point of fragmentation, all too often the patient is blamed for attempting to divide and conquer (Rinsley 1980). What is often forgotten under these circumstances is that splitting is an unconscious process patients employ automatically to maintain their emotional survival. We do not generally blame patients for other defense mechanisms. The unique issue in splitting seems to be the treaters' perception that the patient is being consciously and maliciously destructive. An empathic frame of reference is useful for reminding staff members that splitting is the patient's attempt to ward off destructiveness for personal protection.

To summarize, splitting in a multiple-treater setting involves four primary features: 1) the process occurs at an unconscious level; 2) the patient perceives individual staff members in dramatically different ways, based on projections of the patient's internal object representations, and treats each staff member differentially according to those projections; 3) staff members react to the patient, via projective identification, as though they actually are the projected aspects of the patient; and 4) as a result, treaters assume highly polarized positions in staff discussions about the patient and defend those positions with extraordinary vehemence (Gabbard 1989c).

Management of Splitting in the Multiple-Treater Setting

Any discussion of how to manage splitting must begin with Burnham's (1966) caveat that the complete prevention of splitting is neither possible nor desirable. As with other defense mechanisms, splitting provides a safety valve that protects patients from what they perceive as overwhelming danger. It is a process that will develop regardless of preventive measures implemented by treaters. The essential point is that treatment staff must continuously monitor splitting to prevent it from destroying the treatment, devastating the morale of the staff, and irreparably damaging certain interstaff relationships. Instances of serious psychiatric morbidity and staff resignations have resulted from such situations (Burnham 1966; Main 1957).

Education is one important way to help staff manage splitting. All mental health professionals working with seriously disturbed patients should be thoroughly conversant with the concept of splitting and its variants. If staff members cannot recognize splitting when it develops, managing the situation may be hopeless. In discussions of countertransference, staff members can be encouraged to work toward containing projected aspects of the patient rather than acting on them. Intense feelings toward patients should be viewed as useful material for discussion and supervision rather than as forbidden reactions that must be concealed from supervisors. By developing an understanding of the mechanism of splitting, staff members can learn to avoid exploiting it by refusing to accept idealization that would collude with the devaluation of other staff members (Adler 1973; Shapiro et al. 1977). Staff members must also learn to monitor their countertransference tendencies to project aspects of themselves onto the patient.

Education is only a beginning, however. Regular and frequent staff meetings that include the patient's psychotherapist should be part of the weekly routine of the psychiatric unit. A spirit of open communication about differences should be established and monitored by the staff. Many years ago, Stanton and Schwartz (1954) persuasively demonstrated the prophylactic value of ferreting out and discussing covert staff disagreements. Psychotherapists must view themselves as part of the treatment team and ally themselves with the administrative decisions of the unit team (Adler 1985). Rigid adherence to concerns about confidentiality may feed right into the patient's splitting tendencies.

One primary goal in the treatment of patients with major character pathology is the integration of split self- and object representations. Although interpretation of the splitting mechanism can help patients achieve more moderated and realistic views of themselves and others, it is rarely sufficient to mend the cleavage that occurs at the group level in the hospital. Interpretations to the patient are best viewed as adjuncts to other interventions at the level of staff interactions. Corresponding to the psychotherapist's approach to the internal world of the patient is the staff's goal of integrating and moderating the external objects.

To this end, it is often useful to have the staff member identified with the bad object and the treater identified with the good object meet jointly with the patient to frankly discuss the patient's perception of what is going on. This arrangement makes it more difficult for the patient to maintain polarized views because both treaters are acting human and reasonable. Moreover, treaters who are faced with this situation ordinarily become less polarized and move toward middle ground. The very separateness demanded by the splitting mechanism is undermined. Although this confrontation may temporarily increase the patient's anxiety, it also conveys the message that negative feelings can be contained within interpersonal relationships without disastrous consequences.

When the situation is so emotionally charged that the participants are not willing to meet, an objective consultant can be brought in to mediate the discussion (Gabbard 1986). The consultant can fulfill the role of an observing ego for the group and thereby encourage those individuals involved with the splitting to identify with that function, much as Shapiro et al. (1977) described the function of the psychotherapist when meeting with borderline adolescents and their families.

These meetings presuppose a recognition by all parties of an ongoing splitting process. Such acknowledgment constitutes a major step toward successful management of the splitting. Ordinarily, staff members will be considerably reluctant to see themselves as involved in splitting. When a special meeting is called to discuss the staff dynamics around a particular patient, there may be strong resistance on the part of treaters because such a meeting might make the patient seem too special (Burnham 1966). If the patient's psychotherapist is involved in the split, and willingly attends the staff meeting, it may be with a different agenda. Especially when idealized by the patient, the therapist is likely to assume a condescending attitude as educator so the staff will understand their countertransference reactions and the dynamics of the patient as well as the psychotherapist does. The psychotherapist's implicit message in this situation is that understanding the patient will lead the staff to stop blaming the patient. Rather than viewing the staff meeting as a productive way to discuss a splitting process, the psychotherapist is convinced that he or she is right while everyone else is wrong. Being idealized can be so gratifying that the therapist may not wish to examine the idealization as part of a defensive process in the patient (Finell 1985). This approach will, of course, infuriate the staff even further and widen the split.

When a staff meeting is called to discuss potential splitting, all parties should certainly approach one another with the assumption that they are all reasonable and competent clinicians who care about the patient's welfare. When this approach works, the group feels that each staff member has brought a piece of the puzzle so that the whole becomes more clear (Burnham 1966). However, some splits seem irreparable; and just as the internal objects of the patient cannot be integrated, neither can the external objects reconcile with one another. If the therapist is in the role of the devalued object, such stalemates occasionally end with the staff recommending a new therapist (Adler 1985).

The earlier that splitting is discovered, the less entrenched and the more amenable to change it will be. Certain warning signals should be continually monitored in staff meetings: 1) when a treater is uncharacteristically punitive toward a patient, 2) when a treater is unusually indulgent, 3) when one treater repeatedly defends a patient against critical comments from other staff members, and 4) when one staff member believes that no one else can understand the patient (Gabbard 1989c).

When staff members can swallow their pride and accept that they may be involved in an unconscious identification with projected aspects of the patient, they can begin to empathize with their fellow staff members' feelings and perspectives. This willingness to consider someone else's point of view can lead to collaborative work on behalf of the patient that results in marked improvement in the splitting process. The patient's internal split often begins to mend at the same time the staff's external cleavage heals (Gabbard 1986). These parallel developments may be understood as the third step of projective identification—the previously split-off and projected object representations of the patient have been contained and modified by the treaters and have then been reintrojected (in modified form) by the patient in a meaningful interpersonal context. By approaching their own differences in good faith, staff members can provide an atmosphere in the milieu where good experiences predominate over bad ones—an essential condition for facilitating the integration of love and hate in the patient.

The Multidisciplinary Treatment Team

The typical treatment team is made up of representatives from several mental health disciplines—a psychiatrist, a psychologist, a social worker, an activities therapist, nurses, and mental health technicians. Latent interdisciplinary rivalries are fertile soil for the development of splits within the team. Individual team members must conceptualize their job as subsuming two different tasks: one involves the specific treatment assignment that goes with the discipline, and the other involves serving as a transference object or a container of projections (Kernberg 1984). Observations from both aspects of one's job must be continually brought into staff meetings and shared with the treatment team. All patients should understand that whatever they say will be passed on to other members of the treatment team, to gain a complete picture of the patient and to map out a more effective treatment plan. In this manner, splitting can be identified before it becomes destructive.

The social worker, for example, may bring data to the treatment team from family members and other significant persons who inhabit the environment in which the patient lives. These real individuals may be compared and contrasted with the objects that inhabit the patient's internal world. As social workers perform their usual tasks of gathering data and communicating back and forth between family and patient, they soon find that they are "sucked into" the family matrix. As they allow themselves to contain the projected aspects of the family members and significant others, they gain a greater appreciation of the forces that shape the patient's behavior. Similarly, the social worker's direct contacts with the patient can produce a greater appreciation of the patient's impact on the family. Finally, social workers may contribute a special perspective regarding the manner in which family conflicts are re-created in the milieu.

Members of other disciplines find that the completion of their treatment tasks is similarly affected by the patient's style of relatedness with them. The activities therapist, for example, sets out to assist the patient in completing a task. The patient's performance of that task provides a window into similar problems that the patient may encounter in vocational or educational settings. As the patient attempts to complete the task, characteristic object relations patterns are played out with the activities therapist. Nurses will encounter similar obstacles as they attempt to assist the patient with basic matters of hygiene, and psychologists will confront the same patterns as they encourage the patient to participate in psychological testing. This transference-countertransference model based on object relations theory cuts across all disciplines and forms the basis for a common language among the disciplines.

The Role of Group Treatment in the Milieu

The foregoing descriptions of the introjection and projection of self- and object representations illustrate the need for careful monitoring of group process on every psychiatric unit. Frequent staff meetings are essential for integrating the split-off fragments circulating among staff members and patients. Similarly, regular group meetings with patients promote a careful processing of interactions between the staff and patients, and among patients themselves; they also serve to prevent acting out of conflicts that develop in these relationships. Object relations theory provides a good conceptual framework for understanding group process on the unit (Kernberg 1973, 1984; Oldham and Russakoff 1987). Stanton and Schwartz (1954) illustrated how dynamics in the patient group may directly reflect similar dynamics in the staff group. Specifically, it is commonplace for individual patients to act out covert staff conflicts. Systematic processing of interpersonal conflicts both in staff meetings and in meetings of patients and staff can be valuable in identifying parallel processes in the two groups.

The actual focus of small patient groups in the hospital inpatient unit or day hospital varies, depending on the ego strengths and the diagnostic categories of the patients on a particular unit. In general, however, psychotherapeutic group meetings serve as an interface between the patients' intrapsychic difficulties and their conflicts in the milieu. Kibel (1987) suggested that the focus of such groups should be on the interpersonal difficulties that emerge in daily life on the hospital unit. These difficulties can be linked to the patients' intrapsychic conflicts or deficiencies. He suggested deemphasizing transference in such groups because the anxiety generated by transference work might overwhelm both the individual and collective egos of the group. Horwitz (1987), on the other hand, believed that transference focus may be of value in inpatient groups by serving to strengthen the therapeutic alliance within the group. When small group meetings are properly conducted, they may also become havens or sanctuaries in which patients can ventilate their feelings about the experience of being a psychiatric inpatient and staff members can, in turn, validate those feelings and experiences (Kibel 1987). More specific use of inpatient groups will be discussed in Sections II and III of this volume in the context of distinct diagnostic entities.

Indications for a Dynamically Informed Approach

One might argue that this model of treatment based on transference and countertransference is more applicable to borderline and affectively disturbed patients than it is to schizophrenic patients. The withdrawn schizophrenic patient may not appear to form a transference relationship with treaters. In fact, the schizophrenic patient's internal object relations are re-created in the hospital milieu every bit as much as those of a borderline patient. They are simply less dramatic. Rangell (1982) noted that Freud's assertion that patients suffering from narcissistic neuroses do not form transferences is the only clinical observation he made that has not been validated by subsequent analytic experience. As Brenner (1982) pointed out, the apparent absence of transference *is* the transference. The patient with schizophrenia has re-created his or her internal object world just as the borderline patient has. This relationship vis-à-vis the hospital treaters, which must be understood, clarified, and empathized with, is similar to the process of working with a nonpsychotic patient. Even patients with schizophrenia have their own unique set of characterological defenses. Although many patients do not require the use of this model during a brief hospitalization, this form of treatment is certainly useful for those whose defenses thwart compliance (see Chapter 7).

Another potential objection is that a conceptual framework based on the modification of object relations is not applicable to brief treatment in the same way that it is to extended hospital treatment. The fallacy in this argument is the conceptualization of the hospital treatment as occurring in a vacuum rather than as existing as one segment of a continuous effort over many months or years. There is a cumulative effect of many different disconfirmations of the unconscious expectations of the patient over time. Only with repeated failure to provoke the same pattern of responses in treaters do patients ultimately begin to assimilate and internalize the new object relations presented to them. Long-term follow-up studies of borderline patients (McGlashan 1986; Stone et al. 1987), for example, have indicated that maximal improvement does not occur until the second decade after discharge. Staff members of an inpatient unit or a partial hospitalization service, the psychotherapist, and friends and family may ultimately provide enough new experiences and responses to strengthen the patient's ego and improve his or her object relations to a level of increased functioning in society.

Serious treatment errors can be inflicted on the patient just as easily in a short-term setting as in a long-term setting. A sophisticated psychodynamic understanding of the patient assists the treaters in their efforts to avoid errors of technique. They may avoid, for example, the pitfall of colluding with the patient's passive stance vis-à-vis treatment. A fundamental dynamic notion is that the patient is a collaborator in the treatment process. Psychodynamically informed treatment encourages patients to reflect on connections between their present situation and childhood antecedents so that they can begin to understand how they are perpetuating patterns that were scripted long ago. Intimately connected with this notion is the idea that patients are capable of taking active steps to change their situation.

In Sigmund Freud's (1914/1958) original usage of the term *acting out,* he was noting the transference tendency of patients to repeat in action something from the past rather than to remember and verbalize it. The same phenomenon occurs in inpatient or day hospital treatment, where patients repeat their characteristic mode of engaging others in an attempt to gratify their needs and wishes. Another basic psychodynamic notion is that patients must move in the direction of reflecting and talking about their internal experience rather than automatically allowing it to thrust them into action. Staff members continually remind patients that they will not engage in the "dance" that is being repeated. Instead, they will ask patients to reflect and verbalize the origins of their need for the dance. Those patients who, for reasons of cognitive dysfunction, low intelligence, or psychotic withdrawal, cannot enter into a productive verbal interchange with staff members can nevertheless benefit from the nonverbal experiential aspects of new forms of object relatedness. As Ogden (1986) has stressed, a treatment does not have to be verbal to be psychoanalytic in nature.

In the contemporary psychiatric setting, psychodynamic theory and technique must take its place alongside psychopharmacological interventions, family work, systems theory, and sociocultural considerations. Even with nonresistant patients, the great advantage of this object relations approach is that it provides staff members with a sense of mastery over intense countertransference reactions. The education and understanding provided for the staff by a psychodynamically informed clinician make the job more bearable and more meaningful in the face of the continual emotional onslaughts of highly disturbed patients.

References

Adler G: Hospital treatment of borderline patients. Am J Psychiatry 130:32–36, 1973

Adler G: Borderline Psychopathology and Its Treatment. New York, Jason Aronson, 1985

Adshead G: Psychiatric staff as attachment figures. Br J Psychiatry 172:64–69, 1998

Allen JG, Deering CD, Buskirk JR, et al: Assessment of therapeutic alliances in the psychiatric hospital milieu. Psychiatry 51:291–299, 1988

Bion WR: Experiences in Groups and Other Papers. New York, Basic Books, 1961

Brenner C: The Mind in Conflict. New York, International Universities Press, 1982

Burnham DL: The special-problem patient: victim or agent of splitting? Psychiatry 29:105–122, 1966

Casement PJ: The meeting of needs in psychoanalysis. Psychoanalytic Inquiry 10:325–346, 1990

Cohen RA: Some relations between staff tensions and the psychotherapeutic process, in The Patient and the Mental Hospital: Contributions of Research in the Science of Social Behavior. Edited by Greenblatt M, Levinson DJ, Williams RH. Glencoe, IL, Free Press, 1957, pp 301–308

Finell JS: Narcissistic problems in analysts. Int J Psychoanal 66:433–445, 1985

Freud S: Remembering, repeating and working-through (further recommendations on the technique of psycho-analysis II) (1914), in The Standard Edition of the Complete Psychological Works of Sigmund Freud, Vol 12. Translated and edited by Strachey J. London, Hogarth Press, 1958, pp 145–156

Gabbard GO: The treatment of the "special" patient in a psychoanalytic hospital. International Review of Psychoanalysis 13:333–347, 1986

Gabbard GO: A contemporary perspective on psychoanalytically informed hospital treatment. Hospital and Community Psychiatry 39:1291–1295, 1988

Gabbard GO: On "doing nothing" in the psychoanalytic treatment of the refractory borderline patient. Int J Psychoanal 70:527–534, 1989a

Gabbard GO: Patients who hate. Psychiatry 52:96–106, 1989b

Gabbard GO: Splitting in hospital treatment. Am J Psychiatry 146:444–451, 1989c

Gabbard GO: Comparative indications for brief and extended hospitalization, in American Psychiatric Press Review of Psychiatry, Vol 11. Edited by Tasman A, Riba MB. Washington, DC, American Psychiatric Press, 1992a, pp 503–517

Gabbard GO: The therapeutic relationship in psychiatric hospitalization. Bull Menninger Clin 56:4–19, 1992b

Gabbard GO: Treatment of borderline patients in a multiple-treater setting. Psychiatr Clin North Am 17:839–850, 1994

Gabbard GO: Training residents in psychodynamic psychiatry, in Acute Care Psychiatry: Diagnosis and Treatment. Edited by Sederer LI, Rothschild AJ. Baltimore, MD, Williams & Wilkins, 1997, pp 481–491

Gabbard GO: Treatment-resistant borderline personality disorder. Psychiatric Annals 28:651–656, 1998

Gabbard GO, Wilkinson SM: Management of Countertransference With Borderline Patients. Washington, DC, American Psychiatric Press, 1994

Gabbard GO, Takahashi T, Davidson JE, et al: A psychodynamic perspective on the clinical impact of insurance review. Am J Psychiatry 148:318–323, 1991

Hamilton NG: Self and Others: Object Relations Theory in Practice. Northvale, NJ, Jason Aronson, 1988

Harty MK: Countertransference patterns in the psychiatric treatment team. Bull Menninger Clin 43:105–122, 1979

Hilles L: Changing trends in the application of psychoanalytic principles to a psychiatric hospital. Bull Menninger Clin 32:203–218, 1968

Hoffman IZ, Gill MM: Critical reflections on a coding scheme. Int J Psychoanal 69:55–64, 1988

Horwitz L: Transference issues in hospital groups. Yearbook of Psychoanalysis and Psychotherapy 2:117–122, 1987

Kernberg OF: Psychoanalytic object-relations theory, group processes and administration: toward an integrative theory of hospital treatment. Annual of Psychoanalysis 1:363–388, 1973

Kernberg OF: Severe Personality Disorders: Psychotherapeutic Strategies. New Haven, CT, Yale University Press, 1984

Kibel HD: Inpatient group psychotherapy—where treatment philosophies converge. Yearbook of Psychoanalysis and Psychotherapy 2:94–116, 1987

Kohut H: The Analysis of the Self: A Systematic Approach to the Psychoanalytic Treatment of Narcissistic Personality Disorders. New York, International Universities Press, 1971

Main TF: The ailment. Br J Med Psychol 30:129–145, 1957

McGlashan TH: The Chestnut Lodge follow-up study, III: long-term outcome of borderline personalities. Arch Gen Psychiatry 43:20–30, 1986

Menninger WC: The Menninger Hospital's Guide to the Order Sheet (1939). Bull Menninger Clin 46:1–112, 1982

Ogden TH: Projective Identification and Psychotherapeutic Technique. New York, Jason Aronson, 1982

Ogden TH: The Matrix of the Mind: Object Relations and the Psychoanalytic Dialogue. Northvale, NJ, Jason Aronson, 1986

Oldham JM, Russakoff LM: Dynamic Therapy in Brief Hospitalization. Northvale, NJ, Jason Aronson, 1987

Perry JC, Cooper SH: A preliminary report on defenses and conflicts associated with borderline personality disorder. J Am Psychoanal Assoc 34:863–893, 1986

Pine F: Drive, Ego, Object, and Self: A Synthesis for Clinical Work. New York, Basic Books, 1990

Poggi RG, Ganzarain R: Countertransference hate. Bull Menninger Clin 47:15–35, 1983

Rangell L: The self in psychoanalytic theory. J Am Psychoanal Assoc 30:863–891, 1982

Rinsley DB: Treatment of the Severely Disturbed Adolescent. New York, Jason Aronson, 1980

Rinsley DB: Borderline and Other Self Disorders: A Developmental and Object-Relations Perspective. New York, Jason Aronson, 1982

Sandler J, Sandler AM: On the development of object relations and affects. Int J Psychoanal 59:285–296, 1978

Schlesinger HJ, Holzman PS: The therapeutic aspects of the hospital milieu. Bull Menninger Clin 34:1–11, 1970

Searles HF: Collected Papers on Schizophrenia and Related Subjects. New York, International Universities Press, 1965

Searles HF: The "dedicated physician" in the field of psychotherapy and psychoanalysis (1967), in Countertransference and Related Subjects. Madison, CT, International Universities Press, 1979, pp 71–88

Shapiro ER, Shapiro RL, Zinner J, et al: The borderline ego and the working alliance: indications for family and individual treatment in adolescence. Int J Psychoanal 58:77–87, 1977

Simmel E: Psycho-analytic treatment in a sanatorium. Int J Psychoanal 10:70–89, 1929

Stamm I: Countertransference in hospital treatment: basic concepts and paradigms. Bull Menninger Clin 49:432–450, 1985a

Stamm I: The hospital as a "holding environment." International Journal of Therapeutic Communities 6:219–229, 1985b

Stanton AH, Schwartz MS: The Mental Hospital: A Study of Institutional Participation in Psychiatric Illness and Treatment. New York, Basic Books, 1954

Stone MH, Stone DK, Hurt SW: Natural history of borderline patients treated by intensive hospitalization. Psychiatr Clin North Am 10:185–206, 1987

Symington N: The possibility of human freedom and its transmission (with particular reference to the thought of Bion). Int J Psychoanal 71:95–106, 1990

Weiss J, Sampson H, the Mount Zion Psychotherapy Research Group: The Psychoanalytic Process: Theory, Clinical Observations, and Empirical Research. New York, Guilford, 1986

Wesselius LF: Countertransference in milieu treatment. Arch Gen Psychiatry 18:47–52, 1968

Winnicott DW: The Maturational Processes and the Facilitating Environment: Studies in the Theory of Emotional Development. London, Hogarth Press, 1965

Zee HJ: Purpose and structure of a psychoanalytic hospital. Journal of the National Association of Private Psychiatric Hospitals 84:20–26, 1977

SECTION

II

Dynamic Approaches to Axis I Disorders

C H A P T E R

7

Schizophrenia

There is no developmental period when the human exists outside of the realm of interpersonal relatedness.

Harry Stack Sullivan

Genetic factors play a major role in the development of schizophrenia. The best-controlled studies suggest a concordance for schizophrenia in monozygotic twins of between 40% and 50%, while the concordance in dizygotic twins is roughly similar to that found in siblings (Kety 1996; Plomin et al. 1990). As with virtually all psychiatric disorders, however, clear Mendelian patterns of transmission are not involved. There is likely to be some genetic heterogeneity—in other words, there is probably more than one defective gene involved and more than one genetic picture underlying the disorder. Incomplete penetrance is likely to apply as well, because less than half of monozygotic twin pairs are concordant. Environmental factors also appear to be involved in the development of schizophrenia, although there is not yet a consensus on the exact nature of these environmental insults. Among the possible factors are birth injury, viral infection during gestation, intrauterine blood supply problems, dietary factors, developmental mishaps, and certain kinds of childhood trauma (Kety 1996; Olin and Mednick 1996).

None of the findings of biological research attenuates the impact of one irreducible fact—schizophrenia is an illness that happens to a person with a unique psychological makeup. Even if genetic factors accounted for 100% of the etiology of schizophrenia, clinicians would still be faced with a dynamically complex individual reacting to a profoundly disturbing illness. Sophisticated psychodynamic approaches to the management of the schizophrenic patient will always continue to be vital components of the clinician's treatment armamentarium. Probably no more than 10% of schizophrenic patients are able to function successfully with a treatment approach consisting only of antipsychotic medication and brief hospitalization (McGlashan and Keats 1989). The remaining 90% may benefit from dynamically informed treatment approaches, including dynamic pharmacotherapy, individual therapy, group therapy, family approaches, and skills training, as the crucial ingredients in the successful management of their schizophrenia.

There is no such thing as *the* treatment of schizophrenia. All therapeutic interventions must be tailored to the unique needs of the individual patient. Schizophrenia is a heterogeneous illness with protean clinical manifestations. One helpful organization of the descriptive symptomatology of the disorder is a division into three clusters: 1) positive symptoms, 2) negative symptoms, and 3) disordered personal relationships (Andreasen et al. 1982; Keith and Matthews 1984; Munich et al. 1985; Strauss et al. 1974). First proposed by Strauss et al. (1974), this model distinguishes three discrete psychopathological processes found in schizophrenic patients. This classification is one of several that have been suggested. Some propose that the third cluster should comprise mental or cognitive disorganization symptoms. I have chosen to focus on disordered personal relationships because of their relevance to a psychodynamically informed treatment approach. Positive symptoms include disturbances of thought content (such as delusions), disturbances of perception (such as hallucinations), and behavioral manifestations (such as catatonia and agitation) that develop over a short time and often accompany an acute psychotic episode.

Whereas the florid positive symptoms constitute an undeniable "presence," the negative symptoms of schizophrenia are better categorized as an "absence" of function. These negative symptoms include restricted affect, poverty of thought, apathy, and anhedonia. Patients in whom a negative symptom picture predominates can be characterized by a number of features that suggest structural brain abnormality, including poor premorbid adjustment, poor school performance, greater difficulty holding jobs, poor performance on cognitive testing, poor treatment response, early age at onset, and premorbid difficulties in social and instrumental functioning (Andreasen et al. 1990; McGlashan and Fenton 1992).

Carpenter et al. (1988) suggested a further distinction among negative symptoms. They pointed out that certain forms of social withdrawal, blunted affect, and apparent impoverishment of thought may actually be secondary to anxiety, depression, environmental deprivation, or drug effects. These manifestations should therefore not be labeled *negative symptoms* because they are short-lived and secondary. Carpenter et al. (1988) proposed the term *deficit syndrome* to refer to clearly primary negative symptoms that endure over time. Duration of negative symptoms is also prognostically significant. Whereas negative symptoms were once thought to imply a bleaker prognosis, recent research suggests that only when negative symptoms persist beyond the early phase of illness are they likely to predict a poorer outcome (Kay 1990; McGlashan and Fenton 1992).

Like negative symptoms, disordered personal relationships tend to develop over a long period. These problems grow out of a characterological substrate, and include a myriad of interpersonal difficulties as varied as the range of human personality. Prominent manifestations of disordered interpersonal relationships include withdrawal, inappropriate expressions of aggression and sexuality, lack of awareness of the needs of others, excessive demandingness, and inability to make meaningful contact with other people. This third category is less rigorously defined than the other two because essentially every schizophrenic patient struggles with problems in interpersonal relationships. Indeed, all three categories overlap extensively, and one schizophrenic patient may move from one group to another during the course of the illness. The most useful aspect of these three models is that they facilitate categorizing the predominant manifestations of the illness at any one time so that treatment can be adjusted accordingly. These distinctions are of heuristic and practical value not only at the level of descriptive symptoms but also in weighing dynamic considerations.

Psychodynamic Understanding of Schizophrenia

Many psychodynamic models have been proposed to assist clinicians in understanding the schizophrenic process. The conflict versus deficit controversy (described in Chapter 2) is a prominent feature in discussions of theories of schizophrenia. Freud himself vacillated between a conflict model and a deficit model of schizophrenia as his own conceptualization evolved (Arlow and Brenner 1969; Grotstein 1977a, 1977b; London 1973a, 1973b; Pao 1973). Much of Freud's conceptualization (1911/1958, 1914/1963, 1915/1963, 1924a/1961, 1924b/1961) developed out of his notion of *cathexis,* which referred to the quantity of energy attached to any intrapsychic structure or object representation. He was convinced that schizophrenia was characterized by a decathexis of objects. At times he used this concept of decathexis to describe a detachment of emotional or libidinal investment from intrapsychic object representations; at other times he used the term to describe social withdrawal from real persons in the environment (London 1973a). Freud defined schizophrenia as a regression in response to intense frustration and conflict with others. This regression from object relatedness to an autoerotic stage of development was accompanied by a withdrawal of emotional investment from object representations and from external figures, which explained the appearance of autistic withdrawal in schizophrenic patients. Freud (1914/1963) postulated that the patient's cathexis was then reinvested in the self or ego.

Some authors (London 1973a, 1973b; Wexler 1971) have viewed Freud's decathexis theory as an acknowledgment of a deficit model of schizophrenia, although Freud clearly attempted to take conflict into account as well. After developing the structural model, he revised his view of psychosis accordingly (1924a/1961, 1924b/1961). While he viewed neurosis as a conflict between the ego and the id, he regarded psychosis as a conflict between the ego and the external world. Psychosis involved a disavowal and subsequent remodeling of reality. Despite this revision, Freud continued to speak of the withdrawal of cathexis and its reinvestment in the ego. He used the withdrawal of object cathexis to explain his observation that, compared with neurotic patients, schizophrenic patients were incapable of forming transferences.

Freud's notion that schizophrenic patients do not form transference attachments was undoubtedly related to the fact that he did not attempt intensive therapeutic efforts with such patients. Harry Stack Sullivan, on the other hand, devoted his life to the treatment of schizophrenia and arrived at very different conclusions. He believed that the etiology of the disorder resulted from early interpersonal difficulties (particularly in the child-parent relationship), and he conceptualized the treatment as a long-term interpersonal process that attempted to address those early problems. According to Sullivan (1962), faulty mothering produced an anxiety-laden self in the infant and prevented the child from having its needs satisfied. This aspect of the self-experience was then dissociated, but the damage to self-esteem was profound. The onset of the schizophrenic illness, in Sullivan's view, was a resurgence of the dissociated self that led to a panic state and then psychotic disorganization. Sullivan always considered the capacity for interpersonal relatedness to be present in even the most withdrawn schizophrenic patient. His pioneering work with schizophrenic patients was carried on by his disciple, Frieda Fromm-Reichmann (1950), who stressed that schizophrenic persons are not happy with their withdrawn state. They are fundamentally lonely people who cannot overcome their fear and distrust of others because of adverse experiences early in life.

While Sullivan and his followers were developing their interpersonal theories, early ego psychologists were observing that a faulty ego boundary is one of the chief deficits in schizophrenic patients. Federn (1952) did not agree with Freud's assertion that object cathexis was withdrawn in schizophrenia. Instead, Federn emphasized the withdrawal of ego boundary cathexis. He noted that schizophrenic patients characteristically have no barrier between what is inside and what is out-side, because their ego boundary is no longer psychologically invested (as it is in neurotic patients).

Many of these early psychoanalytic formulations created profound difficulties between the clinicians treating patients with schizophrenia and the families of those patients. Terms such as *schizophrenogenic mother* generated an atmosphere in which mothers felt blamed for causing schizophrenia in their children. In recent decades, more sophisticated psychodynamic formulations of schizophrenia have appeared (Arlow and Brenner 1969; Blatt and Wild 1976; Grand 1982; Grotstein 1977a, 1977b; Mahler 1952; Ogden 1980, 1982). Most of these theories are based on reconstructions from working with adult patients. In other words, the clini-cians have studied the mental processes in the psychotherapeutic setting and then extrapolated backward into childhood developmental issues. Unfortunately, many of the psychoanalytic formulations do not integrate findings from biological re-search into their theories of etiology.

Several psychological configurations reflect the interface between the neuro-biological and the psychological. Children who ultimately develop schizophrenia have an aversion to object relations that make bonding with them difficult. Hyper-sensitivity to stimulation and difficulties with attention and concentration also are common preschizophrenia personality traits. Recent research has suggested that regionally diffuse losses of normal sensory gating in the central nervous system may be characteristic of schizophrenia (Freedman et al. 1996; Judd et al. 1992), so that patients find it difficult to screen out irrelevant stimuli and feel a chronic sense of sensory overload. Robbins (1992) has suggested a correlation between emo-tional states of mental oblivion and findings of cortical atrophy and decreased ac-tivity in the frontal lobes of schizophrenic patients. This cluster of features taken together leads to pathological forms of symbiosis with caretakers who are unable to adapt to the demands of such children. The notion of a diathesis in childhood that is present long before the onset of schizophrenic symptoms has been supported by creative research involving study of the home movies of adult-onset schizophrenia patients and their healthy siblings (Walker and Lewine 1990). Judges who viewed the films and who were blind to the psychiatric outcomes of the subjects were able to identify the preschizophrenic children reliably and distinguish them from their healthy siblings.

Theories of etiology and pathogenesis must take into account the substantial evidence that genetic factors play a key role. In the absence of such factors, even highly dysfunctional family situations will not produce schizophrenic illness in the offspring (Wahlberg et al. 1997). One of the most compelling hypotheses is that of Kendler and Eaves (1986), who postulated that genes control the degree to which an individual is sensitive to the environment's predisposing, risk-increasing aspects versus its risk-reducing and protective aspects. This theory of genetic control of sensitivity to the environment was supported by a Finnish study in which a group of 58 adoptees with schizophrenic biological mothers was compared with a group of 96 comparison adoptees at ordinary genetic risk (Wahlberg et al. 1997). Among the offspring of adoptive parents with high levels of communication deviance, a higher proportion of those adoptees at high genetic risk showed evidence of thought disorder compared with the group of comparison adoptees. In this conceptual model, emphasis is placed on the "fit" between child and family. A subgroup of adoptees at high genetic risk did not "fit" with their adoptive parents who were characterized by high communication deviance.

One of the implications of this conceptual model is that a positive rearing experience can protect high-risk individuals against future development of schizophrenia. This view was supported by the Finnish Adoptive Family Study (Tienari et al. 1994). In this investigation, the children of schizophrenic mothers who had a positive adoptive experience were protected from later schizophrenia, while the genetically vulnerable individuals who experienced a disturbed adoptive family tended to develop the disorder. Other studies, however, have not linked family disturbance to the development of the illness.

In a comprehensive review of the literature, Olin and Mednick (1996) identified premorbid characteristics that appear to be risk markers for future psychosis. These characteristics fall into two categories: 1) early etiological factors, including perinatal complications, family history of schizophrenia, maternal exposure to influenza, neurobehavioral deficits, parental separation in the first year of life, distressed family functioning, and institutional rearing; and 2) behavioral and social precursors of mental illness identified by clinicians and teachers and personality variables revealed by interviews and questionnaires. In other words, an interaction occurs among genetic vulnerability, environmental attributes, and individual traits.

Much of the psychodynamic literature on schizophrenia is focused on treatment considerations. Indeed, psychodynamic understanding is relevant to the treatment of schizophrenia, regardless of its etiology. Certain common threads run through many of the psychodynamic theories that inform the clinician's approach to the patient. First, psychotic symptoms have meaning (Karon 1992). Grandiose delusions or hallucinations, for example, often immediately follow an insult to a schizophrenic patient's self-esteem (Garfield 1985; Garfield et al. 1987). The grandiose content of the thought or perception is the patient's effort to offset the narcissistic injury.

A second common thread is that human relatedness is fraught with terror for these patients. The intense anxieties involving contact with others are apparent even though the etiology cannot be entirely explained. Concerns about the integrity of one's ego boundaries and the fear of fusion with others represent an ongoing problem that is often resolved by isolation. Treatment relationships present a challenge for the patient to be able to trust that catastrophe will not result from becoming connected with others. Finally, a third common thread involves the conviction of all psychodynamically oriented authors that dynamically informed therapeutic relationships with sensitive clinicians can fundamentally improve the quality of life for schizophrenic patients. In a study of fully recovered schizophrenic patients (Rund 1990), 80% had been in long-term psychotherapy and had attached great importance to it. Even when full recovery is not achieved, the therapeutic relationship may still be of extraordinary value in the patient's overall adaptation to life.

Treatment Approaches

Pharmacotherapy

Well-designed controlled studies abundantly demonstrate that antipsychotic medication is highly efficacious in managing the positive symptoms of schizophrenia. The schizophrenic patient's accessibility to all other forms of therapeutic intervention is greatly enhanced by the judicious use of antipsychotics. Keith and Matthews (1984) even asserted that "freedom from positive symptoms approaches a *sino qua non* status for psychosocial treatments" (p. 71). Negative symptoms and disordered interpersonal relationships, however, are much less affected by medication and thus require psychosocial approaches. Some of the new and atypical antipsychotic agents (such as clozapine, risperidone, and olanzapine) appear to make a greater impact on negative symptom constellations.

Because numerous outstanding psychopharmacology texts are available, I will focus on psychosocial approaches to treatment. As discussed in Chapter 5, noncompliance with prescribed medication is an ongoing problem in the treatment of many schizophrenic patients. Dynamic psychiatrists involved in the long-term management of patients suffering from schizophrenia must view medication compliance as a treatment concern. Each patient must be educated about the likelihood of relapse if medication is stopped, about signs of tardive dyskinesia, and about management of the more benign side effects. In addition, the meaning of the medication to the patient must be explored from time to time, particularly at the first sign of noncompliance. As emphasized in Chapter 5, the prescribing of antipsychotic medication must occur in the context of a therapeutic alliance that is carefully fostered through sensitivity to the patient's internal experience of all treatments.

The new atypical antipsychotics that have been become widely used in the last decade have revolutionized the treatment of schizophrenia. These agents, including risperidone, clozapine, olanzapine, quetiapine, and ziprasidone, are at least as effective as conventional antipsychotic medications for positive symptoms, and they are more effective than conventional antipsychotics for negative symptoms. Clozapine has also been shown to relieve psychotic symptoms in a significant percentage of treatment-resistant patients. Moreover, these agents often relieve patients of a number of uncomfortable side effects, so that they are more willing to stay on their medications and to participate in psychosocial treatments. Treatment with risperidone has been shown to exert a more favorable effect on verbal working memory than treatment with a conventional antipsychotic agent, thus making collaboration in a psychotherapeutic or psychosocial treatment more of a possibility (Green et al. 1997). In a study comparing patients who received clozapine with those receiving a conventional antipsychotic, clozapine-treated patients were much more likely to participate in psychosocial rehabilitation treatment (Rosenheck et al. 1998).

The advent of the atypical antipsychotics has also resulted in new psychotherapeutic challenges for the clinician. Some patients who have been chronically ill for many, many years because of nonresponse to conventional agents will suddenly find themselves in a remitted state. Some observers (Degen and Nasper 1996; Duckworth et al. 1997) have compared these dramatic remissions to what Oliver Sacks (1990) described as "awakenings." Psychosis may come to serve a defensive function for many patients, so that they do not have to face the uncertainties of relationships, the complexities of the work situation, and the meaning of existence. The entire identity of the individual may be wrapped in the notion of having a chronic illness. When one's symptoms are finally remitted, there is often a grief process related to what has been lost and a bewildering sense of not knowing who one is in a nonpsychotic state of mind. As Degen and Nasper (1996) noted, "Despite unequivocal improvements, sudden symptom relief has turned out to be at least as painful as psychosis for some people" (p. 9). Psychotherapeutic intervention may help the patient to integrate the old self and the new self.

Patients with chronic psychoses may also have been insulated from the risks of intimacy. The remission of psychotic symptoms may open up the possibility of romantic and sexual involvement for the first time in years. Many patients may experience extraordinary anxiety at this prospect. The inherent risks of loss and rejection must be faced when these patients begin to reach out to others (Duckworth et al. 1997). Finally, emergence from psychosis may present patients with an existential crisis about purpose and meaning in life. They recognize that a good portion of their lives has been lost to chronic illness, and they are forced to reassess their personal and spiritual values. Those who enter the workforce are confronted with integrating the meaning of work into a sense of purpose and personal identity after having been unable to work for extended periods of time.

In addition to skills training, rehabilitation, and other modalities, patients who respond well to atypical antipsychotics also require a supportive human relationship in which these adjustments can be explored.

Individual Psychotherapy

Despite a rich clinical tradition of individual psychoanalytically oriented psychotherapy of schizophrenia, research studies have been hard pressed to demonstrate that the average schizophrenic patient is likely to reap significant benefit from such efforts (Gomez-Schwartz 1984). The Camarillo State Hospital Study (May 1968) is often cited because it was the first large-scale study that compared outcomes of schizophrenic patients according to whether they were treated with psychotherapy or with antipsychotic medication. The patient groups who received medication showed significantly greater improvement than both those who did not receive it and those who received psychotherapy alone. Moreover, no interactive effect was noted between psychotherapy and antipsychotic medication. This study has been criticized, however, because it relied on inexperienced therapists who had no particular commitment to the type of psychotherapy they were instructed to practice with their research subjects. Also, the outcome measures were not sensitive enough to pick up changes in interpersonal and general psychological functioning that might specifically respond to psychotherapy (Conte and Plutchik 1986). Two other studies that were also fraught with methodological problems (Grinspoon et al. 1972; Rogers et al. 1967) found questionable benefit from psychotherapy. Karon and VandenBos (1981) demonstrated more improvement in schizophrenic patients treated by experienced therapists, as compared with a control group of patients who received routine treatment with phenothiazines and supportive therapy, but this study has also been criticized for methodological problems such as a lack of random assignment and early transfer of patients in the drug treatment group to a chronic unit (Keith and Matthews 1984; Klein 1980).

By far the most elegantly designed study on the effects of psychotherapy with schizophrenic patients is the Boston study reported by Stanton, Gunderson, and colleagues (Gunderson et al. 1984; Stanton et al. 1984). A principal failure in previous studies had been the lack of definition in the form of psychotherapy being administered by project therapists. In the Boston study, nonchronic schizophrenic patients from diverse institutional and outpatient settings were assigned either to reality-adaptive, supportive psychotherapy (RAS) or to exploratory, insight-oriented psychotherapy (EIO). Those included in the analysis (95 of the original

164 patients) remained in their assigned treatment situation for at least 6 months. At 2-year follow-up, the investigators obtained complete data on 47 of the original sample. At this point in the data analysis, patients receiving RAS showed less recidivism and better role performance. On the other hand, patients who received EIO had greater improvements in cognition and ego functioning. The investigators concluded that overall differences between the two groups were relatively minor.

Unfortunately, despite the sophisticated methodology and design of the Boston study, generalizability of the results must be limited for several reasons. First, only 47 patients completed the 2-year course of the project; thus, many of the definitive comparisons were based on approximately 20 subjects in each treatment group (Carpenter 1984). Second, the data collection stopped after 2 years. Many experienced therapists of schizophrenic patients would consider 2 years to be merely the beginning of the middle phase of therapy. Schizophrenic patients are notoriously difficult to engage in a psychotherapeutic process. Moreover, expecting a therapist to adhere to either a more-or-less expressive or a more-or-less supportive model in the treatment of a schizophrenic patient introduces an artificiality into the treatment being evaluated. Nowhere is flexibility more important than in the psychotherapy of schizophrenia. As stressed in Chapter 4, in a naturalistic setting, the psychotherapist will shift back and forth from expressive to supportive interventions, depending on the needs of the patient at a given moment.

The investigators themselves (Glass et al. 1989) subsequently blindly rated the actual process of therapy from audiotaped transcripts and concluded that the earlier finding of little overall differences between the two groups "concealed discrete processes within the therapies that have important and specific effects" (p. 607). Therapists who were rated as skilled in dynamic exploration produced greater improvements in global psychopathology, denial of illness, and retardation-apathy.

Finally, one other irreducible difference between the needs of research and the ambience of clinical practice should be taken into account in interpreting the data from the Boston study. The motivations, both conscious and unconscious, that lead a psychotherapist to enter into what could become a lifelong commitment to treating a schizophrenic patient are both mysterious and highly personal. Whatever forces lead a therapist and patient to "choose" each other are ignored by large-group designs that require scientifically rigorous random assignment of patient to therapist (Müller 1984). Only intensive study of individual cases can shed light on this significant contributor to psychotherapeutic success.

In a subsequent report, Gunderson (1987) acknowledged the difficulty of engaging schizophrenic patients in a long-term psychotherapy process. He noted that his study and others have suggested that about two-thirds of schizophrenic patients will drop out of psychotherapy when assigned nonspecifically as part of a research study. Gunderson carefully examined the data from the Boston study to determine the typical characteristics of those who continued in psychotherapy. His surprising finding was that they were characterized by social isolation, emotional flatness, and internal disorganization. However, they tended to have more consistent role performance than the dropout group. He also determined that dropout rate is affected by cultural norms within the hospital milieu. For example, patients from the Veterans Administration hospital used in the study were much more likely to drop out than those hospitalized at McLean Hospital, where psychotherapy is a standard part of treatment. Gunderson also concluded that longer-term hospitalization may be helpful in engaging patients. When he divided the patients according to whether they received RAS or EIO therapy, he determined that emotionally distant, thought disordered patients with an optimistic view of their illness were most likely to continue with the former modality, while patients who were more likely to continue with the latter treatment had fairly intact reality testing, reasonably good interpersonal relatedness, and a view of their psychotic episode as an unfortunate event.

Gunderson's findings are consistent with those of McGlashan's (1984, 1987) long-term follow-up study of patients treated at Chestnut Lodge. In this study, 163 schizophrenic patients previously hospitalized at Chestnut Lodge while receiving intensive psychoanalytically oriented psychotherapy were followed up an average of 15 years after discharge. About one-third of these patients had moderate-to-good outcomes (McGlashan 1984). Of the two identifiable groups whose psychosis remitted, one group attempted to integrate the psychotic experience into their life. They believed that they had gained important information from the psychotic episode, and they were curious about the meaning of their symptoms. The second group showed another pathway to stable recovery, namely, that of "sealing over" the illness. These patients tended to have a fixed, negative view of their illness and no interest in understanding their psychotic symptoms. Although both groups had achieved reasonably stable adjustments, those who integrated their experiences appear to have had somewhat superior outcomes.

These findings suggest that patients who can integrate a psychotic experience into their life may benefit from exploratory work in the context of psychotherapy, while those who seal over a psychotic episode will probably not benefit and may perhaps even be harmed by persistent exploratory attempts. Even psychotherapies that involve some insight will require significant support by the therapist. The expressive-supportive distinction is certainly less rigid in the psychotherapy of schizophrenia than in the treatment of higher-functioning patients.

Personal therapy (Hogarty et al. 1995, 1997a, 1997b) is the most rigorously tested of the individual psychosocial interventions with schizophrenia. In contrast to psychodynamic therapies, which are generally not specific to a disorder, personal therapy is disorder-specific. It is also grounded in research on the illness;

hence, it is based on the stress-vulnerability model and considers stress-related affect dysregulation as central to symptom exacerbation. Some psychodynamic therapists have based their assumptions about the illness on psychoanalytic theories that may have no empirical basis. On the other hand, a range of therapeutic techniques characterize personal therapy, and many dynamic therapists are similarly flexible in adjusting their approach to the patient's needs.

Personal therapy proceeds in phases. In the initial phase, the focus is on clinical stabilization of symptoms, development of the therapeutic alliance, and provision of basic psychoeducation. This phase usually occurs during the first few months after discharge from the hospital. The intermediate phase is geared toward helping the patient become aware of internal affective cues associated with stressors. Some patients might also begin social skills training, exercises in relaxation, and training to enhance social perception at this point. The advanced phase of the therapy is designed to provide opportunities for introspection. In addition, the patient receives instruction in principles of conflict resolution and criticism management. In each phase, the therapy is tailored to the patient's individual needs.

Hogarty et al. (1997a, 1997b) randomly assigned 151 patients with schizophrenia to personal therapy or to one of two comparison treatments: family therapy or supportive individual therapy. They followed the patients for 3 years after hospital discharge. Only 18% prematurely terminated the study, and of those, most were not in the personal therapy group. Personal therapy was found to be more effective than family and supportive therapies in preventing psychotic and affective relapse as well as medication noncompliance; however, this greater effectiveness was seen only in those patients living with their families. Among patients who did not live with a family, those who received personal therapy did worse—they had significantly more psychotic decompensations than did those receiving supportive therapy. The investigators concluded that personal therapy should probably be delayed until patients have achieved residential stability and symptomatic improvement.

Personal therapy appeared to be highly beneficial for role performance or social adjustment, but its effects on symptoms were not significantly greater than those of the comparison treatments. In fact, patients who received personal therapy actually had *more* anxiety than those who received supportive therapy or family treatment. Also, personal therapy seemed to be more durable in its impact than supportive therapy. Patients who received personal therapy continued to improve in social adjustment during the second and third years after discharge, whereas those receiving supportive therapy, with or without family intervention, experienced adjustment effects that peaked at 12 months after discharge and then plateaued.

In keeping with our contemporary understanding of the optimal treatment strategy for schizophrenia, personal therapy was only one modality in the overall treatment plan. Patients received antipsychotic medications, and various rehabilitation approaches were also used in conjunction with the personal therapy. As Fenton and McGlashan (1997) have noted, personal therapy provides the ideal context in which to consider *"the specific combination of interventions that will be most helpful for this particular patient with this particular type of schizophrenia at this particular phase of illness or recovery"* (p. 1495). This effort to tailor the choice of interventions to the patient's specific needs makes good clinical sense. Personal therapy can certainly be applied within a framework of psychodynamic understanding of the patient's defenses, object relations, and sense of self.

In addition, randomized controlled trials of cognitive-behavioral therapy have shown that psychotherapeutic interventions can be a useful component of an overall treatment plan for schizophrenia (Kuipers et al. 1998; Tarrier et al. 1998). In one study, patient improvements resulting from cognitive-behavioral therapy were largely sustained at 18-month follow-up (Kuipers et al. 1998). Strategies such as training in problem solving and relapse prevention appeared to be particularly useful in this study and should be incorporated in any psychotherapeutic approach.

After the patient's symptoms have stabilized, the therapist's main challenge is to begin to build a treatment alliance. Because of these patients' lack of insight into their illness, this is often an extraordinarily difficult task. As a result, therapists must be innovative in finding some common ground. Selzer and Carsky (1990) have stressed the importance of finding an organizing object—a person, an idea, or an inanimate object—that allows the patient and the therapist to talk about what is going on between them. In this early stage of treatment, patients are often unable to acknowledge that they are ill and in need of treatment, and the main focus must be establishing relatedness. For example, Frese (1997) cautions clinicians to avoid challenging patients' delusional beliefs. He points out that when patients have delusions, they naturally assume them to be true, even in the face of evidence to the contrary. Frese, who has himself suffered from schizophrenia for many years while pursuing a successful career as a psychologist, advises clinicians to think of patients as speaking poetically and metaphorically. He suggests that it is useful to help patients see how others regard their beliefs, so that patients can avoid certain actions that may cause them to be admitted to a psychiatric hospital. By allying with the patient's need to avoid hospitalization, the therapist may gain the patient's cooperation and compliance with other aspects of the treatment plan, such as medication.

Much of the early work of psychotherapy must be directive and designed to repair deficits of the patient that impede development of a therapeutic alliance (Selzer 1983; Selzer and Carsky 1990; Selzer et al. 1989). The ensuing work on building an alliance may have significant payoffs. When Frank and Gunderson (1990) examined the role of the therapeutic alliance in the courses and outcomes of the 143 schizophrenic patients in the Boston Psychotherapy Study, they discovered that it was a key predictor of treatment success. Patients with good therapeutic alliances were more likely to remain in psychotherapy, more likely to comply with prescribed medication, and more likely to achieve good outcomes at the end of 2 years.

The treatment alliance can also be facilitated by supporting and restoring the patient's defenses, focusing on the patient's strengths, and providing a safe haven for the patient. McGlashan and Keats (1989) emphasized that above all, psychotherapy should offer asylum. Feelings and thoughts that others do not understand are accepted by the psychotherapist. Withdrawal or bizarre behavior is accepted and understood without any demand that the patient change to be acceptable. Much of this aspect of technique consists of "being with" (McGlashan and Keats 1989)—a willingness to consistently put oneself in the company of another human being without making inordinate demands. As Karon (1992) has pointed out, terror is the primary affect in the person with schizophrenia. Therapists must be able to accept feelings of terror when they are projected onto them and avoid withdrawing and being overwhelmed in the face of such powerful affects.

As the alliance becomes solidified, the therapist can then begin to identify individual-specific relapse factors and help the patient to accept the fact that he or she has a serious illness. The therapist must also serve as an auxiliary ego for the patient. When profound ego weaknesses, such as poor judgment, are in evidence, the therapist may help the patient to anticipate the consequences of his or her actions.

The therapist must strive to be open and genuine with the patient. If all negative feelings are denied and split off in the therapeutic relationship, the patient will experience the therapist as unreal. Moreover, the therapist's apparent ability to transcend all feelings of anger, boredom, hatred, and frustration will simply increase the patient's envy of the therapist (Searles 1967/1979). This posture does not imply that the therapist should engage in extensive self-disclosure, but some therapists may wish to share items of personal interest with the patient and may wish to validate the patient's perception of feelings such as irritation, sadness, boredom, and other unpleasant affects.

The therapist must be attuned to deficits. Some patients will have substantial neurocognitive limitations that the therapist may tactfully point out. When these deficits are addressed, the therapist may also wish to provide advice on how to compensate for the deficits so that the patient does not feel hopeless about them.

Some excellent work based on cognitive-behavioral therapy, with empirical research demonstrating its efficacy, has been described in detail by Kingdon and Turkington (1994). Much of their approach is closely related to dynamically informed supportive therapy, which recognizes fragility and seeks to strengthen ego functioning. For example, in discussing a patient's hallucinations, the therapist may wish to explore the idiosyncratic quality of the perception. Questions such as "Can anybody else hear what is said?" may be asked, and the therapist might inquire about the patient's beliefs regarding the origin of the voices. In working with delusions, the therapist may tactfully ask if there are other possible explanations for the phenomena the patient believes. Is it possible that the patient is taking things personally or reading things into behaviors of others? It is also worth exploring an inference chain. For example, if the patient believes that a silicon chip is in his brain, the therapist might want to know how electricity would get to the chip. The patient's experience should generally be accepted, and a positive atmosphere should be created for exploration that may lead to some critical thinking by the patient about other possibilities.

Only after a solid alliance is established, individual-specific relapse factors have been noted and discussed, deficits have been addressed, and the patient is well established in a residential situation with family or others should the therapist attempt an expressive approach in which insight or interpretation is central. Some patients may never reach that point. When supportive and rehabilitative strategies are sufficient, the therapist may wish to leave well enough alone. The fantasy of rescuing the patient from schizophrenia must be avoided—it is the worst possible psychological attitude for a therapist. Therapists must be comfortable with the possibility that patients will choose "the devil they know" in preference to facing the uncertainties of change and improvement. Effective psychotherapy requires an attitude in the therapist that allows the patient's wish to remain ill to be an acceptable alternative to psychotherapeutic change (Searles 1976/1979). Nonetheless, a substantial subgroup of persons with schizophrenia will want to collaborate with a therapist to gain an understanding their illness and how it has shattered their sense of who they are. In the professional literature, schizophrenic patients have spoken eloquently about the benefits of individual psychotherapy (Anonymous 1986; Ruocchio 1989). These patients comment on the importance of having one consistent figure in their lives who is there through any adversity over many years. These patients convey how their subjective experiences of themselves and of their lives were significantly altered by a long-term psychotherapeutic relationship, even though outcome measures may not be sensitive enough to record such alterations. In the words of one patient (Anonymous 1986), "A fragile ego left alone remains fragile. Medication or superficial support alone is not a substitute for the feeling that one is understood by another human being" (p. 70).

Group Psychotherapy

Studies of group psychotherapy with schizophrenic patients suggest that this modality may be useful, but emphasize the timing of its implementation. The optimal time appears to be after positive symptoms are stabilized through pharmacological intervention (Kanas et al. 1980; Keith and Matthews 1984). The acutely disorganized patient is unable to screen out environmental stimuli, and the multiple inputs from a group setting may overwhelm the patient's already beleaguered ego just when it is attempting to reestablish itself. One review of controlled studies of group therapy for schizophrenia (Kanas 1986) found considerable evidence for the efficacy of inpatient group psychotherapy but a clear trend for greater success on long-term chronic units than on acute wards. After positive symptomatology is controlled, inpatient groups can be highly supportive for schizophrenic patients as they are reorganizing and as they see others preparing for discharge. Efficacy studies suggest that, as an outpatient modality, group therapy may be as effective as individual therapy (O'Brien 1983). For the patient who is stabilized on medication, weekly sessions of 60–90 minutes can serve to build trust and can provide a support group where patients can freely discuss concerns such as how to manage auditory hallucinations and how to deal with the stigma of mental illness.

Family Intervention

In the empirical research literature on the efficacy of psychosocial interventions with schizophrenia, no modality has been more substantiated than family interventions. Numerous studies (Falloon et al. 1982; Goldstein et al. 1978; Hogarty 1984; Leff et al. 1982) have demonstrated that family treatment plus antipsychotic medication is three times as effective as medication alone in preventing relapse. These investigations used a factor known as expressed emotion (EE), first identified by Brown et al. (1972). This term was coined to describe a style of interaction between family members and the patient that is characterized by intense overinvolvement and excessive criticism. Although this concept does not blame parents for causing schizophrenia in their children, it does acknowledge that families are affected by schizophrenia and that they may become secondary contributors to relapse through an intensification of their interactions with the schizophrenic patient. In brief, high-EE families produce a greater frequency of relapse in a schizophrenic member than low-EE families.

A meta-analysis of 27 studies of the EE-outcome relationship with schizophrenia confirmed that EE is a significant and robust predictor of relapse (Butzlaff and Hooley 1998). The relationship between high EE and relapse appeared to be strongest for patients with more chronic forms of schizophrenia.

The extensive research on EE has led to development of a sophisticated psychoeducational approach with families of schizophrenic persons. The families are trained to recognize prodromal signs and symptoms that presage relapse, are taught to reduce criticism and overinvolvement, and are helped to see that a consistent medication program can preserve optimal functioning. Other areas of education include instruction about the side effects of medications and their management, the long-term course and prognosis of schizophrenia, and the genetic and biological basis of schizophrenia. Clinicians using this approach can effectively enlist the family's help as collaborators in the prevention of relapse.

The rigor of the research on family interventions with persons who have schizophrenia is admirable. Studies generally use randomization, well-established inclusion criteria, systematically collected outcomes, evidence of adherence to the intervention, and suitable controls. Reviews of the efficacy of these family treatments suggest that long-term family intervention is effective for lowering relapse rate, reducing EE, and improving outcome (Dixon and Lehman 1995; Penn and Mueser 1996). The treatment gains appear to be fairly stable as well, often enduring for as long as 2 years.

The impressive results obtained with this conceptual model of family intervention have been challenged, however. Some investigators have questioned whether controlling EE is the exclusive factor involved in relapse prevention. One study (MacMillan et al. 1986) found that the regular ingestion of antipsychotic medication and the preadmission duration of illness were factors that, when taken into account, canceled out the effect of EE in predicting relapse. Another study (Parker et al. 1988) examined 57 schizophrenic patients from the standpoint of the EE level of the household. Relapse was predicted by a one-parent household and by a poor course of prior illness, but the level of EE was not predictive. The investigators speculated that those patients with a poor course may evoke responses in relatives that are high in EE, particularly if the patient lives in a one-parent household. Falloon (1988) has pointed out that the research on EE has not included serial measures of EE that would help determine whether behavior disturbances in schizophrenic patients *provoke* high-EE responses in parents or *result from* the stress of high-EE relatedness.

Additional questions have been raised about the high-EE construct and the family interventions that it informs. Many families of schizophrenic patients feel that they are being blamed for relapse when they are merely responding to a difficult situation in the best way they can (Lefley 1992). As Kanter et al. (1987) have noted, if families are strongly urged to remain nonintrusive, they may fail to respond appropriately when provocative behavior and lack of control are exhibited by the schizophrenic family member. Moreover, in some cases it may be assumed that a switch from high to low EE has caused patient improvement when in fact the family has simply lowered its EE as a *result* of the improvement in the patient (Hogarty et al. 1986). Researchers also question whether EE is a construct that is stable over time (Lefley 1992). Other concerns include the observation that high

EE is related to other illnesses besides schizophrenia, the fact that only a certain proportion of people with schizophrenia are influenced at all by high EE, and the realization that the entire construct is essentially cultural (Jenkins and Karno 1992).

Given the controversy surrounding the relationship between relapse and EE, clinicians may be puzzled about the most useful interventions to make with families. Kanter et al. (1987) stressed that psychoeducational efforts involving information about the illness, support, and advice may produce results that are just as impressive as the data from the EE studies. Hatfield (1990) stressed that education is probably more helpful than treatment in working with families and that specific interventions are not necessary. Nevertheless, because highly stimulating environments tend to be difficult for schizophrenic patients to deal with, there is sound wisdom in reducing the intensity of environmental stimuli. Moreover, recent research suggests that the two elements of EE—namely, emotional overinvolvement and excessive criticism—should not be lumped together (King and Dixon 1996). In this investigation of 69 patients and 108 relatives, emotional overinvolvement appeared to be associated with a *better* social outcome in patients, suggesting that excessive criticism may be the factor that promotes relapse.

Psychosocial Skills Training

Psychosocial rehabilitation, which is usually defined as a therapeutic approach that encourages patients to develop their fullest capacities through environmental supports and learning procedures (Bachrach 1992), should be a major part of contemporary treatment for any person suffering from schizophrenia. This individually tailored approach involves capitalizing on the patient's strengths and competencies, restoring hope to the patient, maximizing the patient's vocational potential, encouraging the patient's active involvement in his or her own treatment, and helping the patient develop social skills. These assorted goals are often subsumed under the heading of psychosocial skills training. Hogarty et al. (1991) found that recipients of psychosocial skills training made substantial improvements in social adjustment measures and had a lower rate of relapse at 1-year follow-up compared with a control group. However, this gain eroded within 2 years after the treatment.

Cognitive rehabilitation or remediation has also been incorporated into these strategies. Through repeated practice of related techniques, various cognitive deficits are modified. In social skills training, patients participate in role-playing and other exercises to improve their functioning in interpersonal settings. The research on these approaches is not yet compelling regarding efficacy. Although there seem to be clear improvements in specific motor performance behaviors when training takes place, these skills may erode over time. Also, evidence for the generalizability of psychosocial skills training from the clinical setting to everyday life is rather weak (Penn and Mueser 1996; Scott and Dixon 1995). Nevertheless, there is a general view that teaching specific skills and modifying cognitive deficits show promise as part of an overall treatment plan.

Hospital Treatment

For the schizophrenic patient who has an acute psychotic break, brief hospitalization provides "time out"—a chance to regroup and gain new direction for the future. Antipsychotic medication relieves most of the positive symptoms. The structure of the hospital unit provides a safe haven to prevent patients from hurting themselves or others. Nursing staff members in the milieu perform auxiliary ego functions for the patient. The treatment team can also identify stressors from Axis IV of DSM-IV (American Psychiatric Association 1994) that might contribute to a psychotic episode at this particular time in the patient's life. A psychoeducational effort can begin with the patient and family to establish an optimal posthospital environment. They should be prepared for the fact that they are dealing with a lifelong disease, and that the goal is to minimize disability, not effect a lasting cure. The importance of staying on medication is emphasized, and the concept of EE may be explained as well. At the same time, the treatment team needs to convey a sense of hope. It is often useful to point out that although the disease is chronic, considerable research suggests that some schizophrenic patients become more and more functional as they age (Harding et al. 1987).

The thrust of brief hospitalization is counterregressive. Defenses are restored, and the patient should be returned to functioning as expeditiously as possible. If the patient is not established in psychotherapy, the hospital may be used as a preparatory phase to get the patient ready for an outpatient psychotherapy process (Selzer 1983). The patient's omnipotence is challenged by the necessity of accommodating to the needs of others. By enforcing a routine schedule in patients' lives, some frustration of their needs and wishes is unavoidable. This optimal level of frustration helps patients improve reality testing and other ego functions (Selzer 1983). If psychotherapy can be started during the hospitalization, the patient can then maintain a sense of continuity by seeing the therapist outside the hospital. After the patient's positive symptomatology is relieved to some extent, group treatment may be instituted and may also be continued on an outpatient basis, depending on the patient's amenability to the group format. For some isolated outpatients, group meetings may be their only significant social contact.

For those patients with predominantly negative symptoms, diagnosis and medication can be reassessed. Are there secondary reasons, such as depression, anxiety, and medication side effects, that might account for the negative symptoms? Similarly, the psychotherapy process, if ongoing, can be reevaluated with the collaboration of the therapist to determine whether to make a shift in strategy. Family work can proceed in a psychoeducational fashion, and family members can be enlisted in the search for ongoing stressors that prevent the patient from responding to conventional treatment. Most of all, the negative-symptom group requires psychosocial skills training and vocational rehabilitation. Social skills groups that focus on behavioral improvement in such simple daily behaviors as eating, conversation, walking, and manners can be extraordinarily valuable for the negative-symptom group. Similarly, a careful vocational evaluation in a supervised setting in which concrete job skills are taught and developed may be an essential component.

Research on posthospital adjustment and rehospitalization rates demonstrates that patients are more likely to stay out of the hospital when they have been taught adaptive behaviors and skills and have learned to control symptomatic and maladaptive behaviors during their inpatient stay (Mosher and Keith 1979). Although the behavioral focus of such milieu programs may seem antithetical to dynamic psychiatrists, this focus actually may work synergistically with dynamic approaches. Patients who improve their interpersonal relations as a result of behaviorally oriented social skills training will begin to experience changes in their object relations, which then produce material for discussion in psychotherapy.

Schizophrenic patients who are treatment resistant may also display a predominant picture of disordered interpersonal relatedness. These patients frequently have serious characterological difficulties that coexist with schizophrenia. Clinicians are sometimes prone to forget that every schizophrenic patient also has a personality. These characterological problems may therefore result in noncompliance with medication, alienation of family members and other supportive persons in the environment, denial of illness, and inability to function in a vocational setting. An inpatient unit or day hospital may be the ideal setting in which to address the characterological dimension accompanying the schizophrenia and to examine the underpinnings of the patient's noncompliance.

To a large extent, the hospital or partial hospital treatment of such patients follows the model outlined in Chapter 6. Via projective identification, patients attempt to reestablish their internal object world in the milieu. Staff members contain those projections and provide new models of relatedness for reinternalization. In addition, patients are informed about maladaptive interactional patterns as they occur in the here and now of the treatment setting.

Many of the treatment principles described in this chapter are illustrated in the following detailed case example:

Mr. H, a 22-year-old single man from the southeastern United States, had a 3-year history of schizophrenia that had not responded either to outpatient treatment with medication or to brief hospitalization. Referred for psychiatric hospitalization, he came for admission accompanied by his parents. When asked to describe his problems, he recited a litany of physical complaints involving virtually every anatomic area of his body, but steadfastly denied any psychiatric problems. When he learned that he was being admitted to a psychiatric facility, he was reluctant to sign himself into the hospital. Only with repeated reassurances that a complete physical and neurological workup was part of the psychiatric evaluation would he consent to hospitalization.

The patient's somatic preoccupations precluded any history taking of his psychiatric disorder. Fortunately, his parents were able to fill in the gaps. Mr. H was the third of three children born to highly successful parents. The patient's father was a respected business executive, and his mother had a prominent administrative position in the school system. His older brother was a graduate of a prestigious medical school, and his older sister was an honors student in her MBA program. The patient himself had briefly attended college, but was forced to drop out after the onset of his illness. He complained of hypersensitivity to noise in his dormitory, and he expressed concern that others were talking about him. He finally demanded to be taken home so that he would not be humiliated by the other young men in the dormitory, who he claimed were calling him "loser," "fag," and "crazy" in the middle of the night.

After leaving college, Mr. H returned to live with his parents, where he became increasingly demanding of their time. When his father attempted to leave for work in the morning, the patient would run out the door after him and sometimes jump on the hood of his car to prevent him from leaving. He would also wake his father in the middle of the night to demand that he listen to a recital of his physical complaints. He repeatedly accused his father of neglect by saying, "What are you going to do about my pain?" Mr. H had been seen by numerous specialists, and often several specialists in one field, without any diagnosis of physical disease. He insisted that he needed continual "monitoring" from his parents so that they would be aware of the waxing and waning of his physical symptoms. Mr. H was blessed with loving and concerned parents, who attempted to accommodate his pleas for attention by spending long periods with him. On one occasion, the patient's father sat and listened to the patient's somatic preoccupations for 10 hours without a break.

Mr. H also continued to hear voices condemning him, and in one instance he assaulted a stranger on the street because he was convinced that the stranger was saying unpleasant things about him. Mr. H had been hospitalized for a few weeks each on two different occasions and had been prescribed four different antipsychotic medications at various times. Each time, the patient discontinued the medication because of his denial that he had a psychiatric condition that warranted psychotropic medication and because of anticholinergic side effects that bothered him.

Shortly after admission, a mental status examination revealed that the patient continued to suffer from auditory hallucinations, although he did not complain of "hearing voices." Rather, he was convinced that people were actually talking about him. On several occasions during the first few days of his hospitalization, he angrily confronted other patients because he thought that they were ridiculing him. All of them vehemently denied talking about him. In addition, Mr. H found it difficult to complete a thought because of a formal thought disorder that consisted of blocking and derailment. He would stop in midsentence, change the subject, then begin another sentence.

Mr. H displayed much anxiety in the hospital because none of the staff members would "monitor" his physical symptoms as his parents had. As expected, the patient attempted to re-create his family situation in the milieu. He developed intense transference attachments to his doctor and his primary nurse, whom he expected to be with him at all times. When his doctor left the unit after a meeting with him, Mr. H attempted to run out the door after him just as he had tried to stop his father from going to work.

Physical and neurological examinations revealed no significant findings. After a careful psychiatric evaluation, the treatment team developed an explanatory formulation. The patient's paranoid concerns and somatic preoccupations masked an extraordinarily low sense of self-esteem. Mr. H had grown up feeling like the "black sheep" of the family, because his limitations had precluded competition with the high achievers surrounding him. To preserve some degree of self-esteem, he formed an identity as a "victim" of disabling physical problems that kept him from performing at an acceptable level. Mr. H was then able to attribute his failures in school and in various jobs to physical illnesses.

The somatic concerns also provided an organizing focus for the patient's thoughts, thereby preventing a more profound state of psychotic fragmentation or self-dissolution. This severe somatic preoccupation was linked to his paranoid perception of ridicule from others through the mechanisms of introjection and projection. Early in life, Mr. H had internalized (as persecuting objects) the expectations and demands of his parents. Thus, strangers on the street or in the hallway who were perceived as talking about him had become these persecuting objects that he had projected onto the environment. When the persecutors were reintrojected, they became internal persecutors in the form of various aches and pains requiring immediate attention. Hence, the patient felt constantly under siege by a host of tormentors, both in his environment and within his body.

On a neurophysiological level, Mr. H's inability to screen out various stimuli may have compounded his feeling of numerous sources of pain and torment. Finally, the somatizing performed yet another function: it was the only way the patient knew to maintain object relatedness and therefore defend against severe separation anxiety. This patient clearly had little interest in any diagnostic evaluations or treatment suggestions from consultants. Such findings and recommendations were far less significant to him than his concern that he needed to be continuously "monitored." The patient's litany of physical complaints was not truly designed to elicit an ameliorating response from those around him; rather, its purpose was to maintain a continual external presence so that he would not have to face his anxieties about abandonment. Paradoxically, his barrage of complaints tended to evoke the opposite response, namely, to alienate and drive away others. Initially, the treatment team attempted to control Mr. H's positive symptoms through medication. However, the patient adamantly refused the medication because he associated it with previous doctors who had told him that his pain was "all in your head."

Respecting Mr. H's need to preserve self-esteem and organize his thinking through intense investment in physical symptoms, his hospital doctor assured him that no one was questioning the severity of Mr. H's pain. The doctor explained that the patient's illness had both psychological and physical aspects. The doctor further explained that one physical manifestation of the illness was difficulty filtering out various stimuli in the environment and within the body (Freedman et al. 1996; Spohn et al. 1977). Through this educational approach, Mr. H's doctor thus convinced the patient that the antipsychotic medication might be worth a trial because it often had a beneficial effect on the "filtering" system. After the patient agreed to take the medication, his thought disorder greatly improved, allowing him to talk more coherently with staff members and other patients. His auditory hallucinations continued despite the medication, but abated somewhat in frequency and severity.

The treatment team then attempted to repair some of the patient's ego deficits by functioning as auxiliary egos. On one occasion, for example, a nurse was meeting with Mr. H in a closed room on the hospital unit when he began to claim that people were talking about him outside in the hallway. To demonstrate that no one was there, the nurse opened the door and walked with Mr. H into the hallway. She then explained to the patient that his illness involved voices that originated on the inside, which were then perceived as though coming from outside sources. This approach was reinforced by feedback from fellow patients in group meetings.

This patient had initially been held out of group meetings on the unit because of the overstimulating nature of that treatment modality. After being stabilized on medication, however, Mr. H began to attend the groups and frequently brought up his concern that others were talking about him. The other patients steadfastly denied these accusations, and they all encouraged him to "check it out" whenever he heard the voice. The patient's hostile accusations toward other patients and toward staff members gradually shifted to gentle inquiries as he realized that the voices did indeed emanate from within.

As Mr. H gained greater control over his positive symptoms, the treatment focus shifted to his disordered interpersonal relatedness. The patient attempted to establish the same relationship with his hospital doctor that he had with his father. The hospital doctor found himself spending more time in interaction with Mr. H than with any of his other patients. The urgency with which Mr. H presented his complaints of diarrhea, stomachaches, joint pain, and so on, made his hospital doctor reluctant to disengage from Mr. H and leave the unit. One day when Mr. H frantically followed him out of the unit and continued to walk down the sidewalk with him, the doctor realized the extent to which the patient had replicated his family situation in the hospital. Mr. H felt as though he deserved the complete attention of his doctor and was oblivious to the needs of other patients who shared the same physician. The doctor then told Mr. H that he should lower his expectations of how much time the doctor would spend with him. The doctor explained to Mr. H that he would set up specific 30-minute appointments with him and would not meet with him at other times. This limit-setting approach addressed the patient's sense of entitlement.

This approach also presented a new form of object relatedness for the patient to internalize. The object relationship paradigm of a complaining, demanding self linked to an indulgent object was modified by Mr. H's experience of a new object that was caring but also limit setting. The experience with this new object correspondingly brought about changes in the patient's self-representation. Although initially frustrated, the patient became more tolerant of the doctor's absences and more accepting of limitations on his expectations of others. Moreover, the limitations Mr. H encountered in this relationship led him to discuss his separation anxiety with his doctor. Mr. H began to express concern that in the absence of a caretaking figure, his basic needs would go unmet.

When the patient was able to address these and other psychological concerns, he was referred to an individual psychotherapist not connected with the unit. The early phase of this psychotherapy was characterized by the patient's extensive reports about his physical symptoms. The patient's therapist listened to these reports with interest and concern, empathizing with his need to focus on the somatic rather than the psychological. Periodically, however, the therapist would comment that he was really unable to help the patient with any physical ailments because he had nothing to add to the extensive work of the treatment team and the consultants. As trust developed, the patient began to discuss his profound feelings of inferiority within his family context. Although his brother and sister had distinguished themselves academically, his only distinction was that he suffered from a variety of bizarre ailments that prevented him from similar success. The patient's denial of psychiatric illness, his lack of psychological mindedness, and his lack of curiosity about his symptoms all led the therapist to take a predominantly supportive approach. Within that context, then, the patient was finally able to explore a surprisingly broad range of feelings about himself and his place in his family.

As part of the overall treatment plan, the patient became involved in a social skills group with a small number of his peers. In this setting, he received gentle confrontation about his hygiene problems, his failure to answer conversational questions, his self-absorption, and his obliviousness to the needs of others. He began to improve in all these areas in addition to generally improving his interpersonal functioning. For example, he began to say "good morning" to others who spoke to him, and he would even inquire as to their well-being. The patient also entered a vocational assessment and training program where he had to perform simple tasks under supervision. The activities therapist in charge of the program was careful to gear the level of complexity of the tasks to the patient's ability so that his self-esteem was not seriously threatened. Finally, a psychoeducational approach was employed with the patient's parents to help them accept their son's limitations. They were told that overinvolvement and excessive expectations would be counterproductive because the patient would experience them as pressure to succeed beyond his capacities.

This fragment of dynamically informed treatment illustrates how the different theoretical frameworks discussed in Chapter 2 may be useful in the treatment of one patient. Self psychological principles led the treatment team to an empathic awareness of this patient's need to maintain self-esteem, and his treaters therefore chose not to challenge his somatization. An object relations theoretical framework facilitated the doctor's understanding of this patient's problematic relationship with the doctor. Finally, the ego psychological perspective was helpful in two ways: 1) an ego-deficit model was applied in the form of the nursing staff's ego-building techniques, and 2) a conflict model was used to understand the auditory hallucinations. The persecutory voices this patient heard calling him a "loser" or "crazy" grew out of a painful conflict between the internalized expectations of his parents (in the form of his ego ideal and superego) and the reality of his limitations (realistic ego functioning). These voices always seemed more evident after the patient experienced any failure in his vocational program.

In summary, patients with schizophrenia need therapeutic figures in their lives. They need help navigating through the complicated realities of the mental health system. They also need someone to facilitate their understanding of the fears and fantasies that prevent them from complying with the various components of their overall treatment plan. Indeed, a central role of the psychotherapist is to explore compliance problems that arise in other areas of treatment. In contemporary practice, this role is often assigned to a clinical case manager, usually because the patient is not interested in therapy or because community resources cannot provide psychotherapy. Case managers serve as patient advocates, guides to mental health resources, and coordinators of the total treatment plan. Even though case management is oriented to reality and to adaptation, transference and countertransference issues arise; case managers must thus be capable of providing effective psychotherapeutic interventions (Kanter 1989). What schizophrenic patients most need, whether they are called case managers or psychotherapists, are concerned individuals who can offer compassionate human relationships for sanctuary from a confusing and threatening world.

References

American Psychiatric Association: Diagnostic and Statistical Manual of Mental Disorders, 4th Edition. Washington, DC, American Psychiatric Association, 1994

Andreasen NC, Olsen SA, Dennert JW, et al: Ventricular enlargement in schizophrenia: relationship to positive and negative symptoms. Am J Psychiatry 139:297–302, 1982

Andreasen NC, Flaum M, Swayze VW, et al: Positive and negative symptoms in schizophrenia: a critical reappraisal. Arch Gen Psychiatry 47:615–621, 1990

Anonymous: Can we talk? The schizophrenic patient in psychotherapy: a recovering patient. Am J Psychiatry 143:68–70, 1986

Arlow JA, Brenner C: The psychopathology of the psychoses: a proposed revision. Int J Psychoanal 50:5–14, 1969

Bachrach LL: Psychosocial rehabilitation and psychiatry in the care of long-term patients. Am J Psychiatry 149:1455–1463, 1992

Blatt SJ, Wild CM: Schizophrenia: A Developmental Analysis. New York, Academic Press, 1976

Brown GW, Birley JLT, Wing JK: Influence of family life on the course of schizophrenic disorders: a replication. Br J Psychiatry 121:241–258, 1972

Buztlaff RL, Hooley JM: Expressed emotion and psychiatric relapse: a meta-analysis. Arch Gen Psychiatry 55:547–552, 1998

Carpenter WT Jr: A perspective on the Psychotherapy of Schizophrenia Project. Schizophr Bull 10:599–602, 1984

Carpenter WT Jr, Henrichs DW, Wagman AMI: Deficit and nondeficit forms of schizophrenia: the concept. Am J Psychiatry 145:578–583, 1988

Conte HR, Plutchik R: Controlled research and supportive psychotherapy. Psychiatric Annals 16:530–533, 1986

Degen K, Nasper E: Return From Madness: Psychotherapy With People Taking the New Antipsychotic Medications and Emerging From Severe, Lifelong, and Disabling Schizophrenia. Northvale, NJ, Jason Aronson, 1996

Dixon LB, Lehman AF: Family interventions for schizophrenia. Schizophr Bull 21:631–643, 1995

Duckworth K, Nair V, Patel JK, et al: Lost time, found hope and sorrow: the search for self, connection, and purpose during "awakenings" on the new antipsychotics. Harv Rev Psychiatry 5:227–233, 1997

Falloon IRH: Expressed emotion: current status. Psychol Med 18:269–274, 1988

Falloon IRH, Boyd JL, McGill CW, et al: Family management in the prevention of exacerbations of schizophrenia: a controlled study. N Engl J Med 306:1437–1440, 1982

Federn P: Ego Psychology and the Psychoses. New York, Basic Books, 1952

Fenton WS, McGlashan TH: We can talk: individual psychotherapy for schizophrenia. Am J Psychiatry 154:1493–1495, 1997

Frank AF, Gunderson JG: The role of the therapeutic alliance in the treatment of schizophrenia: relationship to course and outcome. Arch Gen Psychiatry 47:228–236, 1990

Freedman R, Adler LE, Myles-Worsley M, et al: Inhibitory gating of an evoked response to repeated auditory stimuli in schizophrenic and normal subjects: human recordings, computer simulation, and an animal model. Arch Gen Psychiatry 53:1114–1121, 1996

Frese FJ: Recovery: Myths, mountains, and miracles. Presentation to Menninger Clinic staff, May 30, 1997

Freud S: Psycho-analytic notes on an autobiographical account of a case of paranoia (dementia paranoides) (1911), in The Standard Edition of the Complete Psychological Works of Sigmund Freud, Vol 12. Translated and edited by Strachey J. London, Hogarth Press, 1958, pp 1–82

Freud S: On narcissism: an introduction (1914), in The Standard Edition of the Complete Psychological Works of Sigmund Freud, Vol 14. Translated and edited by Strachey J. London, Hogarth Press, 1963, pp 67–102

Freud S: The unconscious (1915), in The Standard Edition of the Complete Psychological Works of Sigmund Freud, Vol 14. Translated and edited by Strachey J. London, Hogarth Press, 1963, pp 159–215

Freud S: Neurosis and psychosis (1924a), in The Standard Edition of the Complete Psychological Works of Sigmund Freud, Vol 19. Translated and edited by Strachey J. London, Hogarth Press, 1961, pp 147–153

Freud S: The loss of reality in neurosis and psychosis (1924b), in The Standard Edition of the Complete Psychological Works of Sigmund Freud, Vol 19. Translated and edited by Strachey J. London, Hogarth Press, 1961, pp 181–187

Fromm-Reichmann F: Principles of Intensive Psychotherapy. Chicago, IL, University of Chicago Press, 1950

Garfield D: Self-criticism in psychosis: enabling statements in psychotherapy. Dynamic Psychotherapy 3:129–137, 1985

Garfield D, Rogoff M, Steinberg S: Affect-recognition and self-esteem in schizophrenia. Psychopathology 20:225–233, 1987

Glass LL, Katz HM, Schnitzer RD, et al: Psychotherapy of schizophrenia: an empirical investigation of the relationship of process to outcome. Am J Psychiatry 146:603–608, 1989

Goldstein MJ, Rodnick EH, Evans JR, et al: Drug and family in the aftercare of acute schizophrenics. Arch Gen Psychiatry 35:1169–1177, 1978

Gomez-Schwartz B: Individual psychotherapy of schizophrenia, in Schizophrenia: Treatment, Management, and Rehabilitation. Edited by Bellack AS. Orlando, FL, Grune & Stratton, 1984, pp 307–335

Grand S: The body and its boundaries: a psychoanalytic view of cognitive process disturbances in schizophrenia. International Review of Psychoanalysis 9:327–342, 1982

Green MF, Marshall BD Jr, Wirshing WC, et al: Does risperidone improve verbal working memory in treatment-resistant schizophrenia? Am J Psychiatry 154:799–804, 1997

Grinspoon L, Ewalt JR, Shader RI: Schizophrenia: Pharmacotherapy and Psychotherapy. Baltimore, MD, Williams & Wilkins, 1972

Grotstein JS: The psychoanalytic concept of schizophrenia, I: the dilemma. Int J Psychoanal 58:403–425, 1977a

Grotstein JS: The psychoanalytic concept of schizophrenia, II: reconciliation. Int J Psychoanal 58:427–452, 1977b

Gunderson JG: Engagement of schizophrenic patients in psychotherapy, in Attachment and the Therapeutic Process: Essays in Honor of Otto Allen Will, Jr. Edited by Sacksteder JL, Schwartz DP, Akabane Y. Madison, CT, International Universities Press, 1987, pp 139–153

Gunderson JG, Frank AF, Katz HM, et al: Effects of psychotherapy in schizophrenia, II: comparative outcome of two forms of treatment. Schizophr Bull 10:564–598, 1984

Harding CM, Zubin J, Strauss JS: Chronicity in schizophrenia: fact, partial fact, or artifact? Hospital and Community Psychiatry 38:477–486, 1987

Hatfield AB: Family Education in Mental Illness. New York, Guilford, 1990

Hogarty GE: Depot neuroleptics: the relevance of psychosocial factors—a United States perspective. J Clin Psychiatry 45(5 pt 2):36–42, 1984

Hogarty GE, Anderson CM, Reiss DJ, et al: Family psychoeducation, social skills training, and maintenance chemotherapy in the aftercare treatment of schizophrenia, I: one-year effects of a controlled study on relapse and expressed emotion. Arch Gen Psychiatry 43:633–642, 1986

Hogarty GE, Anderson CM, Reiss DJ, et al: Family psychoeducation, social skills training, and maintenance chemotherapy in the aftercare treatment of schizophrenia, II: two-year effects of a controlled study on relapse and adjustment. Arch Gen Psychiatry 48:340–347, 1991

Hogarty GE, Kornblith SF, Greenwald D, et al: Personal therapy: a disorder-relevant psychotherapy for schizophrenia. Schizophr Bull 21:379–393, 1995

Hogarty GE, Greenwald D, Ulrich RF, et al: Three-year trials of personal therapy among schizophrenic patients living with or independent of family, II: effects on adjustment of patients. Am J Psychiatry 154:1514–1524, 1997a

Hogarty GE, Kornblith SJ, Greenwald D, et al: Three-year trials of personal therapy among schizophrenic patients living with or independent of family, I: description of study and effects on relapse rates. Am J Psychiatry 154:1504–1513, 1997b

Jenkins JH, Karno M: The meaning of expressed emotion: theoretical issues raised by cross-cultural research. Am J Psychiatry 149:9–21, 1992

Judd LL, McAdams LA, Budnick B, et al: Sensory gating deficits in schizophrenia: new results. Am J Psychiatry 149:488–493, 1992

Kanas N: Group therapy with schizophrenics: a review of controlled studies. Int J Group Psychother 36:339–351, 1986

Kanas N, Rogers M, Kreth E, et al: The effectiveness of group psychotherapy during the first three weeks of hospitalization: a controlled study. J Nerv Ment Dis 168:487–492, 1980

Kanter J: Clinical case management: definition, principles, components. Hospital and Community Psychiatry 40:361–368, 1989

Kanter J, Lamb HR, Loeper C: Expressed emotion in families: a critical review. Hospital and Community Psychiatry 38:374–380, 1987

Karon BP: The fear of understanding schizophrenia. Psychoanalytic Psychology 9:191–211, 1992

Karon BP, VandenBos G: Psychotherapy of Schizophrenia. New York, Jason Aronson, 1981

Kay SR: Significance of the positive-negative distinction in schizophrenia. Schizophr Bull 16:635–652, 1990

Keith SJ, Matthews SM: Schizophrenia: a review of psychosocial treatment strategies, in Psychotherapy Research: Where Are We and Where Should We Go? Edited by Williams JBW, Spitzer RL. New York, Guilford, 1984, pp 70–88

Kendler KS, Eaves LJ: Models for the joint effect of genotype and environment on liability to psychiatric illness. Am J Psychiatry 143:279–289, 1986

Kety SS: Genetic and environmental factors in the etiology of schizophrenia, in Psychopathology: The Evolving Science of Mental Disorder. Edited by Matthysse H, Levy DL, Kagan J, et al. New York, Cambridge University Press, 1996, pp 477–487

King S, Dixon MJ: The influence of expressed emotion, family dynamics, and symptom type on the social adjustment of schizophrenic young adults. Arch Gen Psychiatry 53:1098–1104, 1996

Kingdon DG, Turkington D: Cognitive-Behavioral Therapy of Schizophrenia. New York, Guilford, 1994

Klein DF: Psychosocial treatment of schizophrenia, or psychosocial help for people with schizophrenia? Schizophr Bull 6:122–130, 1980

Kuipers E, Fowler D, Garety P, et al: London–East Anglia randomised controlled trial of cognitive-behavioural therapy for psychosis, III: follow-up and economic evaluation at 18 months. Br J Psychiatry 173:61–68, 1998

Leff J, Kuipers L, Berkowitz R, et al: A controlled trial of social intervention in the families of schizophrenic patients. Br J Psychiatry 141:121–134, 1982

Lefley HP: Expressed emotion: conceptual, clinical, and social policy issues. Hospital and Community Psychiatry 43:591–598, 1992

London NJ: An essay on psychoanalytic theory: two theories of schizophrenia, part I: review and critical assessment of the development of the two theories. Int J Psychoanal 54:169–178, 1973a

London NJ: An essay on psychoanalytic theory: two theories of schizophrenia, part II: discussion and restatement of the specific theory of schizophrenia. Int J Psychoanal 54:179–193, 1973b

MacMillan JF, Gold A, Crow TJ, et al: Expressed emotion and relapse. Br J Psychiatry 148:133–143, 1986

Mahler M: On child psychosis and schizophrenia: autistic and symbiotic infantile psychoses. Psychoanal Study Child 7:286–305, 1952

May PRA: Treatment of Schizophrenia: A Comparative Study of Five Treatment Methods. New York, Science House, 1968

McGlashan TH: The Chestnut Lodge follow-up study, II: long-term outcome of schizophrenia and the affective disorders. Arch Gen Psychiatry 41:586–601, 1984

McGlashan TH: Recovery style from mental illness and long-term outcome. J Nerv Ment Dis 175:681–685, 1987

McGlashan TH, Fenton WS: The positive-negative distinction in schizophrenia: review of natural history validators. Arch Gen Psychiatry 49:63–72, 1992

McGlashan TH, Keats CJ: Schizophrenia: Treatment Process and Outcome. Washington, DC, American Psychiatric Press, 1989

Mosher LR, Keith SJ: Research on the psychosocial treatment of schizophrenia: a summary report. Am J Psychiatry 136:623–631, 1979

Müller C: Psychotherapy and schizophrenia: the end of the pioneers' period. Schizophr Bull 10:618–620, 1984

Munich RL, Carsky M, Appelbaum A: The role and structure of long-term hospitalization: chronic schizophrenia. Psychiatric Hospital 16:161–169, 1985

O'Brien C: Group psychotherapy with schizophrenia and affective disorders, in Comprehensive Group Psychotherapy, 2nd Edition. Edited by Kaplan HI, Sadock BJ. Baltimore, MD, Williams & Wilkins, 1983, pp 242–249

Ogden TH: On the nature of schizophrenic conflict. Int J Psychoanal 61:513–533, 1980

Ogden TH: The schizophrenic state of nonexperience, in Technical Factors in the Treatment of the Severely Disturbed Patient. Edited by Giovacchini PL, Boyer LB. New York, Jason Aronson, 1982, pp 217–260

Olin SS, Mednick SA: Risk factors of psychosis: identifying vulnerable populations premorbidly. Schizophr Bull 22:223–240, 1996

Pao P-N: Notes on Freud's theory of schizophrenia. Int J Psychoanal 54:469–476, 1973

Parker G, Johnston P, Hayward L: Parental "expressed emotion" as a predictor of schizophrenic relapse. Arch Gen Psychiatry 45:806–813, 1988

Penn DL, Mueser KT: Research update on the psychosocial treatment of schizophrenia. Am J Psychiatry 153:607–617, 1996

Plomin R, Defries JC, McClearn GE: Behavioral Genetics: A Primer, 2nd Edition. New York, WH Freeman, 1990

Robbins M: Psychoanalytic and biological approaches to mental illness: schizophrenia. J Am Psychoanal Assoc 40:425–454, 1992

Rogers CR, Gendlin ET, Kiesler DJ, et al (eds): The Therapeutic Relationship and Its Impact: A Study of Psychotherapy With Schizophrenics. Madison, WI, University of Wisconsin Press, 1967

Rosenheck R, Tekell J, Peters J, et al: Does participation in psychosocial treatment augment the benefit of clozapine? Arch Gen Psychiatry 55:618–625, 1998

Rund BR: Fully recovered schizophrenics: a retrospective study of some premorbid and treatment factors. Psychiatry 53:127–139, 1990

Ruocchio PJ: How psychotherapy can help the schizophrenic patient. Hospital and Community Psychiatry 40:188–190, 1989

Sacks O: Awakenings. New York, Harperperennial, 1990

Scott JE, Dixon LB: Psychological interventions for schizophrenia. Schizophr Bull 21:621–630, 1995

Searles HF: The "dedicated physician" in the field of psychotherapy and psychoanalysis (1967), in Countertransference and Related Subjects: Selected Papers. New York, International Universities Press, 1979, pp 71–88

Searles HF: Psychoanalytic therapy with schizophrenic patients in a private-practice context (1976), in Countertransference and Related Subjects: Selected Papers. New York, International Universities Press, 1979, pp 582–602

Selzer MA: Preparing the chronic schizophrenic for exploratory psychotherapy: the role of hospitalization. Psychiatry 46:303–311, 1983

Selzer MA, Carsky M: Treatment alliance and the chronic schizophrenic. Am J Psychother 44:506–515, 1990

Selzer MA, Sullivan TB, Carsky M, et al: Working With the Person With Schizophrenia: The Treatment Alliance. New York, New York University Press, 1989

Spohn HE, Lacoursiere RB, Thompson K, et al: Phenothiazine effects on psychological and psychophysiological dysfunction in chronic schizophrenics. Arch Gen Psychiatry 34: 633–644, 1977

Stanton AH, Gunderson JG, Knapp PH, et al: Effects of psychotherapy on schizophrenic patients, I: design and implementation of a controlled study. Schizophr Bull 10: 520–563, 1984

Strauss JS, Carpenter WT, Bartko JJ: The diagnosis and understanding of schizophrenia, part III: speculations on the process that underlie schizophrenic symptoms and signs. Schizophr Bull 11:61–69, 1974

Sullivan HS: Schizophrenia as a Human Process. New York, WW Norton, 1962

Tarrier N, Yusupoff L, Kinney C, et al: Randomised controlled trial of intensive cognitive-behaviour therapy for patients with chronic schizophrenia. BMJ 317:303–307, 1998

Tienari P, Wynne LC, Moring J, et al: The Finnish Adoptive Family Study of Schizophrenia: implications for family research. Br J Psychiatry 164 (suppl 23):20–26, 1994

Wahlberg K-E, Lyman CW, Oja H, et al: Gene-environment interaction in vulnerability to schizophrenia: findings from the Finnish Adoptive Family Study of Schizophrenia. Am J Psychiatry 154:355–362, 1997

Walker E, Lewine RJ: Prediction of adult-onset schizophrenia from childhood home movies of the patients. Am J Psychiatry 147:1052–1056, 1990

Wexler M: Schizophrenia: conflict and deficiency. Psychoanal Q 40:83–99, 1971

C H A P T E R
8

Affective Disorders

Affective disorders, like schizophrenia, are illnesses that are strongly influenced by genetic and biological factors. Because stressors and the meaning of those stressors appear to be involved etiologically in affective disorders, these illnesses are also ideal models to study the interaction of genes and environment in a clinically relevant way.

A large Australian twin study (Bierut et al. 1999) found that there was a moderate familial aggregation of depression in women, primarily related to genetic factors. These factors seemed to play a smaller role in men with depression. Moreover, for *both* men and women, individual environmental experiences played a major role in the development of depression.

Kendler and his colleagues (1993) followed 680 female-female twin pairs of known zygosity to determine whether an etiological model could be developed to predict major depressive episodes. They found that the role of genetic factors was substantial but not overwhelming. The most influential predictor was the presence of recent stressful events. Two other factors, interpersonal relations and a temperament characterized by neuroticism, also played a significant etiological role. Neuroticism appeared to alienate social support in many cases.

In a subsequent report from an expanded sample of the twin study, Kendler and his colleagues (1995) gained further insight into the etiology of depression. The most compelling model to emerge from their findings was the following: Sensitivity to the depression-inducing effects of stressful life events appears to be under genetic control. For example, when the individuals at lowest genetic risk for major depression were examined, they had a probability of onset of major depression per month of only about 0.5% in the absence of a stressful life event. When these individuals were exposed to a stressor, however, the probability went up to 6.2%. In those individuals who were at the highest genetic risk, the probability of onset of depression per month was only 1.1% without exposure to a life stressor, but the risk rose dramatically, to 14.6%, when a stressful life event was present. In a subsequent analysis (Kendler et al. 1999), the investigators found that about one-third of the association between stressful life events and onsets of depression was *noncausal,* because those individuals predisposed to major depression select themselves into high-risk environments. For example, persons with a neuroticism temperament may alienate others and thus cause a breakup of a significant relationship.

The most powerful stressors appeared to be death of a close relative, assault, serious marital problems, and divorce/breakup. However, there is also considerable evidence that early experiences of abuse, neglect, or separation may create a neurobiological sensitivity that predisposes individuals to respond to stressors in adulthood by developing a major depressive episode. For example, Kendler et al. (1992) documented an increased risk for major depression in those women who had experienced maternal or paternal separation in childhood or adolescence. The kindling response model derived from studies of seizure thresholds has been suggested as a useful paradigm for understanding the mechanisms involved in this increased vulnerability (Gold et al. 1988a, 1988b; Post et al. 1982).

Corticotropin-releasing factor (CRF), which induces the pituitary to secrete adrenocorticotropic hormone (ACTH), is consistently elevated in the cerebrospinal fluid of depressed patients compared with nondepressed control subjects (Nemeroff 1998a). When CRF is injected directly into the brains of laboratory animals, these animals have exhibited behaviors similar to depression in humans. These observations suggest a stress-diathesis model for mood disorders. In other words, a genetic substrate might serve to diminish monoamine levels in synapses or to increase reactivity of the hypothalamic-pituitary-adrenal (HPA) axis to stress. If there is no serious stress on the individual, the genetically determined threshold is not necessarily sufficient to induce depression. However, experiences of neglect or abuse in childhood may activate the stress response and induce elevated activity in CRF-containing neurons, which are known to be stress responsive and to be excessively active in depressed persons (Nemeroff 1998a). These cells can become supersensitive in certain individuals, reacting dramatically to even mild stressors.

In a pilot study designed to explore this model, women who had a history of childhood abuse, with and without current major depression, were compared with healthy control subjects who lacked a history of early neglect or trauma (Heim et al. 1998). Women with a history of childhood abuse had markedly increased ACTH responses to standardized psychosocial laboratory stress compared with healthy control women. On average, the ACTH response was highest in women who had both current major depression and a history of childhood abuse. Cortisol responses and net ACTH were positively correlated with the degree of childhood abuse and with the severity of depression and of PTSD. When CRF stimulation tests were performed, the women who had a history of childhood abuse and current major depression showed blunted ACTH responses, a finding that was most likely related to chronic overexposure of the pituitary to CRF. The investigators concluded that both the HPA axis and extrahypothalamic CRF systems are sensitized in response to early childhood abuse, resulting in an increased vulnerability to the development of depression.

Research from the United Kingdom on the relationship between childhood abuse or neglect and depression in adult women provides some evidence to support such a hypothesis. A prospective study (Bifulco et al. 1998) found that women with a history of childhood abuse or neglect are twice as likely as those without such a history to have negative relationships and low self-esteem in adulthood. Those abused or neglected women who have these negative relationships and low self-esteem in adulthood are then 10 times more likely to experience depression. In a recent review of studies of childhood sexual abuse, Weiss et al. (1999) found a clear relationship between such abuse and adult-onset depression. These authors suggested that gonadal steroids may play a key role in the modulation of the HPA axis and may therefore contribute to the higher sensitivity of that axis to stress in females. This sexual dimorphism may help explain the higher prevalence of depression in women. One of the clinical implications of those findings is that exploration of the impact of childhood trauma or neglect may be crucial in the psychodynamic therapy of depressed patients.

These early stressors of childhood separation, neglect, or abuse appear to make individuals more vulnerable to adult stressors that may lead to depression. However, from a psychodynamic perspective, the clinician must always consider the meaning of a particular stressor: What may seem like a relatively mild stressor to an outside observer may have powerful conscious or unconscious meanings to the patient that greatly amplify its impact. Hammen (1995) noted that "the field has reached considerable consensus that it is not the mere occurrence of a negative life event but rather the person's interpretation of the meaning of the event and its significance in the context of its occurrence" (p. 98). In a longitudinal study of the link between depressive reactions and stressors, Hammen and her colleagues found that those stressors whose content matched the patient's area of self-definition were particularly likely to precipitate depressive episodes (Hammen et al. 1985). In other words, in someone whose sense of self is partly defined by social connectedness, loss of a significant interpersonal relationship may precipitate a major depression. On the other hand, if someone's self-worth is especially linked to mastery and achievement, such a person might be more likely to have a depressive episode in response to a perceived failure in school or at work.

These advances in research on mood disorder suggest that both medication and psychotherapy may be necessary in the treatment of major affective disorders. Psychodynamic exploration of the meaning of stressors may be of particular importance.

Depressed patients may also benefit from dynamic pharmacotherapy. Some depressed patients will not comply with their prescribed medication for a variety of reasons, including that they feel they do not deserve to get better or they feel that taking medication stigmatizes them as mentally ill. In addition to being indicated for patients with noncompliance problems, psychotherapy must be used for those who cannot take antidepressants because of preexisting medical conditions, those who cannot tolerate side effects, and those who are partially or completely refractory to any somatic treatment.

One must also keep in mind that depression spans the entire spectrum of pathology and health and can be present in milder forms at certain times of stress even in basically healthy people. Individuals with minor depression that does not meet the DSM-IV (American Psychiatric Association 1994) criteria for a major depressive episode or dysthymia account for more disability days in the community than do persons with major depression (Broadhead et al. 1990). Physicians provide more services to persons with depressive *symptoms* than to those with formally defined depressive disorders (Johnson et al. 1992). Hence, even when these milder forms of depression lack DSM-IV criteria to be classified as major disorders, they are not necessarily benign. Medication is often ineffective in minor depression, and these patients may need psychotherapy to be restored to normal functioning.

For many patients, the combination of psychotherapy and medication appears to be especially useful. In a mega-analysis of 595 patients with major depressive disorder enrolled in six standardized treatment protocols, Thase et al. (1997) found a highly significant advantage for combined psychotherapy and medication in the more severe recurrent depressions. However, when the milder forms of depression were studied, combined therapy was not more effective than psychotherapy alone. In addition, Nemeroff (1998b) noted that whereas approximately 65% of depressed patients respond to a single antidepressant with a 50% decline on severity rating scales, only 30% return to a fully euthymic state based on their scores on such standard scales.

Psychodynamic understanding in treatment is also extremely useful in dealing with the interface of personality and depression. This interface can be subdivided into three discrete categories: 1) Axis I major depression with Axis II comorbidity, 2) depressive personality, and 3) characterological depression in the context of personality disorders.

A review of the literature provides ample evidence that personality disorders complicate the treatment of Axis I depressive disorders (Reich and Green 1991). In the National Institute of Mental Health (NIMH) collaborative study, patients with personality disorders had significantly worse outcomes in social functioning and were more likely to have residual symptoms of depression than patients without personality disorders (Shea et al. 1990). In a British study involving an 18-year follow-up of 89 depressed patients, an interactive effect of melancholia and the personality measure of neuroticism led to poor outcomes in those with both features (Duggan et al. 1991). These studies suggest that certain personality disorders may contribute to a tendency to maintain depression once it has already occurred, and characterological factors may also be responsible for poor medication compliance. Psychotherapy may be necessary in combination with medication to treat these patients effectively.

The second category, depressive personality, has been controversial despite a long-standing psychoanalytic tradition. In Appendix B of DSM-IV, the criteria for depressive personality disorder emphasize a constellation of personality traits, in contrast to the criteria for dysthymia, which focus on somatic symptoms. These traits include a mood dominated by unhappiness, dejection, and gloominess; a self-concept centered on worthlessness and low self-esteem; a tendency to blame and criticize oneself; a proneness to feel guilt or remorse; a pessimistic attitude; a negativistic and judgmental stance toward others; and a tendency to brood and worry.

Much of the controversy has revolved around whether depressive personality disorder is truly distinct from dysthymia. However, data are emerging that suggest that the distinction between the two is valid and clinically useful. In a study of 54 patients with early-onset long-standing mild depressive features, Phillips et al. (1998) identified 30 subjects with and 24 without depressive personality disorder. Sixty-three percent of the subjects with depressive personality disorder did not have dysthymia, while 60% did not have current major depression. The depressive personality disorder patients were more likely than those in the comparison group to have another personality disorder, but 40% of them had no such disorder. Those who *were* comorbid for a personality disorder tended to have Cluster C or anxious personality disorders, suggesting that defenses and conflicts at a neurotic level were most prominent, which is in keeping with the traditional psychoanalytic understanding of depressive personality disorder (Kernberg 1984). Finally, the duration of psychotherapy was significantly longer for subjects who had depressive personality disorder than for those who did not.

The third category subsumes those patients with severe personality disorders, especially borderline, who present with complaints of "depression" yet fail to meet DSM-IV criteria for an Axis I disorder. Many of these patients describe a feeling of pervasive loneliness or emptiness associated with the perception that their emotional needs are not being met by others. They may also have a conscious sense of rage and frustration that separates them from the typical Axis I patient. Because this form of characterological depression is primarily associated with borderline personality disorder, it will be discussed at greater length in Chapter 15.

For all the foregoing reasons, psychodynamic understanding and treatment still play a major role in the treatment of mood disorders, despite impressive advances in the biological understanding of mania and depression. The psychiatrist who combines psychodynamic approaches with psychopharmacological measures will be better equipped to treat the broad range of affectively disturbed patients seen in clinical practice.

Psychodynamic Understanding of Depression and Mania

In Freud's classic 1917 paper, "Mourning and Melancholia," he differentiated between grief and melancholic depression. In the former, the precipitating event is the real loss of a significant figure. In melancholia, by contrast, the lost object is *emotional* rather than real. Moreover, the melancholic patient feels a profound loss of self-esteem, accompanied by self-reproach and guilt, while the mourner maintains a reasonably stable sense of self-esteem. Freud explained the marked self-depreciation common in depressed patients as the result of anger turned inward. More specifically, the rage is directed internally because the self of the patient has identified with the lost object. In 1923, Freud noted that such introjection may be the only way for the ego to give up an object. That same year, in "The Ego and the Id," he postulated that melancholic patients have a severe superego, which he related to their guilt over having shown aggression toward loved ones.

Klein (1940/1975) linked depression to the depressive position (see Chapter 2). She understood manic-depressive states as a reflection of childhood failure to establish good internal objects. Depressed people, in other words, have never overcome the depressive position common to childhood. She contrasted this state with normal mourning, in which the depressive position is reactivated as a result of losing a loved one, but is then overcome and worked through by reestablishing the lost figure as an internal object, as well as by reinstating the good parents in the process. In Klein's view, then, depressed patients are desperately concerned that they have destroyed the loved good objects within themselves as a result of their own greed and destructiveness. As a consequence of that destruction, they feel persecuted by the hated bad objects that remain. This feeling of being persecuted by bad objects while "pining" for the lost good objects is what constitutes the essence of the depressive position, which is reactivated in melancholic states. In other words, patients may feel worthless because they sense that they have changed their good internal parents into persecutors as a result of their own destructive impulses and fantasies.

Klein noted that manic defenses, such as omnipotence, denial, contempt, and idealization, develop in response to the painful affects produced by "pining" for the lost love objects. These defenses are used in the service of 1) rescuing and restoring the lost love objects, 2) disavowing the bad internal objects, and 3) denying slavish dependency on love objects. Clinically, patients may express these manic operations through a denial of any aggression or destructiveness toward others, a euphoric disposition that is contrary to their actual life situation, an idealization of others, or a scornful, contemptuous attitude toward other people that serves to disavow the need for relationships. An integral aspect of the manic defensive posture is often a wish to triumph over parents and thus reverse the child-parent relationship. This desire for triumph may in turn give rise to guilt and depression. In Klein's view, this mechanism is partly responsible for the depression that frequently develops after success or promotion.

Klein's formulation is useful because it helps clinicians to understand how the psychological function of a manic episode can coexist with biological determinants. The defensive function of mania is most clearly evident in dysphoric manic patients (Post et al. 1989), whose anxiety and depression "break through" a manic episode, necessitating a resurgence of manic denial. Moreover, in a much more attenuated form, hypomanic defenses are typically enlisted to defend against the threat of depressive affects or grief. One patient, for example, described feeling "high" after learning of his mother's death. He felt powerful, expansive, and liberated from dependency. Despite these feelings, he was able to note how odd it was that he was not grief stricken.

Although both Freud and Klein saw aggression as pivotal to the understanding of depression, Bibring (1953) believed that depression was a primary affective state unrelated to aggression turned inward. He viewed depression as arising from the tension between ideals and reality. Three highly invested narcissistic aspirations—to be worthy and loved, to be strong or superior, and to be good and loving—are held up as standards of conduct. However, the ego's awareness of its actual or imagined inability to measure up to these standards produces depression. As a result, the depressed person feels helpless and powerless. Bibring thought that, in certain cases, the ego's awareness of its helplessness may lead to aggression turned inward, but only as a secondary phenomenon. He believed that any narcissistic frustration or injury that lowers self-esteem might precipitate a clinical depression. Alone among all authors writing on the psychodynamics of depression, Bibring (1953) did not postulate that the superego played a key role. Rather, he postulated that tension arises within the ego itself, not between the ego and another intrapsychic agency. He succinctly described this depression as "a partial or complete collapse of the self-esteem of the ego, since it feels unable to live up to its aspirations (ego ideal, superego) while they are strongly maintained" (p. 26). He understood manic elation either as a compensating secondary reaction to depression or as an expression of the fantasy fulfillment of the individual's narcissistic aspirations.

Revising Freud's formulation, Jacobson (1971a) suggested that melancholic patients actually act as if they were the worthless, lost love object, even though they do not assume all the characteristics of that object. The self, then, is experienced as the bad object, and eventually this bad internal object or the lost external love object is transformed into the sadistic superego. The ego then becomes "a victim of the superego, as helpless and powerless as a small child who is tortured by his cruel, powerful mother" (p. 252).

> Ms. I was a 49-year-old homemaker who became psychotically depressed. She became convinced that she was thoroughly worthless, and she was preoccupied with how her father had beaten her as a child because she was such a "bad little girl." At times the bad introject of the abusive, hated father was absorbed into the patient's self-view, and she would cut herself both as self-punishment and as a way of attacking the internal object. At other times, the father would be experienced as a separate internal object, or a harsh superego, who would rebuke her for being bad. In these instances, Ms. I would hear a hallucinated voice, saying, "You are bad" and "You deserve to die."

The internal object world of Ms. I indicates how, in psychotic depression, there may be a fusion of the self with the object, on the one hand, or a reactivation of an internal object relationship in which a tormenting bad object, or primitive superego, persecutes a bad self, on the other. Jacobson believed that mania could be understood as a magical reunion of the self with the harsh superego figure, thus changing that figure from a punitive tormenter into a loving, all-good, forgiving figure. This idealized object may then be projected onto the external world to establish highly idealized relationships with others whereby all aggression and destructiveness are denied.

Based on extensive experience in the psychotherapy of severely depressed patients, Arieti (1977) postulated a preexisting ideology in persons who become severely depressed—namely, living not for oneself, but for another person—what Arieti termed the *dominant other*. Most commonly, the spouse is the dominant other, but an organization or an ideal may also serve that function. When a transcendent purpose or aim occupies this place in the individual's psychological world, it is referred to as the dominant goal or dominant ideology. Arieti's concept is somewhat reminiscent of Bibring's, because of its emphasis on the patient's helplessness upon realizing that the goal is unattainable. These patients generally cannot imagine or accept any alternate frameworks that might allow them to give up the dominant goal. They realize that living for someone or something else is not working out for them, but they feel unable to change. They believe that life is worthless if they cannot elicit the response they wish from the dominant other or if they cannot achieve their impossible goal. They adhere rigidly to an unrealistic life plan that they cannot give up.

We can summarize the various theoretical formulations of depression by concluding that whatever biochemical contributions there may be, patients experience depression psychologically as a disturbance of self-esteem in the context of failed interpersonal relationships. These childhood relationships are internalized and reactivated in adulthood with the onset of major affective disorders. The tormenting internal world of object relationships is then also externalized into current relationships in the patient's world. Depression illustrates the close relationship between an individual's intimate interpersonal interactions and the maintenance of self-esteem (Strupp et al. 1982). In self psychological terms, depression may be viewed as the despair resulting from the failure of selfobjects to gratify the self's needs for mirroring, twinship, or idealization.

Blatt (1998) has suggested that from a psychoanalytic perspective, these various theoretical views represent two underlying types of depression. *Anaclitic* depression is characterized by feelings of helplessness, loneliness, and weakness related to chronic fears of being abandoned and unprotected. Individuals with this type of depression have longings to be nurtured, protected, and loved. *Introjective* depression, on the other hand, is characterized by feelings of unworthiness, failure, inferiority, and guilt. Individuals with this variant are also highly self-critical and suffer from a chronic fear of criticism and disapproval from others. They are exceedingly perfectionistic and competitive and are excessively driven to achieve in work and school. Anaclitic depression is characterized by vulnerability to disruptions of interpersonal relationships, and the depression is primarily manifested as dysphoric feelings of abandonment, loss, and loneliness. Introjective depression involves vulnerability to disruptions of a positive and effective sense of self and is manifested primarily by dysphoric feelings of guilt, failure, and worthlessness and by a sense that one's autonomy and control have been lost.

Psychodynamics of Suicide

Many different psychiatric disorders can culminate in the tragic outcome of suicide. Suicide is most prominently associated with major affective disorders, however, so it is therefore considered in detail in the context of this chapter. Before examining the psychodynamic perspective on suicide, a caveat is in order. Determinants of suicidal behavior may be biological as well as psychological. The psychodynamics revealed by psychotherapeutic work with suicidal patients may in some respects be *secondary* to neurochemical changes, so all available somatic treatment modalities must be used aggressively along with the psychotherapeutic approach. In many cases, psychotherapy alone is insufficient with seriously suicidal patients. In one comparison study (Lesse 1978), only 16% of the severely depressed psychotherapy patients had a positive outcome, while 83% of the patients who received both psychotherapy and pharmacotherapy and 86% of those who received electroconvulsive therapy (ECT) had good results. Saving the patient's life is far more important than theoretical purity.

Suicidal behavior and ideation, like all other acts and thoughts, are the end products of the principles of overdetermination and multiple function (see Chapter 1). Motivations for suicide are highly varied and often obscure (Meissner 1986). The clinician must therefore listen carefully to each patient, noting the particular transference-countertransference developments before reaching any closure on the dynamic underpinnings of suicide.

In keeping with his understanding of the dynamics of depression, Freud (1917/1963) assumed that the ego could kill itself only by treating itself as an object, so he postulated that suicide results from displaced murderous impulses—that is, destructive wishes toward an internalized object are directed instead against the self. After the development of the structural model (1923/1961), Freud redefined suicide as the victimization of the ego by a sadistic superego. Karl Menninger's (1933) view of suicide was a bit more complex. He believed that at least three wishes might contribute to a suicidal act—the wish to kill, the wish to be killed, and the wish to die. The wish to kill may be directed not only toward an *internal* object. Clinical experience confirms again and again that suicide is often designed to destroy the lives of the survivors. Depressed patients often feel, for example, that suicide is the only satisfactory revenge against their parents. The patient's spouse may similarly be the "target" of a suicide.

A recurring theme in the object relations of suicidal patients is the drama between a sadistic tormentor and a tormented victim. As in the case of Ms. I, there is often a persecuting internal object that makes the patient miserable. Alternatively, the patient who identifies with the persecutor may torment everyone in his or her environment. In some cases, the patient may believe that the only possible outcome of the drama is to submit to the tormentor through suicide (Meissner 1986). This internal persecuting figure has been referred to as the "hidden executioner" (Asch 1980).

In other cases, aggression plays a far less prominent role in the motivation for suicide. Fenichel (1945) noted that suicide may be the fulfillment of a reunion wish, that is, a joyous and magical rejoining with a lost loved one, or a narcissistic union with a loving superego figure. Object loss frequently lies behind suicidal behavior, and many suicidal patients reveal strong dependency yearnings toward a lost object (Dorpat 1973). In this regard, suicide may be a regressive wish for reunion with a lost maternal figure. The last words of the Reverend Jim Jones in the 1978 mass homicide and suicide in Guyana were "Mother . . . Mother," spoken just before he shot himself in the head. A pathological grief process is often involved in suicides, particularly those that occur on the anniversary of the death of a loved one. Research has demonstrated, for example, that there is a statistically significant correlation between suicide and the anniversary of a parent's death (Bunch and Barraclough 1971). When an individual's self-esteem and self-integrity depend on attachment to a lost object, suicide may seem to be the only way to restore self-cohesion.

> Ms. J was a 24-year-old psychotically depressed woman who, 2 years earlier, had lost her twin brother to suicide. Following his death, she had withdrawn from life, intent on killing herself. Moreover, she had become psychotically identified with her brother to the point that she identified herself as male and as having his first name. She had been refractory to antidepressant medication, lithium carbonate, and ECT. She felt that she could not continue living in the absence of her brother. Ms. J ultimately committed suicide on the anniversary of her brother's death.

To assess suicide risk with any given patient, these psychodynamic themes must be put in the context of a set of predictors of suicide risk. A prospective examination of 954 patients (Clark and Fawcett 1992) revealed that it was useful to differentiate short-term from long-term risk factors in attempting to predict suicide. Seven factors predicted suicide within 1 year of entry into the study: panic attacks, psychic anxiety, severe loss of pleasure and interests, depressive turmoil involving a rapid switching of mood from anxiety to depression to anger or vice versa, alcohol abuse, diminished concentration, and global insomnia. Long-term risk factors included hopelessness, suicidal ideation, suicidal intent, and a history of previous suicide attempts. Hopelessness, which has repeatedly been shown to be a better predictor of suicide risk than depression, may be linked to a rigidly held view of the self that cannot be shifted despite repeated disappointments. If one cannot live up to rigidly held expectations of what the self should be, hopelessness may result, and suicide may seem the only way out. In a similar vein, Arieti (1977) noted that certain patients who cannot shift their dominant ideology or their expectation of the dominant other may also be at high risk for suicide. In assessing suicidal ideation, a higher risk exists when the ideation is *ego-syntonic*—these patients find suicidal ideation acceptable and appear to have given up the fight against the urge to kill themselves.

To put suicide in a psychodynamic context, clinicians must understand the nature of the precipitating event, the conscious and unconscious motivations, and the preexisting psychological variables that increase the likelihood of acting on suicidal thoughts. Through the use of projective psychological testing, researchers (Smith 1983; Smith and Eyman 1988) have studied and identified four patterns of ego functioning and internal object relations paradigms that differentiate individuals who made serious attempts from those who merely made gestures to control significant others. The serious attempters exhibited 1) an inability to give up infantile wishes for nurturance, associated with conflict about being openly dependent; 2) a sober but ambivalent view toward death; 3) excessively high self-expectations; and 4) overcontrol of affect, particularly aggression. Although this pattern applies more to men than to women (Smith and Eyman 1988), an inhibitory attitude toward aggression distinguishes serious female attempters from those who make mild gestures. These test findings imply that the preexisting psychological structures that favor suicide are more consistent across individual patients than are the various motivations behind a particular suicidal act.

Treatment Considerations

Research Findings

While interpersonal therapy and cognitive-behavioral therapy have been studied rather extensively with depressed patients, brief psychodynamic therapy of depression has less of a research base. In early studies of brief dynamic therapy, it was generally used as a comparison modality for a control group by investigators committed to other approaches. The majority of these studies also looked at brief dynamic therapy in a *group* format rather than in a one-to-one situation.

More recently, however, rigorous controlled studies have shown promising results for brief dynamic therapy of depressed patients. In one investigation of depressed caregivers of elderly family members (Gallagher-Thompson and Steffen 1994), random assignment was made to one of two treatment cells: brief psychodynamic therapy or cognitive-behavioral therapy. After 20 sessions, 71% of the caregivers were no longer clinically depressed. Overall, no differences were found between the two treatment groups.

In the second Sheffield Psychotherapy Project (Shapiro et al. 1994, 1995) in the United Kingdom, similar findings were reported in a randomized controlled trial. One hundred twenty depressed patients were assigned to either 8 or 16 sessions of psychodynamic-interpersonal therapy or cognitive-behavioral therapy. Both treatments were found to be equally effective and to exert their effects with equal rapidity. Patients who had only mild or moderate depression had the same outcome regardless of whether they were treated with 8 or 16 weeks of therapy. However, in the severely depressed patients, significantly superior outcomes were noted when 16 weeks of therapy were provided, regardless of whether the treatment was psychodynamic-interpersonal or cognitive-behavioral. At 1-year follow-up, no overall differences were found in either outcome or maintenance of gains between the two types of therapy. Longer periods of therapy *did* appear to be associated with better long-term outcomes, particularly in the case of psychodynamic-interpersonal therapy.

Brief psychodynamic-interpersonal therapy may also be cost-effective. In a study of 110 nonpsychotic patients who had been unresponsive to routine treatment with a mental health specialist over a 6-month period (Guthrie et al. 1999), 75.5% were found to have a depressive illness. All patients were randomized to 8 weekly sessions of psychodynamic-interpersonal psychotherapy or a control condition of usual care from their psychiatrist. At 6-month follow-up, those receiving therapy had significantly greater improvement than control subjects in social functioning and psychological distress. They also showed significant reductions in health care utilization in the 6 months after treatment compared with control subjects. The additional cost of the therapy was made up by the reductions in health care expenditures in 6 months.

Randomized controlled studies of long-term psychodynamic therapy and psychoanalysis with depressed patients are not available. However, many clinicians recognize that there is a subgroup of depressed patients who will require such treatment. Blatt et al. (1995) reanalyzed the data from the NIMH Treatment of Depression Collaborative Research Program and found that highly perfectionistic and self-critical patients (i.e., the *introjective* subtype of depressed patients) did not respond well to any of the four treatment cells, which included 16 weeks of cognitive therapy, 16 weeks of interpersonal therapy, 16 weeks of imipramine plus clinical management, and 16 weeks of placebo plus clinical management. Two naturalistic follow-along studies (Blatt 1992; Blatt et al. 1994) suggest that long-term psychodynamic therapy may be effective with the self-critical and perfectionistic patients who do not respond to brief modalities. Many of these patients probably have significant obsessive-compulsive or narcissistic characterological traits. These perfectionistic patients may also be at high risk for suicide (Blatt 1998; Hewitt et al. 1997), so the investment of time, energy, and resources may be well justified.

Treatment Principles

Mania. Most manic patients will not benefit from psychotherapeutic interventions until their mania is first pharmacologically controlled. Much of the subsequent treatment involves preventing relapse by focusing on problems with noncompliance and lack of insight into the illness. Several major psychodynamic themes often present in bipolar patients must be addressed. In keeping with the general denial of their illness, these patients often argue that their manic or hypomanic symptoms are not part of an illness but rather a reflection of who they really are. Patients with bipolar illness are notoriously lacking in insight. In a study of 28 manic patients treated on an inpatient unit (Ghaemi et al. 1995), measures of insight were made at admission and discharge. The investigators found that even when all other symptoms of mania had improved or remitted, insight remained notably absent.

Often related to this denial is another psychodynamic theme involving splitting or psychic discontinuity. Many bipolar patients continue to deny the significance of their prior manic episodes when they are euthymic. They may claim that the behavior was simply the result of not taking good care of themselves, and they often adamantly insist that what happened before will never happen again. In this form of splitting, the self-representation involved in the manic episode is viewed as entirely disconnected with the self in the euthymic phase. This lack of continuity of self does not appear to bother the patient, while family members and clinicians may be quite exasperated with it. The clinician managing the patient needs to work psychotherapeutically to piece together the self-fragments into a continuous narrative in the patient's life so that the need for maintenance pharmacotherapy becomes more compelling to the patient. Sometimes tape-recording manic episodes (with the patient's permission) and playing back the recordings when the patient is euthymic may help convince the patient of the connection between the manic self and the euthymic self.

From a Kleinian perspective, the fundamental psychotherapeutic task with the bipolar patient may be to facilitate the work of mourning. There is a strong linkage between childhood physical trauma and mania in adulthood (Levitan et al. 1998), and it is possible that the need to deny aggression has roots in the earliest years of life. The threat of aggressive, persecutory feelings leads to the need for manic defenses to deny them. Following a manic episode, patients may be acutely aware of their own destructiveness and may feel remorseful about the harm they have caused others during the manic phase. Psychotherapists may then be presented with an optimal moment to help patients integrate the loving and aggressive sides of their internal self- and object representations. Continuing to split off these aspects of themselves offers patients temporary relief from the pain but no chance of ultimately resolving their depressive anxieties. Klein (1940/1975) noted that as feelings of persecution and aggression decrease, manic defenses become less necessary to the patient. Hence, another goal is to help the patient to become more capable of internalizing a relationship in which good predominates over bad and love predominates over hate.

In a 2-year prospective study of relapse in 61 outpatients with bipolar illness (Ellicott et al. 1990), relapse could not be explained by changes in lithium levels or medication compliance. However, there was a significant association between stressful life events and relapse. The investigators concluded that psychological interventions at times of high stress are crucial to preventing recurrences. The dynamic psychiatrist must be tuned in to the significance of specific stressors in the patient's life and monitor them while also managing the mood stabilizer.

Lithium and other mood stabilizers often take on special meanings to bipolar patients. For some patients, the medication represents a method of depriving them from the ego-syntonic euphoria of their manic periods. Medication may also remind patients of family members who have suffered from bipolar illness and had adverse consequences such as suicide. Jamison (1995) described her own battle with bipolar illness and commented on the extraordinary value of psychotherapy in helping her to continue taking lithium and understand her fears of complying with the medication regimen. Through psychotherapy, she discovered her secret fears about medication: "In fact, underneath it all, I was actually secretly terrified that lithium might *not* work: What if I took it, and I still got sick? If, on the other hand, I didn't take it, I wouldn't have to see my worst fears realized" (1995, p. 103).

Although problems with noncompliance must be vigorously addressed, the pharmacotherapy of bipolar disorder has limited effectiveness in preventing recurrences over time. Only about 40% of patients who take lithium are relapse-free at 5-year follow-up (Maj 1999). High rates of employment problems and family difficulties are the rule rather than the exception (Miklowitz and Frank 1999). Hence, there is a consensus that psychotherapy must have broader goals than simply improving compliance; it should include identifying stressors, enhancing family functioning, and processing the impact of the illness on the patient and others.

Salzman (1998) has argued persuasively for the integration of pharmacotherapy and psychotherapy in the treatment of bipolar patients. Building a therapeutic alliance is the first order of business and is accomplished through psychotherapeutic exploration, empathy, and education rather than use of debating tactics. Creation of a mood chart may also be helpful. Transference shifts from idealization to devaluation are common, and countertransference acting-out in response to frustration and anger is an ongoing risk.

Jamison (1995) shares the view that combined treatment is necessary: "Ineffably, psychotherapy heals. It makes some sense of the confusion, reins in the terrifying thoughts and feelings, returns some control and hope and possibility of learning from it all. . . . No pill can help me deal with the problem of not wanting to take pills; likewise, no amount of psychotherapy alone can prevent my mania and depressions. I need both" (p. 89).

Depression. Contrary to conventional wisdom, the usefulness of psychodynamic approaches to depression are not limited to the milder, more neurotic forms of the condition. Psychotherapeutic intervention may, in fact, be essential to the treatment of more severe, psychotic forms of depression, especially in those cases where somatic treatments have been ineffective or refused by the patient. Arieti (1977) reported on the intensive psychotherapy of 12 severely depressed patients for whom he had follow-up data for 3 years or more. Seven had shown full recovery and an additional 4 were markedly improved. Regarding the severity of the depression, however, certain fundamental technical principles should guide the clinician.

The first step in treatment, regardless of whether the patient is in a hospital or is an outpatient, is the establishment of a therapeutic alliance. To build the necessary rapport, the clinician must simply listen and empathize with the patient's point of view. Perhaps the most common error both of family members and of beginning mental health professionals is to try to cheer up the patient by focusing on the positive. Comments, such as "You have no reason to be depressed—you have so many good qualities" or "Why should you be suicidal? There's so much to live for," are likely to backfire. These "cheerleading" comments are experienced by depressed patients as profound failures of empathy, which may lead patients to feel more misunderstood and alone and therefore more suicidal.

On the contrary, clinicians who work with these patients must convey their understanding that there is indeed a reason to be depressed. They can empathize with the painfulness of the depression, while also enlisting the patient's help in a collaborative search for its underlying causes. The initial approach must be supportive but firm (Arieti 1977; Lesse 1978). Premature interpretations, such as "You're not really depressed—you're angry," will also be experienced as unempathic and as off the mark. The clinician will be most helpful simply by listening and attempting to comprehend the patient's understanding of the illness.

During the early phases of information gathering, the clinician develops an explanatory formulation of the patient's depression. What events apparently precipitated the depression? What narcissistically valued aspiration has the patient failed to achieve? What is the patient's dominant ideology? Who is the dominant other for whom the patient is living and from whom the patient is not receiving the desired responses? Is there guilt connected with aggression or anger, and if so, toward whom is the patient angry? Is there frustration of the self's strivings for selfobject responses? Does the patient have primarily an anaclitic type of depression, in which therapeutic change will involve interpersonal relationships? Or does the patient have more of an introjective depression, in which self-definition and self-worth will be more central?

While the clinician listens to the patient's story and develops hypotheses about the psychodynamic basis of the depression, the patient forms a transference attachment to the therapist. In Arieti's (1977) terms, the therapist becomes a "dominant third," in addition to the dominant other in the patient's life. Many of the same concerns that are problematic in the patient's primary relationships will also surface in the transference. Arieti pointed out that building a therapeutic alliance may require therapists to conform to certain of the patient's expectations during the initial stages of psychotherapy, thus facilitating the repetition of the patient's pathology in the therapeutic relationship. When enough information has been gathered, the therapist may have to shift to a more expressive approach and interpret to the patient the "dominant other" pattern that has caused so much difficulty. Arieti observed that "the patient must come to the conscious realization that he did not know how to live for himself. He never listened to himself; in situations of great affective significance he was never able to assert himself. He cared only about obtaining the approval, affection, love, admiration, or care of the dominant other" (p. 866). After this realization, a good deal of anger toward the dominant other may surface.

After the dominant ideology has been laid bare, the therapist's task is then to help the patient conceive of new ways of living. In Bibring's (1953) terms, either the idealized aspirations must be modified sufficiently to be realized, or they must be relinquished and replaced with other goals and objectives. At the prospect of developing new life patterns and purposes, these patients may depend on their therapist for answers. If therapists collude by telling their patients what to do, they will simply reinforce any feelings of low self-esteem and ineffectiveness (Betcher 1983; Maxmen 1978). Pleas from patients to solve their dilemmas can simply be turned back to them with the explanation that they are in the best position to make alternative life plans.

Central to the psychodynamic approach with depressed patients is the establishment of the interpersonal meaning and context of their depression. Unfortunately, patients often tenaciously resist these interpersonal implications (Betcher 1983). They frequently prefer to view their depression and their suicidal wishes as occurring in a vacuum, fervently insisting that no one is to blame but themselves. Careful attention to transference-countertransference developments may lead to breakthroughs with this form of resistance. In both psychotherapy and hospital treatment, patients recapitulate their internal object relationships as well as their patterns of relatedness with external figures. Depressed patients, in particular, engender strong feelings. In the course of such treatment, the therapist may experience despair, anger, wishes to be rid of the patient, powerful rescue fantasies, and a myriad of other feelings. All these emotional responses may reflect how others in the patient's life feel as well. These interpersonal dimensions of the depression may be involved in causing or perpetuating the condition. To examine the impact of the patient's condition on others, the therapist must enlist the patient's collaboration by using these feelings constructively in the therapeutic relationship. Many refractory cases of depression have become deadlocked in the repetition of a characteristic pattern of object relatedness that has strong characterological underpinnings and is therefore difficult to alter.

Mr. K was a respected chemist who required hospitalization when he became suicidally depressed at the age of 41. While Mr. K had been an outpatient, every known antidepressant medication had been tried in therapeutic doses with monitored serum levels, and ECT had been used during the first weeks of his hospital stay. None of these somatic interventions had alleviated his depression in the least. Nevertheless, the patient continued to maintain that he was a victim of a "chemical imbalance" which was the doctor's responsibility to restore. Mr. K complained of self-doubt, feelings of worthlessness, inability to sleep, inability to work or concentrate, and hopelessness about the future. He felt that all his accomplishments were meaningless and that he had driven his wife to distraction by his repeated demands to comfort him. Mrs. K despaired because everything she offered her husband seemed to be of no help whatsoever. Whenever she attempted to point out positive aspects of her husband's life, he would respond with a "yes, but" comeback, dismissing her points as irrelevant.

The resident in charge of Mr. K's treatment and the other unit staff members on the treatment team shared Mrs. K's frustration. Mr. K demanded that they attend to his needs, but then dismissed all their suggestions and insights as useless. The entire treatment staff felt de-skilled, impotent, and exhausted in the face of Mr. K's depression. Whenever the various residents on call during the evening hours made rounds on the hospital unit, Mr. K engaged them in long discussions about his depression. He would list the medications that had been tried and would expound on the role of neurotransmitters in depression. He would then ask for advice on his condition. Inevitably, the resident making rounds would be drawn into this discussion in an attempt to alleviate the suffering of this obviously intelligent and well-informed individual. Every suggestion made by any resident, however, would be discounted by Mr. K as "not helpful." By the end of these discussions, the on-call residents would feel that all the time spent with Mr. K was for naught, and they would leave feeling drained and devalued.

The resident in charge of Mr. K's treatment and the staff of the hospital team presented their dilemma with Mr. K to the resident's supervisor, who pointed out how the patient's internal world was being re-created in the milieu. By assuming the role

of the "help-rejecting complainer," Mr. K was reestablishing an internal object relationship characterized by a long-suffering and victimized self-representation connected to an impotent and useless object representation. Mr. K used the reactivation
of this internal object relationship to torment everyone around him. He was thus
able to discharge an enormous reservoir of rage stemming from his childhood interactions with his mother, who he felt had failed to provide for his needs.

As a result of this consultation, a dramatic shift took place in the treatment approach. The resident and the nursing staff primarily involved with Mr. K were able
to disengage from their heroic therapeutic efforts and began to enlist the patient's
collaboration in figuring out what was happening. No longer a passive recipient of
"medical" treatment, the patient was now involved as an active collaborator in a psychological process of reflection and understanding.

The object relations paradigm that was being acted out in the milieu was clarified
and described for the patient. At the same time, the case social worker explained the
psychoanalytically based understanding to Mrs. K to facilitate alleviation of her extraordinary guilt and to help her understand that the present situation was a recapitulation of an unresolved childhood experience. When the treatment team stopped
responding like Mr. K's internal object representation, Mr. K began presenting himself differently. He was initially enraged at their suggestion that he should accept any
responsibility for his condition. The resident explained to him, however, that everything possible in terms of pharmacological interventions had been tried and that
now Mr. K would have to consider his own contributions to the feeling that he was
"stuck" in the depths of despair. This change in approach presented Mr. K with a
new object relationship to contend with. After his initial stubbornness, he did a good
deal of psychological work. He got in touch with his rage at his mother for not giving
him the validation and love that he felt he required, as well as his delight in tormenting his wife to get back at his mother.

The case of Mr. K illustrates how a severe depression that is refractory to conventional somatic treatments may be related to formidable characterological resistances that cause the patient to become "stuck" in an unresolved self–object
relationship. As described in Chapter 6, a breakthrough in such treatment can occur when the treatment staff begins to disconfirm the patient's expectation that
they will respond like the projected object representation; instead, the staff members provided a new model of understanding as well as a new series of objects and
interactions for internalization by the patient.

Another aspect of the breakthrough with Mr. K was that staff members realized
that he was not only a victim of an illness but also a victimizer of those around him.
In discussing the secondary gain frequently associated with depression, Bibring
(1953) noted that some depressed patients exploit their illnesses to justify their
veiled expressions of destructive and sadistic impulses toward others. Mr. K had
forced his wife into a maternal role with him, only to deem her maternal treatment

of him worthless. In commenting on the hidden sadism frequently found in the depressed patient, Jacobson (1971b) noted: "The depressive never fails to make his partner, often his whole environment, and especially his children feel terribly guilty, pulling them down into a more and more depressed state as well" (p. 295). Indeed, the entire treatment staff had begun to feel like Mrs. K. They felt increasingly guilty because they could not find any way to intervene therapeutically with Mr. K, and they became more depressed and drained as a result of each successive failure. Jacobson also pointed out that some depressed patients (such as Mr. K) may establish a vicious cycle that drives their partners away just when their love is most needed. Spouses of such patients rapidly get fed up and may begin to act cruelly or neglectfully as a result of their feelings of inadequacy, thus hurting these patients when they are most needy and vulnerable. Treaters may fall into a similar pattern by becoming sarcastic or cold because their patients repeatedly reject their help.

The clinical vignette regarding Mr. K also underscores the importance of involving the family when treating a severely depressed patient. The literature on families of depressed patients clearly indicates that relapse rates, the course of depression, and suicidal behavior are all affected by family functioning (Keitner and Miller 1990). In one study (Hooley and Teasdale 1989), the single best predictor of relapse was the depressed patient's perception that his or her spouse was highly critical. Paralleling the research on families of schizophrenic patients, studies have also shown that high expressed emotion in family members of depressed patients may be influential in contributing to relapse (Hooley et al. 1986; Vaughn and Leff 1976). Depressed patients provoke a good deal of hostility and sadism in their family members, and clinicians must help relatives overcome their guilt feelings about such reactions so that they can appreciate them as understandable responses to a depressed family member.

Treatment of the Suicidal Patient

Few events in a psychiatrist's professional life are more disturbing than a patient's suicide. In one study (Chemtob et al. 1988), approximately half of those psychiatrists who had lost a patient to suicide experienced stress levels comparable to persons recovering from a parent's death. A completed suicide is a reminder of the limitations inherent in our craft. The natural tendency, whether in hospital practice or in psychotherapy, is for clinicians to go to great lengths to prevent suicide. To implement reasonable measures to prevent patients from taking their life is certainly good judgment from a clinical standpoint, responsible behavior from an ethical standpoint, and sound defensive medicine from a medicolegal standpoint.

However, when the role of savior becomes all-consuming, the results may be countertherapeutic.

First, clinicians must always keep in mind one unassailable fact—patients who are truly intent on killing themselves will ultimately do so. No amount of physical restraint, careful observation, and clinical skill can stop the truly determined suicidal patient. One such patient was placed in a seclusion room with nothing but a mattress. All his clothing and possessions were taken away, and he was checked at regular 15-minute intervals around the clock. Between the 15-minute rounds, the patient began jumping on the mattress so hard that he was able to repeatedly bang his head against the ceiling until he finally broke his neck. Such incidents illustrate that hospital staff members must acknowledge to themselves that they cannot prevent all suicides from occurring on an inpatient unit. Olin (1976) has even suggested that if suicides never occur in a particular hospital, the staff members in the milieu may be taking too much responsibility for the behavior of the patients. Instead, clinicians should repeatedly stress that it is ultimately each patient's responsibility to learn to verbalize suicidal impulses rather than act on them.

After completed suicides, clinicians often feel guilty for not having detected warning signs that would have allowed them to predict an imminent suicide attempt. Despite an accumulating body of literature on short-term and long-range risk factors for suicide, our ability to predict the suicide of an individual patient is still severely limited. Goldstein et al. (1991) studied a group of 1,906 inpatients with affective disorders. Using data on risk factors, the researchers applied stepwise multiple logistic regression to develop a statistical model that would successfully predict suicide. This model failed to identify a single patient who committed suicide. The investigators reluctantly concluded that even among a high-risk group of inpatients, predicting suicide based on our current understanding of the phenomenon is not possible. The primary means of assessing imminent suicide risk in a clinical setting is the verbal communication of intent by a patient or an action that is clearly suicidal in intent. Clinicians cannot read minds and must not berate themselves for their perceived failures when no clear verbal or nonverbal indications of suicidality were present. One study (Isometsä et al. 1995) found that of 571 cases of suicide, only 36% of those in psychiatric care communicated suicidal intent.

Treatment of suicidal depression must begin with an adequate dosage of an antidepressant drug that is not lethal when taken in an overdose. Several other risk factors should also be assessed, including the following: feelings of hopelessness, severe anxiety or panic attacks, substance abuse, recent adverse events, financial problems or unemployment, living alone, being widowed or divorced, male sex, and an age of 60 years or older (Clark and Fawcett 1992; Hirschfeld and Russell 1997). If the patient has a definite plan and appears to be intent on taking immediate action, emergency psychiatric hospitalization is required. If the risk of suicide is substantial but not imminent, a family member or other close person should be in-volved. The availability of firearms in the home or elsewhere should be assessed. Literature reviews (Cummings and Koepsell 1998; Miller and Hemenway 1999) provide strong evidence that the availability of a gun increases the risk of suicide to a substantial degree. Regular communication is essential in such circumstances, and substance abuse must be investigated as well. In cases of intense anxiety or panic, the use of a benzodiazepine should be considered (Hirschfeld and Russell 1997). Psychotherapy may also be of extraordinary importance in understanding why the patient wants to die and what he or she expects will happen following death.

Psychodynamic clinicians tend to agree that treaters who fall prey to the illusion that they can save their patients from suicide are actually decreasing their chances of doing so (Hendin 1982; Meissner 1986; Richman and Eyman 1990; Searles 1967/1979; Zee 1972). One salient psychological concern in the seriously suicidal patient is the desire to be taken care of by an unconditionally loving mother (Richman and Eyman 1990; Smith and Eyman 1988). Some therapists err in at-tempting to gratify this fantasy by meeting the patient's every need. They may ac-cept phone calls from the patient any time of the day or night and throughout their vacations. They may see the patient 7 days a week in their office. Some have even become sexually involved with their patients in a desperate effort to gratify the un-ending demands associated with the depression (Twemlow and Gabbard 1989). This kind of behavior exacerbates what Hendin (1982) described as one of the most lethal features of suicidal patients—namely, their tendency to assign others the responsibility for their staying alive. By attempting to gratify these ever-escalating demands, the therapist colludes with the patient's fantasy that there re-ally is an unconditionally loving mother out there somewhere who is different from everyone else. Therapists cannot possibly sustain that illusion indefinitely; those who attempt to do so are setting up the patient for a crushing disappoint-ment that may increase the risk of suicide.

Clinicians who are drawn into the role of savior with suicidal patients often op-erate on the conscious or unconscious assumption that they can provide the love and concern that others have not, thus magically transforming the patient's wish to die into a desire to live. This fantasy is a trap, however, because, as Hendin (1982) noted, "The patient's hidden agenda is an attempt to prove that nothing the thera-pist can do will be enough. The therapist's wish to see himself as the suicidal pa-tient's savior may blind the therapist to the fact that the patient has cast him in the role of executioner" (pp. 171–172). Therapists are more useful to suicidal patients when they diligently try to understand and analyze the origin of the suicidal wishes instead of placing themselves in bondage to the patient.

Therapists should be on the lookout for idealizing transferences, which often form rapidly when patients are looking for a rescuer. Predicting and interpreting transference disappointments early in the process may be helpful. Some therapists openly acknowledge that they cannot stop the patient from committing suicide and offer instead the opportunity to understand why the patient thinks that suicide is the only option (Hendler 1991). Often this admission has a calming effect and may produce greater collaboration in the psychotherapeutic task.

It is useful to distinguish between *treatment* and *management* of the suicidal patient. The latter includes measures such as continuous observation, physical restraints, and removal of sharp objects from the environment. Although these interventions are useful in preventing the patient from acting on suicidal urges, management techniques do not necessarily decrease a patient's future vulnerability to resorting to suicidal behavior. *Treatment* of suicidal patients—consisting of a psychotherapeutic approach to understanding the internal factors and external stressors that make the patient suicidal—is needed to alter the fundamental wish to die.

The countertransference elicited by the suicidal patient presents a formidable obstacle to treatment. Some clinicians simply avoid any responsibility for seriously depressed patients who are at risk for killing themselves. Those who do attempt to treat such patients often believe that their *raison d'être* is negated by the patient's wish to die. A patient's suicide is also the ultimate narcissistic injury for the treater. Clinicians' anxiety about the suicide of the patient may stem more from the fear that others will blame them for the death than from concern for the individual patient's welfare (Hendin 1982). It is commonplace for therapists to set one standard for others and another for themselves. The therapist who assures other clinicians that they are not responsible for a patient's suicide may feel an exaggerated sense of responsibility for keeping his or her own patients alive, often with the assumption that other therapists will be critical if a patient dies.

Therapists who treat seriously suicidal patients will eventually begin to feel tormented by the repeated negation of their efforts. Countertransference hate is likely to develop at such times, and treaters will often harbor an unconscious wish for the patient to die so that the torment will end. Maltsberger and Buie (1974) have noted that feelings of malice and aversion are among the most common countertransference reactions connected with the treatment of severely suicidal patients. The inability to tolerate their own sadistic wishes toward such patients may lead treaters to act out countertransference feelings. The authors caution that while malice may be more unacceptable and uncomfortable, aversion is potentially more lethal because it can lead clinicians to neglect their patients and provide an opportunity for a suicide attempt. On an inpatient unit, this form of countertransference may be manifested by simply "forgetting" to check on the patient as dictated by the suicidal observation ordered.

Countertransference hatred must be accepted as part of the experience of treating suicidal patients. It often arises in direct response to the patient's aggression. Suicide threats may be held over the therapist's head like the mythical sword of Damocles, tormenting and controlling the therapist night and day. Similarly, the family members of patients may be plagued with the concerns that if they make one false move or one unempathic comment, they will be responsible for a suicide. If countertransference hate is split off and disavowed by the therapist, it may be projected onto the patient, who then must deal with the therapist's murderous wishes in addition to the preexisting suicidal impulses. Clinicians may also deal with their feelings of aggression by reaction formation, which may lead to rescue fantasies and exaggerated efforts to prevent suicide. Searles (1967/1979) has warned therapists of the perils of this defensive style:

> And the suicidal patient, who finds us so unable to be aware of the murderous feelings he fosters in us through his guilt- and anxiety-producing threats of suicide, feels increasingly constricted, perhaps indeed to the point of suicide, by the therapist who, in reaction formation against his intensifying, unconscious wishes to kill the patient, hovers increasingly "protectively" about the latter, for whom he feels an omnipotence-based physicianly concern. Hence, it is, paradoxically, the very physician most anxiously concerned to *keep the patient alive* who tends most vigorously, at an unconscious level, to drive him to what has come to seem the only autonomous act left to him—namely, suicide. (p. 74)

Psychotherapists who treat suicidal patients must help them come to terms with their dominant ideology (Arieti 1977) and their rigidly held life fantasies (Richman and Eyman 1990; Smith and Eyman 1988). When there is a disparity between reality and the patient's constricted view of what life should be like, the therapist can help the patient mourn the loss of the life fantasy. This technique may paradoxically require the therapist to acknowledge the patient's hopelessness so that the lost dreams can be mourned and replaced by new ones that are more realistic. For example, one 23-year-old man became suicidal when he realized that he would never be accepted to Harvard, a dream he had cherished since early childhood. The therapist acknowledged that admission to Harvard was highly unlikely and then helped the patient accept the loss of that dream. At the same time, he helped the patient consider alternative pathways to an education that would build the patient's self-esteem. Thus the therapist helped the patient see how much misery is caused by unrealistically high expectations (Richman and Eyman 1990).

To treat suicidal patients effectively, clinicians must distinguish the patient's responsibility from the treater's responsibility. Physicians in general and psychiatrists in particular are characterologically prone to an exaggerated sense of responsibility (Gabbard 1985). We tend to blame ourselves for adverse outcomes beyond our control. Ultimately, we must reconcile ourselves to the fact that there are terminal psychiatric illnesses. Patients must bear the responsibility for deciding whether they will commit suicide or work collaboratively with their therapist to understand the wish to die. Fortunately, the vast majority of patients contemplate suicide with some ambivalence. The part of the suicidal individual that questions the suicidal solution may lead these patients to choose life over death.

References

American Psychiatric Association: Diagnostic and Statistical Manual of Mental Disorders, 4th Edition. Washington, DC, American Psychiatric Association 1994

Arieti S: Psychotherapy of severe depression. Am J Psychiatry 134:864–868, 1977

Asch SS: Suicide and the hidden executioner. International Review of Psychoanalysis 7:51–60, 1980

Betcher RW: The treatment of depression in brief inpatient group psychotherapy. Int J Group Psychother 33:365–385, 1983

Bibring E: The mechanism of depression, in Affective Disorders: Psychoanalytic Contributions to Their Study. Edited by Greenacre P. New York, International Universities Press, 1953, pp 13–48

Bierut LJ, Heath AC, Bucholz KK, et al: Major depressive disorder in a community-based twin sample: are there different genetic and environmental contributions for men and women? Arch Gen Psychiatry 56:557–563, 1999

Bifulco A, Brown GW, Moran P, et al: Predicting depression in women: the role of past and present vulnerability. Psychol Med 28:39–50, 1998

Blatt SJ: The differential effect of psychotherapy and psychoanalysis with anaclitic and introjective patients: the Menninger Psychotherapy Research Project revisited. J Am Psychoanal Assoc 40:691– 724, 1992

Blatt SJ: Contributions of psychoanalysis to the understanding and treatment of depression. J Am Psychoanal Assoc 46:723–752, 1998

Blatt SJ, Ford R, Berman WH, et al: Therapeutic Change: An Object Relations Perspective. New York, Plenum, 1994

Blatt SJ, Quinlan DM, Pilkonis PA, et al: Impact of perfectionism and the need for approval in the brief treatment of depression: the National Institute of Mental Health Treatment of Depression Collaborative Research Program revised. J Consult Clin Psychol 63:125–132, 1995

Broadhead WE, Blazer DG, George LK, et al: Depression, disability days, and days lost from work in a prospective epidemiological survey. JAMA 264:2524–2528, 1990

Bunch J, Barraclough B: The influence of parental death and anniversaries upon suicide dates. Br J Psychiatry 118:621–626, 1971

Chemtob CM, Hamada RS, Bauer G, et al: Patients' suicides: frequency and impact on psychiatrists. Am J Psychiatry 145:224–228, 1988

Clark DC, Fawcett J: An empirically based model of suicide risk assessment for patients with affective disorder, in Suicide and Clinical Practice. Edited by Jacobs D. Washington, DC, American Psychiatric Press, 1992, pp 55–73

Cummings P, Koepsell TD: Does owning a firearm increase or decrease the risk of death? JAMA 280:471–473, 1998

Dorpat TL: Suicide, loss, and mourning. Suicide Life Threat Behav 3:213–224, 1973

Duggan CF, Lee AS, Murray RM: Do different subtypes of hospitalized depressives have different long-term outcomes? Arch Gen Psychiatry 48:308–312, 1991

Ellicott A, Hammen C, Gitlin M, et al: Life events and the course of bipolar disorder. Am J Psychiatry 147:1194–1198, 1990

Fenichel O: The Psychoanalytic Theory of Neurosis. New York, WW Norton, 1945

Freud S: Mourning and melancholia (1917), in The Standard Edition of the Complete Psychological Works of Sigmund Freud, Vol 14. Translated and edited by Strachey J. London, Hogarth Press, 1963, pp 237–260

Freud S: The ego and the id (1923), in The Standard Edition of the Complete Psychological Works of Sigmund Freud, Vol 19. Translated and edited by Strachey J. London, Hogarth Press, 1961, pp 1–66

Gabbard GO: The role of compulsiveness in the normal physician. JAMA 254:2926–2929, 1985

Gallagher-Thompson D, Steffen AM: Comparative effects of cognitive-behavioral and brief psychodynamic psychotherapies for depressed family caregivers. J Consult Clin Psychol 62:543–549, 1994

Ghaemi SN, Stoll SL, Pope HG: Lack of insight in bipolar disorder: the acute manic episode. J Nerv Ment Dis 183:464–467, 1995

Gold PW, Goodwin FK, Chrousos GP: Clinical and biochemical manifestations of depression: relation to the neurobiology of stress, part I. N Engl J Med 319:348–353, 1988a

Gold PW, Goodwin FK, Chrousos GP: Clinical and biochemical manifestations of depression: relation to the neurobiology of stress, part II. N Engl J Med 319:413–420, 1988b

Goldstein RB, Black DW, Nasrallah A, et al: The prediction of suicide: sensitivity, specificity, and predictive value of a multimyriad model applied to suicide among 1,906 patients with affective disorders. Arch Gen Psychiatry 48:418–422, 1991

Guthrie E, Moorey J, Margison F, et al: Cost-effectiveness of brief psychodynamic-interpersonal therapy in high utilizers of psychiatric services. Arch Gen Psychiatry 56:519–526, 1999

Hammen CL: Stress and the course of unipolar and bipolar disorders, in Does Stress Cause Psychiatric Illness? Edited by Mazure CM. Washington, DC, American Psychiatric Press, 1995, pp 87–110

Hammen C, Marks T, Mayol A, et al: Depressive self-schemas, life stress, and vulnerability to depression. J Abnorm Psychol 94:308–319, 1985

Heim C, Graham YP, Heit SC, et al: Increased sensitivity of the hypothalamic-pituitary-adrenal axis to psychosocial stress in adult survivors of childhood abuse. Soc Neurosci Abstr 28:201.12, 1998

Hendin H: Psychotherapy and suicide, in Suicide in America. New York, WW Norton, 1982, pp 160–174

Henseler H: Narcissism as a form of relationship, in Freud's On Narcissism: An Introduction. Edited by Sandler J, Person ES, Fonagy P. New Haven, CT, Yale University Press, 1991, pp 195–215

Hewitt PL, Newton J, Flett GL, et al: Perfectionism and suicide ideation in adolescent psychiatric patients. J Abnorm Child Psychol 25:95–101, 1997

Hirschfeld RMA, Russell JM: Assessment and treatment of suicidal patients. N Engl J Med 337.910–915, 1997

Hooley JM, Teasdale JD: Predictors of relapse in unipolar depressives: expressed emotion, marital distress, and perceived criticism. J Abnorm Psychol 98:229–235, 1989

Hooley JM, Orley J, Teasdale JD: Levels of expressed emotion and relapse in depressed patients. Br J Psychiatry 148:642–647, 1986

Isometsä ET, Heikkinen ME, Marttunen MJ, et al: The last appointment before suicide: is suicide intent communicated? Am J Psychiatry 152:919–992, 1995

Jacobson E: Psychotic identifications, in Depression: Comparative Studies of Normal, Neurotic, and Psychotic Conditions. Edited by Jacobson E. New York, International Universities Press, 1971a, pp 242–263

Jacobson E: Transference problems in depressives, in Depression: Comparative Studies of Normal, Neurotic, and Psychotic Conditions. Edited by Jacobson E. New York, International Universities Press, 1971b, pp 284–301

Jamison KR: An Unquiet Mind. New York, Vintage Books, 1995

Johnson J, Weissman MM, Klerman GL: Service utilization and social morbidity associated with depressive symptoms in the community. JAMA 267:1478–1483, 1992

Keitner GI, Miller IW: Family functioning and major depression: an overview. Am J Psychiatry 147:1128–1137, 1990

Kendler KS, Neale MC, Kessler RC, et al: Childhood parental loss and adult psychopathology in women: a twin study perspective. Arch Gen Psychiatry 49:109–116, 1992

Kendler KS, Kessler RC, Neale MC: The prediction of major depression in women: toward an integrated etiological model. Am J Psychiatry 150:1139–1148, 1993

Kendler KS, Kessler RC, Walters EE, et al: Stressful life events, genetic liability, and onset of an episode of major depression in women. Am J Psychiatry 152:833–842, 1995

Kendler KS, Karkowski LM, Prescott CA: Causal relationship between stressful life events and the onset of major depression. Am J Psychiatry 156:837–841, 1999

Kernberg OF: Severe Personality Disorders: Psychotherapeutic Strategies. New Haven, CT, Yale University Press, 1984

Klein M: Mourning and its relation to manic-depressive states (1940), in Love, Guilt and Reparation and Other Works 1921–1945. New York, Free Press, 1975, pp 344–369

Lesse S: Psychotherapy in combination with antidepressant drugs in severely depressed outpatients—20-year evaluation. Am J Psychother 32:48–73, 1978

Levitan RD, Parikh SV, Lesage AD, et al: Major depression in individuals with a history of childhood physical or sexual abuse: relationship to neurovegetative features, mania and gender. Am J Psychiatry 155:1746–1752, 1998

Maj M: Lithium prophylaxis of bipolar disorder in ordinary clinical conditions: patterns of long-term outcome, in Bipolar Disorders: Clinical Course and Outcome. Edited by Goldberg JF, Harrow M. Washington, DC, American Psychiatric Press, 1999, pp 21–37

Maltsberger JT, Buie DH: Countertransference hate in the treatment of suicidal patients. Arch Gen Psychiatry 30:625–633, 1974

Maxmen JS: An educative model for inpatient group therapy. Int J Group Psychother 28: 321–338, 1978

Meissner WW: Psychotherapy and the Paranoid Process. Northvale, NJ, Jason Aronson, 1986

Menninger KA: Psychoanalytic aspects of suicide. Int J Psychoanal 14:376–390, 1933

Miklowitz DJ, Frank E: New psychotherapies for bipolar disorder, in Bipolar Disorders: Clinical Course and Outcome. Edited by Goldberg JF, Harrow M. Washington, DC, American Psychiatric Press, 1999, pp 57–84

Miller M, Hemenway D: The relationship between firearms and suicide: a review of the literature. Aggression and Violent Behavior 4:59–75, 1999

Nemeroff CB: The neurobiology of depression. Sci Am 278:42–49, 1998a

Nemeroff CB: Polypharmacology in psychiatry: good or bad? CNS Spectrums 3:19, 1998b

Olin HS: Psychotherapy of the chronically suicidal patient. Am J Psychother 30:570–575, 1976

Phillips KA, Gunderson JG, Triebwasser J, et al: Reliability and validity of depressive personality disorder. Am J Psychiatry 155:1044–1048, 1998

Post RM, Ballenger JC, Uhde TW, et al: Kindling and drug sensitization: implications for the progressive development of psychopathology and treatment with carbamazepine, in Psychopharmacology of Anticonvulsants. Edited by Sandler M. Oxford, Oxford University Press, 1982, pp 27–53

Post RM, Rubinow ER, Uhde TW, et al: Dysphoric mania: clinical and biological correlates. Arch Gen Psychiatry 46:353–358, 1989

Reich JH, Green AI: Effect of personality disorders on outcome of treatment. J Nerv Ment Dis 179:74–82, 1991

Richman J, Eyman JR: Psychotherapy of suicide: individual, group, and family approaches, in Understanding Suicide: The State of the Art. Edited by Lester D. Philadelphia, PA, Charles C Thomas, 1990, pp 139–158

Salzman C: Integrating pharmacotherapy and psychotherapy in the treatment of a bipolar patient. Am J Psychiatry 155:686–688, 1998

Searles HF: The "dedicated physician" in the field of psychotherapy and psychoanalysis (1967), in Countertransference and Related Subjects. Madison, CT, International Universities Press, 1979, pp 71–88

Shapiro DA, Barkham M, Rees A, et al: Effects of treatment duration and severity of depression on the effectiveness of cognitive-behavioral and psychodynamic-interpersonal psychotherapy. J Consult Clin Psychol 62:522–534, 1994

Shapiro DA, Barkham M, Rees A, et al: Effects of treatment duration and severity of depression on the maintenance of gains after cognitive-behavioral and psychodynamic-interpersonal psychotherapy. J Consult Clin Psychol 63:378–387, 1995

Shea MT, Pilkonis PA, Beckham E, et al: Personality disorders and treatment outcome in the NIMH Treatment of Depression Collaborative Research Program. Am J Psychiatry 147:711–718, 1990

Smith K: Using a battery of tests to predict suicide in a long term hospital: a clinical analysis. Omega 13:261–275, 1983

Smith K, Eyman J: Ego structure and object differentiation in suicidal patients, in Primitive Mental States of the Rorschach. Edited by Lerner HD, Lerner PM. Madison, CT, International Universities Press, 1988, pp 175–202

Strupp HH, Sandell JA, Waterhouse GJ, et al: Psychodynamic therapy: theory and research, in Short-Term Psychotherapies for Depression. Edited by Rush AJ. New York, Guilford, 1982, pp 215–250

Thase ME, Greenhouse JB, Frank E, et al: Treatment of major depression with psychotherapy or psychotherapy-pharmacotherapy combinations. Arch Gen Psychiatry 54:1009–1015, 1997

Twemlow SW, Gabbard GO: The lovesick therapist, in Sexual Exploitation in Professional Relationships. Edited by Gabbard GO. Washington, DC, American Psychiatric Press, 1989, pp 71–87

Vaughn CE, Leff JP: The influence of family and social factors on the course of psychiatric illness: a comparison of schizophrenic patients and neurotic patients. Br J Psychiatry 129:125–137, 1976

Weiss EL, Longhurst JG, Mazure CM: Childhood sexual abuse as a risk factor for depression in women: psychosocial and neurobiological correlates. Am J Psychiatry 156:816–828, 1999

Zee HJ: Blindspots in recognizing serious suicidal intentions. Bull Menninger Clin 36:551–555, 1972

CHAPTER
9

Anxiety Disorders

As a rule, what is out of sight disturbs men's minds more seriously than what they see.

Julius Caesar

Anxiety is an affect that was instrumental in the birth of psychoanalysis and psychodynamic psychiatry. Freud (1895/1962) coined the term *anxiety neurosis* and identified two forms of anxiety. One form was the diffuse sense of worry or dread that originated in a repressed thought or wish and was curable through psychotherapeutic intervention. The second form of anxiety was characterized by an overwhelming sense of panic, accompanied by manifestations of autonomic discharge, including profuse sweating, increased respiratory and heart rates, diarrhea, and a subjective sense of terror. This latter form, in Freud's view, did not result from psychological factors. Rather, it was conceptualized as the result of the physiological buildup of libido related to a lack of sexual activity. He referred to this form as *actual neurosis*.

By 1926 Freud had further refined his understanding of anxiety as a result of his recent creation, the structural model (Freud 1926/1959). Anxiety was now viewed as the result of psychic conflict between unconscious sexual or aggressive wishes stemming from the id and corresponding threats of punishment from the superego. Anxiety was understood as a *signal* of the presence of danger in the unconscious. In response to this signal, the ego mobilized defense mechanisms to prevent unacceptable thoughts and feelings from emerging into conscious awareness. If signal anxiety failed to adequately activate the ego's defensive resources, then intense, more persistent anxiety or other neurotic symptoms would result. In this sense, anxiety was conceptualized by Freud as both a symptomatic manifestation of neurotic conflict and an adaptive signal to ward off awareness of neurotic conflict.

In Freud's model, anxiety is an ego affect. The ego controls access to consciousness and, through repression, divorces itself from any association with instinctual impulses from the id. It censors both the impulse itself and the corresponding intrapsychic representation. A repressed instinctual wish or impulse may still find expression as a symptom, although it is likely to be displaced and disguised by the time it reaches symptomatic expression. Depending on the defensive operations and symptomatic manifestations, the resulting neurosis might take the form of an obsessional thought, a hysterical paralysis, or a phobic avoidance.

One unfortunate consequence of the deliberate effort to be atheoretical in the development of the DSM-III (American Psychiatric Association 1980), DSM-III-R (American Psychiatric Association 1987), and DSM-IV (American Psychiatric Association 1994) nosology is the sacrifice of classical neurotic entities and the psychodynamic model of symptom formation associated with them. These have been replaced by three separate categories: anxiety disorders, somatoform disorders, and dissociative disorders. The first of these categories, anxiety disorders, has been further subdivided into panic disorder, phobias, obsessive-compulsive disorder, posttraumatic stress disorder, acute stress disorder, and generalized anxiety disorder. Although this classification accommodates the recent biological research delineating different kinds of anxiety, it also encourages clinicians to think about anxiety as an *illness* rather than as an overdetermined *symptom* of unconscious conflict. In many cases, patients presenting with anxiety have no idea what they are anxious about.

In other cases, the anxiety may be attached to a conscious, acceptable fear that masks a deeper, less acceptable concern. The task of the psychodynamic clinician is to understand the unconscious origins of such anxiety. Freud originated the idea that each successive developmental period in a child's life produces a characteristic fear associated with that phase. Based on Freud's discoveries and those of subsequent psychoanalytic investigators, a developmental hierarchy of anxiety (Table 9–1) can be constructed to assist the psychodynamic clinician in determining the unconscious sources of a patient's symptomatic anxiety.

At the most mature level, anxiety originating in the superego can be understood as guilt feelings or pangs of conscience about not living up to an internal standard of moral behavior. During the oedipal phase, anxiety focuses on potential damage to or loss of the genitals at the hands of a retaliatory parental figure. This fear may be expressed metaphorically as loss of another body part or any other form of

TABLE 9-1.	A developmental hierarchy of anxiety

Superego anxiety
Castration anxiety
Fear of loss of love
Fear of loss of the object (separation anxiety)
Persecutory anxiety
Disintegration anxiety

physical injury. Moving back in the developmental hierarchy to a somewhat earlier anxiety, we find the fear of losing the love or approval of a significant other (originally a parent). A developmentally more primitive source of anxiety is the possibility of losing not just the object's love but also the object itself—what is usually referred to as separation anxiety. The most primitive forms of anxiety are persecutory anxiety and disintegration anxiety. The former derives from the Kleinian paranoid-schizoid position, in which the primary anxiety is that persecuting objects from outside will invade and annihilate the patient from within. Disintegration anxiety may derive either from the fear of losing one's sense of self or boundedness through merger with an object or from concern that one's self will fragment and lose its integrity in the absence of mirroring or idealizing responses from others in the environment.

Whenever anxiety forms part of the clinical picture, the psychodynamic psychiatrist must enlist the patient's collaboration in identifying the developmental origins of the anxiety. This information may be ascertained within a 1-hour interview, or it may take an extensive evaluation. Anxiety, like most symptoms, is often multiply determined by issues deriving from a variety of developmental levels (Gabbard and Nemiah 1985).

The hierarchical organization of these variants of anxiety may lead to the mistaken assumption that more primitive levels of anxiety are "outgrown" as development proceeds. In fact, the most primitive levels of anxiety persist in everyone and can be easily triggered in traumatic or stressful situations or in large groups. For example, persecutory anxieties about "outsiders" or those who are different have historically been major factors in wars, geographical and political tensions, and racial prejudice. This developmental hierarchy is only a guideline to assist the clinician. Each person will have a unique blend of anxieties, and some may have anxieties that do not neatly fit into these categories. The clinician must be creative in understanding each patient's specific fears and their origins.

A growing body of empirical evidence links biological mechanisms to the generation of some forms of anxiety. An infusion of lactate will induce panic attacks in patients who have panic disorder. There are higher concordance rates for certain anxiety disorders in monozygotic twins than in dizygotic twins. Some research suggests that acute panic attacks arise in the brain stem and reflect spontaneous hyperactivity of noradrenergic nuclei in conjunction with lowered firing thresholds in medullary respiratory chemoreceptors. Other brain-based disturbances have been linked with specific disorders, and many of these will be discussed when we consider each of the separate anxiety disorders.

Although the advances in neuroscience research on anxiety disorders have been impressive, there is nonetheless a risk of a kind of biological reductionism in understanding anxiety. Neurophysiological mechanisms may produce an adaptive form of signal anxiety as well as the more pathological forms of chronic symptomatic anxiety. Moreover, psychotherapeutic treatments may have significant effects on brain functioning, as discussed in Chapter 1, and therefore may influence the underlying biological mechanisms of anxiety.

Genetic research (Lesch et al. 1996) has demonstrated that individuals who have a somewhat shorter version of the gene involved in serotonin transport may have greater anxiety associated with the neuroticism temperament than those who have the longer version of the gene. The shorter gene is less capable of transporting serotonin compared with the longer gene. Nearly 70% of people have the shorter and less vigorous version of the gene, which results in greater anxiety. One interpretation of this finding is that this distribution may well reflect natural selection, in that individuals with greater anxiety might be better equipped to survive the dangers in their environment than those who are less worried or concerned.

By categorizing anxiety as an illness rather than also viewing it as an overdetermined symptom of unconscious conflict, one may overlook this adaptive aspect of anxiety. Worrying about what will happen in the future can lead to highly creative thinking. Solutions to problems are found as a result of worry. Healthy self-doubt may also be linked to worrying. If anxiety is seen as a problem that must be eradicated psychopharmacologically, the human psyche may suffer a substantial loss.

In the Menninger Foundation Psychotherapy Research Project, 18 of 35 patients showed increased anxiety at the termination of psychoanalysis or psychotherapy, even though 13 of these 18 patients were judged by independent raters to have achieved substantial improvement (Appelbaum 1977). In evaluating these results, the investigators (Appelbaum 1977; Siegal and Rosen 1962) differentiated between primary anxiety, which is disorganizing to the patient (analogous to panic disorder), and signal anxiety, which may be adaptive. The researchers noted that an increase in anxiety tolerance—defined as the capacity to experience anxiety without having to discharge it—often occurs as a result of dynamic psychotherapy and reflects expansion of the ego. Many of the improved patients showed striking improvements in their capacity to make efficient use of ideational activity in the service of binding anxiety. The investigators concluded that the mere presence or absence of anxiety after treatment was an insufficient basis for assessing change. It may well be that greater ego mastery over anxiety allows one to confront certain existential concerns inherent in life in a more forthright manner. Anxiety can be adaptive or maladaptive, and the assumption that all anxiety should be eradicated is certainly unwarranted based on clinical and life experience.

One final problem should be mentioned by way of introducing the DSM-IV anxiety disorders. There is a growing concern among researchers and clinicians that the taxonomy associated with anxiety disorders in DSM-IV is more illusory than real. Comorbidity studies of anxiety disorders are finding that patients are more likely to have two or more anxiety disorders than a pure form of any of the specific diagnostic entities. Hence, a clinician developing a comprehensive treatment plan must keep in mind that more than one anxiety disorder is likely to be the focus of treatment.

Panic Disorder

Although panic attacks generally last only a matter of minutes, they produce considerable distress within the patient. In addition to alarming physiological symptoms, such as choking, dizziness, sweating, shaking, and tachycardia, patients with panic disorder often sense imminent doom. Most patients with panic disorder also have agoraphobia (i.e., a fear of being in a location or situation from which escape would be difficult or extremely embarrassing). Because panic attacks are recurrent, patients often develop a secondary form of anticipatory anxiety, worrying constantly about when and where the next attack will occur. Panic disorder patients with agoraphobia often restrict their travel to try to control the dreaded situation of having a panic attack in a place they cannot leave easily.

Panic disorder may appear psychologically contentless. The attacks may seem to come "out of the blue," without apparent environmental or intrapsychic precipitants. As a result, the psychodynamic psychiatrist's role is often—and unfortunately—deemed irrelevant in treating these patients. A significant percentage of patients with panic disorder have such attacks because of psychodynamic factors and thus may respond to psychological interventions (Milrod et al. 1997; Nemiah 1984). Psychodynamic clinicians should thoroughly investigate the circumstances of the attacks and the history of each panic disorder patient to determine how psychological factors are relevant.

Although the evidence for neurophysiological factors in panic disorder is impressive, these observations are more persuasive regarding pathogenesis than regarding etiology. None of the neurobiological data explains what triggers the onset of a panic attack. In a pilot study involving psychodynamic interviews with nine consecutive patients with panic disorder, an objective research psychiatrist was able to identify meaningful stressors preceding the onset of the panic attacks in every case (Busch et al. 1991). These stressors tended to be connected with an alteration in the level of expectations placed on the patient. Changes in expectations related to job situations were common, as were losses associated with central figures in the patients' lives. Many of the loss events were associated with childhood experiences in which attachment to a parent or other important person had been threatened. Another common denominator among the patients investigated was the perception of parents as threatening, temperamental, critical, controlling, and demanding. More extensive analysis of the interviews demonstrated a pattern of anxiety about socializing with others during childhood, unsupportive parental relationships, and feelings of being trapped. Anger and aggression were difficult to handle for most of the patients.

Many of the observations in this exploratory study have been confirmed by empirical research. Panic disorder patients have been found to have a higher incidence of stressful life events, particularly loss, compared with control subjects in the months preceding the onset of panic disorder (Faravelli and Pallanti 1989). In another controlled study of patients with panic disorder (Roy-Byrne et al. 1986), the experimental group not only experienced significantly more stressful life events in the year preceding the onset of panic but also felt greater distress about these events in their lives than did the control subjects. In a large study of 1,018 female twin pairs (Kendler et al. 1992a), panic disorder was strongly and significantly associated with both parental separation and death. Early maternal separation, in particular, was linked to panic disorder.

One pathogenetic theory with some degree of empirical support is that panic disorder patients have a predisposing neurophysiological vulnerability that may interact with specific environmental stressors to produce the disorder. Kagan et al. (1988) identified an inborn temperamental characteristic in a number of children that they termed *behavioral inhibition to the unfamiliar*. These children tend to be easily frightened by anything that is strange in their environment. As a way of coping with their fear, they rely on their parents to protect them. As they grow and mature, however, they learn that their parents will not always be available to protect and comfort them. They may then externalize their own inadequacies by projecting them onto their parents, whom they then regard as unreliable and unpredictable. These children may become angry at their parents' inconsistent availability, but the anger creates new problems in that they worry that their angry fantasies will be destructive and drive their parents away, leaving them with the loss of a parent on whom they depend to provide safety (Busch et al. 1991; Milrod et al. 1997). A vicious cycle results in which the child's anger threatens the connection with the parent and thus increases the child's fearful and hostile dependence.

Understanding the pathogenesis of panic disorder from an attachment theory perspective is also helpful in a psychodynamic approach to the treatment (Shear 1996). A small preliminary study of attachment style in 18 women suffering from anxiety disorder suggested that all had problematic attachment styles (Manassis et al. 1994). Fourteen of the 18 patients were diagnosed with panic disorder; these patients tended to have higher rates of preoccupied attachment. Patients with panic disorder often view separation and attachment as mutually exclusive. They have difficulty modulating the normal oscillation between separation and attachment because they have a heightened sensitivity to both loss of freedom and loss of safety and protection. This difficulty results in their operating within an extremely narrow range of behavior that attempts to simultaneously avoid separation that is too frightening and attachment that is too intense. This constricted comfort zone often manifests in an overcontrolling style of interaction with others.

The extreme level of panic seen in these patients may reflect a signal anxiety function inadequate to activate the ego's defensive resources. Threats to attachment, in particular, appear to trigger this kind of overwhelming panic. Milrod (1998) suggests that those who develop panic disorder are prone to feelings of self-fragmentation and may need a therapist or other companion to help them feel that they have a firm sense of identity. The presence of ego defects involving self/other confusion may be related to these difficulties in using anxiety as a signal.

Another etiological factor in women patients that also relates to attachment difficulties is childhood physical and sexual abuse. In one investigation, childhood sexual abuse was found to occur at a rate of 45.1% in women with anxiety disorders, compared with a rate of 15.4% in a group of women without anxiety disorders (Stein et al. 1996). When panic disorder, in particular, was examined, 60% of the women with panic disorder had a history of childhood sexual abuse, compared with 31% of women with other anxiety disorders. Because childhood trauma interferes with the child's attachment to the parents, sexual abuse could account for some of the difficulties that panic disorder patients have in feeling safe and secure with significant objects in their lives. Internalization of abusive representations of parents also interferes with development of trust in adult life.

Taken together, all of these data suggest that the etiology of panic disorder may well involve multiple factors, including the unconscious meaning of events, while the pathogenesis may involve neurophysiological factors triggered by the psychological reaction to the events. Busch et al. (1991) concluded: "Since each individual interprets the meaning of these events differently, an external stressor may or may not lead to the onset of panic in a neurophysiologically susceptible individual. This suggests that there is a crucial psychological variable that mediates between external events and panic onset" (p. 321).

These research findings are borne out by clinical experience with patients who suffer from poorly developed object constancy (see Chapter 15). Such patients cannot summon an internal image of their therapist in times of distress to help them soothe their anxiety. Over long weekends or during their therapist's vacations, these patients may develop full-blown panic attacks triggered by the thought of losing their therapist. They may fear that their therapist has died or is on the verge of rejecting or abandoning them. In such circumstances, just hearing their therapist's voice over the telephone can completely eliminate the panic within a few seconds. One psychiatrist in private practice routinely left a message on his answering machine over the weekend so that his patients would know where to reach him. Upon hiring a secretary, he relegated to her the task of recording the answering machine message. On the first Monday morning after the secretary recorded the message, three patients called him to complain. One patient angrily stated, "I need to hear *your* voice, not hers! It's either your voice or a Xanax!"

As poignantly illustrated by this comment, the *sound* of the therapist's voice was enough to reassure this patient that he was truly still available. Indeed, in this case the therapist's voice had a therapeutic effect as potent as a pharmacological agent. Often patients suffering from a lack of object constancy are able to ultimately develop an internalized image of their therapist over the course of long-term, expressive-supportive psychotherapy. As a result of this internalization process, both the separation anxiety and the panic attacks may improve considerably.

One study (Shear et al. 1991) has demonstrated that lactate induction of panic can be effectively reversed with successful cognitive therapy. This finding, coupled with a variety of case reports of successful treatment of panic disorder with either psychoanalysis or psychodynamic psychotherapy (Abend 1989; Milrod and Shear 1991; Milrod et al. 1997; Sifneos 1972), provides evidence that psychological interventions have a major role to play in the treatment of panic disorder.

In the course of psychodynamic therapy, the patient's difficulties in relationships often become centered in the transference to the therapist. Conflicts around anger, independence, and separation are especially prominent. It usually behooves the therapist to explore the patient's fears of becoming overly dependent on the therapist as the treatment progresses. Similarly, there may be undue anxiety about the loss of the therapist, either temporarily through vacations or permanently through termination of the treatment.

In many cases, fantasies of uncontrollable anger, or even murderous rage, may be central to the therapy. Parental anger may have been so intense that any eruption of anger is seen as potentially destructive. Some children may have experienced their parents as emotionally abandoning them when they expressed their anger. Examining characteristic defense mechanisms designed to avoid anger is often of considerable value. Patients with panic disorder typically use any combination of the following defenses: reaction formation, undoing, somatization, and externalization (Busch et al. 1995). Both undoing and reaction formation can help the patient disavow negative affects such as anger. Psychotherapists may need to help patients become aware of their anxiety about expressing anger and the associated need to defend against it.

Defenses of somatization and externalization often work synergistically to prevent internal reflection. In somatization, the patient's attention is focused on physiological phenomena rather than on psychological causes or meaning. In externalization, problems are attributed to external persons, who are viewed as mistreating the patient in some way. Used in combination, these defenses may create a specific form of object relationship in which others (e.g., family, friends, doctors) are enlisted as healers who are expected to fix something in the patient's body. This pattern of object relatedness frequently plays itself out in the transference as well.

Panic disorder patients frequently require a combination of drug therapy and psychotherapy (Nemiah 1984). Even when patients with panic attacks and agoraphobia have their symptoms pharmacologically controlled, they are often reluctant to venture out into the world again and may require psychotherapeutic interventions to help them overcome this fear (Cooper 1985; Zitrin et al. 1978). At least one study has suggested that the combination of dynamic therapy and medication may help reduce relapse in patients with panic disorder. Patients in Wiborg and Dahl's (1996) study were randomized to treatment with either 9 months of clomipramine alone or 9 months of clomipramine combined with 15 weekly sessions of brief dynamic therapy. Although all patients in both groups were free of panic attacks when assessed 20 weeks after beginning treatment, patients in the group that received only clomipramine had a much higher relapse rate when assessed after the pharmacotherapy had ended. The researchers suggested that brief dynamic therapy may serve to reduce the psychosocial vulnerability connected with panic disorder.

Some patients present with major resistances to medication, often because they believe it stigmatizes them as being mentally ill, so psychotherapeutic intervention is required to help them understand and eliminate their reservations about pharmacotherapy. Still others discontinue medications on their own because of their inability to tolerate side effects. Finally, characterological difficulties in patients may interfere with compliance. The presence of personality disorders, particularly those in Cluster B (i.e., antisocial, borderline, narcissistic, histrionic), has been shown to adversely affect the treatment outcomes of patients with panic disorder (Reich 1988). For a comprehensive and effective treatment plan, these patients require psychotherapeutic approaches in addition to appropriate medications. In all patients with symptoms of panic disorder or agoraphobia, a careful psychodynamic evaluation will help weigh the contributions of biological and dynamic factors.

Mr. L, a 27-year-old office worker, came to an outpatient clinic with a complaint of panic attacks that occurred whenever he attempted to leave town. He was initially unable to link the panic to any psychological content, but further exploration by the evaluating psychiatrist revealed a number of contributing factors. Mr. L had just purchased a new house, and his wife was pregnant with their first child. When the psychiatrist commented on the increased responsibility associated with these events, the patient replied that he felt more like 7 than 27. He went on to say that he was not sure that he was prepared to shoulder the responsibilities of a husband and father accountable for the mortgage on a house. The psychiatrist asked Mr. L to describe in more detail the circumstances of the panic attacks. Mr. L again explained that he had them whenever he started to leave town. The psychiatrist asked about the purpose of these trips, which Mr. L explained was to go hunting with his father. The psychiatrist asked if anything unpleasant had ever happened on these trips. After a few moments' reflection, Mr. L replied that he had accidentally shot his father in two different hunting accidents, although fortunately his father had sustained only minor wounds on each occasion.

The psychiatrist then developed a tentative explanatory formulation based on his evaluation that Mr. L's panic disorder was related to psychological conflict. Recent events in his life had placed him more squarely in competition with his father as a husband, father, and breadwinner. These events activated long-standing aggressive wishes toward his father that were based on repressed and unconscious oedipal rivalry. The impulse to destroy his father had emerged in the form of accidents on two previous hunting trips. Now whenever Mr. L planned to leave town with his father to go hunting, the threatened emergence of the aggressive impulses created signal anxiety that was transformed into a full-blown panic attack because this particular patient had the underlying neural substrate necessary to transform anxiety into panic. The result was an avoidance of situations in which the destructive wishes and the imagined retaliation (castration) would be activated.

To understand the dynamic factors involved in triggering the panic, the patient began expressive-supportive psychotherapy with an expressive emphasis. As the process proceeded, Mr. L began to talk more and more about his attachment to his mother. It soon emerged that his mother had also been terrified of separations. As a child, each time Mr. L went outside, his mother would warn him about the many dangers he might encounter. Through the psychotherapy process, Mr. L eventually realized that he shared his mother's anxiety about separations. He noted that whenever his wife was away on business, he worried the entire time because he feared that she might die and thus abandon him. The patient's oedipal anxieties were clearly compounded by more primitive anxieties about object loss, originally of his mother but now of his wife.

After approximately 2 years of psychotherapy, Mr. L was free from panic attacks and from anticipatory anxiety as well. He had received a promotion at work that he was able to handle without anxiety. His new job necessitated driving out of town almost every workday, and he was able to do so without experiencing any panic.

Several years later, Mr. L returned for further treatment when two life events reactivated the underlying neural structure that mediated his panic attacks. A private business he had started had become enormously successful, resulting in a much more affluent lifestyle. Moreover, his father had been diagnosed as having incurable cancer. This time a combination of medication (alprazolam) and psychotherapy was required to reduce Mr. L's panic attacks to manageable proportions.

Phobias

Anxiety disorders as a group are the most prevalent of all major groups of mental disorders (Regier et al. 1988), and among anxiety disorders, phobias are by far the most common. Phobias are divided into three categories in DSM-IV: 1) agoraphobia without history of panic disorder, 2) specific phobia, and 3) social phobia. The DSM-III-R term *simple phobia* was replaced by *specific phobia* in DSM-IV because of the ambiguous relationship of phobic symptoms to panic attacks and because a subtyping scheme involving the phobic stimulus (e.g., situational type, natural environment type) seemed to improve specificity. Similarly, a subtyping scheme has been developed in DSM-IV for social phobia because the growing literature on the condition indicates that social phobia may be either generalized or limited.

The psychodynamic understanding of phobias illustrates the neurotic mechanism of symptom formation described at the beginning of this chapter. When forbidden sexual or aggressive thoughts that might lead to retaliatory punishment threaten to emerge from the unconscious, signal anxiety is activated, which leads to the deployment of three defense mechanisms—displacement, projection, and avoidance (Nemiah 1981). These defenses eliminate the anxiety by once again repressing the forbidden wish, but the anxiety is controlled at the cost of creating a phobic neurosis. A clinical example illustrates the phobic symptom formation more concretely:

Mr. M was a 25-year-old junior executive who had just completed an MBA and taken his first position with a corporation. He had developed a social phobia that involved an intense fear of meeting new people at work or in social situations. He also developed intense anxiety whenever he had to speak in front of a group of people at work. When forced to confront the feared situations, he would become short of breath and stumble over his words to such an extent that he could not complete sentences.

Brief dynamic therapy was recommended for Mr. M because of his notable ego strengths, the focal nature of his symptom, his good overall functioning, a high level of motivation, and considerable psychological mindedness. In the third session, Mr. M clarified for the therapist that the worst part of meeting new people was having to introduce himself. The following exchange took place:

> Therapist: What's difficult about saying your name?
> Mr. M: I have no idea.
> Therapist: If you reflect about your name for a minute, what comes to mind?
> Mr. M: (after a pause) Well, it's also my father's name.
> Therapist: How does that make you feel?
> Mr. M: A bit uncomfortable, I guess.
> Therapist: Why is that?
> Mr. M: Well, I haven't had a great relationship with him. Ever since he left my mom when I was 4 years old, I've seen very little of him.
> Therapist: So you had to live alone with your mother after he left?
> Mr. M: That's right. My mom never remarried, so I had to be the man of the house from an early age, and I didn't feel ready to take on so much responsibility. I've always resented that. When I was a kid, everybody always said that I acted like such an adult. That used to bother me because I felt like I was just pretending to be an adult when I was really a child inside. I felt like I was fooling everybody, and if they found out, they would be mad at me.
> Therapist: I wonder if that's how you feel now when you introduce yourself.
> Mr. M: I think that's exactly how I feel. To say my name is to say I'm trying to be my father.

The therapist's interpretation helped Mr. M realize that his anxiety was related to guilt and shame about prematurely filling his father's shoes. He imagined that others would see through this charade, or deceit, and disapprove of him. After 10 sessions of brief dynamic therapy, the patient overcame his social phobia and was able to function well at work and in social settings.

At the height of Mr. M's oedipal phase of development, his father left him alone with his mother. In that original anxiety-generating situation, he had feared castration or retaliatory punishment (from his father) for taking his father's place with his mother. As an adult, Mr. M dealt with anxiety by displacing the original feared situation onto an insignificant and seemingly trivial derivative of that situation, namely, saying his name during introductions. Symbolically, this simple social grace had taken on the meaning of replacing his father. The patient's second defensive maneuver was to project the feared situation outward onto the environment so that the threatened punishment or disapproval came from external rather than internal sources (i.e., the superego). The patient's third and final defense mechanism was avoidance. By avoiding all situations in which he had to introduce himself or speak in front of others, Mr. M could maintain control over his anxiety, but at the cost of restricting his social life and jeopardizing his performance at work.

Mr. M's anxiety about speaking in front of others is widely shared. In one metropolitan survey (Pollard and Henderson 1988), one-fifth of the individuals contacted in the city of St. Louis had a social phobia about public speaking or performing. When the investigators modified that figure by including the "significant distress" criteria of DSM-III, the prevalence rate fell to 2%. Exact figures on social phobia are difficult to ascertain, however, because the diagnosis is often applied to general interpersonal patterns of shyness and avoidance of the opposite sex because of fear of rejection. The continuum ranges from social phobia at one end to a generalized characterological style of relating, known as avoidant personality disorder (see Chapter 19), at the other.

Phobias fit nicely into a model of genetic-constitutional diathesis in interaction with environmental stressors. Kendler et al. (1992b) studied 2,163 female twins and concluded that the best model for the disorder is an inherited phobia proneness that requires environmental etiological factors specific to the individual to produce a full-blown phobic syndrome. In their study population, one of the clear environmental stressors associated with an increased risk for phobia was parental death before age 17 years (Kendler et al. 1992a).

The work of Kagan et al. (1988) on behavioral inhibition appears to be applicable to social phobia in much the same way that it is relevant to panic disorder. Although Kagan and colleagues found that infants with this temperament are born with a lower threshold for limbic-hypothalamic arousal in response to unexpected changes in the environment, they also concluded that some form of chronic environmental stress must act on the original temperamental disposition to result in shy, timid, and quiet behavior at 2 years of age. They postulated that stressors such as humiliation and criticism from an older sibling, parental arguments, and death of or separation from a parent were probably among the chief contributory environmental factors.

Rosenbaum et al. (1992) extended the work of Kagan et al. (1988) by evaluating parents of behaviorally inhibited children from a nonclinical cohort studied by Kagan. Parents of these children were at greater risk for anxiety disorders, mainly social phobia. Parents of those children with behavioral inhibition and anxiety had significantly higher rates of two or more anxiety disorders as compared with two different sets of parents in control groups. One possible interpretation of their findings is that those children with behavioral inhibition who go on to develop manifest anxiety disorders are exposed to parents with greater anxiety who may convey to the children that the world is a dangerous place.

Social phobia is a condition with a high rate of comorbidity. In a study of 13,000 adults (Schneier et al. 1992), lifetime major comorbid disorders were present in 69% of subjects with social phobia. These investigators made the point that in the absence of comorbidity, social phobia is rarely treated by mental health professionals. One can postulate that the genetic-constitutional diathesis described by Kagan et al. (1988), Rosenbaum et al. (1992), and others may predispose to a number of anxiety disorders.

Clinical work with socially phobic patients reveals that certain characteristic internal object relationships are present. Specifically, these patients have internalized representations of parents, caretakers, or siblings who shame, criticize, ridicule, humiliate, abandon, and embarrass (Gabbard 1992). These introjects are established early in life and then repeatedly projected onto persons in the environment who are then avoided. Although these patients may have a genetic predisposition to experience others as hurtful, positive experiences can mitigate those effects to some extent. It is as though a genetically programmed template is present at birth. To the extent that caretakers behave like the programmed template, the individual will become increasingly fearful of others and develop social phobia. To the extent that caretakers are sensitive to the child's fearfulness and compensate, the introjects will be more benign, less threatening, and less likely to produce the adult syndrome of social phobia.

Although many patients with social phobia respond well to selective serotonin reuptake inhibitors (SSRIs) and/or cognitive therapy, dynamic therapy can be useful as well. Some patients are particularly treatment resistant because they fear any situation in which they might be judged or criticized. Because the therapeutic setting is viewed as just such a situation, a transference fear of being humiliated or judged may lead patients to miss appointments frequently or to stop coming to treatment altogether. In fact, because of the disorder's high rates of comorbidity, social phobia may only be discovered when a patient seeks treatment for another reason. Embarrassment and shame are central affective states, and the therapist who tunes in to these affects may have a better chance of forming a therapeutic alliance in the initial visits with the patient. Exploring their fantasies of how the therapist and others might react to them will also help these patients begin to appreciate that their *perceptions* of how others feel about them may be different from how others *actually* feel about them. Treatment resistance should be dealt with aggressively, because without treatment, these patients often avoid school or work, and many end up on welfare or disability (Schneier et al. 1992).

The interpersonal ramifications of phobias often benefit from a dynamic approach as well. By virtue of being housebound, severely agoraphobic individuals often require caretaking from another significant person, such as a spouse or parent. It is common, for example, for an agoraphobic woman and her husband to have accommodated to her condition over a period of many years. The husband may actually feel more secure knowing that his wife is always in the house. If the agoraphobia is treated, the couple's equilibrium may destabilize. The husband may become more anxious because of a fear that his wife will begin to seek out other men now that she is leaving the house. Adequate assessment and treatment of phobias must include a careful assessment of how the phobia fits into the patient's network of relationships. A psychodynamic understanding of the interpersonal context of a phobia may thus be crucial to dealing with resistances to conventional treatments such as behavioral desensitization and medication.

Obsessive-Compulsive Disorder

Obsessions are defined as recurrent ego-dystonic thoughts, whereas compulsions are ritualized actions that *must* be performed to relieve anxiety. The complaints of these patients fit into five primary categories: 1) rituals involving checking, 2) rituals involving cleaning, 3) obsessive thoughts unaccompanied by compulsions, 4) obsessional slowness, and 5) mixed rituals (Baer and Jenike 1986). Those patients who are involved in cleaning rituals or obsessive thoughts about germs and contamination bear considerable resemblance to phobic patients. Recent research has suggested that obsessive-compulsive disorder (OCD) is much more common than had been previously thought (Karno et al. 1988). The lifetime prevalence is between 1.2% and 2.4%, a figure many times greater than all previous estimates. OCD is often complicated by depression and by serious impairment in occupational and social functioning so that family members and co-workers of OCD patients may be significantly affected by the illness as well.

Despite the long-established tradition of the diagnosis of obsessive-compulsive neurosis, DSM-III reclassified OCD as an anxiety disorder because the primary function of an obsession or ritual seems to be regulation of anxiety. The classical formulation of the defensive regression inherent in obsessive-compulsive neurosis has been succinctly summarized by Nemiah (1988):

> In the face of stimuli that arouse anxiety-provoking oedipal libido, instead of repressing the drive and converting the energy into somatic symptoms as in hysteria or displacing and projecting it as in the phobic neurosis, the patient with an obsessive-compulsive neurosis retreats from the oedipal position and regresses along the path of psychosexual development to the anal phase, a regression often aided by the presence of anal fixations resulting from disturbances in the patient's initial passage through that developmental stage during early childhood. (p. 243)

The psychodynamic explanation of OCD has been challenged by recent biological research. A number of investigators have suggested that a biological basis exists for the disorder because of several observations, including a higher rate of concordance for OCD in monozygotic than dizygotic twins, an increased prevalence in patients with Tourette's disorder and in their families, and a dramatic response in some patients to psychosurgery (Elkins et al. 1980; Lieberman 1984; Turner et al. 1985). Another study compared 41 medication-free OCD patients with 29 nonpsychiatrically ill control subjects on tasks involving fine motor coordination, involuntary movement, and sensory and visuospatial function (Hollander et al. 1990). The OCD group showed significantly more signs of central nervous system dysfunction than did the control subjects, providing further evidence for a neurological deficit in some patients with OCD. A subsequent study demonstrated that neuropsychological deficits observed in patients with OCD are not observed in matched control patients with panic disorder or unipolar depression (Purcell et al. 1998). Finally, patients with OCD have significantly less total white matter but significantly greater total cortex and opercular volumes compared with healthy control subjects (Jenike et al. 1996).

The literature on treatment outcomes also suggests a biological component. Medications such as clomipramine and fluvoxamine have been found to be effective with some OCD patients (Jenike et al. 1986; Perse 1988; White and Cole 1988). Also, the symptoms of OCD patients are notoriously refractory to psychoanalysis and insight-oriented psychotherapy (Jenike et al. 1986; Nemiah 1988; Perse 1988; Zetzel 1970). (Obsessive-compulsive personality disorder appears to respond well to these treatments, as discussed in Chapter 19.) Pharmacological response, however, does not provide definitive answers to questions of etiology or pathogenesis (Zetin and Kramer 1992). Neurotransmitter changes associated with medications may relate either directly or indirectly to the primary cause of the condition. Moreover, as with panic disorder, OCD may be precipitated by environmental stressors. In one investigation (Buttolph and Holland 1990), 69% of patients with OCD were able to relate the onset or exacerbation of their symptoms to pregnancy, childbirth, or parental care of their children. In another study of 106 female OCD patients (Neziroglu et al. 1992), pregnancy—more than any other life event—was associated with the onset of OCD. Thirty-nine percent of the patients in the sample who had children experienced symptom onset during pregnancy. In addition, four of the five women who had had an abortion or a miscarriage had experienced the onset or exacerbation of OCD symptoms during pregnancy. That the symptoms wax and wane according to the presence or absence of stress in the patient's life is also well known. Improvement may occur when tension is reduced, whereas increased stress or recurrence of the original precipitating situation will worsen symptoms (Black 1974).

Although most clinicians would agree that pharmacotherapy is a crucial part of a comprehensive treatment plan for patients with OCD, medication such as clomipramine should not be regarded as the sole treatment. The Clomipramine Collaborative Study Group (1991) studied 520 OCD patients in 21 centers and found that the mean reduction in symptoms at the end of 10 weeks of treatment with clomipramine was only 38%–44%. Multicenter, placebo-controlled trials of fluoxetine, fluvoxamine, sertraline, and paroxetine have found all of these SSRIs to be more effective than placebo (Greist and Jefferson 1995). However, incomplete improvement was the rule in these trials as well, so the combination of SSRIs and behavior therapy is usually considered the treatment approach of choice. Nevertheless, psychodynamic strategies may be extremely helpful in a number of situations.

Many OCD patients seem to hang onto their symptoms, tenaciously resisting treatment efforts. The symptoms themselves may fend off psychotic disintegration in some patients, thereby performing a highly useful function in terms of psychological homeostasis. Because the symptoms of OCD may accompany any level of underlying personality or ego organization (Cornfield and Malen 1978), a careful psychodynamic evaluation should also focus on the function of the symptoms in the patient's overall intrapsychic structure. Despite the refractory nature of many obsessive-compulsive symptoms, psychodynamic therapy may considerably improve the interpersonal functioning of OCD patients. Dynamic approaches may also be crucial in helping patients overcome resistances to taking medication, as described in the following case:

> Mr. N was a 29-year-old single man with OCD. At the time he presented for psychiatric hospitalization, he reported a 10-year history of obsessive-compulsive symptoms, and he complained of having been totally housebound for the last 8 years because of constant incapacitating, "grotesque, horrific" thoughts that never ceased. Eight years before admission, when Mr. N had become housebound, his mother had retired from her job so that she could take care of him at home and meet his demands for cleanliness. Her life revolved around him.
>
> Mr. N was obsessed with the need to avoid contamination. He also worried about making women pregnant, because he feared he might have semen on his hands. Hence, he became a compulsive hand washer. He insisted that his mother be with him 24 hours per day. Although she did not sleep with him or go into the shower with him, she did help him dress so that he would not have to touch his clothes and become contaminated. He also required her to follow an elaborate 58-step ritual while cooking his food and placing it on the table. If she did not follow this ritual precisely, she had to discard the entire meal and start over again. She threw out thousands of dollars' worth of food each year in order to respond to these demands. Mr. N also insisted that his father had to either stay away from home or remain in another part of the house so that he would not be contaminated by the germs his father brought home from work.

Mr. N's early childhood development was reportedly unremarkable, but he did recall a very unpleasant memory from when he was approximately 5 years old. He remembered seeing his father grab his mother by the breasts while she cried for the patient to rescue her. He tried to stop his father, but he was overpowered by the older man. He remembered feeling terrible about the incident, and he cried because he was unable to rescue his mother.

Although Mr. N had been to numerous psychiatrists, he always refused to go back after the first visit. At one time, he agreed to take clomipramine, but he stopped after the first dose because he said the side effects bothered him. His functioning grew worse, and his parents finally made the decision to hospitalize him. When he came to the hospital, his doctor asked him why he was seeking treatment. He responded, "I'm determined to be dependent—I mean independent." The doctor commented on the fact that he had first said "dependent," and inquired, "Is there perhaps a part of you that would like to be dependent?" Mr. N responded, "You mean on my mother?" His doctor replied that Mr. N would know better than he. Mr. N reflected a moment and said, "Well, she does take pretty good care of me."

Mr. N's slip of the tongue provided a glimpse into the unconscious motivations for his resistance to treatment. Any kind of successful treatment threatened his dependent relationship with his mother. If clomipramine were likely to help him, then he would not take it. Similarly, he would defeat all other outpatient or inpatient treatment efforts as well.

After about a week of hospitalization, Mr. N defied the staff members' expectations. He began to make dramatic improvements. He could touch doorknobs without fearing contamination, he could read magazines that others had touched, and he greatly decreased the time he spent washing his hands. This improvement occurred without medication. Mr. N commented that he felt "a lot less nervous" in the hospital than he had expected. As he explored how the hospital setting might have reduced his anxiety, it became apparent that he was increasingly worried about his sexual wishes toward his mother. He commented that when his mother dressed him, he felt that "there was something sexual about that." Removing him from the emotionally charged household made his sexual wishes toward his mother much less problematic for him. Similarly, aggressive wishes to keep his father out of his life were less troubling. Because his anxiety about both sexual and aggressive wishes had diminished, his obsessive-compulsive symptoms were not needed so extensively to bind his anxiety.

However biologically driven Mr. N's obsessive-compulsive symptoms may have been, they also revealed a symbolic wish to win his mother's affection away from his father, as poignantly depicted in his early childhood memories. His compulsive rituals served as a defense against his sexual longings for his mother by consuming all his time in hand washing and various other exercises. However, these symptomatic rituals also resulted in his being dressed by his mother and receiving all of her attention while his father stayed away from home. Hence, the compromise formation unconsciously constructed contained both the direct expression of an underlying wish and a defense against that wish. Taking medication or receiving any other treatment threatened this triumph over father by placing him in a position in which he no longer needed his mother. On the other hand, this oedipal victory created enormous anxiety and guilt, which increased his recourse to rituals and obsessions. When removed from the triangle he had established with his parents at home, Mr. N had much less need of his obsessive-compulsive symptoms to deal with the anxiety and showed remarkable improvement.

Although Mr. N's treatment did not involve formal dynamic psychotherapy, the psychiatrist's dynamic understanding of this patient's resistance to treatment in general was essential in helping Mr. N address his refusal to take medication and to otherwise cooperate with treatment. Mr. N's slip of the tongue led to his awareness that any improvement in his symptoms might cause him to lose his privileged position with his mother.

Mr. N's case also reflects a common problem that occurs in the families of OCD patients. A study of 34 parents or spouses of OCD patients examined the extent to which these relatives would accommodate the patient through active participation in rituals or significant modifications of their daily routines (Calvocoressi et al. 1995). Of these relatives, 88.2% reported accommodating the patient in some way. This form of family accommodation was clearly correlated with stress in the family, rejecting attitudes toward the patient, and poor family functioning. These accommodations often involve an effort to reduce the patient's anxiety or to control the patient's expressions of anger. Many relatives described feeling "bullied" by the patient into doing things to accommodate the patient's obsessions or compulsions. Similarly, this pattern of relatedness becomes internalized and often is recreated when OCD patients are admitted to partial hospital or inpatient units. A characterological posture entitlement often accompanies the tendency of some OCD patients to insist that everyone—without exception—must accommodate their illness.

Symptoms of OCD often lead to extraordinary relationship problems for these patients, and the diagnosis of OCD is associated with a high risk of divorce or separation (Zetin and Kramer 1992). Psychodynamic therapy therefore may be the only effective modality for addressing the relationship problems secondary to the symptoms. Dynamic group or family psychotherapy, in particular, may be useful in this realm.

Another useful contribution the psychodynamic clinician can make in treating OCD is to investigate the precipitants that initiate or exacerbate symptoms. By helping patients and their families to understand the nature of these stressors, the symptoms can be managed more effectively.

Posttraumatic Stress Disorder

The final decades of the 20th century witnessed a much greater appreciation of the pervasiveness of posttraumatic stress disorder (PTSD) in the general population. The estimated lifetime prevalence is approximately 7.8% (Kessler et al. 1995). More than one-third of the people with an index episode of PTSD fail to recover even after many years. In a survey of 2,181 persons in the Detroit area, the conditional risk of PTSD following exposure to trauma was 9.2% (Breslau et al. 1998). Moreover, the most common precipitating event reported among persons with PTSD was the sudden, unexpected death of a loved one, suggesting that the emphasis on rape, assaultive violence, and combat addresses only a portion of the population who experience PTSD.

In concert with the increasing awareness that PTSD is common, studies have documented the effects of trauma on the individual. In 1976, Horowitz published his landmark work on the impact of trauma on personality. He observed that trauma victims alternate between denying the event and compulsively repeating it through flashbacks or nightmares. Thus the mind attempts to process and organize overwhelming stimuli. Horowitz identified eight common psychological themes that follow severe trauma: 1) grief or sadness, 2) guilt about one's angry or destructive impulses, 3) fear that one will become destructive, 4) guilt about surviving, 5) fear that one will identify with the victims, 6) shame about feeling helpless and empty, 7) fear that one will repeat the trauma, and 8) intense anger directed toward the source of the trauma.

Whereas the severity of the posttraumatic symptoms was once thought to be directly proportional to the severity of the stressor, empirical studies suggest otherwise. In a prospective investigation of 51 burn patients (Perry et al. 1992), PTSD was predicted by *smaller* burns, by less perceived emotional support, and by greater emotional distress. More severe or extensive injury did *not* predict posttraumatic symptoms. The findings of this study are in keeping with the growing consensus that PTSD is perhaps more dependent on subjective factors than on the severity of the stressor. Hence, a majority of the DSM-IV Advisory Committee supported a revision of the stressor criterion that would emphasize the individual's subjective response to the event (Kilpatrick and Resnick 1993).

Despite the DSM-IV Advisory Committee's recommendation to create a new stress response category, PTSD was retained in the anxiety disorder section. However, the stressor criterion was significantly changed so that both of the following criteria are required: "1) the person has experienced, witnessed, or been confronted with an event or events that involve actual or threatened death or serious injury, or a threat to the physical integrity of self or others; 2) the person's response involved intense fear, helplessness, or horror. Note: In children, it may be expressed instead by disorganized or agitated behavior." These changes address both the importance of subjective factors and the fact that traumatic events are experienced by a greater proportion of the general population than was previously thought.

This revision in DSM-IV reflects the importance of careful psychodynamic evaluation of both the meanings the patient assigns to the event and the patient's specific psychological vulnerabilities when assessing various environmental triggers (Ursano 1987; West and Coburn 1984). In one study (Breslau et al. 1991), it was determined that the risk for developing PTSD could be linked to early separation from parents, neuroticism, family history of anxiety, and preexisting anxiety or depression. The authors concluded that a personal predisposition to develop PTSD was necessary for the symptoms to emerge. The aspects of subjective perception that have been most widely documented involve the experience of extreme fear, the attribution of personal helplessness, the perception of life threat, and the perception of potential for physical violence (March 1993).

Most people do not develop PTSD even when faced with horrifying trauma. Moreover, events that seem to be relatively low in severity may trigger PTSD in certain individuals because of the subjective meaning assigned to the event. Old traumas may be reawakened by present-day circumstances. Davidson and Foa (1993) suggest that the following predisposing vulnerability factors influence whether or not PTSD develops: 1) genetic-constitutional vulnerability to psychiatric illness; 2) adverse or traumatic experiences in childhood; 3) certain personality characteristics (such as those found in antisocial, dependent, paranoid, and borderline patients); 4) recent life stresses or changes; 5) a compromised or inadequate support system; 6) recent heavy alcohol use; and 7) a perception that the locus of control is external rather than internal. A study of 105 male Vietnam combat veterans also suggested that lower full-scale IQs may be a risk factor for PTSD (McNally and Shin 1995). Greater severity of PTSD symptoms was associated with lower intelligence, suggesting that cognitive variables may affect the individual's ability to cope with trauma. Peritraumatic dissociation may also predict a greater likelihood of developing PTSD (Griffin et al. 1997).

Although dissociative defenses may be activated to keep intense, painful affects out of awareness, the salience of traumatic memories causes them to be maintained at a high state of cognitive activation. Thus, cognitive and affective factors may work at cross-purposes and lead to the oscillation between memory intrusion and memory failure so common in PTSD. Although Freud postulated the repetition compulsion as the source of intrusive traumatic memories, we can now conclude that unresolved traumatic memories remain cognitively activated precisely because they are *affectively* inhibited by defense mechanisms such as dissociation. The unconscious monitoring system that keeps traumatic memories at bay because of their associations with painful affective states also assumes that they cannot be worked through.

The DSM-IV criteria focus primarily on circumscribed traumatic events. They do not capture the more complex form of PTSD in which the victim is subjected to prolonged and repeated trauma while in captivity under total control of the perpetrator (Herman 1992). Whereas this syndrome may coexist with the more simple forms of PTSD, a variety of symptoms extend beyond the DSM-IV definition: somatization, dissociation, protracted depression, pathological changes in identity and in relationships, repetition of harm through self-mutilation, and revictimization.

The modern psychodynamic view of PTSD has been greatly influenced by the work of Krystal (1968, 1984, 1988). Through extensive investigations of survivors of Nazi persecution, Krystal has connected impairment in the expression and tolerance of affects to psychic trauma. He noted a high prevalence of psychosomatic diseases both in concentration camp survivors and in veterans of war. Like most psychosomatic patients, these individuals also suffer from alexithymia—the inability to identify or verbalize feeling states. In Krystal's view, psychic trauma in childhood results in an *arrest* of affective development, whereas trauma in adulthood leads to a *regression* in affective development. The end result in both cases is that survivors of trauma cannot use affects as signals. Because any powerful emotion is viewed as a threat that the original trauma will return, these patients somatize affects or medicate them by abusing prescription drugs. Krystal also observed that in posttraumatic states, these individuals may suffer impairment in their ability to perform self-caring and self-soothing functions. They can no longer relax and calm themselves sufficiently to fall asleep naturally.

The treatment of choice is still unclear at this point. One implication of Krystal's observations about PTSD is that exploratory psychotherapy designed to help "reenact" the trauma may be harmful to these patients. Those with alexithymia will experience only the physiological correlates of the emotional states without registering feelings in the psychological realm, resulting in further deterioration in their psychosomatic condition (Sifneos 1973). Even getting patients to talk about the trauma may be a formidable task. Krystal (1988) pointed out that in situations of incest or child abuse, the victimized children have usually been threatened with disaster if they break their silence. He also has observed characteristic countertransference reactions to victims of disasters (Krystal 1988). Psychiatrists and other mental health professionals may avoid such patients or regard them with scorn, resulting in less-than-adequate treatment. This countertransference may be exacerbated by a certain subgroup of trauma survivors who feign the syndrome of PTSD or who fiercely hold on to their symptoms with no wish to change. For those patients with preexisting personality disorders, a stressor may represent a convenient nidus for externalizing their problems and disavowing any responsibility for their situation. If PTSD is associated with reimbursement or restitution by the government or other agency, the resistance may intensify. The devastating effects of psychic trauma may well be so unpleasant to confront that treaters will conveniently lump together genuine victims and assorted malingerers.

No treatment is wholly satisfactory for PTSD, but several authors (Brom et al. 1989; Gaston 1995; Lindy et al. 1983) have given considerable thought to the use of dynamic therapy. Massive trauma compels the ego to marshal primitive defenses—for example, denial, minimization, and projective disavowal. The sense of rage at being victimized is often projected onto others, leading some trauma survivors to become hypervigilant in an effort to protect themselves from the aggression they perceive in those around them. Other patients may use anger as a defense against more disturbing feelings of vulnerability. Litigation is sometimes pursued as a way of dealing with that anger, suggesting a powerful revenge motive as well as a wish to master feelings of helplessness by gaining some form of compensation for the suffering induced by the trauma. Guilt may be used as a defense as well. Rape victims often believe that they themselves are responsible for the rape, a defensive posture that masks the more disturbing thought that they are completely helpless in a universe where violence is random.

One well-controlled study of brief psychodynamic therapy with survivors of fires (Lindy et al. 1983) demonstrated significant improvement in the 30 patients who participated, 19 of whom met DSM-III criteria for PTSD alone or with co-morbid depression. The therapy itself consisted of 6–12 sessions of a manualized protocol that encouraged exposure to feared situations.

Most investigators agree that medication is most useful as an adjunct to psychotherapy (Friedman 1991; Solomon et al. 1992). Different forms of psychotherapy may have different effects. Brom et al. (1989) compared patients receiving dynamic therapy, hypnotherapy, and systematic desensitization. All three treatment groups showed more improvement in symptom scores than a control group. Dynamic therapy achieved greater reduction in avoidance symptoms but had less impact on intrusive symptoms. The desensitization and hypnotherapy groups showed the reverse pattern. Behavioral techniques have proven to be effective, but the relaxation necessary for behavioral modalities may be difficult for PTSD patients to achieve because of their impaired self-soothing abilities (Krystal 1984).

Individual psychotherapy must be highly personalized for patients suffering from PTSD. Reconstructions of traumatic experiences with accompanying emotional catharsis may be helpful (West and Coburn 1984), but a careful assessment of the patient's ego capacities must precede such therapeutic work. Certain patients will be overwhelmed by such reconstruction and will react with clinical deterioration. The integration of split-off traumatic experiences must be titrated in keeping with a particular patient's capacity for such integration. The therapist may have to contain projected aspects of the traumatized self until the patient is ready to reintegrate them (Peebles 1989). Clinicians must be aware that suicide attempts and suicidal preoccupation may occur with PTSD. In one study of Vietnam veterans suffering from PTSD, Hendin and Haas (1991) found that combat-related guilt was the most significant predictor of the wish to kill oneself. Many of these patients felt that they deserved to be punished because they had been transformed into murderers.

Because of these considerations, the dynamic psychotherapy of patients with PTSD must strike a balance between an observing, detached posture that allows the patient to withhold distressing information and a stance of gentle encouragement of the patient to reconstruct a complete picture of the trauma. Integrating the memory of the trauma with the patient's continuous sense of self may be an unrealistic goal, because the patient must not be forced to proceed at a pace that becomes overwhelming and disorganizing. The building of a solid therapeutic alliance in which patients feel safe is critical for the therapy to succeed. Education about common reactions to trauma may facilitate such an alliance. An empathic validation of patients' right to feel the way they do may also further the alliance.

Lindy (1996) has identified four kinds of transferences that are common with PTSD patients: 1) the transfer of figures involved in the traumatic event onto the therapist, 2) the transfer of specific disavowed memories of the traumatic event onto the treatment situation, 3) the transfer onto the therapist of intrapsychic functions in the patient that had been distorted as a result of the trauma (with the hope that healthier function will be restored), and 4) the transfer onto the therapist of an omnipotent and wise role in which the therapist can help the patient sort out what happened and restore a sense of personal meaning.

All of these transferences, of course, evoke corresponding countertransferences. The therapist, intent on rescuing the patient from the horrible trauma he or she has experienced, may develop fantasies of omnipotence. Alternatively, the therapist may feel overwhelmed, angry, and helpless in response to the patient's seeming resistance to letting go of the trauma. When the patient is particularly tenacious in holding on to memories of the trauma, the therapist may become indifferent and hopeless.

Goals of psychotherapy with these patients should be modest in most cases—cure or complete removal of symptoms may be too ambitious. A more reasonable ambition is to halt any further decline, support areas of adequate functioning, and reestablish the patient's personal integrity (Lindy et al. 1984). Some reason for optimism may be construed in the finding that natural remission occurs within 3 months in more than half of all acute PTSD cases following rape (Davidson and Foa 1993), and provision of support may be all that is necessary.

Acute Stress Disorder

Acute stress disorder (ASD) has the same stressor criteria as PTSD—the person must have experienced an event that involves threat of death or serious injury and must have responded to it with intense feelings of helplessness, horror, or fear. However, the symptoms resulting from the stressor must have emerged within 4 weeks of the traumatic event and must have lasted for a minimum of 2 days and a maximum of 4 weeks. In other words, this category allows for PTSD-like syndromes that may appear sooner than PTSD, last for a briefer time, or serve as a prodrome to a more typical case of PTSD.

In addition to criteria that reflect PTSD symptoms (such as reexperiencing the event, avoiding stimuli that arouse memories of the trauma, and displaying hyperarousal), the diagnosis of ASD also requires at least three of the following dissociative symptoms: amnesia for important aspects of the trauma; depersonalization; derealization; a decreased awareness of one's surroundings; or a subjective sense of detachment, numbing, or lack of emotional responsiveness. The treatment for this condition is fundamentally the same as that for other forms of dissociative disorder covered in Chapter 10 under "General Considerations."

Generalized Anxiety Disorder

The DSM-IV criteria for generalized anxiety disorder (GAD) have sought to clarify the boundary between this disorder and normal worry. The anxiety must be excessive, difficult to control, and frequent enough that it occurs more days than not for at least a 6-month period. It must also cause clinically significant distress or impair occupational, social, or other important areas of functioning. The diagnosis requires that the focus of the anxiety not be confined to features of other Axis I disorders, such as worry about having a panic attack, concern about contamination, fear of being embarrassed in public, and so forth. The anxiety must be pervasive enough that the patient focuses on a number of activities or events as targets of the anxiety. The quality of life for GAD patients is materially affected by their continual apprehensions about their future, their current life circumstances, their financial situation, the possibility of harm coming to their family members, and assorted other aspects of life. They may experience physical tension and mild symptoms of sympathetic discharge, but nothing approaching the level of panic disorder.

GAD continues to be controversial. Of all the anxiety disorders, it is associated with the highest rate of comorbidity. In a multicenter study (Goisman et al. 1995), almost 90% of patients with GAD had a lifetime history of at least one other anxiety disorder. Although GAD may represent a temperamental vulnerability on Axis II, as some critics of DSM-IV suggest, it nevertheless has a fairly high degree of construct validity (Brown et al. 1994). At any rate, clinicians commonly encounter patients who are chronic worriers, and because many of these patients have difficulty working because of their pervasive anxiety, treatment may be extremely important for them.

When psychodynamic clinicians evaluate patients whose chief complaint is anxiety, they must make a critical decision about which treatment to prescribe—a decision that is likely to be influenced by theoretical bias, by political forces in contemporary psychiatry, and by concerns about cost-effectiveness. Shectman et al. (1989) have nicely captured the nature of this dilemma:

> Are we growth facilitators, or are we removers and suppressors of circumscribed psychological distress? Just what is the object of our efforts? In its most extreme form, do we address the problem (i.e., the symptom) in a patient or deal with a patient who has a problem? And who is to make the determination about such matters: the patient? us? both of us together? But what if there is a difference of opinion about what ought or should be done? (p. 494)

Turning to the literature can, of course, provide essential information to help with such decisions. Numerous studies demonstrate the efficacy of behavioral techniques, pharmacotherapeutic techniques, and even brief dynamic psychotherapy in treating patients with anxiety. However, large-scale group designs tell clinicians nothing about how to determine which individual is likely to benefit from which treatment (Barlow and Beck 1984).

Anxiety appears in response to numerous situations over the course of the life cycle. Whether patients should resort to medication each time they are anxious should be a question of considerable concern to psychiatrists. One can eliminate physiological components of anxiety with medication without addressing the cognitive aspects of the worry that remain. The following clinical vignette is illustrative:

> Ms. O was a 23-year-old graduate student who came for consultation because of periodic episodes of intense anxiety. About three times a month she would begin worrying about death while lying in bed. Typically, she would start ruminating in the following manner: "I am 23 now; in only 7 years, I'll be 30. Then I'll be 40, and my kids will be grown. Then I'll be a grandparent and retire, and then I'll die." These thoughts led to concerns that her parents, both of whom were alive and well, would soon die. As these thoughts escalated, the anxiety she experienced increased to the point where her heart was racing and she could not fall asleep.

After a diagnostic evaluation, several possible interventions were discussed with her: prescription of antianxiety medication, psychotherapeutic exploration of the causes of anxiety, or a combination of the two. She replied pointedly that she had no interest in medication. "How can a pill make my fear of death go away?" she inquired. She made it clear that she wanted to understand the origins of her anxiety so she could master her fears.

She embarked on a course of psychotherapy that led to increasing ideational mastery over the disturbing affect. Her therapist empathized with Ms. O regarding the frightening nature of death but also noted that concerns about living often contributed to fears about death. He asked her what was going on in her life that might contribute to her anxiety. She immediately replied that it had nothing to do with her husband's being stationed overseas. Her eyes started to tear up, and her therapist handed her a box of tissues.

Ms. O ignored the box of tissues and continued talking about how young people were dying of AIDS and cancer. Her therapist asked her why she had not taken a tissue when it was offered to her. She said she thought it would have been a sign of weakness. Her therapist inquired if it had always been difficult for her to acknowledge that she needed the help of other people. She responded that all her life everyone had told her their problems, and she could never acknowledge that she had problems and needed help from others. Her therapist suggested to her that she might need to present a pseudoindependent facade as a way of denying her neediness. She readily acknowledged that she dreaded the feeling of weakness associated with being vulnerable and needy. Her therapist pointed out to her that death was the ultimate situation of vulnerability and neediness. She then responded that the worst thing about death, in her mind, would be having to go through it alone.

As Ms. O continued to explore sources of her anxiety, she revealed a history of having significant difficulties with the expression of anger. She feared that her anger would come out in an explosion that would drive others away from her. Her nighttime anxiety often arose after seeing violent movies. She said it bothered her a great deal that others expressed their anger in such a violent, forthright manner while she worked so diligently to control hers. Further psychotherapeutic exploration led to the uncovering of a good deal of anger at her father that she had been unable to express. Her unconscious concern was that her anger would be so explosive that it would destroy him.

After 2 months of psychotherapy, the episodes of intense anxiety disappeared. Ms. O still worried about death to some extent, but she had developed greater mastery over the fear as she understood the underlying concerns about the impact of her anger and her fears of being abandoned and alone. In other words, a broadened ideational mastery of the affect enabled her to control her symptoms

The case of Ms. O illustrates the time-honored principle that in clinical psychiatry we must adapt the treatment to the patient. Contrary to the point of view of some third-party payers, the most appropriate treatment for a patient is not necessarily the most cost-effective. While some clinicians would argue that an anti-anxiety agent might have more quickly and more cheaply eliminated the patient's symptom, Ms. O was asking for something other than symptom relief. As Barber and Luborsky (1991) have argued, specific anxiety disorder diagnoses require different treatments in different circumstances with different patients. Psychodynamic psychotherapy may be the treatment of choice for the patient who is psychologically minded, motivated to understand the matrix from which the symptom arises, and willing to invest the time, money, and effort in a therapy process. Ms. O did not ask for medication and would probably not have taken it if it had been prescribed.

Antianxiety agents may decrease or remove anxiety, but they may ultimately prove to be a dead-end solution. The most obvious problem is that medication is likely to be effective only as long as the patient continues to take it. The frequency of relapse after patients stop taking benzodiazepines, for example, is estimated at 63%–81% (Rickels et al. 1980, 1986). Pharmacotherapeutic measures also fail to address the underlying factors that create the anxiety.

Medication may at times be a crucial short-term adjunct to psychotherapeutic interventions for GAD. However, it must not be oversold to patients as a definitive treatment for anxiety. Patients need to learn to tolerate anxiety as a meaningful signal in the course of psychotherapy. Those with reasonably good ego strength come to view anxiety as a window into the unconscious.

The treatment of anxiety must begin with a thoughtful and thorough psychodynamic evaluation, with anxiety conceptualized as a multidetermined "tip of the iceberg." The clinician must diagnose the nature of the patient's underlying fear (see Table 9–1). In addition, the role of anxiety in the patient's personality organization must be assessed. What is the ego's capacity to tolerate anxiety and to endure an exploration of the anxiety's origins? Do particular constellations of internal object relations seem to evoke anxiety? Is the anxiety connected with concerns about dissolution of the self? Prescribing the appropriate psychodynamic intervention depends partly on the patient's clinical situation and interests. Some patients may quickly respond well to brief educational and clarifying comments and then require no further treatment. Others who have highly focal symptoms and certain notable ego strengths may have their anxiety ameliorated with brief dynamic therapy. Neurotic patients with fewer focal complaints and a more thoroughgoing interest in fundamental personality change may require psychoanalysis. Finally, patients with serious character pathology who complain of anxiety will need long-term expressive-supportive psychotherapy before they are likely to experience symptom relief.

When psychodynamic therapy is undertaken with GAD patients, the therapist needs to be tolerant of the patient's focus on somatic symptoms and other worries that sound rather superficial. A working hypothesis regarding the defensive function is that focusing on these worries distracts the patient from more disturbing underlying concerns. This characteristic defensive pattern of avoidance may be linked to insecure conflicted attachment in childhood, as well as to early traumas (Crits-Christoph et al. 1995). After listening empathically to the patient's presenting concerns, the therapist can begin to inquire about family relationships, interpersonal difficulties, and the patient's work situation. The therapist then can make linkages among the various situations of worry so that patterns of core conflicts in relationships begin to emerge. As in all dynamic therapy, some of the most persuasive evidence of these patterns may emerge in the transference relationship. As the sources of anxiety become linked to recurrent conflicts, the patient comes to realize that the anxiety can be mastered through an understanding of the unconscious expectations of failure in relationships and at work. A positive outcome may also be a capacity to use anxiety as a signal of a recurrent conflict that leads to introspection and further understanding.

References

Abend SM: Psychoanalytic psychotherapy, in Handbook of Phobia Therapy: Rapid Symptom Relief in Anxiety Disorders. Edited by Lindemann C. Northvale, NJ, Jason Aronson, 1989

American Psychiatric Association: Diagnostic and Statistical Manual of Mental Disorders, 3rd Edition. Washington, DC, American Psychiatric Association, 1980

American Psychiatric Association: Diagnostic and Statistical Manual of Mental Disorders, 3rd Edition, Revised. Washington, DC, American Psychiatric Association, 1987

American Psychiatric Association: Diagnostic and Statistical Manual of Mental Disorders, 4th Edition. Washington, DC, American Psychiatric Association 1994

Appelbaum SA: The Anatomy of Change: A Menninger Report on Testing the Effects of Psychotherapy. New York, Plenum, 1977

Baer L, Jenike MA: Introduction, in Obsessive-Compulsive Disorders: Theory and Management. Edited by Jenike MA, Baer L, Minichiello WE. Littleton, MA, PSG Pub Co, 1986, pp 1–9

Barber JP, Luborsky L: A psychodynamic view of simple phobia and prescriptive matching: a commentary. Psychotherapy 28:469–472, 1991

Barlow DH, Beck JG: The psychosocial treatment of anxiety disorders: current status, future directions, in Psychotherapy Research: Where Are We and Where Should We Go? Edited by Williams JBW, Spitzer RL. New York, Guilford, 1984, pp 29–69

Black A: The natural history of obsessional neurosis, in Obsessional States. Edited by Beech HR. London, Methuen, 1974, pp 19–54

Breslau N, Davis GC, Andreski P, et al: Traumatic events and posttraumatic stress disorder in an urban population of young adults. Arch Gen Psychiatry 48:216–222, 1991

Breslau N, Kessler RC, Chilcoat HD, et al: Trauma and posttraumatic stress disorder in the community: the 1996 Detroit Area Survey of Trauma. Arch Gen Psychiatry 55:626–632, 1998

Brom D, Kleber RJ, Defares PB: Brief psychotherapy for posttraumatic stress disorders. J Consult Clin Psychol 57:607–612, 1989

Brown TA, Barlow DH, Liebowitz MR: The empirical basis of generalized anxiety disorder. Am J Psychiatry 151:1272–1280, 1994

Busch FN, Cooper AM, Klerman GL, et al: Neurophysiological, cognitive-behavioral, and psychoanalytic approaches to panic disorder: toward an integration. Psychoanalytic Inquiry 11:316–332, 1991

Busch FN, Shear MK, Cooper AM, et al: An empirical study of defense mechanisms in panic disorder. J Nerv Ment Dis 183:299–303, 1995

Buttolph ML, Holland AD: Obsessive-compulsive disorders in pregnancy and childbirth, in Obsessive-Compulsive Disorders: Theory and Management, 2nd Edition. Edited by Jenike MA, Baer L, Minichiello WE. Chicago, IL, Year Book Medical, 1990, pp 89–95

Calvocoressi L, Lewis B, Harris M, et al.: Family accommodation in obsessive-compulsive disorder. Am J Psychiatry 152:441–443, 1995

Clomipramine Collaborative Study Group: Clomipramine in the treatment of patients with obsessive-compulsive disorder. Arch Gen Psychiatry 48:730–738, 1991

Cooper AM: Will neurobiology influence psychoanalysis? Am J Psychiatry 142:1395–1402, 1985

Cornfield RB, Malen RL: A multidimensional view of the obsessive character. Compr Psychiatry 19:73–78, 1978

Crits-Christoph P, Crits-Christoph K, Wolf-Palacio D, et al.: Brief supportive-expressive psychodynamic therapy for general anxiety disorder, in Dynamic Therapies for Psychiatric Disorders (Axis I). Edited by Barber JP, Crits-Christoph P. New York, Basic Books, 1995, pp 43–83

Davidson JRT, Foa EB (eds): Epilogue, in Posttraumatic Stress Disorder: DSM-IV and Beyond. Washington, DC, American Psychiatric Press, 1993, pp 229–235

Elkins R, Rapoport JL, Lipsky A: Obsessive-compulsive disorder of childhood and adolescence: a neurobiological viewpoint. Journal of the American Academy of Child Psychiatry 19:511–524, 1980

Faravelli C, Pallanti S: Recent life events and panic disorder. Am J Psychiatry 146:622–626, 1989

Freud S: On the grounds for detaching a particular syndrome from neurasthenia under the description "anxiety neurosis" (1895), in The Standard Edition of the Complete Psychological Works of Sigmund Freud, Vol 3. Translated and edited by Strachey J. London, Hogarth Press, 1962, pp 85–117

Freud S: Inhibitions, symptoms and anxiety (1926), in The Standard Edition of the Complete Psychological Works of Sigmund Freud, Vol 20. Translated and edited by Strachey J. London, Hogarth Press, 1959, pp 75–175

Friedman MJ: Biological approaches to the diagnosis and treatment of post-traumatic stress disorder. J Trauma Stress 4(1):67–91, 1991

Gabbard GO: Psychodynamics of panic disorder and social phobia. Bull Menninger Clin 56 (2, suppl A):A3–A13, 1992

Gabbard GO, Nemiah JC: Multiple determinants of anxiety in a patient with borderline personality disorder. Bull Menninger Clin 49:161–172, 1985

Gaston L: Dynamic therapy for post-traumatic stress disorder, in Dynamic Therapies for Psychiatric Disorders (Axis I). Edited by Barber JP, Crits-Christoph P. New York, Basic Books, 1995, pp 161–192

Goisman RM, Goldenberg I, Vasile RG, et al: Comorbidity of anxiety disorders in a multicenter anxiety study. Compr Psychiatry 36:303–311, 1995

Greist JH, Jefferson JW: Obsessive-compulsive disorder, in Treatments of Psychiatric Disorders, 2nd Edition, Vol 2. Washington, DC, American Psychiatric Press, 1995, pp 1477–1498

Griffin MG, Resick PA, Mechanic MB: Objective assessment of peritraumatic dissociation: psychophysiological indicators. Am J Psychiatry 154:1081–1088, 1997

Hendin H, Haas AP: Suicide and guilt as manifestations of PTSD in Vietnam combat veterans. Am J Psychiatry 148:586–591, 1991

Herman JL: Complex PTSD: a syndrome in survivors of prolonged and repeated trauma. J Trauma Stress 5:377–391, 1992

Hollander E, Schiffman E, Cohen B, et al: Signs of central nervous system dysfunction in obsessive-compulsive disorder. Arch Gen Psychiatry 47:27–32, 1990

Horowitz MJ: Stress Response Syndromes. New York, Jason Aronson, 1976

Jenike MA, Baer L, Minichiello WE (eds): Obsessive-Compulsive Disorders: Theory and Management. Littleton, MA, PSG Pub Co, 1986

Jenike MA, Breiter HC, Baer L, et al: Cerebral structural abnormalities in obsessive-compulsive disorder: a quantitative morphometric magnetic resonance imaging study. Arch Gen Psychiatry 53:625–632, 1996

Kagan J, Reznick JS, Snidman N: Biological bases of childhood shyness. Science 240: 167–171, 1988

Karno M, Golding JM, Sorenson SB: The epidemiology of obsessive-compulsive disorder in five U.S. communities. Arch Gen Psychiatry 45:1094–1099, 1988

Kendler KS, Neale MC, Kessler RC, et al: Childhood parental loss and adult psychopathology in women: a twin study perspective. Arch Gen Psychiatry 49:109–116, 1992a

Kendler KS, Neale MC, Kessler RC, et al: The genetic epidemiology of phobias in women: the interrelationship of agoraphobia, social phobia, situational phobia, and simple phobia. Arch Gen Psychiatry 49:273–281, 1992b

Kessler RC, Sonnega A, Bromet E, et al: Posttraumatic stress disorder in the National Comorbidity Survey. Arch Gen Psychiatry 52:1048–1060, 1995

Kilpatrick DG, Resnick HS: Appendix III: a description of the posttraumatic stress disorder field trial, in Posttraumatic Stress Disorder: DSM-IV and Beyond. Edited by Davidson JRT, Foa EB. Washington, DC, American Psychiatric Press, 1993, pp 243–250

Krystal H (ed): Massive Psychic Trauma. New York, International Universities Press, 1968

Krystal H: Psychoanalytic views on human emotional damages, in Post-Traumatic Stress Disorder: Psychological and Biological Sequelae. Edited by van der Kolk BA. Washington, DC, American Psychiatric Press, 1984, pp 1–28

Krystal H: Integration and Self-Healing: Affect, Trauma, Alexithymia. Hillsdale, NJ, Analytic Press, 1988

Lesch KP, Bengel D, Heils A, et al: Association of anxiety-related traits with a polymorphism in the serotonin transporter gene regulatory region. Science 274:1527–1531, 1996

Lieberman J: Evidence for a biological hypothesis of obsessive-compulsive disorder. Neuropsychobiology 11:14–21, 1984

Lindy JD: Psychoanalytic psychotherapy of posttraumatic stress disorder: the nature of the therapeutic relationship, in Traumatic Stress: The Effects of Overwhelming Experience on Mind, Body, and Society. Edited by van der Kolk BA, McFarlane AC, Weisaeth L. New York, Guilford, 1996, pp 525–536

Lindy JD, Green BL, Grace MC, et al: Psychotherapy with survivors of the Beverly Hills Supper Club fire. Am J Psychother 37:593–610, 1983

Lindy JD, Grace MC, Green BL: Building a conceptual bridge between civilian trauma and war trauma: preliminary psychological findings from a clinical sample of Vietnam veterans, in Post-Traumatic Stress Disorder: Psychological and Biological Sequelae. Edited by van der Kolk BA. Washington, DC, American Psychiatric Press, 1984, pp 43–57

Manassis K, Bradley S, Goldberg S, et al: Attachment in mothers with anxiety disorders and their children. J Am Acad Child Adolesc Psychiatry 33:1106–1113, 1994

March JS: What constitutes a stressor? the "criterion A" issue, in Posttraumatic Stress Disorder: DSM-IV and Beyond. Edited by Davidson JRT, Foa EB. Washington, DC, American Psychiatric Press, 1993, pp 37–54

McNally RJ, Shin LM: Association of intelligence with severity of posttraumatic stress disorder symptoms in Vietnam combat veterans. Am J Psychiatry 152:936–938, 1995

Milrod B: Unconscious pregnancy fantasies as an underlying dynamism in panic disorder. J Am Psychoanal Assoc 46:673–790, 1998

Milrod B, Shear MK: Psychodynamic treatment of panic: three case histories. Hospital and Community Psychiatry 42:311–312, 1991

Milrod BL, Busch FN, Cooper AM, et al: Manual of Panic-Focused Psychodynamic Psychotherapy. Washington, DC, American Psychiatric Press, 1997

Nemiah JC: A psychoanalytic view of phobias. Am J Psychoanal 41:115–120, 1981

Nemiah JC: The psychodynamic view of anxiety, in Diagnosis and Treatment of Anxiety Disorders. Edited by Pasnau RO. Washington, DC, American Psychiatric Press, 1984, pp 115–137

Nemiah JC: Psychoneurotic disorders, in The New Harvard Guide to Psychiatry. Edited by Nicholi AM Jr. Cambridge, MA, Belknap Press of Harvard University Press, 1988, pp 234–258

Neziroglu F, Anemone R, Yaryura-Tobias JA: Onset of obsessive-compulsive disorder in pregnancy. Am J Psychiatry 149:947–950, 1992

Peebles MJ: Posttraumatic stress disorder: a historical perspective on diagnosis and treatment. Bull Menninger Clin 53:274–286, 1989

Perry S, Difede J, Musngi G, et al: Predictors of posttraumatic stress disorder after burn injury. Am J Psychiatry 149:931–935, 1992

Perse T: Obsessive-compulsive disorder: a treatment review. J Clin Psychiatry 49:48–55, 1988

Pollard CA, Henderson JG: Four types of social phobia in a community sample. J Nerv Ment Dis 176:440–445, 1988

Purcell R, Maruff P, Kyrios M, et al: Neuropsychological deficits in obsessive-compulsive disorder: a comparison with unipolar depression, panic disorder, and normal controls. Arch Gen Psychiatry 55:415–423, 1998

Regier DA, Boyd JH, Burke JD, et al: One-month prevalence of mental disorders in the United States. Arch Gen Psychiatry 45:977–986, 1988

Reich JH: DSM-III personality disorders and the outcome of treated panic disorder. Am J Psychiatry 145:1149–1152, 1988

Rickels K, Case WG, Diamond L: Relapse after short-term drug therapy in neurotic outpatients. International Pharmacopsychiatry 15:186–192, 1980

Rickels K, Case WG, Downing RW, et al: One-year follow-up of anxious patients treated with diazepam. J Clin Psychopharmacol 6:32–36, 1986

Rosenbaum JF, Biederman J, Bolduc EA, et al: Comorbidity of parental anxiety disorders as risk for childhood-onset anxiety in inhibited children. Am J Psychiatry 149:475–481, 1992

Roy-Byrne PP, Geraci M, Uhde TW: Life events of the onset of panic disorder. Am J Psychiatry 143:1424–1427, 1986

Schneier FR, Johnson J, Hornig CD, et al: Social phobia: comorbidity and morbidity in an epidemiological sample. Arch Gen Psychiatry 49:282–288, 1992

Shear MK: Factors in the etiology and pathogenesis of panic disorder: revisiting the attachment-separation paradigm. Am J Psychiatry 153 (suppl):125–136, 1996

Shear MK, Fyer AJ, Ball G, et al: Vulnerability to sodium lactate in panic disorder patients given cognitive-behavioral therapy. Am J Psychiatry 148:795–797, 1991

Shectman F, Ross JL, Simpson W: Controversial issues in psychodynamic and symptom-focused treatment. Bull Menninger Clin 53:493–500, 1989

Siegal RS, Rosen IC: Character style and anxiety tolerance: a study of intrapsychic change, in Research in Psychotherapy, Vol 2. Edited by Strupp H, Luborsky L. Baltimore, MD, French-Bray Printing Co, 1962, pp 206–217

Sifneos PE: Short-Term Psychotherapy and Emotional Crisis. Cambridge, MA, Harvard University Press, 1972

Sifneos PE: The prevalence of "alexithymic" characteristics in psychosomatic patients. Psychother Psychosom 22:257–262, 1973

Solomon SD, Gerrity ET, Muff AM: Efficacy of treatment of posttraumatic stress disorder: an empirical review. JAMA 268:633–638, 1992

Stein MB, Walker JR, Anderson G, et al: Childhood physical and sexual abuse in patients with anxiety disorders and in a community sample. Am J Psychiatry 153:275–277,1996

Turner SM, Beidel DC, Nathan RS: Biological factors in obsessive-compulsive disorder. Psychol Bull 97:430–450, 1985

Ursano RJ: Posttraumatic stress disorder: the stressor criterion (commentary). J Nerv Ment Dis 175:273–275, 1987

West LJ, Coburn K: Posttraumatic anxiety, in Diagnosis and Treatment of Anxiety Disorders. Edited by Pasnau RO. Washington, DC, American Psychiatric Press, 1984, pp 79–133

White K, Cole JO: Is there a drug treatment for obsessive-compulsive disorder? (forum). Harvard Medical School Mental Health Letter 5(3):8, 1988

Wiborg IM, Dahl AA: Does brief dynamic psychotherapy reduce the relapse rate of panic disorder? Arch Gen Psychiatry 53:689–694, 1996

Zetin M, Kramer MA: Obsessive-compulsive disorder. Hospital and Community Psychiatry 43:689–699, 1992

Zetzel ER: The Capacity for Emotional Growth. New York, International Universities Press, 1970

Zitrin CM, Klein DF, Woerner MG: Behavior therapy, supportive psychotherapy, imipramine, and phobias. Arch Gen Psychiatry 35:307–316, 1978

C H A P T E R
10

Dissociative Disorders

At the dawn of dynamic psychiatry, two men, Janet and Freud, were perplexed by a variety of hysterical phenomena they were observing. To explain altered states of consciousness such as amnesia and fugue, Janet postulated that memories of trauma persist as relatively unassimilated fixed ideas that serve as foci for the development of such states. He suggested that under specific circumstances, nervous energies holding mental functions together could be lowered sufficiently that certain functions would escape central control, a process he referred to as dissociation.

Freud, on the other hand, postulated the concept of repression, an active banishment of certain mental contents from conscious awareness into the domain of the dynamic unconscious. While these unacceptable feelings remained out of awareness, they continued to be active in the unconscious mind and might reemerge in the form of symptoms. Freud and Janet parted ways on this point, in that Freud postulated that hysterical phenomena resulted from active mental processes, while Janet argued for the role of passive mental processes (Nemiah 1989).

In recent years, psychiatric interest in dissociation has grown in conjunction with the interest in posttraumatic stress disorder (PTSD) and responses to trauma in general. Psychoanalytic thinking traditionally focused on unconscious needs, wishes, and drives in concert with the defenses against them. Intrapsychic fantasy played a greater role than external trauma. Dissociative disorders and PTSD have leveled the playing field so that contemporary psychodynamic clinicians now give equal weight to the pathogenetic influences of real events.

Pathological forms of dissociation are identified by disturbances or alterations in the normally integrative functions of memory, identity, or consciousness (Putnam 1991). DSM-IV (American Psychiatric Association 1994) includes the following diagnostic entities within the category of dissociative disorders: dissociative identity disorder (multiple personality disorder), depersonalization disorder, dissociative disorder not otherwise specified, dissociative amnesia, and dissociative fugue (these last two disorders have been changed from psychogenic amnesia and psychogenic fugue.

General Considerations

Before delving into the specific dissociative disorders, some general considerations about the phenomenon of dissociation are necessary to provide a background context for understanding the individual dissociative disorders. The link between hypnotizability and dissociation has been observed for many years, and it has been well documented that hysterical patients who manifest dissociative symptoms are also highly hypnotizable (Bliss 1980; Spiegel 1984; Spiegel and Fink 1979; Steingard and Frankel 1985). However, there are currently conflicting views about the conceptual relationship between hypnosis and dissociation (Bremner and Marmar 1998). Frankel (1990) suggested that dissociation and hypnotizability are closely related but different phenomena that are difficult to distinguish in groups high in both capacities. Many symptoms typical of dissociative disorders can be elicited with hypnosis in certain subjects who are highly hypnotizable (Putnam 1991). Although some experts view the idea of hypnotic trance as a metaphor for dissociative states, Spiegel (1990) referred to hypnosis as "controlled dissociation elicited in a structured setting" (p. 247). Hypnosis and severe states of dissociation have in common the characteristic of complete absorption in certain aspects of experience combined with complete obliviousness to other aspects.

In essence, dissociation represents a failure to integrate aspects of perception, memory, identity, and consciousness. Minor instances of dissociation, such as "highway hypnosis," transient feelings of strangeness, or "spacing out," are common phenomena in the general population. Extensive empirical evidence suggests that dissociation occurs especially as a defense against trauma. High frequencies of dissociative symptoms have been documented in the wake of firestorms (Koopman et al. 1994), earthquakes (Cardeña and Spiegel 1993), and war combat (Marmar et al. 1994) and in those who have witnessed an execution (Freinkel et al. 1994). Dissociation allows individuals to retain an illusion of psychological control when they experience a sense of helplessness and loss of control over their bodies. Dissociative defenses serve the dual function of helping victims remove themselves from a traumatic event while it is occurring and delaying the necessary working through that places the event in perspective with the rest of their lives.

Trauma itself can be regarded as a sudden discontinuity in experience (Spiegel 1997). Dissociation during trauma leads to a discontinuous memory storage process as well. Data are accumulating that suggest physiological differences between those who dissociate and those who do not. In a study of 85 rape victims (Griffin et al. 1997), individuals who were rated as high in peritraumatic dissociation manifested a significantly different pattern of physiological response compared with those who were rated low in dissociation. The high-dissociation group showed suppression of autonomic physiological responses, which is consistent with the numbing phenomenon typical of dissociative disorders. The victims who were high in dissociation were also more likely to have PTSD symptoms, a finding providing further evidence of a link between dissociation and the pathogenesis of PTSD, as noted in Chapter 9.

Approximately 25%–50% of trauma victims experience some kind of detachment from the trauma, while others have partial to total amnesia for the event (Spiegel 1991). These mental mechanisms allow victims to compartmentalize the experience so that it is no longer accessible to consciousness—it is as though the trauma did not happen to them.

Magnetic resonance imaging (MRI) studies of Vietnam veterans have demonstrated reduced right hippocampal volume in those who have PTSD compared with those who do not (Bremner et al. 1995). The hippocampus is pivotal in the storage and retrieval of memory, leading some researchers to hypothesize that the memory difficulties associated with dissociation are linked to damage in that region (Spiegel 1997). Yehuda (1997) has suggested that heightened responsiveness of the hypothalamic-pituitary-adrenal axis leads to an increase in the glucocorticoid receptor responsiveness that results in hippocampal atrophy. If high degrees of stress associated with a traumatic event effectively shut down the hippocampus, then autobiographical memory for that event will be compromised (Allen et al. 1999; LeDoux 1996). A common defensive response to trauma is dissociative detachment as a way of warding off intensive affects. Allen et al. (1999) have pointed out that this detachment greatly narrows the individual's field of awareness, so that decreased recognition of the context may interfere with the process of elaborative encoding of the memory. Without the reflective thinking required for storage, the memory is not integrated into autobiographical narrative. These authors also suggest that dissociative detachment may involve a problem with cortical disconnectivity (Krystal et al. 1995) that interferes with higher cognitive functions such as language production. Rauch and Shin (1997) have found that PTSD is associated with hypoactivity in Broca's area on positron emission tomography (PET) scans. The combination of hippocampal damage and hypoactivity in Broca's area suggests an impaired ability to cope with memories in lexical terms. Hence, dissociative phenomena may be helpful initially as a defense mechanism but may ultimately limit the brain's ability to cope with traumatic memories (Spiegel 1997).

Physiological correlations with dissociation also raise the possibility of genetic influences on vulnerability to dissociation. In a study of 177 monozygotic and 152 dizygotic volunteer twin pairs from the general population (Jang et al. 1998), subjects completed two measures of dissociative capacity taken from the Dissociative Experiences Scale (DES), a 28-item self-report questionnaire with established reliability and validity (Putnam 1991). The results showed that genetic influences accounted for 48% and 55% of the variance in scales measuring pathological and nonpathological dissociative experience, respectively. The investigators concluded that common genetic factors underlie pathological and nonpathological dissociative capacity. On the other hand, a similar twin study (Waller and Ross 1997) found no evidence for heritability.

The link between dissociation and childhood trauma has been established in a number of studies. In one investigation (Brodsky et al. 1995), among the 50% of subjects who had DES scores indicating pathological levels of dissociation, 60% reported a history of childhood physical and/or sexual abuse. In another study (Mulder et al. 1998) of 1,028 randomly selected individuals, 6.3% were found to suffer from three or more frequently occurring dissociative symptoms, and these individuals had a five-times-higher rate of childhood physical abuse and a two-and-a-half-times-higher rate of childhood sexual abuse. However, logistic regression modeling showed that although physical abuse and current psychiatric illness were directly related to high rates of dissociative symptoms, the influence of sexual abuse was indirect and appeared to be due to its associations with current psychiatric illness and with physical abuse. The investigators concluded that childhood physical abuse was directly related to dissociation, whereas childhood sexual abuse had a much weaker correlation. Hence, although a defensive use of dissociation is clearly linked to trauma, the parameters of that defense are complex and in need of further research.

Dissociative Disorders

Psychodynamic Understanding

Both repression and dissociation are defense mechanisms, and in both, the contents of the mind are banished from awareness. They differ, however, in the way the dismissed mental contents are handled. In the case of repression, a horizontal split is created by the repression barrier, and the material is transferred to the dynamic unconscious. By contrast, a vertical split is created in dissociation so that mental contents exist in a series of parallel consciousnesses (Kluft 1991a). Moreover, the repression model has usually been invoked as a response to forbidden wishes, such as oedipal desires for the opposite-sex parent, rather than to external events. Hence, dissociation may be mobilized by trauma, whereas repression is activated by highly conflictual wishes (Spiegel 1990). Once mobilized, however, dissociation can be reactivated by wishes and desires.

In most cases of dissociation, disparate self-schemas, or representations of the self, must be maintained in separate mental compartments because they are in conflict with one another (Horowitz 1986). Memories of the traumatized self must be dissociated because they are inconsistent with the everyday self that appears to be in full control. One manager of a convenience store, for example, had dissociated a trauma involving anal rape during a holdup of the store because the image of himself as subjugated and humiliated in that situation was completely in conflict with his usual sense of himself as a manager who could "take charge" of all situations.

Dissociative amnesia, dissociative fugue, dissociative identity disorder, and acute stress disorder (classified with the anxiety disorders [see Chapter 9]) have common psychodynamic underpinnings. Dissociative amnesia involves one or more episodes of inability to recall an important personal trauma; dissociative fugue involves sudden, unexpected travel away from home associated with the inability to recall one's past and confusion about one's personal identity. Dissociative identity disorder (DID), formerly known as multiple personality disorder, involves the presence of two or more distinct identities or personality states, each with its own relatively enduring pattern of perceiving, relating to, and thinking about the environment and the self. At least two of these identities or personality states must recurrently take control of the person's behavior. DID is also characterized by a gap in recollection of important personal information that is too extensive to be explained by ordinary forgetfulness.

All of these disorders are frequently misdiagnosed. In a typical case of DID, an average of 7 years of treatment elapses before the DID diagnosis is established (Loewenstein and Ross 1992; Putnam et al. 1986). Diagnosis of DID is particularly problematic because 80% of DID patients have only certain "windows of diagnosability" during which their condition is clearly discernible to clinicians (Kluft 1991a). Diagnostic rigor has been improved by the DES, which can be used effectively to identify high-risk patients. However, a definitive diagnosis requires the use of a structured interview such as the Structured Clinical Interview for Dissociative Disorders (SCID-D) (Steinberg et al. 1991).

Dissociative amnesia may be the most common of the dissociative disorders (Coons 1998), but the diagnosis is often complicated by the fact that almost all patients with this condition have additional psychiatric diagnoses. Moreover, unless specifically asked, many patients do not report periods of amnesia because of the very nature of amnestic episodes. The patient may well feel that everyone experiences memory gaps, so that the lost time periods are not remarkable or worth reporting to the clinician.

Allen et al. (1999) stress the need to distinguish between the reversible memory failures associated with DID and dissociative amnesia and the irreversible memory discontinuities (during which autobiographical memories were not encoded and are therefore not retrievable) associated with dissociative detachment. There is a risk of overdiagnosing DID if all memory gaps are assumed to be attributable to dissociative amnesia, which entails recoverable memories.

Sensationalized cases of DID in the media do not reflect the fact that most patients with this disorder are highly secretive and prefer to conceal their symptoms. The separate dissociated self-states, or "alters," are first deployed adaptively in an attempt on the part of the abused child to distance him- or herself from the traumatic experience. The alters soon gain secondary forms of autonomy, and a patient may hold a quasi-delusional belief in their separateness. The patient's personality actually consists of the sum total of all the personalities, of course, and Putnam (1989) clarified that alters are highly discrete states of consciousness that are organized around a prevailing affect, a sense of self and body image, a limited repertoire of behaviors, and a set of state-dependent memories. The old designation of multiple personality disorder was confusing, because the fundamental problem in the disorder is the state not of having *more* than one personality but of having *less* than one personality (Spiegel and Li 1997).

The precise role of childhood trauma in the etiology and pathogenesis of DID is fraught with controversy. Most experts agree that trauma alone is not sufficient to cause DID. Kluft (1984) proposed a four-factor theory of etiology: 1) the capacity to dissociate defensively in the face of trauma must be present; 2) traumatically overwhelming life experiences, such as physical and sexual abuse, exceed the child's adaptational capacities and usual defensive operations; 3) the precise forms taken by the dissociative defenses in the process of alter formation are determined by shaping influences and available substrates; and 4) soothing and restorative contact with caretakers or significant others is unavailable, so that the child experiences a profound inadequacy of stimulus barriers.

One clear implication of the four-factor etiological model is that trauma is necessary but not sufficient to cause DID. At the risk of stating the obvious, not everyone who is abused as a child develops DID. Psychodynamic thinking has a significant contribution to make in furthering our understanding of the factors that lead to the full-blown syndrome. The concepts of intrapsychic conflict and deficit are relevant in DID just as they are in other conditions (Marmer 1991). Traumatic experience may lead to a variety of conflicts around such issues as guilt over sexual arousal or guilt over collusion with abusers. Kluft's fourth factor, the lack of soothing caretakers to whom the child can turn, is a major contributor to deficit in DID. In van der Kolk's (1987) extensive study of trauma in primates and human beings, he concluded that the availability of a soothing caretaker who can be unconditionally trusted when self-soothing capacities are inadequate is by far the most important factor in overcoming the impact of psychological trauma. Marmer (1991) suggested that in the absence of nurturing adults, children who ultimately develop DID must use themselves (or their alters) as transitional objects.

Ganaway (1989) expanded on Kluft's third factor, regarding the formation of dissociative defenses, by focusing on how characterological features and specific aspects of memory and cognition converge in highly hypnotizable individuals. Moreover, dissociation can occur in the absence of trauma in individuals who are highly fantasy prone and suggestible (Brenneis 1996; Target 1998). Hence, the presence of dissociation does not, in and of itself, confirm a history of early childhood trauma. Although sexual abuse, and specifically incest, is often reported by patients with DID, it is clear that only about 20% of patients with childhood sexual abuse have serious adult psychopathology (Browne and Finkelhor 1986).

Nash et al. (1993) stressed that retrospective studies of women who report childhood abuse cannot definitively establish cause-and-effect relationships between the trauma and psychological symptoms in adulthood. In their analysis of studies seeking to determine the deleterious effects of abuse, these investigators concluded that much of the adult psychopathology seen in childhood sexual abuse victims is related to a generally pathogenetic family environment. They emphasized, however, that childhood sexual abuse in and of itself leaves a child vulnerable to experiencing her body and her sense of self as damaged and inadequate. Although Nash and colleagues did not argue that sexual victimization was irrelevant in the absence of family disturbances, they did note that they took "a very skeptical stance with regard to the relative merit of traumagenic theories of psychopathology that attribute acute and especially long-term impacts of trauma to isolated and objectively defined events without taking into account social and cognitive mediators in the lives of survivors" (Nash et al. 1998, p. 570).

Attachment theory has much to offer in furthering our understanding of the differential impact of childhood sexual abuse. In a study of 92 adult female incest survivors (Alexander et al. 1998), attachment style and abuse severity each appeared to make significant contributions to the prediction of posttrauma symptoms and distress, as well as to the presence of personality disorders. Abuse severity was not significantly related to adult attachment. In this sample, secure attachment was higher among women who had been abused by a father figure than among women who had been abused by someone other than a father figure. Only intrusiveness of thoughts of the abuse and avoidance of memories of the abuse, both classic PTSD symptoms, could be uniquely explained by abuse severity. The investigators concluded that the specific abuse experience and the relational context appeared to have distinct effects on the long-term functioning of incest survivors. Some of the most devastating and long-lasting effects of the incest appeared to be related to the family context and the meaning the patient attributed to intimate relationships overall.

The child's attachment is influenced almost entirely by the relationship with the parents and is relatively independent of genetic influence (Fonagy et al. 1991a, 1991b). Expectant parents' mental models of attachment predict subsequent patterns of attachment between infant and mother and between infant and father. Each parent has an internal working model of relationships that appears to determine that parent's propensity to engender secure—as opposed to insecure—attachments in his or her children. Moreover, the mother's capacity to reflect on the mental state of another human being appears to be a predictor of the evolving relationship between infant and parent. Parents who can use constructs such as internal representations of attachment relationships are three to four times more likely to have secure children than are parents whose reflective capacity is poor.

This research on trauma and attachment may help us understand some of the difficulties faced by severely traumatized patients as a result of their reduced ability to think reflectively about themselves and about relationship experiences. These patients cope with the intolerable prospect of conceiving of the mental state of their tormentors by defensively disrupting the depiction of feelings and thoughts (Fonagy 1998). They avoid thinking about thinking. Nevertheless, attachment research suggests the encouraging possibility that abused children who can establish *mentalization,* or the capacity to understand the representational nature of one's own and others' thinking, often through the assistance of a caring adult, might avoid developing severe psychopathology. The therapist must make clear to the patient that recovery of traumatic memories is not the goal of the psychotherapy. The memory dysfunction typical of patients with dissociative disorders actually makes them less-than-ideal subjects for therapy aimed at recovering memories. A more reasonable goal is to help them recover normal mental functions, particularly the capacity to reflect and mentalize, so that they can develop a more coherent representation of self and others. In the context of a strong attachment relationship to the therapist, the traumatized patient can benefit from the therapist's capacity to reflect on what is happening between them. Ultimately, patients may internalize the therapist's reflective process and become able to bring dissociated aspects of themselves back into awareness so that they experience a greater sense of continuity. Integration of the alters may be possible only for some patients with DID.

Self-destructive behaviors in DID patients cry out for psychodynamic explanation. Revictimization is a pattern of behavior that DID patients share with other victims of incest and childhood abuse (Browne and Finkelhor 1986; van der Kolk 1989). Rape, prostitution, and sexual exploitation by therapists all occur at higher rates with incest victims than with others. Some gender differences exist in this pattern of re-creation of victimization. Abused men and boys tend to identify with their aggressors and later victimize others as adults, whereas women who were abused become attached to abusive men and allow themselves and their offspring to be victimized further (Carmen et al. 1984).

Often, children who grow up in families in which parents abuse them do not have soothing caretakers to whom they can turn to mitigate the trauma. In the absence of such persons, the victims turn to their tormentors (van der Kolk 1989), and this pattern of object relationships persists into adulthood when they look for partners who will continue the "dance" they established as children. Abused children come to believe that an abusive parent is better than no parent at all. The predictability of such relationships helps them defend against the threat of abandonment: the devil one knows is often better than the devil one does not know. The repetition of traumatic relationships is also an example of an attempt to actively master passively experienced trauma. The victims seek to have more control over what was completely outside their control as children.

The intergenerational dimensions of sexual abuse are well known (Carmen et al. 1984; Gelinas 1986; van der Kolk 1989). Parents who abuse their children tend to be abuse victims themselves. In many cases these parents are outraged that their innocence was taken away from them at such a tender age. They may experience profound envy of their own children's innocence, so through the abuse of their children, they enviously attack and spoil what was similarly taken from them (Grotstein 1992).

When DID patients recall their childhood sexual abuse, they often blame themselves for the events that occurred to them. It is commonplace to hear them refer to themselves as "sluts" or "whores" who deserve what they got. As children they frequently held on to the belief that they received such punishment because they were bad children who had misbehaved. Although to some extent this shame and guilt can be explained by introjective identifications with "bad" parents, the self-blame can also be understood as a desperate attempt to make sense out of a horrific situation. If they maintain some capacity to mentalize, they can make sense of the situation by convincing themselves that their parents are basically good people who have their children's interests at heart. The fact that their parents treat them the way they do must reflect that they are bad and deserve it. When clinicians try to persuade these patients that what happened was not their fault, the patients often feel that they are misunderstood. There may be an adaptive aspect to this posture in abuse victims, because the locus of control is perceived as internal rather than external, and as a result, there is a diminished sense of helplessness (van der Kolk 1989).

There is a general tendency within the DID literature to stress the ways in which dissociation is different from splitting. Young (1988) noted that alters tend not to be polarized around contradictory ego states, but rather have many overlapping characteristics. Marmer (1991) argued that whereas in DID the self is split more than the objects, the reverse is true in borderline personality disorder. Kluft (1991b) pointed out that dissociation differs from splitting in three ways: first, it is associated with a psychobiological switching process; second, the different states that result have significantly different psychophysiological characteristics; and finally, in contrast to splitting, amnestic barriers are often constructed between alters. Davies and Frawley (1992) distinguished dissociation from splitting on the basis that the former involves a cleavage of ego states, whereas the latter involves a division between a good object and a bad object—a point also made by Kluft (1991c).

A careful examination of the mechanisms of dissociation and splitting suggests that they have both similarities and differences (P. Lerner, "Some Thoughts on Dissociation" [unpublished manuscript], 1992). Both are characterized by active separation and compartmentalization of mental contents. Both are used defensively to ward off unpleasant experiences and affects. Both are disruptive to the formation of a smooth and continuous sense of self. On the other hand, they differ in terms of which ego functions are disrupted. Kernberg (1975) made it clear that impulse control and tolerance for anxiety and frustration are specifically impaired in splitting. By contrast, in dissociation, memory and consciousness are affected. Finally, dissociation is a broader mechanism than splitting—a variety of divisions occur in dissociation, not simply separations into polarized extremes of affective valence.

The literature on dissociation in DID has focused almost exclusively on the divisions in the self while taking little notice of the corresponding division of objects linked to the self-representations. Fairbairn (1940/1952, 1944/1952) was the first to stress that the child internalizes not an object but an *object relationship*. Davies and Frawley (1992) made note of this dimension when they commented that dissociation is not only a defense but also a process that protects and preserves the entire internal object world of the abused child in split-off form. Citing Fairbairn's thinking, Grotstein (1992) reached similar conclusions: "All mental cleavages are based ultimately on the divisions of perceptions and experiences in regard to objects—and the selves related to each of them. Thus, the dissociation that typifies the multiple personality disorder constitutes, from this point of view, a division of the ego into vertical splits based upon corresponding vertical splits in one's incompatible experiences of the object" (p. 68).

One of the practical implications of this conceptualization is that each alter presents a self in relationship to a fantasied internal object. Ganaway (1989) recognized this linkage in his observation that two common transference-countertransference scenarios based on internal object relationships are 1) a safe and loved child self in relation to an unconditionally loving, good parent, and 2) a victimized, disbelieved, and betrayed child self in relation to an abusive or abuse-enabling parent. In some cases an alter may also represent an internal object rather than a self. This state of affairs is most prominent when one of the alters clearly plays the role of the abusive internalized parent. In this case the alter exists with a corresponding fantasy of a self to which it relates. Although this view of the DID patient's internal world is highly complex, it is of crucial importance in effective psychotherapy.

Treatment Considerations

The psychotherapy of patients with DID and other dissociative disorders is generally long and arduous. There is no definitive brief psychotherapy for these conditions. To be successful, psychotherapy of DID must begin with the establishment of a firm and secure treatment frame. Because of the history of boundary violations in these patients, such details as length of session, payment of fees, appointment times, and use of words rather than touch must all be established from the beginning. A strong therapeutic alliance is crucial for the treatment to proceed, and this may be facilitated by a self psychological approach of empathizing with the patient's subjective experience during the opening phase of the therapy.

A common theme in patients with childhood trauma, especially incest victims, is difficulty determining *who* is doing *what* for *whom*. For example, a daughter who has had an incestuous relationship with her father begins to see her role as that of gratifying the father's needs. Her father may rationalize that he is teaching something to his daughter. In addition, the daughter may feel that she is special to her father because he has singled her out as the object of his desire. At the same time, she may be terribly conflicted about such feelings. She expects that parents should look after the needs of their children, but her experience is the reverse of that. She feels like she must attune herself to the needs of her parents. She will then enter psychotherapy with the same sense of confusion: *Who* is doing *what* for *whom* in the therapeutic setting?

Such a patient would understandably be skeptical of the idea that the therapist is there to be helpful or to care about her. There may be distrust about what will really happen if she asserts herself. She may simply try to figure out what the therapist wants and attempt to meet the therapist's needs instead of her own.

The therapist's major thrust must be to engage the patient's sense of agency. In other words, the therapist must help the patient to recognize that he or she is actively re-creating past patterns in the present. In a recent reconsideration of Frau Emmy von N, the subject of Freud's first published case of hysteria, Bromberg (1996) made the following observation: "We do not treat patients such as Emmy to cure them of something that was done to them in the past; rather, we are trying to cure them of what they still do to themselves and to others in order to *cope* with what was done to them in the past" (p. 70).

Interpretive interventions must be used sparingly with DID patients, particularly in the early phases of the therapy. Traumatized patients often experience interpretations as a challenge to their sense of reality (Gabbard 1997). Although interpretation of conflict-based pathology revolves around a concealed meaning that the therapist attempts to reveal to the patient, severely traumatized patients often feel retraumatized and invalidated by that approach. Killingmo (1989) recommended affirmative interventions to remove doubt in such patients. Affirmation that patients have the right to feel what they are feeling may serve to build a solid alliance, thereby creating a climate in which interpretations can be heard and valued.

There is a broad consensus among clinicians who write about the treatment of DID that a solid grounding in the principles of psychodynamic psychotherapy is essential for successful treatment (Ganaway 1989; Kluft 1991a; Loewenstein and Ross 1992; Marmer 1991). Simple catharsis and abreaction will result in neither integration nor recovery. In fact, repeating the trauma over and over again in psychotherapy may even reinforce the preoccupation and fixation of the patient with the trauma (van der Kolk 1989). Without proper understanding of psychodynamic principles, therapy may become stalemated in a state of "status abreacticus" (Ganaway 1992).

Attention to psychodynamic concepts such as transference, resistance, countertransference, and working through is required to achieve satisfactory recovery. A common finding in the treatment of patients with DID is that they are intensely loyal to the abusive internal object and reluctant to give up the attachment through the processes of integration and mourning. A great deal of working through is necessary to undo the adhesiveness of the libido to this powerful introject. Marmer (1991) also has emphasized the need to help patients rewrite their autobiographies to revise the meaning of the trauma. For example, even though the fact of incest cannot be altered, a patient may come to understand that her only way of surviving was to submit to her father's advances. Effective psychotherapy recovers much of what has been lost and helps the patient to piece together a chronological narrative or autobiography that provides the basis for a newly formed self (Putnam 1990).

When a patient with DID presents different alters in the clinical setting, the therapist must treat them matter-of-factly as aspects of one person. Moreover, the therapist must be alert to the moment of switching from one alter to another and seek to explore with the patient what precipitated the switch. Dissociation in the context of the therapy is generally a defensive flight from something that produces pain or anxiety. This need to flee can ultimately be brought to the patient's awareness.

Psychodynamic therapy of patients with severe dissociative disorders is often compromised by these patients' lack of reflective capacity. Their thinking may be excessively concrete, and they may be unable to sustain a sense of the "as if" nature of the transference. In other words, DID patients may be unable to distinguish between a perception of the therapist as a representation and the way the therapist really is. Instead, they tend to believe that their perceptions are absolute facts rather than ideas that can be "played with" and understood. Moreover, their experience of themselves may be similarly concrete. Their role as passive victims of trauma may be regarded as "bedrock" (Gabbard 1997).

Countertransference dimensions.   Few disorders create countertransference reactions of the intensity witnessed with DID patients. Ganzarain and Buchele (1988) have pointed out that at home, incest victims are often treated as either favorites or objects of violence and sadism. Similarly intense reactions, polarized in the same directions, occur in the treatment of adult DID patients. Much of the emotional reaction to these patients is linked to a dialectic involving belief versus skepticism. At one extreme, many mental health professionals still do not believe that DID is a bona fide psychiatric disorder. Some clinicians view the disorder as iatrogenically created by gullible therapists who misuse hypnosis. In one survey of clinicians who treat DID patients (Dell 1988), over half had encountered such severe skepticism in colleagues that malicious harassment of the therapist and interference with the treatment of the patient had occurred. Skeptical directors of inpatient units forbade therapists to admit their DID patients.

At the other extreme, some therapists uncritically believe everything their DID patients tell them, no matter how outlandish. They become fascinated by the condition and completely lose track of professional boundaries. They attempt to love the patient back to health and to be a better parent than the original parents. They may treat the patients with a "chimney sweeping" mentality of endlessly forcing abreaction of traumatic memories with the naive expectation that all will be well once the patient is "cleaned out." The following vignette illustrates this pattern:

> Ms. P was a 26-year-old DID patient who was referred to a tertiary care dissociative disorders unit after having been in psychotherapy for 1 year with a male therapist who reported no improvement in the patient's suicidality and self-mutilation despite treatment. He had seen the patient 5–6 hours per week throughout the year of ther-

apy. When the patient required hospitalization, he spent hours with the patient in the security of a seclusion room abreacting memories of past trauma. He had allowed the patient's bill to accumulate to several thousand dollars because he had not asked Ms. P to pay for several months. He also indicated that Ms. P and he were writing a book together about the treatment.

After Ms. P's hospitalization on the dissociative disorders unit to which she had been referred, she began to reveal horrific stories about satanic cult abuse in her past. She would provide grisly details of human sacrifice and react with an affective display that was compelling to watch. She "recalled" that she had been a "breeder" for the cult so they would have babies to sacrifice. She reported that after giving birth to the babies, the cult members would grind them up in a meat grinder and then mix them in with the soil used in their garden so that corroborating evidence of the murders could not be found. When Ms. P was sent for a routine gynecological exam, it was discovered that she had in fact never delivered a child.

The doctor in charge of Ms. P's treatment called her previous therapist to explain these findings. He discounted the gynecological evidence and said it was of paramount importance for the staff to believe Ms. P. He said if the staff did not believe her reports, they were simply repeating the past trauma when adults did not believe her tales of abuse.

Ganaway (1989) pointed out that satanic cult abuse offers a clear distinction between good and evil that can help incest victims make sense out of the confusing experience of being betrayed by their parents. Fantasies and pseudomemories can play a crucial role in the development of a network of dissociated alters, and these patients, because of their high suggestibility, are also likely to produce material they think their therapist expects. As children, DID victims often vainly try to please and win the approval of the abusive parent, and this internalized object relationship can be enacted in the transference-countertransference paradigm of the psychotherapy by dutifully reenacting one detailed abuse scene after another for a therapist who is fascinated by such data.

The question of whether memories of trauma are accurate has unfortunately become the centerpiece of a highly politicized debate within our field. The polarization of this issue into an "either/or" controversy is entirely unnecessary and ignores the broad middle ground where well-trained psychodynamic clinicians reside and practice. Most patients who were abused have clearly remembered memories that are lifelong, and in these cases, the therapist can empathize with their experiences and explore the specific personal meanings of the trauma.

When memories are recovered during the course of therapy, the therapist and the patient simply do not know how accurate those memories are. Extensive research has suggested that memory is definitely not a fixed record of experience, inextricably embedded in the mind in the way that an event is recorded on film.

Rather, it is like a theatrical production in which each run-through of the play is somewhat different from the previous one as the play evolves. There is no such thing as pure recapitulation or revival of the past, only reconstructions based on individual meanings that the patient attributes to the event (Edelman 1992; Modell 1996; Novick and Novick 1994).

Memories may be true but inaccurate (Barclay 1986). As Spiegel and Scheflin (1994) have suggested, a memory may have false details but still derive from a real incident. Perception and memory are always active processes of construction. We cannot imagine a memory that is not influenced by the observer. Hence, there is a wide spectrum of accuracy in memories that we see clinically, ranging from totally false memories induced by therapists who are either poorly trained or unscrupulous to reasonably accurate memories in which the details are more or less intact (Table 10–1). Between these two extremes is a continuum involving varying degrees of accuracy (Allen 1995).

In his 1914 paper "Remembering, Repeating and Working-Through," Freud noted that what the patient cannot remember is repeated in the analytic setting (Freud 1914/1958). He was referring to patterns of unconscious, internalized object relations that unfold before the analyst's eyes because the patient does not recall them and cannot speak about them.

The distinctions between implicit versus explicit and procedural versus declarative memory systems are relevant to Freud's observations (Clyman 1991; Squire 1992). As described in Chapter 1, explicit declarative memory involves autobiographical narratives of one's life. When trauma occurs before the age of 3 or 4 years, it is not remembered in the explicit memory system but may be encoded in the implicit procedural memory system (see Table 1–1 in Chapter 1). Trauma occurring after 4 years of age is usually retained as explicit memory to some extent,

---

TABLE 10–1.   The spectrum of accuracy in memory of trauma

Actual trauma history
- Continuously/clearly remembered with corroboration
- Delayed/fragmentary memory with corroboration
- Continuously/clearly remembered without corroboration
- Delayed/fragmentary memory without corroboration
- Exaggerated/distorted memory

No trauma history
- False memory—Patient constructed
- False memory—Therapist suggested

Source.   Based on Allen 1995.

although research suggests that some adults are unable to remember childhood sexual abuse or other traumas for long periods of time (Brown et al. 1998; Williams 1994).

Traumatic reenactments appear to be driven by implicit procedural memory (Siegal 1995). Included in this category would be many of the transference-countertransference enactments that Freud was referring to when he stated that memories are repeated rather than verbalized. In other words, unconscious internal object relationships are stored in the implicit memory system and appear in the therapy in the way the patient relates to the therapist (Gabbard 1997; Target 1998). Hence, the kind of data that unfold in the psychological drama between therapist and patient is not readily available through other means. Through projection and introjection between therapist and patient, the therapist has a unique perspective on the patient's past and internal world. Although the therapist cannot know with certainty that the implicit memories unfolding in the relationship between therapist and patient provide an accurate glimpse of what happened in the patient's childhood, such memories can at least reveal what was experienced by the child at the time, including the child's fantasies about the interactions.

With this new understanding of memory, we now consider an archeological search for convincing relics of the trauma from the buried past to be a misguided strategy in therapy. This approach is often a form of countertransference collusion with the patient to avoid the patient's direct expression of aggression or rage at the therapist and the therapist's identification with the abusive introject, a phenomenon I have called "disidentification with the aggressor" (Gabbard 1997, p. 7). Use of such an approach may also pressure the patient to come up with abuse memories that in fact may reflect the patient's unconscious experience of being intruded upon by the therapist (Brenneis 1997). Another difficulty with pressuring the patient to recover memories is that in cases of dissociative detachment, the memory may never have been encoded in the first place, so that what is retrieved is a confabulated or constructed memory related to the patient's effort to please the therapist by producing meaningful material for the treatment.

Moreover, a change in autobiographical or explicit declarative memory does not appear to be necessary for therapeutic improvement. The therapist observes and interprets the unconscious enactments fueled by equally unconscious patterns of internal object relations. Memories consistent with these patterns may be secondarily activated, but their return is best viewed as merely an epiphenomenon, and their accuracy is impossible to ascertain (Fonagy and Target 1997; Gabbard 1997). What appears to be critical is the change in patterns of living with oneself and others that results from the patient's insight about these previously unconscious patterns. In addition, there are changes that occur unconsciously as the interaction with the therapist is internalized.

The therapist must avoid the role of "arbiter of historical truth." What people remember is always a complex mixture of fantasy and reality (Arlow 1969; Gediman 1991; Grotstein 1992). Therapists must listen to the material with a nonjudgmental attitude of curiosity without being coerced into declaring that what they have heard is 100% accurate or totally false. Kluft (1988) cautioned that clinicians must avoid "the expression of fascination, surprise, excitement, dismay, belief, disbelief, or the voicing of any opinion that could cause the alters to feel the need to demonstrate their authenticity" (p. 53).

A useful way to look at the transference-countertransference developments in the psychotherapy of DID patients is to conceptualize them as episodes in an unfolding drama involving four principal characters: a victim, an abuser, an idealized omnipotent rescuer, and an uninvolved mother (Davies and Frawley 1992; Gabbard 1992). These characters oscillate in various complementary pairings between patient and therapist through the transference-countertransference enactments that develop in the psychotherapy. The first three characters in the cast—the victim, the abuser, and the idealized omnipotent rescuer—interact in a predictable pattern that represents a convergence of countertransference in the narrow sense and countertransference in the broad sense via projective identification. When a history of victimization emerges in a patient, something powerful tugs on the heartstrings of therapists that urges them to somehow try to repair the damage by becoming the good parents that the patient never had.

This rescuer-victim paradigm with which the psychotherapy begins, however, is fraught with problems. The patient is not likely to see the therapist's motives in the same way the therapist sees them. Patients who have been abused as children often assume that everyone will abuse them because they have no reason to think otherwise. Given this perspective, these patients are inherently mistrustful of reassurances from therapists who assert that they will not abuse the patient. Reassurances may make therapists feel better, but they rarely make patients feel better. Professions of caring are intrinsically suspect to patients who have been exploited under the guise of being loved.

Most DID patients have not had the benefit of growing up with generational boundaries and limits enforced by effective, caring parents. They often experience the professional boundaries of the therapeutic situation as a cruel form of withholding. They may demand demonstrations of caring that involve extended sessions, physical contact, self-disclosure from the therapist, and round-the-clock availability. If therapists begin to "go the extra mile" to gratify these requests, their efforts are doomed to failure. The attempt to become a parental substitute bypasses the patient's need to mourn and raises false hopes that a parental relationship is available if only the patient can find the right person.

When a therapist attempts to gratify a patient's escalating demands for evidence that the therapist cares, the patient's sense of entitlement is activated. Treatment of most DID patients sooner or later reveals their underlying conviction that they are entitled to compensation in the present for the abuse they experienced in the past (Davies and Frawley 1992). As the demands further escalate, the therapist may quickly develop a feeling of being tormented. Through processes of introjective and projective identification, the cast of characters has changed in such a way that the therapist has become the victim and the patient has become an abuser. Abusive or malevolent introjects residing within the patient have taken hold, while the victim-self of the patient is projected onto the therapist. Moreover, therapists may create a fertile field for this identification with the patient's/victim's self-representation as a result of guilt feelings related to their growing resentment and hatred of the patient. Patients may sense this development and accuse the therapist of not really caring. In an effort to deny their feelings of resentment at being asked to do too much and to go too far, therapists try even harder to prove that their motives are pure. At such moments therapists may secretly feel that they have been "found out" and react by trying to mask their irritation. An acknowledgment of one's limits may be the most therapeutic way to manage one's countertransference feelings when things reach this point (Gabbard 1986; Gabbard and Wilkinson 1994).

The third act of the drama unfolds in certain instances when the escalating pattern of increasing demands by the patient is accompanied by increasing efforts by the therapist to gratify those demands. At the height of their exasperation with the failure of all therapeutic efforts, therapists may resort to drastic boundary crossings with the patient that in effect repeat the childhood abuse. The therapist then has become the abuser with the patient once again in the role of victim. The most tragic—and, unfortunately, all-too-frequent—manifestation of this third paradigm is overt sexual contact between therapist and patient. Other common examples include sadistic verbal abuse of the patient, attempts to provide nurturance by sitting the patient on the therapist's lap and "re-parenting" the patient, taking the patient on family outings with the therapist's family, and so forth. In such situations the therapist's rage at being thwarted is often completely disavowed. What began as a rescue effort has ended up as a reenactment of exploitation and abuse.

Many DID patients suffer from a form of learned helplessness in which they believe that no effort on their part can change their fate. They assume that when trapped, they have no recourse. These patients have no sense of agency or efficacy to call upon. In this sense they are what Kluft (1990) termed "sitting ducks" for all forms of abuse and boundary violations by therapists who use their patients to gratify their own needs.

The three roles of victim, abuser, and idealized omnipotent rescuer are the most dramatic and obvious manifestations of the introjective-projective processes at work in the psychotherapy of DID patients. The fourth role, the uninvolved mother, shows itself in a somewhat more subtle way (Gabbard 1992). Patients will often perceive this persona in the therapist's silence, which is interpreted as indifference and rejection. In response to this perception of indifference, the patient may feel a sense of nonbeing—described by Bigras and Biggs (1990) as "negative incest"—a deadness or emptiness related to the absent mother who made no attempt to intervene in the incestuous relationship between her husband and her daughter.

The deadness or emptiness experienced by the patient may foster complementary feelings of helplessness and despair in the psychotherapist. There may be long periods in the psychotherapy when the patient remains aloof and distant from the therapist and evokes feelings of deadness or nonbeing in the countertransference (Levine 1990; Lisman-Pieczanski 1990).

The following excerpt from a psychotherapy session with an DID patient depicts this countertransference identification with the uninvolved mother:

> Ms. Q: If I could just leave this damn hospital, everything would be fine. My only problem is I hate to be confined like this, and it makes me want to mutilate.
>
> Therapist: But I wonder if confinement is really your only problem. You certainly mutilated a great deal before you were admitted to the hospital.
>
> Ms. Q: But I need to see my children and my husband. Don't you understand? They won't let them visit me here.
>
> Therapist: The last time they visited you here, you ended up making a serious suicide attempt.
>
> Ms. Q: (blandly) I wanted to cut the artery in my wrist and end everything.
>
> Therapist: Well, then, I can imagine that the staff would be reluctant to have you leave the structure and protection of the hospital.
>
> Ms. Q: I need to give it a try out of here for a while. I think if I could just be with my family outside the hospital, then I'd be fine.
>
> Therapist: What would you do if anxiety came over you and you felt like mutilating?
>
> Ms. Q: (with utter seriousness) I could have a beer or two to settle myself down.
>
> Therapist: It's very important that you see that your problems are not external. You carry your problems within you wherever you go, and no matter whether you're confined to a hospital or home with your family, you'll still have them. Until you make some effort to integrate and face the painful experiences from the past, you'll continue to mutilate yourself and wish to commit suicide.
>
> Ms. Q: I don't want to face the pain of integrating the personalities. It would be unbearable.
>
> Therapist: But you're in considerable pain now. Can it be that much worse?
>
> Ms. Q: (blandly) I don't know, but I don't want to find out.

As the therapist continued to get nowhere with this line of reasoning, he found him-self getting increasingly drowsy. Associated with the sleepy feeling, he felt as though he were withdrawing further and further away from the patient. He began looking at the clock and wishing the time was up. He found himself thinking about what he would do later in the day. He even felt that he no longer really cared if the patient got better or not. The patient also seemed to be drifting further and further away from him. As he observed this remarkable lapse in empathic attunement, it dawned on the therapist that he was becoming the absent, uninvolved mother of her childhood. His efforts to help had been thwarted, and he had a deep sense of despair and hopeless-ness about anything ever changing. He wondered if the patient's mother, too, had felt that way when she realized that she was forever excluded from the bond between her daughter and her husband and felt powerless or helpless to change anything about it.

Countertransference responses such as the one described by Ms. Q's therapist may also reflect an empathic identification with a sense of nonbeing at the core of the patient's self in response to the distant maternal identification in the patient (Gabbard 1992). There comes a time in the psychotherapy of DID patients when the demandingness of the patient is so overwhelming that therapists find them-selves wishing the patient would disappear or go elsewhere for treatment. In such reactions an identification with the uninvolved mother is easily detected, and ther-apists must be mindful that such unconscious collusions may lead unwittingly to suicide attempts on the part of the patient.

The primitive states of psychological deadness depicted in this transference-countertransference paradigm may relate to profound maternal deprivation that severely compromised the infant's developing sense of self. In the absence of the maternal provision of soothing sensory experience, the infant may not establish a secure feeling of sensory boundedness. The self-mutilation so common in DID pa-tients can be understood as a way of reestablishing boundedness at the skin border to deal with anxiety about losing intactness of the ego boundary. Ogden (1989) characterized this mode of generating experience as the autistic-contiguous posi-tion. In this primitive state the process of attributing meaning to experience ceases. Therapists may experience DID patients as imprisoned in such a primitive state that they are completely unreachable. Therapists may then be imbued with a sense of hopelessness in dealing with the patient's anxiety about lack of body integrity secondary to deprivation of close sensory experiences with mother.

Hospital treatment.   Depending on their level of ego organization and the de-gree of comorbidity, many DID patients will require hospitalization at some point in the course of psychotherapy (Kluft 1991d).

DID patients who enter general psychiatry units often find themselves in the role of the classic "special" patient (Burnham 1966; Gabbard 1986). They are regarded both by staff members and by other patients as having special relationships with their psychotherapists and often become scapegoated as a result. Skeptical staff members will begin arguments about what name to use with the patient, the validity of the abuse history, whether or not the patient is responsible for his or her actions, and a myriad of other issues. Matters may be made worse when other patients in milieu groups react with disbelief and contempt when a DID patient denies behavior that others have witnessed.

Kluft (1991d) provided several helpful guidelines. A contractual agreement must be made with the patient at the beginning of the stay stipulating consent to respond to his or her legal name when addressed by it in the milieu. The patient should be told that staff cannot be expected to respond to different alters in different ways when they emerge on the unit. Only the individual therapist will address the separate alters. A patient who cannot make a contract on behalf of all alters must be structured at the level of the most dangerous or self-destructive alter. This agreement avoids the inevitable confusion in staff members about privileges and responsibilities given the variability of functioning of the different alters. Kluft (1991d) also suggested that nursing staff must continually explain rules and policies to patients, as some alters will not be familiar with them.

Group psychotherapy. Kluft (1991d) cautioned that DID patients may have considerable difficulty with unstructured verbal group psychotherapy on hospital inpatient units. If a patient cannot contract to attend as an alter that will conform to the rules of the group, Kluft suggested that the patient should be excluded from group work. Another problem that frequently emerges stems from the suggestibility of this patient population. When one patient hears another speak of the abuse she suffered as a child, there may be a "contagion" effect, in which the first patient believes that everything reported by the second patient also happened to her. As a result, reports of cult abuse may grow increasingly fantastic if they are discussed in inpatient groups. Clearly, the underlying competitive themes in such groups need to be addressed.

On the other hand, homogeneous outpatient group psychotherapy may be useful. Coons and Bradley (1985) reported on a 2½-year program of outpatient group psychotherapy for eight DID patients who met weekly for 75 minutes. Although the process started out slowly because of difficulties with trust, much hope was generated, and the group experience was viewed as a valuable adjunct to individual psychotherapy (all patients had to be in concomitant individual processes to be accepted into the group). The patients mistrusted the male co-therapist for some time, and approximately a year passed before the patients finally discussed their childhood abuse experiences. Themes of negative self-worth and anger at parents were prevalent. Dissociation was sometimes used avoidantly, although less often than expected. In a typical session, no more than one dissociative episode was observed. The patients in the group were able to gain considerable insight by viewing the dissociation of other group members. In this regard, witnessing the dissociative episodes of others helped some patients accept their own diagnosis.

Depersonalization Disorder

Depersonalization disorder differs significantly from the other dissociative disorders. It is generally characterized by persistent or recurrent experiences of feeling detached from one's body or mental processes or of observing them from outside. Reality testing remains intact, but the experience causes significant distress and, to some degree, impairment in occupational or social functioning.

Derealization is ordinarily part of the depersonalization disorder and refers specifically to a sense of being estranged from one's environment. Depersonalization may take a multitude of forms, including a feeling that one's body is numb or dead, a feeling that certain body parts (such as the feet or hands) are not connected with the rest of the body, feelings of being detached from one's self-image so that one seems unfamiliar, and the sense of observing oneself at a distance (Gabbard and Twemlow 1984). The subjective experience of frank detachment from one's body is actually rather infrequent in depersonalization, characterizing only 19% of psychiatric patients with the disorder (Noyes et al. 1977). Although déjà vu experiences are commonly linked with depersonalization, they are actually the obverse of depersonalization and should be maintained as distinct entities (Nemiah 1989). In other words, in déjà vu, what is new is experienced as being familiar, while in depersonalization what is familiar is experienced as being new or unreal.

The DSM-IV criteria stress persistence and severity, because as many as 50% of the general population will have an occasional isolated experience of depersonalization (Nemiah 1989). Other demographic features of depersonalization include its occurrence twice as often in women as in men and predominantly in persons under the age of 40 years (Nemiah 1989). Transient depersonalization may also appear as a response to life-threatening danger such as accidents, serious illnesses, and the like (Gabbard and Twemlow 1984; Noyes et al. 1977; Steinberg 1991). There may be survival value in developing a split between an observing self and a participating self in a moment of crisis, so that a person has the necessary detachment to think of ways to maneuver out of a perilous situation.

Depersonalization occurring in psychiatrically healthy persons exposed to danger has no essential differences from episodes that occur in the context of psychiatric illness (Noyes et al. 1977). Among psychiatric patients, depersonalization is the third most common complaint, following depression and anxiety (Cattell and Cattell 1974). In fact, depersonalization is relatively uncommon as a pure disorder and is more frequently a symptom connected with other illnesses such as schizophrenia, DID, depression, or anxiety disorders (Nemiah 1989). The experience of depersonalization, whether accompanying an illness or not, is typically unpleasant and mobilizes affects such as anxiety, panic, and emptiness. It is experienced as pathological, strange, and dreamlike and often leads people to seek medical attention (Gabbard and Twemlow 1984). Depersonalization has a chronic course in about half the cases but may be highly variable in terms of the degree of dysfunction it causes the individual (Steinberg 1991).

Comorbidity seems to be common in patients with depersonalization disorder. In one study of 30 patients, the lifetime prevalence of major depression and social phobia was 53% for each disorder (Simeon et al. 1997). A 37% lifetime prevalence for panic disorder was also found. Axis II disorders were common in these patients as well, with 30% having avoidant, 27% borderline, and 23% obsessive-compulsive personality disorder. Among the total sample, 60% had at least one personality disorder.

Psychodynamic Understanding

Although the etiology of depersonalization remains obscure in most cases, psychodynamic explanations evolving from treatment situations have been shown to be clinically useful. Rosenfeld (1947/1966) viewed depersonalization as a defense against primitive destructive impulses and persecutory anxieties stemming from the paranoid-schizoid position. Blank (1954) regarded depersonalization as a defense against primitive anxiety stemming from oral rage and oral deprivation. Stamm (1962) concurred with Rosenfeld and Blank regarding the deeply regressive aspects of depersonalization as a defense.

The most current psychodynamic view of depersonalization is that it represents the internalization of conflicting identifications. Jacobson (1959) observed that unacceptable identifications are defended against by disowning and denying the undesirable part of the ego. Sarlin (1962) shared the view of Jacobson and pointed out that depersonalization may reflect a conflict between the patient's parents that has become internalized as two conflicting aspects of the child. Arlow (1966) viewed depersonalization as a defensive means of attributing warded-off impulses in a dangerous situation to the participating self, which is then experienced as estranged by the observing self. In this manner the dangerous conflict is viewed as taking place within a stranger rather than within the self.

This wish to distance oneself from a dangerous situation that conflicts with one's predominant ego identification may be highly relevant to situations when depersonalization occurs in the context of childhood abuse.

Ms. R was a 19-year-old woman who was in psychiatric treatment for chronic suicidality and uncontrollable self-mutilating tendencies. She had been involved in incestuous sexual relations with her stepfather since the age of 8 and had only recently stopped the behavior. She frequently complained of depersonalization and was able to identify its origins at age 8 years when the sexual involvement began. When her stepfather would begin to have sexual relations with her, the anxiety created by the sexual contact was so great that she would find herself in a detached position across the room observing the sexual acts as though she were a spectator. Her body would seem unreal to her, like a "rubber manikin."

Although the depersonalization began under these incestuous circumstances, it soon generalized to any situation when stress or anxiety was prominent, such as a family argument at the dinner table. By the time she was 19, it had become a chronic state in which she felt unreal and dead much of the time. She cut on her forearms to feel a sense of relief from this unpleasant depersonalized state. The pain of the cut was preferable to the estrangement that she experienced.

The defensive function of Ms. R's depersonalization could be stated in the form of an inner reassurance: "That is not me who is experiencing the sexual molestation. That is not my body, because I am over here in another part of the room watching it happen to a stranger." The sexual relations with her stepfather could then be attributed to a bad, degraded self that was split off and not part of her. She also was able to defend against her own instinctual pleasure inherent in the gratification of the oedipal wish and the triumph over her mother.

The role of a trauma history in the etiology of depersonalization disorder is not entirely clear. The literature suggests that patients with depersonalization disorder have somewhat higher childhood trauma rates than do nonpsychiatrically ill control subjects (Simeon et al. 1997), but they tend to be less seriously traumatized than patients with other kinds of dissociative disorders. Nevertheless, depersonalization is frequently described when patients who experienced childhood sexual abuse recall the details of their victimization.

Depersonalization may not always be a defense against danger from without or drive pressures from within. From a self psychological perspective, depersonalization may also be a reflection of disturbances in the consolidation of a cohesive and stable sense of self (Gabbard 1983; Stolorow 1979). The depersonalization state in these patients may reflect their panic over the fragmenting of the self when mirroring and affirming selfobject responses are not forthcoming from others.

Treatment Considerations

Discussions of treatment must begin with the recognition that transient or normal depersonalization requires little more than reassurance. In some cases of chronic depersonalization, patients who have accommodated to the disorder will not particularly feel a need for treatment (Steinberg 1991; Torch 1981). If the depersonalization is secondary to an underlying primary disorder, the clinical improvement of the primary disorder in response to appropriate treatment may also resolve the depersonalization.

In cases of depersonalization disorder in which patients experience significant distress and impairment in interpersonal functioning, the depersonalization symptom is typically treatment refractory (Simeon et al. 1997). A typical history is one in which the patient has taken many different medications and undergone many forms of psychotherapy. Only selective serotonin reuptake inhibitors and benzodiazepines appear to have any benefit for depersonalization symptoms (Simeon et al. 1997). Although most patients who undergo psychotherapy report improvement in many aspects of their lives, they tend not to report a significant decrease in the depersonalization symptoms per se. Nevertheless, dynamic therapy is sometimes useful to examine underlying problems of conflicting ego identifications, particularly as such identifications reflect stresses in the family of origin.

References

Alexander PC, Anderson CL, Brand B, et al: Adult attachment and long-term effects in survivors of incest. Child Abuse Negl 22:45–61, 1998

Allen JG: The spectrum of accuracy in memories of childhood trauma. Harv Rev Psychiatry 3:84–95, 1995

Allen JG, Console DA, Lewis L: Dissociative detachment and memory impairment: reversible amnesia or encoding failure? Compr Psychiatry 40:160–171, 1999

American Psychiatric Association: Diagnostic and Statistical Manual of Mental Disorders, 4th Edition. Washington, DC, American Psychiatric Association, 1994

Arlow JA: Depersonalization and derealization, in Psychoanalysis—A General Psychology: Essays in Honor of Heinz Hartmann. Edited by Loewenstein RM, Newman LM, Schur M, et al. New York, International Universities Press, 1966, pp 456–478

Arlow JA: Fantasy, memory, and reality testing. Psychoanal Q 38.28–51, 1969

Barclay CR: Schematization of autobiographical memory, in Autobiographical Memory. Edited by Rubin DC. New York, Cambridge University Press, 1986, pp 82–99

Bigras J, Biggs KH: Psychoanalysis as incestuous repetition: some technical considerations, in Adult Analysis and Childhood Sexual Abuse. Edited by Levine HB. Hillsdale, NJ, Analytic Press, 1990, pp 173–196

Blank HR: Depression, hypomania, and depersonalization. Psychoanal Q 23:20–37, 1954

Bliss EL: Multiple personalities: report of 14 cases with implications for schizophrenia and hysteria. Arch Gen Psychiatry 37:1388–1397, 1980

Bremner JD, Marmar CR (eds): Trauma, Memory, and Dissociation. Washington, DC, American Psychiatric Press, 1998

Bremner JD, Randall P, Scott TM, et al: MRI-based measurement of hippocampal volume in patients with combated-related posttraumatic stress disorder. Am J Psychiatry 152:973–981, 1995

Brenneis CB: Multiple personality: fantasy proneness, demand characteristics, and indirect communication. Psychoanalytic Psychology 13:367–387, 1996

Brenneis CB: Recovered Memories of Trauma: Transferring the Present to the Past. Madison, CT, International Universities Press, 1997

Brodsky BS, Cloitre M, Dulit RA: Relationship of dissociation to self-mutilation and childhood abuse in borderline personality disorder. Am J Psychiatry 152:1788–1792, 1995

Bromberg PM: Hysteria, dissociation, and cure: Emmy von N revisited. Psychoanalytic Dialogues 6:55–71, 1996

Brown D, Scheflin AW, Hammond DC: Memory, Trauma Treatment, and the Law. New York, WW Norton, 1998

Browne A, Finkelhor D: Impact of child sexual abuse: a review of the research. Psychol Bull 99:66–77, 1986

Burnham DL: The special-problem patient: victim or agent of splitting? Psychiatry 29:105–122, 1966

Cardeña E, Spiegel D: Dissociative reactions to the Bay Area earthquake. Am J Psychiatry 150:474–478, 1993

Carmen EH, Reiker PP, Mills T: Victims of violence and psychiatric illness. Am J Psychiatry 141:378–379, 1984

Cattell JP, Cattell JS: Depersonalization: psychological and social perspectives, in American Handbook of Psychiatry, 2nd Edition, Vol 3. Edited by Arieti S, Brody EB. New York, Basic Books, 1974, pp 766–799

Clyman RB: The procedural organization of emotions: a contribution from cognitive science to the psychoanalytic theory of therapeutic action. J Am Psychoanal Assoc 39 (suppl):349–382, 1991

Coons PM: The dissociative disorders: rarely considered and underdiagnosed. Psychiatr Clin North Am 21:637–648, 1998

Coons PM, Bradley K: Group psychotherapy with multiple personality patients. J Nerv Ment Dis 173:515–521, 1985

Davies JM, Frawley MG: Dissociative processes and transference-countertransference paradigms in the psychoanalytically oriented treatment of adult survivors of childhood sexual abuse. Psychoanalytic Dialogues 2:5–36, 1992

Dell PF: Professional skepticism about multiple personality. J Nerv Ment Dis 176:528–531, 1988

Edelman G: Bright Air, Brilliant Fire: On the Matter of the Mind. New York, Basic Books, 1992

Fairbairn WRD: Schizoid factors in the personality (1940), in Psychoanalytic Studies of the Personality. London, Routledge & Kegan Paul, 1952, pp 3–27

Fairbairn WRD: Endopsychic structure considered in terms of object-relationships (1944), in Psychoanalytic Studies of the Personality. London, Routledge & Kegan Paul, 1952, pp 82–136

Fonagy P: An attachment theory approach to treatment of the difficult patient. Bull Menninger Clin 62:147–169, 1998

Fonagy P, Target M: Perspectives on the recovered memories debate, in Recovered Memories of Abuse: True or False? Edited by Sandler J, Fonagy P. London, Karnac Books, 1997, pp 183–216,10N

Fonagy P, Steele M, Steele H, et al: The capacity for understanding mental states: the reflective self in parent and child and its significance for security of attachment. Infant Mental Health Journal 12:201–218, 1991a

Fonagy P, Steele H, Steele M: Maternal representations of attachment during pregnancy predict the organization of infant-mother attachment at one year of age. Child Dev 62:891–905, 1991b

Frankel FH: Hypnotizability and dissociation. Am J Psychiatry 147:823–829, 1990

Freinkel A, Koopman C, Spiegel D: Dissociative symptoms in media eyewitnesses of execution. Am J Psychiatry 151:1335 1339, 1994

Freud S: Remembering, repeating and working-through (further recommendations on the technique of psycho-analysis II) (1914), in The Standard Edition of the Complete Psychological Works of Sigmund Freud, Vol 12. Translated and edited by Strachey J. London, Hogarth Press, 1958, pp 145–156

Gabbard GO: Further contributions to the understanding of stage fright: narcissistic issues. J Am Psychoanal Assoc 31:123–441, 1983

Gabbard GO: The treatment of the "special" patient in a psychoanalytic hospital. International Review of Psychoanalysis 13:333–347, 1986

Gabbard GO: Commentary on "Dissociative processes and transference-countertransference paradigms . . . " by Jody Messler Davies and Mary Gail Frawley. Psychoanalytic Dialogues 2:37–47, 1992

Gabbard GO: Challenges in the analysis of adult patients with histories of childhood sexual abuse. Canadian Journal of Psychoanalysis 5:1–25, 1997

Gabbard GO, Twemlow SW: With the Eyes of the Mind: An Empirical Analysis of Out-of-Body States. New York, Praeger, 1984

Gabbard GO, Wilkinson SM: Management of Countertransference With Borderline Patients. Washington, DC, American Psychiatric Press, 1994

Ganaway GK: Historical versus narrative truth: clarifying the role of exogenous trauma in the etiology of DID and its variants. Dissociation 2:205–220, 1989

Ganaway GK: Hypnosis, dissociation and multiple personality disorder: a psychodynamic clinician's perspective. Paper presented at the annual meeting of the Society of Clinical and Experimental Hypnosis, Washington, DC, October 24, 1992

Ganzarain RC, Buchele BJ: Fugitives of Incest: A Perspective From Psychoanalysis and Groups. Madison, CT, International Universities Press, 1988

Gediman HK: Seduction trauma: complemental intrapsychic and interpersonal perspectives on fantasy and reality. Psychoanalytic Psychology 8:381–401, 1991

Gelinas DJ: Unexpected resources in treating incest families, in Family Resources: The Hidden Partner in Family Therapy. Edited by Karpel MA. New York, Guilford, 1986, pp 327–358

Griffin MG, Resick PA, Mechanic MB: Objective assessment of peritraumatic dissociation: psychophysiological indicators. Am J Psychiatry 154:1081–1088, 1997

Grotstein JS: Commentary on "Dissociative processes and transference-countertransference paradigms . . . " by Jody Messler Davies and Mary Gail Frawley. Psychoanalytic Dialogues 2:61–76, 1992

Horowitz MJ: Stress Response Syndromes, 2nd Edition. Northvale, NJ, Jason Aronson 1986

Jacobson E: Depersonalization. J Am Psychoanal Assoc 7:581–610, 1959

Jang KL, Paris J, Zweig-Frank H, et al: Twin study of dissociative experience. J Nerv Ment Dis 186:345–351, 1998

Kernberg OF: Borderline Conditions and Pathological Narcissism. New York, Jason Aronson, 1975

Killingmo B: Conflict and deficit: implications for technique. Int J Psychoanal 70:65–79, 1989

Kluft RP: Treatment of multiple personality disorder: a study of 33 cases. Psychiatr Clin North Am 7:9–29, 1984

Kluft RP: The phenomenology and treatment of extremely complex multiple personality disorder. Dissociation 1:47–58, 1988

Kluft RP (ed): Incest-Related Syndromes of Adult Psychopathology. Washington, DC, American Psychiatric Press, 1990

Kluft RP: Multiple personality, in American Psychiatric Press Review of Psychiatry, Vol 10. Edited by Tasman A, Goldfinger SM. Washington, DC, American Psychiatric Press, 1991a, pp 161–188

Kluft RP: Thoughts on the psychodynamic psychotherapy of the dissociative disorders. The Psychodynamic Letter 1(4):1–5, 1991b

Kluft RP: Clinical presentations of multiple personality disorder. Psychiatr Clin North Am 14:605–629, 1991c

Kluft RP: Hospital treatment of multiple personality disorder: an overview. Psychiatr Clin North Am 14:695–719, 1991d

Koopman C, Classen C, Spiegel DA: Predictors of posttraumatic stress symptoms among survivors of the Oakland/Berkeley, Calif., firestorm. Am J Psychiatry 151:888–894, 1994

Krystal JH, Bennett AL, Bremner JD, et al: Toward a cognitive neuroscience of dissociation and altered memory functions in post-traumatic stress disorder, in Neurobiological and Clinical Consequences of Stress: From Normal Adaptation to Post-Traumatic Stress Disorder. Edited by Friedman MJ, Charney DS, Deutch AY. New York, Lippincott-Raven, 1995, pp 239–269

LeDoux J: The Emotional Brain: The Mysterious Underpinnings of Emotional Life. New York, Simon & Schuster, 1996

Levine HB: Clinical issues in the analysis of adults who were sexually abused as children, in Adult Analysis and Childhood Sexual Abuse. Edited by Levine HB. Hillsdale, NJ, Analytic Press, 1990, pp 197–218

Lisman-Pieczanski N: Countertransference in the analysis of an adult who was sexually abused as a child, in Adult Analysis and Childhood Sexual Abuse. Edited by Levine HB. Hillsdale, NJ, Analytic Press, 1990, pp 137–147

Loewenstein RJ, Ross DR: Multiple personality and psychoanalysis: an introduction. Psychoanalytic Inquiry 12(1):3–48, 1992

Marmar CR, Weiss DS, Schlenger WE, et al: Peritraumatic dissociation and posttraumatic stress in male Vietnam theater veterans. Am J Psychiatry 151:902–907, 1994

Marmer SS: Multiple personality disorder: a psychoanalytic perspective. Psychiatr Clin North Am 14:677–693, 1991

Modell AH: Trauma, memory, and the therapeutic setting, in Understanding Therapeutic Action: Psychodynamic Concepts of Cure (Psychoanalytic Inquiry book series, Vol 15). Edited by Lifson LE. Hillsdale, NJ, Analytic Press, 1996, pp 41–50

Mulder RT, Beautrais AL, Joyce PR, et al: Relationship between dissociation, childhood sexual abuse, childhood physical abuse, and mental illness in a general population sample. Am J Psychiatry 155:806–811, 1998

Nash MR, Hulsey TC, Sexton MC, et al: Long-term sequelae of childhood sexual abuse: perceived family environment, psychopathology, and dissociation. J Consult Clin Psychol 61:276–283, 1993

Nash MR, Neimeyer RA, Hulsey TL, et al: Psychopathology associated with sexual abuse: the importance of complementary designs and common ground. J Consult Clin Psychol 66:568–571, 1998

Nemiah JC: Dissociative disorders (hysterical neuroses, dissociative type), in Comprehensive Textbook of Psychiatry, 5th Edition. Edited by Kaplan H, Sadock B. Baltimore, MD, Williams & Wilkins, 1989, pp 1028–1044

Novick KK, Novick J: Postoedipal transformations: latency, adolescence, and pathogenesis. J Am Psychoanal Assoc 42:143–169, 1994

Noyes R Jr, Hoenk PR, Kuperman S, et al: Depersonalization in accident victims and psychiatric patients. J Nerv Ment Dis 164:401–407, 1977

Ogden TH: The Primitive Edge of Experience. Northvale, NJ, Jason Aronson, 1989

Putnam FW: Diagnosis and Treatment of Multiple Personality Disorder. New York, Guilford, 1989

Putnam FW: Disturbances of "self" in victims of childhood sexual abuse, in Incest-Related Syndromes of Adult Psychopathology. Edited by Kluft RP. Washington, DC, American Psychiatric Press, 1990, pp 113–131

Putnam FW: Dissociative phenomena, in American Psychiatric Press Review of Psychiatry, Vol 10. Edited by Tasman A, Goldfinger SM. Washington, DC, American Psychiatric Press, 1991, pp 145–160

Putnam FW, Guroff JJ, Silberman EK, et al: The clinical phenomenology of multiple personality disorder: review of 100 recent cases. J Clin Psychiatry 47:285–293, 1986

Rauch SL, Shin LM: Functional neuroimaging studies in posttraumatic stress disorder. Ann N Y Acad Sci 821:83–98, 1997

Rosenfeld H: Analysis of a schizophrenic state with depersonalization (1947), in Psychotic States: A Psycho-Analytic Approach. New York, International Universities Press, 1966, pp 13–33

Sarlin CN: Depersonalization and derealization. J Am Psychoanal Assoc 10:784–804, 1962

Siegal DJ: Memory, trauma, and psychotherapy: a cognitive science view. J Psychother Pract Res 4:93–122, 1995

Simeon D, Gross S, Guralnik O, et al: Feeling unreal: 30 cases of DSM-III-R depersonalization disorder. Am J Psychiatry 154:1107–1113, 1997

Spiegel D: Multiple personality as a post-traumatic stress disorder. Psychiatr Clin North Am 7:101–110, 1984

Spiegel D: Trauma, dissociation, and hypnosis, in Incest-Related Syndromes of Adult Psychopathology. Edited by Kluft RP. Washington, DC, American Psychiatric Press, 1990, pp 247–261

Spiegel D: Dissociation and trauma, in American Psychiatric Press Review of Psychiatry, Vol 10. Edited by Tasman A, Goldfinger SM. Washington, DC, American Psychiatric Press, 1991, pp 261–275

Spiegel D: Trauma, dissociation, and memory. Ann N Y Acad Sci 821:225–237, 1997

Spiegel D, Fink R: Hysterical psychosis and hypnotizability. Am J Psychiatry 136:777–781, 1979

Spiegel D, Li D: Dissociated cognition and disintegrated experience, in Cognitive Science and Unconscious. Edited by Stein DJ. Washington, DC, American Psychiatric Press, 1997, pp 177–187

Spiegel D, Scheflin AW: Dissociated or fabricated? psychiatric aspects of repressed memory in criminal and civil cases. Int J Clin Exp Hypn 42:411–432, 1994

Squire LR: Declarative and nondeclarative memory: multiple brain systems supporting learning and memory. J Cogn Neurosci 4:232–243, 1992

Stamm J: Altered ego states allied to depersonalization. J Am Psychoanal Assoc 10:762–783, 1962

Steinberg M: The spectrum of depersonalization: assessment and treatment, in American Psychiatric Press Review of Psychiatry, Vol 10. Edited by Tasman A, Goldfinger SM. Washington, DC, American Psychiatric Press, 1991, pp 223–247

Steinberg M, Rousaville B, Cicchetti D: Detection of dissociative disorders in psychiatric patients by a screening instrument and a structured diagnostic interview. Am J Psychiatry 148:1050–1054, 1991

Steingard S, Frankel FH: Dissociation and psychotic symptoms. Am J Psychiatry 142:953–955, 1985

Stolorow RD: Defensive and arrested developmental aspects of death anxiety, hypochondriasis and depersonalization. Int J Psychoanal 60:201–213, 1979

Target M: Book review essay: the recovered memories controversy. Int J Psychoanal 79:1015–1028, 1998

Torch EM: Depersonalization syndrome: an overview. Psychiatr Q 53:249–258, 1981 van der Kolk BA: Psychological Trauma. Washington, DC, American Psychiatric Press, 1987

van der Kolk BA: The compulsion to repeat the trauma: re-enactment, revictimization, and masochism. Psychiatr Clin North Am 12:389–411, 1989

Waller NG, Ross CA: The prevalence and biometric structure of pathological dissociation in the general population: taxometric and behavior genetic findings. J Abnorm Psychol 106:499–510, 1997

Williams LM: Recall of childhood trauma: a prospective study of women's memories of child sexual abuse. J Consult Clin Psychol 62:1167–1176, 1994

Yehuda R: Sensitization of the hypothalamic-pituitary-adrenal axis in posttraumatic stress disorder. Ann N Y Acad Sci 821:57–75, 1997

Young WC: Psychodynamics and dissociation: all that switches is not split. Dissociation 1:33–38, 1988

CHAPTER
11

Paraphilias and Sexual Dysfunctions

Paraphilias

Few psychiatric disorders are fraught with as many moralistic overtones as the paraphilias. To determine that an individual is deviant in the area of sexuality implies the establishment of a clear norm for sexual behavior. Who will establish such norms? Shall psychiatry be the moral guardian of sexual behavior? Can we use terms such as *sexual deviation, perversion,* or even *paraphilia* without sounding pejorative?

The evolution of the definition of perverse activity reveals the extent to which psychiatric nosology mirrors the society from which it emanates. In the context of a culture that viewed normal sexuality in relatively narrow terms, Freud (1905/ 1953) defined sexual activity as perverse according to several criteria: 1) it focused on nongenital regions of the body; 2) rather than coexisting with the standard practice of genital intercourse with an opposite-sex partner, it superseded and replaced such practice; and 3) it tended to be the exclusive sexual practice of the individual. Freud noted that traces of perversion could be found in virtually anyone whose unconscious was subject to psychoanalytic exploration.

Since Freud's early paper, cultural attitudes about sexuality have undergone dramatic changes. As sexuality became a legitimate area for scientific study, it became apparent that "normal" couples engage in a variety of sexual behaviors. Oral-genital relations, for example, became widely accepted as healthy sexual behavior. Homosexuality and anal intercourse similarly were removed from the list of perverse activities.

Psychoanalytic writers have repeatedly confirmed Freud's observation that there is a latent perverse core in all of us (Chasseguet-Smirgel 1983; McDougall 1980, 1986; Stoller 1975, 1985). Thus a more accepting attitude about perverse sexuality has accompanied psychoanalytic advances. McDougall (1986) pointed out that perverse fantasies are regularly found in all adult sexual behavior, but tend to cause few problems because they are not experienced as compulsive. She suggested using the term *neosexuality,* to reflect the innovative nature of the practice and the individual's intense investment in its pursuit. She stressed that clinicians must be empathic with their patients, who experience these sexual demands as necessary for emotional survival. In her view, the term *perversion* should be reserved for instances in which one person imposes personal wishes on a partner who is reluctant to engage in that individual's sexual scenario or seduces a nonresponsible individual, such as a child or mentally handicapped adult (McDougall 1995).

Stoller (1975, 1985) has advocated a narrowed definition of perverse activity. Referring to perversion as "the erotic form of hatred" (1975, p. 4), he asserted that cruelty and the wish to humiliate and degrade one's sexual partner as well as oneself are the crucial determinants of whether a behavior is perverse. From this perspective, the individual's intent is a critical variable in defining perversion. As his view evolved (1985), Stoller added another dimension to this definition. Recognizing that in normal sexual arousal there is a touch of hostility and a desire to humiliate, he concluded that intimacy was a critical differentiating factor. An individual is perverse only when the erotic act is used to avoid a long-term, emotionally intimate relationship with another person. Conversely, sexual behavior is not perverse when it is in the service of establishing a stable intimate relationship.

In an effort to be nonjudgmental in its definition of paraphilias, the DSM-IV (American Psychiatric Association 1994) has suggested restricting the term to situations in which nonhuman objects are used, in which actual humiliation or pain is inflicted on oneself or one's partner, or in which children or nonconsenting adults are involved. To deal with the continuum between fantasy and action, DSM-IV has developed a spectrum of severity. In "mild" forms, patients are quite distressed about their paraphilic sexual urges but do not act on them. In "moderate" degrees of severity, patients translate their urges into action, but only occasionally. In "severe" cases, patients repeatedly act on their paraphilic urges. Finally, in an effort to be more scientific and less pejorative, DSM-IV uses the term *paraphilia* rather than *perversion* or *deviation.*

Although the intent of DSM-IV is admirable, Stoller (1985) argued that the movement to change the official term from *perversion* to *paraphilia* (which occurred in DSM-III-R [American Psychiatric Association 1987]) was a misguided attempt to "sanitize" perversions. *Perversion,* in his view, is useful precisely because it has nasty and sinful connotations:

Perversion is so pejorative. It reeks of sin, accusation, vindictiveness, and righteous-
ness. It has its absoluteness. In it thunder God and his agents on earth. (p. 4)

Stoller has argued for retaining the term *perversion* because a sense of sinning is
a prerequisite for a perverse activity to create erotic excitement. Since both points
of view have merit, the two terms will be used interchangeably in this chapter.

Psychodynamic Understanding

To a large extent, the etiology of paraphilias remains shrouded in mystery. Although certain studies have suggested that biological factors contribute to the
pathogenesis of perversions (Berlin and Meinecke 1981), the data are far from definitive. Even if biological factors are present, psychological issues obviously play a
crucial role in determining the choice of paraphilia and the underlying meaning of
the sexual acts. Psychoanalytic understanding has greatly illuminated the dark recesses of the perverse psyche. However, we must appropriately and modestly note
that psychodynamic models can shed light on the meaning of a perversion without
necessarily establishing a definitive etiology (Person 1986).

The classical view of perversions is deeply embedded in drive theory. Freud
(1905/1953) believed that these disorders illustrated how instinct and object are divorced from one another: "It seems probable that the sexual instinct is in the first
instance independent of its object" (p. 148). Moreover, he defined perversions in
part by contrasting them with neuroses. In the latter condition, neurotic symptoms represent a transformation of repressed perverse fantasies. In perversions,
however, the fantasies become conscious and are directly expressed as ego-
syntonic, pleasurable activities. Hence, Freud described neuroses as the negative of
perversions: neurotic symptoms were desexualized perverse fantasies. In the classical view, perversions may be fixations or regressions to infantile forms of sexuality
persisting into adult life (Fenichel 1945; Sachs 1986). Some remnant of infantile
experience is preserved in consciousness and is the carrier of all infantile sexuality
through the process of displacement. A perverse act becomes a fixated and ritualized procedure that is the only route to genital orgasm. In the classical formulation
(Fenichel 1945), the decisive factor that prevents orgasm through conventional
genital intercourse is castration anxiety. Perversions thus serve the function of denying castration. (Because the overwhelming majority of patients suffering from
paraphilias are male, the formulations presented here will presume male gender.)

Freud (1905/1953) appreciated the complexity of perversions, which are multi-
layered. He noted, for example, the myriad unconscious determinants of voyeurism and exhibitionism, which are opposite sides of the same coin. In his clinical

work, he observed that any "active" perversion was always accompanied by a "passive" counterpart. In this formulation, the sadist would have a masochistic core, whereas the voyeur would suffer from unconscious exhibitionistic desires.

More recent psychoanalytic investigators have concluded that drive theory alone is insufficient to explain much of the perverse fantasies and behavior seen clinically and that the relational aspects of perversions are crucial for a comprehensive understanding (McDougall 1980, 1986; Mitchell 1988). According to Stoller (1975, 1985), the essence of perversion is a conversion of "childhood trauma to adult triumph" (1975, p. 4). Patients are driven by their fantasies of avenging humiliating childhood traumas caused by their parents. Their method of revenge is to dehumanize and humiliate their partner during the perverse act or fantasy.

Perverse sexual activity may also be a flight from object relatedness (Mitchell 1988). Many persons suffering from paraphilias have incompletely separated and individuated from their intrapsychic representations of their mothers. As a result, they feel that their identity as a separate person is constantly being threatened by fusion or engulfment from internal or external objects. Sexual expression may be the one domain in which they can assert their independence. Whereas Stoller (1975, 1985) viewed perversions as expressions of the desire to humiliate, Mitchell (1988) understood them as a defiance of the overbearing influence of the internal mothering figure. One aspect of the relief experienced by paraphilic patients after they have acted on their sexual desires is their feeling of triumph over the controlling mother within.

McDougall (1986) noted other object relational meanings of the *neosexualities*. She suggested that sexual behavior evolves from a complicated matrix of identifications and counteridentifications with our parents. Each child is involved in an unconscious psychological drama that stems from the parents' unconscious erotic desires and conflicts. Hence, the obligatory nature of any neosexuality is programmed by parental scripts internalized by the child. In McDougall's view, deviant sexual behavior may function partly to protect the introjected objects from the patient's aggression by acting out the unconscious drama "written" by the parents.

Kohut (1971, 1977) offered a self psychological perspective on the function of perversions. In his view, perverse activity involves a desperate attempt to restore the integrity and cohesiveness of the self in the absence of empathic selfobject responses from others. The sexual activity or fantasy may help the patient feel alive and intact when threatened by abandonment or separation. Perverse behavior in the course of psychotherapy or analysis may thus be a reaction to failures of empathy by the therapist, leading to a temporary disruption of the self-selfobject matrix established between patient and therapist (Miller 1985). In Kohut's (1977) view, the behavioral manifestations of perversions are secondary phenomena: "After the breakup of the primary psychological unit (assertively demanded empathy-merger with the selfobject), the drive appears as a disintegration product; the drive is then enlisted in the attempt to bring about the lost merger (and thus the repair of the self) by pathological means, i.e., as enacted in the fantasies and actions of the pervert" (p. 128).

Although not a self psychologist, McDougall (1986) also noted a profound fear of loss of identity or sense of self at the core of much perverse activity. Certain sexual practices or sexual objects become like a drug that the patient uses to "medicate" a sense of inner deadness and a fear of self-disintegration. In these patients, McDougall observed a faulty internalization process that impeded their use of transitional objects in childhood during their efforts to separate from maternal figures.

Goldberg (1995) has extended the self psychological view of perversions. He believes that sexualization is an attempt to repair a structural defect in the self that is connected to an incapacity to manage and experience painful emotional states. He also links perversion to a vertical split within the personality between the "real me" part and a disavowed sector that is seen to initiate and promulgate perverse acts. However, Goldberg also stresses that generalizations about psychodynamic themes in perversion are unwarranted because a wide variety of dynamics may be involved in any particular sexualized scenario.

Traditional clinical wisdom has suggested that perversions are rare in women. This point of view has been changing in recent years as the result of empirical research and clinical observation demonstrating that perverse fantasies are actually common in women. In a comprehensive study of female perversions, Louise Kaplan (1991) pointed out that clinicians have failed to identify perversions in women because they involve more subtle dynamics than the more obvious sexuality of men's perversions. Sexual acts stemming from female paraphilias involve unconscious themes of separation, abandonment, and loss. For example, some women who have been sexually abused as children adopt an exaggerated stereotype of female sexiness in an effort to wreak vengeance on men and reassure themselves about their femaleness.

Before considering the dynamics of each individual paraphilia, we should note that the reasons remain obscure for individual preference of one perverse fantasy or act over another. Also, different paraphilias often coexist in the same person. Although the traditional view of perversion held that the perverse individual is fixated on one type of sexual scenario, a study of 561 men seeking evaluation and treatment for paraphilia found that fewer than 30% of subjects (excluding transsexuals) had confined their deviant behavior to only one perversion (Abel et al. 1988). Finally, a wide range of psychiatric diagnoses and levels of personality organization may be present in a paraphilic individual. Perversions have been observed, for example, in psychotic patients, in those with personality disorders, and in relatively intact or neurotic patients. Polymorphous perverse sexuality is commonly found in patients with borderline personality organization (Kernberg 1975). Paraphilias that involve overt cruelty to others are often present in patients with antisocial personality disorder. Thus, the psychodynamic understanding of any individual patient involved in perverse sexual activity implies a thoroughgoing comprehension of how the perversion interacts with the patient's underlying character structure. For example, patients with neurotic organization may use a paraphilic activity to facilitate genital potency, whereas patients near the psychotic border may use the same activity to fend off a sense of dissolution of the self (Person 1986).

Exhibitionism and voyeurism. By publicly exposing his genitals to strange women or girls, the exhibitionist reassures himself that he is not castrated (Fenichel 1945; Freud 1905/1953). The reaction of shock that his actions produce helps him deal with castration anxiety and gives him a feeling of power over the opposite sex. Stoller (1985) has pointed out that exhibitionistic acts typically follow a situation in which the offender felt humiliated, often at the hands of a woman. In turn, the exhibitionist avenges this humiliation by shocking strange women. Moreover, displaying his genitals enables the man to regain some sense of worth and positive masculine identity. Frequently these men reveal a profound insecurity about their sense of maleness. Stoller (1985) noted that castration anxiety does not completely capture the motivation for the exhibitionistic act. In his view, the threat "is best put in identity terms; for humiliation is about 'existence anxiety,' threat to core gender identity" (p. 20). Exhibitionists often feel that they made no impact on anyone in their family, and thus they have had to resort to extraordinary measures to be noticed (Mitchell 1988). Each exhibitionistic act may therefore be an attempt to reverse a childhood traumatic situation.

The flip side of exhibitionism—voyeurism—also involves a violation of a strange woman's privacy, an aggressive but secretive triumph over the female sex. Fenichel (1945) linked voyeuristic tendencies to a fixation on the primal scene of childhood, in which the child either witnesses or overhears parental intercourse. This early traumatic experience could arouse the child's castration anxiety and then lead him to reenact the scene again and again as an adult in an attempt to actively master a passively experienced trauma. Fenichel also identified an aggressive component in looking, conceptualizing it as a guilt-avoiding displacement of the wish to be directly destructive to women. Even patients who are not prone to overtly voyeuristic activities may exhibit common derivatives such as curiosity and anxiety about looking. Some patients are even reluctant to glance around their therapist's office for fear that their curiosity will be construed as destructive or that they will see something forbidden. Mitchell (1988) observed that exhibitionism and voyeurism capture an essential quality typical of all perversions: "a dialectic between surface and depth, between the visible and the secret, between the available and the withheld" (p. 111).

Sadism and masochism. Persons who require sadistic fantasies or actions to achieve sexual gratification are often unconsciously attempting to reverse childhood scenarios in which they were the victim of physical or sexual abuse. By inflicting on others what happened to them as children, they gain revenge and a sense of mastery over the childhood trauma at the same time. Stoller (1991) found that a rather large percentage of members of sadomasochistic clubs who practiced body piercing had been hospitalized children who had continually received injections in order to treat their childhood illnesses. Masochistic patients who require humiliation and even pain to achieve sexual pleasure may also be repeating childhood experiences of abuse. Fenichel (1945) believed that masochistic patients are making a sacrifice—accepting a "lesser evil" in place of castration. They may also be firmly convinced that they deserve punishment for their conflictual sadistic wishes. In some cases, these patients defend against separation anxiety by submitting to abuse. They are frequently convinced that a sadomasochistic relationship is the only available form of object relatedness: an abusive relationship is better than no relationship.

Sadism and masochism are unique in that they are the only classical perversions that are acknowledged to occur regularly in both sexes (Person 1986). Although masochism has been stereotypically linked to women, muted forms of sadistic and masochistic fantasies are regularly found in almost everyone. The practices of male homosexuals and the reports of female prostitutes even suggest that masochistic sexual activities may be more common in men. Sacher-Masoch, the 19th century Austrian writer from whom the term derives, was, in fact, a poet of male masochism. All sexual arousal may indeed be linked to aggressive wishes (Stoller 1985). Patients who come to psychotherapy or psychoanalysis with sexual inhibitions often reveal highly sadistic fantasies that prevent them from becoming sexually involved with other people.

In relational terms, sadism often develops from a particular internal object relationship in which the withholding and distant object requires a forceful effort to overcome its resistance to the corresponding self-representation (Mitchell 1988). Similarly, masochistic surrender may be an enactment of an internal object relationship in which the object will respond to the self only when humiliated.

From a self psychological perspective, masochistic behavior is a frantic effort to restore a sense of aliveness or self-cohesion. Although apparently self-destructive, masochism may be experienced by the patient as self-restorative. Stolorow et al. (1988) reported the treatment of a highly disturbed 19-year-old patient who repeatedly asked the therapist to hit her. In response to the therapist's persistent inquiries about why she would want him to strike her, she wrote: "Physical pain is better than spiritual death" (p. 506). In the absence of physical pain and abuse at the hands of others, this patient felt that she did not exist and was not connected with anyone else. These authors noted that masochistic patients often organize their entire lives to meet their parents' needs. As a result, their own internal affective experience becomes remote and unavailable because it has been sacrificed in the service of their parents.

Fetishism.   To achieve sexual arousal, fetishists require the use of an inanimate object, often an article of women's underwear, or a shoe, or a nongenital body part. Freud originally explained fetishism as stemming from castration anxiety. The object chosen as a fetish symbolically represented the "female penis," a displacement that helped the fetishist overcome castration anxiety. Following the premise that male awareness of the female genitals increased a man's fear of losing his own genitals and becoming like a woman, Freud thought that this unconscious symbolization explained the relatively common occurrence of fetishism. He also used this formulation to develop his concept of the splitting of the ego (1940/1964)—coexisting in the fetishist's mind are two contradictory ideas: denial of castration and affirmation of castration. The fetish represents both.

Although Greenacre (1970, 1979) also viewed castration anxiety as central to the understanding of fetishism, she noted that it has its origins in earlier pregenital disturbances. Chronic traumatic interactions in the first few months of life may thus be instrumental in producing fetishism. Because of severe problems in the mother-infant relationship, the infant is unable to be soothed by the mother or by transitional objects. To experience bodily integrity, the child thus requires a fetish, something "reassuringly hard, unyielding, unchanging in shape, and reliably durable" (1979, p. 102). These early pregenital disturbances are reactivated later when the male child or adult is concerned about genital integrity. In essence, Greenacre saw the fetish as functioning like a transitional object.

Kohut (1977) held a somewhat similar view about fetishism, although couched in self psychological terms. He described a male patient whose childhood was characterized by the traumatic unavailability of his mother. The patient made a fetish of underpants, which served as a substitute for the unavailable selfobject. In contrast to this patient's feelings of helplessness about his mother, he could maintain total control over this nonhuman version of a selfobject. Thus what appears to be an intense sexual need for a fetishistic object may actually reflect severe anxiety about the loss of one's sense of self (Mitchell 1988).

More recent writing on fetishism has broadened the concept to include fetishism as part of a spectrum of phenomena that control anxiety by bestowing magic and illusion on an outside object (Nersessian 1998). Fetishism has also been expanded beyond inanimate objects and is thought to exist in females as well as males. Rather than attempting to link fetishism to anxiety connected with a specific developmental moment, contemporary views focus more on the ego's need for an outside object to master anxiety. In a prospective longitudinal study, Massie and Szajnberg (1997) describe a case of amputee fetishism in which a 30-year-old man recalled the onset of a sexual fetish in his fifth or sixth year of life. The historical information and parent-infant film data in the research record, coupled with the patient's historical recollections, provided a complex and illuminating view of the evolution of a fetish. Several factors were clearly at work, including an unusually intense and sexually exciting relationship with both mother and father, a propensity for strong psychophysiological arousal, difficulties with self-soothing, an overstimulating and highly sensitive alertness on the part of both parents to the child's psychological life, and the early experience of the loss of the father for 10 weeks in the child's third year. This actual trauma appeared to contribute to a vulnerability to separation anxiety. The specific form of the fetish, involving amputee images, could also be related to a caretaker who had her leg in a cast and the boy's anxieties about the cast "coming off." Massie and Szajnberg speculate that fetishism in this case may have been linked to a form of intrapsychic posttraumatic play.

Pedophilia. Of all the perversions, pedophilia is the most likely to create feelings of disgust and contempt in treaters. In fulfilling his sexual desires, the pedophile may irreparably damage innocent children. Some conceptual framework or psychodynamic formulation can enable clinicians to maintain a degree of empathy and understanding when attempting to treat these patients. According to the classical view (Fenichel 1945; Freud 1905/1953), pedophilia represents a narcissistic object choice—that is, the pedophile sees a child as a mirror image of himself as a child. Pedophiles were also regarded as impotent and weak individuals who sought children as sexual objects because they would offer less resistance or create less anxiety than adult partners, thus enabling pedophiles to avoid castration anxiety.

In clinical practice, many pedophiles are found to suffer from narcissistic character pathology, including psychopathic variants of narcissistic personality disorder (see Chapter 17 for a detailed discussion of the interface between narcissistic and antisocial personality disorders). Sexual activity with prepubescent children may shore up the pedophile's fragile self-esteem. Similarly, many individuals with this perversion choose professions in which they can interact with children because the idealizing responses of children help them maintain their positive self-regard. In return, the pedophile often idealizes these children; thus, sexual activity with them involves the unconscious fantasy of fusion with an ideal object or restoration of a youthful, idealized self. Anxiety about aging and death may be warded off through sexual activity with children.

When pedophilic activity occurs in conjunction with a narcissistic personality disorder with severe antisocial features, or as part of an outright psychopathic character structure (see Chapter 17), the unconscious determinants of the behavior may be closely linked to the dynamics of sadism. Sexual conquest of the child is the tool of vengeance. Pedophiles were frequently victims of childhood sexual abuse themselves, and a sense of triumph and power may accompany their transformation of a passive trauma into an actively perpetrated victimization.

Power and aggression are also prominent concerns of pedophiles whose sexual activity is limited to incestuous relationships with their own children or stepchildren. These men often feel unloved by their wives, and they elicit caretaking responses from their children by portraying themselves as victims (Ganzarain and Buchele 1990). The flip side of their martyred self-presentation, however, is a sense of control and power over their sexual partners. These incestuous fathers harbor extraordinary hostility toward women, and they often think of the penis as a weapon to be used in acts of vengeance against women. Some have even acknowledged that feelings of intense anger produce erections (Ganzarain and Buchele 1990).

Pedophiles are often differentiated according to whether they are fixated or regressed (Groth and Birnbaum 1979; McConaghy 1998). The fixated pedophile is sexually attracted to younger persons from the time of adolescence, whereas the regressed pedophile usually does not show sexual attraction to younger people until adulthood. Fixated pedophiles generally commit their offenses against boys, while their regressed counterparts more often than not sexually exploit girls. Those who offend against girls typically carry out their offenses in the home as part of an incestuous relationship, and tend to have very few victims. The fixated pedophile, who chooses boys as the object of sexual desire, tends to have many victims and preys on boys who live outside the home. Because the regressed pedophile may also be attracted to adult women, the prognosis is much better than that for the fixated pedophile, who mainly focuses on boys.

Transvestism.   In this common paraphilia, the male patient dresses as a woman to create sexual arousal in himself that leads to heterosexual intercourse or masturbation. The patient may behave in a traditionally masculine manner while dressed as a man but then become effeminate when dressed as a woman. The classic psychoanalytic understanding of cross-dressing involves the notion of the phallic mother. By imagining that his mother possesses a penis, even if it is not clearly visible, the male child overcomes his castration anxiety. The act of cross-dressing may thus be an identification with the phallic mother (Fenichel 1945).

At a more primitive level, the little boy may identify with his mother to avoid anxiety about separation. His awareness of genital differences between him and his mother may activate anxiety that he will lose her because they are separate individuals. Clinical work with transvestites reveals that when they cross-dress, they commonly experience some degree of fusion with an intrapsychic maternal object. This reassures them that they are not in danger of losing the soothing maternal presence within. These men are always heterosexual (Person 1986), and most are otherwise well-adjusted. In a study of 188 cross-dressing men (Brown et al. 1996), transvestites were found to be indistinguishable from the average man on tests of sexual functioning, personality, and emotional distress. These individuals rarely seek psychiatric treatment. On the other hand, transgender and transsexual men have many more psychiatric symptoms, less sexual drive, and a poorer body image than transvestites. Although transvestites are ordinarily quite convinced that they are heterosexual and male, some may appear at clinics at midlife convinced that they have become transsexuals. Little is known about transsexualism because most of these individuals seek sex-change surgery rather than psychotherapy or psychoanalysis.

Treatment Considerations

Patients with paraphilias are notoriously difficult to treat. Over many years, they have developed a carefully crafted erotic solution to their problems, and they are rarely interested in giving it up (McDougall 1986). Why would someone wish to halt a practice that produces great pleasure? Most perversions are ego-syntonic; only exceptional patients who are distressed by their symptoms willingly seek treatment. Persons with fetishes generally view their fetishism as nothing more than a personal idiosyncrasy—certainly not a psychiatric symptom (Greenacre 1979). They typically seek treatment for other reasons, and the fetishism emerges in the course of therapy or analysis.

The vast majority of paraphilic patients come to treatment under pressure. A marital crisis may bring a transvestite to clinical attention under threat of divorce. In instances of voyeurism, exhibitionism, and particularly pedophilia, legal pressures often mandate treatment as a condition of probation or as an alternative to incarceration. A court date may be pending, so the patient will go through the motions of treatment to "look good" in court and to influence the judge to drop any charges. In every case of paraphilia, the first order of business is to clarify the legal situation. The clinician may decide to defer a decision on long-term treatment until after the disposition of the case in court. Those patients who continue to seek treatment after all legalities have been resolved may have better prognoses (Reid 1989).

Another major impediment to the treatment of patients with perversions is the countertransference responses they evoke. If indeed we all struggle with unconscious perverse wishes, as Freud and many others since his time have repeatedly suggested, then it is reasonable to assume that we may react to the perverse patient as we would to our own perverse impulses. We are filled with disgust, anxiety, and contempt. Our natural impulse is to respond punitively—to moralize, to chide, to lecture, and to do what we can to "stamp out" the perversity. We also recoil in horror at the prospect of anyone allowing full rein to such impulses when we ourselves carefully control them. Another countertransference tendency is to collude with the patient's avoidance of the perversion by talking about other aspects of his life. Clinicians can avoid their own feelings of disgust and contempt by avoiding the whole area of sexual pathology. With some patients—pedophiles, in particular— certain therapists may feel that they simply cannot be effective because of their intense countertransference hatred. In these instances, it is best to refer the patient elsewhere.

One final reason for treatment difficulty with persons suffering from perversions is the associated psychopathology. Perverse fantasy and behavior are difficult enough to alter, but when the patient's condition is complicated by borderline, narcissistic, or antisocial character pathology, the prognosis becomes even more guarded.

Whether or not treatment of paraphilias, especially those involving pedophilia and other criminal offenses, is truly effective remains highly controversial (Hall 1995; Marshall and Pithers 1994; McConaghy 1998; Prentky et al. 1997; Rice et al. 1991). Although some studies are encouraging, the validity of the outcome measures used at follow-up is highly problematic. Using recidivism, as measured by arrest records, casts a narrow net. Because round-the-clock observation of pedophiles, for example, is impossible, researchers cannot be certain whether they continue to act on their impulses to molest children.

Most treatment programs involve integrated models that are individually tailored to the patient. There is a substantial psychoanalytic and psychotherapeutic literature on the treatment of some forms of paraphilia (Fogel and Myers 1991; Goldberg 1995; L. J. Kaplan 1991; McDougall 1980, 1986, 1995; Person 1986; Rosen 1964, 1979; Stoller 1985). In addition to the use of psychodynamic approaches, cognitive-behavioral therapy, behavioral reconditioning, and relapse prevention are also commonly employed and have been useful with certain patients. The treatment goals generally include assisting patients in overcoming their denial and helping them develop empathy for their victims; identifying and treating deviant sexual arousal; identifying social deficits and inadequate coping skills;

challenging cognitive distortions; and developing a comprehensive relapse prevention plan that includes avoidance of situations in which the patient is likely to be tempted.

Antiandrogen medications, such as cyproterone acetate and medroxyprogesterone acetate (Depo-Provera), are also popular treatment modalities. Their usefulness is limited, however, by a number of significant drawbacks. First, they have serious side effects, including pulmonary embolism, weight gain, hypertension, and thrombophlebitis. Second, the problem of noncompliance is formidable—one study (Berlin and Meinecke 1981) had a dropout rate of greater than 50%. The same study also revealed that 15% of the subjects had recurrent perverse behavior even while taking the medication. Testosterone injections can be illegally purchased on the street without much difficulty. A final disadvantage of antiandrogen agents is that they lower the sexual drive by reducing plasma testosterone levels, but do nothing to alter the deviation itself. If the medication is discontinued, within a week or so the patient's deviant behavior recurs (Travin et al. 1985). Despite having been used for 30 years, these drugs are still considered investigational in these disorders.

Psychotherapeutic treatments. Individual expressive-supportive psychotherapy with an expressive emphasis is often the preferred method of treatment, but a therapist's expectations must nevertheless be modest. Although many patients will make considerable gains in object relatedness and ego functioning, their underlying perverse tendencies may be modified to a lesser degree. In general, those patients with higher-level character organizations have a better outcome than those with borderline levels of organization (Person 1986).

Similarly, those patients who are psychologically minded, who possess some degree of motivation, who have some distress about their symptoms, and who are curious about the origins of their symptoms are likely to do better than those who lack such qualities.

Certain problems typically arise when paraphilic persons are treated with dynamic psychotherapy. These patients rarely wish to focus on the perversion itself and often actively assert that it is no longer a problem for them. Although psychotherapists must treat disorders associated with the paraphilia, they must also vigorously confront such denial from the beginning. One therapeutic task is to integrate the perverse behavior with the central sector of the patient's personality functioning so that it can be addressed along with the rest of the patient's life. The vertical split in the patient's personality may give rise to parallel but distinct transference phenomena. Each transference will produce corresponding countertransferences, often involving a form of collusion with the perversion. Goldberg (1995) suggests that the therapist must both recognize the behavior as essential for the patient's emotional survival and regard the perverse behavior as something to be understood and diminished. He notes that in this regard the vertical split in the transference is met with a corresponding split response in the therapist.

Another frequently encountered dilemma in psychotherapy centers around the avoidance of a punitive stance vis-à-vis the patient's perverse activity. Some states have reporting laws that require a therapist to break confidentiality if pedophilic activity is uncovered during psychiatric treatment. Even apart from the legal and ethical considerations, perverse behavior is likely to evoke highly disapproving responses in therapists. Sensitive patients often detect the therapist's struggle to refrain from being punitive. Clever patients may exploit this countertransference struggle by accusing their therapist of being harsh and cruel because of the therapy's focus on the perverse symptom. Patients may also avoid discussing the symptom by instead professing their feelings of shame, embarrassment, and humiliation.

If the patient can overcome his initial resistance to forming a therapeutic alliance in the service of understanding the perverse symptom, then both patient and therapist can begin to search for unconscious meanings of the symptom and its function within the patient's personality. Most paraphilias operate in an object relations context outside the patient's awareness. Many patients with paraphilias experience their fantasies and behavior as essentially nonpsychological, and they are unaware of any connections between their symptoms and feeling states—or between their symptoms and life events—that may increase their need for the symptoms. Much of the therapist's effort must therefore go into explaining these connections.

Mr. S, a 22-year-old college student, was hospitalized following an arrest for exposing himself to female students on the campus. He would sit in his car in the parking lot of the women's dormitory with his genitals exposed. As female students walked by, some would look in the car and react with shock, which substantially excited him. During his brief hospitalization, Mr. S agreed to start psychotherapy, but he was basically a reluctant participant. He told his therapist that his embarrassment and depression upon being arrested and hospitalized would prevent him from ever resorting to exhibitionism again. He preferred to use the therapy to talk about other problems, such as his difficulties with self-esteem and with applying himself to his studies at college.

The therapist confronted this denial and suggested that the problem of exhibitionism had not disappeared simply because Mr. S had been hospitalized. Following discharge from the hospital, Mr. S continued to struggle with exhibitionistic impulses, occasionally giving in to them. Each time he reported such impulses in therapy, his therapist would invite reflection on possible precipitants of the impulses or actions. Mr. S seemed genuinely perplexed as he searched his memory for antecedent events or feelings. The wish to expose himself was so integral to his identity that he did not think of it as developing out of any affective or relational context.

On one occasion after Mr. S exposed himself, his therapist pointed out that the episode of exposure had occurred immediately after a young woman in one of his classes had turned him down when he asked her out for a date. Mr. S acknowledged that he had felt rebuffed and humiliated and that he could understand the possibility that exposing himself was an expression of his anger and revenge when women failed to respond to him. He began to notice a pattern of increasing exhibitionistic impulses whenever he experienced a rebuff or rejection from any woman he pursued romantically. With help from the therapist, Mr. S was able to link his anger at women with his deep resentment of his mother for returning to full-time work outside the home when Mr. S was 2 years old.

When the therapy began to address these sensitive aspects of Mr. S's relationships with women, he abruptly terminated treatment. Several years later, however, he wrote to his therapist, indicating that he had found the key to overcoming his urge to expose himself. Although his exhibitionistic tendency still haunted him once in a while, he had managed to control it by teaching himself "to learn to love women." He had discovered, through a positive relationship with a young woman, that some women actually did care about him. He thanked the therapist for helping him see that he had been distorting the feelings women had toward him. When he realized that women did not automatically resent him because he was a man, he felt less fearful around them and less compelled to take revenge against them through exhibitionistic activity.

Marital therapy may be critical to the successful treatment of paraphilias. A marital crisis may precipitate the patient's seeking of treatment in the first place. Marital therapy can often help delineate how the perverse activity reflects sexual and emotional difficulties in the marital dyad. It may also alleviate the wife's unwarranted feelings of guilt and responsibility for the behavior and can instead facilitate a sense that she is part of its solution rather than part of its cause (Kentsmith and Eaton 1978). An exploration of marital discord may also reveal that the paraphilia is a container or "scapegoat" that deflects the focus from other more problematic areas in the marriage (Reid 1989). Clinicians must therefore be innovative in using the patient's spouse as an adjunctive therapist in refractory cases of paraphilia. For example, one man who was unresponsive to a number of treatments for his exhibitionism was able to control the symptom only when his wife agreed to drive him everywhere he went. In cases of transvestism, the main focus of treatment may be helping the patient's wife accept that the cross-dressing behavior is unlikely to change and assisting her in becoming more tolerant of her husband's need to wear women's clothing.

In cases of pedophilia that occur in the context of incest, family therapy is ordinarily an integral part of the overall treatment plan. Mothers typically collude in these incestuous arrangements by scotomizing the abundant evidence of father-daughter (or occasionally father-son) sexual relations. These mothers frequently grew up as parentified children who never received the nurturance they needed in childhood because they were too busy taking care of their own parents and siblings (Gelinas 1986). They tend to marry highly needy, dependent men as a continuation of their propensity for caretaking. Because of chronic feelings of neglect, the mother in such a family is likely to be highly ambivalent about raising children, and when they arrive, she may feel overwhelmed and neglect her husband as a result. As mother and father become more estranged, the father turns to one of the children—usually the eldest daughter—for nurturance, leading to a second generation of the parentified-child pattern. This child is likely to feel responsible for filling the mother's shoes, and when part of that responsibility entails sexually satisfying her own father, she may subordinate her own needs and rights to his. She exists to satisfy the needs of others. Indeed, family therapy in cases of incest often reveals that the victim protects the offender and maintains loyalty toward him. Effective family therapy requires careful attention to these dynamics. The victim's loyalty to the offender must be acknowledged and respected. It is also helpful to focus on the father's wish for relatedness and emotional connectedness rather than on sexuality or perversion (Gelinas 1986). Incest victims often report that the only warmth they ever received in their family of origin was from the father. The depletion of the mother's emotional resources must also be addressed empathically, and the therapist must bolster her ego capacities. The therapist who approaches the family by identifying and seeking to punish villains will be met with massive resistance—the family members will "circle the wagons" to exclude an outside attacker who does not appreciate the homeostatic balance within the family system.

Dynamic group psychotherapy is another modality that has been used effectively with patients suffering from perversions. Voyeurs and exhibitionists may respond well to group modalities. In one study (Rosen 1964), 21 of 24 patients were recovered or improved at follow-up 6–36 months later. Legally enforced group therapy with sex offenders, such as pedophiles, has also obtained satisfactory results, even on an outpatient basis (Ganzarain and Buchele 1990; Rappeport 1974). These groups provide a mixture of support and confrontation from other offenders who are intimately familiar with the patient's problem, just as homogeneous groups of drug addicts and alcoholics bring group pressure to bear to change destructive behavior. Ganzarain and Buchele (1990) found that excluding severely disturbed pedophiles—those with organic brain syndrome, psychosis, substance abuse, pure sociopathy, and exclusive perversions—can facilitate identification of a subgroup of pedophiles who will respond well to expressive group psychotherapy. Although patients in their group of offenders frequently denied responsibility and externalized blame, many suffered from unconscious guilt feelings and a profound sense of shame and humiliation about having been discovered. Typically, however, these feelings were fended off by considerable resistance to psychotherapeutic exploration. Because the treatment was legally mandated, many of the offenders viewed the group therapists as agents of the court and therefore assumed the posture of "doing time." Those patients with lower degrees of sociopathy and greater unconscious guilt feelings ultimately were able to use the group therapy process to understand that their hatred of women grew out of their wish to be loved. This understanding led to greater control of sexual impulses and general improvement in their capacity for object relations.

Hospital treatment.   Those paraphilic patients most likely to be hospitalized are pedophiles and, to a lesser extent, exhibitionists, who are simply unable to control their behavior on an outpatient basis. Many of the same countertransference problems described for psychotherapeutic treatments also arise in hospital treatment. The patient's denial of his perversion may lead staff members to collude with him by focusing on other problems. One exhibitionist would regularly sit in the lounge of the hospital unit with an erection visible underneath his sweatpants. However, no one on the nursing staff reported noticing this behavior until the doctor pointed out that one manifestation of countertransference with this patient was a fear of looking. This same patient would also often stand nude in his room until a female nurse made rounds; he would then act surprised and indignant when she saw him. When the patient's doctor brought up this behavior in a group meeting on the unit, the patient tried to marshal support from his fellow patients by accusing the doctor of being insensitive and cruel by embarrassing him in front of his peers.

In general, patients with paraphilias will object to discussing their problems in group meetings or community meetings on an inpatient unit. However, when staff members comply with requests to avoid sexual issues in treatment meetings, they are colluding with the patient's tendency to go through an entire hospitalization without dealing with the perversity that necessitated the hospitalization. Many pedophiles are extraordinarily smooth individuals who will charm other patients into avoiding confrontations.

Mr. T, a 41-year-old teacher, had been extensively involved in pedophilic sexual activities for many years. When the hospital staff insisted that he mention his child-molesting in the community meeting on the unit, Mr. T complied, but in such a manner that he received no feedback from any of the other patients. He began by saying that he loved children and was concerned about the future of America. He talked at great length about his love for his own two daughters and his concern about how his hospitalization might affect them. He admitted to sexual behavior with children, but made it sound benign. He explained that he had never forced any sexual activity on any child and he claimed that, in fact, all his victims had enjoyed their physical contact with him. He spoke of it in terms of "hugging" and "stroking," and he maintained that it had always occurred in the context of a loving friendship. By the time he finished his narrative account, the other patients were quite sympathetic. The psychiatrist in charge of the meeting asked if anyone was shocked or repulsed by Mr. T's behavior. Everyone denied any such reaction.

Pedophiles on a hospital unit may virtually paralyze patient groups from giving them the effective feedback given other patients. In addition, those with striking antisocial personality features may simply lie so that their perverse behavior is never dealt with during their hospitalization. One such patient maintained for all 6 weeks of his hospitalization that he had been falsely accused. On the day of his discharge, he acknowledged to his doctor with a chuckle that he actually had molested a child but had not wanted to admit it. As this patient packed his bags to leave the unit, his doctor was left feeling frustrated and impotent to do anything to improve the patient's condition.

Other pedophiles may convince staff members that they are complying with treatment by going through the motions required by it. They appear to use the insights gained in psychotherapy about the origin of their impulses and desires but secretly have no interest in changing themselves. They "play the game" of treatment because it is far preferable to prison, where pedophiles are often subject to gang rape. One pedophile who was a model patient during his hospitalization reported that his pedophilic impulses were thoroughly under control at discharge. He even said that he was no longer turned on by children. Upon transfer to a halfway house after discharge, he continued to report that he was no longer troubled by his pedophilic desires. This illusion was shattered when the police issued a warrant for his arrest stemming from two instances of child molestation. This pattern of deceiving staff members while going through the motions of treatment is all too common among this patient population. Some pedophiles may therefore do far better in correctional facilities with specialized programs for sex offenders that involve group confrontational approaches.

Sexual Dysfunctions

The increased popularity of behavioral techniques in the treatment of sexual dysfunctions (Masters and Johnson 1970) may have led some clinicians to view psychodynamic approaches as less relevant to the treatment of these disorders.

Over the past two decades, however, sex therapists have encountered numerous individuals and couples who, for a variety of reasons, are unsuited for brief behavioral sex therapy. As a result, the prescription of specific treatments for specific sexual dysfunctions has become increasingly sophisticated. Moreover, these disorders have served as models for the development of combined therapeutic techniques that include mixtures of behavioral and dynamic interventions (H. S. Kaplan 1974, 1979, 1986).

There is little question that certain patients can benefit from the techniques of Masters and Johnson. These researchers originally reported an 80% success rate with their 2-week intensive sex therapy program in St. Louis (1970). Data on the efficacy of psychodynamic psychotherapy in the treatment of sexual dysfunctions, however, are less available. One study that appeared shortly after the original Masters and Johnson report suggested less-impressive results (O'Connor and Stern 1972). Ninety-six patients who were treated 2–4 times a week for at least 2 years with psychoanalysis or psychoanalytically oriented psychotherapy for functional disorders had a success rate of 25% for the female subgroup and 57% for the males. Helen Singer Kaplan (1986) has pointed out that comparisons such as these are inappropriate since the patients in the O'Connor and Stern study probably had a much greater degree of associated psychopathology. Much of the effectiveness of the Masters and Johnson approach can be attributed to the select group of patients who sought their treatment. By and large, they were highly motivated, financially secure professional couples who could take 2 weeks out of their lives to devote themselves intensively to a sex therapy program. Kaplan also noted that specific diagnoses greatly influenced the success of sex therapy. Problems intrinsic to the desire phase are often resistant to sex therapy, and most results for this disorder would be comparable to those reported in the O'Connor and Stern (1972) study. Discrepancy of sexual desire between partners is the most commonly treated sexual dysfunction, and one survey of sex therapists revealed that only half of such couples were cured with sex therapy (Kilmann et al. 1986).

The fact that the most common sexual dysfunction is effectively treated by sex therapy only half the time reflects the need for dynamic approaches in addition to behavioral treatments. Clinicians have long known that when a sexual problem is the chief complaint in an initial interview, it is often only the tip of the iceberg. In some cases, the sexual problem may be a "red herring" to distract the clinician from far more serious and urgent problems. In other cases, it may serve to "contain" a variety of intimately related intrapsychic, marital, and family problems. When Viagra (sildenafil) was released on the American market in 1998, skyrocketing sales to men with erectile dysfunction led to the emergence of a variety of marital problems in couples who had achieved a stable equilibrium regarding physical and emotional intimacy on the basis of cessation of sexual relations. Many couples found themselves having to renegotiate their relationship and to seek out marital therapy to help clarify the nature of the intimacy problems that had been masked by the erectile dysfunction. Similarly, some women became worried that their husbands would engage in extramarital flings because they were no longer anxious about their capacity to achieve or maintain an erection.

Patients most likely to respond to brief sex therapy are usually suffering from mild performance anxiety in the context of a reasonably healthy personality structure and a reasonably gratifying marital relationship. Patients whose sexual problems are associated with severe character pathology (e.g., borderline and narcissistic personality disorders) or serious Axis I syndromes (e.g., panic disorder, schizophrenia, and major affective disorder) will not benefit from brief behavioral sex therapy and should therefore not be assigned that form of treatment (H. S. Kaplan 1986). Similarly, couples with entrenched patterns of pathological relatedness and chronic feelings of resentment and bitterness are not suitable candidates for brief sex therapy. Typically, these couples will not practice the assigned sex therapy exercises but will instead become more openly conflictual (Lansky and Davenport 1975). Even couples with greater psychological health may resist practicing the sensate focus exercises that are often part of behavioral sex therapy treatment because the exercises activate unconscious anxiety (H. S. Kaplan 1986). The treatment of sexual symptoms must therefore be highly individualized and must be based on a careful psychiatric and psychodynamic evaluation. Organic causes, especially for erectile disorders, must be ruled out, thereby facilitating an accurate psychiatric diagnosis.

Psychodynamic Understanding

Most of the cataloged sexual dysfunctions may be categorized as disorders of desire, arousal, or orgasm. In a national probability sample of 1,749 women and 1,410 men ages 18–59 years (Laumann et al. 1999), 43% of women and 31% of men reported some degree of sexual dysfunction. Among women, the prevalence of low sexual desire was about 22%, and the prevalence of arousal problems was 14%. Among men, the prevalence of premature ejaculation, erectile dysfunction, and low sexual desire was 21%, 5%, and 5%, respectively. Brief sex therapy may be the most cost-effective treatment for individuals and couples who have difficulty attaining orgasm but who have no serious associated psychopathology. Disorders associated with desire and arousal tend to be more refractory to brief sex therapy because they are anchored in more deep-seated psychopathological factors (H. S. Kaplan 1986; Reid 1989). This discussion will focus on problems in these areas.

The psychodynamic understanding of the male or female patient who has no desire for sex, or of the male patient who has desire but is unable to achieve an erection, begins with a careful understanding of the symptom's situational context. If the patient is involved in an intimate relationship, the clinician must determine whether the problem of desire or arousal is specific to the partner or is generalized to all potential sexual partners. Sexual difficulties that are specific to the couple—as opposed to those representing primarily intrapsychic difficulties that would occur with any partner—must be understood in the context of the interpersonal dynamics of the dyad. Clinicians must remember, though, that desire problems, like all other psychological symptoms, are multiply determined.

The 1999 national probability sample (Laumann et al. 1999) revealed that problematic relationships, in both the present and the past, are highly linked to sexual dysfunctions. In fact, all categories of sexual dysfunction in women in this study showed strong associations with unhappiness and low feelings of emotional and physical satisfaction. Arousal disorder in women was significantly linked to sexual victimization through adult-child contact or forced sexual contact. Male victims of adult-child contact were found to be three times as likely to experience erectile dysfunction as those who had not been victimized. Male victims of childhood sexual abuse were also twice as likely to experience premature ejaculation and low sexual desire compared with control subjects who were free from childhood trauma. The investigators emphasized that long-lasting and profound effects on sexual functioning seem to result from traumatic sexual acts in both sexes.

Levine (1988) has delineated three discrete elements of sexual desire that must function in synchrony for adequate desire and arousal: drive, wish, and motive. Drive is rooted in biology and may be affected by physical factors, such as hormonal levels, medical illnesses, and medications. The wish element is more intimately connected to conscious cognitive or ideational factors. For example, in the presence of a normal drive component, an individual may wish to not have sex because of religious prohibitions or because of a fear of contracting acquired immunodeficiency syndrome (AIDS). The third element, motive, is intimately related to unconscious object relational needs and is the component most likely to be the focus of therapeutic intervention.

The clinician must assess all three elements, according to Levine, and must attempt to understand why these are not integrated into a functional whole. Numerous factors may interfere with an individual's motivation. One partner in the marriage may be having an extramarital affair and may simply have no interest in the spouse. Or one spouse may feel so chronically resentful and angry toward the other that sexual relations are out of the question. Problems in the couple's nonsexual relationship probably account for most instances of inhibited sexual desire. A sexual partner's transference distortions can also play a key role in disturbing motivation. In many couples who enter sex or marital therapy, the spouses are unconsciously relating to one another as if to the opposite-sex parent. When this occurs, sexual relations may unconsciously be experienced as incestuous, so the partners manage the anxiety associated with this taboo by avoiding sex altogether. Simpson (1985) reported a case of sex therapy in which the wife was highly resistant to carrying out the prescribed exercises. When this resistance was explored dynamically, the wife was able to acknowledge to the therapist that part of her wanted her husband to fail in sex therapy. She revealed her fear that her husband would become a "womanizer" like her father if he regained adequate sexual functioning. This transference distortion of her husband threatened to undermine the success of the sex therapy. Even single individuals in therapy or analysis may experience transference-like attachments to a potential sex partner that result in disorders of motivation.

> Mr. U was a 25-year-old, single professional man who entered psychoanalysis because of various problems in his capacity to work and love. The drive component of Mr. U's sexual desire was entirely adequate—he masturbated several times a day to relieve intense sexual tension. The wish component of desire was also intact. He aspired to sexual relations with an appropriate female and fantasized about doing so. However, the motivational element seemed lacking, as evidenced by his characteristic behavior pattern each time he became attracted to a woman. As he talked about the woman in analysis, he would become tearfully convinced that he would ultimately lose the current object of his longings. His anticipation of the loss aroused such intense feelings of grief and so overwhelmed him that he would decide not to pursue a relationship at all but instead to simply retreat into solitary masturbation.
>
> Each time Mr. U experienced these feelings of anticipatory loss, his analyst would try to elicit any associations to previous events or life experiences that might bring up analogous feelings. After a considerable period of analytic work, the patient finally began to make sense of his feelings. When the patient was 5 years old, his father had been away at war for a year. During this time, Mr. U had been "the man of the house," occupying a special position with his mother in the absence of his chief rival for her affections. At times he had even slept in bed with her. When Mr. U's father returned, however, the patient suffered a devastating loss of this special, intimate relationship with his mother.
>
> The patient's memory of this period in his life helped him understand his motives not to pursue sexual relations. As soon as he became infatuated with a woman, he began to form a maternal transference attachment. Reexperiencing her (at an unconscious level) as his mother, he became convinced that she, too, would "dump" him for another man, just as his mother had turned him aside for his father. Mr. U feared confronting that grief again, which led him to avoid sexual relations. This insight also put Mr. U in touch with considerable castration anxiety. He realized that he was deeply worried that his penis might be injured during sex, a concern that he eventually associated with his fear of retaliation for having taken his father's place in his mother's bed.

Our capacity for sexual arousal and desire is clearly connected intimately with our internal object relations. Scharff (1988) developed an object relations model of inhibited sexual desire based on Fairbairn's (1952) theories of development (see Chapter 2). Fairbairn postulated two "bad object" systems, the libidinal ego and object, in which the ego longs for a tantalizing object, and the antilibidinal ego and object, in which the ego feels hatred and anger toward an attacking, abandoning, or negligent object. The rejecting or antilibidinal object attempts to eliminate the exciting or libidinal object. In Scharff's model, then, this antilibidinal system interferes with sexual excitement, which derives from the libidinal system.

These metapsychological abstractions can be more easily understood by examining the development of a typical relationship. Individuals are attracted to one another as a result of activation of the libidinal or need-exciting object system. Via mutual projective identification, each regards the other as the exciting object. To maintain the idealized "in love" state, each must repress the antilibidinal or rejecting object. However, as the luster and freshness of the relationship wear off, the repressed object relations unit begins to surface, particularly when needs are inevitably frustrated. At this point, the rejecting object of the antilibidinal system is projected into the partner, and sexual excitement is contaminated by the perception of the partner as persecuting or abandoning.

In Scharff's model, clinicians must evaluate disturbances of desire according to three different areas of internal and external object relations: 1) the external realities of the couple's current marital relationship; 2) the internal object world of each individual and how it affects the capacity for sexual intimacy; and 3) the current family constellation (including children, elderly parents, and other factors) and how it affects sexual desire. Scharff has noted that sexual desire is greatly affected by the developmental stage of the marriage itself.

A psychodynamic assessment of inhibited sexual desire must acknowledge the possibility that the "designated patient" may not be the one who needs the treatment. Helen Singer Kaplan (1988) has studied couples in which one partner is so exquisitely sensitive to rejection that the other partner will lose interest in having sexual relations. In many of these cases, the female partner suffers from panic disorder, in which the man's absorption in pleasure is perceived as an abandonment of her. No amount of reassurance from the male partner will convince the woman of his commitment to her. Kaplan recommended that the apparently "asymptomatic" partner may need to realize that her efforts at control instead lead her partner to withdraw from sexual intimacy.

Primitively disturbed patients, especially those with schizophrenia and severe borderline features, may find the prospect of genital fusion overwhelming to their fragile ego. Motivational factors in these patients that lead to inhibited sexual desire are related to the primitive anxiety states described in Chapter 9, including dis-

PSYCHODYNAMIC PSYCHIATRY IN CLINICAL PRACTICE

integration anxiety, persecutory anxiety, and a fear of fusing with one's partner. Abstaining from sexual relations may thus appear to safeguard the integrity of the self.

Treatment Considerations

The clinician who assesses functional sexual disorders must decide whether to prescribe brief behavioral sex therapy, couples therapy, psychoanalysis or expressive-supportive psychotherapy, pharmacotherapy, or any combination of these. Lief (1981) estimated that 30%–40% of all sexual dysfunctions will improve symptomatically with brief behavioral techniques. Of those who do not benefit from behavioral therapy, 20% will require marital therapy, 10% will need long-term individual expressive-supportive psychotherapy, and about 30% will need some combination of marital and sex therapy. Helen Singer Kaplan's (1986) estimates are similar, but she has also advocated pharmacotherapy. Approximately one-fourth of the patients at her sex clinic whose problems involved sexual aversion or phobic sex avoidance also met the diagnostic criteria for panic disorder. However, she found that prescribing sensate focus techniques for those patients only increased their anxiety, and thus defeated the treatment. Antipanic medications may be helpful for these patients. But Kaplan (1988) also concluded that these medications do not cure the patient and stressed that attention to dynamic issues should accompany pharmacotherapeutic intervention. A number of medications have been developed to enhance sexual desire, including bupropion, which is often prescribed for depression and may overwhelm certain female patients with intense sexual desire that feels almost uncontrollable (Bartlik et al. 1999). A sudden increase in sexual desire related to the prescribing of bupropion may send a marriage into turmoil. Viagra (sildenafil) may also disrupt the sexual and psychological equilibrium between members of a couple. Nevertheless, such medications may be useful adjuncts to psychotherapeutic measures.

Indications for the various modalities may not always be clear during the initial evaluation. Brief behavioral sex therapy is likely to be successful if a couple is highly motivated, if neither partner suffers from serious psychopathology, if each partner is reasonably satisfied with the relationship, and if the dysfunction is based on performance anxiety and related to the orgasm phase. Couples who have inhibited sexual desire and are generally disillusioned with the relationship may require marital therapy for a time to address basic problems in their relationship. If the couple decides to stay together after marital therapy, then sex therapy techniques can be more appropriately recommended.

Couples who seem appropriate candidates for brief sex therapy techniques but who undermine the process by not practicing the exercises may require a hybrid treatment that Helen Singer Kaplan (1979) labeled *psychosexual therapy*. In this treatment, the therapist prescribes behavioral exercises and then addresses any resistances to practicing the exercises with dynamic psychotherapy. Kaplan found this combination of techniques to be critical to successful treatment with certain patients. The dynamic portion of the treatment allows exploration of themes such as the patient's intense guilt feelings about sexual pleasure. Parental transferences to the partner can also be uncovered and explored. In addition, many patients have unconscious conflicts about being successful in any endeavor—including sexual performance—that may have to be examined. Kaplan (1986) also found that some patients unconsciously act out the role of "loser" or "failure" that they have been assigned in their family of origin.

Patients suffering from severe character pathology or deeply ingrained neurotic conflicts about sexuality should be treated in psychoanalysis or expressive-supportive psychotherapy (H. S. Kaplan 1986; Levine 1988; Reid 1989; Scharff 1988). Sometimes these problems surface only during an extended evaluation with sex therapy (Scharff 1988). Certain patients may remain unconvinced of the need for long-term intensive individual psychotherapy until they have tried brief methods and found them ineffective. Extended sex therapy also allows the therapist to gain a greater grasp of the internal object relations of each member of the couple. As described in the section on object relations family and marital therapy in Chapter 5, the therapist "contains" the various projective identifications from both spouses. Therapists who are open to this process can diagnose problematic patterns of object relatedness in the couple through "firsthand experience." When there is deep-seated neurotic conflict about sexuality or when there is severe character pathology, however, sex therapy will often exacerbate these problems (Lansky and Davenport 1975). The prescribed sensate focus exercises will force the couple to confront issues that are habitually avoided because of the way their relationship has been organized. Particularly in cases where there is a history of sexual trauma, the prescription of sex therapy may be experienced as a form of trauma itself and have far-reaching antitherapeutic effects on the couple.

Mrs. V was a 46-year-old homemaker who entered sex therapy with her husband because of her total lack of interest in sexual relations. After several unproductive sessions, the sex therapist referred Mrs. V for individual expressive-supportive psychotherapy. She felt relieved when she first saw her individual psychotherapist because she realized that she would not be "forced into sexual relations" with her husband.

She described her marital relationship as involving a caretaking role for herself that produced no gratitude from her husband. He had retired 4 years earlier and now spent his days lying around the house watching television. She was not happy with their relationship, but she seemed to have little interest in changing it. She repeatedly berated herself, saying that she did not deserve a better life than what she had. When this pattern of self-denigration and resignation was pointed out to her by the therapist, Mrs. V confided that every time she had felt good in her life, she had been "zapped." She then recounted numerous examples, including the death of one of her children, to illustrate how she had always been punished for any positive feelings she had had about events in her life.

Although Mrs. V talked about a wide range of topics in her psychotherapy, she steadfastly refused to mention anything about her sexuality or the sexual problems that brought her to treatment in the first place. Her therapist began to feel as though he were coercing her into dealing with her sexual problems. When he gently asked her about them, she responded as though to a rapist, feeling violated and withdrawing into silence. The therapist used his countertransference feelings to diagnose an internal object relation that had been externalized in the psychotherapy. He said to Mrs. V, "You seem to react as though I am traumatizing you with my questions about sexuality. Is this repeating any sexually related trauma from your past?" Mrs. V broke down and tearfully acknowledged a history of early sexual trauma at the hands of an uncle. She also opened up further about her first marriage, explaining that she had had a number of extramarital affairs that led to two illegal abortions. She had always been a "daddy's girl," and she wondered if she had been looking for her father in all those affairs. This insight was coupled with an awareness that she had stopped having affairs when her father died about 18 years earlier. Her father had been involved in some of her marital problems that had resulted from her promiscuity, and he had seemed highly distressed by her unfaithfulness to her husband. She even speculated that her promiscuous behavior in her first marriage might have caused her father's death. With interpretations from the therapist, Mrs. V began to understand that her self-sacrifice and selfless devotion to caring for her husband was a form of psychological reparation for the damage she believed she had inflicted on her father. She also began to understand that she denied herself sexual pleasure to punish herself for her promiscuity and the two abortions.

The case of Mrs. V illustrates how deeply ingrained sexual problems may be ego-syntonic because they fulfill certain psychological needs. Many patients with sexual dysfunctions are actually convinced that they should *not* experience sexual pleasure, so they are therefore invested in maintaining their symptomatology. The treatment of sexual dysfunctions is a highly value-laden area of psychiatry. Clinicians must temper their countertransference need to cure with a respect for the patient's right to choose a particular pattern of sexual adjustment. Helen Singer Kaplan (1986) noted that some women who fail to reach orgasm nevertheless report satisfying sexual relations; such women usually do not seek treatment for sexual dysfunction. In addition, many voluntary celibates in religious orders lead happy and productive lives. Finally, clinicians must keep in mind that, for some patients, a sexual symptom is nothing more than an admission ticket to psychotherapy. Once inside the door, these patients become more interested in other areas of their life and the sexual symptoms lose significance.

References

Abel GG, Becker JD, Cunningham-Rathner J, et al: Multiple paraphilic diagnoses among sex offenders. Bulletin of the American Academy of Psychiatry and the Law 16:153–168, 1988

American Psychiatric Association: Diagnostic and Statistical Manual of Mental Disorders, 3rd Edition, Revised. Washington, DC, American Psychiatric Association, 1987

American Psychiatric Association: Diagnostic and Statistical Manual of Mental Disorders, 4th Edition. Washington, DC, American Psychiatric Association 1994

Bartlik B, Kaplan P, Kaminetsky J, et al: Medications with the potential to enhance sexual responsivity in women. Psychiatric Annals 29:46–52, 1999

Berlin FS, Meinecke CF: Treatment of sex offenders with antiandrogenic medication: conceptualization, review of treatment modalities, and preliminary findings. Am J Psychiatry 138:601–607, 1981

Brown GR, Wise TN, Costa PT, et al: Personality characteristics and sexual functioning of 188 cross-dressing men. J Nerv Ment Dis 184:265–273, 1996

Chasseguet-Smirgel J: Perversion and the universal law. International Review of Psychoanalysis 10:293–301, 1983

Fairbairn WRD: Psychoanalytic Studies of the Personality. London, Routledge & Kegan Paul, 1952

Fenichel O: The Psychoanalytic Theory of Neurosis. New York, WW Norton, 1945

Fogel GI, Myers WA (eds): Perversions and Near-Perversions in Clinical Practice: New Psychoanalytic Perspectives. New Haven, CT, Yale University Press, 1991

Freud S: Three essays on the theory of sexuality (1905), in The Standard Edition of the Complete Psychological Works of Sigmund Freud, Vol 7. Translated and edited by Strachey J. London, Hogarth Press, 1953, pp 123–245

Freud S: Splitting of the ego in the process of defence (1940), in The Standard Edition of the Complete Psychological Works of Sigmund Freud, Vol 23. Translated and edited by Strachey J. London, Hogarth Press, 1964, pp 271–278

Ganzarain RC, Buchele BJ: Incest perpetrators in group therapy: a psychodynamic perspective. Bull Menninger Clin 54:295–310, 1990

Gelinas DJ: Unexpected resources in treating incest families, in Family Resources: The Hidden Partner in Family Therapy. Edited by Karpel MA. New York, Guilford, 1986, pp 327–358

Goldberg A: The Problem of Perversion: The View of Self Psychology. New Haven, CT, Yale University Press, 1995

Greenacre P: The transitional object and the fetish: with special reference to the role of illusion. Int J Psychoanal 51:447–456, 1970

Greenacre P: Fetishism, in Sexual Deviation, 2nd Edition. Edited by Rosen I. Oxford, Oxford University Press, 1979, pp 79–108

Groth AN, Birnbaum HJ: Men Who Rape: The Psychology of the Offender. New York, Plenum, 1979

Hall GCN: Sexual offender recidivism revisited: a meta-analysis of recent treatment studies. J Consult Clin Psychol 63:802–809, 1995

Kaplan HS: The New Sex Therapy: Active Treatment of Sexual Dysfunctions. New York, Brunner/Mazel, 1974

Kaplan HS: Disorders of Sexual Desire and Other New Concepts and Techniques in Sex Therapy. New York, Simon & Schuster, 1979

Kaplan HS: The psychosexual dysfunctions, in Psychiatry, Revised Edition. Edited by Cavenar JO Jr. Vol 1: The Personality Disorders and Neuroses. Edited by Cooper AM, Frances AJ, Sacks MH. Philadelphia, PA, JB Lippincott, 1986, pp 467–479

Kaplan HS: Intimacy disorders and sexual panic states. J Sex Marital Ther 14:3–12, 1988

Kaplan LJ: Female Perversions: The Temptations of Emma Bovary. New York, Doubleday, 1991

Kentsmith DK, Eaton MT: Treating Sexual Problems in Medical Practice. New York, Arco, 1978

Kernberg OF: Borderline Conditions and Pathological Narcissism. New York, Jason Aronson, 1975

Kilmann PR, Boland JP, Norton SP, et al: Perspectives of sex therapy outcome: a survey of AASECT providers. J Sex Marital Ther 12:116–138, 1986

Kohut H: The Analysis of the Self: A Systematic Approach to the Psychoanalytic Treatment of Narcissistic Personality Disorders. New York, International Universities Press, 1971

Kohut H: The Restoration of the Self. New York, International Universities Press, 1977

Lansky MR, Davenport AE: Difficulties of brief conjoint treatment of sexual dysfunction. Am J Psychiatry 132:177–179, 1975

Laumann EO, Paik A, Rosen RC: Sexual dysfunction in the United States: prevalence and predictors. JAMA 281:537–544, 1999

Levine SB: Intrapsychic and individual aspects of sexual desire, in Sexual Desire Disorders. Edited by Leiblum SR, Rosen R. New York, Guilford, 1988, pp 21–44

Lief HI (ed): Sexual Problems in Medical Practice. Monroe, WI, American Medical Association, 1981

Marshall WL, Pithers WD: A reconsideration of treatment outcome with sex offenders. Criminal Justice and Behavior 21:10–27, 1994

Massie H, Szajnberg N: The ontogeny of a sexual fetish from birth to age 30 and memory processes: a research case report from a prospective longitudinal study. Int J Psychoanal 78:755–771, 1997

Masters WH, Johnson V: Human Sexual Inadequacy. Boston, MA, Little, Brown, 1970

McConaghy N: Paedophilia: a review of the evidence. Aust N Z J Psychiatry 32:252–265, 1998

McDougall J: Plea for a Measure of Abnormality. New York, International Universities Press, 1980

McDougall J: Identifications, neoneeds and neosexualities. Int J Psychoanal 67:19–31, 1986

McDougall J: The Many Faces of Eros: A Psychoanalytic Exploration of Human Sexuality. New York, WW Norton, 1995

Miller JP: How Kohut actually worked. Progress in Self Psychology 1:13–30, 1985

Mitchell SA: Relational Concepts in Psychoanalysis: An Integration. Cambridge, MA, Harvard University Press, 1988

Nersessian E: A cat as fetish: a contribution to the theory of fetishism. Int J Psychoanal 79:713–725, 1998

O'Connor JF, Stern LO: Results of treatment in functional sexual disorders. New York State Journal of Medicine 72:1927–1934, 1972

Person ES: Paraphilias and gender identity disorders, in Psychiatry, Revised Edition. Edited by Cavenar JO Jr. Vol 1: The Personality Disorders and Neuroses. Edited by Cooper AM, Frances AJ, Sacks MH. Philadelphia, PA, JB Lippincott, 1986, pp 447–465

Prentky RA, Knight RA, Lee AFS: Risk factors associated with recidivism among extrafamilial child molesters. J Consult Clin Psychol 65:141–149, 1997

Rappeport JR: Enforced treatment—is it treatment? Bulletin of the American Academy of Psychiatry and the Law 2:148–158, 1974

Reid WH: The Treatment of Psychiatric Disorders: Revised for the DSM-III-R. New York, Brunner/Mazel, 1989

Rice ME, Quinsey VL, Harris GT: Sexual recidivism among child molesters released from a maximum security psychiatric institution. J Consult Clin Psychol 59:381–386, 1991

Rosen I (ed): Pathology and Treatment of Sexual Deviation: A Methodological Approach. London, Oxford University Press, 1964

Rosen I (ed): Sexual Deviation, 2nd Edition. London, Oxford University Press, 1979

Sachs H: On the genesis of perversions. Translated by Goldberg RB. Psychoanal Q 55:477–488, 1986

Scharff DE: An object relations approach to inhibited sexual desire, in Sexual Desire Disorders. Edited by Leiblum SR, Rosen R. New York, Guilford, 1988, pp 45–74

Simpson WS: Psychoanalysis and sex therapy: a case report. Bull Menninger Clin 49:565–582, 1985

Stoller RJ: Perversion: The Erotic Form of Hatred. New York, Pantheon, 1975

Stoller RJ: Observing the Erotic Imagination. New Haven, CT, Yale University Press, 1985

Stoller RJ: Pain and Passion: A Psychoanalyst Explores the World of S and M. New York, Plenum, 1991

Stolorow RD, Atwood GE, Brandchaft B: Masochism and its treatment. Bull Menninger Clin 52:504–509, 1988

Travin S, Bluestone H, Coleman E, et al: Pedophilia: an update on theory and practice. Psychiatr Q 57:89–103, 1985

Substance-Related Disorders and Eating Disorders

In this chapter I consider two diagnostic categories that involve discrete self-destructive symptoms. Substance abuse is defined by the ingestion of chemicals that may lead to addiction, life-threatening physical problems, and a host of emotional problems. Eating disorders are defined by overeating, voluntary purging, and starvation. Both groups of disorders present a complex problem for psychodynamic clinicians: What is the role of dynamic approaches in disorders that require symptom control as a major thrust of the therapeutic effort? In some quarters, psychodynamic understanding is considered irrelevant to the management of addiction and eating disorders. However, a considerable body of clinical and research literature suggests otherwise.

Substance-Related Disorders

Because psychodynamic psychiatrists often become frustrated in their efforts to treat alcoholic patients, they may abandon or avoid such efforts. Relapse is common, and interpretations of unconscious motivations often seem to have little impact on the drinking behavior itself. Psychodynamic models of alcoholism are regarded with skepticism both by mental health professionals and by society at large.

Two other models—the moral model and the disease model—receive much greater support (Cooper 1987). The moral model views alcoholic individuals as bearing complete responsibility for their alcoholism. From this point of view, alcoholic persons are hedonistic individuals interested only in their own pursuit of pleasure, with no regard for the feelings of others. This model has its roots in the fundamentalist religious belief that alcoholism is a sign of moral turpitude. Failings of willpower are closely linked to notions of sin, and punishment through the legal system is often regarded as the appropriate way to deal with alcoholic individuals. Eliminating drinking behavior is a matter of overcoming weak willpower to "pull oneself up by the bootstraps."

The success of Alcoholics Anonymous (AA) has led to the increasing popularity of the disease model of alcoholism. In contrast to the moral model, this paradigm relieves the alcoholic person of responsibility for his or her illness. Just as a diabetic person is not held responsible for diabetes, the alcoholic individual is not held responsible for alcoholism. Alcoholic persons are viewed as having an inherent predisposition to addiction to exogenous substances; psychological factors are irrelevant. Although this model originated as a backlash to moralizing reactions to—and inhumane treatment of—alcoholic persons, it has recently gained support from genetic studies of the offspring of alcoholic individuals. Even when raised apart from their alcoholic parents, these children have an increased risk of developing alcoholism as adults (Goodwin 1979; Schuckit 1985). Twin studies in both male and female twin pairs (Kendler et al. 1992; Prescott and Kendler 1999) suggest that genetic factors play a major role in the development of alcoholism, with similar influence for alcohol abuse and alcohol dependence.

Further support for the disease model has come from Vaillant's (1983) prospective study of male alcoholic patients throughout the course of their adult lives. He found that the eventual development of alcoholism could not be predicted from adverse childhood experiences or even from psychological profiles of these subjects as young adults. The only reliable predictor of adult alcoholism was antisocial behavior. Vaillant concluded that depression, anxiety, and other psychological characteristics often associated with alcoholic persons were *consequences,* rather than causes, of the disorder. Furthermore, psychotherapy and psychological conceptualizations of alcoholism play a minor role in clinical understanding and treatment planning. Vaillant thus decided that enforced abstinence through AA has the greatest likelihood of success.

A shift in focus from alcoholic patients to those who abuse drugs reveals wide usage of the same two models. The moral model is more widely applied to drug abusers than to alcoholic persons, however, largely because of the extensive overlap between crime and drug abuse. Much of the controversy over the appropriate response to the national drug problem involves whether addicted persons are more effectively handled through legalistically oriented punitive approaches or medically oriented therapeutic approaches. Drug abusers have sought to replicate the success of AA by developing organizations such as Narcotics Anonymous (NA). But the disease model and its associated self-help groups have been less successful with drug abusers, as Vaillant himself (1988) has pointed out, because of apparent fundamental differences between alcoholic persons and polydrug abusers that require differential approaches. In view of these essential differences, the following section will examine the psychodynamic understanding of alcoholic persons and drug abusers in turn.

Psychodynamic Approaches to Alcoholism

The AA approach to the problem of alcoholism has been highly effective in the treatment of many individuals. Although the AA organization itself promotes the disease model, its methods address psychological needs and facilitate lasting structural personality changes (Mack 1981). Abstinence is achieved in an interpersonal context where alcoholic individuals can experience a caring and concerned community of fellow sufferers. These caring figures can be internalized in the same manner that a psychotherapist is internalized, and they can assist the alcoholic individual with affect management, impulse control, and other ego functions, also as a psychotherapist would. Hence, the psychodynamic model can facilitate an understanding of some of the changes rendered by the AA approach (Mack 1981).

For many alcoholic persons, the psychological changes encouraged by AA and the abstinence associated with commitment to its ideals and regular attendance at the meetings are sufficient treatment. The psychodynamically sensitive clinician, understanding the value of this approach, must have the good judgment to leave well enough alone. Clinical experience has repeatedly demonstrated, however, that AA is not suitable for all patients who suffer from alcoholism. It apparently works best for those who can accept the idea that they have no control over their drinking and thus need to surrender to a "higher power," and for those who are essentially free of other psychiatric disorders.

Most alcoholism experts would agree that alcoholism is a heterogeneous disorder with a multifactorial etiology (Donovan 1986). What works for one patient may not work for another, and all the treatments are surrounded with controversy. A review of treatment studies (McCrady and Langenbucher 1996) suggested that specific treatments appear to have differential effectiveness with different patient groups. No one type of therapy is consistently better than any other type of therapy. In a nationwide project sponsored by the National Institute on Alcohol Abuse and Alcoholism (Project MATCH Research Group 1997), three types of therapy were compared: cognitive-behavioral therapy, 12-step facilitation to prepare subjects for a commitment to AA, and motivational enhancement therapy aimed at improving readiness and willingness to change drinking habits. Overall, all three treatments had reasonably good results, and none was more successful than any other. Clearly, no treatment is definitive, and clinicians must consider each patient individually, making a careful psychiatric evaluation before developing an individually tailored treatment plan.

Unfortunately, the disease model has promulgated the "de-psychologizing" of alcoholism. The conclusions drawn by Vaillant (1983) are in conflict with those based on other longitudinal studies, which suggest that personality factors may be important to an understanding of vulnerability to alcoholism (Sutker and Allain 1988). Moreover, Vaillant's conclusions are only as valid as his instruments of measurement. Dodes (1988) observed that Vaillant's methods are not capable of identifying a critical feature in alcoholic patients—namely, their disturbance in self-esteem as revealed by an inability to care for themselves.

Perhaps the major difficulty with the treatment approach suggested by Vaillant and other strict adherents to the disease model is that it ignores the heterogeneity of the disorder. Alcoholism is not a monolithic entity. In fact, one might more accurately refer to the "alcoholisms" (Donovan 1986). Numerous studies attest that there is no single "alcoholic personality" that predisposes to alcoholism (Donovan 1986; Nathan 1988; Sutker and Allain 1988). Nonetheless, personality variables and psychological issues are highly relevant in the treatment of many alcoholic patients. A narrow interpretation of the disease model might lead clinicians to ignore how these factors contribute to relapse in the course of the illness.

Although no specific personality traits are connected with alcoholism, psychoanalytic observers have repeatedly noted structural defects, such as ego weakness and difficulty in maintaining self-esteem (Donovan 1986). Both Kohut (1971) and Balint (1979) noted that alcohol serves the function of replacing missing psychological structures and thereby restores some sense of self-regard and inner harmony. Unfortunately, these effects last only as long as the intoxication. Khantzian (1982) also observed that alcoholic patients had problems with self-esteem, the modulation of affect, and the capacity for self-care. Investigators of borderline personality disorder have consistently noted parallels between alcoholic patients and patients with borderline personality disorder (Hartocollis 1982; Kernberg 1975; Knight 1953; Rinsley 1988); in particular, they share such traits as poor anxiety tolerance, poor affective control, and the use of splitting as a predominant defense (see Chapter 15). This linkage of alcoholism with borderline personality disorder has been further substantiated by empirical studies (Nace et al. 1983; Vaglum and Vaglum 1985) that suggest that 30%–39% of alcoholic persons have coexisting borderline pathology. A review of 12 studies of alcoholic patients in whom a specific attempt was made to diagnose personality disorder found that the prevalence of comorbid Axis II conditions varied from 14% to 78% (Gorton and Akhtar

1994). Other common diagnoses accompanying alcoholism are depression (Weissman and Myers 1980) and sociopathy (Schuckit et al. 1970).

These studies are cited not to convince readers that all alcoholic persons suffer from coexisting psychiatric disorders or preexisting intrapsychic deficits, but rather to highlight the obvious fact that addiction to alcohol occurs in a *person*. An individual may develop alcoholism as the final common pathway of a complex interaction between structural deficits, genetic predisposition, familial influences, cultural contributions, and other assorted environmental variables. A thorough psychodynamic evaluation of the patient will consider the alcoholism and all its contributing factors in the context of the total person. Whether depression, for example, is a cause or a consequence of alcoholism, or a completely separate disease state, is of more interest to researchers than to clinicians. When alcoholic individuals sober up and look back at the wreckage caused by their alcoholic existence, they are commonly faced with a good deal of depression. This depression stems from the painful recognition that they have hurt others (frequently those most important to them). They must also mourn the things (e.g., relationships, possessions) that they have lost or destroyed as the result of their addictive behavior. Although antidepressant medication may alleviate the depression, psychotherapy can assist in the process of working through these painful issues. Also, assessment and treatment of suicide risk must be part of the overall planning in the treatment of alcoholic patients. Twenty-five percent of all suicides occur in alcoholic individuals, and an alcoholic person's likelihood of suicide is between 60 and 120 times higher than that of a person who is not psychiatrically ill (Murphy and Wetzel 1990). When depression and alcoholism are found together, they appear to have a synergistic or additive effect that results in a disproportionately high level of acute suicidality (Cornelius et al. 1995; Pages et al. 1997).

Another implication of the observation that alcoholism occurs in an individual is that each person will prefer and accept different treatment options. Dodes (1988) noted: "Some patients are able to use only psychotherapy, others can use only AA, and there are those who will best be treated with a combination of the two. Accurate prescription of treatment requires individual clinical judgment" (pp. 283–284). Many alcoholic individuals find AA unworkable either because of their embarrassment at having to speak in front of a group or because of their philosophical opposition to the notion of a "higher power." Although Vaillant (1981) has declared psychotherapy to be wasteful in the treatment of alcoholism, some patients are able to maintain sobriety with psychotherapy alone (Dodes 1984; Khantzian 1985a). An unfortunate "straw man" stereotype often applied to the dynamic psychotherapy of alcoholic patients is that the therapist uncovers unconscious motivations for drinking while ignoring the patient's actual drinking behavior. The fact that psychotherapy can be misused by some patients and by some therapists does not mean, however, that it should be written off as a treatment (Dodes 1988).

Patients involved in AA are often in psychotherapy as well. In one study, more than 90% of the abstinent alcoholic patients in AA who sought psychotherapy found it helpful (Brown 1985). Psychotherapy and AA often work synergistically. Dodes (1988) observed that alcoholic patients may develop, in self psychological terms, an idealizing or mirror transference to the AA organization. They view it as a caring, idealized figure in their life that sustains and supports them. This transference may be split off from the psychotherapeutic transference, and the psychotherapist is wise to delay analyzing it. Eventually, the selfobject functions of AA can be internalized enough to improve self-care and heighten self-esteem. After some degree of internalization, psychotherapists can shift the therapy from a supportive to a more expressive emphasis.

Other researchers have argued that abstinence is not an absolute requirement for effective psychotherapy (Dodes 1984; Pattison 1976). If a therapist demands abstinence, some patients will refuse treatment altogether. In fact, it is naive to expect total abstinence in the course of long-term psychotherapy. Very few alcoholic individuals are unambivalent about giving up their symptomatic drinking; any lack of motivation should be viewed as a symptom rather than as a contraindication for psychotherapy (Cooper 1987). However, if patients continue to drink heavily, with no capacity for or interest in exploring their reasons for drinking, they may be unable to use the psychotherapeutic process and may instead require hospitalization to be effectively treated.

Group psychotherapy is also commonly used in both inpatient and outpatient treatment of alcoholism. In a randomized controlled trial of psychodynamic group therapy and cognitive-behavioral therapy for alcohol-dependent patients (Sandahl et al. 1998), patients in both treatment groups improved with 15 weekly 90-minute group sessions. Most of the patients in the psychodynamic group therapy were able to maintain a more positive drinking pattern during the 15-month follow-up period, in contrast to the patients in cognitive-behavioral treatment, who appeared to relapse over time.

Other therapists (e.g., Khantzian 1986) have cautioned against a confrontational approach. Because of the difficulty that many alcoholic patients have in regulating affects such as anxiety, depression, and anger, confrontation in a group setting can be counterproductive or even harmful. Cooper (1987) shared Khantzian's view that confrontation should be used judiciously. He believed that the therapist should empathize with the alcoholic individual's defensive need to avoid painful affect. Cooper advocated inpatient groups that focus on the here and now but are less confrontational. He reported a 55% abstinence rate with patients in such groups, compared with 16% for patients in an inpatient group program without group psychotherapy. Those patients who remained in group therapy for at least 25 hours also demonstrated greater compliance with other aspects of the program.

Psychodynamic Approaches to Drug Abuse

Although the disease model is popular in many drug rehabilitation programs, psychodynamic approaches are more widely accepted and valued in the treatment of drug abusers than in the treatment of alcoholic persons. Vaillant (1988), for example, noted that polydrug abusers, in contrast to alcoholic individuals, are more likely to have had unstable childhoods, more likely to use drugs as "self-medication" for psychiatric symptoms, and more likely to benefit from psycho-therapeutic efforts to address their underlying symptomatology and character pathology.

A considerable body of research literature supports the association of personality disorder and depression with the development of drug addiction (Blatt et al. 1984a; Kandel et al. 1978; Paton et al. 1977; Treece 1984; Treece and Khantzian 1986). These studies suggested that whereas initiation to marijuana use may be related to peer pressure in adolescence, use of and eventual addiction to hard drugs are not. One study found impaired relationships with parents and depression to be highly significant predictors of eventual abuse of illicit drugs, whereas sociodemographic variables were not (Kandel et al. 1978). Another study of high school students who became involved in heavy drug use identified depression as the most potent predictor of all personality variables (Paton et al. 1977). Treece (1984) concluded that the key factor differentiating the chronic drug-addicted person from the controlled or casual abuser is the presence in the former of a severe personality disorder. Gorton and Akhtar (1994) conducted a review of 24 studies to examine the interrelationship between drug abuse and personality disorder. Comorbidity was found to range between 18% and 100%.

Compared with alcoholic persons, drug abusers are much more likely to have significant coexisting psychiatric disorders. In a large epidemiological study involving interviews with 20,291 persons (Regier et al. 1990), drug abusers had a 53% rate of comorbidity, compared with only 37% for alcoholic individuals. Studies of narcotic-addicted individuals have found other psychiatric diagnoses in as many as 80%–93% (Khantzian and Treece 1985; Rounsaville et al. 1982). The comorbidity rate is also high among cocaine abusers. As many as 73% of those seeking treatment meet lifetime criteria for another psychiatric disorder, with anxiety disorders, antisocial personality disorder, and attention deficit disorder ordinarily preceding the onset of the cocaine abuse, and affective disorders and alcohol abuse usually following the onset of the cocaine abuse (Rounsaville et al. 1991). The investigators pointed out that a uniform approach to the treatment of substance abusers is inadequate because those with personality disorders require different treatment approaches. Substance abusers with personality disorders are more depressed, more impulsive, more isolated, and generally less satisfied with their lives than are substance abusers without such disorders.

These research findings have played a key role in the development of sophisticated psychodynamic formulations of substance abuse problems. The early psychoanalytic interpretation of all substance abuse as a regression to the oral stage of psychosexual development has been replaced by an understanding of most drug abuse as *defensive* and *adaptive* rather than regressive (Khantzian 1985b, 1986, 1997; Wurmser 1974). Drug use may actually reverse regressive states by reinforcing defective ego defenses against powerful affects such as rage, shame, and depression. The early psychoanalytic formulations often depicted persons with drug addictions as pleasure-seeking hedonists bent on self-destruction. Contemporary psychoanalytic investigators understand addictive behavior more as a reflection of a deficit in self-care than as a self-destructive impulse (Khantzian 1997). This impairment in self-care results from early developmental disturbances that lead to an inadequate internalization of parental figures, leaving the addicted person without the capacity for self-protection. Hence, the majority of chronic drug-addicted individuals exhibit a fundamental impairment in judgment about the dangers of drug abuse.

Equally important in the pathogenesis of drug addiction is the impaired regulatory function in affect and impulse control and in maintenance of self-esteem (Treece and Khantzian 1986). These deficits create corresponding problems in object relations. Heavy polydrug use has been related directly to the addicted person's incapacity for tolerating and regulating interpersonal closeness (Nicholson and Treece 1981; Treece 1984). Contributing to these relationship problems are the narcissistic vulnerability inherent in interpersonal risks and the inability to modulate the affects associated with closeness. Dodes (1990) noted that addicted individuals tend to feel powerless as a reflection of a specific narcissistic impairment. Their addictive behavior wards off a sense of powerlessness or helplessness by controlling and regulating their affective states. Narcissistic rage and humiliation impel them to use drugs as a way of reestablishing a sense of power. The ingestion of a drug can thus be viewed as a desperate attempt to compensate for deficits in ego functioning, low self-esteem, and related interpersonal problems.

Many drug-addicted patients knowingly perpetuate their pain and suffering by continuing to use drugs. Khantzian (1997) regarded this pain-perpetuating aspect of substance abuse as a manifestation of a repetition compulsion of early trauma. In some cases, the repetitive infliction of pain on oneself represents an attempt to work out traumatic states that cannot be remembered. These states exist as pre-symbolic and unconscious configurations. Thus, the motive for the drug use can be viewed as control of suffering rather than relief from it.

The notion that drug-addicted individuals are medicating themselves leads directly to another observation of contemporary psychodynamic investigators—namely, that specific substances are chosen for specific psychological and pharmacological effects according to each abuser's needs. The most painful affect is likely to be what determines the choice of drug. Khantzian (1997) noted that cocaine appears to relieve distress associated with depression, hyperactivity, and hypomania, while narcotics apparently tone down feelings of rage.

An in-depth study of narcotic-addicted individuals led Blatt et al. (1984a, 1984b) to conclude that heroin addiction is multiply determined by 1) the need to contain aggression, 2) a yearning for gratification of longings for a symbiotic relationship with a maternal figure, and 3) a desire to alleviate depressive affects. Although the research data indicate that a small subgroup of individuals with narcotic addictions also suffers from antisocial personality disorder (Rounsaville et al. 1982), Blatt et al. identified a larger group of severely neurotic opiate-addicted persons, which may represent the majority. These individuals struggle with feelings of worthlessness, guilt, self-criticism, and shame. Their depression appears to intensify when they attempt to become close to others, so they withdraw into isolated "bliss" brought on by heroin or other narcotics, which has both regressive and defensive dimensions. The depressive core of the opiate-addicted individual was further substantiated by a comparison study (Blatt et al. 1984a, 1984b), which found persons with opiate addictions to be significantly more depressed than polydrug abusers. This study also identified self-criticism as a main component of their depression.

The finding of Blatt and his colleagues of a high correlation between superego-ridden, self-critical, depression-prone personality features and opiate addiction has received support from Wurmser's (1974, 1987a, 1987b) psychoanalytic work with addicted patients. He argued that those addicted individuals amenable to psychoanalytic therapy do not suffer from underdeveloped superegos, like antisocial persons with addictions, but rather from an excessively harsh conscience. The intoxicating substance is sought as an escape from a tormenting superego. Many drug abusers employ the defense of splitting to disavow a drug-abusing self-representation that alternates with a non-drug-abusing self-representation. These individuals often feel as if someone else has taken over for a brief period. Wurmser identified success as a prominent trigger for an episode of drug abuse. Positive feelings associated with successful achievement seem to produce an altered state of consciousness characterized by feelings of guilt and shame. Impulsive drug use is seen as the solution to these painful affects. Recurring crises of this kind are characterized by an overbearing conscience that becomes so intolerable that temporary defiance seems the only means of relief.

Although early studies with narcotic-addicted patients suggested that psychotherapy materially contributes to the recovery of addicted persons, much of this research was subsequently discounted because of methodological problems. More recently, a number of reports from the Veterans Administration–Penn Study (Woody et al. 1983, 1984, 1985, 1986, 1987, 1995) have persuasively demonstrated with rigorous methodology that adding psychotherapy to the overall treatment plan of narcotic-addicted patients produces clear benefits. Narcotic-addicted patients in a methadone maintenance program were randomly assigned to one of three treatment conditions: 1) drug counseling alone with paraprofessionals, 2) expressive-supportive psychotherapy plus drug counseling, or 3) cognitive-behavioral psychotherapy plus counseling. Of 110 patients who completed the full treatment program, those receiving psychotherapy improved considerably more than those who received counseling alone. Expressive-supportive psychotherapy based on dynamic principles resulted in greater improvement in psychiatric symptoms and more success in finding and holding a job than did cognitive-behavioral psychotherapy (Woody et al. 1983). Those patients who were depressed showed the most improvement, followed by patients who had opiate dependency but no other psychiatric disorder. Those with antisocial personality disorder alone did not benefit from psychotherapy (Woody et al. 1985). Patients with antisocial personality disorder improved only when depression was also a symptom.

When the researchers divided the 110 psychotherapy patients into groups according to the severity of their psychiatric symptoms, they noted that patients in the low-severity group made equal progress with counseling or with psychotherapy, while patients with a medium degree of severity had better outcomes with treatment plans combining both of these approaches (although some improved just with counseling). However, the group with extremely severe psychiatric symptoms achieved little progress with counseling alone, but made considerable progress when psychotherapy was added: at 7-month follow-up, those patients in the group who received psychotherapy used both illicit and prescribed drugs far less often than did those who did not receive psychotherapy. These changes were sustained at 12-month follow-up (Woody et al. 1987), even though the subjects were no longer in psychotherapy (the duration of psychotherapeutic treatment was 6 months).

The investigators (Woody et al. 1986) drew several conclusions about the psychotherapy of patients with opiate addictions: 1) Both expressive-supportive and cognitive-behavioral psychotherapy can help those narcotic-addicted persons who can become engaged in and will regularly attend such a treatment program. 2) Patients with significant psychiatric disturbances are the best candidates for psychotherapy and will benefit from it the most. 3) The psychotherapist must be integrated into the overall treatment program and must collaborate with other staff members in the treatment. The researchers believed that there were clear benefits to locating the psychotherapy sessions in the same facility as the rest of the methadone maintenance program. Psychotherapy that is fragmented from the rest of the treatment is unlikely to succeed.

Woody et al. (1995) conducted a partial replication study involving psychiatrically symptomatic opiate-dependent patients receiving methadone maintenance treatment. Patients were randomly assigned to 24 weeks of counseling or to counseling plus supportive-expressive psychotherapy. Follow-ups were conducted at 1 month and 6 months after treatment ended. Patients receiving supportive-expressive therapy had fewer cocaine-positive urine samples and required lower doses of methadone. Although both groups made significant gains in 1 month, by 6-month follow-up, many of the gains made by the drug counseling patients had begun to deteriorate. On the other hand, most of the gains made by the supportive-expressive therapy patients remained or were still evident. All significant differences favored the supportive-expressive psychotherapy group.

This comprehensive treatment approach is also highly cost-effective (Gabbard et al. 1997). McLellan et al. (1993) found that adding psychotherapy to standard methadone maintenance treatment led to greater earning power, less welfare income, and strikingly lower hospitalization rates for patients.

Psychotherapy with drug abusers is a treatment approach that indirectly addresses the addiction by focusing on the associated psychopathology. Most clinicians believe that abstinence from the abused substance is a prerequisite to adequate treatment through psychotherapeutic technique of the underlying disturbances—anxiety, depression, personality disorder, self-esteem problems, or ego deficits. The exception would be a drug substitution program such as methadone maintenance. Once abstinence is achieved, the addicted person often feels despair at having given up something more than a drug—a valued part of the self (Treece and Khantzian 1986). Both therapist and patient realize that abstinence alone does not automatically lead to changes in other areas of life. As abstinent persons with addictions struggle with their longing for the drug and their grief over its loss, the therapist must address their tenaciously defended belief that drug use is an adaptive solution to life's problems. The therapist must identify the underlying problems of modulating affects, of regulating self-esteem, and of relating to others, so as to help the addicted person discover alternative answers to those problems. A study of 240 methadone maintenance patients with the self-report Bell Object Relations Reality Testing Inventory found that these patients exhibited specific impairments in object relations (Rutherford et al. 1996). Scores were poorest for those with Axis II disorders in association with the addiction.

One difficulty that psychotherapists will most likely encounter is the alexithymia common in many addicted patients (Krystal 1982–1983). In other words, most of these patients are unable to recognize and identify their internal feeling states. A good deal of education may have to occur during the early phases of therapy, with the therapist explaining how the experience of unpleasant feelings initially leads to drug abuse. These patients must be helped to contain and tolerate their affects so that they can substitute words describing their inner states for actions such as the ingestion of a drug. The therapist can assist patients in this regard by identifying feelings that occur during the therapy hour.

An individual psychotherapy process is much more likely to be successful in the context of a comprehensive program. Khantzian (1986) suggested the concept of the primary care therapist—an individual who facilitates the addicted patient's involvement with all treatment modalities. The therapist analyzes the patient's resistance to accepting other forms of treatment, such as NA or group therapy, but also provides a holding environment for dealing with the strong affects mobilized in the treatment process. The primary care therapist must also participate in treatment decisions involving other modalities. In this model, the emphasis is more supportive than expressive at the beginning of treatment, and the therapist's role is similar to that of a hospital doctor working with an inpatient.

Treece and Khantzian (1986) identified four essential components of a treatment program for mastery of drug dependence: 1) a substitute for the dependency on chemicals (e.g., NA, an alternative system of beliefs, or a benign dependency on a person or religious institution); 2) adequate treatment for other psychiatric disorders, including appropriate psychotropic medication and psychotherapy; 3) enforced abstinence (e.g., drug antagonists, urine surveillance, probation, drug substitutes such as methadone, external support systems) during a psychological maturational process; and 4) promotion of growth and structural personality change through psychotherapy.

Wurmser (1987b) also advocated a multi-pronged approach, but with more expressive psychotherapy. Because he conceptualized an overbearing superego as central to the pathogenesis of compulsive drug use, he cautioned therapists to avoid being punitive or critical with their patients and to refrain from "preaching" to them about drug abuse. A more appropriate role for therapists, in Wurmser's view, is to attempt to understand the superego pressures on the patient, much as in working with a severely neurotic patient. He also believed that therapists should devote their time to looking at underlying issues rather than just focusing on the drug abuse, which can be taken up by other members of the treatment team.

Although no major controlled studies of dynamic group psychotherapy with addicted patients share the methodological sophistication of the Veterans Administration–Penn Study on individual psychotherapy, group psychotherapy has become a component of many programs because of the clinical impression that it is helpful to many patients. Because group psychotherapy is rarely the only treatment modality used in these programs, it is difficult to determine whether any specific therapeutic aspects of group therapy are not also present in other modalities. However, practically speaking, many addicted persons are helped by talking with others who have had the same problem. Also, because denial is a prominent defense in all substance abusers, a group setting of peers facilitates a powerful confrontation of denial and compels addicted individuals to accept the seriousness of their substance abuse. The same caveats about the negative effects of overly aggressive confrontation that were mentioned in the section on group psychotherapy of alcoholic patients also apply to group psychotherapy of addicted persons. Effective groups provide as much support as they do confrontation. Inpatient programs often rely more on groups for the practical reason that enforcing attendance is easier with inpatients than with outpatients (Woody et al. 1986). A commonly encountered resistance to groups in both inpatient and outpatient facilities is that many members may have committed crimes and are therefore reluctant to open up in groups for fear that confidentiality will be breached.

In summary, the indications for expressive-supportive psychotherapy can be conceptualized as the following: 1) serious psychopathology other than drug abuse; 2) engagement in an overall treatment program that includes NA or another support group, enforced abstinence, possibly a drug substitute such as methadone, and appropriate psychotropic medication; 3) no diagnosis of antisocial personality disorder (unless depression is also present) (treatment considerations with antisocial personality disorder are discussed in detail in Chapter 17); and 4) sufficient motivation to keep session appointments and become engaged in the process. The indications for an expressive or supportive emphasis after the process is well launched are largely determined by the same factors that determine the emphasis in any other psychotherapeutic process (see Table 4–1 in Chapter 4).

Eating Disorders

Anorexia nervosa and bulimia nervosa appear to be disorders of our time. The electronic media bombard the public with images of slender women who "have it all." In many areas of Western culture, food is in abundance, a precondition for binge eating behavior. Individuals affected by these disorders tend to be Caucasian, educated, female, economically advantaged, and ensconced in Western cultures (Johnson et al. 1989). Anorexia nervosa is virtually unknown in countries where thinness is not considered a virtue (Powers 1984). Media images of females, moreover, suggest that external appearance is far more important than internal identity. Although intrapsychic and biological factors should not be minimized in the etiology and pathogenesis of eating disorders, those factors clearly interface with a particular sociocultural period in Western civilization to produce a syndrome that reflects the culture. Anorexia nervosa has more than doubled in incidence since the 1960s, while the prevalence of bulimia nervosa has been found to be approximately 1% in adolescent and young adult females (Fairburn and Beglin 1990). These disturbing figures indicate that the disorder may be an increasingly common solution to a variety of intrapsychic, familial, and environmental stressors.

Anorexia Nervosa

The label *anorexia nervosa* can be misleading, since the first word of the phrase implies that loss of appetite is the central problem. The diagnostic hallmark of anorexia nervosa is actually a fanatical pursuit of thinness related to an overwhelming fear of becoming fat. An arbitrary cutoff of less than 85% of minimal normal body weight for age and height is often used to make the diagnosis. Amenorrhea is a prominent feature of anorexia nervosa in females. Although 5%–10% of cases are male, their clinical features and psychodynamics are remarkably similar to those of females.

Psychodynamic understanding.   For the last few decades, the seminal contributions of Hilde Bruch (1973, 1978, 1982, 1987) have served as a beacon in the darkness for clinicians treating anorexic patients. She observed that the preoccupation with food and weight is a relatively late occurrence emblematic of a more fundamental disturbance in self-concept. Most patients with anorexia nervosa have a thoroughgoing conviction that they are utterly powerless and ineffective. The illness often occurs in "good girls" who have spent their life trying to please their parents, only to suddenly become stubborn and negativistic in adolescence. The body is often experienced as separate from the self, as though it belongs to the parents. These patients lack any sense of autonomy to the point that they do not even feel in control of their bodily functions. The premorbid defensive posture of being a perfect little girl ordinarily defends against a profound underlying feeling of worthlessness. Anorexia nervosa develops as "an attempt at self-cure, to develop through discipline over the body a sense of selfhood and interpersonal effectiveness. Anorexics transform their anxiety and psychological problems through manipulation of food intake and size" (Bruch 1987, p. 211).

Bruch traced the developmental origins of anorexia nervosa back to a disturbed relationship between the infant and its mother. Specifically, the mother appears to parent the child according to her own needs rather than those of the child. When the child-initiated cues do not receive confirming and validating responses, the child cannot develop a healthy sense of self. Instead, the child experiences herself simply as an extension of her mother, not as a center of autonomy in her own right. This understanding is in keeping with early psychoanalytic formulations about the pathogenesis of psychosomatic disorders in children in which an "appersonation" of the child was noted (Sperling 1944). The child is not perceived as a separate individual, but rather as the "right arm" of the mother.

Bruch, then, understood the behavior of the anorexic patient as a frantic effort to gain admiration and validation as a unique and special person with extraordinary attributes. More recently, Bruch (1987) suggested that the clinical picture may be changing somewhat because it is more and more difficult for the anorexic patient to feel unique, given the increasing prevalence of the disorder and the media attention on eating disorders of all kinds. The illness has now become imbued with a sense of competition to be the thinnest or the most unique.

Family therapists, such as Selvini Palazzoli (1978) and Minuchin (Minuchin et al. 1978), have confirmed and elaborated some of the dynamic concepts of Bruch. Minuchin and his colleagues described a pattern of enmeshment in the families of anorexic patients, where there is a general absence of generational and personal boundaries. Each family member is overinvolved in the life of every other family member to the extent that no one feels a sense of separate identity apart from the family matrix. Selvini Palazzoli (1978) also noted that patients with anorexia nervosa have been unable to psychologically separate from their mothers, which results in a failure to achieve any stable sense of their own bodies. The body is thus often perceived as if it were inhabited by a bad maternal introject, and starvation may be an attempt to stop the growth of this hostile, intrusive internal object. Williams (1997) similarly stressed that the parents of an anorexic patient tend to project their anxiety onto their child rather than contain it. These projections may be experienced as inimical foreign bodies within the child. To protect herself from the unmetabolized experiences and fantasies projected onto her by her parents, the young girl may develop a "no entry" system of defenses, concretized by not eating.

The extreme defensive posture of anorexia nervosa suggests that a powerful underlying impulse warrants such a strategy. Indeed, Boris (1984b) noted that intense greed forms the core of anorexia nervosa. Oral desires are so unacceptable, however, that they must be dealt with projectively. Through projective identification, the greedy, demanding self-representation is transferred to the parents. In response to the patient's refusal to eat, the parents become obsessed with whether or not the patient is eating; they become the ones who have desires. In a formulation influenced by Kleinian thinking, Boris conceptualized anorexia nervosa as an inability to receive good things from others because of an inordinate desire to possess. Any act of receiving food or love confronts these patients squarely with the fact that they cannot possess what they desire. Their solution is to not receive anything from anyone. Envy and greed are often closely linked in the unconscious. The patient envies the mother's good possessions—love, compassion, nurturance—but to receive them simply increases the envy. Renouncing them supports the unconscious fantasy of spoiling what is envied, not unlike the fox in Aesop's fable who concluded that the grapes he couldn't reach were sour. The patient conveys the following message: "There is nothing good available for me to possess, so I will simply renounce all my desires." Such renunciation makes the anorexic patient the object of the desire of others and, in her fantasy, the object of their envy and admiration, because they are "impressed" by her self-control. Food symbolizes their positive qualities that she desires in herself; being enslaved by hunger is preferable to desiring to possess the maternal figure.

Most developmental formulations of the origins of anorexia nervosa focus on the mother-daughter dyad. Bemporad and Ratey (1985), however, observed a characteristic pattern of paternal involvement with anorexic daughters. The typical father was superficially caring and supportive but emotionally abandoning of his daughter whenever she truly needed him. In addition, many fathers of anorexic patients seek emotional nurturance from—rather than give it to—their daughters. Both parents often are experiencing serious disappointment in their marriage, leading each parent to seek emotional sustenance from the daughter.

In self psychological terms, the daughter may be treated as a selfobject that provides mirroring and validating functions for each parent but is denied her own sense of self. The child, in turn, cannot rely on human beings to meet her selfobject needs. The anorexic child seriously doubts that parents or any other significant figures in her life will even temporarily give up their own interests and needs to attend to her needs for soothing, affirmation, and mirroring (Bachar et al. 1999). The child may escalate the starvation and restriction in a desperate attempt to force her parents to pay attention to her suffering and recognize her need for help.

To summarize our psychodynamic understanding of anorexia nervosa, the overt behavior of self-starvation is a multiply determined symptom. It is 1) a desperate attempt to be special and unique, 2) an attack on the false sense of self fostered by parental expectations, 3) an assertion of a nascent true self, 4) an attack on a hostile maternal introject viewed as equivalent to the body, 5) a defense against greed and desire, 6) an effort to make others—rather than the patient—feel greedy and helpless, 7) a defensive attempt to prevent unmetabolized projections from the parents from entering the patient, and 8) an escalating cry for help to shake the parents out of their self-absorption and make them aware of the child's suffering.

These psychodynamic factors are also accompanied by certain characteristic cognitive features. These features include misperception of one's own body image, all-or-nothing thinking, magical thinking, and obsessive-compulsive thoughts and rituals. The presence of obsessive-compulsive symptoms has led some researchers to wonder whether obsessive-compulsive personality disorder coexists with anorexia nervosa. This assumption is confounded by the notorious unreliability of personality disorder diagnoses in the presence of starvation (Kaplan and Woodside 1987; Powers 1984). Many symptoms, including obsessive-compulsive behavior, appear secondary to starvation. Also, premorbid personality characteristics are accentuated in states of nutritional deficiency. The fear of being fat has itself been shown to moderate when the patient begins to eat and gain weight (Garfinkel and Garner 1982).

Treatment approaches. Clinicians who treat patients who have anorexia nervosa are in consensus that the treatment goals must not be focused narrowly on weight gain (Boris 1984a, 1984b; Bruch 1973, 1978, 1982, 1987; Chessick 1985; Dare 1995; Hsu 1986; Hughes 1997; Powers 1984). A "two-track" approach, advocated by Garner et al. (1986), includes a first step of restoration of eating for weight gain. Once this step is accomplished, the second step of psychotherapeutic intervention can begin. Anorexic patients show much greater improvement when provided with a mixture of family therapy and dynamic individual therapy than when they are simply managed with educational measures designed to control weight (Dare 1995; Hall and Crisp 1983). Long-term, individual expressive-supportive psychotherapy is the cornerstone of the treatment. Unless the patient's underlying disturbance of the self and the associated distortions of internal object relations are addressed, the patient will follow a course of repeated relapse and revolving-door hospital admissions (Bruch 1982). For those patients living at home, family therapy may be a valuable adjunct to individual therapy. Although some patients appear to benefit from group psychotherapy (Lieb and Thompson 1984; Polivy 1981), the limited data suggest that those who benefit most do not have associated personality disorders (Maher 1984).

Hospitalization may also be a beneficial adjunct to individual psychotherapy. Although no indications for inpatient treatment are universally agreed on, a weight loss of 30% of normal body weight is a good rule of thumb to use in determining whether inpatient treatment is necessary (Garfinkel and Garner 1982). Approximately 80% of all anorexic patients will gain weight with hospital treatment (Hsu 1986), provided that the hospital staff can create a specific milieu. As described in Chapter 6, the hospital staff must be wary of the patient's unconscious efforts to reenact the family struggle in the hospital milieu. They must convey an interest in helping the patient restore weight without becoming excessively concerned about it and without making demands similar to those the patient's parents would make. The patient can be helped to cope with the fear of losing control by arranging an eating plan of frequent but small meals with a member of the nursing staff who is available to discuss the patient's anxiety about eating. Weight gains should be reported to the patient with concomitant positive reinforcements. Any surreptitious vomiting or purging should be confronted and controlled with structural measures such as locking the bathroom door. Members of the treatment staff may need to reassure the patient that they will not allow too much weight gain, thus helping the patient develop a sense of trust in them.

If individual and family therapy were being conducted prior to admission, these should continue during hospitalization. If the patient's hospitalization is her first treatment contact, however, these adjunctive therapies should be implemented as part of the hospital treatment. Antidepressant medication is helpful with patients who meet the criteria for major depression. (Milder forms of depression improve with weight gain.) Brief hospitalizations are rarely curative, nor are treatment programs that demand a normal average weight and then ignore the intense anxiety aroused by such a demand (Bruch 1982). At least 50% of the patients who successfully control their anorexia nervosa with inpatient treatment will relapse within a year (Hsu 1980). For the 20% who do not respond to brief hospitalization, extended hospitalization is indicated.

Individual expressive-supportive psychotherapy often takes several years of painstaking work because of the formidable resistance posed by the anorexic patient. Four guiding principles of technique are useful (Table 12–1).

1. *Avoid excessive investment in trying to change the eating behavior.* As Boris (1984b) observed, "What we call their symptoms they call their salvation" (p. 315). The patient views anorexia nervosa as the solution to an internal problem. Psychotherapists who immediately define it as a problem that must be changed reduce their chances of forming a viable therapeutic alliance. The behavior associated with anorexia nervosa elicits demands and expectations for change from the patient's parents. Through projective identification, the therapist is likely to experience powerful pressure to identify with the patient's projected internal objects that are associated with the parents. Instead of acting on that pressure and becoming a parental figure, the therapist must try to under-

---

TABLE 12–1. Technical guidelines in the psychotherapy of anorexic patients

Avoid excessive investment in trying to change the eating behavior.

Avoid interpretations early in the therapy.

Carefully monitor countertransference.

Examine cognitive distortions.

---

stand the patient's internal world. One form of this reenactment is the equation of eating with talking. Just as the patient provokes her parents by refusing to eat, she will attempt to provoke the therapist by refusing to talk (Mintz 1988). At the beginning of the therapy, it may thus be helpful to clarify that the primary goal of the treatment is to understand the patient's underlying emotional disturbance rather than the problem of not eating (Bruch 1982; Chessick 1985). Although Boris (1984a) advocated complete avoidance of psychotherapeutic focus on eating, Bruch (1982) suggested that psychotherapy is not feasible unless the patient weighs in the neighborhood of 95 pounds. She explains to her patients that their capacity for thinking and communicating will improve if they can get their weight at least to that level.

2. *Avoid interpretations early in the therapy.* Interpretations of unconscious wishes or fears will be experienced by the anorexic patient as a repetition of her life story. *Someone else* is telling her what she really feels, while her conscious experience is minimized and invalidated. Rather, the therapist's task should be to validate and empathize with the patient's internal experience (Bruch 1987; Chessick 1985). The therapist should take an active interest in what the patient thinks and feels, conveying the message that the patient is an autonomous person entitled to her own ideas about her illness. Of major importance is helping the patient define her own feeling states. The actions and decisions stemming from these feelings must be legitimized and respected. The therapist can help the patient explore various options but should refrain from telling her what to do (Chessick 1985). This empathic, ego-building, supportive approach in the early phases of therapy will facilitate introjection of the therapist as a benign object. Bruch (1987) suggested emphasizing the positive and conceptualizing the therapy as an experience in which patients will discover their positive qualities. She acknowledged that her approach has many similarities to Kohut's (1984) self psychological approach. Chessick (1985) shared this view that insight into unconscious conflict is unlikely to be curative with these patients. Although slightly more optimistic about the use of interpretations, Boris (1984a) recommended withholding interpretations until the patient finds herself. Even then, he advocated talking "to the air" instead of directly to the patient, thereby providing some distance in the relationship and respecting her boundaries. Such interpretations should be delivered as hypotheses, as though talking to an imaginary colleague rather than as making a definitive pronouncement directly to the patient.

3. *Carefully monitor countertransference.* Anorexic patients commonly believe that their parents want them to gain weight so that other people won't view the parents as failures (Powers 1984). The therapist is likely to become anxious about similar matters. Therapists who work within the framework of a com-

prehensive treatment team, in particular, may begin to feel that others are negatively judging their work if their patients fail to gain weight. This counter-transference concern may lead the therapist to fall into the trap of identifying with the patient's parents. The ideal situation for individual psychotherapy is for another treater to monitor weight gain, leaving the therapist free to explore the patient's underlying psychological issues. When hospitalization is required for weight control, the admitting psychiatrist can manage food intake while the psychotherapist continues the psychotherapeutic work in the hospital. In this setting, the psychotherapist can work productively with the team.

Hughes (1997) has beautifully described some of the typical countertrans-ference dilemmas confronted in the treatment of patients with anorexia nervosa. Just as the patient keeps the parents involved in trying to help but always failing, she also engages the therapist in that role. Frequently, the patient presents herself as wanting to cooperate with treatment but then sabotages the therapist's help. With anorexia patients, the therapeutic alliance is typically much more tenuous than it appears, and the therapist must cope with the frus-tration of feeling duped by the patient. To handle the countertransference, it is useful to remember that the patient understands progress as equivalent to sep-aration from family and growing up, both of which are highly threatening. Anxiety is stirred up in the therapist by the patient's flirtation with death, which is made all the more frustrating because of the patient's frequent denial of suicidal wishes. Just as families may get exhausted and angry and even de-velop unconscious murderous wishes toward the anorexic patient, the thera-pist may also experience despair, murderous rage, and a sense that no one else fully appreciates the lethality of the patient. This unfolding transfer-ence-countertransference drama is the core of the illness as manifested in the therapeutic relationship and thus provides enormously valuable information for the therapist that can ultimately be shared and understood with the patient.

4. *Examine cognitive distortions.*   Misperceptions of body size and illogical cog-nitive beliefs should be explored with the patient nonjudgmentally (Powers 1984). The therapist thus serves as an auxiliary ego to help the patient sharpen her powers of observation and her critical thinking (Chessick 1985). Clearly, the psychotherapist must assume an educative role with these patients, helping them understand the effects of starvation on cognition. However, the therapist must seek to educate while making no demand for change. Alternatively, the therapist can simply explore the consequences of the patient's choices.

These technical guidelines, while useful, are not to be taken as a "cookbook" formula for the psychotherapy of anorexic patients. Therapists must be flexible, persistent, and stable in the face of the patient's tendency to "wait out" the therapy process until she can once again be left alone. Body image distortions, which often approach delusional proportions, may be particularly refractory to educational and therapeutic efforts. Therapists must be wary of countertransference despair and frustration that might lead them to attempt to force the patient to "see things as they really are."

Although patients with anorexia nervosa may seem highly treatment resistant in the short run, many of them ultimately improve. In one long-term follow-up study (Sullivan et al. 1998), only 10% of patients followed up a mean of 12 years after initial referral still met criteria for anorexia nervosa. However, many still struggled with some of the features of the illness, including perfectionism and a relatively low body weight. On the other hand, in a review of 300 patients in four different series, Hsu (1991) calculated that about 1 in 7, or 14% of the patients, had subsequently died from suicide or complications of the illness. In a 5-year follow-up comparison of family therapy and individual supportive therapy (Eisler et al. 1997), both treatments produced significant improvements. Patients with early onset and a short history of anorexia nervosa appeared to do better with family therapy, whereas those with late onset appeared to do better with individual supportive therapy. Psychoanalytic psychotherapy also appears to be as effective as supportive therapy (Dare 1995). In a randomized controlled study comparing self psychological therapy with cognitive orientation treatment, five of six anorexia nervosa patients treated with self psychological therapy remitted, while neither of the two patients treated with cognitive orientation therapy remitted. In a different study (Robin et al. 1995), anorexic patients ages 12–19 years were treated with either family therapy or individual ego treatment. After a year of therapy, all patients from both groups were menstruating, and 82% from family therapy and 50% from the ego treatment met the dual criteria of target weight and menstruation.

Bulimia Nervosa

Patients with bulimia nervosa are generally distinguished from those with anorexia nervosa on the basis of relatively normal weight and the presence of binge eating and purging. Emaciated patients who are also binge eating and purging are often classified as anorexics, bulimic subgroup (Hsu 1986). This diagnostic classification reflects how the concept of anorexia nervosa has become blurred by the cultural fascination with bulimia (Bruch 1987). In Bruch's view, the two syndromes have little in common—the rigid self-discipline and harsh conscience of the anorexic patient contrast sharply with the impulse-ridden, irresponsible, and undisciplined behavior of the bulimic person. The condensed term *bulimarexia* is thus a "semantic atrocity" (Bruch 1987) in that it mistakenly implies similarity.

Bruch's view, however, is not supported by accumulating data that suggest considerable linkage between the two disorders (Garner et al. 1986). At least 40%–50% of all anorexic patients also have bulimia (Garfinkel et al. 1980; Hall et al. 1984; Hsu et al. 1979). Long-term follow-up data suggest that over a long period of time, anorexia nervosa may give way to bulimia nervosa, but that the reverse pattern is much rarer (Hsu 1991). In light of these findings, DSM-IV (American Psychiatric Association 1994) subtypes anorexia nervosa according to the presence or absence of bulimic symptoms and precludes the diagnosis of bulimia nervosa in the presence of anorexia nervosa when the bulimia occurs only during episodes of anorexia nervosa.

Part of the reason for the blurring of diagnostic boundaries between anorexic and bulimic behavior is that the clinical picture can be so varied. Concurrent psychiatric disorders are common (Yager 1984), and over half of all bulimic patients may suffer from associated personality disorders (Johnson et al. 1989). As Yager (1984) eloquently observed,

> Bulimia is not a disease. Nor is it a simple habit. Bulimia is heterogeneous and, like pneumonia, it may result from a variety of causes. I have found it useful to conceptualize bulimia as a habit or behavioral pattern embedded in a personality, in turn embedded in a biology, and all this embedded in a culture in which bulimia seems to be developing at an increasing rate. (p. 63)

Psychodynamic understanding.   When considering the psychodynamics of bulimia, therapists must keep in mind this heterogeneity. The various contributors to our dynamic understanding of bulimia are likely to be analogous to the proverbial blind men reporting their perceptions of an elephant based on their particular vantage points. As always, dynamic understanding must be individualized. A clinical picture of bulimia may be observed in patients with vastly different character structures, ranging from psychotic through borderline to neurotic (Wilson 1983). Anorexia and bulimia are essentially opposite sides of the same coin (Mintz 1988). Whereas the anorexic patient is characterized by both greater ego strength and greater superego control, the bulimic patient may suffer from a generalized inability to delay impulse discharge, based on a weakened ego and a lax superego. Binge eating and purging are not usually isolated impulse problems; rather, they typically coexist with impulsive, self-destructive sexual relationships and with polydrug abuse.

Some empirical evidence suggests which psychodynamic factors might be at work in patients with bulimia nervosa. In a multivariate genetic analysis, Kendler et al. (1995) found that family and environmental factors play key roles in the development of the disorder. In a community-based case-control study involving

102 subjects with bulimia nervosa and 204 healthy control subjects (Fairburn et al. 1997), parental problems, sexual or physical abuse, and negative self-evaluation were all associated with the development of the illness. The investigators suggested that negative self-evaluation might encourage dieting by distorting the girls' views of their appearance. These empirical findings are supported by observations stemming from psychoanalytic treatment. Reich and Cierpka (1998) found disturbances in the emotional dialogue between the bulimic patients and their parents and a consistent pattern of conflict between contradictory parts of the self that was undoubtedly influenced by conflicting identifications with parents. These authors also suggested that many bulimic patients experience a lack of respect for boundaries and a tactless intrusion into their privacy, which would apply to both sexual abuse and psychological abuse. Reich and Cierpka noted that these patients frequently used defenses involving reversal of affects and turning passive to active, and they also experienced contradictory superego demands.

Those authors who have studied the developmental origins of bulimia have identified extensive difficulty with separation both in the parents and in the individual patient. A common theme in the developmental history of bulimic patients is the absence of a transitional object, such as a pacifier or blanket, to help the child separate psychologically from her mother (Goodsitt 1983). This developmental struggle to separate may be played out instead by using the body itself as a transitional object (Sugarman and Kurash 1982), with the ingestion of food representing a wish for symbiotic merger with the mother and the expulsion of food an effort at separation from her. Like the mothers of anorexic patients, the parents of children who grow up to be bulimic often relate to their children as extensions of themselves (Humphrey and Stern 1988; Strober and Humphrey 1987). These children are used as selfobjects to validate the self of the parent. Each member of the family depends on all the other members to maintain a sense of cohesion. Although this pattern characterizes the families of anorexic patients, a particular mode of managing unacceptable "bad" qualities is predominant in bulimic families. The bulimic family system apparently involves a strong need for everyone to see themselves as "all good." Unacceptable qualities in the parents are often projected onto the bulimic child, who becomes the repository of all "badness." By unconsciously identifying with these projections, she becomes the carrier of all the family's greed and impulsivity. The resulting homeostatic balance keeps the focus on the "sick" child rather than on conflicts within or between the parents.

The psychodynamic observations about difficulties with separation in bulimic patients have been confirmed by empirical research (Patton 1992). A group of 40 patients with eating disorders was compared with a control group of 40 women with normal eating patterns to see how they would respond to subliminal or supraliminal stimuli. Each group was shown an abandonment or a control stimulus at exposure durations that was either subliminal or supraliminal. Following exposure to an abandonment stimulus, the group with eating disorders ate significantly more crackers than did subjects in the control group. The investigators concluded that binge eating was indeed a defense against an unconscious fear of abandonment.

In many instances, then, bulimic patients concretize the object relations mechanisms of introjection and projection. Ingestion and expulsion of food may directly reflect the introjection and projection of aggressive, or "bad," introjects. In many cases, this splitting process is further concretized by the patient. She may regard protein as "good" food, which is therefore retained rather than purged, and carbohydrates or junk food as "bad" food, which is consumed in huge quantities, only to be regurgitated. On the surface, this strategy of managing aggression may be compelling—the expulsion of badness in the form of vomit leaves the patient feeling good. However, the residual feeling of "goodness" is unstable because it is based on splitting, denial, and projection of aggression rather than on integration of the bad with the good.

Treatment considerations.   The most important single principle in the treatment of bulimia is individualization of the treatment plan. Concurrent psychiatric disorders, such as depression, personality disorders, and drug abuse, should be addressed as part of comprehensive treatment planning. "Assembly line treatment programs" (Yager 1984) that treat all bulimic patients alike will only help a fraction of them because of a failure to recognize and appreciate the inherent heterogeneity of the bulimic population. About one-third of all bulimic patients represent a relatively healthy subgroup who will respond well to a time-limited approach involving brief cognitive-behavioral therapy and a psychoeducational program (Johnson and Connors 1987; Johnson et al. 1989). Support groups such as Overeaters Anonymous (OA) may also sustain this subgroup of patients without further treatment.

Follow-up studies suggest that the temporal stability of bulimic symptoms may be a problem for many patients (Joiner et al. 1997). In a review of 88 studies conducting follow-up assessments with bulimic subjects, Keel and Mitchell (1997) found that approximately 50% of women had fully recovered from the disorder 5–10 years after presentation. However, 20% continued to meet full criteria for bulimia nervosa, and approximately 30% had relapsed into bulimic symptoms. In a follow-up of 173 women more than 10 years following presentation, the same investigators (Keel et al. 1999) reported that nearly 70% of their sample were either in full or partial remission, but 30% continued to engage in recurrent binge eating or purging behaviors.

Although dynamic approaches may not be indicated or necessary for all patients, they still may benefit the majority. Among nonresponders, as many as two-thirds may have borderline personality disorder (Johnson et al. 1989), while others may have other personality disorders or significant depression. These patients usually require long-term, expressive-supportive psychotherapy and often need psychopharmacological intervention as well. Many patients also frankly resent a behavioral approach to their bulimic symptoms (Yager 1984). Focusing on the patient's overt behavior while neglecting her internal world may recapitulate the patient's experience of growing up with parents who are more concerned about surface than substance. Yager (1984) suggested that as many as 50% of all bulimic patients are dissatisfied with behavior modification techniques. Some patients will even experience the task of writing a daily diary about their eating habits as demeaning, because they may view their eating problems as symptomatic of more fundamental disturbances. Treatment that does not match the patient's interests and belief system is doomed to failure (Yager 1984).

Bulimia nervosa can be life-threatening. Patients have been known to alter their electrolyte balance sufficiently to precipitate cardiac arrest. Blood chemistry monitoring should therefore be part of the outpatient management of these patients, with hospitalization as a backup strategy. Since many bulimic patients also suffer from borderline personality disorder or major affective disorders, hospitalization may be required in the face of a suicide attempt or severe self-mutilation. The hospital treatment must follow an individualized comprehensive treatment plan, in addition to the task of gaining symptom control through locking bathrooms, implementing a normal meal schedule, providing psychoeducational assistance from a dietitian, and encouraging the keeping of a diary. Hospitalization often provides the therapist with an opportunity to better understand the patient's internal object relations; thus, it facilitates more sophisticated diagnostic understanding and more precise treatment planning:

Ms. W was a 19-year-old college student with a mixture of bulimic and anorexic symptoms. She was hospitalized after "firing" her psychotherapist and completely losing control of her binge eating and purging. Her parents, who were quite exasperated with her behavior, brought her to the hospital because they felt hopeless about ever getting her to eat properly. During the first week of hospitalization, Ms. W informed her hospital doctor that she planned to remain aloof and distant because she did not want to get attached to a doctor again only to be disappointed. Regular meals and group meetings were immediately implemented, but the patient refused to go to meals or to attend the group. She insisted that she was capable of dieting only by eating when and what she wanted. She pointed out to her doctor that her weight was remaining constant, so there was no need for concern.

The nursing staff became increasingly irritated with Ms. W for her utter lack of cooperation. The more stubborn and resistant the patient became, the more the staff insisted that she follow the structure of the hospital program. In one staff meeting, the hospital doctor observed that the patient had succeeded in recapitulating her family situation. By asserting that she should have control over her diet, she provoked others into attempting to take control of her eating. She could then feel victimized by the controlling forces around her, just as she felt victimized by her parents.

Ms. W's doctor met with her and pointed out to Ms. W that she was attempting to provoke the hospital staff into a reenactment of her family situation. She asked the patient to reflect on what she might gain from this reenactment. Ms. W responded by indicating to her doctor that she was not interested in talking. Three days later, she told her doctor that she had been hoarding medications and sharp objects in a locked drawer in her hospital room so that she might attempt suicide. She said that she had decided to tell her doctor because she really did not want to die. She also indicated that it was terribly difficult for her to communicate feelings to her doctor because she believed that she would become uncontrollably dependent and would lose any sense of her own self. She was certain that dependency on her doctor would lead to her being exploited and mistreated according to the doctor's needs rather than her own treatment needs.

This information helped the hospital staff understand Ms. W's resistance to the treatment structure. By refusing to cooperate, this patient was attempting to establish a sense of self independent of the demands and expectations of others. Cooperation with the nursing staff and collaboration with her hospital doctor carried the risk that she would become a mere extension of others, as she had in her family. Once this underlying anxiety surfaced, the staff members allowed Ms. W to have more say in her eating program. With a member of the nursing staff, she was able to collaborate on and then follow a program that was acceptable to both of them.

Just when Ms. W seemed to be improving, however, her hospital doctor received a call at home on Christmas morning as her family was opening presents. A hospital nurse was calling to inform her that Ms. W had smuggled in and then taken a large number of laxatives and had been having diarrhea all morning. The nurse was worried that Ms. W might require emergency medical treatment, so Ms. W's doctor felt compelled to go to the hospital to see the patient. Two days later, when Ms. W was medically stable, her doctor confronted her about the transference hostility involved in her purging, then suggested that perhaps Ms. W had wished to spoil her doctor's Christmas morning. Although the patient blandly denied any such possibility, her doctor had to suppress intense anger at Ms. W for the timing of her acting-out. It gradually dawned on the doctor that the act of purging had enabled the patient to expel her own aggression. As a result, she could not relate to the doctor's interpretation of her act as hostile; the doctor unconsciously served as a container of the patient's projected anger.

Although this case illustrates a more refractory patient with borderline personality disorder as part of the clinical picture, the transference/countertransference struggles are not atypical of what individual therapists commonly encounter with bulimic patients. Therapists may find themselves repeatedly provoked into accepting the "badness" the patient is attempting to expel. They may also feel "vomited on" when the patient repeatedly spits back at them all their therapeutic efforts. The recapitulation of the family pattern in hospital treatment or in individual psychotherapy helps the clinician understand the patient's role within the family system. Because bulimia is so often part of a homeostatic balance in the family, family therapy or family intervention in association with individual therapy is frequently needed. By ignoring the family system, the therapist runs the risk that the patient's improvement will be terribly threatening to other family members. Defensive reactions to this threat may include an insidious undermining of the bulimic patient's treatment or the development of a serious dysfunction in another family member. The family's need for the bulimic patient's illness must be respected, and the parents must feel "held" and validated so that they will not sabotage the treatment (Humphrey and Stern 1988).

Because of their intense ambivalence and their concern about upsetting the family equilibrium, many bulimic patients will try to avoid intensive psychodynamic therapy. They may consider themselves to be defective, and psychotherapeutic exploration involves a risk that this defectiveness will be exposed (Reich and Cierpka 1998). Introducing an eating diary and pointing out the association between certain eating patterns and emotional states may be an extremely effective way to build a therapeutic alliance with the patient. One of the common countertransference difficulties encountered is the desire to cure the patient quickly, which leads the therapist to begin "overfeeding" the patient by introducing too many interpretive interventions too soon. As Reich and Cierpka (1998) cautioned, interpretations and confrontations may be handled in a bulimic way by greedily consuming but not properly digesting them. A self psychologically based empathic approach in which interpretation is postponed appears to help many bulimic patients. In a randomized controlled study of self psychological therapy versus cognitive orientation treatment, 4 of the 8 bulimic patients treated with the former intervention remitted, while only 2 of 10 treated with the cognitive orientation treatment did so (Bachar et al. 1999).

Dynamic group psychotherapy may also be a useful adjunctive treatment. A growing empirical literature testifies to the efficacy of group psychotherapy for patients with bulimia nervosa (Harper-Giuffre et al. 1992; Liedtke et al. 1991; Mitchell et al. 1990). In a review of 18 different reports of this modality with bulimic patients in an outpatient setting, Oesterheld et al. (1987) found reason for guarded optimism. The consensus was that group psychotherapy effectively reduced bulimic symptoms by an average of 70%. However, these figures appear inflated because most studies excluded dropouts from their calculations. Dropout rates tended to be high even though most groups had excluded patients with borderline personality disorder and other severe character pathology. Long-term follow-up data were also lacking. The group therapists appeared to agree, much as did the individual therapists, that a stable remission requires both insight and symptom control.

In summary, the indication for a dynamic approach to bulimia nervosa is a lack of response to time-limited psychoeducational and cognitive-behavioral methods. Family interventions in the form of support, education, and possibly family therapy are also generally necessary. Some form of symptom control is required in conjunction with the other approaches. Brief hospitalization, support groups such as OA, and group psychotherapy can all assist the patient with symptom control. Some individual psychotherapists also consider symptom control as part of the treatment process. A substantial subset of bulimic patients with associated severe character pathology, suicidal tendencies, and propensities toward life-threatening electrolyte disturbances will require psychotherapy in the context of long-term hospitalization. These patients defy the most diligent efforts of treaters to structure their lives. They seem bent on a self-destructive course that may indeed be fatal without extended hospital treatment.

References

American Psychiatric Association: Diagnostic and Statistical Manual of Mental Disorders, 4th Edition. Washington, DC, American Psychiatric Association, 1994

Bachar E, Latzer Y, Kreitler S, et al: Empirical comparison of two psychological therapies: self psychology and cognitive orientation in the treatment of anorexia and bulimia. J Psychother Pract Res 8:115–128, 1999

Balint M: The Basic Fault: Therapeutic Aspects of Regression. New York, Brunner/Mazel, 1979

Bemporad JR, Ratey J: Intensive psychotherapy of former anorexic individuals. Am J Psychother 39:454–466, 1985

Blatt SJ, McDonald C, Sugarman A, et al: Psychodynamic theories of opiate addiction: new directions for research. Clin Psychol Rev 4:159–189, 1984a

Blatt SJ, Rounsaville B, Eyre SL, et al: The psychodynamics of opiate addiction. J Nerv Ment Dis 172:342–352, 1984b

Boris HN: On the treatment of anorexia nervosa. Int J Psychoanal 65:435–442, 1984a

Boris HN: The problem of anorexia nervosa. Int J Psychoanal 65:315–322, 1984b

Brown S: Treating the Alcoholic: A Developmental Model of Recovery. New York, Wiley, 1985

Bruch H: Eating Disorders: Obesity, Anorexia Nervosa, and the Person Within. New York, Basic Books, 1973

Bruch H: The Golden Cage: The Enigma of Anorexia Nervosa. Cambridge, MA, Harvard University Press, 1978

Bruch H: Psychotherapy in anorexia nervosa. Int J Eat Disord 1(4):3–14, 1982

Bruch H: The changing picture of an illness: anorexia nervosa, in Attachment and the Therapeutic Process. Edited by Sacksteder JL, Schwartz DP, Akabane Y. Madison, CT, International Universities Press, 1987, pp 205–222

Chessick RD: Clinical notes toward the understanding and intensive psychotherapy of adult eating disorders. Annual of Psychoanalysis 22/23:301–322, 1985

Cooper DE: The role of group psychotherapy in the treatment of substance abusers. Am J Psychother 41:55–67, 1987

Cornelius JR, Salloum IM, Mezzich J, et al: Disproportionate suicidality in patients with comorbid major depression and alcoholism. Am J Psychiatry 152:358–364, 1995

Dare C: Psychoanalytic psychotherapy, in Treatments of Psychiatric Disorders, 2nd Edition, Vol 2. Edited by Gabbard GO. Washington, DC, American Psychiatric Press, 1995, pp 2129–2152

Dodes LM: Abstinence from alcohol in long-term individual psychotherapy with alcoholics. Am J Psychother 38:248–256, 1984

Dodes LM: The psychology of combining dynamic psychotherapy and Alcoholics Anonymous. Bull Menninger Clin 52:283–293, 1988

Dodes LM: Addiction, helplessness, and narcissistic rage. Psychoanal Q 59:398–419, 1990

Donovan JM: An etiologic model of alcoholism. Am J Psychiatry 143:1–11, 1986

Eisler I, Dare C, Russell GF, et al: Family and individual therapy in anorexia nervosa: a 5-year follow-up. Arch Gen Psychiatry 54:1025–1030, 1997

Fairburn CG, Beglin SJ: Studies of the epidemiology of bulimia nervosa. Am J Psychiatry 147:401–408, 1990

Fairburn CG, Welch SL, Doll HA, et al: Risk factors for bulimia nervosa: a community-based case-control study. Arch Gen Psychiatry 54:509–517, 1997

Gabbard GO, Lazar SG, Hornberger J, et al: The economic impact of psychotherapy: a review. Am J Psychiatry 154:147–155, 1997

Garfinkel PE, Garner DM: Anorexia Nervosa: A Multidimensional Perspective. New York, Brunner/Mazel, 1982

Garfinkel PE, Moldofsky H, Garner DM: The heterogeneity of anorexia nervosa: bulimia as a distinct subgroup. Arch Gen Psychiatry 37:1036–1040, 1980

Garner DM, Garfinkel PE, Irvine MJ: Integration and sequencing of treatment approaches for eating disorders. Psychother Psychosom 46:67–75, 1986

Goodsitt A: Self-regulatory disturbances in eating disorders. Int J Eat Disord 2(3):51–60, 1983

Goodwin DW: Alcoholism and heredity. Arch Gen Psychiatry 36:57–61, 1979

Gorton GE, Akhtar S: The relationship between addiction and personality disorder: reappraisal and reflections. Integrative Psychiatry 10:185–198, 1994

Hall A, Crisp AH: Brief psychotherapy in the treatment of anorexia nervosa: preliminary findings, in Anorexia Nervosa: Recent Developments in Research. Edited by Darby PL, Garfinkel PE, Garner DM, et al. New York, Alan R Liss, 1983, pp 427–439

Hall A, Slim E, Hawker F, et al: Anorexia nervosa: long-term outcome in 50 female patients. Br J Psychiatry 145:407–413, 1984

Harper-Giuffre H, MacKenzie KR, Sivitilli D: Interpersonal group psychotherapy, in Group Psychotherapy for Eating Disorders. Edited by Harper-Giuffre H, MacKenzie KR. Washington, DC, American Psychiatric Press, 1992, pp 105–145

Hartocollis P: Borderline syndrome and alcoholism, in Encyclopedic Handbook of Alcoholism. Edited by Pattison EM, Kaufman E. New York, Gardner, 1982, pp 628–635

Hsu LK: Outcome of anorexia nervosa: a review of the literature (1954 to 1978). Arch Gen Psychiatry 37:1041–1046, 1980

Hsu LK: The treatment of anorexia nervosa. Am J Psychiatry 143:573–581, 1986

Hsu LK: Outcome studies in patients with eating disorders, in Psychiatric Treatment: Advances in Outcome Research. Edited by Mirin SM, Gossett JT, Grob MC. Washington, DC, American Psychiatric Press, 1991, pp 159–180

Hsu LK, Crisp AH, Harding B: Outcome of anorexia nervosa. Lancet 1(8107):61–65, 1979

Hughes P: The use of the countertransference in the therapy of patients with anorexia nervosa. European Eating Disorders Review 5:258–269, 1997

Humphrey LL, Stern S: Object relations and the family system in bulimia: a theoretical integration. J Marital Fam Ther 14:337–350, 1988

Johnson C, Connors ME: The Etiology and Treatment of Bulimia Nervosa: A Biopsychosocial Perspective. New York, Basic Books, 1987

Johnson C, Tobin DL, Enright A: Prevalence and clinical characteristics of borderline patients in an eating-disordered population. J Clin Psychiatry 50:9–15, 1989

Joiner TE, Heatherton TF, Keel PK: Ten-year stability and predictive validity of five bulimia-related indicators. Am J Psychiatry 154:1133–1138, 1997

Kandel DB, Kessler RC, Margulies RZ: Antecedents of adolescent initiation into stages of drug use: a developmental analysis, in Longitudinal Research on Drug Use. Edited by Kandel DB. New York, Hemisphere, 1978, pp 73–78

Kaplan AS, Woodside DB: Biological aspects of anorexia nervosa and bulimia nervosa. J Consult Clin Psychol 55:645–653, 1987

Keel PK, Mitchell JE: Outcome in bulimia nervosa. Am J Psychiatry 154:313–321, 1997

Keel PK, Mitchell JE, Miller KB, et al: Long-term outcome of bulimia nervosa. Arch Gen Psychiatry 56:63–69, 1999

Kendler KS, Heath AC, Neale MC, et al: A population-based twin study of alcoholism in women. JAMA 268:1877–1882, 1992

Kendler KS, Walters EE, Neale MC, et al: The structure of the genetic and environmental risk factors for six major psychiatric disorders in women: phobia, generalized anxiety disorder, panic disorder, bulimia, major depression, and alcoholism. Arch Gen Psychiatry 52:374–383, 1995

Kernberg OF: Borderline Conditions and Pathological Narcissism. New York, Jason Aronson, 1975

Khantzian EJ: Psychopathology, psychodynamics, and alcoholism, in Encyclopedic Handbook of Alcoholism. Edited by Pattison EM, Kaufman E. New York, Gardner, 1982, pp 581–597

Khantzian EJ: Psychotherapeutic interventions with substance abusers—the clinical context. J Subst Abuse Treat 2:83–88, 1985a

Khantzian EJ: The self-medication hypothesis of addictive disorders: focus on heroin and cocaine dependence. Am J Psychiatry 142:1259–1264, 1985b

Khantzian EJ: A contemporary psychodynamic approach to drug abuse treatment. Am J Drug Alcohol Abuse 12.213–222, 1986

Khantzian EJ: The self-medication hypothesis of substance use disorders: a reconsideration and recent applications. Harv Rev Psychiatry 4:231–244, 1997

Khantzian EJ, Treece C: DSM-III psychiatric diagnosis of narcotic addicts: recent findings. Arch Gen Psychiatry 42:1067–1071, 1985

Knight RP: Borderline states. Bull Menninger Clin 17:1–12, 1953

Kohut H: The Analysis of the Self: A Systematic Approach to the Psychoanalytic Treatment of Narcissistic Personality Disorders. New York, International Universities Press, 1971

Kohut H: How Does Analysis Cure? Edited by Goldberg A. Chicago, IL, University of Chicago Press, 1984

Krystal H: Alexithymia and the effectiveness of psychoanalytic treatment. International Journal of Psychoanalytic Psychotherapy 9:353–378, 1982–1983

Lieb RC, Thompson TL II: Group psychotherapy of four anorexia nervosa inpatients. Int J Group Psychother 34:639–642, 1984

Liedtke R, Jäger B, Lempa W, et al: Therapy outcome of two treatment models for bulimia nervosa: preliminary results of a controlled study. Psychother Psychosom 56:56–63, 1991

Mack JE: Alcoholism, AA, and the governance of the self, in Dynamic Approaches to the Understanding and Treatment of Alcoholism. Edited by Bean MH, Zinberg NE. New York, Free Press, 1981, pp 128–162

Maher MS: Group therapy for anorexia nervosa, in Current Treatment of Anorexia Nervosa and Bulimia. Edited by Powers PS, Fernandez RC. Basel, Switzerland, Karger, 1984, pp 265–276

McCrady BS, Langenbucher JW: Alcohol treatment and healthcare system reform. Arch Gen Psychiatry 53:737–746, 1996

McLellan AT, Arndt IO, Metzger DS, et al: The effects of psychosocial services in substance abuse treatment. JAMA 269:1953–1959, 1993

Mintz IL: Self-destructive behavior in anorexia nervosa and bulimia, in Bulimia: Psychoanalytic Treatment and Theory. Edited by Schwartz HJ. Madison, CT, International Universities Press, 1988, pp 127–171

Minuchin S, Rosman BL, Baker L: Psychosomatic Families: Anorexia Nervosa in Context. Cambridge, MA, Harvard University Press, 1978

Mitchell JE, Pyle RL, Eckert ED, et al: A comparison study of antidepressants and structured intensive group psychotherapy in the treatment of bulimia nervosa. Arch Gen Psychiatry 47:149–157, 1990

Murphy GE, Wetzel RD: The lifetime risk of suicide in alcoholism. Arch Gen Psychiatry 47:383–392, 1990

Nace EP, Saxon JJ Jr, Shore N: A comparison of borderline and nonborderline alcoholic patients. Arch Gen Psychiatry 40:54–56, 1983

Nathan PE: The addictive personality is the behavior of the addict. J Consult Clin Psychol 56:183–188, 1988

Nicholson B, Treece C: Object relations and differential treatment response to methadone maintenance. J Nerv Ment Dis 169:424–429, 1981

Oesterheld JR, McKenna MS, Gould NB: Group psychotherapy of bulimia: a critical review. Int J Group Psychother 37:163–184, 1987

Pages KP, Russo JE, Roy-Byrne PP, et al: Determinants of suicidal ideation: the role of substance use disorders. J Clin Psychiatry 58:510–515, 1997

Paton S, Kessler R, Kandel D: Depressive mood and adolescent illicit drug use: a longitudinal analysis. J Genet Psychol 131:267–289, 1977

Pattison EM: Nonabstinent drinking goals in the treatment of alcoholism: a clinical typology. Arch Gen Psychiatry 33:923–930, 1976

Patton CJ: Fear of abandonment and binge eating: a subliminal psychodynamic activation investigation. J Nerv Ment Dis 180:484–490, 1992

Polivy J: Group psychotherapy as an adjunctive treatment for anorexia nervosa. Journal of Psychiatric Treatment and Evaluation 3:279–283, 1981

Powers PS: Psychotherapy of anorexia nervosa, in Current Treatment of Anorexia Nervosa and Bulimia. Edited by Powers PS, Fernandez RC. Basel, Switzerland, Karger, 1984, pp 18–47

Prescott CA, Kendler KS: Genetic and environmental contributions to alcohol abuse and dependence in a population-based sample of male twins. Am J Psychiatry 156:34–40, 1999

Project MATCH Research Group: Matching alcoholism treatments to client heterogeneity: Project MATCH posttreatment drinking outcomes. J Stud Alcohol 58:7–29, 1997

Regier DA, Farmer ME, Rae BS, et al: Comorbidity of mental disorders with alcohol and other drug abuse: results from the Epidemiologic Catchment Area (ECA) Study. JAMA 264:2511–2518, 1990

Reich G, Cierpka M: Identity conflicts in bulimia nervosa: psychodynamic patterns and psychoanalytic treatment. Psychoanalytic Inquiry 18:383–402, 1998

Rinsley DB: The Dipsas revisited: comments on addiction and personality. J Subst Abuse Treat 5:1–7, 1988

Robin AL, Siegel PT, Moye A: Family versus individual therapy for anorexia: impact on family conflict. Int J Eat Disord 17:313–322, 1995

Rounsaville BJ, Weissman MM, Kleber H, et al: Heterogeneity of psychiatric diagnosis in treated opiate addicts. Arch Gen Psychiatry 39:161–166, 1982

Rounsaville BJ, Anton SF, Carroll K, et al: Psychiatric diagnoses of treatment-seeking cocaine abusers. Arch Gen Psychiatry 48:43–51, 1991

Rutherford MJ, Cacciola JS, Alterman AI, et al: Assessment of object relations and reality testing in methadone patients. Am J Psychiatry 153:1189–1194, 1996

Sandahl C, Herlitz K, Ahlin G, et al: Time-limited group psychotherapy for moderately alcohol dependent patients: a randomized controlled clinical trial. Psychotherapy Research 8:361–378, 1998,12N

Schuckit MA: Genetics and the risk for alcoholism. JAMA 254:2614–2617, 1985

Schuckit MA, Rimmer J, Reich T, et al: Alcoholism: antisocial traits in male alcoholics (abstract). Br J Psychiatry 117:575–576, 1970

Selvini Palazzoli M: Self-Starvation: From Individual to Family Therapy in the Treatment of Anorexia Nervosa. Translated by Pomerans A. New York, Jason Aronson, 1978

Sperling O: On appersonation. Int J Psychoanal 25:128–132, 1944

Strober M, Humphrey LL: Familial contributions to the etiology and course of anorexia nervosa and bulimia. J Consult Clin Psychol 55:654–659, 1987

Sugarman A, Kurash C: The body as a transitional object in bulimia. Int J Eat Disord 1(4).57–67, 1982

Sullivan PF, Bulik CM, Fear JL, et al: Outcome of anorexia nervosa: a case-control study. Am J Psychiatry 155:939–946, 1998

Sutker PB, Allain AN: Issues in personality conceptualizations of addictive behaviors. J Consult Clin Psychol 56:172–182, 1988

Treece C: Assessment of ego functioning in studies of narcotic addiction, in The Broad Scope of Ego Function Assessment. Edited by Bellak L, Goldsmith LA. New York, Wiley, 1984, pp 268–290

Treece C, Khantzian EJ: Psychodynamic factors in the development of drug dependence. Psychiatr Clin North Am 9:399–412, 1986

Vaglum S, Vaglum P: Borderline and other mental disorders in alcoholic female psychiatric patients: a case control study. Psychopathology 18:50–60, 1985

Vaillant GE: Dangers of psychotherapy in the treatment of alcoholism, in Dynamic Approaches to the Understanding and Treatment of Alcoholism. Edited by Bean MH, Zinberg NE. New York, Free Press, 1981, pp 36–54

Vaillant GE: The Natural History of Alcoholism. Cambridge, MA, Harvard University Press, 1983

Vaillant GE: The alcohol-dependent and drug-dependent person, in The New Harvard Guide to Psychiatry. Edited by Nicholi AM Jr. Cambridge, MA, Belknap Press of Harvard University Press, 1988, pp 700–713

Weissman MM, Myers JK: Clinical depression in alcoholism. Am J Psychiatry 137:372–373, 1980

Williams G: Reflections on some dynamics of eating disorders: "no entry" defenses and foreign bodies. Int J Psychoanal 78:927–941, 1997

Wilson CP (ed): Fear of Being Fat: The Treatment of Anorexia Nervosa and Bulimia. New York, Jason Aronson, 1983

Woody GE, Luborsky L, McLellan AT, et al: Psychotherapy for opiate addicts: does it help? Arch Gen Psychiatry 40:639–645, 1983

Woody GE, McLellan AT, Luborsky L, et al: Severity of psychiatric symptoms as a predictor of benefits from psychotherapy: the Veterans Administration–Penn Study. Am J Psychiatry 141:1172–1177, 1984

Woody GE, McLellan AT, Luborsky L, et al: Sociopathy and psychotherapy outcome. Arch Gen Psychiatry 42:1081–1086, 1985

Woody GE, McLellan AT, Luborsky L, et al: Psychotherapy for substance abuse. Psychiatr Clin North Am 9:547–562, 1986

Woody GE, McLellan AT, Luborsky L, et al: Twelve-month follow-up of psychotherapy for opiate dependents. Am J Psychiatry 144:590–596, 1987

Woody GE, McLellan AT, Luborsky L, et al: Psychotherapy in community methadone programs: a validation study. Am J Psychiatry 152:1302–1308, 1995

Wurmser L: Psychoanalytic considerations of the etiology of compulsive drug use. J Am Psychoanal Assoc 22:820–843, 1974

Wurmser L: Flight from conscience: experience with the psychoanalytic treatment of compulsive drug abusers, I: dynamic sequences, compulsive drug use. J Subst Abuse Treat 4:157–168, 1987a

Wurmser L: Flight from conscience: experience with the psychoanalytic treatment of compulsive drug abusers, II: dynamic and therapeutic conclusions from the experiences with psychoanalysis of drug users. J Subst Abuse Treat 4:169–179, 1987b

Yager J: The treatment of bulimia: an overview, in Current Treatment of Anorexia Nervosa and Bulimia. Edited by Powers PS, Fernandez RC. Basel, Switzerland, Karger, 1984, pp 63–91

CHAPTER
13

Dementia and
Other Cognitive Disorders

It is faulty in principle to try to make a distinction between so-called organic and functional diseases, as far as symptomatology and therapy are concerned. In both conditions, one is dealing with abnormal functioning of the same psychophysical apparatus and with the attempts of the organism to come to terms with that. If the disturbances—whether they are due to damage to the brain or to psychological conflicts—do not disappear spontaneously or cannot be eliminated by therapy, the organism has to make a new adjustment to life in spite of them. Our task is to help the patients in this adjustment by physical and psychological means; the procedure and goal of the therapy in both conditions is, in principle, the same.

Kurt Goldstein

In this classic cautionary statement against mind/brain dualism, Goldstein reminds us of the fundamental interdependence of psychology and biology. The traditional distinction between organic and functional syndromes implies that psychology is irrelevant to the former and biology irrelevant to the latter. Because the term *organic* generally denotes the presence of actual anatomic damage to neuronal and glial structures, some psychiatrists view such disorders as outside their purview and therefore refer patients with them to neurologists. Dynamic psychiatrists in particular may view patients with structural brain damage as so lacking in the capacity for abstraction that they are inaccessible to psychotherapeutic intervention. This abdication is unfortunate because dynamic clinicians have much to contribute to the cognitively impaired patient.

With increasing knowledge of how the central nervous system functions, the notion of "organic" versus "nonorganic" psychiatric disorders has become less meaningful. Referring to major psychiatric disorders such as schizophrenia and bipolar affective disorder as "nonorganic" or "functional" fails to connote the biological substrate of both diseases. In addition, contributors to DSM-IV (American Psychiatric Association 1994) had some concern that the organic/nonorganic distinction might encourage continued stigmatization of people with psychiatric disorders by suggesting that no true medical or biological basis existed for their illnesses.

The personality is the end result of a series of complex functions occurring in cortical (and subcortical) structures. Psychodynamic factors in disorders involving brain damage can most productively be discussed by dividing the conditions into those present from birth and those involving insult to brain tissue later in the life cycle (Lewis 1986). In those conditions present from birth, the psychological issues of each developmental phase throughout the life cycle are shaped by the patient's neuroanatomic deficits. In those conditions occurring later, development has been unencumbered by neural dysfunction, so the major issue is adjustment to the loss of a previous level of functioning. The discussion in this chapter will focus on those cognitive impairment disorders for which dynamic approaches are particularly useful. Attention-deficit/hyperactivity disorder (ADHD) is one disorder present from birth in which the dynamic psychiatrist may play a key role. Brain injury and dementia are conditions of later onset that will also be discussed.

Conditions Present From Birth:
Attention-Deficit/Hyperactivity Disorder

Genetic-constitutional and perinatal sources of brain damage play a key role in each subsequent developmental phase throughout the life cycle. Although at one time children were believed to "outgrow" the syndrome of ADHD, it is now clear that the condition may persist into adult life (Bellak 1977; Biederman 1998; Biederman et al. 1993; Hartocollis 1968). Clinicians should therefore have a high index of suspicion when a patient presents with a history of poor response to conventional psychiatric or psychological treatments, a chronic inability to perform at the level expected by teachers and parents, a history of repeated life frustrations, problems with spatial orientation (such as getting lost or experiencing difficulty distinguishing between left and right), emotional outbursts, restlessness, a spotty job history, memory impairment, and marked discrepancies between performance and verbal IQ scores.

Patients who grow up with ADHD frequently have a host of subtle deficits that can be categorized according to specific ego functions (Bellak 1977). Primary autonomous functions (such as perception, memory, and motor abilities) are the most commonly affected ego capacities. Next are impairments in the ability to regulate and control impulses and affects, which will be manifested as frequent temper outbursts, assaults, and poor tolerance for frustration. The ego function involved with providing a barrier to internal and external stimuli is also easily overloaded. Although the thought processes of such patients may be formally intact, their ability to think abstractly is typically compromised. The ego function known as *sense of reality* will often show several characteristic deficits, including spatial disorientation, unclear body boundaries, and difficulty discriminating between right and left. Finally, because these patients suffer a fundamental impairment in synthetic-integrative functioning, they may struggle to bring contradictory ideas or feelings together into a unified whole.

Psychodynamic Understanding

The diagnostic criteria of ADHD as defined in DSM-IV focus almost entirely on behavioral phenomena. The mental experience of individuals with this disorder is rarely discussed, in part because of the relative paucity of psychoanalytic contributions on ADHD and learning disabilities. More recently, however, psychoanalysts and psychoanalytically informed clinicians have begun to conceptualize these conditions from a psychodynamic vantage point (Gilmore, in press; Rothstein 1998; Rothstein and Glenn 1999).

To understand adult patients with congenital forms of brain impairment, clinicians must consider the impact of a compromised neural substrate on the achievement of normal developmental tasks. The growing infant struggles daily with an underlying tension between the pressure of drives and affects, on the one hand, and cortical control, on the other. Drive pressures resist mastery when the infant lacks the usual endowment of functioning cortex (Weil 1978). Similarly, the conflict-free or autonomous spheres of ego functioning (such as intellect, thinking, perception, motility, and language) are dependent on constitutional endowment (Hartmann 1939/1958).

Numerous authors have commented on the effects of structurally based cognitive deficits on the development of the self and on the internalization of object relations (Allen et al. 1988; Buchholz 1987; Gilmore, in press; Kafka 1984; Lewis 1986;

Palombo 1979; Pickar 1986; Rothstein 1998; D. N. Stern 1985; Weil 1978). As Daniel Stern (1985) noted, the development of the self depends on mutual cueing between mother and infant that derives from an empathic bond formed by their sensitive attunement to the emotional reactions of one another. Infants with structurally based cognitive dysfunction will be unable to perceive accurately or to integrate effectively the affective signals from the mother. When the child fails to respond to the mother as she expects, the mother may become anxious, thus inserting tension and discord into the infant-mother interactions. Parents may experience an infant or child who responds abnormally or who is otherwise defective as a profound narcissistic injury (Buchholz 1987). The parents may recoil from the child and convey their sense of disappointment and anxiety in all their subsequent interactions, leading to a disturbance of the child's feelings of self-esteem (Abrams and Kaslow 1976). Alternatively, the parents may become overinvolved and overprotective. As these children grow and develop, they continue to fall short of parental expectations, resulting in further feelings of failure and humiliation. Such children have poorer cortical control of impulses, leading to more parental reprimands, to more interactions in which others are angry and punitive, and to experiences with parents who convey, through their excessive anxiety, that separation from a parental figure is dangerous (Pickar 1986; Weil 1978). Because these children are often unable to effectively appreciate cause-effect sequences, they do not link the rejection responses of others to their own behavior, resulting in feelings of victimization and helplessness (T. Bryan 1977).

Defects in an individual's primary autonomous ego functions of visual and auditory perception and memory will adversely affect that person's ability to achieve object constancy. Children with learning disabilities and ADHD often suffer from an incapacity to soothe themselves because they have never been able to internalize and maintain comforting maternal figures as affectively meaningful images. As a result, they may struggle to maintain a stable sense of self. Their inability to accurately perceive social signals from others contributes to their frequently observable ineptitude in relating to others in a socially appropriate manner (J. H. Bryan et al. 1980).

To compensate for their profound feelings of inadequacy and incompetence, individuals with ADHD may develop a defensive grandiosity. Kafka (1984) reported on one such patient who came to analysis. Having grown up with a host of learning disabilities and other cognitive deficits, the patient had felt like a "faker" all his life. To deal with his sense that something fundamental was missing, he assumed a defensive posture of independence and grandiosity. He was embarrassed and humiliated about his dependency on others for help with his spatial disorientation. Because he associated these disabilities with a lack of masculinity, he felt deeply ashamed.

Some individuals can compensate for their neuropsychological deficits by over-developing other areas of ego functioning. The inventor Thomas Edison, who suffered from learning disabilities, is one famous example. However, when compensatory efforts fail, the young person may avoid dealing with the enormous frustration of repeated failure by turning to juvenile delinquency (Pickar 1986). Instead of dealing with the shame and humiliation associated with trying but failing to meet the academic and social expectations of others, the adolescent may adopt a posture of contempt toward the values of parents, teachers, and society in general.

Treatment Considerations

Therapeutic nihilism with brain-damaged patients is unwarranted. As Lewis (1986) noted: "The unqualified belief that brain damage renders a person inaccessible to meaningful psychological change through psychotherapy is erroneous and derives from the misconception that brain damage is a monolithic entity" (p. 78). The therapist cannot expect the tendency toward concrete thinking to completely disappear, but many patients achieve substantial gains in their ability to think symbolically or abstractly (Buchholz 1987). Even in a highly expressive treatment like psychoanalysis, Kafka (1984) found that no significant modifications of technique were necessary for such a patient. He did note that his patient responded with narcissistic mortification to minor slips of the tongue because such incidents seemed to expose his defects. In addition, Kafka often had to repeat interpretations patiently and tactfully in various contexts using different examples.

Adapting the treatment approach to patients who suffer from more severe cognitive deficits requires a precise understanding of how those deficits affect these patients' ability to use psychotherapy. For example, Lewis (1986) described a patient who had suffered since early childhood from memory disturbances that impaired her ability to evoke a soothing mental image of her therapist. She was unable to maintain continuity between her twice-weekly hour-long sessions because she couldn't recall the therapist's words or appearance. Simply changing the appointment time to one half hour each weekday allowed the patient to internalize the therapeutic process more effectively because she could now remember how the therapist looked and sounded.

Repeated failures of empathy characterize the life stories of such patients. Beginning with parents, other people do not understand the nature or extent of these cognitive limitations and repeatedly expect more than these patients can deliver. Because of this life pattern, some clinicians (Buchholz 1987; Palombo 1979) have suggested using a self psychological approach. The repeated experiences of self-fragmentation and deflation connected with the lack of mirroring responses from others can be addressed as these feelings develop in the transference. The therapist can empathically reflect the patient's strivings for admiration and approbation and can give meaning to how the cognitive impairments have interfered with those strivings. Thus the therapist serves as a selfobject who helps the patient grieve, assists the patient in building a more cohesive self, and encourages self-forgiveness as well.

Although empathizing with the patient's experience of being defective may be helpful, in doing so the therapist runs the risk of ignoring intrapsychic conflict. Rothstein (1998) stresses the importance of exploring how the patient's *specific* cognitive difficulties become interwoven with intrapsychic conflicts. She points out that neuropsychological dysfunction cannot truly be separated from internal conflict and unconscious fantasies about oneself and others. Gilmore (in press), who shares this concern, suggests that the therapist should view ADHD as a disturbance in the organizing, synthetic, and integrative function of the ego. From this perspective, psychoanalytically oriented therapy may be of considerable usefulness with such patients. Gilmore notes that adults with ADHD may develop stereotypic ways of relating to others as a defense against their anxiety about failing to recognize the demands of an interpersonal situation. Psychodynamic therapy may assist such patients in developing greater self-esteem and self-confidence and a more flexible capacity to relate to others in nonprogrammed and spontaneous ways. Narcissistic fragility and a need to be in control often dominates adult patients with ADHD, and dynamic therapy in conjunction with stimulant medications may strengthen their sense of self-esteem and improve their capacity to respond and interact with others in a way that allows for spontaneity and flexibility.

When behavioral dyscontrol is a major feature of the patient's clinical picture, hospitalization may be required. Conventional psychiatric treatments usually have proved ineffective for these patients. Frequently, diagnosticians have missed the brain-based dimension because of its subtlety and because of more florid symptoms of personality disorder. Clinicians who assume that all the symptomatology is related to character pathology may develop considerable countertransference frustration when patients react to interventions with wandering attention, poor memory, and failure to reflect on meanings. As the treater's irritation grows, the patient feels increasingly like a failure for not responding properly to treatment, thus recapitulating past experiences with parents, teachers, and employers.

One study of treatment-refractory inpatients drew a psychological profile of patients who suffered from severe psychiatric disorders complicated by "organic" features (Allen et al. 1988; Colson and Allen 1986). Problems with self-esteem and affect modulation are two commonalities in this group of patients. Rarely do these patients have clear-cut neurological disorders, and they are therefore difficult to diagnose. The cumulative diagnostic picture of neurological soft signs, borderline abnormalities on electroencephalogram (EEG), and spotty deficits on neuropsychological testing implicates central nervous system dysfunction. Subcortical involvement, manifested by episodes of behavioral dyscontrol and affective storms, appears of greater relevance than cortical impairment. These patients feel powerless in the face of overwhelming eruptions of affect. In a desperate attempt to gain some sense of mastery and control, they pretend that their episodes are volitional acts designed to intimidate others—a response similar to a grandiose delusion. Their explosions lead to increased isolation from others, great embarrassment, and decreased self-esteem. These patients live in fear of further loss of control. To deal with this threat, they develop extreme defensive postures against any affect whatsoever by becoming constricted and superficial, much like persons with alexithymia. To ward off feelings, they commonly employ the defenses of denial and externalization.

The high expectations of treaters and parents for academic and vocational performance contribute to a vicious cycle with these patients. Because they are unable to live up to such high expectations, their self-esteem plummets and their frustration grows, leading to further vulnerability to affective explosions. These episodes of dyscontrol elicit additional negative feedback from parents and treaters and further erode their self-esteem. The diagnosis of the brain-based contribution often is therapeutic in and of itself, and these patients generally respond with relief to it. The diagnosis also leads to lowered expectations from both parents and clinicians. As a result, the vicious cycle is interrupted, and the patients develop better self-esteem and an increased sense of mastery as their episodes of dyscontrol decrease and their sense of chronic failure diminishes.

Mr. X, a 20-year-old single male, was hospitalized after repeated episodes of temper outbursts leading to physical altercations with fellow employees. The patient's father, a prosperous factory owner, had given Mr. X a job because all previous attempts at gainful employment had failed. At work, Mr. X was viewed as "the boss's son." Minor allusions to preferential treatment of Mr. X by his father provoked outbursts of aggression by Mr. X. At admission, Mr. X's father clearly indicated that he was fed up with his son. He cataloged a long list of life failures, including poor school performance, athletic failures, and "laziness" manifested by an inability to keep a job. Mr. X hung his head in shame as this list was rattled off, and he seemed particularly wounded when his father compared him with an older brother who had recently attained a graduate professional degree.

On the hospital unit, Mr. X related to others in a formal, constricted manner that made his occasional outbursts seem to come from out of the blue. In one typical instance, he was returning to the unit after an activities therapy session when he suddenly started shoving another male patient walking beside him. With a look of rage, he pinned the patient to the ground, snatched his wallet from his pants pocket, and threw it onto the roof of the hospital. Mr. X was returned to the unit and confined to his room. In a subsequent group meeting, the other patient and the staff member who had accompanied them described the incident in detail, particularly noting its inexplicability because there was no apparent trigger. With much bravado, Mr. X claimed that the other patient had provoked him by making fun of him. He maintained that the attack was justified. As a result of this and other incidents, the other patients on Mr. X's team (and several staff members) began to feel intimidated and frightened by Mr. X.

Of course, Mr. X's violent outbursts led to further isolation from the patient community. He was confined to his room for much of the time to decrease stimulation and to protect the other patients. In a one-to-one session with his psychiatrist, he allowed his defensive facade to yield to other feelings. He confided that after each episode of dyscontrol, he felt "like an idiot." He said that he had no idea why he had attacked his male peer on the way back to the hospital unit. His psychiatrist asked Mr. X what had happened in the activity period preceding the assault. He replied that he had been asked to make a wooden bowl in the wood shop. Asked how his bowl had turned out, Mr. X responded, "As usual, I screwed up." His psychiatrist then asked if it was possible that attacking the other patient was his way of dealing with his frustration. Mr. X acknowledged that it probably was, and then added that he would do anything to prevent future outbursts but that he was pessimistic about any treatment being helpful. He had dealt with such outbursts all his life and doubted that anything could control them.

A detailed neuropsychiatric evaluation revealed the following findings, which suggested a brain-based component to Mr. X's problems: 1) a history of learning disabilities from early grade school through high school, 2) difficulties with right/left discrimination, 3) a childhood history of hyperactivity and other symptoms of attention deficit disorder, and 4) moderate perceptual deficits on neuropsychological testing. A 24-hour sleep-deprivation EEG with nasopharyngeal leads was entirely normal, and even an ambulatory EEG monitor failed to reveal any abnormalities in the temporal lobes. Results of a computed tomography (CT) scan were also within normal limits.

Carbamazepine was tried on an empirical basis and seemed to reduce the frequency and intensity of Mr. X's behavioral dyscontrol episodes. The main thrust of the treatment, however, was a careful explanation to Mr. X and his family of the implications of these findings. Initially, Mr. X's parents were quite resistant to the idea that their son had a subtle form of brain damage from early in life. Eventually, though, they were persuaded when the neuropsychologist discussed the testing in detail with them and explained the nature of the physical impairment. The parents' anger and frustration with their son gradually diminished as they began to understand the extent of his limitations. This diagnosis helped put the patient's history in perspective, and it led Mr. X's parents to rethink their expectations for his vocational future. After the psychiatrist explained that Mr. X's lowered stimulus barrier led to his overstimulation when he was around other people, the father arranged for a job for Mr. X at a satellite facility where he could do repetitive menial tasks in isolation from other workers. This arrangement not only lowered the expectations of high job performance but also removed interpersonal triggers of the dyscontrol episodes.

Mr. X responded favorably to the reports of the diagnostic evaluation and particularly to the lowered expectations of his parents. He said he felt like "the pressure was off." The new job arrangement worked satisfactorily for him. Although he remained socially isolated, his self-esteem increased considerably because of his improved mastery of the episodes of dyscontrol and because of his ability to perform adequately at his new job.

Conditions of Later Onset: Brain Injury and Dementia

The human brain that receives an insult later in the developmental life cycle involves a different set of therapeutic issues. In these instances, the patient has deteriorated from a previous level of functioning, and both the patient and the family must adjust to the change. These conditions fall into two broad categories: 1) acute brain injuries with a sudden alteration of functioning and 2) progressive degenerative diseases with a gradual decline. Both forms of insult will be considered in the ensuing discussion. Excluded from consideration are delirium, states of drug intoxication or withdrawal, and other acute insults that rapidly clear when the medical condition or toxic agent has been dealt with, because psychodynamic issues are less relevant to such conditions.

Psychodynamic Understanding

The self, at the most fundamental level, is a product of brain functioning. Damage to brain tissue may produce significant alterations in an individual's sense of identity, thus causing family and loved ones to feel that the patient is no longer the same person. Brain trauma typically affects the frontal and temporal lobes, dramatically influencing the patient's ability to interpret the meaning of stimuli and to connect them with relevant feelings (Prigatano 1989). Such alterations strike at the very heart of the personality.

The awareness of the self is difficult to localize to one area of the brain. Studies of patients whose cerebral hemispheres have been surgically disconnected (Sperry et al. 1979) have suggested that the sense of self is present in both halves of the brain. It appears to be a complex schema to which different brain regions make different contributions.

Patients react to their loss of identity in certain characteristic ways. Goldstein

(1952), one of the first investigators of the psychological effects of brain damage, described an anxiety state that he termed the *catastrophic condition* or *reaction*. When brain-injured patients were asked to perform a simple task that had been no problem for them prior to the trauma, they became angry, agitated, and extremely anxious. Goldstein observed that they perceived their failure to complete the task as a danger to their very existence. As a reaction to this threat, patients characteristically restrict their lives so that they are not exposed to unfamiliar situations or impossible tasks. Thus they defend against catastrophic anxiety by avoiding awareness of their defects. These patients commonly become excessively orderly to the point of being obsessive-compulsive. Keeping everything in place gives them the illusion of control over their environment. It also transforms passivity into activity and provides a concrete solution to a complex, abstract problem.

When brain-injured patients can restrict their lives sufficiently, they may appear remarkably free of anxiety and oblivious to their deficits. Despite showing evidence of memory problems, childish behavior, and a short temper, they often may deny any limitations. In fact, one study (Oddy et al. 1985) found that 40% of patients studied 7 years after an insult to the brain disavowed any disability whatsoever. Clinicians may struggle to differentiate between neurogenic and psychogenic denial in such patients. Lewis (1991) has pointed out that, in contrast to psychological forms of denial, neurogenic denial remits within hours or days of the injury, appears as a pattern of overall deficits rather than as an isolated symptom, and does not produce anxiety or agitation in patients who are confronted with it.

The gradual loss of functioning typical of dementia syndromes generally presents a somewhat different picture. People with dementia preserve a sense of who they are until relatively late in the course of the illness. They may be able to perform their usual work and conduct their usual social routines reasonably well. About two-thirds of all dementia cases involve Alzheimer's disease, and the average duration of the decline in such cases is about 10 years (Small et al. 1997). During this period of decline, which may last as long as 20 years, a variety of mood and personality disturbances may emerge in addition to the cognitive decline. As the illness progresses, the patient is likely to experience increasing difficulty with calculation, performance of complex tasks, and fluency of language. At this point in the illness, when patients realize that they cannot perform the tasks they were once able to, catastrophic reactions may emerge that are similar to those in brain-injured patients. Similarly, eruptions of anger and even combativeness may develop as the disease progresses.

From a psychodynamic perspective, the loss of mental faculties associated with progressive dementia can be understood as a regressive process in the ego, in which more mature defense mechanisms give way to more primitive modes of defense (Weiner 1991). Aspects of the personality that have been partially suppressed by a biologically intact cortex gradually emerge as defensive layers are eroded. High-level defenses such as altruism are replaced by self-absorption, for example. Denial and projection are perhaps the two most common primitive defenses used by persons with dementia. When a memory failure occurs, patients with dementia blame others rather than acknowledge responsibility for the error themselves.

In many aging patients with dementia of the Alzheimer's type, the tragedy of the illness is that self-awareness may remain intact as a number of the mental faculties deteriorate. Because recent memory tends to be sacrificed before remote memory, many patients can clearly recollect how they used to be, which makes their current dysfunctional state all the more disturbing to them. To a large extent, the continuity of the self over time depends on the capacity of memory. When remote memories begin to fade as the illness progresses, then the patient's identity begins to disappear along with the memories. Ultimately, the patient cannot recognize loved ones and family members and can no longer remember significant life events.

Internal objects—particularly, soothing introjects—may also be sacrificed as part of the dementia process. Memory involves others as much as the self. The following case example demonstrates how the loss of memory may be associated both with the loss of a soothing introject and with the recurrence of anxieties from early in life.

Mr. Y was a 75-year-old man who requested psychiatric consultation because his difficulty with memory and cognition associated with Alzheimer's disease made him feel that he was "losing his mind." Three years prior to seeing a psychiatrist, he had been told by his internist that he would need to stop trying to work part time because of difficulties with cognition. Following that conversation, Mr. Y had noted increasing problems with memory, abstraction, computation, and verbal expressive language, all of which were limiting his daily activities. He was also feeling intensely anxious at night when he went to bed.

When asked about previous episodes of anxiety, Mr. Y recounted his early history. At the age of 2½ years, he was sent to live with his grandmother after the death of his parents. The first time he remembered having an anxiety attack was shortly thereafter. Mr. Y recalled listening at night to his grandmother's breathing on the other side of his bedroom wall. He heard her stop breathing and then experienced a sense of panic, which led him to assume a fetal position, rock himself, and call her name. He was filled with a sense of dread that his grandmother would die as his parents had. Mr. Y subsequently experienced anxiety when he had to leave his grandmother and enter kindergarten. Throughout his childhood and adolescence, he experienced anxiety verging on panic each time he faced any form of separation, geographical move, or role change.

Throughout his adult life, Mr. Y had maintained connections with nurturing figures in his environment to ward off any feelings of separation anxiety or panic. For example, he married a woman 20 years younger than he as a way of assuring that she would not abandon him through death and leave him alone and isolated. He had been largely free of anxiety symptoms until the age of 72, when his internist informed him that he was suffering from Alzheimer's disease. The dementia process upset an equilibrium that he had achieved through considerable struggle early in life. His feeling that he was beginning to "lose his mind" was associated with the loss of his grandmother's soothing internal presence. As he lay in bed at night, he once again experienced a terror of abandonment associated with his failing memory. As a result, he became increasingly dependent and clinging in relationship to his wife.

Treatment Considerations

Treatment planning depends on a careful assessment of several factors (Lewis 1986; Prigatano and Klonoff 1988): 1) the exact manner in which the brain insult has affected the sensory, motor, and cognitive spheres; 2) the patient's psychological reaction to the organic deficits; 3) the impact of both the brain insult and the patient's reaction on the patient's psychological and social adjustment; 4) the contribution of the patient's premorbid personality structure to the clinical picture; and 5) differentiation of those symptoms that are direct sequelae of the brain damage from those that are associated with previously defended conflicts or ego deficits, now released as a result of the trauma. This type of assessment requires a detailed history from a family member or a significant other in the patient's life.

Part of the assessment of such patients should include an evaluation of their suitability for expressive-supportive psychotherapy. Lewis and Rosenberg (1990) delineated five useful indicators for selecting which neurologically impaired patients can benefit from dynamic therapy: 1) personal motivation, both to begin and to remain in a psychotherapeutic process; 2) a history of at least one meaningful interpersonal relationship; 3) a degree of success and active mastery in some area of life; 4) absence of serious language problems of either an expressive or receptive type; and 5) absence of frontal lobe symptoms, such as anosognosia, severe apathy, or marked impulsiveness, that would make psychotherapy impossible. Another factor that may be critical in determining suitability for psychotherapy is the patient's financial situation as a result of the brain injury. When workers' compensation substantially reimburses patients for their injuries, psychotherapy may be ineffective. If patients are rewarded financially for remaining disabled, their conditions frequently deteriorate and their motivation to change through psychotherapy may be severely compromised (Prigatano and Klonoff 1988).

A growing literature documents the value of dynamic psychotherapy for brain-injured patients (Ball 1988; Lewis 1986; Lewis and Langer 1994; Lewis and Rosenberg 1990; Morris and Bleiberg 1986; Prigatano and Klonoff 1988; J. M.

Stern 1985). A major goal of any psychotherapeutic process with these patients is to help them accept the extent of their deficits and their limitations in terms of returning to work. To accomplish this goal, the therapist must be sensitive to the narcissistic injury inherent in accepting the irreparable damage to one's skills, intellectual capabilities, talents, and even the very essence of one's personality. It is essential for the therapist to respect and empathize with the patient's need to use denial (Lewis 1991). Blunt confrontations of denial are likely to accomplish nothing and may even destroy any hope of developing a therapeutic alliance. Promoting self-acceptance of these cognitive limitations requires therapists to gradually expose their patients to the reality of the deficits in a way that allows the patients to briefly mourn week by week, over an extended period. Even patients with brain injury may have the capacity to use symbols metaphorically in a restorative way. Symbolization may assist in the mourning process (Lewis and Langer 1994). A psychoeducational model in which the nature of the deficits and their implications are explained in small units of information that the patient is capable of assimilating may be useful at the beginning of therapy (Prigatano and Klonoff 1988). Drawings or diagrams may help patients with these limitations to visualize what the therapist is describing. As patients mourn the loss of their previous identity and their previous level of functioning, anger at themselves and others connected with the accident is likely to surface. Therapists can then help patients forgive themselves and others so that they can get on with their life.

Both individual dynamic psychotherapy and family or marital therapy may be necessary to help patients adjust to changes in intimate relationships. Spouses may be upset or bewildered by the new behaviors of their brain-damaged partners, such as childishness, concretistic thinking, paranoid accusations, and uninhibited passion (Prigatano and Klonoff 1988). Psychoeducational approaches may help family members understand the organic contribution to these behaviors. However, explorations of themes such as guilt and anger at the patient for having the accident must also be addressed. Frequently, families will completely rearrange their lifestyles to provide round-the-clock companionship and assistance to the brain-injured patient (Ball 1988). If this unnecessarily smothering behavior goes unchecked, it will lead to increasing resentment. Interpretations of reaction formation that defend against anger may help family members return to a closer approximation of their normal lives before the accident. Family members may also find it helpful to explore guilt feelings related to fantasies of causing the accident by what they did or did not say. Reasonable expectations of the spouse and other family members should be discussed individually with the patient during the psychotherapeutic process.

The dynamic therapist of a brain-injured patient must also be cognizant of the time course of the recovery and its effect on the therapeutic process. Three general phases can be identified (J. M. Stern 1985). In the first phase, the patient is unable to process what has happened. The usual ego defenses are overwhelmed, and the therapist must serve as a consistent, supportive, auxiliary ego that provides missing functions to the patient and explains what the patient is going through. In the second phase, patients start to understand what has happened to them and are prone to feel that they have been victimized by a menacing and malevolent world. All "badness" is split off and projected onto others, including the therapist. In this phase, therapists must contain the destructive impulses and the malevolent self- and object representations projected onto them and yet continue to be an observing ego for the patient. Developing trust in others is a major task in the recovery of brain-injured patients, and a trusting alliance with a therapist can be a first step in this direction. Therapists can promote trust by explaining the meaning of the patient's experience and by sharpening the differentiation between what is happening inside the patient and what is actually going on in external reality. As cognitive functioning improves, patients enter the third phase, in which intrapsychic conflicts become more prominent. The therapist's task in this phase is to help patients form a new identity by connecting past experiences and self-representations with current experiences of themselves. The patient's idealization of the past may be questioned by the therapist to facilitate integration of the past with the present. Grief and loss are central themes during this phase.

Several authors (Lewis 1986; Lewis and Rosenberg 1990; Prigatano and Klonoff 1988; Prigatano et al. 1984) have emphasized the necessity for psychotherapy to address characterological issues that predate the injury. These premorbid personality dispositions may profoundly affect the patient's rehabilitation process. For example, Morris and Bleiberg (1986) described a patient who became oppositional to a rehabilitation therapist whom he experienced as a controlling mother. This patient's characterological tendency to see others as controlling was diagnosed through the transferential relationship to the therapist. A dynamically informed decision was then made to allow the patient more control over rehabilitation and treatment planning.

Problems with self-esteem and affect modulation almost invariably surface in the psychotherapy and rehabilitation of patients suffering from brain trauma. However, these two areas are also problematic for many persons suffering from personality disorders. Psychotherapists must avoid being seduced into thinking that all psychological symptoms are directly related to the brain injury. It is common for narcissistic, antisocial, and borderline patients to place themselves in situations that involve risk of injury, and these characterological dimensions may have to be addressed during psychotherapy. Also, characterological tendencies are often exacerbated by brain damage, causing patients to become "more like they already are." To deal with the loss of control arising from the destruction of brain tissue, an obsessive-compulsive patient may become increasingly obsessive-compulsive. Hysterical or histrionic patients may become more cognitively diffuse and affectively labile in response to brain injury. Psychotherapists must not abandon their treatment of personality disorders simply because of a patient's brain injury.

Many clinicians are guardedly optimistic about the treatment of brain-injured patients. Progressive dementia, on the other hand, often elicits profound pessimism in treaters. When treatable causes of dementia (e.g., depression, hypothyroidism, vitamin deficiencies, porphyria, neoplasm, and encephalitides) are ruled out, some clinicians reluctantly diagnose Alzheimer's disease and withdraw from a therapeutic role. This unfortunate withdrawal is associated with the view that Alzheimer's disease is untreatable. From a psychodynamic perspective, however, there is no such thing as an untreatable dementia. Much can be done to help these patients and their families deal with Alzheimer's on a daily basis.

Psychotherapy is often not seen as a helpful modality by Alzheimer's patients or their families. Clinicians may need to initiate the psychotherapeutic process rather than waiting for a request from the patient. Psychotherapists may wish to encourage patients with dementia to tell and retell their individual life stories so that as the disease progresses, the therapist may serve in an auxiliary ego function by helping the patient recall significant memories that are beginning to be lost (Hausman 1992). The stories that these patients tell may be rich in metaphorical allusions that are therapeutically useful (Cheston 1998). A crucial aspect of a psychodynamic approach to dementia is to recognize that these patients can be reached emotionally long after they have experienced major cognitive losses. Fifty-one people with a probable diagnosis of Alzheimer's disease were studied in the aftermath of the Kobe earthquake in 1995 (Ikeda et al. 1998). Their memories of the earthquake, measured at 6 and 10 weeks afterward, were compared with their memories of undergoing a magnetic resonance imaging (MRI) scan immediately following the earthquake. Whereas only 31% of the subjects remembered the MRI scan, fully 86% remembered the earthquake, including subjects with severe dementia. One of the implications of these findings are that patients with dementia can be engaged around emotionally meaningful events in their lives. In an editorial accompanying this landmark study, Williams and Garner (1998) emphasized that "these people have islands of memory, which, if discovered and utilized, can have an activating effect and release further memories" (p. 379). The authors also advocated the introduction of meaningful stimulation into the daily activity pattern of patients with dementia to help decrease the rate of memory loss and maintain an affective connection to treaters.

Another key principle in psychodynamically informed treatment is to do what one can to preserve the self-esteem of the patient who is slipping cognitively and reinforce adaptive defenses.

The following case example illustrates some useful principles of management:

Mr. Z was a 59-year-old Protestant minister with a 4-year history of deterioration in his mental functioning. Members of his congregation had noticed a sense of apathy about him and a sloppiness in his administrative functioning. Church bulletins were poorly organized, and he seemed to be less conscientious about carrying out his commitments to various parishioners. Mr. Z's wife noticed that he often failed to fulfill simple requests. She would become angry at him for "selective hearing" when he indicated to her that he had forgotten what she said.

Mrs. Z brought her husband for psychiatric evaluation, complaining that he was "just not the same." Mr. Z conceded that he felt as if something was happening to him, but he was unable to be more specific than to say that he could not remember as well as he used to. Mrs. Z complained that their marital relationship was deteriorating because her husband did not attend to her needs as he had in the past. Mr. Z expressed hurt at the feedback from members of his congregation, and he noted that he was starting to feel like a failure.

Mental status examination revealed problems with short-term memory and calculation and minor difficulties with orientation to time. Mr. Z also showed signs of mental inertia, as he was unable to move from one subject to another or from one task to another unless given considerable time. Extensive diagnostic studies ruled out causes of dementia stemming from trauma, infection, neoplasm, and normal-pressure hydrocephalus, or from autoimmune, metabolic, hematologic, vascular, and toxic factors. Also negative were findings from a CT scan, skull X rays, and EEG. Neuropsychological testing was more productive, with the following results noted: 1) mild-to-moderate deficits in manual dexterity, 2) mild-to-moderate deficits in perceptual functioning, 3) mild-to-moderate deficits in recent memory, 4) diffuse organic dysfunction typical of progressive neurological disease, and 5) a decrease in attention span.

After the diagnosis of dementia of unknown origin was determined (Alzheimer's in a 59-year-old man is unusual but not unheard of), the diagnostic findings were explained to the patient and his wife. When Mrs. Z could accept her husband's structural brain damage, she was able to lower her expectations for his responses to her. Instead of assuming that he would always react to her verbal comments as he had in the past, she tried new ways of relating to him. At the psychiatrist's suggestion, she slowed her rate of speech and repeated comments that did not seem to register. She also tried rewording comments that Mr. Z did not seem to understand. Above all, she no longer was so easily irritated with him, leading to more positive interactions between the two of them and a corresponding increase in Mr. Z's self-esteem.

Mr. Z had always been an orderly, fastidious person with prominent obsessive-compulsive character traits. To deal with his sense that his intellectual and administrative capacities were deteriorating, he had begun to read the Bible 2 or 3 hours a day, both to encourage divine intervention and to attempt to gain mastery over the information he hoped to impart to his congregation. The evaluating psychi-

atrist helped Mr. Z marshal his obsessive-compulsive character traits more effectively. As a result, Mr. Z began to sit down with his wife each morning to write out a
daily schedule of what he had to do between breakfast and bedtime. Moreover, he began to carry a notebook at all times so he could write down what other people told
him and thereby remember what he had to do.

Mr. Z's self-esteem had depended on his role as minister, and his inability to continue in that capacity inflicted a deep narcissistic wound. Initially, he protested when
the psychiatrist advised him to reduce his responsibilities. However, with Mr. Z's
permission, his associate minister was enlisted as an ally in devising ways for Mr. Z to
continue to serve the church without being placed in situations where he was faced
with impossible tasks. For example, the associate minister began to prepare and type
the weekly bulletin, but Mr. Z continued to operate the printer to produce the required number for the Sunday service. Thus Mr. Z continued to feel productive,
which helped him preserve some degree of self-esteem. By avoiding tasks that were
beyond his capabilities, he also avoided repeated narcissistic injuries.

The case of Mr. Z illustrates several useful principles in the dynamically informed management of dementia: 1) attend to self-esteem issues; 2) assess characteristic defense mechanisms and help the patient use them constructively; 3) find
ways to replace defective ego functions and cognitive limitations, such as keeping
calendars for orientation problems, taking notes for memory problems, and making schedules for problems of secondary autonomous functioning; and 4) assist
family members in developing new ways of relatedness that shore up the patient's
self-esteem by decreasing negative interactions.

Patients in the early stages of Alzheimer's dementia may use denial to prevent
the full impact of the illness from entering conscious awareness. Clinicians treating
such patients must respect their need for denial but also help them to tie up loose
ends with business and family before it is too late (Martin 1989). Those who treat
Alzheimer's patients are apt to face countertransference struggles that interfere
with such planning. They must be alert to feelings of helplessness, guilt, failure,
wishes to abandon the patient, and hopelessness.

Although these measures do not prevent the ultimate deterioration associated
with dementia of the Alzheimer's type, they do result in an improved quality of life
during the gradual but inevitable downhill course of the disease. Ultimately, the
patient's family members are the main focus of intervention, as they struggle with
anger, guilt, grief, and exhaustion in the face of the patient's inexorable decline. In
fact, family therapy is probably the dynamic treatment of choice in Alzheimer's dementia (Lansky 1984). Blaming of self and others is a frequent development in
family members. Also, the readjustment of family roles may require intervention.
The final task, of course, involves the acceptance of death. Clinicians who struggle
along with these families in such situations will often find the treatment process a

trying one, but they can pride themselves on having made a significant impact on the lives of all involved.

References

Abrams JC, Kaslow FW: Learning disability and family dynamics: a mutual interaction. Journal of Clinical Child Psychology 5:35–40, 1976

Allen JG, Colson DB, Coyne L: Organic brain dysfunction and behavioral dyscontrol in difficult-to-treat psychiatric hospital patients. Integrative Psychiatry 6:120–130, 1988

American Psychiatric Association: Diagnostic and Statistical Manual of Mental Disorders, 4th Edition. Washington, DC, American Psychiatric Association, 1994

Ball JD: Psychotherapy with head-injured patients. Medical Psychotherapy 1:15–22, 1988

Bellak L: Psychiatric states in adults with minimal brain dysfunction. Psychiatric Annals 7:575–589, 1977

Biederman J: Attention-deficit/hyperactivity disorder: a life-span perspective. J Clin Psychiatry 59 (suppl 7):4–16, 1998

Biederman J, Faraone SV, Spence T, et al: Patterns of psychiatric comorbidity, cognition, and psychosocial functioning in adults with attention-deficit hyperactivity disorder. Am J Psychiatry 150:1792–1798, 1993

Bryan JH, Sherman RE, Fisher A: Learning disabled boys' nonverbal behaviors within a dyadic interview. Learning Disability Quarterly 3:65–72, 1980

Bryan T: Learning disabled children's comprehension of nonverbal communication. J Learn Disabil 10:501–506, 1977

Buchholz ES: The legacy from childhood: considerations for treatment of the adult with learning disabilities. Psychoanalytic Inquiry 7:431–452, 1987

Cheston R: Psychotherapeutic work with people with dementia: a review of the literature. Br J Med Psychol 71:211–231, 1998

Colson DB, Allen JG: Organic brain dysfunction in difficult-to-treat psychiatric hospital patients. Bull Menninger Clin 50:88–98, 1986

Gilmore K: A psychoanalytic perspective on attention deficit/hyperactivity disorder. J Am Psychoanal Assoc (in press)

Goldstein K: The effect of brain damage on the personality. Psychiatry 15:245–260, 1952

Hartmann H: Ego Psychology and the Problem of Adaptation (1939). Translated by Rapaport D. New York, International Universities Press, 1958

Hartocollis P: The syndrome of minimal brain dysfunction in young adult patients. Bull Menninger Clin 32:102–114, 1968

Hausman C: Dynamic psychotherapy with elderly demented patients, in Care-Giving in Dementia. Edited by Jones GMM, Miesen BML. London, Tavistock/Routledge, 1992, pp 181–198

Ikeda M, Mori E, Hirono N, et al: Amnestic people with Alzheimer's disease who remembered the Kobe earthquake. Br J Psychiatry 172:425–428, 1998

Kafka E: Cognitive difficulties in psychoanalysis. Psychoanal Q 53:533–550, 1984

Lansky MR: Family psychotherapy of the patient with chronic organic brain syndrome. Psychiatric Annals 14:121–129, 1984

Lewis L: Individual psychotherapy with patients having combined psychological and neurological disorders. Bull Menninger Clin 50:75–87, 1986

Lewis L: The role of psychological factors in disordered awareness, in Awareness of Deficit After Brain Injury: Clinical and Theoretical Issues. Edited by Prigatano GP, Schachter DL. New York, Oxford University Press, 1991, pp 223–239

Lewis L, Langer KG: Symbolization in psychotherapy with patients who are disabled. Am J Psychother 48:231–239, 1994

Lewis L, Rosenberg SJ: Psychoanalytic psychotherapy with brain-injured adult psychiatric patients. J Nerv Ment Dis 17:69–77, 1990

Martin RL: Update on dementia of the Alzheimer type. Hospital and Community Psychiatry 40:593–604, 1989

Morris J, Bleiberg J: Neuropsychological rehabilitation and traditional psychotherapy. International Journal of Clinical Neuropsychology 8:133–135, 1986

Oddy M, Coughlan T, Tyreman A: Social adjustment after closed head injury: a further follow-up seven years after injury. J Neurol Neurosurg Psychiatry 48:564–568, 1985

Palombo J: Perceptual deficits and self-esteem in adolescence. Clinical Social Work Journal 7:34–61, 1979

Pickar DB: Psychosocial aspects of learning disabilities: a review of research. Bull Menninger Clin 50:22–32, 1986

Prigatano GP: Work, love, and play after brain injury. Bull Menninger Clin 53:414–431, 1989

Prigatano GP, Klonoff PS: Psychotherapy and neuropsychological assessment after brain injury. J Head Trauma Rehabil 3:45–56, 1988

Prigatano GP, Fordyce DJ, Zeiner HK, et al: Neuropsychological rehabilitation after closed head injury in young adults. J Neurol Neurosurg Psychiatry 47:505–513, 1984

Rothstein AA: Neuropsychological dysfunction and psychological conflict. Psychoanal Q 67:218–239, 1998

Rothstein A, Glenn J (eds): Learning Disabilities and Psychic Conflict: A Psychoanalytic Casebook. Madison, CT, International Universities Press, 1999

Small GW, Rabins PV, Barry PB, et al: Diagnosis and treatment of Alzheimer disease and related disorders: consensus statement of the American Association for Geriatric Psychiatry, the Alzheimer's Association, and the American Geriatric Society. JAMA 278:1363–1371, 1997

Sperry RW, Zaidel E, Zaidel D: Self-recognition and social awareness in the deconnected minor hemispheres. Neuropsychologia 17:153–166, 1979

Stern DN: The Interpersonal World of the Infant: A View From Psychoanalysis and Developmental Psychology. New York, Basic Books, 1985

Stern JM: The psychotherapeutic process with brain-injured patients: a dynamic approach. Isr J Psychiatry Relat Sci 22:83–87, 1985

Weil AP: Maturational variations and genetic-dynamic issues. J Am Psychoanal Assoc 26: 461–491, 1978

Weiner MF: Dementia as a psychodynamic process, in The Dementias: Diagnosis and Management. Edited by Weiner MF. Washington, DC, American Psychiatric Press, 1991, pp 29–46

Williams DDR, Garner J: People with dementia can remember: implications for care. Br J Psychiatry 172:379–380, 1998

SECTION

III

Dynamic Approaches to Axis II Disorders

Cluster A Personality Disorders

Paranoid, Schizoid, and Schizotypal

Paranoid Personality Disorder

Paranoid thinking is not in and of itself pathological. As described in Chapter 2, the paranoid-schizoid position is a basic mode of organizing experience that persists in the human psyche throughout the life cycle. In this mode, dangerous or unpleasant thoughts and feelings are split off, projected outward, and attributed to others. This mode is readily accessible in all kinds of group experiences, such as political conventions, sporting events, and institutional dynamics. At certain historical junctures, entire cultures have been pervaded by paranoid thinking, as in the "witch hunts" of the McCarthy era in this country.

The paranoid personality disorder, however, is a distinct pathological entity that is independent of cultural factors and is not a transient state growing out of the nexus of group dynamics. It involves a pervasive style of thinking, feeling, and relating to others that is extraordinarily rigid and unvarying. These individuals live within the paranoid-schizoid position. Seven common features comprise the diagnostic criteria; at least four must be present to make the diagnosis (Table 14–1). Moreover, the patient's suspicious beliefs must stop short of being delusional and must occur independently of an Axis I psychotic diagnosis such as schizophrenia or delusional disorder.

As with most personality disorders, the key features of the paranoid personality disorder are ego-syntonic. A psychodynamic understanding of these individuals is

| **TABLE 14–1.** | DSM-IV criteria for paranoid personality disorder |

A. A pervasive distrust and suspiciousness of others such that their motives are interpreted as malevolent, beginning by early adulthood and present in a variety of contexts, as indicated by four (or more) of the following:

   1. suspects, without sufficient basis, that others are exploiting, harming, or deceiving him or her

   2. is preoccupied with unjustified doubts about the loyalty or trustworthiness of friends or associates

   3. is reluctant to confide in others because of unwarranted fear that the information will be used maliciously against him or her

   4. reads hidden demeaning or threatening meanings into benign remarks or events

   5. persistently bears grudges, i.e., is unforgiving of insults, injuries, or slights

   6. perceives attacks on his or her character or reputation that are not apparent to others and is quick to react angrily or to counterattack

   7. has recurrent suspicions, without justification, regarding fidelity of spouse or sexual partner

B. Does not occur exclusively during the course of schizophrenia, a mood disorder with psychotic features, or another psychotic disorder and is not due to the direct physiological effects of a general medical condition.

Note: If criteria are met prior to the onset of schizophrenia, add "premorbid," e.g., "paranoid personality disorder (premorbid)."

Source. Reprinted from DSM-IV (American Psychiatric Association 1994), pp. 637–638. Used with permission.

based on limited experience of psychoanalytic or psychotherapeutic work with this population. In a study of 100 patients applying for psychoanalysis at the Columbia Psychoanalytic Center (Oldham and Skodol 1994), only 4 were diagnosed by rigorous personality disorder instruments as having paranoid personality disorder. The diagnosis is more likely to be made when patients present with Axis I symptoms and are found to be comorbid for paranoid personality disorder. For example, in a pilot study of panic disorder patients (Reich and Braginsky 1994), paranoid personality disorder was found in 54% of subjects with panic disorder presenting to a community mental health center.

    Paranoid patients are often brought to treatment by family members or coworkers who are fed up with the patient's constant allegations and accusations. A boss, for example, may insist that an employee seek treatment—or look elsewhere for a job. A spouse who is tired of accusations of infidelity may use the threat of divorce to force the paranoid individual into treatment. Even when paranoid patients enter treatment willingly, they usually remain unconvinced that they are psychiatrically disturbed. Their presenting problems revolve around how others have mistreated and betrayed them.

The diagnostic criteria reflect a way of thinking that can be conceptualized as a distinctly paranoid cognitive style (Shapiro 1965). This style of thinking is characterized by an unrelenting search for hidden meanings, for clues to uncover the "truth" behind a situation's face value. The obvious, the superficial, and the apparent merely mask the reality. This endless search involves an intense hyperalertness of attention, evidenced by a guardedness related to this continuous attentional monitoring. A paranoid individual constantly scans the environment for anything out of the ordinary—a style of thinking that takes a considerable toll in physical and emotional tension. The paranoid patient is simply unable to relax.

Paranoid thinking is also characterized by a lack of flexibility. The most persuasive argument will generally have no impact on the rigid and unswerving beliefs of the paranoid person. In fact, those persons who attempt to argue with a person who has a paranoid personality disorder will simply find themselves becoming the target of suspicion. The paranoid person's thinking differs from that of the paranoid schizophrenic person in that it is not delusional. In fact, patients with paranoid personality disorder tend to have remarkably accurate perceptions of their environment. However, their judgments about those perceptions are generally impaired. Reality itself is not distorted; rather, the *significance* of apparent reality is misconstrued (Shapiro 1965). This characteristic cognitive style may be difficult to diagnose because the paranoid individual is often closemouthed and guarded. In fact, even projective testing may only identify the paranoid individual as a more-or-less normal person who is simply inhibited.

Psychodynamic Understanding

An understanding of the characteristics of the paranoid-schizoid position is essential to an understanding of the paranoid patient. As noted in Chapter 2, splitting is a central defense mechanism in this mode of organizing experience. Feelings of love and hate toward the same object must be separated from one another. Any movement toward integration creates intolerable anxiety that stems from the fear that the hatred will overpower and destroy the love. From the standpoint of the paranoid patient, emotional survival requires the patient to split off all "badness" and project it onto outside figures. One manifestation of this defensive maneuver is that the normal internal world of aggressor and victim is transformed into a life experience in which the paranoid individual is constantly in the role of victim vis-à-vis external aggressors or persecutors. The view that paranoid patients have of the world thus relieves their internal tension between introjects. If a paranoid individual is forced to reinternalize what has been projected, the heightened internal tension will result in increased rigidity and defensiveness (Shapiro 1965).

Another characteristic of the paranoid-schizoid position is that the patient's experience of others is discontinuous; no relationship is perceived as enduring over time. Rather, the patient has only the perception of the moment. Patients with paranoid personality disorder approach every relationship with the belief that the other person will eventually "slip up" and confirm their suspicions. In the paranoid-schizoid mode of existence, the patient lives in a state of unremitting anxiety stemming from a conviction that the world is peopled with untrustworthy and unpredictable strangers (Ogden 1986). Even when a stable, helpful therapist has worked with a paranoid patient over a long period, one minor disappointment can lead the patient to completely disregard the therapist's previous behavior and to feel—with unswerving conviction—that the therapist is untrustworthy. The therapist has been "unmasked." Thus, good experiences with a person in the past can be totally erased by the present situation.

Experience is literally taken at face value. Patients with paranoid personality disorder are unable to think, "It is *as if* this other person is trying to hurt me." Instead, they *know* that the other person harbors malevolent intentions. Similarly, in the transference relationship with the therapist, the paranoid patient is unable to say, "I feel that I am reacting to you *as if* you are as sadistic as my father was." The patient simply experiences the therapist as sadistic. Feelings are not personal creations of the patient, but rather things-in-themselves. When patients develop a mediating self that is able to interpret accurately and to think symbolically in "as if" terms, then they have achieved the depressive position (Ogden 1986).

Projection and projective identification are two key defense mechanisms of the paranoid personality disorder. Projection substitutes an external threat for an internal one; projective identification goes a step further. In addition to externalizing threats, projective identification "controls" persons in the environment by binding them to the paranoid person in highly pathological ways. The need to control others reflects the terribly low self-esteem at the core of paranoia (Meissner 1986). Deep down, the paranoid patient feels inferior, weak, and ineffectual. Thus, the grandiosity or sense of "specialness" often seen in these patients can be understood as a compensatory defense that makes up for feelings of inferiority. Those who actually seek treatment may have some feelings of depression or anxiety as a result of the failure of paranoid and grandiose defenses and a breakthrough of these underlying feelings of inadequacy (Meissner 1995).

The low self-esteem at the heart of the paranoid personality disorder leads these individuals to develop a keen sense of attunement to issues of rank and power. They are intensely concerned that persons in authority will humiliate them or expect them to be submissive (Shapiro 1965). They perceive threats to their autonomy as omnipresent. A recurring fear about their interpersonal relationships is that they will result in subjection to external control; they fear that anyone who tries to be close to them is secretly trying to take over. This concern may surface as a dread of passive homosexual impulses, originally described by Freud (1911/1958) in the case of the psychotically disturbed Judge Schreber. However, all paranoid individuals are not necessarily concerned about passive homosexual impulses. Overt homosexuality and paranoid personality disorder can and do exist in the same person. The main point is rather that these patients are concerned about *all* passive surrender to *all* impulses and to all persons (Shapiro 1965).

Successful treatment can provide a glimpse of what lies beneath the projective system: a good deal of depressive content (Meissner 1976) and diametrically opposing self-representations. Coexisting with the special, entitled, grandiose version of the self is a weak, worthless, inferior polar opposite. Akhtar (1990) has systematically examined these coexisting self-representations and characterized them as follows: "Outwardly, paranoid individuals are demanding, arrogant, mistrustful, driven, unromantic, moralistic, and acutely vigilant towards the external environment. Internally, however, they are frightened, timid, self-doubting, gullible, inconsiderate, vulnerable to erotomania, and cognitively unable to grasp the totality of actual events" (pp. 21–22). Therapists who are aware of this other dimension of the paranoid personality can more easily empathize with these difficult patients.

The developmental failure to achieve object constancy is a characteristic of paranoid patients that organizes much of their behavior and thinking (Auchincloss and Weiss 1992; Blum 1981). Because they cannot maintain a loving connection with an internal object representation, they are convinced that love relationships are dangerous and unstable. To deal with the terrors associated with object inconstancy, the paranoid patient constructs fantasies of concrete and magical connectedness to objects (Auchincloss and Weiss 1992). Paranoid individuals impose an extreme either/or requirement on relationships. Either the object of their attention is thinking about them continuously or that person is emotionally indifferent to them—a thought paranoid patients find intolerable. This set of anxieties concerning indifference and connectedness is largely responsible for the willingness of paranoid patients to constrict their freedom in the service of feeling a concrete and magical connection to objects.

Treatment Approaches

Because of their suspiciousness, paranoid patients usually do poorly in group psychotherapy. Most treatment efforts must therefore be initiated in the context of individual therapy, despite the formidable challenge to the individual psychotherapist. As noted earlier, these patients often enter treatment under some external pressure, and they have the utmost difficulty trusting anyone. In light of these obstacles, the first step in psychotherapy should be to build a therapeutic alliance.

This process is made more difficult by the tendency of paranoid patients to evoke defensive responses in others. The therapist is no exception, as the following vignette illustrates:

> Patient: I'm really angry with you because I've been sitting in the waiting room for half an hour. You told me to be here at 9:30 today.
> Therapist: No, that's not true. I said 10 A.M.
> Patient: You said 9:30.
> Therapist: (a little louder and more forcefully) I said 10 o'clock. I wrote it down in my book.
> Patient: You're trying to trick me! You won't admit you're wrong, so you try to make me think that I'm the one who's wrong.
> Therapist: (louder still) If I were wrong, I would admit it. On the contrary, I think you are the one who won't admit to being wrong, and you attribute that to me!
> Patient: I'm not going to take this harassment. I'll find another therapist!

This slightly caricatured interaction illustrates the projective identification cycle that is extraordinarily common in paranoid patients. The patient treats the therapist as a persecuting bad object. The therapist feels coerced into being defensive and ends up giving an interpretation that attempts to force the projection back onto the patient. The patient responds by feeling attacked, misunderstood, and deceived. To avoid this escalating cycle, the therapist must empathize with the patient's need to project as a means of emotional survival. The therapist must be willing to serve as a container for feelings of hatred, badness, impotence, and despair (Epstein 1979; Gabbard 1991, 1996). Attempting to return such feelings prematurely will simply lead the patient to feel an increased internal tension and to become more rigid. The therapist must be able to accept blame, even to the point of acknowledging a lack of ability to help the patient (Epstein 1984). Most therapists have strong countertransference resistances to accepting responsibility for a failing treatment; they just naturally become defensive when their patients accuse them of incompetence. However, by acknowledging the low self-esteem that creates the need to see fault in others, therapists can empathize with their patient's point of view and genuinely seek suggestions for how to make the treatment more productive. Becoming defensive is also a natural reaction to being accused of dishonesty. Defensiveness, however, may be misinterpreted as confirmation that the therapist has something to hide. Openness is by far the best policy with paranoid patients. If they act suspicious about the therapist's records or process notes, then the therapist would do well to share those notes with the patients and to thereby use them as a therapeutic intervention. Refusal to share notes will simply incite further paranoia.

Throughout the psychotherapy, particularly during the early phases of building an alliance, the therapist must avoid responding defensively—like everyone else in the patient's environment. The therapist should not challenge the patient's construction of events or the patient's perception of the therapist, no matter how negative. The therapist should merely ask for more detail and should empathize with the patient's feelings and perceptions. Above all, the therapist must resist the frequent countertransference tendency to be rid of undesirable projections by forcing them back onto the patient via premature interpretations (Epstein 1979). As in the previous example, interpretations of this kind will simply confirm the perception that the therapist is highly invested in attacking the patient. The same situation might be handled quite differently using these principles of technique:

> Patient: I'm really angry with you because I've been sitting in the waiting room for half an hour. You told me to be here at 9:30 today.
> Therapist: Let me see if I understand you correctly. Your understanding was that you were to see me today at 9:30 instead of 10 o'clock?
> Patient: You said 9:30.
> Therapist: I can certainly see why you might be angry at me then. Having to wait for someone for 30 minutes would make most people angry.
> Patient: You admit that you told me to come at 9:30?
> Therapist: Frankly, I don't remember saying that, but I'd like to hear more about your recall of that conversation so I can find out what I said to give you that impression.

In this scenario, the therapist accepts blame nondefensively without admitting to any fault. The therapist contains the patient's projection and seeks to find out more information about how it arose. By being willing to entertain the possibility of having indeed misled the patient, the therapist validates the patient's perception as legitimate and worthy of further discussion. Finally, the therapist does not attempt to return what has been projected in the form of an interpretation.

Therapists also need to empathize with the patient's tendency to be guarded. There is a certain adaptive quality in guardedness; paranoid patients who talk extensively about their perceptions are likely to alienate others. Therapists who allow for periods of silence and constriction instead of intrusively asking questions may help the patient to open up a bit more. Another technique for building an alliance is to focus on the patient's state of tension secondary to the extraordinary vigilance necessary to maintain the paranoid cognitive style. Comments such as, "Your nerves must be shot," or "You must be exhausted after all of this," may help the patient feel understood. When the patient is willing to talk, the therapist should encourage elaboration, which may reveal historical antecedents to the current situation of stress (Meissner 1976).

Countertransference exasperation and impatience may develop as these patients describe how others are constantly thinking about them and scrutinizing their behavior in an unrelenting manner. Therapists may have to fight off urges to confront the grandiosity and to deflate the notion that the patient is the center of the universe. An appreciation of the defensive function of this perception in terms of its role in maintaining connectedness may be helpful to the therapist struggling with countertransference. Challenging the paranoid construct of magical connectedness prematurely will rupture any semblance of a developing therapeutic alliance. Over time, however, the fear of indifference and the need to feel connected with others can be gently interpreted in the service of establishing greater object constancy (Auchincloss and Weiss 1992).

The overall goal of psychotherapeutic work with paranoid patients is to help them shift their perceptions of the origin of their problems from an external locus to an internal one. This shift can only follow an unhurried timetable that is unique to each patient. A second shift that is intimately connected with the first is the transformation of a paranoid mode of thinking into a depressive mode in which the patient allows him- or herself to experience feelings of vulnerability, weakness, inferiority, and defectiveness (Meissner 1995). The therapist must withstand repeated barrages of accusations and suspicions without becoming exasperated or despairing. As the patient opens up more, the therapist can begin to label the patient's feelings and thereby help the patient distinguish between emotions and reality (Meissner 1976). Therapists can also help their patients define gaps in their knowledge. For example, a therapist might ask, "Did your boss say that he hates you?" When the patient responds negatively to the question, the therapist can comment matter-of-factly about the patient's limited knowledge of the boss's feelings. Such questions must be worded tactfully and neutrally so as not to inordinately challenge the patient's view of the world. The therapist need not take a pro or con position in the matter, but should only indicate that more information is necessary (Meissner 1976).

Throughout the entire psychotherapy process, the therapist must contain feelings rather than act on them. This containment will provide the patient with a new object relationship different from those previously encountered. The different experience is eventually internalized over time. This relationship model of change is complemented by gradual changes in thinking. The key is for such patients to entertain a "creative doubt" (Meissner 1986) about their perceptions of the world. As patients move from the paranoid-schizoid position to encounter the depressive elements within, they begin to experience a sense of self that can mediate and interpret experience. Things may become "as if" they are a certain way rather than as *really* a certain way. Patients may also allow longer glimpses of their feelings of worthlessness and inferiority so that depressive elements can be worked through in the transference. In the most optimal circumstances, these patients can reveal a yearning for acceptance, love, and closeness that is associated with their frustration and disappointment with early figures in their lives (Meissner 1976, 1995). As a result, they can begin the process of mourning those attachments.

A brief report of the early stages of psychotherapy with a patient suffering from paranoid personality disorder will illustrate some of the technical principles described in the foregoing paragraphs. The bracketed comments below indicate how theory and technique relate in this case.

Mr. AA was a 42-year-old accountant who had been on disability for a year because of his continual complaints of allergies to substances in the work environment. After receiving a promotion, he had moved into a new office where he had experienced a sudden onset of several troublesome physical symptoms, including headaches, sluggish thinking, tightening in the chest, blurred vision, generalized aching, weakness, easy fatigability, and lack of motivation. Mr. AA attributed these symptoms to the new paneling and carpeting in the office and to vibrations in the floor from the blower system. The ill effects began to dissipate whenever he left the office and were often gone by the time Mr. AA visited a doctor. He had had numerous diagnostic evaluations by various specialists, only one of whom had thought that there was any physical basis for the complaints. Mr. AA used this isolated opinion to vindicate his own view. He was pressured into psychotherapy by the management of his firm, who were concerned that his disability was becoming permanent. In the initial stages of therapy, Mr. AA denied any emotional problems other than marital tension, for which he blamed his wife. He spoke at length about his symptoms and maintained that he was convinced of their physical origin regardless of the negative findings of most of the specialists. [The patient reveals himself to be totally impervious to rational arguments from experts. He also displays grandiosity by believing that he knows more than the doctors.]

When asked about his interpersonal relationships, Mr. AA said that he and his father were not on speaking terms because his father had deceived him in business deals. Moreover, he complained that his father was always harder on him than on all his brothers. He summarized his description of his father by saying that he was an unfair and untrustworthy man. Mr. AA went on to describe his wife as deceitful. She had "tricked" him into having a child by failing to use birth control and becoming pregnant. He said that he had never forgiven his wife for her trickery—8 years previously—and he said that their marriage had been a disaster ever since. He said that the only way this situation could change would be for her to become more trustworthy. [The patient has projected malevolent persecuting objects onto close figures in his family and sees them as the source of all his problems. The patient himself acknowledges no contributions to these difficulties in family relationships and suggests that the only possible solutions involve change in others instead of in him.]

Throughout the first psychotherapy session, Mr. AA listened intently to the therapist, often asking for further clarification of comments. He seemed to be listening for hidden messages in the most benign communications. Mr. AA was also hyper-alert to any slight body movements of the therapist, often misinterpreting them as indications of boredom or disinterest. After listening for some time, the therapist commented empathically, "You must feel awful right now. Your boss is on your back to get therapy, you feel physically miserable, and your wife and you are not speaking to each other." The patient responded to this empathic comment by opening up a lit-tle more, admitting that he had always been "thin-skinned." He acknowledged that he was often considerably disturbed by minor things that did not bother other peo-ple. [The therapist's empathic validation of Mr. AA's beleaguered self-esteem allowed him to feel understood. This beginning alliance allowed the patient to ac-knowledge a problem in himself for the first time, namely, that he was "thin-skinned."]

Mr. AA described his relationship with his son in cold, calculating terms by say-ing, "We're together more than average for the population at large." [This descrip-tion reveals the inability of the paranoid personality to feel emotional warmth and tenderness in relationships because having such feelings would make him vulnerable to rejection or attack.] Mr. AA changed the subject to his concerns about the doctors who had examined him. He expressed a strong belief that all doctors are basically in-competent, and he seemed convinced that one doctor had almost caused him to have a cerebral hemorrhage with a certain medication. He described three psychiatrists who had previously examined him as all incompetent. He then asked the therapist if he knew of a particular nonpsychiatric medication. When the therapist admitted to being unfamiliar with the drug, Mr. AA quickly responded that the therapist was probably as much of a "quack" as the other doctors. [The paranoid person's fear of being controlled, allied with feelings of inferiority in "one-down" relationships, often leads to devaluation and demeaning of other people. By devaluing the thera-pist, Mr. AA reassures himself that he has nothing to envy and no reason to feel inferior.]

When Mr. AA continued to disparage the opinions of the many specialists he had seen, the therapist noted, "This must be very demoralizing for you." Mr. AA re-sponded sharply, "You're trying to lead me on!" [Here the therapist's attempt to em-pathize by introducing a new feeling exceeded the patient's ability to admit to that feeling. The patient's reaction might have been more positive if the therapist had stayed closer to the words and feeling states that the patient himself had described.]

As Mr. AA continued to talk about his current state of affairs, he was able to ac-knowledge that he had found it difficult to adjust to disability and unemployment af-ter being in an executive position. Sensing an opening regarding the self-esteem issue, the therapist noted that being unable to work must have been quite a blow. Mr. AA responded by asking the therapist, "Do you think I am weak?" [Again the therapist's ability to empathize with the patient's low self-esteem rather than becom-ing defensive allowed Mr. AA to reveal concern about his underlying weakness and inferiority.]

Prevention of Violence

Although patients who suffer from any of a broad variety of psychiatric disorders may become violent, paranoid patients pose a particular threat to psychiatrists. An understanding of the dynamics of paranoia may help avert assault. To prevent the escalation of aggression, psychiatrists should keep in mind several principles of management:

1. *Do everything possible to help the patient save face.* The core of paranoia is low self-esteem, so psychiatrists should empathize with the patient's experience and not challenge the truth of what the patient says. As in any treatment setting with a paranoid patient, the first task is to build a therapeutic alliance. In a study of 328 patients hospitalized on inpatient units (Beauford et al. 1997), patients who had a weaker therapeutic alliance at the time of admission were significantly more likely to display violent behavior during hospitalization. In a busy outpatient clinic, a resident who saw a paranoid patient for the first time suspected that he was not telling the truth about his current living situation. He told the patient that he was going to check up on his statement by calling the halfway house where the patient said he lived. As the resident reached in his desk drawer for the telephone book, the patient struck him in the face with his fist. This unfortunate incident leads directly into another major principle of violence prevention.
2. *Avoid arousing further suspicion.* Because of the basic distrust of these patients, all interventions must be geared to avoiding any increase in their paranoia. Each movement should be explained slowly and carefully. The movements themselves should be performed slowly and in clear view. You might say, for example, "Now I'm going to reach in my desk and get an appointment slip so that you'll know when our next meeting is." You should also avoid being overly friendly to these patients, since such behavior is in stark contrast to their usual experience and will simply further arouse their suspicions.
3. *Help the patient maintain a sense of control.* Control is of extraordinary importance to paranoid patients, who are likely to fear loss of control as much as the therapist fears it. The therapist must avoid panic at all costs. A therapist who displays fear that the patient will lose control will only heighten the patient's own fears of losing control. Much of the anxiety among paranoid individuals stems from a fear that others will try to be in control; for this reason, anything the therapist can do to indicate respect for these patients' autonomy will help reduce their anxiety about passive surrender. Interventions should acknowledge their right to view the situation as they see it. For example, the therapist might tell such a patient, "I think your feelings are legitimate about

the situation, given what you've been through, and I respect your right to feel that way."

4. *Always encourage these patients to verbalize rather than to violently act out anger.* Get them to discuss their anger in as much detail as possible. Encourage a consideration of the logical consequences of becoming violent. If possible, provide constructive alternatives to violence so that these patients can begin to see that there are other options. Supporting the anger as a legitimate reaction does not mean endorsing aggressive action. The therapist who feels immediately threatened may attempt to translate this threat into words. When one psychiatry resident sensed that a new patient was about to erupt in violence, he said, "I wonder if you're feeling like you want to hit me right now." The patient nodded in assent. The resident then replied, "Maybe if we go take a walk and you tell me about the feelings you're having, you'll be able to avoid acting on those feelings." This calm, matter-of-fact approach taken helped the patient feel more in control, and the patient actually thanked the resident for his help.

5. *Always give paranoid individuals plenty of breathing room.* Their fear of passive surrender to others is heightened by physical proximity. Avoid a seating arrangement where they feel trapped in the office. Violent individuals have been shown to need greater distance from others to feel secure (Kinzel 1971). Avoid sitting too close, as well as touching them, even in the most benign manner. One paranoid woman began carrying a gun to her therapy sessions after her therapist persisted in hugging her at the end of each session.

6. *Finally, be attuned to your own countertransference in dealing with potentially violent patients* (Felthous 1984). Countertransference denial is common both in hospital staff members and in therapists who work with paranoid individuals. They may fail to ask important historical questions for fear of confirming their worst fears about their patients' potential for violence. Treaters must acknowledge their own fears and then must avoid situations of jeopardy with patients who have been assaultive in the past. Denial may be more prominent with female patients because of gender stereotypes maintaining that men are more likely to be assaultive than women. In fact, the patterns of violence of male and female inpatients are similar, and women are just as likely as men to have attacked another person in the month before admission (Tardiff et al. 1997). Therapists may also use countertransference projection to disavow their own aggression and externalize it onto their patients. Projective identification may provoke patients to violence when therapists see destructiveness and aggression only in their patients and not in themselves. One study of psychiatrists who have been assaulted by patients (Madden et al. 1976) found that 53% of the psychiatrists had in some way been provocative toward the patient prior to being assaulted.

Schizoid and Schizotypal Personality Disorders

In addition to paranoid personality disorder, Cluster A in Axis II of DSM-IV (American Psychiatric Association 1994) subsumes schizoid and schizotypal personality disorders. Although these are distinct entities, they will be considered together here because both the dynamic understanding of and the therapeutic approaches to these disorders have much in common.

The decision to separate schizoid and schizotypal personality disorders seems to have been largely related to genetic studies (Kendler et al. 1981; Kety et al. 1971; Rosenthal et al. 1971) that suggested a muted version of schizophrenia characterized by more or less intact reality testing, difficulties in relationships, and mild thought disturbances. The link between schizotypal personality and schizophrenia was further bolstered by McGlashan's (1983) long-term follow-up study, which demonstrated that schizotypal and schizophrenic patients had similar outcomes. The outcomes of borderline patients, on the other hand, were more typical of those associated with affective disorders. The designation of certain close relatives of schizophrenic individuals as schizotypal replaced the more problematic term *borderline schizophrenia,* which was easily confused with borderline personality disorder. Some critics (Siever and Gunderson 1979) have questioned the appropriateness of classifying a variant of a psychotic condition as a personality disorder. In their view, the diagnosis depends to a large extent on symptoms resembling schizophrenia rather than on sustained patterns of relating to others, which are used to define the other personality disorders.

Between the appearance of DSM-III-R (American Psychiatric Association 1987) and the publication of DSM-IV, further empirical research demonstrated the link between schizotypal personality disorder and schizophrenia. Further analysis of the data from the Chestnut Lodge Follow-Up Study (Fenton and McGlashan 1989) demonstrated that three DSM-III (American Psychiatric Association 1980) criteria for schizotypal personality disorder predicted schizophrenia at long-term follow-up. The predictive power of these three key characteristics—magical thinking, suspiciousness or paranoid ideation, and social isolation—suggested that schizotypal personality disorder belongs in the schizophrenia spectrum. Another study demonstrated that the morbid risk for schizophrenia-related disorders in the first-degree relatives of patients with schizotypal and paranoid personality disorders is significantly higher than in the first-degree relatives of patients with other personality disorders (Siever et al. 1990). More recent research (O'Driscoll et al. 1998; Roitman et al. 1997) has shown linkages between schizotypy and schizophrenia in the areas of attentional deficits and eye tracking as well.

Because of the compelling evidence that schizotypal personality disorder is related to schizophrenia in terms of biological, genetic, phenomenological, outcome, and treatment-response characteristics, serious consideration was given to moving the diagnosis out of Axis II into Axis I as part of the "Schizophrenia and Other Psychotic Disorders" section of DSM-IV. However, because of its resemblance to other personality disorders in regard to factors such as pervasiveness, stability, and onset, schizotypal personality disorder was retained in Axis II.

As Gunderson (1983) pointed out, persons with schizotypal personality disorder are much the same as those with schizoid personality disorder except that the definition of schizotypal personality disorder includes a few symptoms suggestive of an attenuated form of schizophrenia. In actuality, schizoid and schizotypal patients form a continuum, so it is somewhat arbitrary to draw a dividing line between the two entities. An examination of the DSM-IV criteria for schizoid personality disorder (Table 14–2) and schizotypal personality disorder (Table 14–3) reveals that both disorders involve a good deal of social detachment and affective constriction.

Schizotypal patients themselves form a continuum, from those on one end who are much like schizoid patients (except for a few more oddities of behavior and communication) to those closer to schizophrenia who are prone to brief psychotic episodes. The ensuing discussion of the psychoanalytic understanding of these conditions assumes that they are inherently similar.

TABLE 14–2. DSM-IV criteria for schizoid personality disorder

A. A pervasive pattern of detachment from social relationships and a restricted range of expression of emotions in interpersonal settings, beginning by early adulthood and present in a variety of contexts, as indicated by four (or more) of the following:

1. neither desires nor enjoys close relationships, including being part of a family
2. almost always chooses solitary activities
3. has little, if any, interest in having sexual experiences with another person
4. takes pleasure in few, if any, activities
5. lacks close friends or confidants other than first-degree relatives
6. appears indifferent to the praise or criticism of others
7. shows emotional coldness, detachment, or flattened affectivity

B. Does not occur exclusively during the course of schizophrenia, a mood disorder with psychotic features, another psychotic disorder, or a pervasive developmental disorder and is not due to the direct physiological effects of a general medical condition.

Note: If criteria are met prior to the onset of schizophrenia, add "premorbid," e.g., "schizoid personality disorder (premorbid)."

Source. Reprinted from DSM-IV (American Psychiatric Association 1994), p. 641. Used with permission.

TABLE 14–3. DSM-IV criteria for schizotypal personality disorder

A. A pervasive pattern of social and interpersonal deficits marked by acute discomfort
   with, and reduced capacity for, close relationships as well as by cognitive or perceptual distortions and eccentricities of behavior, beginning by early adulthood and
   present in a variety of contexts, as indicated by five (or more) of the following:
   1. ideas of reference (excluding delusions of reference)
   2. odd beliefs or magical thinking that influences behavior and is inconsistent with
      subcultural norms (e.g., superstitiousness, belief in clairvoyance, telepathy, or
      "sixth sense"; in children and adolescents, bizarre fantasies or preoccupations)
   3. unusual perceptual experiences, including bodily illusions
   4. odd thinking and speech (e.g., vague, circumstantial, metaphorical, overelaborate,
      or stereotyped)
   5. suspiciousness or paranoid ideation
   6. inappropriate or constricted affect
   7. behavior or appearance that is odd, eccentric, or peculiar
   8. lack of close friends or confidants other than first-degree relatives
   9. excessive social anxiety that does not diminish with familiarity and tends to be
      associated with paranoid fears rather than negative judgments about self

B. Does not occur exclusively during the course of schizophrenia, a mood disorder
   with psychotic features, another psychotic disorder, or a pervasive developmental
   disorder.

Note: If criteria are met prior to the onset of schizophrenia, add "premorbid," e.g.,
"schizotypal personality disorder (premorbid)."

Source. Reprinted from DSM-IV (American Psychiatric Association 1994), p. 645. Used with permission.

Psychodynamic Understanding

Schizoid and schizotypal patients often live on the fringes of society. They may be
ridiculed as "weirdos," "oddballs," or "misfits," or they may merely be left alone to
pursue a solitary and idiosyncratic existence. Their isolation and anhedonia may
lead others to feel sorry for them and reach out to them. More often than not, however, the individuals who make such gestures give up after being repeatedly rebuffed. Family members may become so exasperated that they force their schizoid
relative into a treatment situation. Parents of adolescents or young adults may
bring their son or daughter to a psychiatrist out of concern that their child is not
getting enough out of life (Stone 1985). Other schizoid and schizotypal patients
come to psychiatric treatment voluntarily because of painful loneliness.

The inner world of the schizoid patient may differ considerably from the individual's outward appearance. Indeed, these people are often a bundle of contradictions. Akhtar (1987) has grouped these contradictions into overt and covert

manifestations: "The schizoid individual is 'overtly' detached, self-sufficient, absent-minded, uninteresting, asexual, and idiosyncratically moral while 'covertly' being exquisitely sensitive, emotionally needy, acutely vigilant, creative, often perverse, and vulnerable to corruption" (p. 510). These polarities do not reflect conscious and unconscious personality traits. Rather, they represent a splitting or fragmentation of the self into different self-representations that remain unintegrated. From a psychodynamic perspective, the "schizoid" designation reflects this fundamental splitting of the self. The result is a diffuse identity—schizoid patients are not sure who they are, and they feel buffeted by highly conflictual thoughts, feelings, wishes, and urges. This identity diffusion makes relating to others problematic. Indeed, perhaps the most striking feature of schizoid and schizotypal patients is their apparent nonrelatedness to others. Psychoanalytic work with these patients suggests that they definitely have feelings and strivings for others, but that the patients themselves are frozen developmentally at an early stage of relatedness (Lawner 1985). These patients seem to base their decision to be isolated on a conviction that their failure to receive what they needed from their mothers means that they can make no further attempt to receive anything else from subsequent significant figures (Nachmani 1984).

Much of our understanding of the inner world of the schizoid patient derives from the work of the British object relations theorists. Balint (1979) viewed these patients as having a fundamental deficit in their ability to relate—a "basic fault" caused by significant inadequacies in the mothering they received as infants. He believed that the schizoid patient's difficulty in relating to others stems from this basic incapacity rather than from conflict (as in neurotic patients). Fairbairn (1954), perhaps the foremost contributor to our understanding of schizoid patients, viewed the schizoid retreat as a defense against a conflict between a wish to relate to others and a fear that one's neediness would harm others. The infant who initially perceives its mother as rejecting may withdraw from the world. However, the infant's neediness grows until it is experienced as insatiable. The infant then fears that its greed will devour the mother and leave it alone again. Hence, the very object that the infant most needs may be destroyed by its own incorporative strivings. Fairbairn termed this concern the "Little Red Riding Hood Fantasy," based on the fairy tale in which the little girl finds, to her horror, that her grandmother has disappeared, leaving her alone with her own projected oral greed—in the form of a devouring wolf.

Just as Little Red Riding Hood may project her greed onto the wolf, infants may project their own greed onto their mothers, whom they then view as devouring and dangerous. This infantile dilemma is frozen in time for schizoid patients, who first fear that they will devour others with their neediness, and then fear being devoured by others. This fundamental dilemma of schizoid patients mandates that they will vacillate between the fear of driving others away by their neediness, on the one hand, and the fear, on the other hand, that others will smother or consume them. As a result, all relationships are experienced as dangerous and to be avoided. Because the decision to be nonrelated leaves the schizoid individual alone and empty, there is often a "schizoid compromise" (Guntrip 1968), in which the patient simultaneously clings to and rejects others.

Schizoid patients live under the constant threat of abandonment, persecution, and disintegration (Appel 1974). To take anything in from someone else risks the triggering of intense longings for dependency and merger. Love is equated with fusing with someone else, losing one's identity, and destroying the other person. Although the writing of the British School has focused on schizoid patients, the descriptions provided by Balint, Guntrip, and others refer to schizotypal patients as well (Stone 1985).

The schizoid patient's characteristic retreat from interpersonal relations may serve an important developmental function. Winnicott (1963/1965) believed that the isolation of the schizoid patient preserves an important authenticity that is absolutely sacred to the evolving self of the patient: "There is an intermediate stage in healthy development in which the patient's most important experience in relation to the good or potentially satisfying object is the refusal of it" (p. 182). The schizoid withdrawal is a way to communicate with the "true self" within instead of sacrificing that authenticity to artificial interactions with others that would lead to a "false self." Winnicott suggested that we all have this noncommunicating core, and that we must respect the schizoid individual's right—and need—to be noncommunicative. Periods of extreme abstinence and isolation may help schizoid individuals get in touch with this sequestered self so that it can be integrated with other self-representations (Eigen 1973).

Schizoid patients who allow their therapists to have access to their inner worlds will often reveal omnipotent fantasies. These usually accompany the reclusive aspects of the self to which the patient retreats. Like other aspects of the hidden self, they serve as a "sanctuary from exposure" (Grotstein 1977) to shore up fragile self-esteem and to allay anxiety about self-disintegration. Like paranoid patients, schizoid patients have omnipotent fantasies that increase in frequency in inverse proportion to their level of self-esteem (Nachmani 1984). Lacking good internal self- and object representations to help accomplish essential work toward success in relationships or careers, schizoid patients employ fantasies of omnipotence to bypass such work and directly achieve their grandiose fantasies. Schizoid patients often feel a great deal of shame about their fantasies and are reluctant to share them with their therapists until they feel secure in the relationship.

Individual Psychotherapy

Like patients with paranoid personality disorder, patients with schizotypal and schizoid personality disorders do not often appear at the therapist's doorstep. In a national survey of clinicians, schizotypal personality disorder was the least widely treated entity of all Axis II disorders (Westen 1997). In the Columbia Psychoanalytic Center Study of 100 patients applying for psychoanalysis (Oldham and Skodol 1994), only 1 was diagnosed as schizoid personality disorder, and none had the diagnosis of schizotypal personality disorder. Hence, much of the data accumulated about the psychotherapy and the psychotherapeutic treatment of these patients has been anecdotal, based on relatively small numbers.

Schizoid and schizotypal patients may be helped with individual expressive-supportive therapy, dynamic group psychotherapy, or a combination of the two. Since the thought of the interactional demands of a group setting usually produces a good deal of anxiety, most of these patients will feel more comfortable beginning with an individual process. Much of the modern literature on the psychotherapy of schizoid and schizotypal personality disorders suggests that the mechanism of therapeutic action is likely to be internalization of a therapeutic relationship rather than interpretation of conflict (Appel 1974; Gabbard 1989; Khan 1983; Nachmani 1984; Stone 1983, 1985; Winnicott 1963/1965).

The task of the therapist is to "thaw" the patient's frozen internal object relations by providing a new experience of relatedness. The schizoid style of relatedness emerges from inadequacies in the patient's earliest relationships with parental figures—what Epstein (1979) referred to as primary maturational failure. Throughout life, the patient has evoked similar reactions from those in the environment, producing secondary maturational failures. In other words, the schizoid patient may go through life distancing everyone. Therapists must figure out how to relate to the patient in a maturationally corrective way. Therapists must not allow themselves to be driven away or alienated like everyone else in the patient's life.

To say that the goal of therapy is to provide a new relationship for internalization is deceptively straightforward and simple. Yet this strategy presents formidable obstacles. First, the patient's basic mode of existence is nonrelatedness. The therapist is asking a nonrelating person to move in the direction of greater relatedness. As expected, the therapist's efforts to provide a new model of relatedness will be met with emotional distance and a good deal of silence.

Therapists who attempt to treat withdrawn schizoid patients must have extraordinary patience because of the slow, painstaking internalization process. They must also adopt a permissive, accepting attitude about silence. Specifically, silence must be viewed as more than simply resistance—it is also a specific form of nonverbal communication that may provide essential information about the patient.

During long periods of silence, the therapist must recognize that a relationship is still occurring. Through projective identification, the patient's behavior will evoke certain responses in the therapist that contain valuable diagnostic information about the patient's internal world (Gabbard 1989). One patient who, throughout childhood, had been given "the silent treatment" by his father, stopped talking in his therapy; his unconscious intent was to induce the therapist to feel what the patient had experienced as a child when his father "shut down." Thus, like a mother who holds and processes the elements projected onto her from her infant, the therapist must contain and modify the patient's projections before the patient can reintroject them.

With this model, the therapist's emotional reactions to the patient, however subtle, are the primary source of information about the patient. When the silence is prolonged, therapists must be wary of turning the tables and projecting their own self- and object representations onto the patient. This state of affairs is beautifully depicted in Ingmar Bergman's moving film *Persona*, in which a mute patient is treated by a nurse. After many unsuccessful attempts to get the patient to speak, the nurse becomes frustrated and begins to project aspects of herself onto the patient. Driven crazy, the nurse begins to treat the patient as an embodiment of her own internal world (Gabbard 1989).

This model of therapy requires therapists to receive their patient's projections and to monitor their own without being swept into countertransference acting-out. When therapists feel like quitting or giving up on a patient, they must view those feelings like any others in the process and attempt to understand them. As mentioned in Chapter 4 in the discussion of psychotherapy, the projective identifications might be diagnosed and understood only after the therapist has been "coerced" into playing a specific role vis-à-vis the patient. Therapists must silently note the interactions taking place between them and their patients and then use that information to inform subsequent interactions. Ogden (1982) summarized the therapist's task in such situations:

> The perspective of projective identification neither requires nor excludes the use of verbal interpretation; the therapist attempts to find a way of talking with and being with the patient that will constitute a medium through which the therapist may accept unintegrable aspects of the patient's internal object world and return them to the patient in a form that the patient can accept and learn from. (p. 42)

Indeed, a decision not to interpret may be the most therapeutically potent strategy with schizoid and schizotypal patients. If silence is interpreted as resistance, these patients may feel responsible and humiliated for their incapacity to communicate (Khan 1983; Nachmani 1984). On the other hand, by refraining from interpretation and accepting silence, the therapist may legitimize the private, non-communicative core of the self referred to by Winnicott (1963/1965). With certain patients, the therapist must respect their silent self. It may be the only viable technical approach to building a therapeutic alliance (Gabbard 1989).

Therapists greatly value interpersonal relatedness. We want to mean something to our patients. Accepting silent nonrelatedness runs counter to our training and psychological predisposition. Our natural tendency is to burden our patients with the expectation that they should be different than they are. Specifically, we want our patients to talk to us and to relate to us. However, that expectation means that we must ask patients to confront the very pain they avoid by schizoid withdrawal. Greater expectations from the therapist will paradoxically lead the patient to further detachment, as Searles (1986) observed:

> Winnicott's (1941/1958) concept of the . . . good-enough holding environment implies that the analyst be not merely relatively stably there, for the patient, but also relatively destructible (psychologically) by the patient, time and again, as the patient's persistent needs for autistic (omnipotent) functioning still require. Hence, the analyst needs intuitively to provide his own absence, perhaps as often as his own presence, to the patient at timely moments. (Searles 1986, p. 351)

Certain patients will respond to this tolerant, empathic acceptance with greater openness in the therapeutic relationship. These patients may begin to speak about hidden aspects of the self, eventually integrating these into a more cohesive sense of self. At the beginning of a psychotherapy process, it is difficult to know which patients are likely to benefit from it. Stone (1983), writing about schizotypal (borderline schizophrenic) patients, suggested that those who do a bit better in psychotherapy have some depressive symptoms or some capacity for emotional warmth and empathy. He warned therapists to be wary of excessive countertransference expectations, because only limited progress can be expected. He also recommended that therapists resign themselves to the fact that many embarrassing topics may have to remain hidden for extended periods of time in the therapy (Stone 1995). Too much eagerness to probe may frighten or shame the patient. In Stone's view, therapists must be able to tolerate the disappointing possibility that their patients will progress only in areas other than relatedness. In general, those patients with better ego functioning (i.e., more intact reality testing, better judgment, smaller amounts of cognitive slippage) will do better in treatment than those patients with more profoundly disturbed ego functioning. With patients in the latter group, therapists may need to function as an auxiliary ego, helping patients supportively with various tasks such as reality testing, judgment, and self–object differentiation. Stone (1985) also pointed out that, like schizophrenic patients (see

Chapter 7), schizotypal patients need more than expressive-supportive psychotherapy. Lower-functioning schizotypal patients also need social skills training, re-education, and various social supports.

Dynamic Group Psychotherapy

In general, schizoid patients are prime candidates for dynamic group psychotherapy (Appel 1974; Azima 1983). Group therapy is oriented toward helping patients with socialization, which is exactly where schizoid patients suffer most. It is also a setting in which a good deal of new parenting can take place. For many schizoid patients, their peers in a group process can function as a reconstructed family, eventually being internalized by these patients to counterbalance their more negative and frightening internal objects (Appel 1974).

Such patients can benefit considerably simply by having regular exposure to others. Some schizoid patients literally have no social outlets beyond their group therapy sessions. As they begin to feel accepted and to find that their worst fears are not realized, they gradually become more comfortable with people. In a manner similar to the individual therapy process described earlier, the reactions of other group members may provide a corrective experience that runs counter to all previous relationship experiences. Some difficulties that arise in the group psychotherapy of schizoid patients include resentment from other patients who have to "spill their guts" while the schizoid patient remains silent. These feelings may lead to a kind of "ganging up" to force the schizoid patient to talk. At such moments, the therapist must support the schizoid member of the group and help the other patients accept that patient's need to be silent (Azima 1983). The other patients may also simply ignore a withdrawn schizoid patient and proceed as if that patient was not there. In these instances, the therapist's task is to bring the patient into the group by pointing out how a pattern that takes place outside the group is repeating itself inside the group. Schizotypal patients tend to benefit from group therapy much as schizoid patients do, but those whose behavior is bizarre or whose thinking is psychotic may become scapegoats because they are simply too different from other members of the group. With such patients, individual therapy alone may be the preferred modality.

A combination of group and individual psychotherapy is ideal for many schizoid patients because the social field they encounter in the group can be discussed and processed with their individual psychotherapist. A significant number of schizoid patients will feel, however, that receiving a recommendation for group therapy is like "being thrown to the lions." They may even feel betrayed when their therapist makes the suggestion. A preliminary step to group referral is often the working through of these patients' fantasies about what will happen in group therapy.

The following case example illustrates some of the unique advantages of group psychotherapy for some schizoid patients.

Mr. BB was a 23-year-old single man with schizoid personality disorder. He worked as a nurse's aide on the night shift in a nursing home and took daytime classes at a local university. He liked working at night because very few interpersonal demands were made on him. His supervisor frequently slept, so he was free to read novels. When he was not sleeping, Mr. BB would spend many hours in vigorous bodybuilding exercises. He would then pose nude in front of the mirror and flex his muscles and admire himself. Much of the posing and flexing was accompanied by omnipotent fantasies of becoming an Olympic decathlon winner. He also imagined that if he achieved a certain level of bodily perfection, he would then be attractive to a girl in one of his college classes that he could never bring himself to speak to.

Mr. BB was deeply concerned about the fact that he had been adopted. He spoke about it with great shame, as though convinced that it reflected some inherent flaw. In his view, the early rejection by his biological mother was a sign that he was so inherently undesirable that others would also certainly reject him if given the chance.

Like many schizoid patients, Mr. BB had a perverse streak that took the form of exhibitionism. He would place himself in situations where women would come upon him in the nude. He would then act surprised and immediately leave the scene so as to avoid prosecution. However, the sexual pleasure he derived from this activity led him into more and more risky adventures. He once switched the men's and women's labels on the locker room doors in a gymnasium so that women would enter the men's locker room and find him standing there nude, drying himself after showering.

Mr. BB eventually came to an outpatient clinic where he sought group psychotherapy. He was concerned that his exhibitionism was getting out of hand and might lead to legal consequences, and he was genuinely disturbed by the loneliness of his existence. He sought group psychotherapy because he had previously tried individual psychotherapy for 2 years. He reported that he had remained silent throughout practically the entire therapy. Finally, he and the therapist had mutually decided that there was no point in continuing. Mr. BB also reported that he had a strong desire to overcome his fear of other people, and he believed that group therapy might be a good way to deal with that fear.

Mr. BB began a dynamic group psychotherapy process with a reasonably high-functioning group of other patients with assorted personality disorders. He attended regularly but sat silently through much of the group's discussion. Little by little, he was able to reveal more and more about himself. Something of a breakthrough occurred when he mustered enough courage to talk about the female classmate who was the object of his fantasies. One female patient in the group responded by saying, "Why don't you ask her out? You're an attractive man." Moved by this comment, Mr. BB replied that no one had ever told him that before.

The support and positive feedback this patient received from other group members bolstered his self-esteem and allowed him to speak more frequently and more openly. When he finally was able to discuss his exhibitionism, he experienced considerable relief that no one recoiled in horror at his revelation.

After several years of group therapy, Mr. BB's anxieties about relationships and his self-regard had improved to the point that he was able to begin dating and to form some appropriate peer relationships with males. The episodes of exhibitionism gradually decreased, although they tended to recur whenever the group took a vacation and Mr. BB felt abandoned by the therapist and his fellow patients.

The case of Mr. BB illustrates how the overt absence of object relations in schizoid personality disorder may be accompanied by intense fantasies of relatedness and by covert sexual activities of a perverse nature. Long periods of exercise are also fairly common in schizoid and schizotypal individuals. Physical activity of this kind may serve to "burn off" sexual energy or, as in the case of Mr. BB, may also be a way to build self-esteem by fantasizing that others will find the individual more attractive as a result of such efforts.

Although a number of perversions are commonly found in schizoid individuals, exhibitionism seems to hold a particular significance for these patients. Fairbairn (1954) observed that schizoid individuals frequently overvalue their mental contents, perceiving them as extraordinarily precious. They fear giving anything of themselves because in so doing they would deplete their narcissistically prized contents. Fairbairn noted that schizoid patients commonly use exhibitionism as a defense against the fear of giving. To be more exact, "showing" becomes a substitute for "giving," since the latter carries the fear of losing something precious while the former does not. Although the exhibitionism was overt in the case of Mr. BB, it frequently appears in sublimated forms, such as involvement in the performing arts.

Group psychotherapy provided Mr. BB with a new series of relationships to internalize. The relatedness with his fellow patients (and with the therapist) disconfirmed his expectations of how others would respond to him. Instead of being alienated by him, the group members accepted him as he was and confirmed his desirability as a person. Thus the validation of other patients in group therapy may have a more powerful impact on a schizoid patient than similar validation by an individual therapist. The schizoid patient may write off the positive regard of the therapist as an attitude contrived for therapeutic effect; the therapist is "just doing his job."

Many schizoid and schizotypal patients are much more refractory to treatment than Mr. BB. As Stone (1985) suggested, therapists must genuinely respect their patient's need to be different and must not feel compelled to transform a patient into someone else. In treating schizoid and schizotypal patients, we would all be well advised to remember the wisdom of Thoreau: "If a man does not keep pace with his companions, perhaps it is because he hears a different drummer. Let him step to the music which he hears, however measured or far away" (Thoreau 1937/1950, p. 290).

References

Akhtar S: Schizoid personality disorder: a synthesis of developmental, dynamic, and descriptive features. Am J Psychother 61:499–518, 1987

Akhtar S: Paranoid personality disorder: synthesis of developmental, dynamic, and descriptive features. Am J Psychother 44:5–25, 1990

American Psychiatric Association: Diagnostic and Statistical Manual of Mental Disorders, 3rd Edition. Washington, DC, American Psychiatric Association, 1980

American Psychiatric Association: Diagnostic and Statistical Manual of Mental Disorders, 3rd Edition, Revised. Washington, DC, American Psychiatric Association, 1987

American Psychiatric Association: Diagnostic and Statistical Manual of Mental Disorders, 4th Edition. Washington, DC, American Psychiatric Association 1994

Appel G: An approach to the treatment of schizoid phenomena. Psychoanal Rev 61:99–113, 1974

Auchincloss EL, Weiss RW: Paranoid character and the intolerance of indifference. J Am Psychoanal Assoc 40:1013–1037, 1992

Azima FJC: Group psychotherapy with personality disorders, in Comprehensive Group Psychotherapy, 2nd Edition. Edited by Kaplan HI, Sadock BJ. Baltimore, MD, Williams & Wilkins, 1983, pp 262–268

Balint M: The Basic Fault: Therapeutic Aspects of Regression. New York, Brunner/Mazel, 1979

Beauford JE, McNiel DE, Binder RL: Utility of the initial therapeutic alliance in evaluating psychiatric patients' risk of violence. Am J Psychiatry 154:1272–1276, 1997

Blum HP: Object inconstancy and paranoid conspiracy. J Am Psychoanal Assoc 29:789–813, 1981

Eigen M: Abstinence and the schizoid ego. Int J Psychoanal 54:493–498, 1973

Epstein L: Countertransference with borderline patients, in Countertransference. Edited by Epstein L, Feiner AH. New York, Jason Aronson, 1979, pp 375–405

Epstein L: An interpersonal–object relations perspective on working with destructive aggression. Contemporary Psychoanalysis 20:651–662, 1984

Fairbairn WRD: An Object-Relations Theory of the Personality. New York, Basic Books, 1954

Felthous AR: Preventing assaults on a psychiatric inpatient ward. Hospital and Community Psychiatry 35:1223–1226, 1984

Fenton WS, McGlashan TH: Risk of schizophrenia in character disordered patients. Am J Psychiatry 146:1280–1284, 1989

Freud S: Psycho-analytic notes on an autobiographical account of a case of paranoia (dementia paranoides) (1911), in The Standard Edition of the Complete Psychological Works of Sigmund Freud, Vol 12. Translated and edited by Strachey J. London, Hogarth Press, 1958, pp 1–82

Gabbard GO: On "doing nothing" in the psychoanalytic treatment of the refractory borderline patient. Int J Psychoanal 70:527–534, 1989

Gabbard GO: Technical approaches to transference hate in the analysis of borderline patients. Int J Psychoanal 72:625–637, 1991

Gabbard GO: Love and Hate in the Analytic Setting. Northvale, NJ, Jason Aronson, 1996

Grotstein JS: The psychoanalytic concept of schizophrenia, I: the dilemma. Int J Psychoanal 58:403–425, 1977

Gunderson JG: DSM-III diagnoses of personality disorders, in Current Perspectives on Personality Disorders. Edited by Frosch JP. Washington, DC, American Psychiatric Press, 1983, pp 20–39

Guntrip H: Schizoid Phenomena, Object-Relations, and the Self. New York, International Universities Press, 1968

Kendler KS, Gruenberg AM, Strauss JS: An independent analysis of the Copenhagen sample of the Danish adoption study of schizophrenia, II: the relationship between schizotypal personality disorder and schizophrenia. Arch Gen Psychiatry 38:982–984, 1981

Kety SS, Rosenthal D, Wender PH, et al: Mental illness in the biological and adoptive families of adopted schizophrenics. Am J Psychiatry 128:302–306, 1971

Khan MR: Hidden Selves: Between Theory and Practice in Psychoanalysis. New York, International Universities Press, 1983

Kinzel AF: Violent behavior in prisons, in Dynamics of Violence. Edited by Fawcett J. Chicago, IL, American Medical Association, 1971

Lawner P: Character rigidity and resistance to awareness of the transference. Issues in Ego Psychology 8:36–41, 1985

Madden DJ, Lion JR, Penna MW: Assaults on psychiatrists by patients. Am J Psychiatry 133:422–425, 1976

McGlashan TH: The borderline syndrome, II: is it a variant of schizophrenia or affective disorder? Arch Gen Psychiatry 40:1319–1323, 1983

Meissner WW: Psychotherapeutic schema based on the paranoid process. International Journal of Psychoanalytic Psychotherapy 5:87–114, 1976

Meissner WW: Psychotherapy and the Paranoid Process. Northvale, NJ, Jason Aronson, 1986

Meissner WW: Paranoid personality disorder, in Treatments of Psychiatric Disorders, 2nd Edition, Vol 2. Edited by Gabbard GO. Washington, DC, American Psychiatric Press, 1995, pp 2249–2259

Nachmani G: Hesitation, perplexity, and annoyance at opportunity. Contemporary Psychoanalysis 20:448–457, 1984

O'Driscoll GA, Lezenweger MF, Holzman PS: Antisaccades and smooth pursuit eye tracking and schizotypy. Arch Gen Psychiatry 55:837–843, 1998

Ogden TH: Projective Identification and Psychotherapeutic Technique. New York, Jason Aronson, 1982

Ogden TH: The Matrix of the Mind: Object Relations and the Psychoanalytic Dialogue. Northvale, NJ, Jason Aronson, 1986

Oldham JM, Skodol AE: Do patients with paranoid personality disorder seek psychoanalysis?, in Paranoia: New Psychoanalytic Perspectives. Edited by Oldham JM, Bone S. Madison, CT, International Universities Press, 1994, pp 151–166

Reich J, Braginsky Y: Paranoid personality traits in a panic disorder population: a pilot study. Compr Psychiatry 35:260–264, 1994

Roitman SEL, Corblatt BA, Bergman A, et al: Attentional functioning in schizotypal personality disorder. Am J Psychiatry 154:655–660, 1997

Rosenthal D, Wender PH, Kety SS, et al: The adopted-away offspring of schizophrenics. Am J Psychiatry 128:307–311, 1971

Searles HF: My Work With Borderline Patients. Northvale, NJ, Jason Aronson, 1986

Shapiro D: Neurotic Styles. New York, Basic Books, 1965

Siever LJ, Gunderson JG: Genetic determinants of borderline conditions. Schizophr Bull 5:59–86, 1979

Siever LJ, Silverman JM, Horvath TB, et al: Increased morbid risk for schizophrenia-related disorders in relatives of schizotypal personality disordered patients. Arch Gen Psychiatry 47:634–640, 1990

Stone MH: Psychotherapy with schizotypal borderline patients. J Am Acad Psychoanal 11:87–111, 1983

Stone MH: Schizotypal personality: psychotherapeutic aspects. Schizophr Bull 11:576–589, 1985

Stone MH: Schizoid and schizotypal personality disorders, in Treatments of Psychiatric Disorders, 2nd Edition, Vol 2. Edited by Gabbard GO. Washington, DC, American Psychiatric Press, 1995, pp 2261–2272

Tardiff K, Marzuk PM, Leon AC, et al: Violence by patients admitted to a private psychiatric hospital. Am J Psychiatry 154:88–93, 1997

Thoreau HD: Walden, in Walden and Other Writings of Henry David Thoreau. Edited by Atkinson B. New York, The Modern Library, 1937/1950, p 290

Westen D: Divergences between clinical and research methods for assessing personality disorders: implications for research and the evolution of Axis II. Am J Psychiatry 154:895–903, 1997

Winnicott DW: The observation of infants in a set situation (1941), in Through Paediatrics to Psycho-Analysis. New York, Basic Books, 1958, pp 52–69

Winnicott DW: Communicating and not communicating leading to a study of certain opposites (1963), in The Maturational Processes and the Facilitating Environment: Studies in the Theory of Emotional Development. New York, International Universities Press, 1965, pp 179–192

C H A P T E R
15

Cluster B Personality Disorders

Borderline

Our consideration of Cluster B personality disorders begins with the borderline patient, because borderline personality disorder serves as a reference point for the entire cluster. Narcissistic, antisocial, and histrionic personality disorders are often defined by how they differ from borderline personality disorder. Moreover, when *borderline* is used in the broad sense of a spectrum (Meissner 1988) or a personality organization (Kernberg 1967), all the personality disorders in Cluster B, along with those in Cluster A, may be subsumed under the general category of borderline conditions. Unfortunately, the increasing popularity of the borderline diagnosis in the last two decades has made it something of a psychiatric "wastebasket"—both overused and misused. Patients who are diagnostically confusing may receive the label *borderline* by default. A brief historical survey of the term *borderline* in American psychiatry may shed light on the place of borderline personality disorder (BPD) in the current nomenclature.

Evolution of the Term

In the late 1930s and throughout the 1940s, clinicians began to describe certain patients who were not sick enough to be labeled schizophrenic but who were far too disturbed for classical psychoanalytic treatment. In an effort to capture the "in between" state typical of these patients, Hoch and Polatin (1949) referred to this group as having pseudoneurotic schizophrenia characterized by a symptomatic pattern of "panneurosis," "pananxiety," and "pansexuality." Robert Knight (1953) further characterized this ill-defined group by focusing on several impairments in ego functioning, including the inability to plan realistically, the incapacity to defend against primitive impulses, and the predominance of primary process thinking over secondary process thinking.

These early contributors were observing a "messy" syndrome that did not fit well into preexisting diagnostic rubrics. Grinker et al. (1968) brought some diagnostic rigor to the syndrome in the early 1960s with their statistical analysis of approximately 60 such patients who were hospitalized in Chicago. A cluster analysis of data on these patients suggested that there were four subgroups of borderline patients (Table 15–1). These patients appeared to occupy a continuum from the "psychotic border" (Type I) all the way to the "neurotic border" (Type IV). In between the two extremes could be found a group with predominantly negative affects and difficulty maintaining stable interpersonal relationships (Type II), and another group (Type III) characterized by a generalized lack of identity, resulting in a need to borrow identity from others.

Grinker and his associates (1968) also attempted to identify common denomi-

---

TABLE 15–1.   Grinker's four subtypes of borderline patients

Type I: Psychotic Border

    A. Inappropriate, nonadaptive behavior
    B. Problems with reality testing and sense of identity
    C. Negative behavior and openly expressed anger

Type II: Core Borderline Syndrome

    A. Pervasive negative affect
    B. Vacillating involvement with others
    C. Anger acted out
    D. Inconsistent self-identity

Type III: As-If Group

    A. Tendency to copy identity of others
    B. Affectless
    C. Behavior more adaptive
    D. Relationships lacking in genuineness and spontaneity

Type IV: Neurotic Border

    A. Anaclitic depression
    B. Anxiety
    C. Neurotic and narcissistic features

Source.   Based on Grinker et al. 1968.

nators in the borderline syndrome that were present regardless of the subtype. They came up with the following four key features: 1) anger as the main or only affect, 2) defects in interpersonal relationships, 3) absence of consistent self-identity, and 4) pervasive depression. One of the most significant contributions of this empirical study was the finding that the borderline syndrome was clearly distinct from schizophrenia. Grinker et al. found that these patients do not deteriorate into frank schizophrenia over time. Rather, they are stably unstable (Schmideberg 1959) throughout the course of their illness. This discovery helped refute the belief some skeptics held that borderline patients were actually schizophrenic.

By 1990, Gunderson and his colleagues (Zanarini et al. 1990) were able to identify clear discriminating features based on research that focused on descriptive characteristics of the borderline syndrome (Table 15–2).

Many of these criteria are interrelated. Borderline patients are consumed with establishing exclusive one-to-one relationships with no risk whatsoever of abandonment. They may demand such relationships with an air of entitlement that overwhelms and alienates others. Moreover, when they do become close with another person, a set of twin anxieties are activated. On the one hand, they begin to worry that they will be engulfed by the other person and lose their own identity in this primitive merger fantasy. On the other hand, they experience anxiety verging on panic related to the conviction that they are about to be rejected or abandoned at any moment. To prevent being alone, borderline patients may resort to wrist-cutting or suicidal gestures, hoping to elicit rescue by the person to whom they are attached. Cognitive distortions, such as quasi-psychotic thought (defined as transient, circumscribed, and/or atypical strains on reality testing), also may occur in the context of interpersonal relationships. Near-delusional perceptions of abandonment by loved ones are common, and psychotic transference regressions may appear when patients become attached to their therapists. Clinicians who witness this kaleidoscopic display of shifting ego states are prone to a variety of intense countertransference reactions, including rescue fantasies, guilt feelings, transgressions of professional boundaries, rage and hatred, anxiety and terror, and profound feelings of helplessness (Gabbard 1993; Gabbard and Wilkinson 1994).

TABLE 15–2. Discriminating characteristics of borderline personality disorder

Quasi-psychotic thought	Demandingness/entitlement
Self-mutilation	Treatment regressions
Manipulative suicide efforts	Countertransference difficulties
Abandonment/engulfment/annihilation concerns	

Source. Based on Zanarini et al. 1990, pp. 165–166.

Whereas Gunderson and Grinker et al. focused primarily on descriptive diagnostic criteria, Otto Kernberg (1967, 1975) sought to characterize borderline patients from a psychoanalytic perspective. Using a combined ego psychological–object relations approach, he coined the term *borderline personality organization* to encompass a group of patients who showed characteristic patterns of ego weakness, primitive defensive operations, and problematic object relations. He observed a variety of symptoms in these patients, including free-floating anxiety, obsessive-compulsive symptoms, multiple phobias, dissociative reactions, hypochondriacal preoccupations, conversion symptoms, paranoid trends, polymorphous perverse sexuality, and substance abuse. Kernberg cautioned, however, that descriptive symptoms were not sufficient for a definitive diagnosis. He believed instead that the diagnosis rested on a sophisticated structural analysis that revealed four key features (Table 15–3).

1. *Nonspecific manifestations of ego weakness.*   One aspect of ego functioning is the capacity to delay the discharge of impulses and to modulate affects such as anxiety. Borderline patients, in Kernberg's view, are unable to marshal ego forces to perform those functions because of inherent nonspecific weaknesses. Similarly, they have a difficult time sublimating powerful drives and using their conscience to guide behavior.
2. *Shift toward primary process thinking.*   Like Robert Knight, Kernberg noted that these patients tend to regress into psychotic-like thinking in the absence of structure or under the pressure of strong affects. However, these shifts primarily occur in the context of generally intact reality testing.

TABLE 15–3.   Kernberg's criteria for borderline personality organization

---

I.   Nonspecific manifestations of ego weakness

    A. Lack of anxiety tolerance
    B. Lack of impulse control
    C. Lack of developed subliminatory channels

II. Shift toward primary process thinking

III. Specific defensive operations

    A. Splitting
    B. Primitive idealization
    C. Early forms of projection, especially projective identification
    D. Denial
    E. Omnipotence and devaluation

IV. Pathological internalized object relations

Source.   Based on Kernberg 1975.

3. *Specific defensive operations.* Foremost among these defenses was splitting, which Kernberg viewed as an active process of separating contradictory introjects and affects from one another (see Chapter 2). Splitting operations in the person with borderline personality organization manifest themselves clinically as follows: 1) an alternating expression of contradictory behaviors and attitudes, which the patient regards with a lack of concern and bland denial; 2) a compartmentalization of all persons in the patient's environment into "all good" and "all bad" camps, with frequent oscillations between camps for a given individual; and 3) coexisting contradictory views and images of oneself (self-representations) that alternate in their dominance from day to day and from hour to hour.

> A 41-year-old Catholic priest was admitted to a psychiatric hospital upon discovery that he had engaged in extensive sexual behavior with children of both sexes. Shortly after admission, his routine laboratory studies revealed a positive test for syphilis. When confronted with the lab result, the priest responded, "I don't know how that's possible. I'm a celibate priest." The resident treating the priest simply pointed out that the patient had been admitted to the hospital because of his extensive sexual activity with minors. The priest blandly responded to this confrontation by saying, "What do you expect? I'm only human."

This clinical vignette illustrates how contradictory self-representations coexist in the borderline patient—a "celibate priest" coexisted with a promiscuous, bisexual pedophile. Moreover, the priest's matter-of-fact response was typical of the bland denial that many borderline patients display when confronted with the splitting maneuvers they employ. Other defenses, such as primitive idealization, omnipotence, and devaluation, similarly reflect splitting tendencies (i.e., others are seen in wholly positive or wholly negative terms). Projective identification, in which self-representations or object representations are split off and projected onto others in an effort to control them, is another prominent defense in borderline personality organization, according to Kernberg.

4. *Pathological internalized object relations.* As a result of splitting, the person with borderline personality organization does not view other people as having a mixture of positive and negative qualities. Instead, others are divided into polar extremes and are regarded, in the words of one patient, as "either gods or devils." These individuals cannot integrate libidinal and aggressive aspects of others, which inhibits their ability to truly appreciate the internal experiences of other people. Their perceptions of others may alternate daily between idealization and devaluation, which can be highly disturbing for anyone in a rela-

tionship with such a person. Similarly, their inability to integrate positive and negative representations of the self results in profound identity diffusion, as illustrated by the previous example of the priest.

Kernberg's concept of borderline personality organization is distinct from the actual phenomenological characteristics that identify a specific personality disorder. In other words, his term encompasses many different personality disorders. In his view, patients with narcissistic, antisocial, schizoid, paranoid, infantile, and cyclothymic personality disorders, for example, are all characterized by an underlying borderline personality organization.

There is considerable controversy over whether the term *borderline* should be applied to a specific personality disorder or should be used broadly, as Kernberg used it, to describe a dimension of personality (Gunderson and Zanarini 1987). Grinker and his associates (1968) clearly believed that there were several subcategories of the borderline syndrome, constituting a spectrum. Meissner (1984, 1988) categorized borderline conditions differently than Grinker et al., but he, too, believed that limiting the usage of the term *borderline* to a specific personality disorder was misleading. He noted that there were clear descriptive groupings within the spectrum, specifically, a hysterical continuum and a schizoid continuum. In a retrospective study of 180 inpatients who had been diagnosed with BPD by DSM-III (American Psychiatric Association 1980) criteria, Fyer et al. (1988) found that 91% had another diagnosis as well, while 42% had two or more additional diagnoses. They speculated that the diagnosis of BPD is often applied to a heterogeneous group of patients whose symptoms overlap extensively with those of other diagnoses. To avoid conceptual confusion (and because related personality disorders, such as paranoid, schizoid, narcissistic, antisocial, and histrionic, are discussed at length in other chapters of this volume), the discussion in this chapter will be confined to those patients with the borderline features described by DSM-IV (American Psychiatric Association 1994) (Table 15–4).

Demographic Features and Course of Illness

At least three-fourths of the patients who are diagnosed with BPD are female (Gunderson et al. 1991). This finding may be due largely to cultural biases stemming from sex role stereotypes, because male patients who have the features of BPD are often diagnosed as having narcissistic or antisocial personality disorders. BPD is by far the most commonly used Axis II diagnosis, with a prevalence somewhere between 15% and 25% in clinical populations (Gunderson and Zanarini 1987). Its prevalence in the general population probably ranges between 1.8% and

---

TABLE 15–4. DSM-IV criteria for borderline personality disorder

---

A pervasive pattern of instability of interpersonal relationships, self-image, and affects, and marked impulsivity beginning by early adulthood and present in a variety of contexts, as indicated by five (or more) of the following:

1. frantic efforts to avoid real or imagined abandonment

(**Note:** Do not include suicidal or self-mutilating behavior covered in criterion 5.)

2. a pattern of unstable and intense interpersonal relationships characterized by alternating between extremes of idealization and devaluation
3. identity disturbance: markedly and persistently unstable self-image or sense of self
4. impulsivity in at least two areas that are potentially self-damaging (e.g., spending, sex, substance abuse, reckless driving, binge eating)

(**Note:** Do not include suicidal or self-mutilating behavior covered in criterion 5.)

5. recurrent suicidal behavior, gestures, or threats, or self-mutilating behavior
6. affective instability due to a marked reactivity of mood (e.g., intense episodic dysphoria, irritability, or anxiety usually lasting a few hours and only rarely more than a few days)
7. chronic feelings of emptiness
8. inappropriate, intense anger or difficulty controlling anger (e.g., frequent displays of temper, constant anger, recurrent physical fights)
9. transient, stress-related paranoid ideation or severe dissociative symptoms

---

Source.   Reprinted from DSM-IV (American Psychiatric Association 1994), p. 654. Used with permission.

4% (Baron et al. 1985; Gunderson and Zanarini 1987; Loranger et al. 1982; Swartz et al. 1990). The legitimacy of the diagnostic category of BPD has been substantiated by long-term follow-up studies demonstrating that, over time, borderline patients continue to manifest consistent clinical symptomatology; in the vast majority of cases, these patients do not shift into other major psychiatric disorders (Gunderson and Zanarini 1987).

Because all the major long-term follow-up studies (McGlashan 1986; Plakun et al. 1985; Stone et al. 1987; Werble 1970) have focused on subjects who have had rather extensive treatment experiences, the untreated course of BPD remains something of a mystery. In fact, the key follow-up studies have been undertaken with patients who have had long-term (1–2 years), psychoanalytically oriented hospital treatment. These studies suggest that BPD usually becomes apparent in late adolescence or young adulthood and that it runs a rocky course during its first decade of treatment, leading many clinicians to become discouraged with the patient's lack of progress. However, after approximately 5 or 6 years of treatment, borderline patients often begin to show substantial improvement that peaks in the second decade after their first hospitalization.

In the sample of 251 borderline patients studied by Stone and his colleagues

(1987), approximately two-thirds were "recovered" or doing reasonably well after a decade or so, although many of these patients continued to receive outpatient treatment. In the Austen Riggs study (Plakun et al. 1985), borderline patients achieved a mean Global Assessment Scale score of 67—which placed them in the "good" range of functioning—after a mean follow-up period of 15 years (comparable to Stone's study). In the Montreal study at the Jewish General Hospital (Paris et al. 1987), borderline patients were also reinterviewed at a mean of 15 years after hospitalization, and the investigators found that 75% of the patients no longer met the criteria for BPD as defined by Gunderson's Diagnostic Interview for Borderlines. In McGlashan's (1986) follow-up study of 81 patients originally hospitalized at Chestnut Lodge, most of the patients were able to live independently and to adjust satisfactorily to work. However, the sample revealed a bimodal distribution when it came to functioning in intimate relationships: whereas one group managed to maintain meaningful intimate relationships over time, the other group adjusted to life by avoiding close interpersonal contact.

All of these studies suggest that clinicians have reason for optimism in the treatment of borderline patients. The patients studied all had better outcomes than did schizophrenic patients who were used in comparison groups, and they were very similar to patients with affective disorders on most measures. This optimism is tempered, however, by the finding that between 3% and 10% of the borderline patients in these studies committed suicide.

In the last decade of the 20th century, encouraging results began to emerge from studies of short-range outcome as well. Mehlum et al. (1991) followed 29 patients with BPD prospectively for an average of 2.8 years. When assessed at follow-up, the patients showed moderate improvement on the Global Severity Index and the Health-Sickness Rating Scale. In addition, 56% of the sample were employed and 38% were self-supporting. Karterud et al. (1992) studied 34 BPD patients for an average duration of 6 months. Patients showed significant improvement on the Global Severity Index but only very modest change on the Health-Sickness Rating Scale after 6 months of day treatment.

Najavits and Gunderson (1995) prospectively followed 37 female BPD patients who were beginning new psychotherapies after inpatient admission. Eight assessment measures were used at four time points: baseline, 1 year, 2 years, and 3 years. The results showed significant improvement in several areas and no significant deterioration. Most patients had a course of erratic improvement. Of interest in this study of the clinical course was that low obsessive and phobic symptoms seemed to be baseline predictors of good 3-year outcome. Also, every significant measure of change was in the direction of improvement. Although these results are encouraging, it is possible that those who completed the research protocol were a more functional subsample of BPD patients.

These promising findings about the course of BPD are given further credence by psychotherapy studies that will be reviewed later in the chapter. Although borderline patients may seem to be chronic and difficult patients in the short run, there is reason to believe that with persistent treatment, substantial improvement may occur.

Psychodynamic Understanding

Kernberg

Kernberg (1975) linked the etiology and pathogenesis of BPD to the developmental scheme of Margaret Mahler (Mahler et al. 1975). Readers may wish to review this scheme, outlined in Chapter 2, before continuing with this discussion. Specifically, Kernberg viewed borderline patients as having successfully traversed Mahler's symbiotic phase so that self and object can be clearly distinguished but also as having become fixated during the separation-individuation phase. Kernberg targeted the rapprochement subphase, between approximately 16 and 24 months, as the chronological site of this developmental crisis. At this stage, the child becomes alarmed about the potential for its mother to disappear and at times displays a frantic concern about her location. From this developmental standpoint, borderline patients can be viewed as repeatedly reliving an early infantile crisis in which they feared that attempts to separate from their mother would result in her disappearance and abandonment of them. In the adult form of this childhood crisis, individuals are unable to tolerate periods of being alone and fear abandonment from significant others. Patients with BPD also may be overwhelmed with anxiety in the face of major separations from their parents or other nurturing figures. The reasons for the fixation at the rapprochement subphase are related, in Kernberg's view, to a disturbance of the mother's emotional availability during this critical period, due either to a constitutional excess of aggression in the child or to maternal problems with parenting, or even a combination of both.

An important component of this fixation is the lack of object constancy typical of the borderline patient. Like other children, throughout the period of separation-individuation, these children are unable to integrate the good and bad aspects of themselves and their mothers. These contradictory images are kept separate via splitting, so that both the mother and the self are seen as alternating between being thoroughly bad and thoroughly good. But whereas most children of nearly 3 years of age will have object constancy solidified sufficiently so that they can embrace a whole-object view of the mother and the self, such is not true of borderline-prone individuals. At that point, children can generally tolerate separation somewhat better because they have internalized a whole, soothing image of their mother that sustains them in times of her physical absence. Since borderline persons lack this internal image, they have little or no object constancy, which contributes significantly to their intolerance of separation and aloneness.

The end result of this developmental fixation is a condition that Kernberg (1966) characterized by its predominance of negative introjects. Although he allowed for environmental sources for these negative internalized self- and object representations, Kernberg's theory emphasized the significance of a constitutional excess of oral aggression in borderline patients. This factor reduces the borderline patient's ability to integrate good and bad images of self and other; these patients are convinced that the overwhelming "badness" will destroy any "goodness" in themselves or in others. When the bad introjects are projected outward, borderline patients feel at the mercy of malevolent persecutors. When reintrojected, the bad introjects make them feel unworthy and despicable, occasionally leading to suicidal thoughts. This innate aggression also impedes the borderline patient's passage through the oedipal phase. Thus, oedipal conflicts in borderline patients often appear more raw and primitive, compared with those in neurotic patients.

Masterson and Rinsley

The formulation of Masterson and Rinsley (1975) also focused on the rapprochement subphase of separation-individuation. However, they stressed the behavior of the mother rather than the innate aggression of the child. They found that the mothers of borderline patients, whom Masterson and Rinsley viewed as typically borderline themselves, were highly conflicted about their children growing up. As a result, the child receives a message from the mother that growing up and becoming one's own person will result in the loss of maternal love and support. A key corollary of this message is that remaining dependent constitutes the only available means of maintaining the maternal bond. This powerful maternal communication provokes "abandonment depression" any time the prospect of separation or autonomy presents itself to the child.

According to Masterson and Rinsley, this rapprochement subphase crisis between child and mother becomes rarefied as two separate split object relations units (Table 15–5). These units consist of three entities: a part–self-representation, a part–object representation, and an affect that connects the two. The rewarding object relations unit is associated with feelings of being loved and gratified. It includes a maternal part-object that is affirming, loving, and supportive. In association with this positively regarded maternal introject, there is a part–self-

TABLE 15–5. Role of the mother in the borderline syndrome (Masterson and Rinsley)

Mother-Infant Interaction in Rapprochement Subphase:

- Reward for regression, clinging
- Withdrawal for separation-individuation

Split Object Relations Units:

- Withdrawing (aggressive) part-unit

Maternal Part-Object	+	Affect	+	Part–Self-Representation
attacking, critical, hostile, withdrawing approval		*anger, frustration, feeling thwarted*		*inadequate, bad, helpless, guilty, ugly, empty*

- Rewarding (libidinally gratifying) part-unit

Maternal Part-Object	+	Affect	+	Part–Self-Representation
approval, support, and reward for regressive, clinging behavior		*feeling good, being fed, gratification of wish for reunion*		*good, passive, compliant*

Source. Based on Masterson and Rinsley 1975.

representation of a "good child" who is obedient and passive. The withdrawing object relations unit is associated with feelings of rage, abandonment, depression, and helplessness. The maternal part-object is malevolent and critical, while the part–self-representation is a "bad child" who is guilty and undesirable.

The fixation at this fragmented level leaves the borderline patient feeling that there are only two choices—you can feel abandoned and bad, or like Peter Pan, you can feel good only by denying reality and never growing up. Rinsley (1988) subsequently found this formulation of split object relations unit to be somewhat oversimplified and limiting in its therapeutic implications. He went on to apply the constructs of Fairbairn (1954) to the borderline personality (Rinsley 1987) and to focus on the developmental differences between borderline and narcissistic personality disorders (Rinsley 1984, 1985, 1989). By so doing, Rinsley moved away from his earlier emphasis, with Masterson, on the conflict-related origin of BPD and toward a deficit or "insufficiency" model.

Adler

Whereas the psychodynamic models of Kernberg and of Masterson and Rinsley are derived essentially from conflict models of psychopathology, Adler's (1985) understanding of BPD is based on a deficit or "insufficiency" model. Inconsistent or unreliable mothering, in Adler's view, causes the borderline patient's failure to develop a "holding-soothing" internal object. Adler, who was heavily influenced by the self psychological theories of Kohut (see Chapter 2), understood the borderline patient as being in search of selfobject functions from external figures because of the absence of nurturing introjects.

Adler emphasized the developmental framework of Selma Fraiberg (1969) in contrast to that of Mahler. He noted that at approximately 18 months of age, according to Fraiberg, the normal child is ordinarily able to summon up an internal image of a maternal figure even in the physical absence of that figure. This capacity for "evocative memory," as Fraiberg termed this cognitive achievement, is only tenuously established in the borderline patient, according to Adler. In situations of stress, or in the throes of an intense transference, borderline patients tend to regress until they can no longer recall important figures in their environment who are not physically present unless an object such as a picture is available as a reminder. Adler conceptualized this observation as a regression to a developmental age between 8 and 18 months, before evocative memory has been achieved.

The borderline patient's lack of a holding-soothing internal object accounts for several aspects of borderline psychopathology. This lack creates feelings of emptiness and depressive tendencies. It is also responsible for the clinging dependency so commonly seen in borderline patients. In the absence of selfobject responses from significant others, borderline individuals have inadequate internal resources to sustain them and are prone to fragmentations of the self. This dissolution of the self is accompanied by a profound emptiness described as "annihilation panic" by Adler. Finally, the absence of a holding-soothing introject leads to a chronic oral rage in borderline patients related to their feeling that mothering figures were not emotionally available during childhood.

Empirical Research and Etiology

Although the discussion of the three psychodynamic models presented here in no way represents a comprehensive overview of the psychoanalytic discourse regarding borderline disorders, it should serve to acquaint readers with the three points of view that lie at the heart of much of the controversy around this diagnostic category. More to the point, each model has specific treatment implications that are themselves perhaps even more controversial than the diagnostic understanding. Much of the literature involves critiques of the positions set forth by these theorists. Those who localize the developmental disturbance to the rapprochement subphase have been taken to task by no less a critic than Margaret Mahler herself (Mahler and Kaplan 1977), who pointed out that focusing on one subphase of separation-individuation is somewhat reductionistic in that such a posture fails to acknowledge or appreciate the influence of other subphases, as well as oedipal influences, in the pathogenesis of BPD. She expressed doubt that a discrete linear relationship exists between disturbances in one subphase of separation-individuation and later adult manifestations of psychopathology. Gunderson (1984) also pointed out that empirical studies of parents of borderline patients suggest that inadequate parenting is not confined to particular developmental subphases, but rather is pervasive throughout all phases of childhood. Moreover, neglect appears to be at least as common as overinvolvement. These studies also indicate that *both* parents, rather than only the mother, are typically neglectful of their parental responsibilities. Masterson and Rinsley were criticized by Esman (1980) for unfairly blaming mothers in their formulation while not sufficiently taking into account constitutional factors, such as organically based cognitive dysfunction, that may contribute to problems in the separation-individuation phase.

Whereas Masterson and Rinsley were accused of blaming mothers, Kernberg was criticized for attributing constitutionally based oral rage to borderline patients. Atwood and Stolorow (1984), for example, suggested that Kernberg's observations of excessive aggression in borderline patients may be viewed as an iatrogenic artifact stemming from Kernberg's early confrontation and interpretation of negative transference.

All of the psychodynamic models have been challenged to some extent by the empirical research literature. For example, the maternal overinvolvement depicted in the Masterson-Rinsley formulation has been questioned in a series of studies (H. Frank and Hoffman 1986; H. Frank and Paris 1981; Goldberg et al. 1985; Gunderson et al. 1980; Paris and H. Frank 1989; Paris and Zweig-Frank 1992; Soloff and Millward 1983; Zweig-Frank and Paris 1991) that collectively suggest three overarching conclusions (Zanarini and Frankenburg 1997): 1) borderline patients generally view their maternal relationships as distant, highly conflictual, or uninvolved; 2) the father's failure to be present is an even more discriminating aspect of the families of origin in BPD than the maternal relationship; and 3) disturbed relationships with both the mother and the father may be more pathogenic as well as more specific for BPD than those with either parent alone.

These findings suggest that neglect may be a more significant etiological factor than overinvolvement. One elegantly designed prospective study (Johnson et al. 1999) found that neglect in childhood was associated with an increase in BPD symptoms as well as those connected with several other personality disorders,

Psychodynamic theories emphasizing the significance of separation and abandonment have received some confirmation from studies measuring the prevalence of early separations and loss in the childhood histories of patients with BPD (Akiskal et al. 1985; Links et al. 1988; Walsh 1977; Zanarini et al. 1989a). In a study (Zanarini and Frankenburg 1997) comparing borderline patients with patients with other Axis II conditions, psychotic patients, and affectively disturbed patients, borderline patients were found to have a significantly higher percentage of early losses and separations in their backgrounds. The figures ranged from 37% to 64% and were highly discriminating for BPD (Zanarini and Frankenburg 1997).

All of the major psychodynamic models seriously understated the role played by childhood trauma in the etiology and pathogenesis of BPD. There is now extensive empirical support for the notion that abuse during childhood is a major contributing factor to the etiology of the disorder (Baker et al. 1992; Gunderson and Sabo 1993; Herman et al. 1989; Ogata et al. 1990; Swartz et al. 1990; Walsh 1977; Westen et al. 1990; Zanarini et al. 1989b, 1997). Childhood sexual abuse appears to be an important etiological factor in around 60% of borderline patients. Although control patients with other personality disorders or depression do not report sexual abuse as often as do borderline patients, the same is not true for physical abuse, where the prevalence is roughly the same. About 25% of borderline patients have a history of parent-child incest. On the other hand, sexual abuse is neither necessary nor sufficient for the development of BPD, and other early experiences, such as neglect by caretakers of both genders and chaotic or inconsistent home environments, also appear to be significant risk factors (Zanarini et al. 1997). This perspective was supported in a prospective study by Johnson et al. (1999), which linked borderline symptoms in adulthood to childhood sexual abuse and neglect, but not to physical abuse.

Expanding on Kernberg's notion that certain constitutional factors are relevant to the etiology of BPD, a variety of studies have explored biological and genetic factors that may influence whether an individual develops BPD. Cloninger et al. (1993) developed a psychobiological model of personality involving four dimensions of temperament and three dimensions of character. Within this model, approximately 50% of personality can be attributed to temperament, which is heavily influenced by genetic variables, and 50% to character, which is largely determined by environmental variables (Figure 15–1).

The four dimensions of temperament are 1) novelty-seeking, characterized by frequent exploratory activity in response to novelty, impulsive decision making, extravagance in the approach to cues and reward, quick loss of temper, and active avoidance of frustration; 2) harm-avoidance, which involves pessimistic worry about the future, avoidant behavior such as fear of uncertainty and shyness regarding strangers, and rapid fatigability; 3) reward-dependence, characterized by sentimentality, social attachment, and dependence on approval of others; and 4) persistence, which refers to the capacity for perseverance despite frustration and fatigue.

The three dimensions of character are shaped by family and social influences, intrapsychic fantasy, trauma, and stressors in the environment. Self-directedness involves acceptance of responsibility for one's choices rather than blaming others,

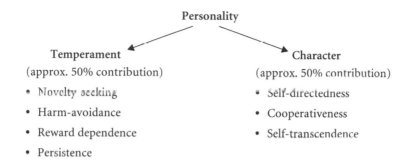

FIGURE 15–1.   A psychobiological model of personality.
Source.   Based on Cloninger et al. 1993.

acceptance of self, resourcefulness, and the identification of life goals and purposes. Cooperativeness is a measure of object relatedness and taps such dimensions as empathy, helpfulness, compassion, and social acceptance. Self-transcendence refers to the individual's spiritual acceptance, identifications beyond the self, and altruistic pursuits.

Cloninger et al. (1993) found that the character dimensions of self-directedness and cooperativeness are critical factors in the diagnosis of personality disorder. In fact, low self-directedness and low cooperativeness are associated with all categories of personality disorder. Certain temperaments are characteristic of specific types of personality disorders. Cloninger and colleagues reported that patients with BPD are unique in being high in *both* novelty-seeking and harm-avoidance. In other words, borderline patients are impulsive and angry and also extremely anxious.

The Cloninger model suggests a genetic-biological diathesis that is acted upon by certain environmental factors to create the combination of low self-directedness and low cooperativeness in conjunction with a temperament characterized by high harm-avoidance and high novelty-seeking. Figueroa and Silk (1997) proposed a related model in which the effects of trauma interact with an underlying predisposition to serotonergic dysfunction. Their hypothesis is based in part on the observation that borderline patients have a significantly decreased level of serotonergic activity. Because serotonin has an inhibitory effect on behavior, the impulsivity characteristic of borderline patients may in part relate to this altered serotonergic activity (Coccaro and Kavoussi 1997; Coccaro et al. 1989; Siever and Davis 1991). The increased vulnerability secondary to lower serotonin is made worse by the effects of trauma, which include alterations in cortisol and catecholamines. The hypersensitive noradrenergic system, related in part to temperament and in part to the hyperreactivity resulting from trauma, leads to self-destructive behaviors, such as mutilation, in an attempt to diminish dysphoric and painful affects.

Further evidence of a biological substrate for BPD derives from data that suggest the presence of neurocognitive deficits. Andrulonis (1991) noted that significant numbers of borderline patients have soft signs of neurological difficulties, including a history of attention-deficit/hyperactivity disorder, learning problems, poor impulse control, and conduct disorder. Studies of neuropsychological impairments report that borderline patients have significantly more signs of such impairments but that some of the difficulties may be subtle and become evident only when BPD subjects are matched with healthy control subjects (O'Leary and Cowdry 1994; Swirsky-Sacchetti et al. 1993; vanReekum et al. 1993). At least one study has also identified a significantly higher rate of head injury prior to diagnosis in BPD patients compared with control subjects (Streeter et al. 1995).

Family studies have noted that BPD is significantly more common among the first-degree relatives of borderline patients than among those of control subjects (Zanarini and Frankenburg 1997). However, whether this tendency for the disorder to run in families is related to environmental factors or to heritability cannot be definitively determined without studies of adopted-away twins.

All of these contributing factors also affect the child's capacity to attach to its mother or caregiver. As noted in Chapter 2, attachment theory posits four categories of child-caregiver bonds: 1) secure/autonomous, 2) insecure/dismissing, 3) preoccupied, and 4) unresolved or disorganized. Patients with BPD tend to be classified as preoccupied or unresolved. As a response to neglect and abuse, children who grow up to develop BPD may defensively disrupt the mental processes necessary for depicting thoughts and feelings both in themselves and in others. This deactivation of mentalization prevents the children from developing reflective function by which they could understand internal states (see Chapter 2). By refusing to think about the contents of their parents' or their caregivers' minds, such children avoid having to think about the hostile intent in individuals who are supposed to be caring for them. The resulting lack of a sense of agency and a cohesive sense of self leads such patients to disavow ownership of their own bodies and actions (Fonagy and Target 1995). The core of the child's self develops from the internalization of the caregiver's perception of the child as an intentional being. In the absence of such caregiving, infants cannot "find themselves" in the caregiver's reactions to them. This interaction between caregiver and child may also contribute to dissociative states in borderline patients (see Chapter 10).

These accumulated data suggest that BPD has a multifactorial etiology. Zanarini and Frankenburg (1997) postulate three overarching factors. One is a traumatic and chaotic home environment, involving prolonged early separations, neglect, emotional discord in the family, insensitivity to the child's feelings and needs, and trauma of varying degrees. The second is a biologically based vulnerable temperament. The third factor relates to triggering events, such as attempting to form an intimate relationship, moving away from home, or experiencing a rape or other traumatic event, any of which may act as a catalyst to produce the symptomatology of the borderline condition. Certain types of genetically based temperaments may increase the likelihood that negative life events will occur, so there is an ongoing interactive effect of genes and environment in the development of BPD (Paris 1998). One conclusion is that each borderline patient may have a unique etiological pathway involving differing degrees of each of the etiological factors.

Some of the contradictory views expressed in the psychodynamic theories may reflect differing developmental experiences and different populations of borderline patients. For example, patients who have experienced early childhood loss or neglect may fail to develop a holding-soothing introject, as described by Adler (1985). The work of Zweig-Frank and Paris (1991) indicated that other patients were subjected to overcontrol in childhood (by both mother and father) and therefore may suffer from abandonment concerns such as those described by Masterson and Rinsley (1975) and Kernberg (1975). Controlled research has also documented a high correlation between separation-individuation issues and borderline psychopathology (Dolan et al. 1992).

Relationship With Affective Disorders

When the term *borderline* first appeared in the psychiatric literature, it clearly denoted a clinical entity that was "on the border" of psychosis or, more specifically, schizophrenia. As time has passed and long-term follow-up data have accumulated on the course of BPD, the disorder has been more closely linked to affective disorders than to schizophrenia (McGlashan 1983; Stone 1980; Stone et al. 1987). The interface between affective disorders and BPD has been the source of ongoing controversy in clinical psychiatry. In one long-term follow-up study (Stone et al. 1987), there was a 69% overlap between major affective disorder and BPD. Another study found an 80% lifetime prevalence of major depression in patients with both dysthymia and BPD (Zanarini et al. 1989a). Most research, though, has suggested that the comorbidity between major affective disorder and BPD is nonspecific in light of findings that other personality disorders have equal or higher frequencies of co-occurrence with major depression (Barasch et al. 1985; Fyer et al. 1988; Gunderson and Phillips 1991; Pfohl et al. 1984; Shea et al. 1987).

Similar shifts have occurred in the thinking about family history data. Whereas earlier studies had suggested a higher prevalence of affective disorder in the relatives of borderline patients, newer data have indicated that these linkages do not hold if borderline probands who also have major affective disorder on Axis I are removed from consideration (Gunderson and Phillips 1991). The rates of co-morbid major depression found in BPD are at least in the range of 40%–60%, but BPD does not appear to be a variant of affective disorder. The current consensual view is that depression and BPD have a modest and nonspecific etiological association but are distinct disorders (Gunderson and Phillips 1991; Gunderson et al. 1999). There are also data indicating that the neuroticism temperament, which is closely related to Cloninger's harm-avoidance temperament, may carry with it a vulnerability for the development of depression. Hence, BPD and major depression may have in common an underlying temperamental vulnerability. In borderline patients, dependent interpersonal relatedness appears to confer susceptibility to an anaclitic type of depression involving feelings of helplessness, unloveability, and a desire to be protected (Gunderson et al. 1999).

A common problem confronting the clinician is differentiating the characterological depression typical of borderline personality from major depressive disorder. A knowledge of the specific characteristics of each type of depression can assist clinicians in making this determination (Table 15–6).

Borderline patients may use the term *depression* to describe chronic feelings of boredom, emptiness, and loneliness, but diagnostically they may lack the vegetative signs of Axis I major depression (Gunderson and Zanarini 1987). Moreover, conscious feelings of rage are often intermingled with the characterological depression of the borderline patient, in contrast to the patient with a more autonomous and endogenous type of depression (Gunderson and Phillips 1991). Rogers et al. (1995) corroborated the notion that the depression associated with BPD is in some respects unique and distinct from that found in nonborderline patients. They studied 50 depressed inpatients, 21 of whom had BPD. The aspects most clearly linked to a diagnosis of BPD were emptiness, self-condemnation, abandonment fears, hopelessness, and self-destructiveness. Clinicians must keep in mind, however, that while these distinctions are helpful, both forms of depression may coexist in the same patient.

Medication has become an increasingly standard part of the overall treatment plan for patients with BPD. Using Cloninger et al.'s psychobiological model, one can postulate that medication may treat temperamental variables while psychotherapy addresses character. Three different double-blind, placebo-controlled studies (Coccaro and Kavoussi 1997; Markovitz 1995; Salzman et al. 1995) have demonstrated some degree of efficacy for selective serotonin reuptake inhibitors (SSRIs) in patients with borderline and other severe personality disorders. These agents seemed to be especially effective in reducing anger and impulsive aggressive

TABLE 15–6.   Differential diagnosis of major depressive disorder and characterological depression typical of borderline personality disorder

Borderline characterological disorder	Shared characteristics	Major depressive disorder
1. Loneliness, emptiness	1. Depressed mood; early onset, sustained	1. Guilt feelings, remorse
2. Anger, neediness	2. Worthlessness, hopelessness	2. Withdrawal/agitation, severe vegetative symptoms
3. Repeated suicidal gestures	3. Object hunger (without gestures)	3. Suicidality
4. Demanding, hostile, dependent relationships	4. Dependency in relationships	4. Stable relationships
5. Concern with interpersonal loss, separation	5. Fragile self-esteem	5. Concern with defeat, failures
6. Illusory self-sufficiency (with history of dependency)		6. Caregiving welcomed (with history of independence)

Source.   Based on Gunderson and Phillips 1991.

behavior, particularly verbal aggression. SSRIs also appeared to be useful even in borderline patients without comorbid affective disorders, which suggests that they may work at the level of temperament. However, in some patients the dosage of fluoxetine had to be pushed up to 80 mg/day to be effective (Markovitz 1995), much higher than one would expect in a pure Axis I major depression.

It should be noted, however, that these agents are not curative and serve only as an adjunct to psychotherapy. In many cases, they reduce background affective "noise" related to anger or rage, allowing the patient to become more reflective about the psychotherapy process. Some patients with BPD do not respond to SSRIs, and Soloff (1998) has developed several tentative algorithms that guide the clinician toward other agents. Soloff's algorithms are based on target symptom clusters: affective dysregulation symptoms, impulsive-behavioral symptoms, and cognitive-perceptual symptoms. For affective dysregulation symptoms, when an SSRI does not seem effective, one can consider switching to nefazodone or venlafaxine or other SSRIs that act on multiple neurotransmitter systems. If anger is a problem, a low-dose antipsychotic may be added, and clonazepam may be useful if anxiety is a major difficulty. Alprazolam should be avoided because it has been shown to produce disinhibition in BPD patients, which may result in violent or self-destructive behavior (Cowdry and Gardner 1988; Gardner and Cowdry 1985). Monoamine oxidase inhibitors (MAOIs) or lithium can be used as a last resort for affective dysregulation symptoms; however, both of these agents have problematic side effects, and clinicians should carefully weigh the risks and benefits of prescribing them for a population known for its noncompliance and abuse of medication. These medication strategies are summarized in Table 15–7.

When the borderline patient's primary target symptoms are in the impulsive-behavioral domain, an SSRI would still be the first-line agent. In this category, in addition to low-dose antipsychotics, lithium carbonate, or MAOIs, the clinician might also consider carbamazepine and divalproex, both of which have been shown in double-blind, placebo-controlled trials to reduce impulsive outbursts (Cowdry and Gardner 1988; Hollander 1999). For self-mutilation and/or alcohol abuse, naltrexone may be worth a try (Gabbard 2000).

If cognitive-perceptual symptoms, such as paranoid ideation or depersonalization, are particularly problematic, low doses of conventional antipsychotics have been shown to help with quasi-psychotic thoughts. Although most of the randomized controlled trials in the literature have focused on conventional antipsychotics, there is growing anecdotal evidence that some of the atypical antipsychotics such as clozapine may be useful as well (Frankenburg and Zanarini 1993). SSRIs may also be useful for some of the cognitive disturbances.

TABLE 15–7. Medication strategies for borderline personality disorder target symptoms

Affective dysregulation symptoms	Impulsive-behavioral symptoms	Cognitive-perceptual symptoms
SSRI[a]	SSRI	Low-dose conventional antipsychotic
Low-dose antipsychotic	Low-dose antipsychotic	SSRI
Clonazepam[b]	Lithium carbonate	Atypical antipsychotic
MAOI[c]	MAOI	
Lithium	Carbamazepine	
	Divalproex	
	Atypical antipsychotic	
	Naltrexone (if self-mutilation and/or alcohol abuse is present)	

[a]SSRI = selective serotonin reuptake inhibitor.
[b]Do not use alprazolam, as it may result in disinhibition.
[c]MAOI = monoamine oxidase inhibitor; should be used with considerable caution because of dietary restrictions.
Source.   Based on Gabbard 2000 and Soloff 1998.

Treatment Approaches

Individual Psychotherapy

Empirical Research

In recent years, many American therapists have found it difficult to conduct extended psychodynamic therapy with borderline patients because managed care companies will often deny reimbursement. Some managed cared companies will flatly state that they do not reimburse for Axis II disorders. Others will assert that there is no evidence that psychotherapy is helpful for patients with BPD. Many such companies view the long-term psychotherapy of such patients as prohibitively expensive. There is actually a growing literature suggesting that extended therapy of a year or more is not only successful in making substantial improvements in borderline patients but also cost-effective (Gabbard 1997; Gabbard et al. 1997).

In the dissertation research of Hoke (1989), 58 borderline patients were followed for up to 7 years. The BPD subjects in this study could be divided into two different groups on the basis of their natural course. The first group (approximately half) received intermittent or inconsistent psychotherapeutic treatments, while the second group received consistent psychotherapy over at least 2 years. Those who remained in a stable psychotherapy process showed greater improvement in mood functioning, a decreased need for more-intensive psychiatric interventions (e.g., emergency room visits, day treatment, and hospitalization), decreased impulsiveness, and improved Global Assessment Scale scores.

In Sydney, Australia, Stevenson and Meares (1992) reported on a study in which 30 borderline patients were given twice-weekly outpatient psychotherapy for 12 months by closely supervised trainee therapists. A specific form of psychodynamic psychotherapy, based on the ideas of Kohut and Winnicott and focused on the development of the patient's self, produced substantial improvements. In this prospective "pre-post" design, the 12 months prior to beginning the 1 year of twice-weekly therapy were compared with the 12 months following the end of therapy. Among the improvements noted was a marked and statistically significant decrease in time spent away from work over the 12 months following therapy (1.37 months per year) compared with the 12 months before therapy (4.47 months per year). This group of borderline patients also demonstrated similarly significant improvement in a number of other outcome measures: 1) number of visits to medical professionals dropped to one-seventh of pretreatment rates, 2) number of self-harm episodes declined to one-fourth of pretreatment rates, 3) number of hospital admissions decreased by 59%, and 4) time spent as an inpatient dropped by half.

These impressive results were largely sustained at 5-year follow-up (Stevenson and Meares 1995). The only outcome measure that suggested loss of the gains achieved in the psychotherapy was the time the patient spent away from work, which again began to increase. The investigators noted that the recession in Australia coinciding with the study period may have influenced this finding.

The same investigators (Meares et al. 1999) subsequently reported on a comparison of their 30 BPD patients with a waiting-list control group consisting of the first 30 patients on the waiting list, all of whom had been waiting 12 months or more. These patients had their usual treatments during the waiting period, which included supportive therapy, crisis intervention, and cognitive therapy. The investigators then compared the results of the treated patients with those of the waiting-list control patients.

Of the 30 treated patients, 30% no longer met criteria for the diagnosis of BPD after 12 months of psychotherapy. The 30 patients who had been on the waiting list for 1 year or more showed no change in diagnosis. Definitive conclusions cannot be drawn from this study because randomization was not employed, but the results are suggestive of substantial gains from the dynamic therapy that was offered.

Promising results were also reported in the Halliwick Day Unit Study by Bateman and Fonagy (1999). These investigators compared 38 borderline patients in a psychoanalytically oriented partial hospital program with those in a control group. The partial hospital condition consisted of once-weekly individual psychoanalytic psychotherapy, three-times-per-week group psychoanalytic therapy, once-weekly expressive therapy informed by psychodrama techniques, a weekly community meeting, regular meetings with the case coordinator, and medication review by a resident psychiatrist. The control treatment consisted of regular psychiatric review an average of two times per month with a senior psychiatrist, inpatient admission as appropriate, outpatient and community follow-up, no psychotherapy, and medication similar to that received by the treatment group.

Bateman and Fonagy found a clear reduction in the proportion of treatment group patients who had attempted suicide in the previous 6 months. That proportion fell from 95% on admission to 5.3% at 18-month follow-up. The average length of hospitalization increased dramatically in the control group during the last 6 months of the study, while it remained stable in the treatment group, at around 4 days per 6 months. Self-reported state and trait anxiety both decreased substantially in the treatment group but remained unchanged in the control group. Depression scores (as measured by the Beck Depression Inventory) also decreased significantly in the treatment group, and there was a statistically significant decrease in severity of symptoms as measured by the Symptom Checklist-90—Revised (SCL-90-R) at 18 months.

The researchers concluded that whereas the improvement in psychiatric symptoms and the reduction in suicide attempts were seen after 6 months of treatment, the reduction in frequency of hospital admissions and length of inpatient stay became apparent only during the final 6 months of the study, indicating a need for longer-term treatment. They also noted that partial hospitalization with psychoanalytic therapy seems to be a promising and cheaper alternative to specialist-inpatient and general psychiatric treatment.

Taken together, these studies illustrate that although there is no "quick fix" for BPD, those patients who stay in dynamic therapy for a substantial period of time may experience significant improvement. Moreover, these studies also demonstrate that financial support for extended weekly psychotherapy may be cost-effective in the long run. Borderline patients, by their very nature, are treatment seeking, and if denied access to psychotherapy, they will incur increased costs by appearing in emergency rooms with overdoses that require intensive care or psychiatric hospitalization, by visiting other medical practitioners, and by running up so-called indirect costs from extensive work disability (Gabbard 1997). The Australian study (Stevenson and Meares 1999) found that borderline patients who were in psychotherapy consumed far fewer health care dollars. On the basis of the decrease in hospital treatment alone, the psychotherapy was a good investment. During the 12 months prior to treatment, hospital treatment alone cost $684,346 (Australian dollars), with a range of $0–$143,756 per patient. The cost of hospital admissions for the year after treatment was $41,424, with a range of $0–$12,333 per patient. The average decrease in cost per patient was $21,431 over 12 months. The average cost of therapy per patient was $13,000, representing a savings per patient of $8,431. Although cost savings were not calculated for the Halliwick Day Unit Study, one can speculate that comparable savings were also made in that setting.

Although Linehan and colleagues' (1991) study demonstrating the efficacy of dialectical behavior therapy for borderline patients was not a dynamic psychotherapy study, it is of interest that similar conclusions could be drawn from that approach. After receiving once-weekly individual and once-weekly group therapy for 1 year, the patients in this study were found to have reduced their psychiatric hospital days to an average of 8.46 per year, whereas those in the control group who received "treatment as usual" had an average of 38.86 hospital days per year. Even when the cost of the group and individual therapy sessions were included, the researchers calculated that dialectical behavior therapy saved $10,000 per patient per year (Heard 1994).

This brief survey of empirical research on the extended dynamic psychotherapy of borderline patients suggests that the treatment is well worthwhile, both from the standpoint of the substantial improvements shown from the therapy and from the standpoint of cost-effectiveness. Perhaps the worst situation for borderline patients in psychotherapy is the frequent managed care arrangement in which patients do not know from week to week whether their psychotherapy will be extended. For patients who are extremely concerned about abandonment, the tenuousness of this arrangement infuses them with an overwhelming separation anxiety based on the fear that they may be cut off from their therapist at any moment.

Expressive Versus Supportive Approaches

Although individual psychodynamic therapy for patients with BPD may be extremely useful, virtually all clinicians would agree that it is extraordinarily challenging and emotionally taxing for the therapist. Clinicians who wish to engage in intensive psychotherapy with borderline patients should either be experienced or be supervised by expert colleagues. Even those with considerable experience should consult regularly with a respected and knowledgeable therapist to ensure that countertransference blind spots have not given rise to unexpected difficulties.

Although clinicians often disagree about whether psychotherapy should be weighted predominantly toward the expressive or the supportive end of the expressive-supportive continuum, they concur that these patients are likely to quit psychotherapy, to act out self-destructively, to make inordinate demands for special treatment from their therapists, to provoke therapists into ill-advised professional boundary crossing, and to torment therapists with unrelenting phone calls at all hours of the day and night. A major problem in the psychotherapy of borderline individuals is the tenuous nature of the therapeutic alliance (Adler 1979; Gabbard et al. 1988; Gorney 1979; Horwitz et al. 1996; Kernberg 1976; Masterson 1976; Modell 1976; Zetzel 1971). These patients have great difficulty viewing their therapist as a helpful figure who is working collaboratively with them toward mutually perceived goals.

In the McLean Borderline Psychotherapy Engagement Project (A. F. Frank 1992), 60% of the first 60 patients studied discontinued their therapy within 6 months. Evaluations of the reasons for this substantial dropout rate suggested that as many as 77% had difficulties in developing an alliance with their therapists. After 6 months of treatment, solid therapeutic alliances were still rather uncommon, even among those patients who continued in therapy.

Much of the controversy in the literature regarding the relative value of expressive versus supportive interventions revolves around which approach is more likely to foster the development and maintenance of the therapeutic alliance. Without a rudimentary therapeutic alliance, the therapist may not have a patient. The borderline patient may rapidly develop an intense negative transference, which mobilizes primitive character defenses that interfere with the establishment of an alliance (Kernberg 1976). Some clinicians (Boyer 1977; Kernberg 1975) believe that these transference distortions should be addressed early through transference interpretations. Such interpretations pave the way for the patient to view the therapist more accurately and allow the therapeutic alliance to develop with fewer psychological obstacles. Interpretation of primitive defensive operations in the here and now of the transference relationship serves to help patients integrate their "good" and "bad" views of the therapist into a more realistic "whole object" perception.

Masterson (1976) and Modell (1976) proposed quite a different technical approach. They suggested that interpretation must be delayed until the patient has developed sufficient trust in the therapist's intentions and reliability. Modell emphasized that a "holding" environment must be established as a prerequisite to interpretive interventions. This point of view is in keeping with Adler's conceptualization of the primary goal of psychotherapy as the establishment of a holding-soothing introject to sustain the patient in times of separation and aloneness. Adler (1979) saw the therapeutic alliance as something of a "myth" in the psychotherapy of borderline patients. These patients are unable to experience psychotherapy as a working collaboration, at least in the early phases. Because borderline patients are initially incapable of appreciating the real qualities of their therapists, they are maintained in psychotherapy by the soothing, supportive experience of a stable selfobject transference. As patients increasingly internalize the relationship, Adler believed, they become capable of allying themselves with the therapist in the service of pursuing common therapeutic goals. Adler viewed as a major therapeutic accomplishment the patient's perception of the therapist as a real and separate person who is invested in helping the patient. Zetzel (1971) was perhaps the strongest advocate of a supportive approach. She believed that interpretive psychotherapy is too disruptive of the therapeutic alliance and that low-frequency supportive psychotherapy (once a week or less) is the only effective way to maintain an alliance with borderline patients.

This controversy over the relative merits of expressive and supportive interventions is reflected in the contradictory findings of the Menninger Foundation Psychotherapy Research Project. The project's quantitative study (Kernberg et al. 1972) revealed that borderline patients treated by skilled therapists who focused intently on the transference showed a significantly better outcome than did those treated by skilled therapists who focused less on the transference. In contrast, the prediction study of the project (Horwitz 1974), using both quantitative and qualitative assessments of the treatment process, suggested that a series of patients, some of whom were borderline and were treated by predominantly supportive methods, showed greater gains in supportive treatment than anticipated. Finally, as reported in Chapter 4, Wallerstein's (1986) examination of the data from this project suggested that all treatments were characterized by a mixture of expressive and supportive interventions. These apparently contradictory findings with regard to transference focus remain unresolved, in part because the original design of the study had several shortcomings relevant to this issue: 1) the specific diagnostic category of BPD was not used; 2) a detailed process study was not undertaken, so that essential treatment developments could only be roughly approximated at the termination of treatment; and 3) the therapeutic alliance was not one of the project's variables. Retrospectively, however, the prediction study found the therapeutic alliance useful in conceptualizing results (Horwitz 1974).

Much of the current controversy surrounding the psychotherapy of borderline patients can be understood as another unfortunate example of the "either/or" approach to the application of theory to clinical practice, discussed at some length in Chapter 1. Both approaches are useful for *some* patients at *some* points in the treatment (Gabbard et al. 1994; Horwitz et al. 1996). We are dealing with a spectrum of highly heterogeneous patients who require individually tailored psychotherapeutic approaches (Meissner 1988). To a large extent, the same indications for expressive or supportive emphasis (see Table 4–1 in Chapter 4) that guide the clinician's work with other diagnostic entities apply to psychotherapy with borderline patients. Stone's (1987) follow-up study of borderline patients who were sufficiently disturbed to require extended hospitalization revealed that only about one-third of those patients who originally appeared amenable to expressive psychotherapy were truly suited for that approach. However, large aggregate studies of this nature, while useful, do not address the nuances of the therapeutic process at a more microcosmic level.

Because of these concerns, the Menninger Clinic Treatment Interventions Project studied the detailed process of representative sessions from three cases of long-term dynamic therapy of borderline patients at The Menninger Clinic (Gabbard et al. 1988, 1994; Horwitz et al. 1996). All sessions of the three psychotherapy processes were audiotaped, and two sets of investigators worked from typed transcripts of randomly selected psychotherapy hours. A team of three clinician-researchers rated the interventions on the basis of their degree of expressiveness or supportiveness. As described in Chapter 4, from the expressive end of the continuum to the supportive end, the interventions were rated as follows: interpretation, confrontation, clarification, encouragement to elaborate, empathic validation, advice and praise, and affirmation. Each of these seven interventions was also classified as having a focus on either transference or extratransference issues. A separate team of three clinical judges assessed the patient's collaboration with the therapist as a measure of the therapeutic alliance. The judges were primarily interested in detecting upward or downward shifts in the patient's collaboration, as measured by the patient's bringing in significant content or making productive use of the therapist's contributions. We were particularly interested in determining whether the shifts could be related to the therapist's interventions.

One of the conclusions we reached was that transference interpretations are a "high-risk, high-gain" intervention in the dynamic psychotherapy of borderline patients. They tend to have greater impact—both positive and negative—than other interventions made with such patients. Whereas in some cases they resulted in substantial improvement in the patient's ability to collaborate with the therapist, in others they led to marked deterioration in that collaboration.

In our efforts to determine which transference interpretations increased collaboration and which resulted in deterioration in the therapeutic alliance, we found several key factors at work. First, paving the way for transference interpretation with affirmative appreciation of the patient's internal experience may be of crucial importance. Surgeons need anesthesia before they can operate. The psychotherapist needs to create a holding environment through empathic validation of the patient's experience before offering an interpretation of unconscious dynamics. Expressive and supportive approaches are often artificially polarized, when in actuality the two work synergistically in most psychotherapeutic situations.

In a study of borderline patients who discontinued psychotherapy prematurely, Gunderson et al. (1989) found that more than half of the dropouts departed in anger following early confrontation by the therapist. These findings led Gunderson and his colleagues to advocate more supportive techniques for alliance-building early in therapy. They also stressed the importance of recognizing the reality of early trauma in the form of child abuse in many borderline patients (Gunderson and Chu 1993; Gunderson and Sabo 1993). They observed that therapists may be able to forge a stronger therapeutic alliance by validating and acknowledging the effects of early trauma on the patient's capacity to form trusting relationships as an adult.

The tendency to force transference interpretations on unprepared patients who are oriented toward externalization and action rather than reflection may result from the inherent bias of many analysts and dynamic therapists toward expressive rather than supportive strategies. Gunderson (1992) candidly reflected on his own tendency to push patients to engage in transference work while insufficiently acknowledging that their functioning outside the therapy has improved dramatically. He recognized that he occasionally made the error of becoming preoccupied with the patient's failure to collaborate in self-examination rather than actively supporting the patient's substantial improvement in functioning.

Although the therapeutic approach varies depending on the needs of the patient, several principles of technique apply rather broadly to most patients with the borderline diagnosis.

Maintain flexibility.   A flexible therapeutic stance is necessary for the optimal treatment of patients with BPD. As a general rule, higher-level borderline patients with greater ego strengths and greater psychological mindedness will be more able to use expressively oriented psychotherapy than those closer to the psychotic border, who will need a supportive emphasis. Most will require a flexible stance on the part of the therapist, with shifts between interpretive and noninterpretive interventions geared to the state of the patient's relatedness to the therapist at a given moment. In this regard, the conceptual frameworks of *both* Kernberg *and* Adler can be useful. Adler and Rhine (1988) used case material to demonstrate how containment of projections from the patient may constitute a selfobject function for the therapist, thus integrating Kernberg's object relations concept of projective identification with Adler's self psychological concept of selfobjects. Finally, no single theory is likely to insulate the therapist from the tumultuous emotional affects experienced by both partners of the dyad. Most therapists find themselves using a trial-and-error approach until they can clearly determine which interventions are most effective with a given patient.

Because of well-founded concerns about the potential to transgress boundaries with borderline patients (Gabbard and Wilkinson 1994; Gutheil 1989), the beginning therapist may take an unyielding position that is experienced by the patient as remote and cold. The patient may then quit the therapy because of the therapist's apparent lack of responsiveness. The therapist needs to strive for a disciplined spontaneity in which professional boundaries and focus are maintained—but in the context of an acknowledged human interaction involving two people struggling to get to know one another. It is useful to think of the character dimension of the borderline patient as involving an ongoing attempt to actualize certain patterns of internal object relations in a current relationship (Gabbard 1998; Sandler 1981). Through his or her behavior, the patient subtly attempts to impose a certain way of responding and experiencing on others. Therapists need to allow themselves sufficient flexibility to respond spontaneously to the form of object relatedness that is being thrust upon them. In other words, the therapist joins in a "dance" based on specific music within the patient that provides a wealth of information about the patient's characteristic difficulties in human relationships outside the transference-countertransference situation. This response must be attenuated and partial, of course, and the therapist must attempt to maintain a reflective stance regarding the "dance."

Establish conditions that make psychotherapy viable.   Because of the chaotic nature of the borderline patient's life, stability must be imposed from external sources early in the process. In the pretherapy consultations and throughout the course of the therapy, the psychotherapist must establish and reestablish what therapy involves and how it differs from other relationships. Among the topics that should be covered are clear expectations about fee payment, consistent appointment times, the need to end sessions on time even though the patient may wish to stay longer, and an explicit policy about the consequences of missed appointments. In addition, with a suicidal borderline patient, the therapist may wish to make it clear that in a situation of acute suicide risk, it is impossible for the therapist to prevent the patient from acting on his or her impulses, and hospitalization may be needed. In a substance-abusing patient, the therapist may need to insist that the patient attend Narcotics Anonymous or Alcoholics Anonymous as a condition of the treatment. When medication is obviously indicated, the therapist may need to make clear that the patient's a willingness to try medication is an essential component of the overall treatment plan. Besides establishing the conditions that will make psychotherapy viable, the therapist is also communicating his or her own limits to the patient. This communication often is at odds with the patient's expectations that the therapist will be an omnipotent rescuer. Hence, this dialogue leads directly into a discussion of what therapy is and what it is not.

In the pretherapy phase of consultations, Kernberg advocated establishing a "contract" with the patient (Kernberg et al. 1989). As part of setting up this contract, the therapist makes clear that it is not within the psychotherapist's role to get involved in the actions of the patient's life outside of the sessions. Hence, the therapist does not expect to receive phone calls between sessions and makes it clear that his or her availability is quite limited. However, this approach may interfere with the development of a stable attachment to the therapist, especially if the conditions of the "contract" seem impossible for the patient. As Gunderson (1996) pointed out, the patient may have recurrent reactions of panic because of poorly developed evocative memory and may need to call the therapist periodically to develop a stable representation that can be internalized. Gunderson suggested that the therapist should discuss between-session availability only *after* the patient initiates an inquiry about it. He suggested, and I concur, that patients be told that the therapist wishes to be contacted in an emergency. This position avoids an adversarial beginning to the process and often makes the patient feel understood and "held" in the Winnicottian sense. If phone calls do occur between sessions, Gunderson recommended that the calls be the focus of exploration in the therapeutic work. As the therapist comes to recognize the patient's fear of aloneness and its developmental meaning, the patient's development of holding-soothing introjects—as described by Adler—may be facilitated. If the phone calls become excessive, clear limits can be imposed while also exploring the meaning and significance of the between-session contacts.

Allow transformation into the bad object.   One of the most difficult challenges in the psychotherapy of borderline patients is to tolerate and contain the patient's intense anger, aggression, and hate. Therapists often feel falsely accused, and an inner voice wants to ask the patient, "How can you possibly accuse me of being worthless when I'm trying so hard to help you?" It is helpful to remember that these patients have internalized a hated and possibly abusive introject that they are desperately trying to externalize through projective identification in the transference-countertransference dimensions of the dyad. Borderline patients are searching for a "bad-enough object" (Rosen 1993). In a paradoxical way, patients find it predictable, familiar, and even soothing to re-create a sadomasochistic internal object relationship from childhood with the therapist. When the therapist resists this transformation, patients may have to escalate their provocativeness and work even harder to transform the therapist (Fonagy 1998).

Therapists who defend against the growing aggression within them may strive to be more and more saintly in response to patients' verbal attacks. They may also make transference interpretations that attempt to force the patient to take back his or her hostility rather than projecting it into the therapist. Alternatively, the therapist may subtly withdraw from an emotional investment in the patient, consciously or unconsciously hoping that the patient will quit therapy and find someone else to torment. Another, more disconcerting alternative is that the therapist may begin to make hostile or sarcastic comments or even explode in anger at the patient. Allowing the transformation into the bad object does not mean that the therapist loses any sense of professional decorum. Rather, it requires that the therapist function as a container who accepts the projections and attempts to understand them and hold them for the patient until the patient is once again able to own these projected aspects for him- or herself, much as was described in Chapter 14 in dealing with paranoid patients. As we have noted elsewhere (Gabbard and Wilkinson 1994), "the optimal state of mind for therapists is when they can allow themselves to be 'sucked in' to the patient's world while retaining the ability to observe it happening in front of their eyes. In such a state, therapists are truly thinking their own thoughts, even though they are under the patient's influence to some extent" (p. 82).

Many instances of mismanagement of suicide threats relate to a countertransference wish to avoid being the bad object. Borderline patients often suggest to the therapist that they will be driven to suicide because of the therapist's insufficiencies (Maltsberger 1999). These accusations fuel therapists' doubts and activate their own abandonment anxiety, so therapists in this situation may attempt to demonstrate their caring through heroic measures to try to save the patient. The result may be that the patient exercises an omnipotent control over the therapist—what Maltsberger (1999) has called *coercive bondage*. In this scenario, the therapist takes full responsibility for the patient's survival instead of allowing the patient to accept most of the responsibility for his or her own living or dying, which is imperative if the patient is to ultimately get better.

Promote reflective function.   An overall thrust in the psychotherapy of patients with BPD is to help them recover reflective function so that they can begin to
think about the internal world of themselves and others. Interpreting the meaning
of enactments may be premature for patients who are unable to mentalize. It may
be much more useful to help such patients elaborate on the emotional state that
may have triggered the enactment (Fonagy 1998). For example, a patient came to
therapy saying that she had binged on 10 candy bars the previous evening. The
therapist asked her to elaborate on what had triggered the binge. Although she initially said that she didn't know, as the therapist continued to gently press for possible precipitating factors and emotional states, the patient eventually recalled that a
man she had met had called her to ask her out on a date. She then said that if she
had gone out to dinner with him, he would have undoubtedly regarded her as "fat
pig" and never asked her out again. So she hung up the phone and then went to the
store to buy candy bars. Through this encouragement to understand the emotional
state that precipitated the enactment, the therapist also helped to establish a connection between feelings and actions. In other words, the bingeing did not come
out of the blue. Rather, it emerged from feelings of self-loathing and anxiety related to the invitation to dinner from the man she had met.

Another way to promote mentalization is to observe the patient's mo-
ment-to-moment changes in feelings so that the patient can eventually internalize
the therapist's observations of his or her internal state. In addition, it is useful to
encourage the patient's fantasy about the therapist's internal state (i.e., in the
broadest sense, the therapist's countertransference). Hence, Gunderson (1996)
suggested that when called in the middle of the night, the therapist may explore the
patient's fantasy in the next session by asking, "How did you think I would feel
about your call?"

Another technique to encourage more reflectiveness is to help the patient think
about the consequences of self-destructive behaviors (Waldinger 1987). Many of
the self-destructive behaviors of borderline patients are enacted in the urgency of
the moment without any consideration of the eventual consequences of these acts.
Through repeated questioning about the potential adverse consequences of such
behaviors, the therapist may help them become less gratifying to the patient. For
example, a male homosexual patient (discussed in Chapter 18) told his therapist
that he felt a strong need for homosexual encounters because having semen injected into his rectum by a virile, masculine male made him feel that he would
become more masculine. His therapist pointed out that despite this fantasy, the
real consequence was that he would risk contracting HIV.

Set limits when necessary.   Many borderline patients experience the usual
professional boundaries as cruel and punitive deprivation by the therapist. They

may demand more concrete demonstrations of caring, such as hugs, extended sessions, decreases in the fee, and round-the-clock availability (Gabbard and Wilkinson 1994). Some therapists who experience guilt feelings about the setting of limits may begin to cross professional boundaries with borderline patients in the name of flexibility or suicide prevention (Gutheil 1989). One male therapist, for example, began seeing a female patient twice a week for psychotherapy, but within a year was seeing the patient seven times a week. On Sundays, he would make a special trip to his office just to see this patient. When a consultant questioned this behavior, the therapist defended it as necessary to prevent the patient from committing suicide. He also acknowledged that he allowed the patient to sit on his lap during their sessions, justifying this behavior as a way to provide the patient with the mothering that she had not received as a child. Many cases of therapist-patient sex involve borderline patients (Gabbard 1989c). One female patient insisted that nothing short of an orgasm induced by her male therapist would result in her improvement. She threatened to kill herself if her therapist would not comply. After two different therapists indulged her demands, she eventually killed herself anyway—their misguided expressions of "caring" failed either to address her basic problems or to relieve her emotional pain (Eyman and Gabbard 1991). The dynamics of erotic and erotized transference are discussed more fully in Chapter 18, but the tragic end of this particular patient underscores the futility of trying to gratify the patient's demands. The more gratification that borderline patients receive, the more insatiable they become.

On the other hand, the therapist cannot maintain emotional distance and complete unresponsiveness to emotional pleas from the patient. A helpful guideline is the distinction drawn by Casement (1985) between "libidinal demands" and "growth needs." The former cannot be gratified without gravely jeopardizing the treatment and committing serious ethical compromises. The latter cannot be frustrated without preventing growth. While consistency is part of creating a holding environment for the patient, empathic response to the changing needs of the patient is also a critical factor in maintaining the therapeutic alliance.

Much of the difficulty is the therapist's feeling of being cruel and sadistic when enforcing reasonable limits on the patient's enactments. Paradoxically, however, many patients who demand greater freedom get worse when it is granted to them. In a spin-off study of the Menninger Foundation Psychotherapy Research Project, Colson et al. (1985) examined the cases with negative outcomes. One common denominator was the therapist's failure to set limits on acting-out behaviors. Instead, the therapist would simply continue to interpret the unconscious motivations for the acting-out while the patient's condition deteriorated.

In a succinct summary of the group of behaviors that require limit setting, Waldinger (1987) identified those that threaten the safety of the therapist or the patient, and those that jeopardize the psychotherapy itself. Suicide is an ever-present risk with borderline patients, and therapists must be ready to hospitalize their patients when these impulses become overwhelming. Therapists often find themselves in the untenable position of heroically attempting to treat lethal patients by having continuous contact with them. One therapist ended up talking on the phone to a borderline patient for an hour every night to prevent her from killing herself.

Establish and maintain the therapeutic alliance. As noted earlier in this chapter, the therapeutic alliance is an elusive construct in the psychotherapy of borderline patients. Because of the patient's chaotic internal object relations, the therapist is likely to be transformed into either an adversary or an idealized rescuer throughout the course of the treatment. It is useful for the therapist to bring the patient back to the commonly held goals of the psychotherapy when the process becomes particularly difficult. A recurrent message to the patient must be that therapy is not coercive. It is a process chosen by the patient in order to work on specific goals that create suffering. Patients frequently lose track of those goals, and revisiting them helps remind patients that the therapist is an ally who is working collaboratively with them.

Manage splitting between psychotherapy and pharmacotherapy. As emphasized in Chapter 5, pharmacotherapy requires the same psychodynamic understanding as psychotherapy. If the same psychiatrist is providing both the pharmacotherapy and the psychotherapy for a borderline patient, that clinician must avoid splitting off the medication as an administrative matter that requires no exploration. The same psychodynamic themes—transference, countertransference, and resistance—that apply to psychotherapy also apply to the prescribing. In one survey of dynamic therapists who were highly experienced in the treatment of borderline patients (Waldinger and Frank 1989), the respondents indicated that they were more likely to prescribe when they were feeling pessimistic about a particular patient's ability to work psychotherapeutically. They also reported that nearly half of their patients misused prescribed medication. This abuse was intimately connected with transference themes, and the investigators suggested that therapists should actively explore the patient's fantasy about the medication to prevent such misuse. There may be an idealizing transference to the medication as a panacea that will solve all the patient's problems. Medication may also be perceived as a means by which the therapist hopes to take control of the patient's life. Therapists who prescribe medications for their patients must help them understand that the goals are modest—namely, to modify affective, impulsive, or cognitive symptoms in such a way as to facilitate the psychotherapy process.

If the pharmacotherapy and the psychotherapy are being provided by two different clinicians, the danger of splitting off the medication from the therapy is even greater. There should be an understanding that the two treaters are part of the same team and will need to discuss the treatment openly. A major impediment to regular communication between therapist and prescriber is the fact that the time spent on such discussions is rarely reimbursed. Nevertheless, the absence of communication provides a fertile ground for splitting. The patient may idealize the pharmacotherapist as a humane and responsive doctor who attempts to alleviate discomfort and distress—in contrast to the psychotherapist, who is continually prodding the patient to reflect on and understand painful emotional material. Conversely, the prescribing doctor may be seen as rushing the patient out of the office in 15 minutes, whereas the psychotherapist takes time to listen and understand. In the absence of regular discussions about the split transference between the two providers, the treatment can become quite chaotic.

From both a clinical and a risk management perspective, the two treaters need to decide whether their relationship is consultative, supervisory, or collaborative (Meyer and Simon 1999a). In the consultative relationship, one clinician may offer an opinion to another without assuming any responsibility for the patient's ongoing care. In a supervisory model, one clinician is responsible for overseeing and directing all aspects of the patient's treatment. Most such relationships, however, are collaborative—that is, both the pharmacotherapist and the psychotherapist share responsibility and are professionally interdependent. In such situations, the pharmacotherapist and the psychotherapist, as well as any other treatment team members, must have a clear agreement about which clinician is assuming the primary overall responsibility for the patient's safety and treatment (Gabbard 2000). This clinician is designated as the final authority on decisions about hospitalization, the introduction or discontinuation of a particular treatment modality, and the monitoring of safety. Ordinarily, this individual should be a psychiatrist, because a considerable range of expertise and knowledge is necessary for this form of responsibility.

Regardless of which mental health professional is designated as the final authority on the treatment team, several matters should be discussed explicitly by the treaters (Meyer and Simon 1999b). The patient should provide consent for the psychotherapist and pharmacotherapist to discuss the treatment as needed. Each clinician should also agree to inform the other about any significant changes being contemplated in the treatment. Both treaters should agree about who should take emergency calls about possible hospitalization during evenings or weekends, who is responsible for coverage during vacations, and who should be communicating with outside parties. In the interest of managing potential splitting, the pharmacotherapist and the psychotherapist should have an understanding that when the patient begins to disparage one of the treaters, the clinician who receives that information should contact the other treater to discuss what is going on rather than to take the information at face value and act on it. Finally, the pharmacotherapist and the psychotherapist should have an understanding that either can choose to terminate participation in the treatment if either one feels that the collaboration is not working. Sufficient notice is needed in these cases so that a replacement for the departing clinician can be found. Before such a drastic measure is taken, however, treaters may wish to meet with a consultant to see if there is a way their differences can be worked out (see Chapter 6).

Help the patient re-own aspects of the self that are disavowed and/or projected elsewhere. Because splitting and projective identification are primary defense mechanisms of patients with BPD, an experience of being incomplete or fragmented is a core phenomenon in borderline psychopathology. Patients may disown behavior that occurred a month ago as though someone else were responsible for that behavior. This lack of self-continuity also emerges in the form of dramatic changes from week to week in how these patients present themselves to the therapist. The therapist's task is to connect these fragmented aspects of the patient's self and interpret the underlying anxieties connected with re-owning and integrating the disparate self-representations into a coherent whole. Similarly, the patient's internal self- and object representations are projected onto the therapist or other individuals. Over time, therapists attempt to help borderline patients understand that they are unconsciously placing aspects of themselves in others as a way of attempting to control those distressing parts of themselves. Much of this effort involves interpretation of patients' fear that if they integrate the good and the bad aspects of themselves and others, the intense hatred they harbor will destroy any remnants of love. Therapists must help borderline patients recognize that hate is a ubiquitous emotion that must be integrated and tempered with love so that aggression is harnessed in more constructive directions. As I have noted elsewhere, "We help patients learn to live within their own skin, squarely within the dialectic created by love and hate and by life and destructiveness" (Gabbard 1996, p. 231).

Monitor countertransference feelings. Implicit in this entire discussion of psychotherapy has been the centrality of attending to the countertransference. Containing the projected parts of the patient and reflecting on the nature of these projections will help the therapist understand the patient's internal world (Gabbard and Wilkinson 1994). Moreover, ongoing attention to one's own feelings prevents countertransference acting-out. Each therapist has personal limits regarding how much hatred or anger is tolerable. If the therapist closely monitors countertransference feelings, this limit can be handled constructively rather than destructively. For example, a therapist might use countertransference feelings therapeutically by saying to the patient, "I'm getting the feeling that you are trying to make me angry at you instead of letting me help you. Let's see if we can understand what's happening here." Alternatively, the therapist may have to set limits on the patient's verbal barrages based on countertransference reactions, as follows: "I really don't feel I can work with you effectively if you continue to shout at me. I think it's important for you to work on controlling your anger so you can express it to me without screaming." Therapists must be real and genuine with borderline patients, or they will only increase the patient's envy of them as saintly figures that are basically nonhuman (Searles 1986).

The following clinical example of a psychotherapy session with Ms. CC, a 22-year-old borderline patient, illustrates some of the principles of technique just described:

> Ms. CC arrives at her session after having missed the previous one. She begins the session by engaging the therapist in banter about a book on his bookshelf.
>
> Ms. CC: Hey, you got a new book.
> Therapist: No, that book's always been there.
> Ms. CC: No, it hasn't. I would have noticed it before.
> Therapist: Oh, I'm quite sure it has been there. But I'd really like to change the subject and find out more about why you didn't show up last time.
> *(The therapist engages in some spontaneous preliminary banter but eventually returns to the serious matter of the patient's absence from the last session.)*
> Ms. CC: I just didn't feel like coming to therapy. I didn't want to have to deal with the feelings that I was having in here.
> Therapist: Did you get my call on your machine?
> *(The therapist, worrying about the patient's suicidality, had called the patient at home when she did not show up for the session.)*
> Ms. CC: Yes. I was there when you left your message on the machine.
> Therapist: Why didn't you pick up the phone?
> Ms. CC: Oh, I didn't pick up any of my calls. I didn't want to talk to anyone.
> Therapist: You remember that I asked you to return my call?
> Ms. CC: I know, but I was too embarrassed to call you back.
> Therapist: What did you imagine about how I might react to that?
> *(The therapist encourages reflective function by inviting the patient to explore her fantasies of his countertransference.)*
> Ms. CC: I didn't really think much about that.
> *(The patient demonstrates lack of reflective function on internal states in self or others.)*
> Therapist: Were you concerned that I might be worried about your hurting yourself?

Ms. CC: Yes, I guess I did worry about that. I'm sorry. I won't do it again.

Therapist: I'd like to get beyond just being sorry about it and see if we can understand what's going on in your mind at those moments, because it really affects our ability to work together when you don't come to the therapy.

(The therapist makes it clear that one of the conditions necessary to make the therapy viable is for the patient to attend the sessions regularly.)

Ms. CC: I was just into myself at the time. I was kind of in a funk.

Therapist: About what?

Ms. CC: I don't know.

Therapist: Well, let's don't accept "I don't know." Let's try to see what reasons there might be.

(The patient does not want to reflect on her internal state, but the therapist encourages further elaboration beyond the knee-jerk dismissal.)

Ms. CC: Well, I just feel like everybody's going to forget about me. Nobody's going to care what I do or what my needs are.

Therapist: But you've been telling me that you can't stand the way your parents intrude into your life and hover over you all the time.

Ms. CC: I know, but that's because I'm always screwing up.

Therapist: Do you imagine that if you stop screwing up and become responsible, then no one will pay any attention to you?

(The therapist poses a possible interpretation or explanation of the patient's behavior as a question for the patient to entertain and reflect upon rather than a forceful declaration of fact.)

Ms. CC: I just think everyone will forget about me.

Therapist: I have an idea about that. I wonder if you forget about people when you're not around them, so you worry that others will do the same about you.

(The therapist presents an interpretive understanding of her concern based on his awareness of her poor object constancy or evocative memory.)

Ms. CC: I can't keep people in my mind. I can't picture your face when I'm not with you. I can't picture either of my parents' face or my brother's face. It's just like they're not there. I've never been able to do that.

Therapist: Then I can imagine that it's hard for you to think about how people are reacting to you when you're away from them. Just like last Thursday when you missed our session. At that time it was probably difficult for you to imagine me sitting here wondering where you were and why you hadn't called.

(The therapist empathically communicates his understanding of the patient's difficulties with mentalization and evocative memory.)

Ms. CC: I just didn't think about it. Part of it was I just get tired of being in treatment. There's something else I haven't told you. I stopped my Prozac.

Therapist: When?

Ms. CC: About a week ago.

Therapist: Why didn't you discuss this with me so we could talk about the pros and cons of doing that?

(The therapist's countertransference frustration emerges as he begins to identify with the policing parent who wants to coerce the patient into doing whatever he says.)

Ms. CC: I just knew you'd say no.

Therapist: I'm still not clear though on why you stopped it.

Ms. CC: I just don't want to be a patient. I like therapy okay, but I don't want to take medication.

Therapist: I guess the thing that bothers me the most about this is that you didn't talk with me about what you were thinking of doing. It's similar to not showing up Thursday, not calling me, not returning my calls when I called you. It's like there's part of you that sees me as an adversary and doesn't want to collaborate with me on major decisions, like stopping your Prozac or coming to therapy.

Ms. CC: It's like everybody is scrutinizing me and watching my every move. Everyone tries to catch me doing something wrong.

Therapist: Well, if you experience me in that way, I can see why you would stay away from therapy.

(The therapist explores the emerging negative transference and the adversarial role in which he has been cast as a way of promoting a therapeutic alliance and returning to the original goals of the therapy.)

I think it's important for us to keep in mind that you're here because you want to get over the suicidality and lead a more productive life.

Hospital and Partial Hospital Treatment

The principles of psychoanalytically informed hospital and partial hospital treatment are outlined in Chapter 6. In addition, the management of splitting, an essential ingredient in work with borderline patients, is also discussed in that chapter. Readers are therefore referred back to Chapter 6 for the basic principles of the milieu treatment of borderline patients. Several other points specific to patients with borderline personality will be covered here.

In the hospital, borderline patients can disrupt units as their internal chaos is externalized into the milieu. Some become "special" patients who create intense countertransference problems related to splitting and projective identification (Burnham 1966; Gabbard 1986; Main 1957). Others are extraordinarily hateful and venomously attack all staff members who attempt to help them (Gabbard 1989b), creating a sense of futility in the staff. Still others may be passively oppositional and refuse to participate in any aspect of the treatment plan (Gabbard 1989a). Although these patients may seem to be treatment-refractory, some may ultimately be treatable through careful attention to the individual dynamics of the patient and the staff countertransference.

A great deal of lore exists on the hospital treatment of borderline patients, much of it based on little or no solid data. Some clinicians think that hospitalization should not be used for borderline patients because it will promote regression and dependency. No hard data support this premise, but at least one controlled study has shown that hospital treatment can be quite beneficial for patients with severe personality disorders. In the United Kingdom, Dolan et al. (1997) examined a group of 137 consecutive patients with severe personality disorder on referral and at 1-year posttreatment at Henderson Hospital. Seventy of those referred were admitted, and 67 were not. The researchers noted a significantly greater reduction of Borderline Syndrome Index (BSI) scores in the admitted group compared with those who were not admitted. Also, the changes in BSI scores were significantly positively correlated with the length of the hospital treatment.

The patient who requires brief hospitalization in the course of psychotherapy is likely to be in a crisis involving a psychotic regression, self-destructive behavior, or suicidal impulses. There may be varying degrees of turmoil in the psychotherapy process as well. Since the goal of short-term hospitalization is rapid restoration of the patient's defenses and adaptive functioning, the inpatient staff must convey a counterregressive expectation. Treaters in the milieu must communicate to such patients that they can control impulses despite their disclaimers. Although external controls, such as restraints and antipsychotic medication, may be necessary at times, the emphasis is on helping these patients take responsibility for self-control. The weakened ego of the patient can be supplemented with a firm, consistent structure involving a regular schedule, clear consequences for impulsive acting-out, and a predictable pattern of group and individual meetings with staff members and other patients.

The usual tendency of the newly admitted borderline patient is to expect, on demand, lengthy individual sessions with members of the nursing staff. When nurses are actually "roped into" attempting to gratify these demands, the patient typically deteriorates in direct proportion to the amount of time spent in these one-to-one "therapy" sessions. Borderline patients do much better when the nursing staff can build into the regular structure brief 5- to 10-minute meetings.

Staff members in the milieu and the unit structure itself function as auxiliary egos for borderline patients. Rather than attempting exploratory or interpretive work, the unit staff can help patients identify precipitants of their crises, delay impulse discharge by seeking alternatives, anticipate consequences of their actions, and clarify their internal object relations (as described in Chapter 6). Another function of brief hospitalization is that it affords a more accurate view of the patient's internal world. Finally, the milieu staff can often assist the psychotherapist in understanding the nature of a crisis or impasse that occurs in the patient's psychotherapy. In addition to addressing any splitting processes (as described in Chapter 6), the milieu staff can help the therapist by validating the therapist's competence and worth as a clinician (Adler 1984). From the self psychological perspective of Adler, the unit nurses and other personnel can perform selfobject functions for both the patient and the therapist (Adler 1987).

There must also be a unit norm that discourages keeping secrets. Anything the patient says to one staff member must be shared with other staff members in meetings. The staff of the unit must be able to repeatedly say "no" to the patient in a matter-of-fact, caring way that conveys no malice. Otherwise, the patient may not be able to integrate the fact that "good" caring figures are the same persons who implement restrictive measures (i.e., "bad" interventions). This integration of internal self- and object representations is another primary goal of extended inpatient treatment.

Limits applied to a patient must always be based on an empathic understanding of the patient's need for limits rather than on any sadistic attempt at control, which is how the patient usually views such restrictions.

Suicidal and self-mutilative behavior is often a significant problem because borderline patients attempt to control the entire treatment staff just as they have controlled their family and loved ones with such behavior. The staff members must stress that each patient is ultimately responsible for controlling such behavior and that realistically no one can prevent a patient from committing suicide. Borderline patients often make superficial cuts on themselves with paperclips, beverage cans, light bulbs, and other objects that are generally available even in hospitals. While the actual damage from such superficial scratching may be minimal, the unit staff should carefully investigate the origins of the mutilation. Is it connected with depersonalization episodes or dissociation? Is there a history of childhood sexual abuse? Does the patient warrant a trial of fluoxetine? Is the behavior primarily manipulative in an effort to gain attention from the staff?

The chronically suicidal borderline patient may engender intense countertransference feelings in staff members, who perceive the attempts and gestures as manipulative and therefore begin to react to the patient's suicidal threats with a lack of concern. The inpatient staff must keep in mind that suicide attempters are 140 times more likely to commit suicide than nonattempters (Tuckman and Youngman 1963), and that roughly 10%–20% of all suicide attempters eventually kill themselves (Dorpat and Ripley 1967).

Family Therapy

Therapeutic modification of the borderline patient's internal object world generally requires an intensive individual psychotherapy process. Work with the family, however, is often an essential adjunct to the overall treatment plan. The use of formal family therapy is far less common than that of one or more family interventions in the course of treatment (Brown 1987). Inpatient treatment, for example, provides clinicians with the opportunity to meet with the patient's family and to understand those interactions as compared and contrasted with a recapitulation of the patient's internal object world in the milieu via splitting and projective identification. In outpatient psychotherapy, the individual process may be undermined by the countertherapeutic efforts of family members who feel threatened by any change in the patient. Family interventions or, in severe cases, family therapy may therefore be required for a successful individual treatment.

The first step of family intervention is to identify the role family interactions play in the pathogenesis and maintenance of the borderline patient's symptomatology. As described in Chapter 5, splitting and projective identification are extremely common mechanisms that serve to maintain a pathological homeostasis in the family system. For example, a parent may ward off bad internal self or object representations and project them onto an adolescent or young adult offspring, who subsequently identifies with these projections and becomes the symptomatic member of the family.

In diagnosing family patterns, therapists should avoid imposing their own theoretical constructs on the family. For example, although certain psychodynamic models (Masterson and Rinsley 1975) might presuppose overinvolvement on the part of the mother, empirical research (Gunderson and Englund 1981; Gunderson et al. 1980) has suggested that overinvolved parents are less common than neglectful ones. Neglectful parents of borderline patients tend to be needy themselves and therefore often fail to provide their children with guidance in the form of rules or "structure."

In families where overinvolvement is a pervasive pattern, family intervention must respect the needs of each family member for the other members. The parents may suffer from borderline psychopathology themselves and may be terribly threatened by the prospect of "losing" their borderline offspring through treatment. Clinicians must take seriously the possibility that a significant improvement in the patient may result in a severe decompensation in a parent, who will be thrown into a panic because of the perceived separation (Brown 1987). In these instances, a family therapist should help the family deal with the dilemmas created by change in the patient as well as in the family system as a whole. The therapist must conscientiously avoid any attempt to "pry apart" the borderline patient and the family. Such efforts will be viewed by both the family and the patient as a highly threatening attack that will simply cause them to "circle the wagons" and increase their enmeshment. Family therapists produce better results when they assume a nonjudgmental, neutral position regarding change, empathizing with the family's need to remain together because of the stability inherent in the overinvolvement (Jones 1987). Any change in the system must come from *within* rather than being imposed by mental health professionals, who traditionally place a high value on separation and autonomy.

Another crucial principle in working with the families of BPD patients is to avoid siding with the patient's vilification of the parents as though every monstrous report is completely accurate. In a study comparing BPD patients' perceptions of their families with the perceptions of their parents and those of normative families, Gunderson and Lyoo (1997) found that borderline patients perceived their family relationships in a significantly more negative light than did either the parents or the normative families. Parents tend to agree with each other but not with the borderline offspring. This schism in the family must be taken seriously. Clinicians should keep in mind that the borderline patient's account may be colored by his or her own psychological propensities while also recognizing that the parents' view must be accepted with caution as well. Many parents will have defensive responses during an assessment and feel like they are being blamed for the child's difficulties. In most cases, the truth lies somewhere between the two viewpoints, and each side's perceptions have some validity. Gunderson and Lyoo also advocated psychoeducational work with families of BPD patients to help them appreciate the complexities of borderline pathology.

Group Psychotherapy

Group psychotherapy may also be a beneficial adjunct to individual psychotherapy of borderline patients. As Ganzarain (1980) and Horwitz (1977) have noted, all groups are prone to employ the borderline defenses of splitting and projective identification. Group psychotherapy affords the borderline individual an opportunity to understand these defenses as they occur in a group context. Most contributors to the literature on group psychotherapy of the borderline patient, however, suggest that the borderline patient is most effectively treated in groups of patients who suffer from neuroses or higher-level personality disorders (Day and Semrad 1971; Horwitz 1977; Hulse 1958; Slavson 1964).

Likewise, the consensus of the literature is that borderline patients in group psychotherapy need concomitant individual psychotherapy (Day and Semrad 1971; Horwitz 1977; Hulse 1958; Slavson 1964; Spotnitz 1957). The dilution of transference in group psychotherapy significantly benefits both the borderline patient and the therapist. The intense rage that is ordinarily mobilized in borderline patients when they are frustrated in treatment may thus be diluted and directed toward other figures besides the individual therapist. Similarly, the strong countertransference reactions to borderline patients may be diluted by the presence of other people.

Horwitz (1977) pointed out that the individual psychotherapist may serve a crucial supportive function when the borderline patient's anxiety escalates in response to confrontation in the group setting. The individual therapist ideally should be someone other than the group therapist, because "it is antitherapeutic for the group therapist to see some patients individually while not seeing others privately as well" (p. 415). Horwitz also identified abrasive characterological traits as an indication for group psychotherapy in addition to individual psychotherapy. He observed that borderline patients seem more willing to accept confrontation and interpretation about such traits from their peers in group psychotherapy than from a therapist. They may also find it easier to accept their therapist's interpretations as part of a group centered theme than when the interpretations single them out as individuals.

Empirical data are emerging that corroborate the widespread clinical impression that group treatment may be quite useful for borderline patients. Although not a psychodynamic modality, dialectical behavior therapy (Linehan et al. 1991) uses groups as its cornerstone and has been shown to reduce self-mutilating and suicidal behaviors. In a randomized controlled trial of interpersonal group psychotherapy versus individual dynamic therapy, Munroe-Blum and Marziali (1995) found that 25 weekly sessions of 90-minute group therapy followed by 5 biweekly sessions leading to termination resulted in significant improvements. Analysis at 12- and 24-month follow-ups showed significant improvements on all major outcomes. Moreover, the group patients did as well as those in individual therapy.

Despite the advantages of working in a group context, therapists will find certain inherent difficulties in the group psychotherapy of borderline patients. Such patients may easily become scapegoated because of their more primitive psychopathology and their greater tendency to express affect in a direct manner. The therapist may be required to support the borderline patient when scapegoating emerges as a group theme. Moreover, borderline patients may also experience an increase in their feelings of deprivation because of competition with the group for the nurturance of the therapist. Finally, borderline patients tend to maintain a certain distance in group psychotherapy because of their primary attachment to the individual therapist.

References

Adler G: The myth of the alliance with borderline patients. Am J Psychiatry 47:642 645, 1979

Adler G: Issues in the treatment of the borderline patient, in Kohut's Legacy: Contributions to Self Psychology. Edited by Stepansky PE, Goldberg A. Hillsdale, NJ, Analytic Press, 1984, pp 117–134

Adler G: Borderline Psychopathology and Its Treatment. New York, Jason Aronson, 1985

Adler G: Discussion: milieu treatment in the psychotherapy of the borderline patient: abandonment and containment. Yearbook of Psychoanalysis and Psychotherapy 2:145–157, 1987

Adler G, Rhine MW: The selfobject function of projective identification: curative factors in psychotherapy. Bull Menninger Clin 52:473–491, 1988

Akiskal HS, Chen SE, Davis GC, et al: Borderline: an adjective in search of a noun. J Clin Psychiatry 46:41–48, 1985

American Psychiatric Association: Diagnostic and Statistical Manual of Mental Disorders, 3rd Edition. Washington, DC, American Psychiatric Association, 1980

American Psychiatric Association: Diagnostic and Statistical Manual of Mental Disorders, 4th Edition. Washington, DC, American Psychiatric Association, 1994

Andrulonis PA: Disruptive behavior disorders in boys and the borderline personality disorder in men. Ann Clin Psychiatry 3:23–26, 1991

Atwood GE, Stolorow RD: Structures of Subjectivity: Explorations in Psychoanalytic Phenomenology. Hillsdale, NJ, Analytic Press, 1984

Baker L, Silk KR, Westen D, et al: Malevolence, splitting, and parental ratings by borderlines. J Nerv Ment Dis 180:258–264, 1992

Barasch A, Frances A, Hurt S, et al: Stability and distinctness of borderline personality disorder. Am J Psychiatry 142:1484–1486, 1985

Baron M, Gruen R, Asnis L, et al: Familial transmission of schizotypal and borderline personality disorders. Am J Psychiatry 142:927–934, 1985

Bateman A, Fonagy P: The effectiveness of partial hospitalization in the treatment of borderline personality disorder: a randomized controlled trial. Am J Psychiatry 156:1563–1569, 1999

Boyer LB: Working with a borderline patient. Psychoanal Q 46:386–424, 1977

Brown SL: Family therapy and the borderline patient, in The Borderline Patient: Emerging Concepts in Diagnosis, Psychodynamics, and Treatment, Vol 2. Edited by Grotstein JS, Solomon MF, Lang JA. Hillsdale, NJ, Analytic Press, 1987, pp 206–209

Burnham DL: The special-problem patient: victim or agent of splitting? Psychiatry 29:105–122, 1966

Casement PJ: On Learning From the Patient. London, Tavistock, 1985

Cloninger CR, Svrakic DM, Pryzbeck TR: A psychobiological model of temperament and character. Arch Gen Psychiatry 50:975–990, 1993

Coccaro EF, Kavoussi RJ: Fluoxetine and impulsive aggressive behavior in personality-disordered subjects. Arch Gen Psychiatry 54:1081–1088, 1997

Coccaro EF, Siever LJ, Klar HM, et al: Serotonergic studies in patients with affective and personality disorders: correlates with suicidal and impulsive aggressive behavior. Arch Gen Psychiatry 46:587–599, 1989

Colson DB, Lewis L, Horwitz L: Negative outcome in psychotherapy and psychoanalysis, in Negative Outcome in Psychotherapy and What to Do About It. Edited by Mays DT, Frank CM. New York, Springer, 1985, pp 59–75

Cowdry RW, Gardner DL: Pharmacotherapy of borderline personality disorder: alprazolam, carbamazepine, trifluoperazine, and tranylcypromine. Arch Gen Psychiatry 45: 111–119, 1988

Day M, Semrad E: Group therapy with neurotics and psychotics, in Comprehensive Group Psychotherapy. Edited by Kaplan HI, Sadock BJ. Baltimore, MD, Williams & Wilkins, 1971, pp 566–580

Dolan BM, Evans C, Norton K: The Separation-Individuation Inventory: association with borderline phenomena. J Nerv Ment Dis 180:529–533, 1992

Dolan B, Warren F, Norton K: Change in borderline symptoms one year after therapeutic community treatment for severe personality disorder. Br J Psychiatry 171:274–279, 1997

Dorpat TL, Ripley HS: The relationship between attempted suicide and committed suicide. Compr Psychiatry 8.74–79, 1967

Esman AH: Adolescent psychopathology and the rapprochement process, in Rapprochement: The Critical Subphase of Separation-Individuation. Edited by Lax RF, Bach S, Burland JA. New York, Jason Aronson, 1980, pp 295–297

Eyman JR, Gabbard GO: Will therapist-patient sex prevent suicide? Psychiatric Annals 21:669–674, 1991

Fairbairn WRD: An Object-Relations Theory of the Personality. New York, Basic Books, 1954

Figueroa E, Silk KR: Biological implications of childhood sexual abuse in borderline personality disorder. J Personal Disord 11:71–92, 1997

Fonagy P: An attachment theory approach to treatment of the difficult patient. Bull Menninger Clin 62:147–169, 1998

Fonagy P, Target M: Understanding the violent patient: the use of the body and the role of the father. Int J Psychoanal 76:487–501, 1995

Fraiberg S: Libidinal object constancy and mental representation. Psychoanal Study Child 24:9–47, 1969

Frank AF: The therapeutic alliances of borderline patients, in Borderline Personality Disorder: Clinical and Empirical Perspectives. Edited by Clarkin JF, Marziali B, Munroe-Blum H. New York, Guilford, 1992, pp 220–247

Frank H, Hoffman N: Borderline empathy: an empirical investigation. Compr Psychiatry 27:387–395, 1986

Frank H, Paris J: Recollections of family experience in borderline patients. Arch Gen Psychiatry 38:1031–1034, 1981

Frankenburg FR, Zanarini MC: Clozapine treatment of borderline patients: a preliminary study. Compr Psychiatry 34:402–405, 1993

Fyer MR, Frances AJ, Sullivan T, et al: Comorbidity of borderline personality disorder. Arch Gen Psychiatry 45:348–352, 1988

Gabbard GO: The treatment of the "special" patient in a psychoanalytic hospital. International Review of Psychoanalysis 13:333–347, 1986

Gabbard GO: On "doing nothing" in the psychoanalytic treatment of the refractory borderline patient. Int J Psychoanal 70:527–534, 1989a

Gabbard GO: Patients who hate. Psychiatry 52:96–106, 1989b

Gabbard GO (ed): Sexual Exploitation in Professional Relationships. Washington, DC, American Psychiatric Press, 1989c

Gabbard GO: An overview of countertransference with borderline patients. J Psychother Pract Res 2:7–18, 1993

Gabbard GO: Love and Hate in the Analytic Setting. Northvale, NJ: Jason Aronson, 1996

Gabbard GO: Borderline personality disorder and rational managed care policy. Psychoanalytic Inquiry 17 (suppl):17–28, 1997

Gabbard GO: Treatment-resistant borderline personality disorder. Psychiatric Annals 28: 651–656, 1998

Gabbard GO: Combining medication with psychotherapy in treatment of personality disorders, in Psychotherapy of Personality Disorders (Review of Psychiatry Series; Oldham JM and Riba MB, series eds.), Vol 19. Edited by Gunderson JG, Gabbard GO. Washington, DC, American Psychiatric Press, 2000, pp 65–90

Gabbard GO, Wilkinson SM: Management of Countertransference With Borderline Patients. Washington, DC, American Psychiatric Press, 1994

Gabbard GO, Horwitz L, Frieswyk S, et al: The effect of therapist interventions on the therapeutic alliance with borderline patients. J Am Psychoanal Assoc 36:697–727, 1988

Gabbard GO, Horwitz L, Allen JG, et al: Transference interpretation in the psychotherapy of borderline patients: a high-risk, high-gain phenomenon. Harv Rev Psychiatry 2:59–69, 1994

Gabbard GO, Lazar SG, Hornberger J, et al: The economic impact of psychotherapy: a review. Am J Psychiatry 154:147–155, 1997

Ganzarain RC: Psychotic-like anxieties and primitive defenses in group analytic psychotherapy. Issues in Ego Psychology 3:42–48, 1980

Gardner DL, Cowdry RW: Alprazolam-induced dyscontrol in borderline personality disorder. Am J Psychiatry 142:98–100, 1985

Goldberg RL, Mann LS, Wise TN, et al: Parental qualities as perceived by borderline personality disorders. Hillside Journal of Clinical Psychiatry 7:134–140, 1985

Gorney JE: The negative therapeutic interaction. Contemporary Psychoanalysis 15:288–337, 1979

Grinker RR Jr, Werble B, Drye RC: The Borderline Syndrome: A Behavioral Study of Ego-Functions. New York, Basic Books, 1968

Gunderson JG: Borderline Personality Disorder. Washington, DC, American Psychiatric Press, 1984

Gunderson JG: Studies of borderline patients in psychotherapy, in Handbook of Borderline Disorders. Edited by Silver D, Rosenbluth M. Madison, CT, International Universities Press, 1992, pp 291–305

Gunderson JG: The borderline patient's intolerance of aloneness: insecure attachments and therapist availability. Am J Psychiatry 153:752–758, 1996

Gunderson JG, Chu JA: Treatment implications of past trauma in borderline personality disorder. Harv Rev Psychiatry 1:75–81, 1993

Gunderson JG, Englund DW: Characterizing the families of borderlines: a review of the literature. Psychiatr Clin North Am 4:159–168, 1981

Gunderson JG, Lyoo K: Family problems and relationships for adults with borderline personality disorder. Harv Rev Psychiatry 4:272–278, 1997

Gunderson JG, Phillips KA: A current view of the interface between borderline personality disorder and depression. Am J Psychiatry 148:967–975, 1991

Gunderson JG, Sabo AN: The phenomenological and conceptual interface between borderline personality disorder and PTSD. Am J Psychiatry 150:19–27, 1993

Gunderson JG, Zanarini MC: Current overview of the borderline diagnosis. J Clin Psychiatry 48 (suppl 8):5–14, 1987

Gunderson JG, Kerr J, Englund DW: The families of borderlines: a comparative study. Arch Gen Psychiatry 37:27–33, 1980

Gunderson JG, Frank AF, Ronningstam EF, et al: Early discontinuance of borderline patients from psychotherapy. J Nerv Ment Dis 177:38–42, 1989

Gunderson JG, Zanarini MC, Kisiel CL: Borderline personality disorder: a review of data on DSM-III-R descriptions. J Personal Disord 5:340–352, 1991

Gunderson JG, Triebwasser J, Phillips KA, et al: Personality and vulnerability to affective disorders, in Personality and Psychopathology. Edited by Cloninger CR. Washington, DC, American Psychiatric Press, 1999, pp 3–32

Gutheil T: Borderline personality disorder, boundary violations, and patient-therapist sex: medicolegal pitfalls. Am J Psychiatry 146:597–602, 1989

Heard H: Behavior therapies for borderline patients. Paper presented at the 147th annual meeting of the American Psychiatric Association, Philadelphia, PA, 1994

Herman JL, Perry JC, van der Kolk BA: Childhood trauma in borderline personality disorder. Am J Psychiatry 146:490–495, 1989

Hoch P, Polatin P: Pseudoneurotic forms of schizophrenia. Psychiatr Q 23:248–276, 1949

Hoke LA: Longitudinal patterns of behaviors in borderline personality disorder (doctoral dissertation). Boston, MA, Boston University Graduate School, 1989

Hollander E: Managing aggressive behavior in patients with obsessive-compulsive disorder and borderline personality disorder. J Clin Psychiatry 17:28–31, 1999

Horwitz L: Clinical Prediction in Psychotherapy. New York, Jason Aronson, 1974

Horwitz L: Group psychotherapy of the borderline patient, in Borderline Personality Disorders: The Concept, the Syndrome, the Patient. Edited by Hartocollis PL. New York, International Universities Press, 1977, pp 399–422

Horwitz L, Gabbard GO, Allen JG, et al: Borderline Personality Disorder: Tailoring the Psychotherapy to the Patient. Washington, DC, American Psychiatric Press, 1996

Hulse WC: Psychotherapy with ambulatory schizophrenic patients in mixed analytic groups. Archives of Neurology and Psychiatry 79:681–687, 1958

Johnson JG, Cohen P, Brown J, et al: Childhood maltreatment increases risk for personality disorders during early adulthood. Arch Gen Psychiatry 56:600–606, 1999

Jones SA: Family therapy with borderline and narcissistic patients. Bull Menninger Clin 51:285–295, 1987

Karterud S, Vaglum S, Friss S, et al: Day hospital therapeutic community treatment for patients with personality disorders: an empirical evaluation of the containment function. J Nerv Ment Dis 180:238–243, 1992

Kernberg OF: Structural derivatives of object relationships. Int J Psychoanal 47:236–253, 1966

Kernberg OF: Borderline personality organization. J Am Psychoanal Assoc 15:641–685, 1967

Kernberg OF: Borderline Conditions and Pathological Narcissism. New York, Jason Aronson, 1975

Kernberg OF: Technical considerations in the treatment of borderline personality organization. J Am Psychoanal Assoc 24:795–829, 1976

Kernberg OF, Burstein ED, Coyne L, et al: Psychotherapy and psychoanalysis: final report of the Menninger Foundation's Psychotherapy Research Project. Bull Menninger Clin 36:3–275, 1972

Kernberg OF, Selzer MA, Koenigsberg HW, et al: Psychodynamic Psychotherapy of Borderline Patients. New York, Basic Books, 1989

Knight RP: Borderline states. Bull Menninger Clin 17:1–12, 1953

Linehan MM, Armstrong HE, Suarez A, et al: Cognitive-behavioral treatment of chronically parasuicidal borderline patients. Arch Gen Psychiatry 48:1060–1064, 1991

Links PS, Steiner M, Offord DR, et al: Characteristics of borderline personality disorder: a Canadian study. Can J Psychiatry 33:336–340, 1988

Loranger AW, Oldham JM, Tulis EH: Familial transmission of DSM-III borderline personality disorder. Arch Gen Psychiatry 39:795–799, 1982

Mahler MS, Kaplan LJ: Developmental aspects in the assessment of narcissistic and so-called borderline personalities, in Borderline Personality Disorders: The Concept, the Syndrome, the Patient. Edited by Hartocollis PL. New York, International Universities Press, 1977, pp 71–85

Mahler MS, Pine F, Bergman A: The Psychological Birth of the Human Infant: Symbiosis and Individuation. New York, Basic Books, 1975

Main TF: The ailment. Br J Med Psychol 30:129–145, 1957

Maltsberger JT: Countertransference in the treatment of the suicidal borderline patient, in Countertransference Issues in Psychiatric Treatment (Review of Psychiatry Series; Oldham JM and Riba MB, series eds). Edited by Gabbard GO. Washington, DC, American Psychiatric Press, 1999, pp 27–43

Markovitz P: Pharmacotherapy of impulsivity, aggression, and related disorders, in Impulsivity and Aggression. Edited by Hollander E, Stein DJ, Zohar J. New York, Wiley, 1995, pp 263–287

Masterson JF: Psychotherapy of the Borderline Adult: A Developmental Approach. New York, Brunner/Mazel, 1976

Masterson JF, Rinsley DB: The borderline syndrome: the role of the mother in the genesis and psychic structure of the borderline personality. Int J Psychoanal 56:163–177, 1975

McGlashan TH: The borderline syndrome, II: is it a variant of schizophrenia or affective disorder? Arch Gen Psychiatry 40:1319–1323, 1983

McGlashan TH: The Chestnut Lodge follow-up study, III: long-term outcome of border-line personalities. Arch Gen Psychiatry 43:20–30, 1986

Meares R, Stevenson J, Comerford A: Psychotherapy with borderline patients, I: a compari-son between treated and untreated cohorts. Aust N Z J Psychiatry 33:467–472, 1999

Mehlum L, Friis S, Irion T, et al: Personality disorders 2–5 years after treatment: a prospec-tive follow up study. Acta Psychiatr Scand 84:72–77, 1991

Meissner WW: The Borderline Spectrum: Differential Diagnosis and Developmental Is-sues. New York, Jason Aronson, 1984

Meissner WW: Treatment of Patients in the Borderline Spectrum. Northvale, NJ, Jason Aronson, 1988

Meyer DJ, Simon RI: Split treatment: clarity between psychiatrists and psychotherapists, part 1. Psychiatric Annals 29:241–245, 1999a

Meyer DJ, Simon RI: Split treatment: clarity between psychiatrists and psychotherapists, part 2. Psychiatric Annals 29:327–322, 1999b

Modell AH: "The holding environment" and the therapeutic action of psychoanalysis. J Am Psychoanal Assoc 24:285–307, 1976

Munroe-Blum H, Marziali E: A controlled trial of short-term group treatment for border-line personality disorder. J Personal Disord 9:190–198, 1995

Najavits LM, Gunderson JG: Better than expected: improvements in borderline personality disorder in a 3-year prospective outcome study. Compr Psychiatry 36:296–302, 1995

Ogata SN, Silk KR, Goodrich S, et al: Childhood sexual and physical abuse in adult patients with borderline personality disorder. Am J Psychiatry 147:1008–1013, 1990

O'Leary KM, Cowdry RW: Neuropsychological testing results in borderline personality dis-order, in Biological and Neurobehavioral Studies of Borderline Personality Disorder. Edited by Silk KR. Washington, DC, American Psychiatric Press, 1994, pp 127–157

Paris J: Does childhood trauma cause personality disorders in adults? Can J Psychiatry 43: 148–153, 1998

Paris J, Frank H: Perceptions of parental bonding in borderline patients. Am J Psychiatry 146:1498–1499, 1989

Paris J, Zweig-Frank H: A critical review of the role of childhood sexual abuse in the etiol-ogy of borderline personality disorder. Can J Psychiatry 37:125–128, 1992

Paris J, Brown R, Nowlis D: Long-term follow-up of borderline patients in a general hospi-tal. Compr Psychiatry 28:530–535, 1987

Pfohl B, Stangle D, Zimmerman M: The implications of DSM-III personality disorders for patients with major depression. J Affect Disord 7:309–318, 1984

Plakun EM, Burkhardt PE, Muller JP: 14-year follow-up of borderline and schizotypal per-sonality disorders. Compr Psychiatry 26:448–455, 1985

Rinsley DB: A comparison of borderline and narcissistic personality disorders. Bull Menninger Clin 48:1–9, 1984

Rinsley DB: Notes on the pathogenesis and nosology of borderline and narcissistic person-ality disorders. J Am Acad Psychoanal 13:317–328, 1985

Rinsley DB: A reconsideration of Fairbairn's "original object" and "original ego" in relation to borderline and other self disorders, in The Borderline Patient: Emerging Concepts in Diagnosis, Psychodynamics, and Treatment, Vol 1. Edited by Grotstein JF, Solomon MF, Lang JA. Hillsdale, NJ, Analytic Press, 1987, pp 291–231

Rinsley DB: A review of the pathogenesis of borderline and narcissistic personality disorders. Adolescent Psychiatry 15:387–406, 1988

Rinsley DB: Developmental Pathogenesis and Psychoanalytic Treatment of Borderline and Narcissistic Personalities. Northvale, NJ, Jason Aronson, 1989

Rogers JH, Widiger TA, Krupp A: Aspects of depression associated with borderline personality disorder. Am J Psychiatry 152:268–270, 1995

Rosen IR: Relational masochism: the search for a bad enough object. Paper presented at scientific meeting of the Topeka Psychoanalytic Society, Topeka, KS, January 21, 1993

Salzman C, Wolfson AN, Schatzberg A, et al: Effect of fluoxetine on anger in symptomatic volunteers with borderline personality disorder. J Clin Psychopharmacol 15:23–29, 1995

Sandler J: Character traits and object relationships. Psychoanal Q 50:694–708, 1981

Schmideberg M: The borderline patient, in American Handbook of Psychiatry, Vol 1. Edited by Arieti S. New York, Basic Books, 1959, pp 398–416

Searles HF: My Work With Borderline Patients. Northvale, NJ, Jason Aronson, 1986

Shea MT, Glass Dr, Pilkonis PA, et al: Frequency and implications of personality disorder in a sample of depressed outpatients. J Personal Disord 1:27–42, 1987

Siever LJ, Davis KL: A psychobiological perspective on the personality disorders. Am J Psychiatry 148:1647–1658, 1991

Slavson SR: A Textbook in Analytic Group Psychotherapy. New York, International Universities Press, 1964

Soloff PH: Algorithms for pharmacological treatment of personality dimensions: symptom-specific treatments for cognitive-perceptual, affective, and impulsive-behavioral dysregulation. Bull Menninger Clin 62:195–214, 1998

Soloff PH, Millward JW: Developmental histories of borderline patients. Compr Psychiatry 24:574–588, 1983

Spotnitz H: The borderline schizophrenic in group psychotherapy: the importance of individualization. Int J Group Psychother 7:155–174, 1957

Stevenson J, Meares R: An outcome study of psychotherapy for patients with borderline personality disorder. Am J Psychiatry 149:358–362, 1992

Stevenson J, Meares R: Borderline patients at 5-year follow-up. Paper presented at the annual Congress of the Royal Australian–New Zealand College of Psychiatrists, Cairns, Australia, May 1995

Stevenson J, Meares R: Psychotherapy with borderline patients, II: a preliminary cost-benefit study. Aust N Z J Psychiatry 33:473–477, 1999

Stone MH: The Borderline Syndromes: Constitution, Personality, and Adaptation. New York, McGraw-Hill, 1980

Stone MH: Psychotherapy of borderline patients in light of long-term follow-up. Bull Menninger Clin 51:231–247, 1987

Stone MH, Stone DK, Hurt SW: Natural history of borderline patients treated by intensive hospitalization. Psychiatr Clin North Am 10:185–206, 1987

Streeter CC, vanReekum R, Shorr RI, et al: Prior head injury in male veterans with borderline personality disorder. J Nerv Ment Dis 183:577–581, 1995

Swartz M, Blazer D, George L, et al: Estimating the prevalence of borderline personality disorder in the community. J Personal Disord 4:257–272, 1990

Swirsky-Sacchetti T, Gorton G, Samuel S, et al: Neuropsychological function in borderline personality disorder. J Clin Psychol 49:385–396, 1993

Tuckman J, Youngman WF: Suicide risk among persons attempting suicide. Public Health Rep 78:585–587, 1963

vanReekum R, Conway CA, Gansler D, et al: Neurobehavioral study of borderline personality disorder. J Psychiatry Neurosci 18:121–129, 1993

Waldinger RJ: Intensive psychodynamic therapy with borderline patients: an overview. Am J Psychiatry 144:267–274, 1987

Waldinger RJ, Frank AF: Clinicians' experiences in combining medication and psychotherapy in the treatment of borderline patients. Hospital and Community Psychiatry 40:712–718, 1989

Wallerstein RS: Forty-Two Lives in Treatment: A Study of Psychoanalysis and Psychotherapy. New York, Guilford, 1986

Walsh F: The family of the borderline patient, in The Borderline Patient. Edited by Grinker RR, Werble B. New York, Jason Aronson, 1977, pp 158–177

Werble B: Second follow-up study of borderline patients. Arch Gen Psychiatry 23:3–7, 1970

Westen D, Ludolph P, Misle B, et al: Physical and sexual abuse in adolescent girls with borderline personality disorder. Am J Orthopsychiatry 60:55–66, 1990

Zanarini MC, Frankenburg FR: Pathways to the development of borderline personality disorder. J Personal Disord 11:93–104, 1997

Zanarini MC, Gunderson JG, Frankenburg FR: Axis I phenomenology of borderline personality disorder. Compr Psychiatry 30:149–156, 1989a

Zanarini MC, Gunderson JG, Marino MF, et al: Childhood experiences of borderline patients. Compr Psychiatry 30:18–25, 1989b

Zanarini MC, Gunderson JG, Frankenburg FR, et al: Discriminating borderline personality disorder from other Axis II disorders. Am J Psychiatry 147:161–167, 1990

Zanarini MC, Williams AA, Lewis RE, et al: Reported pathological childhood experiences associated with the development of borderline personality disorder. Am J Psychiatry 154:1101–1106, 1997

Zetzel ER: A developmental approach to the borderline patient. Am J Psychiatry 127:867–871, 1971

Zweig-Frank H, Paris J: Parents' emotional neglect and overprotection according to the recollections of patients with borderline personality disorder. Am J Psychiatry 148:648–651, 1991

C H A P T E R
16

Cluster B Personality Disorders

Narcissistic

O, you are sick of self-love, Malvolio, and taste with a distemper'd appetite. To be generous, guiltless, and of free disposition, is to take those things for bird-bolts* that you deem cannon bullets.

> Olivia in Act I, Scene v
> of Shakespeare's *Twelfth Night*

*blunt-headed arrows for shooting birds

In Shakespeare's comedy, it is clear to both Olivia and the audience that Malvolio's love of himself and his tendency to experience mild slights as devastating attacks are indications that he is "sick." In contemporary psychiatric practice, however, the distinction between healthy and pathological degrees of narcissism is fraught with difficulty. A certain measure of self-love is not only normal but also desirable. Yet the point on the continuum of self-regard where healthy narcissism turns into pathological narcissism is not easy to identify.

Another confounding factor is that certain behaviors may be pathologically narcissistic in one individual while simply a manifestation of healthy self-regard in another. Let us imagine, for example, a 15-year-old boy who stands in front of the mirror blow-drying his hair for 45 minutes in order to get every hair perfectly in place. Most of us would chuckle to ourselves at this image and realize that vanity of this sort is entirely normal for a pubescent youngster. Now let us shift to an image of a 30-year-old man who spends the same amount of time every morning in front of the mirror with a blow dryer. This visual picture is a bit more disconcerting, because such excessive self-absorption is far from the norm for a man of this age. If we now imagine a 45-year-old man engaged in the same activity, we again become a bit more charitable in our attitude because, as was the case with the adolescent boy, we understand such behavior as part of a developmental phase in the life cycle that we often refer to as midlife crisis. Before making a definitive determination about the relative health or pathology in this individual, however, we would want to know more about his other activities.

The above examples illustrate how narcissism is judged differently depending on the phase of the life cycle through which one is passing. Even though we are aware of these developmental distinctions, the term *narcissistic* is rarely used as a compliment to refer to someone with healthy self-esteem. On the contrary, the term is much more commonly used pejoratively as a synonym for "son of a bitch," especially when referring to colleagues and acquaintances whom we find unpleasant. Also, the term is often invoked to refer to someone whose success and confidence we envy. Since we all struggle with narcissistic issues, we must always be wary of the potential for hypocrisy in labeling others as narcissistic. Some (Lasch 1979) would argue that the history of humankind suggests that we have always been selfish and that nothing is gained by applying a psychiatric label to such qualities.

To complicate things further, we live in a narcissistic culture (Cooper 1998; Lasch 1979; Rinsley 1986; Stone 1998). We are slavishly devoted to electronic media that thrive on superficial images and ignore substance and depth. We view consumption of material goods as the road to happiness. Our fear of aging and death keeps plastic surgeons in business. We are consumed with the glamour of celebrity. Books with titles like *Looking Out for Number One* make the best-seller list. Competitive sports, the great American pastime, teach us that being number one is the most important goal of all.

One of the key diagnostic criteria for narcissistic personality disorder, interpersonal exploitiveness, is highly adaptive in our society. Indeed, the very fabric of our economic system is based on rewarding those who are able to talk others into buying a product (Maccoby 1976; Person 1986). In the corporate world, "making it" has become more important than values of commitment, loyalty, integrity, and interpersonal warmth. College athletic coaches can get away with outrageous treatment of their athletes as long as they continue to bring home conference titles. Winning forgives everything.

Given this cultural ambience, it is often problematic to determine which traits indicate a narcissistic personality disorder and which are simply adaptive cultural traits. Moreover, the difference between a healthy self-esteem and an artificially inflated self-esteem is often ambiguous. Let us visualize, for example, a mental health professional presenting a scientific paper to an audience of peers. The presenter notices that about half the audience are falling asleep during his presentation, while others are getting up and leaving. During the discussion period at the end of the presentation, the presenter is severely criticized for "muddy thinking," "insufficient familiarity with the literature," and "presenting nothing new." He responds to these criticisms by saying to himself, "No matter what they think, I know I'm competent anyway." How do we evaluate this response? Based on the information in this example, we could reach one of two conclusions: 1) this person has a healthy self-regard that does not collapse merely because of one untoward experience, or 2) the presenter's response is reflective of pathological narcissism in that it is a grandiose defensive reaction to compensate for a devastating injury to his self-esteem.

With such a bewildering array of varied usage, developmental differences, and cultural influences, what definitive criteria can be used to differentiate healthy from pathological narcissism? The time-honored criteria of psychological health—to love and to work—are only partly useful in answering this question. An individual's work history may provide little help in making the distinction. Highly disturbed narcissistic individuals may find extraordinary success in certain professions, such as big business, the arts, politics, the entertainment industry, athletics, and televangelism (Gabbard 1983; Rinsley 1985, 1989). In some cases, however, narcissistic pathology may be reflected in a superficial quality to one's professional interests (Kernberg 1970), as though achievement and acclaim are more important than mastery of the field itself.

Pathological forms of narcissism are more easily identified by the quality of the individual's relationships. One tragedy affecting these people is their inability to love. Healthy interpersonal relationships can be recognized by qualities such as empathy and concern for the feelings of others, a genuine interest in the ideas of others, the ability to tolerate ambivalence in long-term relationships without giving up, and a capacity to acknowledge one's own contribution to interpersonal conflicts. People whose relationships are characterized by these qualities may at times use others to gratify their own needs, but this tendency occurs in the broader context of sensitive interpersonal relatedness rather than as a pervasive style of dealing with other people. On the other hand, the person with a narcissistic personality disorder approaches people as objects to be used up and discarded according to his or her needs, without regard for their feelings. People are not viewed as having a separate existence or as having needs of their own. The individual with a narcissistic personality disorder frequently ends a relationship after a short time, usually when the other person begins to make demands stemming from his or her own needs. Most importantly, such relationships clearly do not "work" in terms of the narcissist's ability to maintain his or her own sense of self-esteem (Stolorow 1975).

Phenomenology of
Narcissistic Personality Disorder

The psychodynamic literature on narcissistic personality disorder is somewhat confusing because the label seems to apply equally well to patients with quite different clinical pictures. DSM-IV (American Psychiatric Association 1994) lists nine criteria for the diagnosis of narcissistic personality disorder (Table 16–1).

These criteria identify a certain kind of narcissistic patient—specifically, the arrogant, boastful, "noisy" individual who demands to be in the spotlight. However, they fail to characterize the shy, quietly grandiose, narcissistic individual whose extreme sensitivity to slights leads to an assiduous avoidance of the spotlight (Cooper and Michels 1988).

The literature identifies something of a continuum of narcissistic personality disorder. Kernberg (1970, 1974a, 1974b, 1998) delineated an envious, greedy type who demands the attention and acclaim of others, while Kohut (1971, 1977, 1984) described a narcissistically vulnerable type prone to self-fragmentation. The various types of narcissistic patients described by these authors may be conceptualized as falling between two endpoints on a continuum based on the typical style of in-

---

TABLE 16–1.   DSM-IV criteria for narcissistic personality disorder

A pervasive pattern of grandiosity (in fantasy or behavior), need for admiration, and lack of empathy, beginning by early adulthood and present in a variety of contexts, as indicated by five (or more) of the following:

1. has a grandiose sense of self-importance (e.g., exaggerates achievements and talents, expects to be recognized as superior without commensurate achievements)
2. is preoccupied with fantasies of unlimited success, power, brilliance, beauty, or ideal love
3. believes that he or she is "special" and unique and can only be understood by, or should associate with, other special or high-status people (or institutions)
4. requires excessive admiration
5. has a sense of entitlement, i.e., has unreasonable expectations of especially favorable treatment or automatic compliance with his or her expectations
6. is interpersonally exploitative, i.e., takes advantage of others to achieve his or her own ends
7. lacks empathy: is unwilling to recognize or identify with the feelings and needs of others
8. is often envious of others or believes that others are envious of him or her
9. shows arrogant, haughty behaviors or attitudes

Source.   Reprinted from DSM-IV (American Psychiatric Association 1994), p. 661. Used with permission.

terpersonal relatedness. From a descriptive standpoint, the two opposite extremes on this continuum may be labeled the *oblivious* narcissist and the *hypervigilant* narcissist (Gabbard 1989) (Table 16–2). These terms specifically refer to the person's predominant style of interacting, both in transference relationships with a therapist and in social relationships in general.

Oblivious types appear to have no awareness whatsoever of their impact on others. They talk as though addressing a large audience, rarely establishing eye contact and generally looking over the heads of those around them. They talk "at" others, not "to" them. Persons of this type are oblivious to the fact that they are boring and that some people will therefore leave the conversation and seek companionship elsewhere. Their talk is replete with references to their own accomplishments, and they clearly need to be the center of attention. They are insensitive to the needs of others, even to the point that they do not allow others to contribute to the conversation. These people are often perceived as "having a sender but no receiver." The oblivious type of narcissistic personality disorder closely matches the clinical picture described in the DSM-IV criteria.

The narcissistic issues of the hypervigilant type, on the other hand, are manifested in starkly different ways. These people are exquisitely sensitive to how others react to them. In fact, their attention is continually directed toward others, in contrast to the self-absorption of the oblivious narcissist. Like the paranoid patient, they listen to others carefully for evidence of any critical reaction, and they tend to feel slighted at every turn. One narcissistic patient was so attuned to his therapist's reactions that every time the therapist shifted position in his chair or cleared his throat, the patient viewed it as a sign of boredom. When this therapist removed a dead leaf from an office plant on his desk, the patient felt humiliated and demanded a new therapist. Patients of this type are shy and inhibited to the point of being self-effacing. They shun the limelight because they are convinced that they

---

TABLE 16–2. Two types of narcissistic personality disorder patients

The Oblivious Narcissist	The Hypervigilant Narcissist
1. Has no awareness of reactions of others	1. Is highly sensitive to reactions of others
2. Is arrogant and aggressive	2. Is inhibited, shy, or even self-effacing
3. Is self-absorbed	3. Directs attention more toward others than toward self
4. Needs to be the center of attention	4. Shuns being the center of attention
5. Has a "sender but no receiver"	5. Listens to others carefully for evidence of slights or criticisms
6. Is apparently impervious to having feelings hurt by others	6. Has easily hurt feelings; is prone to feeling ashamed or humiliated

will be rejected and humiliated. At the core of their inner world is a deep sense of shame related to their secret wish to exhibit themselves in a grandiose manner.

Shame has other determinants as well. Shame relates to a self-assessment process in which one feels inadequate (i.e., falling short of a standard or ideal of what one should be). Central to shame is a sense of inherent defect (Cooper 1998). Lewis (1987) distinguished shame from guilt. Whereas guilty persons may feel they are not living up to a standard, they do not have the sense of being irreparably defective in the way that certain individuals with narcissistic personality disorder do. The feeling of being humiliated or painfully exposed when confronted with deficiencies in one's abilities or the recognition of unsatisfied needs is central to the psychopathology of individuals with pathological narcissism, and many of the defenses such persons develop are designed to prevent themselves from becoming aware of the feelings associated with these experiences.

Although both types struggle with maintaining their self-esteem, they deal with that issue in extremely different ways. Oblivious narcissists attempt to impress others with their accomplishments while insulating themselves from narcissistic injury by screening out the responses of others. Hypervigilant narcissists attempt to maintain their self-esteem by avoiding vulnerable situations and by intensely studying others to figure out how to behave. They projectively attribute their own disapproval of their grandiose fantasies onto others (Gabbard 1983). This typology is closely related to Rosenfeld's (1987) distinction between "thick-skinned" and "thin-skinned" narcissistic patients and to Broucek's (1982) categories of *egotistical* and *dissociative*. However, whereas the oblivious narcissist is virtually identical with the egotistical type, the hypervigilant patient does not project his or her grandiosity onto an idealized other, as is the case with Broucek's dissociative type, but instead retains it within and regards the other as a persecutor.

Despite the failure of the DSM-IV criteria to represent the hypervigilant variant of narcissistic personality disorder, there is empirical support for the oblivious-hypervigilant distinction. Wink (1991) performed a principal-components analysis of six Minnesota Multiphasic Personality Inventory (MMPI) narcissism scales and found two orthogonal factors: a Vulnerability-Sensitivity dimension and a Grandiosity-Exhibitionism dimension. He concluded that these two relatively uncorrelated sets, which he referred to as *covert* and *overt* narcissism, confirmed the existence of two distinct forms of pathological narcissism. Although both forms shared the features of disregard for others, self-indulgence, and conceit, the Vulnerability-Sensitivity group was characterized as introverted, defensive, anxious, and vulnerable to life's traumas, whereas the Grandiosity-Exhibitionism group was extraverted, self-assured, exhibitionistic, and aggressive.

Further empirical support for the two subtypes of narcissistic personality disorder has come from a study of 701 college students (Hibbard 1992). The subjects filled out questionnaires containing eight scales measuring narcissism, object relations, masochism, and shame. Narcissism formed two distinct subgroups, a narcissistically vulnerable style and a "phallic," grandiose style. The affect of shame was central in dividing these groups—it correlated positively with the vulnerable style and negatively with the grandiose style.

Although these two types may occur in pure form, many patients present with a mixture of phenomenological features from both types. Between these two endpoints on the continuum will be many narcissistic individuals who are much smoother socially and who possess a great deal of interpersonal charm.

Psychodynamic Understanding

For the past three decades, the principal controversy surrounding the theoretical understanding of narcissistic personality disorder has revolved around the models of Kohut and Kernberg (Adler 1986; Glassman 1988; Heiserman and Cook 1998; Josephs 1995; Kernberg 1974a, 1974b, 1998; Ornstein 1974a, 1998). Because the self psychology theory of Kohut was covered in some detail in Chapter 2, it will be only schematically reviewed here.

Kohut (1971, 1977, 1984) believed that narcissistically disturbed individuals are developmentally arrested at a stage where they require specific responses from persons in their environment to maintain a cohesive self. When such responses are not forthcoming, these individuals are prone to fragmentations of the self. Kohut understood this state of affairs as the result of the parents' empathic failures. Specifically, the parents did not respond to the child's phase-appropriate displays of exhibitionism with validation and admiration, did not offer twinship experiences, and did not provide the child with models worthy of idealization. These failures manifest themselves in the patient's tendency to form a mirror, twinship, or idealizing transference.

Kohut postulated a double-axis theory (see Figure 2–5 in Chapter 2) to explain how both narcissistic needs and object-related needs can coexist in the same individual. Throughout our lives, Kohut argued, we are in need of selfobject responses from the people around us. In other words, at some level we all regard others not as separate persons but as sources of gratification for the self. A need for the soothing, validating functions of selfobjects is never outgrown. The goal of treatment is to move away from a need for archaic selfobjects toward an ability to use more mature and appropriate selfobjects.

A case example may help illustrate how the theory of self psychology manifests itself in a clinical situation.

Ms. DD was a 26-year-old, single woman who came to treatment after her 4-year relationship with her boyfriend ended. She indicated that his rejection of her had been "devastating." While she specifically denied any suicidal thoughts, she did say that she felt she was no longer alive without him. Although it had been a year since the breakup, she was unable to get her life back on track. She sat around feeling empty and lonely. She continued to go to work, but then would return home each evening and just sit in her apartment staring blankly or watching television. Throughout her day at work she felt detached from any activities she pursued, as if she was on "automatic pilot." She repeatedly spoke of needing to be "plugged in" to her boyfriend to feel alive. She desperately missed having him stroke her hair to calm her down when she came home anxious from work. She poignantly stated: "Without him, I am nothing. I can't soothe myself." She lacked the symptoms necessary for a diagnosis of Axis I major depressive episode, but she described herself as depressed and empty.

She met with her therapist for several weeks and reported that she began to "feel alive again." Ms. DD then stated that she felt "plugged in" to her therapist. She tended to misinterpret her therapist's comments to mean that he was about to reject her at any moment. She asked if her therapist would increase the number of sessions from two to five a week so she could see him every weekday. The therapist, on the other hand, believed that all he was doing was listening. He noted to his supervisor: "I don't think she is really interested in anything I say. She's perfectly content if I simply give her my undivided attention."

Kernberg's theoretical formulations (1970, 1974a, 1974b, 1984, 1998) differ sharply from those of Kohut (Table 16–3). The major theoretical differences in their conceptualizations of narcissistic personality disorder may well relate to the different populations of patients that they studied. Kohut's sample consisted of relatively well-functioning outpatients who could afford psychoanalysis. Typically, they were professional people who described vague feelings of emptiness and depression and particular problems in their relationships. They struggled to maintain their professional self-esteem, and they tended to feel slighted by others (Kohut 1971). Kernberg, on the other hand, has always worked in hospitals, and he based his conceptual framework on a mixture of inpatients and outpatients. His clinical descriptions portray patients who are more primitive, more arrogant, more aggressive (often with antisocial features), and more overtly grandiose (although the grandiosity may alternate with shyness) than those depicted by Kohut.

Kohut (1971) differentiated narcissistic personality disorders from borderline conditions. He saw the borderline patient as not having achieved sufficient cohesiveness of the self to be analyzed. His diagnosis of narcissistic personality was based on the development of either the mirror or the idealizing transference in the context of a trial analysis. In contrast, Kernberg (1970) saw the defensive organization of narcissistic personality as strikingly similar to borderline personality disor-

TABLE 16–3.   Dynamic understanding of narcissistic personality disorder—Kohut versus Kernberg

Kohut	Kernberg
1. Bases theory on relatively well-functioning people whose self-esteem is vulnerable to slights—all outpatients	1. Bases theory on a mixture of inpatients and outpatients, most of whom are primitive, aggressive, and arrogant, with haughty grandiosity coexisting with shyness
2. Differentiates narcissistic personality from borderline states	2. Defines narcissistic personality as a strikingly similar subcategory of borderline personality (while most have better ego functioning than borderline patients, some function at an overt borderline level)
3. Does not define inner world of narcissistic personality because emphasis is on internalization of missing functions	3. Delineates primitive defenses and object relations typical of borderline personality disorder
4. Defines archaic "normal" self as one that is developmentally arrested	4. Defines self as a highly pathological structure composed of the fusion of the ideal self, the ideal object, and the real self
5. Views self as nondefensive	5. Views grandiose self as being *defensive* against investment or dependency on others
6. Focuses mainly on libidinal/idealizing aspects, with aggression conceptualized as *secondary* to narcissistic injury	6. Emphasizes envy and aggression
7. Accepts idealization at face value as a normal developmental phase making up for missing psychic structure	7. Views idealization as defensive against rage, envy, contempt, and devaluation

der. In fact, he viewed it as one of several personality types that operate at a borderline level of personality organization (see Chapter 15). He differentiated narcissistic personality disorder from borderline personality on the basis of the narcissist's integrated but pathological grandiose self. This structure is a fusion of the ideal self, the ideal object, and the real self. This fusion results in the destructive devaluation of object images. Patients with narcissistic personality disorder identify themselves with their idealized self-images in order to deny their dependency on external objects (other people) as well as on the inner images of those objects. At the same time, they deny the unacceptable features of their own self-images by projecting them onto others.

The pathological grandiose self explains the paradox of relatively good ego functioning in the presence of the primitive defenses (splitting, projective identification, omnipotence, devaluation, idealization, and denial) typical of the border-line patient. In other words, whereas borderline patients tend to have alternating self-representations that make them look very different from day to day, narcissis-tic patients have a smoother, more consistent level of functioning based on an inte-grated pathological self. Also, the borderline personality is much more likely to have problems related to ego weaknesses, such as poor impulse control and poor anxiety tolerance. These ego weaknesses are much less common in narcissistic per-sonalities because of the smooth-functioning self-structure. However, Kernberg also added that some narcissistic patients function at an overt borderline level. These patients have the grandiosity and haughtiness of the narcissistic personality with the poor impulse control and the kaleidoscopic object relations of borderline patients. It is this subgroup that occasionally requires hospitalization. (Hospital treatment for these patients is similar to that for borderline patients discussed in Chapter 15. Inpatient treatment of narcissistic patients with serious antisocial fea-tures is described in Chapter 17.)

The detailed description of the narcissistic patient's defensive constellation and internal object relations provided by Kernberg is in contrast with Kohut's ten-dency to leave undefined the inner world of the narcissistic patient. Kohut empha-sized the internalization of missing functions from people in the environment and thus was less concerned about the patient's intrapsychic structure. He conceptual-ized the narcissistic self, however, as an archaic "normal" self that is simply frozen developmentally—in other words, the patient is a child in an adult's body. Unlike Kohut, Kernberg (1974a, 1974b) viewed the narcissistic self as a highly pathologi-cal structure that in no way resembles the normal developing self of children. He pointed out that the exhibitionistic self-display of children is charming and en-dearing, in contrast to the greed and demandingness of the narcissist's pathological self.

Another difference in their views of the self relates to the self's defensive func-tioning. Kohut saw the self as essentially nondefensive (i.e., a normally developing self that simply became stuck). Kernberg saw the pathologically grandiose self as defensive against investment in others, and specifically against dependency on oth-ers. This characteristic may manifest itself as a pseudo–self-sufficiency whereby the patient denies any need for nurturance while at the same time attempting to im-press others and gain approval. Narcissistic patients frequently insist, for example, that they have no reactions to their therapists' vacations.

Kohut's view of the narcissistic personality is perhaps more charitable than Kernberg's. He focused mainly on the childhood longing for certain parental re-sponses. Aggression is seen as a *secondary* phenomenon (i.e., narcissistic rage in re-action to not having one's needs for mirroring and idealizing gratified). In that sense, Kohut viewed aggression as an entirely understandable response to parental failures. Kernberg saw aggression as a more primary factor. Inordinately high levels of aggression cause the narcissistic patient to be destructive toward others. In Kernberg's (1970) view, the etiology of this aggression can be either constitutional or environmental. It was seen, however, as arising from within rather than as simply an understandable reaction to the external failures of others. One manifestation of the narcissistic patient's aggression is chronic intense envy (Kernberg 1974b), which causes the patient to want to spoil and destroy the good things of others. Although Kohut did not view envy as having a central role, Kernberg described these patients as constantly comparing themselves with others, only to find themselves tormented with feelings of inferiority and intense yearning to possess what others have. The devaluation of others to deal with one's envy of them is associated with an emptying out of the internal world of object representations and leaves the patient feeling a sense of an internal void (Kernberg 1998). That emptiness can only be compensated for by constant admiration and acclaim from others and an omnipotent control over others so that their free and autonomous functioning and enjoyment do not create further envy.

Idealization was viewed quite differently by Kohut and Kernberg. Kohut viewed idealization in the transference as the recapitulation of a normal developmental phase. Rather than labeling it as a defensive posture, he saw it as a way to make up for missing psychic structure. Fundamental to Kohut's understanding is the notion that the narcissistic individual is incomplete without a selfobject. Kernberg viewed idealization as a defense against a variety of negative feelings, including rage, envy, contempt, and devaluation.

In light of these point-by-point differences between Kohut and Kernberg, it should be clear that Kernberg was describing patients who more closely approximate the oblivious type, while Kohut seemed to be writing about patients who are closer to the hypervigilant type. The narcissistic patients described by Kernberg frequently appear to have nothing but the most superficial forms of object relatedness. If the patient is male, he may have a "Don Juan" syndrome in which he systematically seduces women and discards them when his idealization of them turns to devaluation. Viewing women only as conquests, he has no capacity to empathize with their internal experience. Such a patient seems to have little interest in what others say unless the content is flattering. Although these patients are most commonly male, females may suffer from similar narcissistic pathology.

Ms. EE was an actress who was extraordinarily charming. She was highly successful as an actress because the charisma she exuded on the stage brought her a great deal of acclaim and applause from her audiences. However, she came to treatment because a series of relationships with men had left her feeling that she would never find anyone who would be suitable for her. She described a rapid loss of interest in each lover after an initial period of idealization. She complained that the men seemed to get pre-occupied with their own interests and did not pay her enough attention. Her last relationship had broken up when her boyfriend exploded at her and said, "No man will ever be able to give you the kind of attention you want. The only place you'll ever see that kind of attention is what a mother gives to a baby!" This comment stung Ms. EE and made her begin to think that psychotherapy would be of help. She was basically describing an inability to appreciate the separate subjectivity of her male lovers along with their needs and interests that did not involve her.

The Kohut-Kernberg controversy continues to smolder, with proponents on each side claiming that clinical experience validates their own favorite theoretical perspective. In practice, some narcissistic patients seem to fit one framework better than the other. The broad range of patients encompassed by the term *narcissistic personality disorder* may demand more than one theoretical perspective for explanation. One research effort to validate the two constructs found data consistent with both theories but suggested that the most parsimonious explanation was to view Kohut's model as a special case of Kernberg's more general ego psychological–object relations theory (Glassman 1988).

The theoretical debate between Kohut and Kernberg often obscures other creative contributions to the understanding of narcissistic personality disorder. In a series of papers, Rinsley (1980, 1984, 1985, 1989) linked the origin of narcissistic personality disorder to Mahler's developmental framework (Mahler et al. 1975). He postulated that whereas the borderline patient suffers from a developmental arrest of both separation and individuation subprocesses that reaches a peak during the rapprochement subphase (see Chapters 2 and 15), the narcissistic patient can be characterized as having a developmental *dissociation* of the two subprocesses—individuation was allowed to proceed while separation was arrested. This developmental scenario results in a "pseudo-mature" child who gets the message that he is allowed to separate psychologically from his mother only on the condition that all of his subsequent achievements are ultimately in relation to her. Rinsley's explanation resonates with Kernberg's observation that in certain areas the narcissistic patient may function smoothly and may even be able to achieve impressive gains at work, while still suffering from highly problematic object relations.

Rothstein (1980) attempted to understand the narcissistic personality disorder within the framework of Freud's structural model (see Chapter 2). He defined narcissism as "a felt quality of perfection" that is a universal aspect of the human psyche. This perfect state can be integrated with either a healthy or a pathological ego—the nature of the ego determines whether the narcissism is pathological or healthy.

Modell (1976) used the metaphor of a cocoon to describe the narcissistic individual's sense of nonrelatedness to the environment. This cocoon is like an illusion of omnipotent self-sufficiency, reinforced by grandiose fantasies, which may be initiated by a mother who has an exaggerated grandiose view of her child's capabilities. Modell believed that the noncommunicative and nonrelated facade reflects a fear of merger that the patient must defend against. The therapist's task must be to create a holding environment (Winnicott 1965) to allow development to proceed, much as in the treatment of schizoid personality disorders (described in Chapter 14).

Treatment Approaches

Individual Psychotherapy and Psychoanalysis

Technique

Both Kernberg and Kohut believed that psychoanalysis is the treatment of choice for most patients with narcissistic personality disorder. Because of practical limitations of time and money, many of these patients are also seen in expressive-supportive psychotherapy with a predominance of expressive techniques in once- or twice-weekly sessions. The specific technical suggestions of Kohut and Kernberg reflect their different theoretical conceptualizations.

For Kohut, empathy was the cornerstone of the technique (Ornstein 1974b, 1998). Treaters must empathize with the patient's attempt to reactivate a failed parental relationship by coercing the therapist into meeting the patient's need for affirmation (the mirror transference), for idealization (the idealizing transference), or for being like the therapist (the twinship transference). The emergence of these selfobject transferences should not be prematurely interpreted. Kohut's emphasis on empathizing with the patient as a victim of the empathic failures of others does not imply a predominantly supportive technique. He stressed that the analyst or therapist should interpret—rather than actively gratify—the patient's yearning to be soothed (Kohut 1984). A typical intervention might sound like this: "It hurts when you are not treated the way you feel you deserve to be treated."

Despite Kohut's insistence that his technical approach did not depart radically from classical psychoanalytic technique, his suggestions as described by supervisees (Miller 1985) revealed fundamental differences from that technique. He advised analysts to always take analytic material in a "straight" manner, just as the patient experiences it. The therapist can thus avoid repeating the empathic failures of the parents, who often try to convince a child that his or her actual feelings are *different* from those the child describes. Kohut indicated that, if the face-value approach does not bear fruit, one could always invert material or look for hidden meanings beneath the "experience-near" feelings. This approach is intimately related to Kohut's view of "resistance" as a psychic activity that safeguards the cohesiveness of the self (see Chapter 2).

Kohut was acutely sensitive to evidence of a patient's self-fragmentation in the actual analytic or therapeutic session. When such fragmentations occur, the therapist must focus on the precipitating event rather than on the content of the fragmentation itself (Miller 1985; Ornstein 1974a). For example, after one of Kohut's supervisees sneezed in an analytic session and the patient found it difficult to continue, Kohut advised the analyst to focus on the naturalness of the patient's response to such an unexpected stimulus rather than on the patient's special sensitivity to the stimulus (Miller 1985). This focus is in keeping with a general premise of self psychology that therapists must be continually attuned to how they recapitulate infantile traumas with their patients. Kohut believed that the patient is always right; if the patient feels deflated or hurt, it is reasonable to assume that the analyst or therapist has made an error. He noted that patients frequently feel exposed and ashamed when the analyst calls attention to slips of the tongue, so he did not stress the interpretation of parapraxes. Kohut was always sensitive to the proneness of narcissistic patients to feel shame. The therapist must avoid bypassing the patient's conscious subjective experience to address unconscious material outside the patient's awareness. Interpretations of unconscious motives will only make the patient feel "caught," misunderstood, and ashamed.

Kohut stressed the importance of looking at the *positive* side of the patient's experience, and he scrupulously avoided comments that might be viewed as harshly critical. He called attention to the patient's progress and shunned the asking of questions. He believed that it was the therapist's job to understand, not the patient's (Miller 1985).

Kohut asserted that the goal of psychoanalytic and psychotherapeutic treatment of narcissistic personality disorder is to help the patient identify and seek out appropriate selfobjects. Kohut believed that mental health professionals tend to overvalue separation and autonomy. He was concerned that therapists might use a moralistic tone to convey to patients the expectation that they *should* become more independent.

Kohut's technical approach has been criticized on many counts. His reduction of all psychopathology to empathic failures on the part of parents has been criticized as oversimplified "parent blaming" and as being out of keeping with the core psychoanalytic principle of overdetermination (Curtis 1985; Stein 1979). His emphasis on staying "experience near" in the therapeutic technique has also been challenged as having the potential to overlook important unconscious issues that should be addressed during treatment (Curtis 1985).

Kernberg (1974a, 1974b) observed some of the same transference phenomena as Kohut, but he believed that different technical approaches are indicated. For example, he conceptualized the mirror and idealizing transferences in a more parsimonious manner (Table 16–4). Kernberg saw the patient's grandiose self as being alternately projected and reintrojected so that one idealized figure is always in the room while the other figure is devalued and in the shadow of the idealized person. He also viewed idealization as a frequent defensive operation that involves splitting. In other words, because idealization of the therapist may be the patient's way of defending against split-off feelings of contempt, envy, and rage, the therapist should interpret idealization as a defense rather than simply accepting it as a normal developmental need, as Kohut advocated.

Kernberg's approach in general is much more confrontational than Kohut's. Convinced that the greed and demandingness typical of the narcissistic personality disorder are not simply aspects of normal development, Kernberg believed that these traits must be confronted and examined from the standpoint of their impact

TABLE 16–4. Psychotherapeutic technique—Kohut versus Kernberg

Kohut	Kernberg
1. Views mirror and idealizing transferences as two different poles of bipolar (Kohut 1977) or tripolar (Kohut 1984) self	1. Views mirror and idealizing as aspects of transference related to projection and reintrojection of patient's grandiose self
2. Accepts idealization of patient as normal developmental need	2. Interprets idealization as a defense
3. Empathizes with patient's feeling as an understandable reaction to failures of parents and others	3. Helps patient see his or her own contribution to problems in relationships
4. Accepts patient's comments at face value, viewing resistances as healthy psychic activities that safeguard the self	4. Confronts and interprets resistances as defensive maneuvers
5. Looks at the positive side of patient's experience	5. Examines both positive and negative aspects of patient's experience (if only positive experiences are emphasized, the patient may develop an increased fear of internal envy and rage)
6. Calls attention to patient's progress	6. Focuses on envy and how it prevents patient from acknowledging and receiving help
7. Has treatment goal of helping patient acquire ability to identify and seek out appropriate selfobjects	7. Has treatment goal of helping patient to develop guilt and concern, and to integrate idealization and trust with rage and contempt

on others. Whereas Kohut emphasized the positive side of the patient's experience, Kernberg believed that early, negative transference developments must be systematically examined and interpreted. Specifically, Kernberg stressed that the therapist must focus on envy and how it prevents the patient from receiving or acknowledging help. When patients receive something positive from their therapist, it often escalates their envy because it generates feelings of inadequacy or inferiority in response to the therapist's capacity for nurturing and understanding. A sample interpretation might sound like this: "To avoid painful feelings of envy, you may need to dismiss my comments as being ridiculous or meaningless."

Although Kernberg is often misconstrued as focusing exclusively on negative transference, he in fact advocated a systematic examination of both positive and negative transference developments (Kernberg 1974b). He warned that therapists who address only the positive aspects of the transference may unconsciously increase their patients' fear of their own envy or rage. A patient who believes that the therapist cannot handle those aspects of the patient may therefore split them off and keep them outside the therapeutic process.

Kernberg also differs significantly from Kohut in important ways regarding the goals of treatment. Whereas Kohut's technique implies that the essence of the cure is not in the cognitive sphere, Kernberg believed that a cognitive understanding via the interpretive process is crucial to therapeutic success. The goal of treatment for Kernberg (1970) included developing guilt and concern for others, as well as integrating idealization and trust with rage and contempt (i.e., integrating the "good" aspects of experience with the "bad").

Kernberg viewed persons with narcissistic personality disorder as among the most difficult patients to treat because much of their effort goes into trying to defeat the therapist. For the treatment and the therapist to be effective, these patients must deal with their intense feelings of envy that someone else has good qualities that they lack. The patient defensively uses devaluation and omnipotent control to keep the therapist at a distance. Kernberg believed that for the treatment to be viable, these defensive maneuvers must be continually confronted. A patient with significant antisocial features (which are common in narcissistic patients) may simply be untreatable. (The factors that determine the treatability of antisocial patients are discussed in Chapter 17 in some detail.) However, several factors suggest a favorable prognosis (Kernberg 1970): some ability to tolerate depression and mourning, more guilt than paranoid tendencies in the transference, some ability to sublimate primitive drives, relatively good impulse control, and good motivation. Patients who seek therapy or analysis simply for training purposes or because they think it will confer prestige on them in the eyes of others may present a formidable resistance that contributes to a less favorable prognosis.

In the subgroup of patients just mentioned who operate at an overtly borderline level, Kernberg (1984) suggested that a truly supportive psychotherapy is a much more effective treatment than expressive therapy or analysis. This approach should probably be combined with inpatient treatment if the ego weaknesses, such as lack of impulse control, are particularly severe. The indications for supportive therapy in narcissistic personality disorders include excessive cruelty and sadism, prominent antisocial features, virtually no involvement with other people, intense paranoid reactions to others, and a proneness to chronic rage that is always rationalized as someone else's fault. In these supportive processes, Kernberg (1984) suggested that patients may benefit from "stealing" positive qualities from their therapist. Because this identification with the therapist may help patients function better, the process is best left uninterpreted.

Critics of Kernberg's approach argue that it interferes with the natural development of selfobject transferences. Some have even suggested that aggressively confronting the oral aggression of patients may result in their deteriorated functioning (Brandschaft and Stolorow 1984). In this view, the borderline picture of rage, contempt, and devaluation is an artifact of the narcissistic injury induced by the therapist's "critical interventions." Thus the differences in the kinds of patients described by Kernberg and Kohut could be viewed as partially resulting from iatrogenic factors (Adler 1986).

Psychotherapists faced with the formidable task of treating narcissistic patients must avoid an "either/or" approach to the theories of Kernberg and Kohut. Rather than obsessing about which one is "right," therapists may more usefully apply themselves to listening carefully to their patients, observing the transference and countertransference developments, and particularly noting their responses to trial interventions. In this manner therapists will soon reach a tentative conclusion about which theoretical and technical model is the most helpful with the particular patient under consideration. Some patients will simply not tolerate anything but an empathic, experience-near approach based on Kohut's model. Any deviation from that pattern of interventions will be met with prolonged "shutdowns," with the patient refusing to talk and feeling misunderstood, or even abruptly deciding to quit therapy.

In other cases, the patient may feel understood by interpretations of envy and contempt and may therefore respond better to Kernberg's technique. Some narcissistic patients do not develop any of the selfobject transferences Kohut described, but instead present the therapist with continual devaluation and rage. In some instances, the therapist must interpret and confront these overt verbal attacks or the patient will find it difficult or impossible to persist in the treatment. Mitchell (1988) pointed out that it is erroneous to regard Kohut's approach as more empathic than Kernberg's. Both respond empathically to different dimensions of the patient.

Still other patients can benefit from a combination of technical strategies. Although purists would argue that the two theories are incompatible, the patient is not aware of theories. Moreover, the therapist treats patients, not theories. Many patients require the self psychological approach to technique early in their treatment because it helps build a therapeutic alliance based on a sense that the therapist understands and empathizes with the experience of victimization. After an alliance is established, the therapist may begin to confront patients with their own contributions to their interpersonal difficulties, such as inordinate expectations that others cannot fulfill. Practically speaking, narcissistic pathology can rarely be conceptualized as wholly the fault of either the parents or the patient. More commonly, both parties have contributed to the difficulty, and a comprehensive therapy should address these problems from both angles. Indeed, the majority of analysts and other dynamically oriented clinicians operate from some midpoint between the two extremes (Gabbard 1998; Mitchell 1988). Josephs (1995) suggested that although empathy for the patient's archaic selfobject needs is helpful initially, it ultimately must be counterbalanced by interpretation of the defensive function of the selfobject transferences.

Finally, we must not assume that the etiology and pathogenesis of narcissistic character pathology will always fit neatly into the theoretical frameworks of Kohut and Kernberg. In sharp contrast to the parent with empathic failures, some parents of narcissistic patients tend to be overly indulgent. They seem to encourage grandiosity through a pattern of excessive mirroring. Such parents shower their children with admiration and approval, making them feel truly special and gifted. When these children grow up, they are repeatedly shattered because others do not respond to them as their parents did. In other cases, mother-son incest or variants thereof may produce a narcissistic picture of the hypervigilant type (Gabbard and Twemlow 1994). These patients have a grandiose view of themselves as entitled to occupy a special position with others, combined with a paranoid tendency to anticipate retaliation or abandonment for perceived oedipal transgressions. Hence, therapists can benefit from taking a heuristic approach (see Chapter 4) with narcissistic patients; the therapy should be a collaborative effort in which patient and therapist together discover the origins of the patient's difficulties without rigidly forcing the material to fit one theory or another.

Countertransference

Regardless of a therapist's theoretical framework, certain predictable countertransference problems arise in the treatment of narcissistic patients. Some of these problems are of sufficient magnitude and intensity to undermine the treatment situation irrevocably. Hence, the optimal management of countertransference patterns cannot be stressed enough.

There is little question that psychotherapy as a career provides an opportunity to gratify wishes to be loved, needed, and idealized (Finell 1985). The therapist in the throes of an idealizing transference from a narcissistic patient may enjoy basking in the glow of warmth and love to such an extent as to collude with the patient's wish to exclude hatred and anger from the therapy. A frequent development in the treatment of narcissistic patients is that they will initially idealize their current therapist while devaluing all previous treaters. Instead of viewing this process as a defensive maneuver, therapists who long for idealization may simply accept at face value the notion that they have unique gifts that were lacking in their patients' previous therapists.

Narcissistic issues are not the exclusive province of the narcissistic personality disorder. These issues reside in all patients and in all therapists. Therapists who cannot acknowledge and accept their own narcissistic needs, and then harness them in the service of delivering effective treatment, may instead disavow and externalize them. These defenses contribute to an erroneous view of the patient as the sole carrier of narcissism in the patient-therapist dyad.

Another countertransference problem that regularly surfaces in the treatment of narcissistic patients is boredom. This usually arises from a feeling that the patient is unaware of or oblivious to the therapist's presence. For prolonged periods, the therapist may have to tolerate a sense of being used as a sounding board by the patient. This pattern is particularly typical of the oblivious narcissistic patient who holds forth as though speaking to an audience, ignoring the therapist as a separate person with separate thoughts and feelings.

Mr. FF came to therapy after three previously failed attempts. His last treatment had lasted 3 years with a therapist in another city. Mr. FF denigrated that therapeutic experience as "a complete waste of time" and could not even recall his previous therapist's name. (These two signs, an inability to remember a previous therapist's name and a complete devaluation of the previous therapeutic experience, are often diagnostic clues to narcissistic character pathology.) He said that "doctor what's his name" interrupted him a lot and was not a good listener. Mr. FF talked at great length about his need for a really "special" therapist. He even speculated that there might not be anyone in the city who could really understand him.

As Mr. FF continued to ramble on at some length over many weeks, his therapist began to dread each session. The therapist found his thoughts wandering to his plans for the evening, his financial status, unfinished paperwork, and a variety of other matters with little bearing on Mr. FF and his problems. The therapist also found himself glancing at the clock more often than usual, eagerly awaiting the end of Mr. FF's session. When the therapist intervened, Mr. FF would often ignore his comments and say, "Just let me finish this train of thought first," or, "Oh, yes, I'm already aware of that."

After returning from a 3-week vacation, the therapist resumed his sessions with Mr. FF. In the first session, the patient picked right up where he had left off at the end of their last session, as though no time had elapsed. The therapist, exasperated by his sense that he had no importance whatsoever to Mr. FF, said, "You act as though we saw each other yesterday. Didn't the 3-week separation from me have any impact on you?" Mr. FF detected a critical, sarcastic tone in the therapist's voice and replied, "You have the same problem as my last therapist. You're always inserting yourself into this. I'm not paying you to talk about you or your feelings. I'm here to talk about myself."

All of us have a need to be needed, and it is therefore difficult for therapists to tolerate the "satellite existence" (Kernberg 1970) that many narcissistic patients assign them. This feeling of being excluded by the patient may represent a projective identification process (Adler 1986; Finell 1985) in which the patient excludes the therapist just as he was once excluded by his own parents. Because the narcissistic patient tends to treat the analyst as a self-extension, the patient is likely to evoke certain states in the analyst that reflect the patient's own internal struggles (Groopman and Cooper 1995). In other words, an aspect of the patient is projected onto the therapist, who identifies with that self before helping the patient to reintroject it. The containment of this projected aspect of the patient may be a major part of the psychotherapeutic treatment in narcissistic patients. Understanding this pattern may keep the therapist from withdrawing from the patient, from sadistically confronting the patient, or from feeling hurt and abused by the patient.

The hypervigilant variety of narcissistic personality leads the therapist to struggle with countertransference problems of feeling controlled. When the patient reads every movement as an indication of boredom or rejection, the therapist may feel coerced into sitting still and into focusing attention on the patient every moment. Interventions designed to address this interaction may deal productively with this countertransference development. A therapist working from Kernberg's perspective might say: "You seem to have an unrealistic expectation that you can control others and make them behave as extensions of yourself rather than allowing them to respond from within according to their own needs." A self psychological intervention might consist of "It seems to hurt your feelings when I clear my throat or fidget in my seat because you feel I am not giving you my full attention." Regardless of the pros and cons of these two sample interventions, the main point is that such comments bring a behavioral interaction associated with a countertransference response into the verbal realm, where it can be discussed openly as an issue between therapist and patient.

Finally, the therapist will often have to struggle with countertransference feelings in response to intense devaluation by the patient.

Ms. GG was a narcissistic patient functioning at an overtly borderline level who had been hospitalized for drug abuse. She demanded barbiturates for insomnia and became enraged when her hospital doctor refused to prescribe them. Each time the doctor made daily rounds, Ms. GG would recite her doctor's many shortcomings: "You're only a resident, so you don't understand how to relate to patients. When you try to go into practice after your residency, you won't have any patients because you don't know how to relate to people. Instead of listening to my needs, you practice psychiatry out of a book. You don't even know how to dress. You're a complete joke as a physician." The doctor asked, "Why is it that you feel such hatred for me?" Ms. GG responded, "Hatred? You're not worth hating! You're beneath contempt!"

These verbal barrages are all too common with narcissistic patients. When they go on at some length, the doctor feels useless and impotent, as well as hurt and angry. These patients engender strong countertransference hatred that can lead to vengeful comments or ill-advised management decisions as a way to get back at the patient. Although as therapists we can contain a certain amount of abuse, we all have a limit that only we can determine. When that line is crossed, the therapist may need to confront the patient's contempt forcefully by pointing out how the barrage is destroying the patient's chance of getting effective treatment.

Group Psychotherapy

Dynamic group psychotherapy with narcissistic personality disorders is fraught with difficulties if it is the only treatment used (Azima 1983; Horner 1975; Wong 1979, 1980; Yalom 1985). Oblivious narcissistic patients may enjoy the idea of having an audience in group psychotherapy, but they may also resent the fact that other people take some of the therapist's time and attention. One such patient quit group therapy because he never got enough "air time." The hypervigilant narcissistic patient may be injured at even the suggestion of group therapy. The referral itself is experienced as a rejection or as an indication that the therapist is not interested in the patient. Most narcissistic patients will see group psychotherapy as a situation in which their specialness and uniqueness will be overlooked. Narcissistic patients tend to place extraordinary stress on the group therapist because of their need for narcissistic gratification from the group (Roth 1998). When narcissistic patients do enter group therapy, they often monopolize the group discussions or take on the role of "doctor's assistant," making observations about other people's problems but denying their own (Wong 1979).

Despite the problems inherent in group settings for narcissistic patients, there are clearly some advantages. In groups, narcissistic patients must confront and accept the fact that others have needs and that they themselves cannot expect to be the center of attention at all times. Moreover, narcissistic patients may also benefit from the feedback that others provide about the impact of their character traits on others. Narcissistic patients can have therapeutic effects on others in the group by activating latent feelings of envy and greed in patients with other forms of characterological disturbance (Azima 1983).

Some authors have suggested that combined individual and group psychotherapy may benefit narcissistic patients more than either approach alone (Horwitz 1977; Wong 1979, 1980). Few groups can absorb the narcissistic patient's intense demands for attention, but if an individual process is begun first, the patient may make fewer demands on the group. Wong (1979, 1980) specifically recommended a rather long preparatory period of individual therapy with a technical approach along the lines described by Kohut so that a solid therapeutic alliance exists by the time the patient enters the group. This preparatory period also gives the patient time to explore personal fantasies about group psychotherapy. Wong recommended using the same therapist for both individual and group psychotherapy. Even with the combination, however, the therapist must actively support the patient if the other group members begin to scapegoat the narcissistic member. The group therapist can help the other patients empathize with the narcissistic patient's need to be recognized and admired.

As discussed in Chapter 5, group psychotherapy can serve to dilute intense negative transferences. This principle is certainly applicable to narcissistic patients, and the other patients in the group are often helpful in pointing out the distortions involved in devaluing or idealizing the therapist. Similarly, the countertransference reactions that are so problematic in the treatment of narcissistic patients can also be diluted in group therapy (Wong 1979). However, it is advisable to have only one narcissistic patient at a time in a heterogeneous group, lest the impact of these patients' demandingness overwhelm the other members.

Narcissistic Personality Disorder Over the Life Cycle

Narcissistic patients who come to treatment as young adults often complain about the quality of their intimate relationships. They may have had repeated infatuations that are short-lived and unsatisfying. After the initial luster of the relationship wears off, idealization of the partner turns either to devaluation or to boredom, and they withdraw and seek new partners who can fulfill their needs for admiration, affirmation, unconditional love, and perfect attunement. This pattern of sucking people dry and discarding the empty shells may eventually become tiresome. These patients frequently settle down and marry in their 30s or 40s.

Not surprisingly, characteristic patterns of difficulty occur in the marriages of patients with narcissistic personality disorder. They may first seek marital therapy under the guise of sexual problems, depression, or impulsive behavior (Lansky 1982). Beneath the disguised presentation is often a dread of being shamed or humiliated by the marital partner (i.e., a fear of self-fragmentation, in self psychological terms). A narcissistic husband, for example, may blame his wife for deliberately trying to humiliate him rather than acknowledging that he has a problem with being excessively vulnerable, dependent, and extraordinarily needy of selfobject responses, such as mirroring, from his wife. This same husband may eventually reach a state of chronic narcissistic rage, in which he maintains an intractable resentment and bitterness toward his wife for not treating him in the manner to which he feels entitled. Such marriages may be highly refractory to marital therapy because the narcissistic spouse perceives the injury as so damaging that forgiveness is out of the question and nothing the offending spouse can do could possibly redress the grievances.

Regardless of whether narcissistic patients choose to marry as they travel through life, they are likely to find the aging process highly distressing. In many cases these patients are physically attractive or interpersonally charming and have achieved a certain degree of success during their young adult years. However, although they can postpone facing the emptiness at their core, they cannot ultimately escape it. Kernberg (1974b) noted:

> If we consider that throughout an ordinary life span most narcissistic gratifications occur in adolescence and early adulthood, and that even though the narcissistic triumphs and gratifications are achieved throughout adulthood, the individual must eventually face the basic conflicts around aging, chronic illness, physical and mental limitations, and above all, separations, loss, and loneliness—then we must conclude that the eventual confrontation of the grandiose self with the frail, limited, and transitory nature of human life is unavoidable. (p. 238)

Many narcissistic patients do not age well. Their grandiose fantasies of unending youth and beauty are torn asunder by the vicissitudes of aging. To prove their youth and vigor, they may frantically seek extramarital affairs with partners half their age or take on ill-advised pursuits such as marathon running. Also common are dramatic religious conversions in which the narcissist avoids mourning by a manic flight into the shadow of an idealized object (God).

Much of the pleasure of midlife and old age involves vicarious enjoyment of the success of younger people, such as one's children (Kernberg 1974b). One of the tragedies facing persons who suffer from narcissistic personality disorder is that they are robbed of this source of pleasure because of their envy and despair. These feelings may bring patients to treatment for the first time when they are well into their 40s. Faced with a sense of having missed something and the feeling that their lives are on a faulty course, they may finally be amenable to treatment. They often find themselves lonely, without any supportive relationships, and with a devastating feeling of being unloved. They see themselves confirming the warning of Benjamin Franklin: "He who loves himself will have no rivals."

Some patients with high levels of pathological narcissism may respond favorably to certain life events, so there is reason for hope. Ronningstam et al. (1995) reported on changes in narcissism over a 3-year period in a follow-along study of 20 patients with narcissistic personality disorder. While 40% remained unchanged, 60% showed significant improvement. Examination of life events for the improved patients suggested that three types of experiences had made a difference in their narcissistic orientation. For nine subjects, *corrective achievements* had occurred, leading to an enhanced acceptance of a more realistic self-concept along with a diminution of exaggerated fantasies. For four of the patients, a *corrective relationship* had been instrumental in reducing pathological narcissism. This observation led the investigators to conclude that some narcissistic defenses are not as entrenched as they appear to be in certain individuals who are diagnosed with narcissistic personality disorder. Finally, in three of the patients *corrective disillusionments* occurred that helped the patients gain a more realistic assessment of themselves.

Narcissistic patients provide enormous challenges for therapists. Kernberg (1974b) argued that the effort is well worthwhile, however, because if even partially successful, it will help attenuate the ravages of the second half of life. If, through treatment, narcissistic patients can achieve some degree of empathy, can partially replace their envy with admiration, and can begin to accept others as separate individuals with their own needs, then they may be able to avoid ending their lives in embittered isolation.

References

Adler G: Psychotherapy of the narcissistic personality disorder patient: two contrasting approaches. Am J Psychiatry 143:430–436, 1986

American Psychiatric Association: Diagnostic and Statistical Manual of Mental Disorders, 4th Edition. Washington, DC, American Psychiatric Association, 1994

Azima FJC: Group psychotherapy with personality disorders, in Comprehensive Group Psychotherapy, 2nd Edition. Edited by Kaplan HI, Sadock BJ. Baltimore, MD, Williams & Wilkins, 1983, pp 262–268

Brandschaft B, Stolorow R: The borderline concept: pathological character or iatrogenic myth? In Empathy II. Edited by Lichtenberg J, Bornstein M, Silver D. Hillsdale, NJ, Analytic Press, 1984, pp 333–357

Broucek FJ: Shame and its relationship to early narcissistic developments. Int J Psychoanal 63:369–378, 1982

Cooper AM: Further developments in the clinical diagnosis of narcissistic personality disorder, in Disorders of Narcissism: Diagnostic, Clinical, and Empirical Implications. Edited by Ronningstam EF. Washington, DC, American Psychiatric Press, 1998, pp 53–74

Cooper AM, Michels R: Book review of Diagnostic and Statistical Manual of Mental Disorders, 3rd Edition, Revised (DSM-III-R by the American Psychiatric Association). Am J Psychiatry 145:1300–1301, 1988

Curtis HC: Clinical perspectives on self psychology. Psychoanal Q 54:339–378, 1985

Finell JS: Narcissistic problems in analysts. Int J Psychoanal 66:433–445, 1985

Gabbard GO: Further contributions to the understanding of stage fright: narcissistic issues. J Am Psychoanal Assoc 31:423–441, 1983

Gabbard GO: Two subtypes of narcissistic personality disorder. Bull Menninger Clin 53:527–532, 1989

Gabbard GO: Transference and countertransference in the treatment of narcissistic patients, in Disorders of Narcissism: Diagnostic, Clinical, and Empirical Implications. Edited by Ronningstam EF. Washington, DC, American Psychiatric Press, 1998, pp 125–146

Gabbard GO, Twemlow SW: The role of mother-son incest in the pathogenesis of narcissistic personality disorder. J Am Psychoanal Assoc 42:159–177, 1994

Glassman M: Kernberg and Kohut: a test of competing psychoanalytic models of narcissism. J Am Psychoanal Assoc 36:597–625, 1988

Groopman L, Cooper AM: Narcissistic personality disorder, in Treatments of Psychiatric Disorders, 2nd Edition, Vol 2. Edited by Gabbard GO. Washington, DC, American Psychiatric Press, 1995, pp 2327–2343

Heiserman A, Cook H: Narcissism, affect, and gender: an empirical examination of Kernberg's and Kohut's theories of narcissism. Psychoanalytic Psychology 15:74–92, 1998

Hibbard S: Narcissism, shame, masochism, and object relations: an exploratory correlational study. Psychoanalytic Psychology 9:489–508, 1992

Horner AJ: A characterological contraindication for group psychotherapy. J Am Acad Psychoanal 3:301–305, 1975

Horwitz L: Group psychotherapy of the borderline patient, in Borderline Personality Disorders: The Concept, the Syndrome, the Patient. Edited by Hartocollis PL. New York, International Universities Press, 1977, pp 399–422

Josephs L: Balancing Empathy and Interpretation: Relational Character Analysis. Northvale, NJ, Jason Aronson, 1995

Kernberg OF: Factors in the psychoanalytic treatment of narcissistic personalities. J Am Psychoanal Assoc 18:51–85, 1970

Kernberg OF: Contrasting viewpoints regarding the nature and psychoanalytic treatment of narcissistic personalities: a preliminary communication. J Am Psychoanal Assoc 22: 255–267, 1974a

Kernberg OF: Further contributions to the treatment of narcissistic personalities. Int J Psychoanal 55:215–240, 1974b

Kernberg OF: Severe Personality Disorders: Psychotherapeutic Strategies. New Haven, CT, Yale University Press, 1984

Kernberg OF: Pathological narcissism and narcissistic personality disorder: theoretical background and diagnostic classification, in Disorders of Narcissism: Diagnostic, Clinical, and Empirical Implications. Edited by Ronningstam EF. Washington, DC, American Psychiatric Press, 1998, pp 29–51

Kohut H: The Analysis of the Self: A Systematic Approach to the Psychoanalytic Treatment of Narcissistic Personality Disorders. New York, International Universities Press, 1971

Kohut H: The Restoration of the Self. New York, International Universities Press, 1977

Kohut H: How Does Analysis Cure? Edited by Goldberg A. Chicago, IL, University of Chicago Press, 1984

Lansky MR: Masks of the narcissistically vulnerable marriage. International Journal of Family Psychiatry 3:439–449, 1982

Lasch C: The Culture of Narcissism: American Life in an Age of Diminishing Expectations. New York, WW Norton, 1979

Lewis HB (ed): The Role of Shame and Symptom Formation. Hillsdale, NJ, Lawrence Erlbaum, 1987

Maccoby M: The Gamesman: The New Corporate Leaders. New York, Simon & Schuster, 1976

Mahler MS, Pine F, Bergman A: The Psychological Birth of the Human Infant: Symbiosis and Individuation. New York, Basic Books, 1975

Miller JP: How Kohut actually worked. Progress in Self Psychology 1:13–30, 1985

Mitchell SA: Relational Concepts in Psychoanalysis: An Integration. Cambridge, MA, Harvard University Press, 1988

Modell AH: "The holding environment" and the therapeutic action of psychoanalysis. J Am Psychoanal Assoc 24:285–307, 1976

Ornstein PH: A discussion of the paper by Otto F. Kernberg on "Further contributions to the treatment of narcissistic personalities." Int J Psychoanal 55:241–247, 1974a

Ornstein PH: On narcissism: beyond the introduction, highlights of Heinz Kohut's contributions to the psychoanalytic treatment of narcissistic personality disorders. Annual of Psychoanalysis 2:127–149, 1974b

Ornstein P: Psychoanalysis of patients with primary self-disorder: a self psychological perspective, in Disorders of Narcissism: Diagnostic, Clinical, and Empirical Implications. Edited by Ronningstam EF. Washington, DC, American Psychiatric Press, 1998, pp 147–169

Person ES: Manipulativeness in entrepreneurs and psychopaths, in Unmasking the Psychopath: Antisocial Personality and Related Syndromes. Edited by Reid WH, Dorr D, Walker JI, et al. New York, WW Norton, 1986, pp 256–273

Rinsley DB: The developmental etiology of borderline and narcissistic disorders. Bull Menninger Clin 44:127–134, 1980

Rinsley DB: A comparison of borderline and narcissistic personality disorders. Bull Menninger Clin 48:1–9, 1984

Rinsley DB: Notes on the pathogenesis and nosology of borderline and narcissistic personality disorders. J Am Acad Psychoanal 13:317–328, 1985

Rinsley DB: The adolescent, the family, and the culture of narcissism: a psychosocial commentary. Adolescent Psychiatry 13:7–28, 1986

Rinsley DB: Notes on the developmental pathogenesis of narcissistic personality disorder. Psychiatr Clin North Am 12:695–707, 1989

Ronningstam E, Gunderson J, Lyons M: Changes in pathological narcissism. Am J Psychiatry 152:253–257, 1995

Rosenfeld H: Impasse and Interpretation: Therapeutic and Anti-Therapeutic Factors in the Psychoanalytic Treatment of Psychotic, Borderline, and Neurotic Patients. Edited by Tuckett D. London, Tavistock, 1987

Roth BE: Narcissistic patients in group psychotherapy: containing affects in the early group, in Disorders of Narcissism: Diagnostic, Clinical, and Empirical Implications. Edited by Ronningstam EF. Washington, DC, American Psychiatric Press, 1998, pp 221–237

Rothstein A: The Narcissistic Pursuit of Perfection. New York, International Universities Press, 1980

Stein MH: Book review of The Restoration of the Self by Heinz Kohut. J Am Psychoanal Assoc 27:665–680, 1979

Stolorow RD: Toward a functional definition of narcissism. Int J Psychoanal 56:179–185, 1975

Stone MH: Normal narcissism: an etiological and ethological perspective, in Disorders of Narcissism: Diagnostic, Clinical, and Empirical Implications. Edited by Ronningstam EF. Washington, DC, American Psychiatric Press, 1998, pp 7–28

Wink P: Two faces of narcissism. J Pers Soc Psychol 61:590–597, 1991

Winnicott DW: The Maturational Processes and the Facilitating Environment: Studies in the Theory of Emotional Development. London, Hogarth Press, 1965

Wong N: Clinical considerations in group treatment of narcissistic disorders. Int J Group Psychother 29:325–345, 1979

Wong N: Combined group and individual treatment of borderline and narcissistic patients: heterogeneous versus homogeneous groups. Int J Group Psychother 30:389–404, 1980

Yalom ID: The Theory and Practice of Group Psychotherapy, 3rd Edition. New York, Basic Books, 1985

C H A P T E R
17

Cluster B Personality Disorders

Antisocial

Antisocial patients are perhaps the most extensively studied of all those with personality disorders, but they are also the patients that clinicians tend to avoid the most. In the therapeutic situation, these patients may lie, cheat, steal, threaten, and otherwise act irresponsibly and deceptively. They have been referred to as "psychopaths," "sociopaths," and "character disorders"—terms that, in psychiatry, have traditionally been equated with being untreatable. Some might even argue that such patients should be regarded as "criminals" and should not be included under the purview of psychiatry. Clinical experience suggests, however, that the antisocial label is applied to a broad spectrum of patients, ranging from the totally untreatable to those who are treatable under certain conditions. The existence of this latter group warrants a detailed understanding of these patients so that those amenable to help can receive the best possible treatment.

In his classic work *The Mask of Sanity,* Hervey Cleckley (1941/1976) provided the first comprehensive clinical description of these patients. As his title implies, Cleckley viewed the psychopath as an individual who was not overtly psychotic but whose behavior was so chaotic and so poorly attuned to the demands of reality and society that it indicated a psychosis beneath the surface. Whereas psychopaths seemed to be able to relate superficially to other people, they were completely irresponsible in all their relationships and had no regard for the feelings or concerns of others.

The term *psychopath* fell out of favor during the decades following the appearance of Cleckley's landmark work. *Sociopath* was used for a while, ostensibly as a reflection of the social rather than psychological origins of some of the difficulties faced by these individuals. By the time the American Psychiatric Association's second Diagnostic and Statistical Manual (DSM-II) was published in 1968, the term *antisocial personality* had become the preferred nomenclature. With the arrival of DSM-III in 1980, the antisocial personality disorder had been considerably altered from Cleckley's original description. Although the DSM-III criteria provided more diagnostic detail than those for any other personality disorder, they narrowed the focus of the disorder to a criminal population likely to be connected with oppressed and disadvantaged lower socioeconomic groups (Halleck 1981; Meloy 1988; Modlin 1983).

When the DSM-III criteria were applied to incarcerated offenders, researchers found that the majority of such populations (50%–80%) had diagnosable antisocial personality disorder (Hare 1983; Hart and Hare 1998). Strikingly different results were obtained when researchers used diagnostic criteria that more closely resembled the tradition of Cleckley, in which psychopathy was emphasized. For example, if Hare's Psychopathy Checklist—Revised (PCL-R) were used, only about 25% of the incarcerated offender population would qualify as psychopaths (Hare 1991; Hare et al. 1991). In a study of 137 treatment-seeking cocaine-dependent women (Rutherford et al. 1999), more than a quarter of the women had diagnosable antisocial personality disorder by DSM criteria, but only 1.5% were diagnosed with a moderate level of psychopathy by the PCL-R. This instrument relies on expert clinical ratings rather than self-report and includes items such as irresponsibility; impulsivity; lack of realistic, long-term goals; promiscuous sexual behavior; early behavioral problems; parasitic lifestyle; callousness and lack of empathy; shallow affect; lack of remorse or guilt; need for stimulation and proneness to boredom; grandiose sense of self-worth; and glibness associated with superficial charm. The Axis II Work Group of the Task Force on DSM-IV (American Psychiatric Association 1994) deliberately attempted to provide more emphasis on the personality traits associated with psychopathy and also tried to simplify the criteria set without substantially changing the clinical picture described by the diagnosis (Widiger et al. 1996).

Despite improvements in the DSM-IV criteria (Table 17–1), however, certain problems persist. Although psychopathy traits are somewhat more evident in the new set, the criteria still reflect behavioral rather than psychodynamic constructs. Some of the more dynamically oriented psychopathy items tested in the field trial, such as "inflated and arrogant self-appraisal" and "lacks empathy," did not make it into the final list. The term *psychopath* has grown in popularity in recent years as a diagnostic term that implies particular psychodynamic and even biological features that are not captured in the DSM-IV criteria of antisocial personality disorder (Hart and Hare 1998; Meloy 1988, 1995; Person 1986; Reid et al. 1986). Meloy (1988) used this term to describe persons with a total absence of empathy and a sadomasochistic interactional style based on power rather than emotional attachment. Person (1986) viewed psychopathy as "an impulse disorder in which the short-term relief of anxiety is more important than any long-term consequence" (p. 266). These psychodynamic views are clinically useful because a person can be a psychopath without meeting DSM-IV criteria for an antisocial personality disorder. Conversely, a person can meet the DSM-IV criteria for antisocial personality disorder but not be a psychopath.

One final problem with the DSM-IV criteria is that they are not particularly useful in determining treatability. With antisocial patients, the clinician must determine first and foremost whether a particular patient is treatable under the circumstances. This dilemma can be conceptualized by viewing the antisocial patient as a subcategory of narcissistic personality disorder (Kernberg 1984, 1998; Meloy 1988, 1995; Reid 1985). Indeed, there is a narcissistic continuum of antisocial pathology ranging from the most primitive psychopathy in its purest form, to narcissistic personality disorder with ego-syntonic antisocial features, to narcissistic patients who are simply dishonest in the transference (Kernberg 1984, 1998).

Clinicians will encounter many patients with antisocial features. The dynamic

---

TABLE 17–1.   DSM-IV criteria for antisocial personality disorder

A. There is a pervasive pattern of disregard for and violation of the rights of others occurring since age 15 years, as indicated by three (or more) of the following:
   1. failure to conform to social norms with respect to lawful behaviors as indicated by repeatedly performing acts that are grounds for arrest
   2. deceitfulness, as indicated by repeated lying, use of aliases, or conning others for personal profit or pleasure
   3. impulsivity or failure to plan ahead
   4. irritability and aggressiveness, as indicated by repeated physical fights or assaults
   5. reckless disregard for safety of self or others
   6. consistent irresponsibility, as indicated by repeated failure to sustain consistent work behavior or honor financial obligations
   7. lack of remorse, as indicated by being indifferent to or rationalizing having hurt, mistreated, or stolen from another

B. The individual is at least age 18 years.
C. There is evidence of conduct disorder with onset before age 15 years.
D. The occurrence of antisocial behavior is not exclusively during the course of schizophrenia or a manic episode.

Source.   Reprinted from DSM-IV (American Psychiatric Association 1994), pp. 649–650. Used with permission.

psychiatrist should approach each patient with this narcissistic continuum in mind. Using the dynamic understanding (discussed later in this chapter) related to narcissistic and antisocial pathology, clinicians can make a dynamically informed decision about whether a patient is treatable and what conditions warrant a treatment effort. In this chapter the term *psychopath* is used narrowly to connote that subgroup of patients captured by the Hare PCL-R criteria and the psychodynamic descriptions of Meloy (1988, 1995) and Person (1986). "Antisocial patients" will be used generically to describe patients along the continuum who show varying degrees of antisocial behavior.

Epidemiology

A considerable body of knowledge has been accumulated regarding the epidemiology of antisocial personality disorder (Cadoret 1986), which has a 2%–3% lifetime prevalence in the United States population. Persons with this disorder are more commonly found in impoverished central city areas, and many of them drop out of high school before graduation. There is a downward drift in the lives of antisocial individuals (Person 1986), who tend to make and lose money cyclically until they "burn out" in middle age, often accompanied by severe alcoholism and debilitation (Halleck 1981).

There is a striking correlation between antisocial character pathology and substance abuse (Cadoret 1986; Halleck 1981; Meloy 1988; Modlin 1983; Reid 1985; Vaillant 1983). The current thinking on the interrelationship of the two is that they often coexist but that each has a separate etiology (Cadoret 1986; Reid 1985; Vaillant 1983). It is also well established, of course, that criminal activity is intimately tied to substance abuse (Holden 1986). Fifty-two percent to 65% of felons have also been found to be drug abusers.

It is generally assumed that most patients with antisocial problems are male, and indeed the male-to-female ratio among antisocial personality disorders varies from 4:1 to 7.8:1 (Cadoret 1986). Familial links between psychopathy and somatization disorder (hysteria) have been extensively documented (Cadoret 1978; Cloninger and Guze 1975; Cloninger et al. 1984; Woerner and Guze 1968). One proposed explanation for this correlation is that gender influences whether individuals with hysterical or histrionic personality tendencies will develop antisocial personality or somatization disorder (Lilienfeld et al. 1986).

Psychopathy can and does occur in female patients, despite its much more common occurrence among males. Clinicians may overlook the diagnosis in females because of sex role stereotypes. A seductive and manipulative woman who exhibits considerable antisocial activity is much more likely to be labeled hysterical, histri-onic, or borderline. One 19-year-old hospitalized female patient had been involved in extensive antisocial behavior, including the murder of a man she had said was attempting to rape her, as well as stealing, lying, and undermining the treatment of other patients. At one point during her hospitalization, she convinced two male patients to take a crowbar to her window to help her escape. After flying across country with them (using her parents' credit cards), she abandoned them without money in an airport. Her treatment reached a turning point when she started a fire in her room that threatened the safety of everyone on her hospital unit. Because this patient was attractive, seductive, and not without interpersonal charm, her treaters kept giving her the benefit of the doubt. Some even viewed her behavior as reflecting "depression" rather than antisocial pathology. Yet she met both the DSM-IV criteria for antisocial personality disorder and the psychodynamic criteria for psychopathy.

This tendency to misdiagnose antisocial women may be changing (Reid 1985), however, as women gain increasing social freedom. As more women modify their lifestyles in the direction of traditionally male patterns, more of them may be diag-nosed with antisocial personality disorder.

Psychodynamic Understanding

A comprehensive understanding of the antisocial personality disorder must begin with recognition that biological factors clearly contribute to the etiology and pathogenesis of the disorder. Studies of twins offer convincing evidence that ge-netic factors influence the development of psychopathy (Cadoret 1986). The con-cordance for criminality, for example, is two to three times higher for monozygotic twins than it is for dizygotic twins (Christiansen 1977; Wilson and Herrnstein 1985). In fact, antisocial personality disorder appears to be a model disorder with which to examine the interaction of genes and environment. In a study of 95 male and 102 female adoptees (Cadoret et al. 1995), a biological background of anti-social personality disorder predicted increased adolescent aggressivity, conduct disorder, and adult antisocial behaviors. However, an adverse adoptive home envi-ronment independently predicted an increase in adult antisocial behaviors. A ge-netic predisposition to antisocial personality disorder interacted with problematic adoptive home environments to significantly increase aggressivity and conduct disorder in adoptees.

One of the most elegant studies of the interplay between genes and the environ-ment suggests that the unique environment, *unshared* by siblings in the same family, may have a substantial impact on the development of antisocial behavior. Reiss et al. (1995) studied 708 families with at least two same-sex adolescent siblings involving multiple variations. Ninety-three families had monozygotic twins, 99 had dizygotic twins, 95 had ordinary siblings, 181 had full siblings in stepfamilies, 110 had half-siblings in stepfamilies, and 130 were characterized by genetically unrelated siblings in stepfamilies. Data on parenting styles were collected by video recordings and by questionnaire. Approximately 60% of the variance in adolescent antisocial behavior could be accounted for by negative and conflictual parental behavior directed specifically at the adolescent. The investigators suggested that heritable characteristics of the children evoked harsh and inconsistent parenting. By contrast, siblings without those heritable characteristics did not evoke negative parental behavior, and these siblings seemed to experience a protective effect when harsh parental behavior was directed at the other sibling.

Other investigations have examined the interaction between birth complications and adverse family environments in the development of violent crime. Raine et al. (1996) compared a group of male subjects with obstetric risk factors only, a group with poverty risk factors only, and a group that had both early neuromotor deficits and unstable family environments. They found that those individuals with *both* negative family environments and early neuromotor deficits were significantly more likely to become criminal and violent compared with those who had only the obstetric risk factors or only an impoverished background. In a subsequent report, Raine et al. (1997) found that early maternal rejection interacted with birth complications in predisposing a subject to violence.

Evidence is accumulating about characteristics of the biological substrate for antisocial personality disorder. Levels of 5-hydroxyindoleacetic acid (5-HIAA) are significantly lower in infants with family histories of antisocial personality disorder than in those without such family histories (Constantino et al. 1997). There are also striking linkages between lowered autonomic nervous system responsiveness and risk for criminal behavior (Brennan et al. 1997; Raine et al. 1990, 1995). In fact, heightened autonomic nervous system responsiveness appears to be protective against criminal behavior in prospective follow-along studies of teenagers. From a psychodynamic perspective, individuals who possess strongly internalized standards of right and wrong—often associated with the superego and ego ideal—may experience anxiety and heightened autonomic responsiveness in the form of guilt when they transgress those moral standards. Various neuropsychological deficits in childhood also appear to predict the development of antisocial personality disorder. For example, children with attention-deficit/hyperactivity disorder are at significantly higher risk for subsequent antisocial personality disorder (Mannuzza et al. 1998).

An elegantly designed prospective study (J. G. Johnson et al. 1999) demonstrated that childhood neglect and physical abuse (but not sexual abuse) predicted an increased prevalence of adult antisocial symptoms. Although it is true that experiences of childhood abuse may predict symptoms of antisocial personality disorder in adults, the etiology cannot be reduced to a simple formula that victims become victimizers. In one study (Luntz and Widom 1994), 86% of abused and neglected children did not grow up to have antisocial personality disorder, whereas 7% without such histories did. Likewise, in an investigation of 85 incarcerated women (Zlotnick 1999), childhood abuse was not associated with antisocial personality disorder.

The heritable characteristics of the child, often compounded by perinatal brain injury, may create specific difficulties in parenting. The child may be difficult to soothe and may lack the normal affective responsiveness that the parents long to see. In some cases, parents may already have abusive tendencies because of their own psychopathology; in others, they may grow increasingly impatient and irritated with the child who does not respond as they wish. Meloy (1988) noted two separate processes that often take place in the development of antisocial individuals. One is a profound detachment from all relationships and from affective experience in general. The other is a more object-related path characterized by sadistic attempts to bond with others so as to exercise power and destructiveness. There is also a significant problem in internalization of others because of the genetic/biological deficits in the child and the adverse home environment into which the child is born.

The serious impairment of internalization in the psychopath obviously leads to a massive failure of superego development—the classical hallmark, in a dynamic sense, of the psychopath. The absence of any moral sense in these individuals is one of the chilling qualities that make them seem lacking in basic humanness. Their only value system of any consequence is the exercise of aggressive power, and their only trace of superego development may be the sadistic superego precursors (or stranger selfobjects) manifested by their sadistic and cruel behavior (Kernberg 1984).

Higher-level patients, who do not fit the category of the "pure" psychopath, may exhibit superego lacunae (A. M. Johnson 1949). These individuals, because of their relatively more favorable constitutional factors and environmental experiences with parenting, have some semblance of a conscience but with circumscribed areas in which the superego does not seem to operate. Some of these individuals have been subtly or not-so-subtly encouraged in their antisocial behavior by one or both parents.

Allen was a 10-year-old boy who was admitted to the hospital by his parents. During the admission interview with the psychiatrist and social worker, his mother and father described a long history of aggressive behavior. Allen had repeatedly fought at school, engaged in minor acts of vandalism of neighbors' property, and refused to obey his parents. Allen's father described the incident that finally precipitated his son's admission to the hospital: "This old guy was driving by our house, and Allen was out in the yard with his bow and arrow. Even though the guy was driving 35 miles an hour, Allen was able to shoot an arrow through the car's windshield and hit the guy in the eye. You have to admit that it was a pretty good shot." As a smile flickered across Allen's father's lips, a confused look appeared on Allen's face.

White-collar criminals often fit this category of superego lacunae. Their narcissistic personality structure has allowed them to succeed, but certain defects in their conscience eventually become manifested in antisocial behaviors that are detected by others. It is important in this context to distinguish between antisocial *behavior* and true antisocial personality. Behavior of an antisocial nature may arise from peer pressure, from neurotic conflict, or from psychotic thinking. In these cases, it may bear no relation to antisocial personality disorder.

Another aspect of superego pathology more characteristic of the true psychopath than of the higher-level narcissistic variants is a complete lack of effort to morally justify or rationalize the antisocial behavior (Meloy 1988). When confronted with their antisocial behavior, psychopaths are likely to respond with self-righteousness, declaring that the victims of their antisocial acts deserved what they got. Psychopaths may also choose to lie and to avoid any responsibility for their behavior.

Mr. HH was a 23-year-old man who had been involuntarily committed to long-term hospitalization by the court. Shortly after admission, he was seen by a consultant, and the following dialogue took place:

Consultant: What brings you to the hospital?
Mr. HH: The court sent me.
Consultant: How come?
Mr. HH: I was in a car accident, and my best friend was accidentally killed.
Consultant: How did it happen?
Mr. HH: I was driving down the street, minding my own business, when the guy in front of me slams on his brakes. I plow into his rear end, and the gun in my glove compartment goes off and accidentally shoots my friend through the head.
Consultant: Why did you have a gun in your glove compartment?
Mr. HH: You gotta have a gun in the neighborhood I come from. I gotta protect myself. There's all kinds of drug dealers around.
Consultant: Why did the court commit you to a hospital as the result of an accident?
Mr. HH: Good question.

Consultant: Do you have any emotional problems?

Mr. HH: No, I'm a pretty happy-go-lucky guy.

Consultant: Have you had any other problems with the law?

Mr. HH: The only other thing that happened wasn't my fault either. These buddies of mine ripped off a dollar-changing machine from a laundromat and left it on my porch as a gag. The police thought I did it and arrested me.

Mr. HH's disavowal of responsibility shows his absence of concern about his "best friend" and his complete inability to acknowledge any of his own problems that might have contributed to his situation. This vignette underscores the difficulty therapists may have engaging antisocial patients in treatment because they externalize all problems.

Antisocial and psychopathic behavior is most usefully characterized as a primitive variant of the narcissistic personality disorder continuum (Kernberg 1984, 1998; Meloy 1988, 1995). Table 17–2 illustrates this continuum. At the bottom of the continuum are psychopathic individuals who cannot imagine an ethical quality in others and who are totally incapable of investing themselves in nonexploitative relationships. The next step up on the continuum involves malignant narcissism, characterized by ego-syntonic sadism and a paranoid orientation. Persons in this category differ from psychopathic individuals in that they have some capacity for loyalty and concern for others. They also can imagine that people other than themselves may have moral concerns and convictions. The third category from the bottom in the continuum includes patients with narcissistic personality disorder who show antisocial behavior. These individuals lack the paranoid and sadistic qualities of the malignant narcissist, but they can be ruthlessly exploitative of others in the service of their own goals. However, they do experience guilt and concern at times, and they also may be capable of realistic planning for the future. Their difficulty in making a commitment to in-depth object relations may be reflected in what appears to be antisocial behavior. As one ascends the hierarchy on the continuum,

---

TABLE 17–2. A continuum of antisocial and psychopathic behavior

Antisocial behavior as a part of a symptomatic neurosis
Neurotic personality disorder with antisocial features
Antisocial behavior in other personality disorders
Narcissistic personality disorder with antisocial behavior
Malignant narcissism syndrome
Antisocial personality disorder/psychopathy

Source. Based on Kernberg 1998.

one encounters occasional antisocial behavior in other personality disorders, such as borderline, histrionic, or paranoid personality disorder. These phenomena occur in individuals with much more developed superego structures. At the top two tiers of the continuum, one finds individuals with neurotic characterological traits who may behave in an antisocial manner out of an unconscious sense of guilt, in the hope of being caught and punished. All variations of the narcissistic and antisocial personality disorders may present as individuals who are charming and manipulative in such a way that others are frequently duped.

The psychodynamically based differentiation of the higher-level, treatable narcissistic patient with antisocial features from the untreatable pure psychopath is a highly complicated undertaking because of the tendency of all antisocial patients to deceive clinicians. There are very few studies to guide the clinician, but in the following sections, I will examine some of the criteria that have been found to be useful in determining treatability.

Treatment Approaches

Hospital Treatment

There is a broad consensus that patients with serious antisocial behavior are unlikely to benefit from a treatment approach characterized exclusively by outpatient psychotherapy (Frosch 1983; Gabbard and Coyne 1987; Meloy 1995; Person 1986; Reid 1985). Some form of institutional or residential setting is necessary for even modest improvement. If psychotherapy is employed as a treatment, it must begin while the antisocial patient is contained by the structure of a round-the-clock milieu. These action-oriented individuals will never get in touch with their affective states as long as they have the outlet of behavior to discharge their impulses. It is only when they are immobilized by an inpatient setting that the treatment staff will begin to see them display emotions such as anxiety and emptiness (Frosch 1983; Person 1986).

The decision to hospitalize an antisocial patient in a general psychiatry unit containing patients with a variety of diagnoses usually leads to regret. The psychopath's disruptive behavior may grossly interfere with the treatment of other patients and may bring all therapeutic programs in the milieu to a grinding halt. These patients will steal from, sexually exploit, and assault other patients; they will also lie to and ridicule staff members, smuggle drugs and alcohol into the unit, ridicule the treatment philosophy, and corrupt staff members into dishonest and unethical behavior. Some will systematically destroy any therapeutic alliance that other patients have developed with the treatment staff.

Mr. II was a 46-year-old clergyman forced into hospital treatment by his superiors in the church because his behavior was creating chaos in his congregation. He had seduced a number of women connected with his church and had delighted in "undermining their faith" by challenging the basic tenets of their beliefs. Similar patterns of behavior and object relations occurred in the hospital. Mr. II was silent in most group meetings, but he insidiously "poisoned" the milieu by devaluing staff members in private one-to-one meetings with other patients and by systematically eroding other patients' faith that treatment could be helpful. He viewed all his relationships with female patients and female treaters as sexualized conquests, and even when his sexual acting-out was blocked by the structure of the hospital unit, Mr. II would find other ways to dominate and humiliate women. He often joked with other patients about the relative sexual merits of various female nurses and doctors on the unit, and he devalued the expertise of all staff members regardless of gender. His treatment ended when he planned and executed an elopement with a female inpatient. For several months after Mr. II's departure, however, his impact on the unit was still felt in the patients' pervasive doubt about the value of treatment—a doubt that he had fueled by his comments and actions.

More sophisticated and intelligent psychopaths may present a different problem in the hospital milieu. Because they are aware that hospitalization is far more comfortable than prison, they may deceive the treatment staff into thinking that they are benefiting greatly from treatment. Such patients may be highly skilled charmers who convince the staff that they should be discharged sooner than initially expected. The behavioral changes of antisocial patients that occur during hospitalization, however, do not usually continue beyond discharge (Frosch 1983). These patients often just go through the motions of treatment without being touched by it. When they revert to their antisocial behavior after discharge, the hospital staff may feel outraged because they have been conned.

To avoid wasting an enormous investment of time, money, and energy, hospital clinicians must determine which antisocial patients warrant a trial of psychiatric hospitalization. There is a broad consensus that true psychopaths do not belong on general psychiatry units because they are unable to benefit from such treatment, perhaps because they tend to transform the experience into an exploitative situation of the proverbial "fox in the chicken coop." Specialized units, such as those in prison settings (Kiger 1967; Sturup 1968), nonmedical community residential programs (Reid and Solomon 1981), and wilderness programs (Reid 1985) have had somewhat better success with psychopathic patients and are generally viewed as the only hope for those in this diagnostic category.

In specialized institutional settings, such as the Patuxent Institution in Maryland or the Herstedvester Institution in Denmark, the treatment of the psychopath was enhanced by the homogeneous composition of the milieu. These programs relied heavily on group confrontation by peers. Other psychopaths are familiar with the "con artist" techniques of their cohorts; when these are consistently confronted, their effectiveness is neutralized. These programs also employed a tight structure with clear and rigidly enforced rules. The consequences for rule breaking of any kind were implemented swiftly without any allowance for bargaining or rationalizations on the part of the patients (Reid 1985; Yochelson and Samenow 1977).

Once institutions like these have established control over the lives of the patients and have blocked their usual channels for discharging unpleasant affects through action, these patients may begin to come to terms with their anxiety and aggression. The staff's predictable and consistent responses to all breaks in structure frustrate the usual efforts to get around "the system." These programs depend on court-mandated treatment, however, because the patients may wish to leave the institution as soon as untoward feelings creep into awareness.

A small subsample of patients with antisocial features, usually those with borderline or narcissistic personality disorders, may benefit from voluntary hospitalization in a general psychiatry unit (Gabbard and Coyne 1987). However, differentiating these patients from the pure psychopath may be difficult because of the intense countertransference reactions evoked by antisocial patients. Mental health professionals, by the very nature of their career choice, are inclined to be charitable and kindly toward those they treat. They are prone to give patients the benefit of the doubt and to see them as somehow treatable no matter how resistant they may appear. This tendency may lead treaters to downplay the extent of ruthlessness in psychopathic patients and to assume that antisocial behavior is really a "cry for help." Hospital staff members in particular often have a deep-seated need to see themselves as capable of treating the untreatable patient. They may take extraordinary steps to connect with a patient who has no interest in meaningful human relationships. In reaching out to such patients, they may collude with the tendency of these patients to minimize the extent of their antisocial behavior and superego pathology. One aspect of this countertransference denial is that clinicians may underdiagnose psychopaths and thus view them as more treatable than they actually are. For example, in one study, only half the patients meeting DSM-III-R (American Psychiatric Association 1987) criteria for antisocial personality disorder were given that diagnosis (Gabbard and Coyne 1987).

Underdiagnosis may result in viewing the patient as simply narcissistic rather than psychopathic, as immature—with a character structure that is "not yet crystallized," or as primarily a substance abuser. In fact, substance abuse may be an excuse used by psychopaths themselves. In some cases, treatment staff collude with this excuse by arguing vehemently that a patient's crimes occurred only under the influence of drugs and alcohol so the patient should not be viewed as antisocial. These professionals will often argue that treating the patient's substance abuse will eliminate the problematic antisocial behavior. This point of view fails to consider the extensive overlap between psychopathy and drug abuse, which was described earlier in this chapter. Moreover, some studies have demonstrated that a diagnosis of comorbid substance abuse in no way improves a psychopath's prospects for psychological change (Gabbard and Coyne 1987; Woody et al. 1985).

Because of countertransference contamination in distinguishing between the treatable antisocial patient and the pure psychopath, objective criteria are essential to such determinations. "Gut feelings" about particular patients are notoriously unreliable. The data from one study of hospitalized patients with antisocial features found that there are three predictors of a reasonably positive treatment outcome for these patients in a general psychiatry unit (Gabbard and Coyne 1987) (Table 17–3).

As explained earlier in this chapter, the presence of an Axis I diagnosis of a major depressive episode effectively rules out (by definition) the presence of true psychopathy. Patients who meet the Axis I criteria for depression have some superego development and some capacity, however minimal, for remorse. Similarly, the presence of anxiety represents some concern about one's behavior and its consequences. Finally, the presence of an Axis I psychotic diagnosis, such as mania, suggests that pharmacological treatment may improve the prognosis. It is certainly well known that individuals in the midst of a manic episode often exhibit antisocial behavior. Pharmacological treatment has not been particularly effective for the true psychopath (Halleck 1981).

The same study delineated several predictors of negative treatment response for the same population (see Table 17–3). When there is no other way to keep psycho-

---

TABLE 17–3. Predictors of positive and negative treatment response on a general psychiatric unit

Negative response
1. History of felony arrest
2. History of repeated lying, aliases, conning
3. Unresolved legal situation at admission
4. History of felony conviction
5. Hospitalization forced as an alternative to incarceration
6. History of violence toward others
7. Diagnosis on Axis I of organic brain impairment

Positive response
1. Presence of anxiety
2. Axis I diagnosis of depression
3. Axis I psychotic diagnosis other than depression or organic brain syndrome

Note. Based on Gabbard and Coyne 1987.

pathic patients involved in treatment, they may benefit from involuntary hospitalization in a specialized penal setting. Psychopaths who are forced to seek hospital treatment as an alternative to prison, however, will simply exploit the opportunity to con the staff of the unit, who are predisposed anyway to see such patients as "sick" or "disturbed" rather than as criminals in need of punishment. Under these conditions, the patients will either disrupt the unit or merely go through the motions of treatment. Many patients will use the hospital to "hide out" from an unresolved legal situation that requires a court appearance. A serious history of violence bodes poorly for treatment because, when these patients become frustrated, they may resort to violence, either against staff members or against other patients. Likewise, a serious organic brain impairment may interfere with a patient's ability to understand and benefit from the constructive feedback provided in a hospital milieu, which in turn may increase frustration.

Antisocial patients seldom have all the positive predictors and rarely lack any of the negative predictors in Table 17–3. Although there is no ideal antisocial patient, each additional positive predictor improves a patient's suitability for hospital treatment, and each negative predictor worsens the patient's amenability to hospital treatment (Gabbard and Coyne 1987).

Even with a relatively favorable profile, antisocial patients present a host of difficulties in a typical psychiatric milieu. Only long-term hospital treatment has a chance of producing any lasting change in these patients. They naturally attempt to continue their pattern of impulsively translating their feelings into actions. The cornerstone of treatment must therefore be a tightly controlled structure. From day one, treaters must anticipate and address likely forms of acting-out in the hospital. Certain expectations must be spelled out at admission. For example, the patient must be told that substance abuse, violence, theft, and sexual relationships with other patients will not be tolerated. If the patient is a drug abuser, all mail must be opened in front of staff members to help prevent the smuggling in of drugs. Patients must be clearly told that they will be accompanied by staff whenever they leave the unit and that they will remain at that level of responsibility for a considerable time. Phone calls and access to cash and credit cards also must be restricted. The patient should be made aware that any breaks in structure will result in clear-cut consequences, such as room restriction. Treatment must be viewed initially as being conducted on a trial basis only—as a period of evaluation—to determine the patient's suitability for treatment. All these conditions may be written out as a "contract" at the time of admission, so that the patient will have a copy for reference.

Staff members must scrupulously monitor their countertransference reactions, both as individuals and in the group context. Three common staff reactions are disbelief, collusion, and condemnation (Symington 1980). Disbelief may surface as denial that the patient is really "that bad." Rationalizing antisocial behavior as being due to such problems as drug abuse or adolescent rebellion may cause staff members to deny the presence of psychopathic features and to instead view the patient as depressed or misunderstood.

Collusion is one of the most problematic forms of countertransference. A common development in the hospital treatment of antisocial patients is for the patient to corrupt one or more staff members. In the belief that they are helping the patient, the staff members involved in such countertransference acting-out may commit illegal acts or otherwise behave unethically. Staff members have been known to lie on behalf of such patients; they also have falsified records, been seduced into sexual relationships, and helped these patients to escape from the hospital. These countertransference developments can be understood as part of the projective identification process whereby a corrupt aspect of the patient's self enters the treater and transforms that individual's behavior. Staff members who are involved in such countertransference acting-out often report that "I was not acting like myself."

Another way to conceptualize these countertransference collusions is that they are the result of what Meloy (1988) referred to as *malignant pseudo-identification*. In this process, "the psychopath consciously imitates or unconsciously simulates a certain behavior to foster the victim's identification with this individual, thus increasing the victim's vulnerability to exploitation" (p. 139). Through simulated tearfulness, remorse, or sadness, antisocial patients manipulate clinicians into empathizing with them. If only one clinician sees this simulated self-presentation of the patient, it can lead to splitting among the hospital staff. The staff member involved in the malignant pseudo-identification will adamantly defend the patient against the "attacks" of other staff members. Meloy points out that these simulated affects in the patient can often be identified by sadistic countertransference feelings in the face of the patient's outpouring of sadness and by the patient's apparently rapid recompensation, leaving observers with the impression that they have witnessed a performance.

Condemnation is a third common countertransference reaction. It is often manifested in expressions by hospital staff that a patient is totally untreatable and that no effort should be made to establish a treatment relationship. Such a decision can be made by rationally assessing objective factors, but it is more often a knee-jerk reaction to hearing some history of antisocial activity. This automatic reaction may be countertransference in the narrow sense, because it is based on the treater's past experience with similar individuals. Condemnation that stems from intensive work with the patient may be understood as a projective identification with the aggressive introject of the patient.

Other common countertransference reactions in the treatment of antisocial patients include feelings of helplessness and impotence in the face of a treatment-resistant patient, wishes to destroy the patient that grow out of anger, and feelings of invalidity and loss of identity (Strasberger 1986). The treatment staff may also fear an assault by these patients, who are often threatening and menacing. (Certain psychopathic patients evoke an intense fear of predation in treaters merely by looking at them [Meloy 1988].) Fear of assault may lead staff members to avoid implementing the firm structure that the patient so desperately needs. To avoid arousing the patient's anger or violence, staff members may rationalize their loose structure and indulgence of the patient. Perhaps one of the most problematic countertransferences is the assumption of psychological complexity in a psychopathic individual (Meloy 1995). Institutional treatment staff often have a great deal of difficulty accepting that the psychopath is fundamentally *different* from them. He has no concern for the feelings or safety of others and interacts with treatment staff only in the service of his own interests. The psychopath may exploit this countertransference blind spot by presenting himself as identical to the treaters. This *narcissistic twinship* is a frequent ploy to enlist treaters in a corrupt collusion. By convincing staff members that they and he are fundamentally the same, the patient gains the treaters' trust in ways that allow him greater freedom or power. This attunement to the treatment staff reflects the highly developed sense of empathy possessed by many psychopathic patients despite the traditional view of these patients as unempathic.

A major aspect of the hospital treatment of antisocial patients must be the continual focus on their faulty thought processes (Yochelson and Samenow 1976). When they pose as the victim because of being held accountable for their behavior, they must be confronted with how they are responsible for what happens to them. Staff members must also function as auxiliary egos in terms of judgment. The staff must point out over and over how these patients fail to anticipate the consequences of their behavior.

The antisocial patient tends to move directly from impulse to action. The hospital staff must therefore help these patients insert *thought* between impulse and action. In other words, each time an antisocial patient has an impulse, the staff must encourage the patient to think about what may result from the action. In milieu treatment, patients must also learn that impulses and actions grow out of feelings. Often the language of emotions is so foreign to the patients that they cannot identify their internal states.

All these strategies focus on the "here and now" in the milieu, because exploring the childhood origins of such problems is often useless with antisocial patients. Any attempt by the antisocial patient to corrupt staff members must also be confronted *as it occurs.* If an intervention is not made immediately after the acting-out behavior, then the patient may dismiss it or forget it.

A case example of a treatable antisocial patient will illustrate many of the principles described here.

Mr. JJ was a single 24-year-old who came to a long-term hospital unit after being released from prison, where he had served time for selling cocaine. The hospitalization was not a condition of parole, and Mr. JJ was seeking admission voluntarily. He said that he needed to change his lifestyle so that he would stop abusing drugs and destroying any chance he had to become successful. In addition to a history of selling and abusing cocaine, Mr. JJ also had a history of extensive antisocial behavior, including lying, cheating, stealing, and operating as a building contractor without a license. His object relations were characterized by exploitative and manipulative patterns. Despite this ominous-sounding history, Mr. JJ experienced genuine anxiety about his destructive behavior and was motivated to change it. Moreover, because he was not under pressure to seek hospitalization, he was viewed as having a reasonable chance to improve. Diagnostically, Mr. JJ was best described as having a narcissistic personality with antisocial features.

The cornerstone of Mr. JJ's treatment plan was a contractual agreement between him and the treatment team. This contract stipulated that Mr. JJ would have to adhere to a specific structure in order to be adequately treated. This structure included staff accompaniment to all activities and appointments outside the unit, staff monitoring of telephone calls, a $25-per-week allowance and no access to credit cards, no visits from friends, attendance at all treatment activities and meetings, no violent behavior, no sexual behavior with other patients, no substance abuse, and no negotiation of this structure. By frustrating the various outlets for impulses, the staff forced the patient to deal with his anxiety and internal emptiness rather than to discharge it through acting-out behavior.

The patient found this structure enormously frustrating and restricting, but he seemed to realize that it was necessary. Mr. JJ was repeatedly confronted by staff members about his tendency to externalize problems that occurred in relationships on the unit. He was told that he was not a passive victim under the influence of others but, rather, an active contributor to the problems that occurred with other people on the unit. He was a handsome and charming man who behaved seductively toward a number of female patients but then complained that he could not possibly please them all.

Mr. JJ also devalued the treatment structure, openly saying that it was ridiculous and that he did not require such restrictions. He aroused considerable sympathy from other patients by portraying himself as a victim of an extremely harsh and sadistic treatment team. The clinicians working to deal with this manipulation conducted a good deal of group work on the unit. In the group meetings, Mr. JJ was confronted with his efforts to appear as a victim instead of as a manipulative patient whose history warranted such tight structure. Since he would not mention his antisocial behavior in the treatment meetings, the staff often had to remind him, and the other patients, of the reasons for Mr. JJ's hospitalization. He had developed an artificial split between his "bad self," which he had left outside the hospital, and his "good self," which was in the hospital. He repeatedly minimized his antisocial past as being "past history." The treatment staff, on the other hand, confronted him with the reality that *he* had committed those antisocial acts and that he still had the potential for such behavior. Thus Mr. JJ's splitting maneuvers were challenged, and his "good self" and "bad self" were brought together.

Early in the treatment, Mr. JJ broke the established structure on several occasions by using the phone to call friends who might supply him with cocaine. Whenever this occurred, the staff immediately implemented further restrictions, such as unit confinement, without discussion or negotiation. Mr. JJ also had to open all his mail in front of a staff member, who checked to be sure that no drugs or contraband were being mailed to him.

On one occasion Mr. JJ was able to manipulate a female mental health technician (who found him charming and attractive) into loaning him a dollar to buy a Coke. After buying the Coke, he did not return any change to her. While the mental health technician dealt with her countertransference acting-out in supervision, Mr. JJ was confronted about his actions in a group treatment meeting. He went on at great length about how "totally ridiculous" it was to focus on such a small amount of money. He said that he had fully intended to return the change, but that he had simply forgotten. The treatment team confronted his minimization and denial and pointed out that his behavior outside the hospital was being repeated, only on a smaller scale.

Over time, Mr. JJ became increasingly psychologically minded. He was referred for twice-weekly psychotherapy after he began to show an ability to reflect on the staff's confrontations rather than to respond defensively and automatically. A turning point occurred when a female patient in his "harem" attempted suicide because she could not stand the way he was leading her on while simultaneously sharing his attention with several other women. Only then did Mr. JJ begin to realize that his exploitative relationships with women could be highly destructive. He also eventually realized that he lacked empathy for others and was simply using women to gratify his own needs. By the time he left the hospital, he had begun to piece together how internal anxiety states led him to drug abuse and other impulsive actions as a way to "treat" his anxiety. Specifically, he realized that he was extremely concerned about being rejected or abandoned by women, so he maintained several relationships at a time to reduce his vulnerability. He called this manipulation his "spare tire" strategy.

After discharge, Mr. JJ continued psychotherapy and joined Narcotics Anonymous as well. In his final meeting with his hospital psychiatrist, Mr. JJ noted that his inpatient experience was the first time that he had ever really felt understood. In his own words, "You guys knew what a con artist I was." At 4-year follow-up, Mr. JJ had remained abstinent from cocaine and other drugs and was working full-time in a business-related field. He had become quite active in the stock market, where he was able to sublimate his thrill-seeking and risk-taking tendencies in a legal and socially acceptable manner.

Mr. JJ is unusual among hospitalized antisocial patients. Many will leave treatment when the frustration becomes too great to bear. A small subgroup, however, can benefit from long-term hospitalization. As with borderline patients, milieu treatment combined with psychotherapy provides these patients with an opportunity to internalize new patterns of object relatedness. One reason for Mr. JJ's improvement was the "softening" or modification of his aggressive self- and object representations. Clearly, the enormous expense of such intensive treatment must not be squandered on patients who will misuse the treatment or who will not benefit from it.

Individual Psychotherapy

Outpatient individual psychotherapy of the severely antisocial patient is doomed to failure. Affects will be discharged through action because there is no contained environment in which to control such channeling. In addition, the patient's lies and deceptions are so pervasive that the therapist will have no idea what is really going on in the patient's life. In an institutional or hospital setting, there is some reason for guarded optimism about psychotherapy with a select subgroup of antisocial patients such as Mr. JJ. As with hospital treatment, the clinician's task is to determine which patients are worth the time, energy, and money required by a long-term therapy process with an uncertain outcome.

At present there is no systematic body of controlled empirical research that offers much encouragement for a treatment effort. Meloy (1995) provided the general axiom that the severity of the psychopathy should be inversely proportional to the treatment efforts. He also suggested that the safety of the clinician and the availability of supervision should always be paramount concerns.

The pure psychopath, in the dynamic sense, will not respond to psychotherapy, and so it should not be attempted (Kernberg 1984; Meloy 1988, 1995; Woody et al. 1985). Further along the continuum, the patient who has a narcissistic personality disorder with severe antisocial features is somewhat more amenable to psychotherapy. These patients may subtly reveal dependency in the transference, their antisocial behavior may have an enraged quality about it, and their internal "ideal object" may be somewhat less aggressive than that of the pure psychopath (Kernberg 1984; Meloy 1988). They may attempt to rationalize or justify their behavior, thus reflecting some rudimentary value system. Their treatability will be essentially determined by their ability to form some semblance of an emotional attachment to others and to exercise some rudimentary superego functions.

Projective psychological testing may be extraordinarily helpful in assessing the antisocial patient's superego development and object relations. The Rorschach has been used, for example, to quantitatively evaluate the severity of the antisocial pathology (Exner and Weiner 1986). Although patients may successfully deceive clinicians during an interview by simulating guilt or concern for others, they have much more difficulty with the ambiguous stimuli of an inkblot, where there are no obviously "correct" answers.

The presence of bona fide depression appears to be a sign of amenability to psychotherapy just as it is a positive predictor of hospital treatment response. In a study of patients with antisocial personality disorder who were opiate addicts, the presence of depression appeared to indicate suitability for psychotherapy even if there continued to be behavioral manifestations of psychopathy (Woody et al. 1985). The antisocial patients in the study who were not depressed fared poorly in psychotherapy. In addition, the absence of relatedness to others was the most negative predictor of psychotherapy response.

Clinicians who evaluate antisocial patients must feel comfortable making a recommendation for no treatment. Such a decision may be a perfectly rational determination based on the patient's strengths and weaknesses and the danger that the patient might pose to those attempting to treat him. This manner of evaluating treatability differs greatly from the knee-jerk countertransference response described earlier. Meloy (1988), using his extensive experience in the psychotherapy of psychopaths, has identified five clinical features that absolutely contraindicate any attempt in psychotherapy (Table 17–4). Sadistic cruelty toward others, total absence of remorse, and lack of emotional attachment are three key features that differentiate the psychopath from the more treatable narcissistic patient. The chilling countertransference feelings that lead therapists to fear for their personal safety can paralyze them and preclude any constructive efforts at treatment. Finally, the paradoxical contraindications of both high and low intelligence reflect the extremely bright patient's adeptness at thwarting the process and the dull patient's cognitive inability to grasp the therapist's interventions.

Deceiving or conning others is a way of life for antisocial patients. They experience a powerful sense of delight, or even exhilaration, whenever they "put something over" on their therapist (Bursten 1972; Meloy 1988). Unconscious envy of the therapist's positive qualities often leads to this repetitive cycle of deception. The exhilarating feeling of triumph at a successful con is laced with contempt, which serves as a defense against envy. The patient's avoidance of a meaningful relationship with the therapist also wards off feelings of envy, but leaves the patient feeling empty.

If therapists can accept the fact that these patients will practice deception, they can proceed with psychotherapy based on the recommendations of those therapists who have had extensive experience with this population (Adler and Shapiro 1969; Frosch 1983; Kernberg 1984; Lion 1978; Meloy 1988, 1995; Person 1986;

TABLE 17–4.	Clinical features that contraindicate psychotherapy of any kind

1. A history of sadistic, violent behavior toward others that resulted in serious injury or death
2. A total absence of remorse or rationalization for such behavior
3. Intelligence in either the very superior or the mildly mentally retarded range
4. A historical incapacity to develop emotional attachments to others
5. An intense countertransference fear of predation on the part of experienced clinicians even without clear precipitating behavior on the part of the patient

Source. Based on Meloy 1988.

Reid 1985; Strasberger 1986; Vaillant 1975). These recommendations can be distilled into seven basic principles of technique:

1. *The therapist must be stable, persistent, and thoroughly incorruptible.* More than with any other patient group, the therapist must be absolutely scrupulous about maintaining normal procedures in therapy (Person 1986). Deviating from the structure and usual context of the hours is inadvisable. These patients will do whatever they can to corrupt the therapist into unethical or dishonest conduct. David Mamet's movie *House of Games* (1987) portrays the perils of attempting to help the antisocial patient by departing from the role of therapist and becoming overinvolved in the patient's life.
2. *The therapist must repeatedly confront the patient's denial and minimization of antisocial behavior.* Pervasive denial even infiltrates the antisocial patient's choice of words. If the patient says, "I ripped off this guy," the therapist needs to clarify, "So, you are a thief." If the patient says, "I offed this dude," the therapist may confront the patient by responding, "So, you are a murderer then." This technique of repeated confrontation enables the therapist to help these patients become aware of their tendency to externalize all responsibility, and they can therefore begin to acknowledge and accept responsibility for their antisocial behavior.
3. *The therapist must help the patient connect actions with internal states.* Just as with antisocial patients undergoing hospital treatment, those in individual psychotherapy require education in this regard.
4. *Confrontations of here-and-now behavior are more effective than interpretations of unconscious material from the past.* In particular, the patient's denigration of the therapist and contemptuous devaluation of the process must be repeatedly challenged.
5. *Countertransference must be rigorously monitored to avoid acting-out by the therapist.* Any collusion must also be carefully avoided, despite the tendency to "take the path of least resistance."

6. *The therapist must avoid having excessive expectations for improvement.* Antisocial patients will detect this *furor therapeuticus* and will take great delight in thwarting their therapist's wishes to change them. Therapists whose self-esteem depends on the improvement of their patients should not treat antisocial patients.

7. *Treatable conditions, such as Axis I disorders, should be identified and treated.*

Progress is painstakingly slow with antisocial patients in psychotherapy. At some level, these patients experience therapy as a threat to the grandiose self. They will fight their therapist every step of the way to avoid giving up their cherished grandiosity. Therapists must therefore be cognizant of this resistance and must realize that the patient's internal cohesiveness depends on a grandiose self-concept (Reid 1985). For long periods in the therapy process, the therapist may feel paralyzed by the patient's overt or covert threats (Kernberg 1984). This intimidation may de-skill therapists and effectively stalemate their efforts. To avoid becoming victimized by their patients, therapists must be constantly attuned to these attempts at control.

One final comment about neutrality is in order. Therapists treating antisocial patients cannot reasonably expect to maintain a neutral position regarding the patient's antisocial activities. Attempting to do so would be tantamount to a silent endorsement of or collusion with the patient's actions. More to the point, the therapist's moral outrage will be evident in a myriad of nonverbal communications and vocal intonations, so the patient will view any effort at neutrality as hypocritical. When therapists are shocked at a patient's antisocial behavior, they should simply say so (Gedo 1984). Empathy, in accord with the self psychological approach, is both misguided and collusive in such instances.

Even when therapists are capable of navigating the various obstacles of resistance presented by the antisocial patient, their attempts to be effective can still backfire. Competent therapists who are able to avoid being destroyed by the patient are the ones most likely to evoke intense envy, which may surface as hatred toward the loving or idealized object (i.e., the therapist), eventually leading to an intractable negative therapeutic reaction. Despite these pitfalls, however, many experienced clinicians believe that psychotherapeutic efforts with these patients pay off frequently enough to warrant such heroic treatment.

References

Adler G, Shapiro LN: Psychotherapy with prisoners. Current Psychiatric Therapies 9:99–105, 1969

American Psychiatric Association: Diagnostic and Statistical Manual of Mental Disorders, 2nd Edition. Washington, DC, American Psychiatric Association, 1968

American Psychiatric Association: Diagnostic and Statistical Manual of Mental Disorders, 3rd Edition. Washington, DC, American Psychiatric Association, 1980

American Psychiatric Association: Diagnostic and Statistical Manual of Mental Disorders, 3rd Edition, Revised. Washington, DC, American Psychiatric Association, 1987

American Psychiatric Association: Diagnostic and Statistical Manual of Mental Disorders, 4th Edition. Washington, DC, American Psychiatric Association, 1994

Brennan PA, Raine A, Schulsinger F, et al: Psychophysiological protective factors for male subjects at high risk for criminal behavior. Am J Psychiatry 154:853–855, 1997

Bursten B: The manipulative personality. Arch Gen Psychiatry 26:318–321, 1972

Cadoret RJ: Psychopathology in the adopted-away offspring of biologic parents with antisocial behavior. Arch Gen Psychiatry 35:176–184, 1978

Cadoret RJ: Epidemiology of antisocial personality, in Unmasking the Psychopath: Antisocial Personality and Related Syndromes. Edited by Reid WH, Dorr D, Walker JI, et al. New York, WW Norton, 1986, pp 28–44

Cadoret RJ, Yates WR, Troughton E, et al: Genetic-environmental interaction in the genesis of aggressivity and conduct disorders. Arch Gen Psychiatry 52:916–924, 1995

Christiansen KO: A preliminary study of criminality among twins, in Biosocial Bases of Criminal Behavior. Edited by Mednick SA, Christiansen KO. New York, Gardner, 1977, pp 89–108

Cleckley HM: The Mask of Sanity: An Attempt to Clarify Some Issues About the So-Called Psychopathic Personality, 5th Edition. St. Louis, MO, CV Mosby, 1976 (original work published 1941)

Cloninger CR, Guze SB: Hysteria and parental psychiatric illness. Psychol Med 5:27–31, 1975

Cloninger CR, Sigvardsson S, von Knorring A-L, et al: An adoption study of somatoform disorders, II: identification of two discrete somatoform disorders. Arch Gen Psychiatry 41:863–871, 1984

Constantino JN, Morris JA, Murphy DL: CSF 5-HIAA and family history of antisocial personality disorder in newborns. Am J Psychiatry 154:1771–1773, 1997

Exner JE Jr, Weiner IB: The Rorschach: A Comprehensive System, Vol 1: Basic Foundations, 2nd Edition. New York, Wiley, 1986

Frosch JP: The treatment of antisocial and borderline personality disorders. Hospital and Community Psychiatry 34:243–248, 1983

Gabbard GO, Coyne L: Predictors of response of antisocial patients to hospital treatment. Hospital and Community Psychiatry 38:1181–1185, 1987

Gedo JE: Psychoanalysis and Its Discontents. New York, Guilford, 1984

Halleck SL: Sociopathy: ethical aspects of diagnosis and treatment. Current Psychiatric Therapies 20:167–176, 1981

Hare RD: Diagnosis of antisocial personality disorder in two prison populations. Am J Psychiatry 140:887–890, 1983

Hare RD: The Hare Psychopathy Checklist—Revised. Toronto, Ontario, Multi-Health Systems, 1991

Hare RD, Hart SD, Harpur TJ: Psychopathy and the DSM-IV criteria for antisocial personality disorder. J Abnorm Psychol 100:391–398, 1991

Hart SD, Hare RD: Association between psychopathy and narcissism: theoretical views and empirical evidence, in Disorders of Narcissism: Diagnostic, Clinical, and Empirical Implications. Edited by Ronningstam EF. Washington, DC, American Psychiatric Press, 1998, pp 415–436

Holden C: Growing focus on criminal careers. Science 233:1377–1378, 1986

Johnson AM: Sanctions for superego lacunae of adolescents, in Searchlights on Delinquency: New Psychoanalytic Studies. Edited by Eissler KR. New York, International Universities Press, 1949, pp 225–245

Johnson JG, Cohen PA, Brown J, et al: Childhood maltreatment increases risk for personality disorders during early childhood. Arch Gen Psychiatry 56:600–606, 1999

Kernberg OF: Severe Personality Disorders: Psychotherapeutic Strategies. New Haven, CT, Yale University Press, 1984

Kernberg OF: Pathological narcissism and narcissistic personality disorder: theoretical background and diagnostic classification, in Disorders of Narcissism: Diagnostic, Clinical, and Empirical Implications. Edited by Ronningstam EF. Washington, DC, American Psychiatric Press, 1998, pp 29–51

Kiger RS: Treating the psychopathic patient in a therapeutic community. Hospital and Community Psychiatry 18:191–196, 1967

Lilienfeld SO, VanValkenburg C, Larntz K, et al: The relationship of histrionic personality disorder to antisocial personality and somatization disorders. Am J Psychiatry 143: 718–722, 1986

Lion JR: Outpatient treatment of psychopaths, in The Psychopath: A Comprehensive Study of Antisocial Disorders and Behaviors. Edited by Reid WH. New York, Brunner/Mazel, 1978, pp 286–300

Luntz BK, Widom CS: Antisocial personality disorder in abused and neglected children grown up. Am J Psychiatry 151:670–674, 1994,17N

Mannuzza S, Klein RG, Bessler A, et al: Adult psychiatric status of hyperactive boys grown up. Am J Psychiatry 155:493–498, 1998

Meloy JR: The Psychopathic Mind: Origins, Dynamics, and Treatment. Northvale, NJ, Jason Aronson, 1988

Meloy JR: Antisocial personality disorder, in Treatments of Psychiatric Disorders, 2nd Edition, Vol 2. Edited by Gabbard GO. Washington, DC, American Psychiatric Press, 1995, pp 2273–2290

Modlin HC: The antisocial personality. Bull Menninger Clin 47:129–144, 1983

Person ES: Manipulativeness in entrepreneurs and psychopaths, in Unmasking the Psychopath: Antisocial Personality and Related Syndromes. Edited by Reid WH, Dorr D, Walker JI, et al. New York, WW Norton, 1986, pp 256–273

Raine A, Venables PH, Williams M: Relationships between central and autonomic measures of arousal at age 15 years and criminality at age 24 years. Arch Gen Psychiatry 47:1003–1007, 1990

Raine A, Venables PH, Williams M: High autonomic arousal and electrodermal orienting at age 15 years as protective factors against criminal behavior at age 29 years. Am J Psychiatry 152:1595–1600, 1995

Raine A, Brennan P, Mednick B, et al: High rates of violence, crime, academic problems, and behavioral problems in males with both early neuromotor deficits and unstable family environments. Arch Gen Psychiatry 53:544–549, 1996

Raine A, Brennan P, Mednick SA: Interaction between birth complications and early maternal rejection in predisposing individuals to adult violence: specificity to serious, early-onset violence. Am J Psychiatry 154:1265–1271, 1997

Reid WH: The antisocial personality: a review. Hospital and Community Psychiatry 36: 831–837, 1985

Reid WH, Solomon G: Community-based offender programs, in The Treatment of Antisocial Syndromes. Edited by Reid WH. New York, Van Nostrand Reinhold, 1981, pp 76–94

Reid WH, Dorr D, Walker JI, et al (eds): Unmasking the Psychopath: Antisocial Personality and Related Syndromes. New York, WW Norton, 1986

Reiss D, Hetherington EM, Plomin R, et al: Genetic questions for environmental studies: differential parenting and psychopathology in adolescence. Arch Gen Psychiatry 52: 925–936, 1995

Rutherford MJ, Cacciola JS, Alterman AI: Antisocial personality disorder and psychopathy in cocaine-dependent women. Am J Psychiatry 156:849–856, 1999

Strasberger LH: The treatment of antisocial syndromes: the therapist's feelings, in Unmasking the Psychopath: Antisocial Personality and Related Syndromes. Edited by Reid WH, Dorr D, Walker JI, et al. New York, WW Norton, 1986, pp 191–207

Sturup GK: Treating the Untreatable: Chronic Criminals at Herstedvester. Baltimore, MD, Johns Hopkins University Press, 1968

Symington N: The response aroused by the psychopath. International Review of Psychoanalysis 7:291–298, 1980

Vaillant GE: Sociopathy as a human process: a viewpoint. Arch Gen Psychiatry 32:178–183, 1975

Vaillant GE: Natural history of male alcoholism, V: is alcoholism the cart or the horse to sociopathy? British Journal of Addiction 78:317–326, 1983

Widiger TA, Cadoret R, Hare R, et al: DSM-IV antisocial personality disorder field trial. J Abnorm Psychol 105:3–16, 1996

Wilson JQ, Herrnstein RJ: Crime and Human Nature. New York, Simon & Schuster, 1985

Woerner PI, Guze SB: A family and marital study of hysteria. Br J Psychiatry 114:161–168, 1968

Woody GE, McLellan AT, Luborsky L, et al: Sociopathy and psychotherapy outcome. Arch Gen Psychiatry 42:1081–1086, 1985

Yochelson S, Samenow SE: The Criminal Personality, Vol 1: A Profile for Change. New York, Jason Aronson, 1976

Yochelson S, Samenow SE: The Criminal Personality, Vol 2: The Treatment Process. New York, Jason Aronson, 1977

Zlotnick C: Antisocial personality disorder, affect dysregulation and childhood abuse among incarcerated women. J Personal Disord 13:90–95, 1999

C H A P T E R
18

Cluster B Personality Disorders

Hysterical and Histrionic

In the transition from DSM-II (American Psychiatric Association 1968) to DSM-III (American Psychiatric Association 1980), hysterical personality disorder disappeared from the official diagnostic nomenclature of American psychiatry. This change eliminated a diagnostic entity with a time-honored clinical tradition paralleled by few other psychiatric syndromes. DSM-III replaced it with histrionic personality disorder which, the manual suggests, is synonymous with hysterical personality disorder. In fact, the diagnostic criteria for DSM-III histrionic personality disorder described a much more primitive, much more impulsive, and much less stable variant that sounded remarkably like borderline personality disorder.

Despite the DSM-III-R (American Psychiatric Association 1987) modifications, the diagnostic criteria for histrionic personality disorder still failed to capture the well-integrated and higher-functioning hysterical personality well known to dynamic clinicians for decades. Studies using DSM-III-R criteria continued to find overlap between histrionic and borderline personality diagnoses in the range of 44%–95% (Pfohl 1991).

The DSM-IV (American Psychiatric Association 1994) criteria (Table 18–1) added a new item, "considers relationships to be more intimate than they actually are," based on historical concepts and the favorable ratings of expert consultants (Pfohl 1991). The new criteria, however, still do not capture the well-integrated and higher-functioning hysterical personality. Because both the high-level hysterical personality disorder and the more primitive histrionic personality disorder are

TABLE 18–1. DSM-IV criteria for histrionic personality disorder

A pervasive pattern of excessive emotionality and attention seeking, beginning by early adulthood and present in a variety of contexts, as indicated by five (or more) of the following:

1. is uncomfortable in situations in which he or she is not the center of attention
2. interaction with others is often characterized by inappropriate sexually seductive or provocative behavior
3. displays rapidly shifting and shallow expression of emotions
4. consistently uses physical appearance to draw attention to self
5. has a style of speech that is excessively impressionistic and lacking in detail
6. shows self-dramatization, theatricality, and exaggerated expression of emotion
7. is suggestible, i.e., easily influenced by others or circumstances
8. considers relationships to be more intimate than they actually are

Source. Reprinted from DSM-IV (American Psychiatric Association 1994), pp. 657–658. Used with permission.

commonly encountered in clinical practice, both will be considered in this chapter in an effort to make clinically useful distinctions.

Hysterical Versus Histrionic

The staunchly atheoretical nature of the personality disorder criteria in DSM-IV is particularly problematic when considering patients with hysterical or histrionic tendencies. To determine the appropriate treatment for this diverse group of patients, a careful psychodynamic assessment is far more crucial than a descriptive cataloging of overt behaviors. One primary source of confusion in the related literature has been a tendency to rely on behavioral characteristics instead of dynamic understanding.

A further source of confusion is that the term *hysterical* has been used not only to describe a personality disorder but also to refer to a disease largely of women, characterized by frequent surgeries and multiple somatic complaints, and to denote various conversion symptoms, such as paralysis or blindness, that have no organic basis. The former condition, known as Briquet's hysteria or Briquet's syndrome, is currently subsumed by somatoform disorder in DSM-IV. Conversion symptoms may now be found in Axis I under conversion disorder. Hysterical conversion symptomatology is what opened the gates of the unconscious to Freud and led to the development of psychoanalysis. Freud understood conversion symptoms as symbolic physical symptoms that represented displaced and repressed instinctual wishes. However, there is a broad consensus in modern psychiatry that hysterical conversion symptoms and hysterical personality disorder are not related either clinically or dynamically (Chodoff 1974). Although conversion symptoms can occur in patients with hysterical personality disorder, they also can occur across a wide variety of other character diagnoses.

During the first half of the century, the intrapsychic conflicts associated with the hysterical personality were thought to derive from genital-oedipal developmental issues. Part of the legacy of Freud's work with hysterical conversion symptoms was the more generalized view that repressed sexuality was of paramount importance in both character neuroses and neurotic symptoms. Clinically unsuccessful psychoanalytic efforts to treat these patients led some to question Freud's formulation. Beginning with Marmor's classic 1953 article, the psychiatric literature has strongly identified pregenital (particularly oral) issues as central to the pathogenesis of hysterical personality disorder (Chodoff 1974).

The literature of the last three or four decades has seen a convergence of opinion regarding the existence of both "healthy" and "sick" hysterical patients (Baumbacher and Amini 1980–1981; Blacker and Tupin 1977; Chodoff 1974; Easser and Lesser 1965; Horowitz 1995, 1997; Kernberg 1975; Lazare 1971; Sugarman 1979; Wallerstein 1980–1981; Zetzel 1968). "Healthy" hysterical patients are referred to by a variety of names, including "good," "phallic," and "true." Even more labels have been applied to those in the latter group—"oral hysterics," "so-called good hysterics," "hysteroids," and "infantile personalities." For reasons of clarity, in this chapter I will refer to the healthier group as those with *hysterical personality disorders* and the more disturbed group as those with *histrionic personality disorders*.

Defining the exact interrelationship between the hysterical and the histrionic personality is a controversial process. While some have argued that the two are simply gradations along a continuum (Blacker and Tupin 1977; Lazare 1971; Wallerstein 1980–1981; Zetzel 1968), others have viewed the two groups as so different as to constitute sharply distinct entities (Baumbacher and Amini 1980–1981; Sugarman 1979). Horowitz (1995, 1997) has noted that patients who exhibit an interpersonal style characteristic of a histrionic personality disorder may be psychiatrically healthy, neurotic, narcissistic, or borderline in terms of the coherence of their identity and the continuity of their regard for significant others. These levels are differentiated by the level of integration of self and others in the person schemas of the individual. Person schemas of "all good" and "all bad" that are split off from one another are associated with the borderline level. The histrionic patient organized at a narcissistically vulnerable level has a more cohesive self-schema but is vulnerable to feeling grandiose or extremely impoverished. These individuals also view others as if they were extensions of themselves. The neurotically organized histrionic patient in Horowitz's model has long-standing, unresolved internal conflicts that are enacted in repetitive maladaptive relationship cycles in the sphere of intimacy and work. For purposes of this discussion, the neurotically organized histrionic patient will be considered identical with the patient with hysterical personality disorder, whereas patients who are organized at a narcissistic or borderline level will be subsumed under the group referred to as histrionic personality disorders.

What appears to link hysterical persons and histrionic persons is an overlap in overt behavioral characteristics, such as labile and shallow emotionality, attention seeking, disturbed sexual functioning, dependency and helplessness, and self-dramatization. These qualities have come to be associated with the use of "hysterical" by laypersons to mean *dramatic overreaction.* The paradox is that these characteristics are far more typical of histrionic patients than of hysterical patients. As Wallerstein (1980–1981) noted: "Those who behaviorally look more hysterical in the sense of the dramatic or flamboyant hysterical character type are the very ones who look less hysterical in the sense of the dynamics of the 'good' or 'true' hysteric" (p. 540). Zetzel (1968) similarly observed that the "so-called good hysterics" who appear floridly hysterical are often mistaken for analyzable, high-level hysterical patients although they are actually primitively organized and unanalyzable—what I refer to here as *histrionic personalities.*

The literature distinguishing the two groups can be summarized by listing the characteristics that differentiate hysterical personality disorder from histrionic personality disorder (Easser and Lesser 1965; Kernberg 1975; Lazare 1971; Sugarman 1979; Zetzel 1968) (Table 18–2). The histrionic personality is more florid than the hysterical in virtually every way. All the DSM-IV criteria symptoms are more exaggerated in the histrionic person. Greater lability of affect, more impulsivity, and a more overt seductiveness are all hallmarks. The sexuality of these patients is often so direct and unmodulated that it may actually "turn off" members of the opposite sex. Their demanding, exhibitionistic need to be the center of attention may also fail to engage others because of its ruthless nature. In this regard, these patients clearly have much in common with persons who have narcissistic personality disorder.

By contrast, persons who have true hysterical personality disorder may be much more subtly dramatic and exhibitionistic, and their sexuality may be expressed more coyly and engagingly. In addition, Wallerstein (1980–1981) suggested that a sizable group of high-level hysterics are not dramatic or flamboyant at all. He described these patients as "constricted wallflowers, shy and even tongue-tied in interpersonal encounter, at extremes mousy and totally inhibited in demeanor and interaction" (p. 540). He persuasively pointed out that a focus on overt behavior rather than underlying dynamics can result in a misdiagnosis.

TABLE 18–2.   Differentiation of hysterical personality disorder from histrionic personality disorder

Hysterical Personality Disorder	Histrionic Personality Disorder
1. Restrained and circumscribed emotionality	1. Florid and generalized emotionality
2. Sexualized exhibitionism and need to be loved	2. Greedy exhibitionism with a demanding, oral quality that is "cold" and less engaging
3. Good impulse control	3. Generalized impulsivity
4. Subtly appealing seductiveness	4. Crude, inappropriate, and distancing seductiveness
5. Ambition and competitiveness	5. Aimlessness and helplessness
6. Mature, triangular object relations	6. Primitive, dyadic object relations, characterized by clinging, masochism, and paranoia
7. Separations from love objects can be tolerated	7. Overwhelming separation anxiety occurs when abandoned by love objects
8. Strict superego and some obsessional defenses	8. Lax superego and a predominance of primitive defenses, such as splitting and idealization
9. Sexualized transference wishes develop gradually and are viewed as unrealistic	9. Intense sexualized transference wishes develop rapidly and are viewed as realistic expectations

Patients with hysterical personality disorder are often reasonably successful at work and demonstrate ambition as well as constructive competitiveness. This active mastery can be juxtaposed with the aimless, helpless, dependent quality that keeps histrionic patients from succeeding except in the sense of passively manipulating others to meet their needs. Whereas the true hysterical patient has attained mature whole-object relations characterized by triangular oedipal themes and has been able to form significant relationships with both parents, the histrionic patient is fixated at a more primitive dyadic level of object relations often characterized by clinging, masochism, and paranoia.

Hysterical patients can tolerate separation from their love objects even though they may identify those relationships as their main area of difficulty. Histrionic patients, on the other hand, are often overwhelmed with separation anxiety when apart from their love objects. The strict superego and other obsessional defenses of the hysterical patient contrast with the histrionic patient's typically lax superego and predominantly more primitive defenses, such as splitting and idealization.

When hysterical patients enter psychotherapy or psychoanalysis, sexualized transference wishes develop gradually over a considerable time and are generally viewed as unrealistic by the patients themselves. Histrionic patients, on the other hand, develop intense erotic transference wishes almost immediately and often view these wishes as realistic expectations. When the wishes are frustrated, the patient may become furious with the therapist for not being more gratifying. Zetzel (1968) pointed out that the hysterical patient's capacity to differentiate the therapeutic alliance from transference feelings is intimately linked with the ability to separate internal from external reality, an ego function that is compromised in the histrionic patient.

The distinguishing features of the histrionic personality disorder highlight its close relationship with the borderline personality disorder. Kernberg (1975), for example, explicitly conceptualized the infantile personality as having an underlying borderline personality organization. These patients do not defend against genital sexuality so much as against passive and primitive orality (Lazare 1971).

Patients with hysterical personality disorder, on the other hand, usually present with problems that revolve either around genital sexuality per se or around difficulties with the sexual objects in their lives. Although the hysterical female has classically been described as "frigid" or anorgasmic, she may also be promiscuous or fully orgasmic but basically dissatisfied with her sexual relationships. She may be unable to make a romantic or sexual commitment to a man who is appropriate for her, instead falling hopelessly in love with an unavailable man. Another recurrent problem for the female hysterical patient is that men often misinterpret her actions as sexual advances, and she is continually surprised at this misunderstanding—a fact that reflects the *unconscious* nature of her seductiveness.

Gender and Diagnosis

Throughout the history of psychiatry, the hysterical personality has been associated with the female gender. This tendency to think of the diagnosis only in relation to women probably relates more to cultural sex role stereotypes than to psychodynamics. Halleck (1967) pointed out that deprived males in our society tend to deny their own needs and attack those they believe have rejected them. Women in our society, however, are not expected to deny their dependency needs and have "little opportunity to express aggression directly" (p. 753). Female children "are more likely to adapt to deprivation by seeking to bind people to . . . [them] through relationships in which . . . [the women assume] a highly dependent role" (p. 753). Others (Hollender 1971; Lerner 1974) have noted that the hysterical personality characteristics reflect cultural expectations of how women are supposed to adapt in American society. Another glaring contributor to the overwhelming tendency to view hysterical personality as a female disease is the fact that, with few exceptions, the literature on the disorder has been written entirely by men (Chodoff and Lyons 1958; Luisada et al. 1974).

Despite the predominant association between hysterical personality and femininity, hysterical personality disorder has been extensively documented in males (Blacker and Tupin 1977; Cleghorn 1969; Kolb 1968; Halleck 1967; Luisada et al. 1974; MacKinnon and Michels 1971; Malmquist 1971). The descriptions of male hysterical patients fall into two broad subtypes: the hypermasculine and the passive/effeminate. Those in the hypermasculine subtype are directly analogous to the classical female hysteric in that they are caricatures of masculinity. They may be "Don Juans" who act seductively toward all women and may even engage in antisocial behavior. The latter subtype of passive/effeminate males may be "foppish" (MacKinnon and Michels 1971), flamboyant homosexuals or passive, impotent heterosexuals who are fearful of women. The same distinction between the high-level hysterical personality and the lower-level histrionic personality can be made in male patients, based largely on the same criteria used to distinguish the two groups in females.

In a study of 27 male patients with hysterical personality disorder, Luisada et al. (1974) found that the vast majority were heterosexual, but that all had some form of disturbed sexual relationships. Antisocial behavior, such as lying and unreliability, were common problems in the group, as were alcohol and drug abuse. These investigators identified both passive/effeminate and hypermasculine subtypes, with unstable relationships typical of both. Many of these patients would probably receive a diagnosis of narcissistic personality disorder, some with antisocial features, but as a group they tended to have much more warmth toward and empathy for others than the true narcissist. Nevertheless, empirical research (Hamburger et al. 1996) has demonstrated high rates of psychopathy in at least some patients with histrionic personality disorder.

Despite the overt differences in the behavior of the passive/effeminate subtype and the hypermasculine subtype, the underlying dynamics of these two variants of the male hysterical personality disorder are remarkably similar. These dynamics and their contribution to the behavioral facade of the male hysterical patient will be discussed later in this chapter.

Cognitive Style and Defense Mechanisms

One aspect of intrapsychic functioning that links the hysterical and the histrionic personality disorders is cognitive style. Shapiro (1965) identified the cognitive style typical of these personality disorders as generally "global, relatively diffuse, and lacking in sharpness, particularly in sharp detail. In a word, it is *impressionistic*" (p. 111). When a therapist asks a patient with this cognitive style, "How was your weekend?" the response is likely to be along the lines of "just great" or "really awful," without any supportive detail. The same order of response is likely to apply to significant figures in the patient's life. When one hysterical patient was asked to describe her father, she responded, "He's just super!" Similarly, when patients with this form of cognitive style approach a task, such as psychological testing, they are inclined to avoid concentrating on facts and to instead respond with a hunch. When a highly successful and intelligent professional man was asked to estimate the population of the United States, he hastily replied, "I don't know. I think it's around 5 billion." When the psychologist pressed him for a little more thought about the question, the man recognized that he had given the population of the world rather than the population of the country. The patient was not ignorant, but his histrionic cognitive style made him resent having to concentrate on such details. The therapist may encounter considerable frustration, for example, in getting historical facts about a patient's family background.

This global, impressionistic cognitive style is intimately connected with the use of defense mechanisms by hysterical and histrionic patients (Horowitz 1977b, 1995, 1997). They inhibit information processing to blunt strong emotions. Repression, denial, dissociation, and suppression are defensive strategies that also reduce emotional arousal. These patients may say "I don't know" when what they really mean is "I must not know" (Horowitz 1997). In the early literature on hysteria, this blunting of emotional connection was often described as *la belle indifférence,* referring to the female patient's apparent lack of concern about her conversion symptoms. The hysterical or histrionic cognitive style may account for this failure to integrate or recognize implications, consequences, and details of experience.

On the other hand, this inhibition of emotional arousal generally oscillates with exaggerated emotional displays designed to elicit responses from others. Hysterical/histrionic patients deploy their attention globally and diffusely, but much of their focus is on whether or not others are paying attention to them.

Dissociative states, like conversion symptoms, have often been classified as hysterical phenomena, even though they are found in patients with a variety of diagnoses. The most extreme manifestation of dissociation is dissociative identity disorder, which involves both splitting—in the sense that different self-representations are maintained as separate—and repression—in the sense that the primary personality usually has no memory of the alters. The reactions of histrionic patients to their emotional outbursts resemble dissociation and dissociative identity disorder, albeit in attenuated form. These patients often have poor recall of their actions, which they say seemed to be like those of "someone else."

One histrionic patient who also suffered from dissociative symptoms discovered cuts on her left breast but could not explain how they got there. Shortly after this discovery, her husband found her in the bathroom at 3 A.M.; she was in a dissociated state and was cutting her left breast lightly with a razor blade. Hypnotized for diagnostic purposes, the patient said, "I must suffer as my mother suffered." Her mother had just undergone surgery for breast cancer. This patient also illustrates the defense mechanism of identification, another common hysterical defense (MacKinnon and Michels 1971).

One final defense mechanism that may be found in both hysterical and histrionic patients is emotionality itself. Becoming intensely, yet superficially and shallowly, emotional may defend against deeper, more heartfelt affects that the patient wishes to avoid (MacKinnon and Michels 1971). Knee-jerk emotionality in concert with the global, impressionistic cognitive style serves to keep the histrionic patient from being in touch with any genuine affective states or attitudes toward self and others.

Psychodynamic Understanding

Because a variety of overt behaviors in both genders are subsumed under the categories of hysterical and histrionic personality disorders, a careful psychodynamic assessment is crucial to the informed assignment of the appropriate type of psychotherapy. Female patients with hysterical or histrionic personality styles tend to encounter difficulties at two of the classical psychosexual stages of development: they experience relative maternal deprivation during the oral stage, and they have difficulty resolving the oedipal situation and emerging with a clear sexual identity (Blacker and Tupin 1977). Although both hysterical and histrionic patients have some difficulty with oral and phallic-oedipal issues, the histrionic patient obviously encounters greater difficulty at the earlier stage, whereas the hysterical patient is fixated primarily at the later stage.

In the case of the histrionic female patient, the lack of maternal nurturance leads her to turn to her father for the gratification of dependency needs (Blacker and Tupin 1977; Hollender 1971; MacKinnon and Michels 1971). She soon learns that flirtatiousness and dramatic exhibitionistic displays of emotion are required to gain her father's attention. As she matures, she learns that she must repress her genital sexuality to remain "daddy's little girl." When the little girl grows up, the primitive neediness characteristic of all her sexual relations may be termed the *breast-penis equation*. She often engages in promiscuous sexual behavior that is ultimately unsatisfying since the male penis only serves as a substitute for the maternal breast she unconsciously longs for.

The female with hysterical personality disorder has negotiated the oral stage of development with a reasonable degree of success. She, too, is disappointed with her mother, but the disappointment occurs at a more advanced stage of development. In the phallic stage of development directly preceding the full-blown oedipal situation, the little girl must come to terms with the fact that she cannot physically possess her mother as her father can. The narcissistic injury ensuing from this awareness of genital difference normally leads the little girl to transfer her libidinal phallic strivings from her mother to her father during the oedipal phase of development.

As little girls, these women often idealized their father, perhaps as the only man worth having. This intense attachment led to rivalrous feelings toward the mother and active wishes to replace her. In the course of therapy or analysis, many hysterical patients recover previously repressed fantasies of this nature. If they perceive that their brothers are granted special status with their fathers by virtue of their male gender, they also may develop deep resentment and may become highly competitive with men.

Although anorgasmia has classically been associated with hysteria, sexual symptomatology actually is much more varied in patients with hysterical or histrionic personality disorder. Some may have relatively asymptomatic sexual functioning but are cut off from any authentic inner experience of love or intimacy during sexual relations. Sexual body parts may be exhibited through provocative ways of dressing, even though there is little erotic arousal associated with the provocative behavior. In fact, a common occurrence in female hysterical and histrionic patients is surprise when others respond to them as though they are seductive or sexually provocative. In other words, there is a dissociation between the overtly sexualized behavior unconsciously designed to attract attention and the empathic attunement to how it will affect others. All sexuality may be tinged with incestuous meanings because of the oedipal attachment to the father. These women also may choose inappropriate partners as a further defense against giving up oedipal longings. These dynamics are often covert, however, and often only become clear after a careful evaluation. Although some hysterical patients may have overt, conscious attachments to their father, others will have repressed this dimension of development. Their conscious experience of their father may be tinged with anger as a defense against their underlying longing. Similarly, they may be unaware of their rivalrous feelings toward their mother, whom they consciously love. Evidence of hysterical dynamics in the female patient may come instead from persistent patterns of triangular relationships, such as falling in love with married men, or from slowly emerging developments in the transference, such as intense rivalry with other female patients. Whether or not the dynamics are repressed may depend on the father's response to his daughter's oedipal longings. If he views such feelings as unacceptable, he will convey this attitude to his daughter, who will then feel that she must repress them.

The exaggerated theatrical behavior typical of these patients often relates to a core experience of early childhood that involved not being recognized. In other words, parents who were too self-absorbed, too depressed, or too resentful of their child's developmental needs may have tuned the child out and not recognized the child's internal affective experience. In this regard, caregivers may not have served the necessary containing function to help the child process and metabolize over-whelming and frightening affect states. As Riesenberg-Malcolm (1996) has stressed, the hyperbole or exaggeration may be an effort by patients to distance themselves from what is going on internally while also making others take notice of unrecognized emotions.

The developmental dynamics outlined for the female patient may be similarly applied to the male. The histrionic male patient will have experienced maternal de-privation and will have looked to his father for nurturance. If the father is absent or emotionally unavailable, the boy child is faced with two alternatives: he may model himself after his mother and develop a passive, effeminate identity, or (in the absence of a true masculine role model) he may mimic various cultural stereotypes of hypermasculinity to take flight from any anxiety about effeminacy and to counter-act his regressive pull to be like his mother (Blacker and Tupin 1977).

The male patient with hysterical personality disorder resembles his female counterpart in that he enters the phallic stage intensely attached to his mother. He also experiences feelings of genital inadequacy when comparing himself to his father or other adult males. The narcissistic injury associated with greater genital awareness prevents him—just as it does some females—from entering the compet-itive arena of the Oedipus complex. He remains attached to his mother, and his heterosexual relationships are largely related to efforts to counteract his underly-ing feelings of genital inadequacy. He is always disappointed in women, since none of them can measure up to his mother. Some men with this hysterical configura-tion will choose a celibate lifestyle, such as the priesthood, to unconsciously main-tain unswerving loyalty to their mother. Other boys will deal with their perceived genital inadequacy by indulging in hypermasculine activities, such as bodybuilding and the compulsive seduction of women. Thus they can reassure themselves that they are "real men" with nothing to feel inferior about.

No discussion of female hysteria would be complete without reference to incest and childhood seduction. Freud originally believed that many of his hysterical pa-tients had been seduced by their fathers because he so often heard such reports from his patients. He later became convinced that many of these reports were fantasies stemming from oedipal wishes. Amidst the furor over whether Freud's view was correct, many clinicians have adopted an either/or position. Either little girls are actually seduced, or they merely fantasize seduction. This dichotomy is further complicated by the fact that many women who have been victimized by incest nevertheless have powerful fantasies about and yearnings for the perpetrator of the incest. Even women who have never been violated by their father may still have powerful conscious or unconscious sexual wishes for him. Finally, there is considerable middle ground where erotized interactions occur that do *not* result in overt incest, but that *do* encourage fantasies.

In terms of the developmental pathogenesis of histrionic and hysterical personality disorder, a history of actual incest is much more likely to be found in the histrionic patient. These patients may go through their adult life repeating the original trauma by seeking out men who are forbidden in one way or another, such as therapists, married men, or bosses. They may be unconsciously attempting to actively master a passively experienced trauma by being the one to initiate it rather than the one to passively submit.

The higher-level hysterical patient is much less likely to have a history of overt incest but may have had what she perceived as a special relationship with her father. Hysterical patients frequently have a father who was unhappy with his wife and turned to the patient for fulfillment and gratification not possible in the marriage. The patient may receive an implicit message that she must remain loyal to her father forever to rescue him from an unhappy marriage. Fathers in this situation may give subtle or even overt signs of disapproval whenever their daughters show interest in other men. In this scenario, the hysterical patient will find herself surrounded with dynamics similar to incest, only in attenuated form. Hysterical patients with these dynamics and family constellations may find themselves unable to give up their dependency on their father and get on with their lives.

Treatment Approaches

Individual Psychotherapy

Patients with hysterical personality disorder generally respond well to expressive individual psychotherapy or to psychoanalysis. The discussion here will focus on those patients, since therapeutic strategies appropriate to the lower-level histrionic patient are similar to those used in the treatment of the borderline personality disorder (Allen 1977) discussed earlier (see Chapter 15). Where appropriate, modifications of technique required for the treatment of histrionic personality disorders will be discussed.

Although some patients with hysterical personality disorder will present with a discrete symptom, such as sexual dysfunction, more commonly they enter psychotherapy because of a general dissatisfaction with their relationship patterns. The precipitating event may be the breakup of a marriage or a love relationship. They also may experience vague feelings of depression or anxiety related to disappointment with their current partner (MacKinnon and Michels 1971). Unlike many patients with the personality disorders in Clusters A and B of DSM-IV, the patient with hysterical personality disorder readily becomes attached to the therapist and quickly develops a therapeutic alliance in which the therapist is perceived as helpful. The psychotherapy process will generally go well if the therapist adheres to several general principles.

Principles of Technique

A rule of thumb in expressive work is to address resistance before attempting to interpret the underlying content. In the case of the hysterical patient, this axiom dictates that the patient's cognitive style must be dealt with first, since it is so intimately bound up with the patient's defensive configuration. Hysterical patients often begin psychotherapy with an unconscious expectation that the therapist should be able to understand them intuitively, nonverbally, and globally without details of their intrapsychic world (Allen 1977). This expectation is frequently linked to a poignant wish that mother and/or father would have recognized and understood them in childhood. Thus, the expectation of being seen, heard, and understood is fraught with a mixture of hope and disappointment (Riesenberg-Malcolm 1996). These patients fear that their performance will be dismissed or denigrated by the therapist. Indeed, a frequent countertransference reaction to exaggerated displays of emotionality is exactly that sort of contempt. The therapist must appreciate that something important is being communicated in the hyperbolic display of emotion and also that these exaggerated feelings contain a kernel of truth. Something desperate is being communicated to the therapist—something to the effect of "Please recognize me! Please tune in to my pain!"

Even as the therapist empathizes with the affective communication, he or she must also convey to the patient that more detail is needed for a fuller understanding. This approach encourages the patient to begin to articulate in words what is conveyed in feelings. Some carefully planned questions are useful: What does the patient fear? What does the patient want? What are the conflicts that the patient feels? (Horowitz 1997). The therapist may also attempt to give words to the patient's feelings based on what he or she observes. This outside perspective (Gabbard 1997) may help patients gain a greater sense of self by internalizing how the therapist views them.

The internal experience of the hysterical patient is often that of a leaf in the wind buffeted by powerful feeling states. There may be a complete repression of the ideas that connect one feeling with another. In urging the hysterical patient to reflect and to attend in detail to internal and external reality, the therapist helps the patient retrieve the ideational connections between feelings. As Allen (1977) noted, part of this process involves teaching the hysterical person to feel with more depth and genuineness. Superficial and shallow feelings defend against more disturbing and more deeply experienced affects. As the patient's tolerance for these deeper feeling states increases, a concomitant increase occurs in the patient's ability to attend to details (Horowitz 1977a).

As hysterical patients become able to identify their feelings, attitudes, and ideational states, they develop a greater sense of self-as-agent in effective interaction with the environment rather than self-as-passive-victim of the environment (Horowitz 1977a). Hysterical patients often experience vivid visual images and fantasies, but they will not translate these into words unless the therapist assists in this process. Thus, therapists help their patients identify what they want and feel. Patients also learn that having certain thoughts or feelings is not dangerous.

When threatening thoughts and feelings emerge, hysterical patients frequently express a wish to know all about the therapist's life. They are highly suggestible, and if therapists share a lot about their own life and beliefs, their patients will rapidly adopt similar qualities so as to please their therapists and to thereby avoid the arduous task of getting in touch with their own feelings and beliefs. Therapists should similarly avoid giving a great deal of advice to their hysterical patients, who need to learn that they have considerable resources within themselves with which to approach their problems.

Patients in long-term therapy will find that the process of modifying their cognitive style leads to a modification of object relatedness as well. As these patients begin to attend in more detail to self and others in interpersonal contexts, they develop new patterns of perceiving relationships (Horowitz 1977a). Instead of always seeing themselves as the victim of others, patients begin to understand that they play an active role in perpetuating certain patterns of relating to others. They develop a capacity to compare the actual facts of an interpersonal situation with the internal patterns often superimposed on external situations. Ultimately, the self-representation of the passive child so typical of the hysterical patient is replaced by a more mature representation involving activity and sexuality. This transition may take years, however, because patients frequently experience the loss of the hysterical cognitive style as a threat to a basic sense of identity.

In the psychotherapy of hysterical personality disorder, therapeutic work within the transference is a primary vehicle for change. The problems that the patient encounters in relationships outside the therapy will be reproduced within the transference. Although psychotherapy can be effective and gratifying with hysterical patients, the mishandling of transference, particularly erotic transference, is a common cause of therapeutic failure.

Management of Erotic Transference

Despite the pervasiveness of the phenomenon of erotic transference, not only in hysterical patients but also in others, many therapists do not receive adequate training in the effective and therapeutic management of transference feelings. One female psychiatry resident who was struggling with a male patient's sexual feelings toward her took the problem to her psychotherapy supervisor, an analyst. He responded by scratching his head and replying, "I don't know what you girls do about this problem." Historically, a subtle (or not-so-subtle) sexism has pervaded psychotherapy training programs. Because the vast majority of erotic transference reports in the literature, from Freud to the present, have been of female patients who have fallen in love with their male therapists or analysts, male supervisors have sometimes inadvertently promoted among their male supervisees a casual, denigrating attitude toward female patients who develop an erotic transference. One male resident who was beginning psychotherapy training told his male supervisor that he was uncertain about how to approach his first psychotherapy patient. His supervisor informed him, "It's really very simple. Do you know how to seduce a woman?" The supervisor went on to draw an analogy between "hooking" the patient in a psychotherapy process and seducing a woman. This unprofessional attitude typifies an unfortunate historical trend to "enjoy" the erotic transference rather than analyze and understand it.

Since the term is used loosely to describe a number of different transference developments, a clear definition of the phenomenon is relevant to a discussion of its management. Person (1985) provided a succinct definition that applies to psychotherapy as well as to psychoanalysis:

> The term *erotic transference* is used interchangeably with the term *transference love*. It refers to some mixture of tender, erotic, and sexual feelings that a patient experiences in reference to his or her analyst and, as such, forms part of a positive transference. Sexual transference components alone represent a truncated erotic transference, one that has not been fully developed or is not fully experienced. (p. 161)

In hysterical patients, the erotic transference usually develops gradually and with considerable shame and embarrassment. Sexual longings for the therapist are often experienced as ego-dystonic, and the patient knows that the fulfillment of these wishes would be inappropriate.

Histrionic and borderline patients may develop a subtype of erotic transference often termed the *erotized transference* (Blum 1973). In contrast to ordinary transference love, the patient in the throes of an erotized transference makes a tenacious and ego-syntonic demand for sexual gratification. Because of ego impairments in these patients, their internal and external realities are blurred, and they view their expectation of sexual consummation with their therapist as reasonable and desirable. Their seeming obliviousness to the crossing of symbolically incestuous boundaries may stem from a childhood history of being victimized in actual sexual seductions by parents or parental figures (Blum 1973; Kumin 1985–1986).

The spectrum of transferences ranging from the erotic to the erotized is aptly described by Person (1985) as "both gold mine and minefield" (p. 163). These transferences can set the scene for devastating countertransference acting-out. Therapist-patient sex has severely stigmatized the mental health professions, has ruined the careers of a number of psychotherapists, and has caused severe psychological damage to the patients who are its victims (Gabbard 1989; Gabbard and Lester 1995; Pope and Bouhoutsos 1986). Surveys reveal that as many as 10% of all male therapists have engaged in such behavior (Gabbard 1989), so it cannot be dismissed as an occasional aberration of only the seriously disturbed therapist. Many of these unfortunate therapists appear to be both seeking a cure for themselves and making a desperate attempt to cure their patients (Twemlow and Gabbard 1989).

The "gold mine" aspect of erotic transferences is that they provide the therapist with an in vivo recapitulation of a past relationship in the present situation of the transference relationship. Such patients show their therapists what contributions they bring to similar relationships outside the therapeutic situation. Thus a patient's problems with love and sexuality can be examined and understood as they develop in a safe relationship where the patient will not be exploited or abused. To mine the gold in the experience without being destroyed by the minefield requires therapists to adhere to four principles of technique (Table 18–3). Although there are definite gender differences in the expression of erotic transference, I will first discuss the handling of erotic transference in general and then examine the specific gender-determined aspects of the phenomenon.

TABLE 18–3.   Therapeutic management of erotic transference

1. Examination of countertransference feelings
2. Nonexploitative acceptance of erotic transference as important therapeutic material to be understood
3. Assessment of the multiple meanings of the transference in its function as a resistance to a deepening of the therapeutic process
4. Interpretation of connections between transference and both current and past relationships

---

Examination of countertransference feelings. The therapist's counter-transference reactions to erotic transference feelings in the patient may represent countertransference narrowly as a reactivation of a relationship in the therapist's past, broadly as an identification with a projected aspect of the patient, or as a mixture of both (Kumin 1985–1986; Sandler 1976). Although the patient may well represent a forbidden but sexually arousing object from the therapist's past, the therapist's desire for the patient may also be linked to the actual incestuous desire of a parental figure from the patient's oedipal phase of development. Thus the first step in monitoring countertransference, in keeping with the practice of dynamic psychiatry, is for therapists to assess the relative weight of their own contributions versus those of the patient. Therapists who attempt to manage erotic transference in intensive psychotherapy without a personal treatment experience, however, will be at a serious disadvantage.

Several common countertransference patterns relate to erotic transference. The first, common in male residents treating attractive female patients, is to see erotic transference where none exists. Male therapists may respond to their own sexual arousal by projectively disavowing it and instead seeing it in their patients, whom they label as "seductive." In these circumstances, the resident who is pressed for details about why the patient is seductive or why she is sexually interested in him is often at a loss to present convincing evidence. Because of anxieties about his own sexual feelings, he has avoided them, much as the hysterical patient attempts to avoid her sexual feelings. Although this avoidance may simply reflect beginner's anxiety about having sexual feelings in psychotherapy, it may also be a repetition of the patient's father's response to his own sexual desire for his daughter (Gorkin 1985).

Another possibility is that the projective disavowal of the therapist's own sexual feelings for the patient may subtly influence the patient to develop an erotic transference. The constructivist perspective emphasizes the continuous influence of the therapist's subjectivity on the patient's transference. Erotic transference, in particular, may reflect significant contributions from the therapist (Gabbard 1996). These contributions can involve a variety of factors, including the therapist's expectations, the therapist's needs, the therapist's theoretical viewpoint, the therapist's countertransference, and even quotidian elements like the therapist's gender, physical appearance, and age. All of these factors may partly determine how the patient sees the therapist, and ongoing self-scrutiny will help the therapist sort out what is coming from the patient and what derives from the therapist's influence on the patient. Patients with hysterical and histrionic personalities are highly suggestible, and if they believe that the therapist wants them to fall in love in the transference, they may readily comply.

A second countertransference reaction is cold aloofness in response to the patient's confessions of erotic longings for the therapist (MacKinnon and Michels 1971). To control any sexual countertransference reactions to the patient's feelings, the therapist may become more silent, less empathic, and more distant. This "straitjacketing" of all emotions helps to rigidly maintain control of sexual impulses that seem threatening.

A third common countertransference reaction is anxiety stemming from the fear that sexual feelings—either in the patient or in the therapist—will get out of control. This anxiety may lead the therapist to divert the conversation from the patient's expressions of love or sexual arousal, or to interpret such feelings prematurely as "resistance," a digression from the therapeutic task. When a male therapist inappropriately tells his female patient that he will not allow the therapy to be sidetracked by her feelings for him, he forces her to stick to the problems outside therapy that brought her to treatment. Such anxious attempts to eliminate erotic transference feelings may give patients the message that sexual feelings are unacceptable and possibly disgusting, a view that often mirrors feelings of these patients. The therapist's own underlying disgust relates to the covert message in intense erotic transference that therapy is useless—that only sex or "love" can cure (Gorkin 1985).

In the fourth countertransference pattern, which may be more insidious than the others, therapists may encourage and foster erotic feelings for their personal gratification. These therapists, who listen with voyeuristic delight to the details of their patient's sexual fantasies, may have been drawn to the profession because they long to be idealized and loved. Underneath this wish, they may gain sadistic pleasure from arousing their patients' futile sexual wishes. This pattern can often be traced to these therapists' childhood interactions, in which they felt they were aroused by the opposite-sex parent only to be frustrated. By practicing psychotherapy, these individuals may be trying to reverse that childhood situation. Thus therapists must be aware of their own desires in the therapeutic relationship. As Kumin (1985–1986) noted, "Both the analyst's capacity and incapacity to interpret accurately the patient's wishes in the transference requires an appreciation of not only what and whom the patient desires but also what and whom the analyst desires" (p. 13). Kumin also suggested that the desires of the therapist for the patient may present a more formidable resistance than do the patient's desires for the therapist. Numerous psychotherapy processes have become stalemated in the throes of intense erotic transference because the therapist has been too busy basking in the glow of sexual feelings.

Nonexploitative acceptance of erotic transference as important therapeutic material to be understood.   A therapist may wish to convey to the patient that sexual or loving feelings are acceptable aspects of the therapeutic experience. The therapist may make an educational comment such as "In psychother-apy you are likely to experience a broad range of feelings—hate, love, envy, sexual arousal, fear, anger, and joy—all of which must be dealt with as acceptable topics for discussion and as carriers of important information for the therapy." While it is true that erotic transference may serve as resistance to the emergence of other ma terial in the therapy, it is usually a technical error to immediately interpret such feelings as resistance. To understand what is being repeated from the past, the erotic transference must be allowed to develop fully.

Freud (1914/1958) first used the term *acting-out* to describe a patient's ten-dency to repeat in action something from the past rather than remember and ver-balize it. Patients can be told that the feelings developing in the therapy will provide important information about feelings that develop in their other relation-ships, both past and present. If a patient insists on having the therapist gratify the transference wishes, the therapist can point out that not gratifying the wishes can lead to a better understanding of what happens in other relationships. The thera-pist should keep in mind that erotic transference may be intensely unpleasant for the patient (just as it may be for the therapist), not only because of the frustration it brings but also because it may be embarrassing. The therapist may wish to commu-nicate an empathic understanding of the patient's shame: "I know it is difficult and painful for you to have these feelings without being able to gratify them, but if we can explore them together we may be able to help you understand more fully the problems that brought you here."

Assessment of the multiple meanings of the transference in its func-tion as a resistance.   Erotic transference is a resistance in the sense that some-thing is being repeated rather than remembered and verbalized. Resistance should not be equated, however, with "something bad that must be removed immedi-ately," as it often is by beginning therapists. As just noted, erotic transference is also an important communication that should be understood. Like all other men-tal phenomena, erotic transference is determined by the principle of multiple function. It should not be taken simply at face value, but rather should be explored via the patient's associations, dreams, and memories for all of its multiple mean-ings, some of which may be unconscious. In the psychotherapeutic setting, there is considerable fluidity of gender and sexual orientation (Gabbard and Wilkinson 1996). For example, a male patient's erotic transference to a female therapist may represent passive homosexual longings even though the therapist is of the opposite sex (Torras de Be 1987). Because erotic transference must also be understood in terms of its function at a particular moment in therapy, the therapist must assess what preceded its development and what follows its flourishing.

One male patient began his therapy session with his male therapist by saying that he had been helped enormously in the previous session by the therapist's explanation. After commenting on how much the therapist's interpretation had helped him at work, the patient began to contradict what he had just said by maintaining that his relationships were deteriorating. As he continued to talk, he revealed that he had been having sexual fantasies about the therapist and that he believed the therapist could only help him by ejaculating semen into his rectum to make him more masculine. The therapist pointed out that the patient was devaluing the help of the insights that he had received in the previous session by holding onto a magical belief that a sexual liaison was the only way to be helped. The patient acknowledged that he needed to devalue the therapist's help because he felt so inferior to the therapist, who he said was "on Mt. Olympus." The therapist then explained that the patient's envy had increased as he was helped, so he had sexualized the transference to devalue the help. (If the therapist's insights were not particularly effective or useful, there was much less to envy.) In response, the patient said that his liberating feelings of having been helped had alternated with feelings of humiliation because he had to acknowledge that the therapist knew something the patient did not know, which made him feel vulnerable.

In this instance, the patient's erotic transference was a way to defend against his envy of the therapist's competence by devaluing it. Sexualization in the transference may be a way to defend against other feelings as well.

A male patient was seeing his female therapist for the last time prior to her departure at the end of her residency training program. He told her that he had seen a movie the night before in which a female psychiatrist had kissed one of her male patients. He observed that the patient had seemed to benefit from the therapist's affection, and he asked his therapist if she might do the same with him. After an initially anxious reaction to the request, the therapist asked if the unexpected request might be related to the termination of the therapy. The patient responded that he would rather not think about that subject. The therapist then pointed out to the patient that his wish to sexualize their relationship might be a defense against facing the grief associated with termination.

Sexualizing the end of a relationship is a common phenomenon (in therapy and in life in general). It serves to avoid the mourning process connected with loss of an important figure. In this vignette, the patient's wish to become physically involved with his therapist was also a way to deny the definitive nature of termination: A kiss might lead to a *beginning*, rather than an ending. Indeed, many cases of therapist-patient sexual boundary violations occur around the time of termination (Gabbard and Lester 1995). Sexualization can be a manic defense against loss that leads the two members of the therapeutic dyad to engage in mutual denial.

Therapists who view transference love as a natural and understandable response to their enormous sexual appeal are overlooking the darker side of erotic transference. One of the many stories told about Dr. Karl Menninger illustrates this dilemma:

> A somewhat depressed and hysterical 40-year-old woman was hospitalized at The Menninger Clinic for over a year with essentially no change in her condition. She had developed an intense and intractable erotic transference toward her male psychotherapist. Dr. Menninger was asked to consult on the case because of the therapeutic stalemate that had been reached. Throughout much of the interview, the patient repeatedly commented on her great love for her therapist. After listening to her protestations of love for several minutes, Dr. Menninger reportedly said, "You know, if you really loved him, you would get better for him."

Dr. Menninger was addressing the hostility that often lies just beneath the surface of a patient's transference love. Indeed, erotic transferences frequently mask considerable aggression and sadism, even to the extent that an erotic transference might be considered a form of negative transference (Kumin 1985–1986). Exploration of transference wishes for a sexual relationship regularly reveal wishes to hurt, embarrass, or destroy the therapist. A patient's demands for sexual boundary crossing may be so tormenting, especially in instances of the erotized variant typical of histrionic and borderline patients, that the therapist dreads each session. The therapist may feel used and transformed into a need-gratifying object whose only function is to fulfill the patient's inappropriate demands (Frayn and Silberfeld 1986).

> Ms. KK was a 24-year-old homosexual histrionic patient functioning at a borderline level of ego organization who had a history of sexual abuse by male relatives. She formed an intense erotized transference to her female therapist almost immediately. She flirted with her provocatively in the sessions by touching the therapist's foot lightly with her own foot and asking, "Does this make you nervous?" Ms. KK steadfastly maintained that her therapist could only get to know her if she slept with her. She also demanded to know her therapist's sexual orientation. Although the therapist frustrated the patient's wish to destroy their professional relationship by transforming it into a sexual one, the patient continued her efforts at seduction.
>
> The patient would regularly bring in explicit sexual fantasies about her therapist:
>
>> I am caressing your body—your back, your hips, your thighs. I gently and quickly stroke my hand across your pussy. You moan softly and tighten your grip across my back. I kiss you and whisper softly in your ear that I'm going to make love to you. I softly massage your breasts and kiss them. I kiss your stomach and move down toward your pussy. I kiss

the inside of your thighs while stroking your clitoris with my tongue. I continue to kiss, suck, and caress you with my tongue. You moan with pleasure as you have an orgasm. I kiss your thighs again and lightly squeeze your breasts and run my fingers down your sides to your hips. I begin to lick at your clitoris again and stick my tongue inside you. I then lick and suck on your clitoris while I gently ease one, then two of my fingers into you. You have a long, multiple, satisfying orgasm which ends with you stroking my hair and me lightly kissing your pussy.

Needless to say, the patient's expression of such fantasies made the therapist feel uncomfortable and anxious, as well as controlled. If she interrupted the fantasies, she felt that she was revealing her discomfort and disapproval of the patient's transference feelings. If she remained silent, she felt that she was colluding in an exhibitionist-voyeur pairing.

The patient finally revealed some of the underlying aggressive feelings that were masquerading as erotized transference. She commented to the therapist, "You know I'm aware of still wanting to piss you off. Probably force you into rejecting me. Make you hate me. Am I succeeding? I really want you to like me. But since I know that's out of the question, I'll just drive you away. It's the shits, isn't it? You see, I see our relationship in two ways: either we fuck, or I make you hate my guts."

To a large extent, Ms. KK had induced a paralysis in the therapist, who felt cruel and sadistic by frustrating the patient's wishes. A consultation helped the therapist understand that she was being controlled by a projective identification process so that the normal professional limits of psychotherapy seemed ruthless and unreasonable. In other words, a cold, depriving object from the patient's past had been projected onto the therapist, who unconsciously identified with this projected material. Moreover, her own anger at the patient for her relentless control of the therapy also contributed to her feeling that any intervention would appear cold and ruthless. As the psychotherapy continued, it became clearer that the overt sexual wish was only the tip of an iceberg.

During one session, Ms. KK reported a dream in which she was in a high-tech office. There was a machine that could translate the patient's thoughts, so that she did not have to tell them to her therapist. In the patient's associations to the dream, she acknowledged that her longings for the therapist were not truly sexual, but rather a wish for her therapist to really know her intimately. The therapist eventually helped Ms. KK to see that her wish for sex was really a wish for merger—a wish that her therapist would know her thoughts without her having to voice them.

This regressive longing to return to the mother-infant symbiotic state is often a powerful component of erotic or erotized transferences in the female patient–female therapist dyad. The sexualized wish may be preferable to the more threatening wish for merger.

Interpretation of connections between transference and both current and past relationships. A correct interpretation of the erotic transference will often reduce the desire and the resistance inherent in transference love (Kumin 1985–1986). To avoid premature interpretation, the therapist may need to silently formulate the interpretation to help with countertransference desires even before delivering the interpretation to the patient. The timing of transference interpretations is a matter of judgment. One guideline is to avoid interpreting it until the underlying linkages to past relationships and to current extratransference relationships are near conscious awareness. The therapist can use the model of the triangle of insight described in Chapter 4 to construct connections between the transference feelings and past relationships, as well as between the transference and current extratransference relationships. By pointing out that transference love is a repetition of something from the past, and by asking the patient if the situation is reminiscent of past situations, the therapist can lay the groundwork for interpretive interventions. However, an important caveat is in order. In general, therapists must avoid telling patients with hysterical personality disorder that the love they feel for them, the therapist, is "not real." From the patient's perspective, it is extraordinarily real. It would be much more accurate, not to mention empathic, to help these patients understand that the love they feel for the therapist is *both* real *and* displaced, in the sense that derives, in part, from feelings that were experienced toward objects from the past (Gabbard 1996).

An actual transcript of a psychotherapy session may illustrate some of the technical approaches to interpreting erotic transference.

> Ms. LL was a 26-year-old married patient with a diagnosis of hysterical personality disorder. She was seen twice weekly by a male therapist in expressive-supportive psychotherapy with a predominantly expressive emphasis. She began psychotherapy with complaints of anorgasmia, headaches, constant marital difficulties, fear of "standing on her own two feet," feelings of being unloved and unwanted, and a generalized concern that she was too dependent. Midway through the second year of treatment, the following exchange occurred in one session:
>
> > Ms. LL: My husband and I haven't been getting along. We don't see each other much, and when we do, we argue. I wanted to make you a buddy again today, but when I walked in, something changed. I don't know what to say today. I'd like to get real mad at you, but I don't know why. Probably because I need attention and my husband's not giving me any. When I don't have anything to say, it's usually because I have feelings for you—I

had butterflies just now when I said that. There are two kinds of feelings I get in here—one is when I feel that you're like my dad and I want you to cradle me and give me the pat on the back. The other is when I want you to hold me real tight . . . (patient stops)

Therapist: You had a feeling just now that stopped you in midsentence. What was it?

Ms. LL: I don't want to say it. It's ridiculous. (with great hesitation) I can't just come in here . . . and look at you . . . and think, "I want to make love with you." I can't feel that way. That's not me.

Therapist: To think that you could have sexual feelings is so unacceptable to you that you cannot own the feelings as yours?

Ms. LL: I'm just not like that. Not even with my husband. My subconscious wants to hang on to you and hold you tightly, but my conscious mind wants to pretend I don't have the feelings. I'd rather go back to just having the feeling that you were like my dad and I need a pat on the back.

Therapist: It's particularly unacceptable for you to have sexual feelings for someone that you also view as a dad. I wonder if the same thing happened as a little girl in your relationship with your father.

Ms. LL: I was always very special to my dad. When he walked me down the aisle and gave me away at the wedding, he told me that I was always his favorite of his three daughters. I shouldn't be talking like this. I have to go out and get in the car with my husband and spend the evening with him, but my thoughts are going to be about you.

Therapist: It sounds like there is a similarity between your attachment to me and your attachment to your dad in that both make it difficult for you to invest emotionally in your husband.

In this vignette, the therapist draws a connection between the patient's erotic transference and her feelings for her father. Sexual feelings are forbidden in both relationships because she sees them as incompatible with her otherwise paternal view of the therapist and her father. After linking the transference feelings to the patient's past relationship with her father, the therapist connects these longings to her difficulty with her husband, a current extratransference relationship.

These four principles of technique may be helpful to the psychotherapist who is treating a patient struggling with erotic transference feelings. However, adherence to these principles requires rational, level-headed thinking. As poets have long known, passion clouds judgment. By their very nature, feelings of love and/or lust tend to evoke enactments in both patient and therapist (Gabbard 1994). In other words, both persons are prone to lose their reflective awareness of the transferential and countertransferential characteristics of the feelings because they seem so real and compelling. Therapists must carefully monitor deviations from their standard clinical practice as a way of alerting themselves to countertransference enactment. Several warning signs are particularly useful in this form of boundary monitoring: extending sessions beyond their usual length, reducing the fee or not charging the patient, self-disclosing about one's personal life to the patient, day-dreaming constantly about the patient, paying careful attention to one's appearance on the day of the patient's appointment, hugging the patient or engaging in other forms of physical contact, wishing to meet the patient in a nonclinical setting, and imagining that one can rescue the patient from his or her misery (Gabbard and Wilkinson 1994; Gutheil and Gabbard 1993). When therapists begin to observe that they are deviating along these lines or being swept away by erotic feelings toward the patient, they would be wise to seek out consultation or supervision from a respected colleague. Indeed, it is probably wise for all therapists to make regular use of consultation when they are treating a patient with an erotic transference or experiencing erotic countertransference (Gabbard 1996; Gabbard and Lester 1995). Sexual feelings in the dyad may be "out of sync," and desire may oscillate back and forth between the therapist and patient and only occasionally reside in both together.

Therapists must also be aware that all patients experiencing sexual feelings toward the therapist will not respond to interpretive efforts. Some histrionic and borderline patients may translate their feelings into action and throw themselves at the therapist's feet, sit on the therapist's lap, or passionately hug the therapist as they move toward the office door. In such cases, the therapist must set firm limits. Patients may need to be told that they must return to their chairs and that physical contact is off-limits. Sometimes an educational comment is helpful as well: "Psychotherapy is a verbal treatment that can only work under certain circumstances. One of those circumstances is that you sit in your chair and I sit in mine."

Gender Differences in Erotic Transference

The overwhelming majority of case reports in the literature involving erotic or erotized transferences are of female patients with male therapists. Lester (1985) pointed out that the absence of reports involving male patients and female therapists may reflect the general rarity of transference love in those dyads. She speculated that the male patient's anxiety about the female analyst as a powerful preoedipal phallic mother, who makes "penetrating" interpretations, can overshadow and greatly inhibit his expression of sexual feelings toward the analyst as an oedipal mother. Lester also noted that the regressive passivity in analytic therapy goes against the grain of the traditional active male sexual role.

Lester's experience has not been corroborated by all female therapists. Gornick (1986) viewed Lester's scenario of the phallic mother as only applicable to some male patients working with female therapists. Other male patients, she asserted, find it much more unacceptable to be passive and dependent vis-à-vis a female than to express direct sexual feelings. The shame of being dependent may lead certain male patients to defend against such feelings by "turning the tables" and using sexual feelings in the transference to restore a sense of male dominance.

When a female therapist is treating a male patient, another gender difference is apparent—namely, the risk of assault. If the male patient has a serious antisocial or borderline personality disorder and poor impulse control, a female therapist may be in danger in a locked office. Interpreting transference to an aggressive and impulsive patient may be of no use whatsoever, and limits must be clearly set. In some cases, treatment may even need to be terminated, because it is not possible to work in a context where there is threat of assault.

Because so many more case reports of female patients with erotic transference have appeared in the literature, Person (1985) has observed that clinicians might get the impression that sexual feelings in therapy are specifically and exclusively related to the psychology of women. However, while many male patients being treated by a male therapist may suppress or deny erotic transference because of homosexual anxieties, some do develop full-blown erotic or erotized transference to their male therapist that needs to be systematically understood and interpreted. In many cases, the sexualized transference is a defense against more uncomfortable feelings of love and longing that are difficult to express (Gabbard 1994).

Group Psychotherapy

Clinicians have often noted that patients who are good candidates for dynamic individual psychotherapy are also good candidates for dynamic group psychotherapy. Such is the case with hysterical patients, who often become "stars" in their groups. They are highly valued by other group members for their ability to express feelings directly and for their care and concern about others in the group. The hysterical patient's cognitive style and its associated defenses of repression and denial can be dealt with quite effectively in group psychotherapy. Other patients in the group will help hysterical patients see how they tend to distort their view of self and others by omitting details from interactional situations. For example, when one female hysterical patient described how she was misunderstood as being seductive when she was simply being friendly with a man at work, male patients in the group pointed out that she might be overlooking what she had said (or how she had said it) in the interaction. Furthermore, they pointed out how this patient behaved similarly in the group itself and how she seemed oblivious to the flirtatious signals she gave men in the group as well.

Hysterical patients generally form a positive maternal transference to the group as a whole. They seize group therapy as an opportunity to receive some of the maternal nurturance that they believe they missed during childhood. They are therefore well motivated to attend group therapy and to encourage others to view it as a valuable resource. Histrionic patients, however, can be more problematic in groups, because they will often "upstage" other patients by demanding to be the center of attention through florid displays of emotionality. Such patients can be effectively treated in group psychotherapy only if they are also in individual psycho therapy, much as with group psychotherapy of borderline patients (see Chapter 15).

References

Allen DW: Basic treatment issues, in Hysterical Personality. Edited by Horowitz MJ. New York, Jason Aronson, 1977, pp 283–328

American Psychiatric Association: Diagnostic and Statistical Manual of Mental Disorders, 2nd Edition. Washington, DC, American Psychiatric Association, 1968

American Psychiatric Association: Diagnostic and Statistical Manual of Mental Disorders, 3rd Edition. Washington, DC, American Psychiatric Association, 1980

American Psychiatric Association: Diagnostic and Statistical Manual of Mental Disorders, 3rd Edition, Revised. Washington, DC, American Psychiatric Association, 1987

American Psychiatric Association: Diagnostic and Statistical Manual of Mental Disorders, 4th Edition. Washington, DC, American Psychiatric Association 1994

Baumbacher G, Amini F: The hysterical personality disorder: a proposed clarification of a diagnostic dilemma. International Journal of Psychoanalytic Psychotherapy 8:501–532, 1980–1981

Blacker KH, Tupin JP: Hysteria and hysterical structures: developmental and social theories, in Hysterical Personality. Edited by Horowitz MJ. New York, Jason Aronson, 1977, pp 95–141

Blum HP: The concept of erotized transference. J Am Psychoanal Assoc 21:61–76, 1973

Chodoff P: The diagnosis of hysteria: an overview. Am J Psychiatry 131:1073–1078, 1974

Chodoff P, Lyons H: Hysteria, the hysterical personality and "hysterical" conversion. Am J Psychiatry 114:734–740, 1958

Cleghorn RA: Hysteria—multiple manifestations of semantic confusion. Canadian Psychiatric Association Journal 14:539–551, 1969

Easser BR, Lesser SR: Hysterical personality: a re-evaluation. Psychoanal Q 34:390–405, 1965

Frayn DH, Silberfeld M: Erotic transferences. Can J Psychiatry 31:323–327, 1986

Freud S: Remembering, repeating and working-through (further recommendations on the technique of psycho-analysis II) (1914), in The Standard Edition of the Complete Psychological Works of Sigmund Freud, Vol 12. Translated and edited by Strachey J. London, Hogarth Press, 1958, pp 145–156

Gabbard GO (ed): Sexual Exploitation in Professional Relationships. Washington, DC, American Psychiatric Press, 1989

Gabbard GO: On love and lust in erotic transference. J Am Psychoanal Assoc 42:385–403, 1994

Gabbard GO: Love and Hate in the Analytic Setting. Northvale, NJ, Jason Aronson, 1996

Gabbard GO: A reconsideration of objectivity in the analyst. Int J Psychoanal 78:15–26, 1997

Gabbard GO, Lester EP: Boundaries and Boundary Violations in Psychoanalysis. New York, Basic Books, 1995

Gabbard GO, Wilkinson SM: Management of Countertransference With Borderline Patients. Washington, DC, American Psychiatric Press, 1994

Gabbard GO, Wilkinson SM: Nominal gender and gender fluidity in the psychoanalytic situation. Gender and Psychoanalysis 1:463–481, 1996

Gorkin M: Varieties of sexualized countertransference. Psychoanal Rev 72:421–440, 1985

Gornick LK: Developing a new narrative: the woman therapist and the male patient. Psychoanalytic Psychology 3:299–325, 1986

Gutheil TH, Gabbard GO: The concept of boundaries in clinical practice: theoretical and risk management dimensions. Am J Psychiatry 150:188–196, 1993

Halleck SL: Hysterical personality traits: psychological, social, and iatrogenic determinants. Arch Gen Psychiatry 16:750–757, 1967

Hamburger ME, Lilienfeld SO, Hogben M: Psychopathy, gender, and gender roles: implications for antisocial and histrionic personality disorders. J Psychother Pract Res 10:41–55, 1996

Hollender M: Hysterical personality. Comment on Contemporary Psychiatry 1:17–24, 1971

Horowitz MJ: Structure and the processes of change, in Hysterical Personality. Edited by Horowitz MJ. New York, Jason Aronson, 1977a, pp 329–399

Horowitz MJ: The core characteristics of hysterical personality (Introduction), in Hysterical Personality. Edited by Horowitz MJ. New York, Jason Aronson, 1977b, pp 3–6

Horowitz MJ: Histrionic personality disorder, in Treatments of Psychiatric Disorders, 2nd Edition, Vol 2. Edited by Gabbard GO. Washington, DC, American Psychiatric Press, 1995, pp 2311–2326

Horowitz MJ: Psychotherapy for histrionic personality disorder. J Psychother Pract Res 6:93–107, 1997

Kernberg OF: Borderline Conditions and Pathological Narcissism. New York, Jason Aronson, 1975

Kolb LC: Noyes' Modern Clinical Psychiatry, 7th Edition. Philadelphia, PA, WB Saunders, 1968

Kumin I: Erotic horror: desire and resistance in the psychoanalytic situation. International Journal of Psychoanalytic Psychotherapy 11:3–20, 1985–1986

Lazare A: The hysterical character in psychoanalytic theory: evolution and confusion. Arch Gen Psychiatry 25:131–137, 1971

Lerner HE: The hysterical personality: a "woman's disease." Compr Psychiatry 15:157–164, 1974

Lester EP: The female analyst and the erotized transference. Int J Psychoanal 66:283–293, 1985

Luisada PV, Peele R, Pitard EA: The hysterical personality in men. Am J Psychiatry 131: 518–521, 1974

MacKinnon RA, Michels R: The Psychiatric Interview in Clinical Practice. Philadelphia, PA, WB Saunders, 1971

Malmquist C: Hysteria in childhood. Postgrad Med 50:112–117, 1971

Marmor J: Orality in the hysterical personality. J Am Psychoanal Assoc 1:656–671, 1953

Person ES: The erotic transference in women and in men: differences and consequences. J Am Acad Psychoanal 13:159–180, 1985

Pfohl B: Histrionic personality disorder: a review of available data and recommendations for DSM-IV. J Personal Disord 5:150–166, 1991

Pope KS, Bouhoutsos JC: Sexual intimacy between therapists and patients. New York, Praeger, 1986

Riesenberg-Malcolm R: "How can we know the dancer from the dance?": hyperbole in hysteria. Int J Psychoanal 77:679–688, 1996

Sandler J: Countertransference and role-responsiveness. International Review of Psychoanalysis 3:43–47, 1976

Shapiro D: Neurotic Styles. New York, Basic Books, 1965

Sugarman A: The infantile personality: orality in the hysteric revisited. Int J Psychoanal 60:501–513, 1979

Torras de Be E: A contribution to the papers on transference by Eva Lester and Marianne Goldberger and Dorothy Evans. Int J Psychoanal 68:63–67, 1987

Twemlow SW, Gabbard GO: The lovesick therapist, in Sexual Exploitation in Professional Relationships. Edited by Gabbard GO. Washington, DC, American Psychiatric Press, 1989, pp 71–87

Wallerstein RS: Diagnosis revisited (and revisited): the case of hysteria and the hysterical personality. International Journal of Psychoanalytic Psychotherapy 8:533–547, 1980–1981

Zetzel ER: The so called good hysteric. Int J Psychoanal 49:256–260, 1968

Cluster C Personality Disorders

Obsessive-Compulsive, Avoidant, and Dependent

The three personality disorders classified in Cluster C of DSM-IV (American Psychiatric Association 1994)—obsessive-compulsive, avoidant, and dependent—are grouped together because persons suffering from these disorders usually have anxiety or fear in common as a prominent characteristic. A long clinical-psychoanalytic tradition is associated with the obsessive-compulsive personality disorder(OCPD), but no similar traditions exist for the other two characterological entities of Cluster C. The fact that all three personality disorders are considered here in one chapter reflects the paucity of contributions to the psychodynamic literature regarding avoidant and dependent personality disorders.

Obsessive-Compulsive Personality Disorder

The distinction between obsessive-compulsive disorder (OCD) (or obsessive-compulsive neurosis) and OCPD is based on the difference between symptoms and enduring character traits. As described in Chapter 9, the patient suffering from OCD is plagued with recurring unpleasant thoughts and is driven to perform ritualistic behaviors. These symptomatic manifestations are ego-dystonic in that the patient recognizes them as problems and ordinarily wishes to be rid of them. In contrast, the traits that constitute the DSM-IV diagnosis of OCPD (Table 19–1) are lifelong patterns of behavior that are ego-syntonic. These traits seldom cause distress in the patients themselves and may even be regarded as highly adaptive. Indeed, studies of physicians suggest that certain obsessive- compulsive characteristics contribute significantly to success as a physician (Gabbard 1985; Krakowski 1982; Vaillant et al. 1972). The unswerving devotion to work typical of the obsessive-compulsive person also leads to high achievement in professions other than medicine where attention to detail is essential. However, success in the work sphere often comes at a high price to these people. Their significant others often find them difficult to live with and frequently instigate their coming to psychiatric attention.

Although the distinctions between OCD and OCPD in DSM-IV are clear and useful, there is some controversy over the extent of the overlap between these two diagnostic entities. Symptoms of an obsessive-compulsive nature have also been reported as transitory occurrences during the psychoanalytic treatment of patients with OCPD (Munich 1986). However, empirical studies indicate that a wide range of personality disorders may occur in patients with OCD. In one study, less than

---

TABLE 19–1. DSM-IV criteria for obsessive-compulsive personality disorder

A pervasive pattern of preoccupation with orderliness, perfectionism, and mental and interpersonal control, at the expense of flexibility, openness, and efficiency, beginning by early adulthood and present in a variety of contexts, as indicated by four (or more) of the following:

1. is preoccupied with details, rules, lists, order, organization, or schedules to the extent that the major point of the activity is lost
2. shows perfectionism that interferes with task completion (e.g., is unable to complete a project because his or her own overly strict standards are not met)
3. is excessively devoted to work and productivity to the exclusion of leisure activities and friendships (not accounted for by obvious economic necessity)
4. is overconscientious, scrupulous, and inflexible about matters of morality, ethics, or values (not accounted for by cultural or religious identification)
5. is unable to discard worn-out or worthless objects even when they have no sentimental value
6. is reluctant to delegate tasks or to work with others unless they submit to exactly his or her way of doing things
7. adopts a miserly spending style toward both self and others; money is viewed as something to be hoarded for future catastrophes
8. shows rigidity and stubbornness

Source. Reprinted from DSM-IV (American Psychiatric Association 1994), pp. 672–673. Used with permission.

half of the patients with OCD satisfied the criteria for OCPD (Rasmussen and Tsuang 1986). In fact, the most common characterological diagnosis in this sample was a mixed personality disorder with avoidant, dependent, and passive-aggressive features. In a study (Baer et al. 1990) that assessed 96 patients with OCD, only 6% had an Axis II diagnosis of OCPD. Other investigations have found that OCPD is significantly more common in patients with OCD than in those with panic and major depressive disorder (Diaferia et al. 1997) and that obsessional symptoms are more likely to be associated with traits of OCPD than with traits of other personality disorders (Rosen and Tallis 1995). In a Scandinavian study of comorbidity between OCD and personality disorders (Bejerot et al. 1998), 36% of OCD patients were also diagnosed with OCPD. Despite the uncertainty about whether the two conditions are actually related, OCPD and OCD are usually discussed separately because the treatment implications for the two are quite different.

Psychodynamic Understanding

Early psychoanalytic contributions (Abraham 1921/1942; Freud 1908/1959; Jones 1948; Menninger 1943) connected certain character traits—particularly obstinacy, parsimony, and orderliness—with the anal phase of psychosexual development. Patients with these personality features were viewed as having regressed from the castration anxiety associated with the oedipal phase of development to the relative safety of the anal period. Driven by a punitive superego, they presumably employed characteristic defensive operations of the ego, including isolation of affect, intellectualization, reaction formation, undoing, and displacement (see Chapter 2). Their obsessive orderliness, for example, was conceptualized as a reaction formation against an underlying wish to engage in anal messiness and its derivatives. The considerable difficulty that the obsessive-compulsive personality has expressing aggression was related to early power struggles with maternal figures around toilet training. The stubbornness of the obsessive individual could also be viewed as an outgrowth of those same struggles.

More recent contributions (Gabbard 1985; Gabbard and Menninger 1988; Horowitz 1988; Josephs 1992; McCullough and Maltsberger 1995; Salzman 1968, 1980, 1983; Shapiro 1965) have gone beyond the vicissitudes of the anal phase to focus on interpersonal elements, self-esteem, management of anger and dependency, cognitive style, and the problems of balancing work and emotional relationships. Individuals with OCPD suffer from a good deal of self-doubt. Their experience as children was that they were not sufficiently valued or loved by their parents. In some cases, this perception may relate to actual coldness or distance in parental figures, while in others the children may simply have required more reassurance and affection than the ordinary child to feel a sense of parental approval. Psychodynamic treatment of these patients reveals strong unfulfilled dependent yearnings and a reservoir of rage directed at the parents for not being more emotionally available. Since obsessive-compulsive patients find both anger and dependency consciously unacceptable, they defend against those feelings with defenses such as reaction formation and isolation of affect. In a counterdependent effort to deny any dependency on anyone, many obsessive-compulsive persons go to great lengths to demonstrate their independence and their "rugged individualism." Similarly, they strive for complete control over all anger, and they may even appear deferential and obsequious to avoid any impression of harboring angry feelings.

Intimate relationships pose a significant problem to the obsessive-compulsive patient. Intimacy raises the possibility of being overwhelmed by powerful wishes to be taken care of, with the concomitant potential for frustration of those wishes, resulting in feelings of hatred and resentment, and a desire for revenge. The feelings inherent to intimate relationships are threatening because they have the potential for becoming "out of control," one of the fundamental fears of the obsessive-compulsive person. Significant others frequently complain that their obsessive-compulsive loved one is too controlling. Stalemates and impasses often occur in such relationships because obsessive-compulsive persons refuse to acknowledge that anyone else might have a better way to do things. This need to control others often stems from a fundamental concern that sources of nurturance in the environment are highly tenuous and may disappear at any moment. Somewhere in every obsessive-compulsive person is a child who feels unloved. The low self-esteem connected with this childhood sense of not being valued often leads to an assumption that others would prefer not to put up with obsessive-compulsive persons. The high level of aggression and the intense destructive wishes lurking in the unconscious of the obsessive-compulsive person may also contribute to this fear of losing others. These patients often fear that their destructiveness will drive others away or that it will lead to counteraggression, a projection of their own rage.

Despite OCPD patients' efforts to be dutiful, considerate, and compliant, the fear that they will alienate others often becomes a self-fulfilling prophecy. Obsessive-compulsive behavior tends to irritate and exasperate those who come in contact with it. The person displaying the behavior, however, may be perceived in somewhat different ways, depending on the power differential in the relationship (Josephs 1992). To subordinates, individuals with OCPD come across as domineering, hypercritical, and controlling. To their superiors, they may seem ingratiating and obsequious in a way that rings false. Ironically, then, the very approval and love they seek is undermined, and people with OCPD feel chronically unappreciated as they labor in their own tortured way to gain the longed-for approbation of others.

Obsessive-compulsive persons are also characterized by a quest for perfection. They seem to harbor a secret belief that if they can only reach a transcendent stage of flawlessness, they will finally receive the parental approval and esteem they missed as children. These children often grow up with the conviction that they simply did not try hard enough, and as adults, they chronically feel that they are "not doing enough." The parent who seems never satisfied is internalized as a harsh superego that expects more and more from the patient. Many obsessive-compulsive individuals become workaholics because they are unconsciously driven by this conviction that love and approval can be obtained only through heroic efforts to achieve extraordinary heights in their chosen profession. The irony in this striving for perfection, however, is that obsessive-compulsive persons rarely seem satisfied with any of their achievements. They appear driven more by a wish to gain relief from their tormenting superego than by a genuine wish for pleasure.

These dynamic underpinnings lead to a characteristic cognitive style (Horowitz 1988; Shapiro 1965). Whereas hysterical and histrionic patients tend to overvalue affective states at the expense of careful thought, the reverse is true for obsessive-compulsive persons. Not unlike Mr. Spock of *Star Trek* fame, obsessive compulsive individuals seek to be thoroughly rational and logical in every endeavor. They dread any situation of uncontrolled emotion, and their mechanistic tendency to be totally without affect may drive those around them to distraction. Moreover, their thinking is logical only within certain narrow parameters. Their thought patterns can be characterized as rigid and dogmatic (Shapiro 1965). Dynamically, these qualities can be understood as compensatory for the underlying self-doubt and ambivalence that plague the obsessive-compulsive person.

In contrast with the cognitive style of the hysterical patient, that of the obsessive-compulsive individual involves careful attention to detail but an almost complete lack of spontaneity or flexibility, with impressionistic hunches being automatically dismissed as "illogical." Obsessive-compulsive persons expend extraordinary energy to maintain their rigid cognitive and attentional styles, so that absolutely nothing they do is without effort. Taking vacations, or even relaxing, generally hold no allure whatsoever for the true obsessive-compulsive person. In one survey of 100 self-professed obsessive-compulsive physicians (Krakowski 1982), only 11% took vacations exclusively for the sake of a vacation and only 10% regularly took time away from work to relax.

Although many of these individuals are high achievers, some find that their character style impairs their ability to succeed at work. Obsessive-compulsive persons may ruminate endlessly about small decisions, exasperating those around them. They often get bogged down in details and lose track of the main purpose of the task at hand. Their indecision may be dynamically related to deep feelings of self-doubt. They may feel that the risk of making a mistake is so great as to preclude a definite decision one way or another. Similarly, their concern that the final outcome of a project may be less than perfect may contribute to their indecisiveness. Many obsessive-compulsive persons are extraordinarily articulate verbally but encounter major psychological obstacles in their writing because of this concern that the end result will not be flawless.

The "driven" quality inherent in the actions of the obsessive-compulsive person has been well described by Shapiro (1965) as having "the appearance of being pressed or motivated by something beyond the interest of the acting person. He does not seem that enthusiastic. His genuine interest in the activity, in other words, does not seem to account for the intensity with which he pursues it" (p. 33). These patients are always driven by their own internal overseer who issues commands about what they "should" or "ought to" do. Dynamically speaking, they have little autonomy from their own superego injunctions. They behave the way they do because they must, regardless of how their behavior impinges on others.

The hypertrophied superego of the obsessive-compulsive patient is relentless in its demands for perfection. When those demands are not satisfied over a long period, depression may set in. This dynamic link between the obsessive-compulsive character and depression has been observed by clinicians for many years. The obsessive-compulsive person may be at particularly high risk for depression in middle age, when the idealistic dreams of youth are shattered by the reality of time running out with advancing age. These patients may become suicidal at this point in their life cycle and may require hospitalization, despite a long history of functioning reasonably well in a work situation. Many of the perfectionistic depressed patients described in Chapter 8 as particularly treatment resistant are driven by obsessive-compulsive personality characteristics.

The complex character structure of the OCPD patient can be summarized as involving a public sense of self, a private sense of self, and an unconscious sense of self (Josephs 1992). Each of these has one dimension that is more applicable to superiors and another linked to relationships with subordinates. For example, the public sense of self in relationship to superiors is that of a responsible and conscientious worker who is serious, considerate, socially appropriate in all situations, and predictable. The public sense of self in relation to subordinates is that of a thoughtful mentor or constructive critic who is providing valuable feedback for those who will listen. Unfortunately, this subjectively experienced sense of public selfhood is not always what is perceived by others. The reactions of others, in fact, give rise to a private sense of self that is fully conscious but largely hidden from others. Patients with OCPD frequently have a sense that they are unappreciated and consequently feel hurt and angry. The lack of approval leads them to be tortured by self-doubt. This insecurity must be shielded from those in superior positions, because individuals with OCPD dread the humiliation and shame associated with having this self-doubting side of them exposed. They are often convinced that others will see them as weak and whining. Existing side by side with this aspect of the private sense of self is a thoroughgoing conviction of moral superiority to those who are in subordinate positions. Because OCPD patients are so defended against their own sadism and aggression, they do not want to appear contemptuous. They attempt to mask this aspect of the private sense of self to avoid appearing pretentious, pompous, or hypercritical. They can then feel proud of how considerate and self-contained they are toward those "beneath" them.

The two dimensions of the unconscious sense of self can be summarized as that of an obsequious masochist in relation to superiors and that of a controlling sadist in relation to subordinates (Josephs 1992). The sadistic and mean-spirited unconscious wish to inflict pain on those who do not submit to their control is entirely unacceptable to OCPD patients and must therefore be repressed. To do otherwise would be to compromise their high moral standards. In relationships with authority figures, on the other hand, these patients fear humiliation in the context of being submissive and longing for love, so they masochistically submit to their own excessively harsh moral standards and torture themselves for not living up to these expectations. This self-torture spares them from what they fear—namely, controlling, dominating, and sadistic humiliation by others. The unconscious message given to superiors is "There is no need for you to criticize and attack me, because you can see that I'm already tormenting myself mercilessly."

Psychotherapeutic Considerations

In contrast with the refractory nature of OCD, OCPD is often greatly improved by psychoanalysis or individual psychotherapy with an expressive emphasis (Gunderson 1988; Horowitz 1988; McCullough and Maltsberger 1995; Munich 1986; Salzman 1980). Winston et al. (1994) described a controlled trial of 25 patients with Cluster C disorders who were treated in dynamic therapy, the mean length of which was 40.3 sessions. Although many patients require longer treatment, those in this sample improved significantly on all measures compared with control patients on a waiting list. Follow-up an average of 1.5 years after treatment completion demonstrated continued benefit. In another investigation (Barber et al. 1997), 24 patients with avoidant personality disorder and 14 patients with OCPD were treated in 52 sessions of time-limited expressive-supportive dynamic psychotherapy. By the end of treatment, only 15% of the OCPD patients retained that diagnosis. Compared with avoidant patients, OCPD patients remained in treatment significantly longer and tended to improve more, and the improvements were broad-based, including measures of personality disorder, anxiety, depres-

sion, interpersonal problems, and general functioning. Of course, without a waiting-list control group, one cannot be certain that the treatment was responsible for
the changes that were documented. Dynamic group psychotherapy may also be effective for patients with OCPD. Whether individual or group psychotherapy is
chosen, similar therapeutic problems arise, requiring similar approaches.

In considering the resistances commonly encountered in the psychotherapy of
obsessive-compulsive patients, one must first empathize with the implications that
dynamic psychotherapy has for such patients. The very idea of the unconscious
threatens their sense of control. Psychodynamic theory teaches that we are unconsciously controlled and consciously confused. Hence, the typical obsessive-compulsive patient is going to resent the basic premise of dynamic therapy.
To deal with the feeling of being threatened, the obsessive-compulsive person may
discount all of the therapist's insights as "nothing new." Obsessive-compulsive patients may at first be reluctant to admit that the therapist is saying anything of
which they are not already aware (Salzman 1980). Resistance can be understood as
a patient's typical defensive operations as manifested in the psychotherapeutic
process. These defenses include isolation of affect, intellectualization, undoing, reaction formation, and displacement. Isolation of affect, then, may present itself as
a lack of awareness of any feelings toward the therapist, particularly dependency or
anger. The patient may talk at great length about factual information from both
past and present situations, with no apparent emotional reaction to these events.
When the therapist returns from a lengthy vacation, the obsessive-compulsive patient is likely to be reluctant to admit any emotional reaction to the separation. If
reaction formation is a prominent defense, the patient will probably respond with:
"Oh, no, I wasn't bothered by it. I just hope that you had a wonderful time and feel
refreshed." Using the distinction between public, private, and unconscious presentations of the self, one could describe the chief resistance as attempting to hide the
private sense of self behind the public presentation of self as dutiful and conscientious (Josephs 1992).

Obsessive-compulsive persons also respond to the threat of intense affect by obsessional rambling that serves as a smoke screen to mask their real feelings. More
precisely, it may serve as an anesthetizing cloud that puts others to sleep. As the patient wanders farther and farther afield from the original point, the therapist may
lose track of the thread that links the patient's associations and may begin to "tune
out" the patient. Because these persons may experience thoughts as having as
much power as actions, the patient may feel the need to undo what has already
been said, as follows:

> During the weekend visit with my parents, I became somewhat irritated with my fa-
> ther. Well, I wouldn't really say that I was irritated, in the sense that I truly felt any

anger toward him. It's just that he sat and watched TV and seemed to have no interest in speaking to me. At one point, I had the thought of turning the TV off and confronting him, but of course I didn't really do that. I would never actually be that rude to anyone.

The rambling speech pattern typical of the obsessive-compulsive patient in psychotherapy features the frequent canceling of thoughts or wishes that have just been verbalized. In addition, an overinclusiveness of thinking leads the patient to bring in peripheral events that take the content of the rambling progressively further from the main theme of the session.

Many obsessive-compulsive patients will attempt to become the "perfect patient." They may try to produce exactly what they think the therapist wants to hear, with the unconscious fantasy that they will finally get the love and esteem they feel they missed as children. As McCullough and Maltsberger (1995) noted, "Ritualizing the therapeutic encounter, the patient is likely to fence the therapist in by never coming late, paying the fee immediately, and becoming superficially very 'good' in the service of boxing in the treatment" (p. 2373). Patients with OCPD have a good deal of difficulty learning that spontaneous comments, occasional lateness, or a tardy fee payment may help both members of the dyad deepen their understanding of the process. Because they are certain that any expression of anger will result in disapproval, they may consciously experience no anger while unconsciously expressing it by completely monopolizing the session. One obsessive-compulsive patient talked nonstop for 50 minutes, only to cease exactly on time, without ever letting the therapist get a word in edgewise. In this manner, the patient was able to express his anger without having to acknowledge any angry feelings.

Other obsessive-compulsive patients will manifest their resistance by recreating in the transference relationship with the therapist their power struggle with their parents.

Mr. MM was an obsessive-compulsive printer who came to psychoanalytic therapy twice a week. He initially presented as a rather submissive and passive "good boy," who was completely unable to express any anger within the therapy sessions. However, he developed a pattern of not speaking for approximately half the 50-minute session and of not paying his bill. Although he denied any anger toward the therapist when this behavior was brought out in the open, he developed a pattern of ventilating his anger with an exit line. One day, after failing to voice anger about the therapist "staring" at him during the session, he strode to the door and said, "I guess you didn't catch my cold," referring to a previously expressed concern that he might give his therapist his cold. On another occasion, after he was confronted about his failure to pay his bill, he exited with the following comment: "Don't freeze to death!"

Shortly thereafter, another session ended with, "Don't slip on the ice!"

One of Mr. MM's most remarkable exit lines was delivered after a session where he was largely silent except for an occasional comment on the failure to pay his bill. The therapist connected his failure to produce payment for the bill with his failure to produce verbal material for the sessions. After a prolonged silence, Mr. MM was informed that the time was up. As he went to the door, he turned to the therapist and said, "I almost bought you a book at a sale yesterday. It was by a physician and was entitled *Thirty Years of Rectal Practice.*" Then he rapidly left the room and slammed the door. During the next session, his therapist brought up this comment about his seemingly benevolent wish to buy him a gift. Mr. MM was able to explore his feeling that the therapist's attempt to extract money and words was comparable to an intrusive finger in his anus attempting to extract feces.

In the transference, Mr. MM had re-created a highly ambivalent relationship with his mother, which involved issues of withholding and control. He experienced his therapist as a mother who was demanding that he produce his feces (words and money) when and where she ordered him to. To defy what he felt as a sadistic and unreasonable command, he withheld his productions until the last moment, then let them go under his own control. In so doing, he attempted to make active what was passively experienced, ventilating his sadistic aggression in angry comments. However, as these examples illustrate, his characterological defense of reaction formation got the best of him in each exit line. Seeing through the reaction formation, the exit lines can be heard as follows: "Don't slip on the ice!" would be "I hope you slip on the ice." "Don't freeze to death!" would mean "I wish you would freeze to death." Even Mr. MM's attempt to equate his therapist with a sadistic and intrusive mother who was forcibly extracting his bodily contents had to be cloaked in the thought of buying him a gift. Despite the reaction formation, the anger in these exit lines still came through to the therapist. Because of Mr. MM's omnipotent concerns about the devastating power of his anger, he had to exit immediately after any hostile expression. He feared that his therapist would be so profoundly affected by these comments that he would retaliate in a massive and destructive fashion. Hence, Mr. MM could express his anger only as he left the office, out of danger from retaliation (Gabbard 1982).

Therapeutic approaches to address these characteristic resistances of obsessive-compulsive patients begin with careful attention to countertransference. The therapist may feel a strong pull to disengage from the rambling, mechanistic presentation of factual material. Therapists may begin to isolate affect just as the patient does rather than experience the irritation and anger as an important part of the process that needs to be interpreted to the patient. For example, when the therapist begins to feel bored and distanced by the material, a useful comment might be "Is it possible that you are presenting all this factual material as a way of keeping emotionally distant from me?" Another countertransference pitfall is for the therapist to scotomize certain aspects of the patient's psychopathology because of the therapist's own obsessive-compulsive tendencies. Because obsessive-compulsive traits are highly adaptive in getting through medical school and psychiatry residency training (Gabbard 1985), therapists may be prone to overlook how these same traits might negatively affect a patient's relationships. To acknowledge the relational consequences of obsessive-compulsive tendencies may make therapists feel uncomfortable because the patient's situation may resonate with similar trends in the therapist's own personal relationships.

One effective strategy in the psychotherapeutic treatment of patients with obsessive-compulsive character structure is to cut through the smoke screen of words to go directly after feelings. The therapy process will frequently get bogged down in the patient's search for facts to avoid feelings, as in the following example:

Mr. NN was a 29-year-old graduate student who sought psychotherapy with the chief complaint of not being able to complete his dissertation. His therapist was a psychiatry resident slightly younger than him. In the first few sessions, the patient struggled with his concern about the therapist's age by attempting to establish certain facts.

Mr. NN: You look like you're probably not old enough to be a fully trained psychiatrist. I would guess you're approximately the same age as me. Is that correct?

Therapist: Yes. I'm approximately the same age as you.

Mr. NN: I assume, of course, that you've had considerable training in psychotherapy. Isn't that correct?

Therapist: Yes, I have.

Mr. NN: How long is a psychiatry residency anyway?

Therapist: Four years.

Mr. NN: And what year are you in?

Therapist: I'm in my third year.

Mr. NN: I guess you probably have a supervisor, though, don't you?

At this point, the resident became aware that this question-and-answer approach was bypassing the patient's feelings. Instead of merely answering all the patient's factual questions, the therapist chose to address the process itself.

Therapist: Mr. NN, it seems to me that this attempt to establish the facts of my training is a way of not addressing the feelings you're having about seeing a therapist who is approximately your own age and who is in training. I wonder if there isn't some anger and possibly even a bit of humiliation about having been assigned to a resident.

This vignette illustrates how the therapist should forthrightly address the patient's feelings even when the patient is denying their existence. Obsessive-compulsive patients will also flee from transference feelings by retreating into long discourses about historically distant events. The therapist may have to bring the patient back to the here and now in the transference and attempt to establish what is going on in the present situation that caused the patient to seek refuge in the past (Salzman 1980, 1983). By keeping certain overarching themes and goals of the treatment in mind, often those with which the patient originally came to treatment, the therapist can maintain anchoring points for the process (Salzman 1980, 1983). When the patient endlessly ruminates about seemingly irrelevant minutiae, the therapist may have to interrupt the ruminations and bring the patient back to the central theme or issue that began the session. Group psychotherapy is often highly effective in dealing with this problem, because the patient may accept such feedback from peers without the same power struggle that accompanies feedback from the therapist.

In addition to confronting and interpreting the patient's characteristic defenses and helping the patient to express the feelings behind those defenses, another overall goal of the psychotherapy or psychoanalysis is to soften and modify harsh superego attitudes. In the simplest terms, this means that these patients must accept their humanness. They must accept that their wish to transcend feelings of anger, hatred, lust, dependency, and so forth is doomed to failure. Feelings must finally be embraced as part of the human condition. They must be integrated as part of the person's self-experience rather than suppressed, denied, repressed, or disavowed as belonging to someone else. To accomplish this goal of making the superego a more benign structure, reassurance is rarely useful. Comments such as "You're not really as bad as you think you are" or "You're much too hard on yourself" will sound hollow to the patient.

Superego changes are more likely to occur through detailed interpretation of the patient's conflicts around dependency, aggression, and sexuality, in concert with the therapist's stable neutrality over time. By remaining nonjudgmental, the therapist helps the patient discover that his or her perceptions of the therapist are distorted according to templates forged by past relationships. Although the patient will repeatedly try to view the therapist as critical and judgmental, the therapist can facilitate recognition that the patient is attributing his or her own critical, judgmental attitude to the therapist.

As these patients begin to understand that others are not nearly as critical as they themselves are, their self-esteem may correspondingly increase. They realize that others have accepted them all along much more than they had imagined. As they experience their therapist's acceptance of them for who they are, they also gain an increasing self-acceptance. As they learn that their conflicts over aggression and dependency stem from childhood situations, they gain greater mastery over these feelings and accept them as part of being human. The therapist can use periodic confrontations about the unrealistic expectations these patients so frequently harbor about themselves. One patient, for example, berated himself in a psychotherapy session over his feelings of rivalry with his older brother at a Christmas family gathering. The therapist commented, "You seem to believe that you should be able to transcend all feelings of competition with your brother and that you're a failure if you don't."

As in the psychotherapy of most patients, resistances are interpreted before underlying content. However, failure to respect the patient's defenses can lead to ill-advised, premature interpretations. Therapists who become irritated or exasperated and interpret the patient's private or unconscious sense of self may expose the patient in a way that feels terribly shaming or humiliating to him or her. If the therapist can contain countertransference irritation, the patient may start to express the private doubts and insecurities and the hidden contempt for others. Defenses against anger, such as reaction formation, may have to be addressed for some time before the patient can see the defensive pattern clearly enough to relate it to underlying anger. For example, the therapist might have to deliver an interpretation such as the following: "Each time I announce a vacation, I notice that you say, 'No problem!' I wonder if that response covers up some other feelings that are more unacceptable." When obsessive-compulsive patients can finally experience and express undisguised anger toward the therapist, they learn that it is not nearly as destructive as they had thought. The therapist is a consistent, durable figure who is there week after week, clearly unscathed by expressions of anger. Similarly, these patients discover that they themselves are not transformed by their anger into destructive monsters.

Patients with OCPD tend to be tormented by "thought crimes." In the patient's unconscious, there is little difference between thinking an angry thought and punching someone in the nose. Part of the superego modification that takes place in dynamic therapy or psychoanalysis involves helping the patient to appreciate that hostile impulses, feelings, or thoughts are simply not the same as acts. The patient eventually learns that thoughts and feelings are not subject to the same moral standards as destructive actions. The acceptance of one's inner life also reduces anxiety.

To the obsessive-compulsive patient, sexual feelings are frequently just as unacceptable as anger or dependency. Again, the transference will be the forum for a reenactment of the childhood situation in which the patient sees the therapist as a parent who disapproves of sexuality. By avoiding a position of judgmental disapproval, the therapist allows the patient to eventually see that such prohibitions are internal, not external. The threat (of castration or loss of love) attributed to the therapist can be understood, then, as an illusory one emanating from within the patient.

Finally, the key to successful psychotherapy or psychoanalysis with patients who suffer from OCPD is empathy for the shame and guilt associated with the unacceptable aspects of the private sense of self and the unconscious sense of self that make these patients engage in self-loathing. Interventions acknowledging these patients' fear that others will discover their sadistic impulses, submissive longings, and pervasive insecurity may help create a holding environment in which the darker aspects of the psyche can be explored.

Avoidant Personality Disorder

This controversial disorder was designed to characterize a group of socially withdrawn individuals distinct from schizoid patients. Unlike schizoid patients (discussed in Chapter 14), avoidant patients long for close interpersonal relationships but are also afraid of them. These individuals avoid relationships and social situations because they fear the humiliation connected with failure and the pain connected with rejection. Their desire for relationships may not be readily apparent because of their shy, self-effacing self-presentation.

The distinction between avoidant and schizoid personality disorders has been criticized on several grounds: for having no "clinical, empirical, or even widely accepted theoretical rationale" (Gunderson 1983, p. 23), for impoverishing the historical concept of schizoid personality disorder by obscuring some of its key features (Livesley and West 1986; Livesley et al. 1985), and for not adequately differentiating the two groups of patients (Reich and Noyes 1986). In a study of 82 psychiatric outpatients, Reich and Noyes (1986) found that a large percentage of those with schizoid personality disorder also met the diagnostic criteria for avoidant personality disorder. Their data suggested that schizoid personality might actually be a variant of avoidant personality disorder.

In response to these and other criticisms, the diagnostic criteria have undergone continued revisions. The DSM-IV criteria (Table 19–2) provided clear gains over the DSM-III-R (American Psychiatric Association 1987) criteria from a psychodynamic perspective. By placing greater emphasis on fears of humiliation, embarrassment, and rejection, the new criteria linked this diagnostic entity more closely to the psychoanalytic tradition of the phobic personality as described by Fenichel (1945). Avoidant personality disorder is thus conceptualized as a character neurosis, in contrast to schizoid personality disorder, which is reflective of a more primitive organization that some authors (Akhtar 1986; Kernberg 1975; Meissner 1988) have linked to the borderline spectrum. Recent research (Baillie and Lampe 1998)

TABLE 19–2.   DSM-IV criteria for avoidant personality disorder

A pervasive pattern of social inhibition, feelings of inadequacy, and hypersensitivity to negative evaluation, beginning by early adulthood and present in a variety of contexts, as indicated by four (or more) of the following:

1. avoids occupational activities that involve significant interpersonal contact, because of fears of criticism, disapproval, or rejection
2. is unwilling to get involved with people unless certain of being liked
3. shows restraint within intimate relationships because of the fear of being shamed or ridiculed
4. is preoccupied with being criticized or rejected in social situations
5. is inhibited in new interpersonal situations because of feelings of inadequacy
6. views self as socially inept, personally unappealing, or inferior to others
7. is unusually reluctant to take personal risks or to engage in any new activities because they may prove embarrassing

Source.   Reprinted from DSM-IV (American Psychiatric Association 1994), pp. 664–665. Used with permission.

has confirmed that the seven DSM-IV criteria have reasonably good internal consistency and assess a single dimension.

Controversy continues, however, regarding the distinction between generalized social phobia and avoidant personality disorder. While there has been considerable research on social phobia, relatively few studies have focused on avoidant personality disorder, especially on treatment interventions. There is some indication that selective serotonin reuptake inhibitors such as paroxetine, which has been shown to be effective in treating generalized social phobia (Stein et al. 1998), may also be useful in patients with avoidant personality disorder (Kapfhammer and Hippius 1998). A number of authors (Dahl 1996; Sutherland and Francis 1995; Widiger 1992) have examined the differences between avoidant personality disorder and generalized social phobia and have reached the conclusion that the two are overlapping constructs that are probably part of a spectrum bridging Axis I and Axis II.

The criteria for avoidant personality disorder are frequently present in clinical populations. However, the disorder is rarely the primary or sole diagnosis in clinical practice (Gunderson 1988). It is most commonly a supplementary diagnosis to another personality disorder or is used in conjunction with an Axis I diagnosis. The centrality of shame in the avoidant patient provides a psychodynamic link with certain types of narcissistic patients (particularly the phenomenologically hypervigilant type and some of those described by Kohut). Both narcissistic and avoidant patients may be prone to shame, but the former are also often characterized by a sense of entitlement and a quiet grandiosity.

Psychodynamic Understanding

People can be shy and avoidant for a variety of reasons. They may have a constitutional predisposition to avoid stressful situations based on inborn temperament that is secondarily elaborated into their entire personality style (Gunderson 1988). The dimension referred to as *harm-avoidance* in the psychobiological model of Cloninger et al. (1993), for example, may be a common biological factor in most patients with avoidant personality disorder. Some research data suggest that the trait of shyness is of genetic-constitutional origin but that it requires a specific environmental experience to develop into a full-blown trait (Kagan et al. 1988). Shyness or avoidance defends against embarrassment, humiliation, rejection, and failure. As with any other form of anxiety, the psychodynamic meaning of the anxiety must be explored to understand fully its origins with each individual patient. However, the psychotherapeutic and psychoanalytic treatment of individuals with these concerns often uncovers shame as a central affective experience.

Shame and self-exposure are intimately connected. What avoidant patients generally fear is any situation in which they must reveal aspects of themselves that leave them vulnerable. Whereas guilt involves concerns about punishment for having violated some internal rule, shame relates more to an assessment of the self as somehow inadequate, as not measuring up to an internal standard. In this sense, guilt is more closely related to the superego in the structural model, whereas shame is more closely connected to the ego ideal (see Chapter 2).

Individuals with avoidant personality disorder may feel that social situations must be avoided because they allow their inadequacies to be displayed for all to see. They may feel ashamed about many different aspects of themselves; for instance, they may perceive themselves as weak, as unable to compete, as physically or mentally defective, as messy and disgusting, as unable to control bodily functions, or as exhibitionistic (Wurmser 1981).

Shame is etymologically derived from the verb "to hide" (Nathanson 1987), and the avoidant patient often withdraws from interpersonal relationships and situations of exposure out of a wish to "hide out" from the highly unpleasant affect of shame. Shame cannot be reductionistically linked with one developmental moment in the life of the child, but seems instead to evolve from many different developmental experiences at various ages (Nathanson 1987). Apparently present from very early in life, shame certainly is evident at the onset of stranger anxiety around 8 months of age (Broucek 1982). It is also connected with feelings that arise from bladder and bowel accidents and from an internalization of the parental reprimands often associated with those accidents. The 2-year-old child who is exhilarated by romping in the buff may also develop shame when a stern parent stops such activity by insisting that the child get dressed (Gabbard 1983). All these developmental experiences may be reactivated in the avoidant patient upon exposure to a group of people or an individual who matters a great deal to the patient.

Attachment theory has much to offer our understanding of avoidant patients. Adults with an avoidant attachment style have generally felt rebuffed by parents or caregivers in childhood and are thus frightened to develop love relationships in adulthood (Connors 1997). They often have a sense that their developmental needs were excessive or inappropriate, and they suffer from a failure of adequate selfobject responses (Miliora 1998).

Psychotherapeutic Approaches

Although empirical research on dynamic therapy of avoidant personality disorder is limited, two different studies, both of which were mentioned earlier in this chapter in the discussion of OCPD, suggest that this approach is useful. In the controlled study of Winston et al. (1994), patients with Cluster C personality disorders who were treated with dynamic therapy did better than subjects in a waiting-list control group. In a study of time-limited expressive-supportive therapy in patients with obsessive-compulsive and avoidant personality disorders, Barber et al. (1997) found that 52 sessions of this treatment significantly improved patients' general functioning, interpersonal problems, depression, and anxiety. Moreover, 61% of the patients with avoidant personality disorder no longer retained the diagnosis at the end of treatment.

Patients with avoidant personality disorder may be most responsive to expressive-supportive psychotherapy if it is combined with firm encouragement to expose oneself to the feared situation (Gabbard and Bartlett 1998; Sutherland and Frances 1995). This encouragement to face the feared situation must, of course, be linked with empathic appreciation of the embarrassment and humiliation associated with exposure. One might say that the therapy is expressive-supportive in the sense that the expressive elements involve exploring the underlying causes of shame and their linkages to past developmental experiences, while the supportive elements involve empathically based encouragement to confront the feared situation rather than retreating in fear from it. This approach may be combined with a selective serotonin reuptake inhibitor such as paroxetine to address the biological temperament.

More of the anxieties and fantasies will be activated in the actual situation of exposure than in the defensive posture of withdrawal. This fact can be explained to these patients in an educational intervention to help them see the value of actively seeking out the feared situations.

Initial exploratory efforts may be frustrating because avoidant patients will not be entirely sure what it is that they fear. Avoidant patients often resort to psychiatric clichés, such as "rejection." The therapist must seek more detail of actual situations to help the patient move beyond such vague explanations for avoidance. The therapist may ask, "What was your actual fantasy of what your co-workers might think of you when you sat in the lunchroom with them yesterday?" Similarly, specific fantasies can be explored in the context of the transference. Avoidant patients usually have a good deal of anxiety about the exposure inherent in psychotherapy. When a patient blushes about something that has been verbalized, the therapist might ask, "Can you share with me what's embarrassing you right now? Is there some reaction that you imagine I'm having to what you just said?" By pursuing the details of specific situations, the patient will develop a greater awareness of the cognitive correlates of the shame affect.

Ms. OO was a 24-year-old nursing student who came to psychotherapy because she felt dissatisfied with her life, had difficulty establishing heterosexual relationships, and experienced anxiety in social situations. She described chronic problems with feeling timid and shy around men. Since she was exceptionally attractive, she was frequently asked out, but her anxiety about each date would escalate to the point where she had to drink alcohol to relax. She told her therapist that she felt at risk for developing a dependence on alcohol, because she was only able to "open up" to men when she was under the influence. Ms. OO also noted the same experience of anxiety when she found herself "loosening up" with other people, such as peers in nursing school.

She had tried group psychotherapy for several months, but found herself tongue-tied and self-conscious in the group. She would rarely speak for fear of "saying the wrong thing." When she began missing group psychotherapy sessions, she rationalized her absence by saying that it did not matter since she was not participating anyway. Ms. OO decided to seek individual psychotherapy because she thought it would be easier to open up to one person instead of eight.

In her third session in psychotherapy, she began to fall silent frequently. The therapist was patient during these silences, but after a few more sessions, he noted that her silences seemed to occur when she was about to experience strong feelings. She acknowledged that she was terribly afraid of losing control when she became emotional. The therapist asked Ms. OO if she were concerned about his response to her expression of emotion. Ms. OO said that she felt certain he would criticize her and "shame" her for "acting like a baby."

At this point the therapist asked Ms. OO if this fear was based on any similar past experiences. She launched into an extensive description of how her father had treated her as a child. She said that he was "a big man who couldn't take criticism but could deal it out." Each time she brought home a report card, he would yell at her, demanding, "Why didn't you get an A?" She also remembered spilling her milk at the supper table and being severely reprimanded by her father, who railed at her, "Why can't you be more like your sister?" With considerable embarrassment, she said her father had never made her feel comfortable about being female. He teased her on the day of her first period by telling her she now had an excuse for being "bad" once a month. She recalled being extraordinarily mortified and crying in her room for hours. When she came home one day full of excitement because she had been selected as a cheerleader, her father called her "conceited and spoiled." She held a strong conviction that she would never be able to measure up to her father's expectations.

At one point in the therapy, Ms. OO was talking about her difficulty in attending parties or other social situations. Again the therapist asked about past situations that might be related to this fear. Ms. OO remembered that when she had been a little girl, her mother would dress her up and take her over to a friend's house, and everyone would always comment on how "cute" she was. She remembered her sense of embarrassment at these compliments, as though she had been "showing off." As the therapist helped her explore that feeling further, she realized that to some extent she had enjoyed the exposure because she had received such positive feedback in contrast to the constant criticism from her father. The therapist encouraged her to attend some of the social functions to which she was invited to see what other associations came to mind during an anxiety attack.

When Ms. OO began socializing more without first becoming inebriated, she realized that she feared enjoying herself. If she enjoyed the compliments of the men who hovered around her at a social gathering, then she was convinced that she was "conceited and spoiled," just as her father had used to say. This conviction made her feel that she was a "bad girl."

The case of Ms. OO illustrates that success in interpersonal situations often may be feared every bit as much as failure. The thrill of an exhibitionistic display may automatically trigger earlier parental reprimands about "showing off." Many individuals with avoidant personality disorder fear that they will become intoxicated with themselves when they are in the spotlight. This dynamic is central to the experience of stage fright (Gabbard 1979, 1983). Coexisting with Ms. OO's fear of enjoying her moment at center stage was another fear that she would fall short of the high expectations she had set for herself. These expectations were internalized by living with a father who had excessively high expectations. In the therapy, she was eventually able to acknowledge her intense anger at her father for repeatedly shaming her and making her feel so conflicted about her sexuality and her femaleness. Miller (1985) has noted a consistent connection between the inhibition of anger and the shame experience. Ms. OO could never freely express her anger at her father, and she felt ashamed of even having such feelings.

Dependent Personality Disorder

Dependency, like rejection, has become something of a psychiatric cliché. Everyone is dependent to some degree, and most patients in a clinical setting will have some conflict over their feelings of dependency. Particularly in American culture, where a powerful myth centers on rugged individualism and independence, the word "dependency" is often used pejoratively. Yet self psychologists would argue that true independence is neither possible nor desirable (see Chapter 2). Most of us need various selfobject functions, such as approval, empathy, validation, and admiration, to sustain us and to regulate our self-esteem.

The DSM-IV category of dependent personality disorder (DPD) is meant to capture a dependency so extreme as to be pathological (Table 19–3). These individuals are unable to make decisions for themselves, are unusually submissive, are always in need of reassurance, and cannot function well without someone else to take care of them.

DPD, like avoidant personality disorder, is rarely used as a principal or single diagnosis. Various studies (Bornstein 1995; Loranger 1996; Skodol et al. 1996) have demonstrated high comorbidity rates for patients with DPD. Included among the Axis I conditions frequently found in conjunction with DPD are major depression, bipolar disorder, some anxiety disorders, and eating disorders. Skodol et al. (1996) suggested that there is no specific relationship between DPD and depression. DPD simply presents a set of maladaptive behaviors and traits that cut across

---

TABLE 19–3.   DSM-IV criteria for dependent personality disorder

---

A pervasive and excessive need to be taken care of that leads to submissive and clinging behavior and fears of separation, beginning by early adulthood and present in a variety of contexts, as indicated by five (or more) of the following:

1. has difficulty making everyday decisions without an excessive amount of advice and reassurance from others
2. needs others to assume responsibility for most areas of his or her life
3. has difficulty expressing disagreement with others because of fear of loss of support or approval
   (*Note.*   Do not include realistic fears of retribution.)
4. has difficulty initiating projects or in doing things on his or her own (because of a lack of self-confidence in judgment or abilities rather than a lack of motivation or energy)
5. goes to excessive lengths to obtain nurturance and support from others, to the point of volunteering to do things that are unpleasant
6. feels uncomfortable or helpless when alone because of exaggerated fears of being unable to care for himself or herself
7. urgently seeks another relationship as a source of care and support when a close relationship ends
8. is unrealistically preoccupied with fears of being left to take care of himself or herself

---

Source.   Reprinted from DSM-IV (American Psychiatric Association 1994), pp. 668–669. Used with permission.

a wide range of personality psychopathology and are related to a variety of types of psychological distress. Indeed, most studies demonstrate that a patient diagnosed with DPD will also meet criteria for several other Axis II disorders. Although more than 50% of patients diagnosed with DPD also receive the diagnosis of borderline personality disorder, the two diagnoses can be differentiated based on key aspects of relationship patterns. Borderline patients react to abandonment with rage and manipulation, whereas dependent patients become submissive and clinging (Hirschfeld et al. 1991). Moreover, the intense and unstable quality of the borderline patient's relationships is not found in the relationships of persons with DPD.

The diagnosis of DPD is more frequently applied to women than to men (Bornstein 1996; Gunderson 1988; Loranger 1996). However, this fact may be related to entrenched gender stereotypes in the culture, which suggest that dependency is more acceptable in women than in men and allow women to express dependency more floridly.

Psychodynamic Understanding

Although early psychoanalytic writers believed that problems with dependency were connected with disturbances during the oral phase of psychosexual development, this view is not widely held today (Gunderson 1988). Such a formulation has the same problem as other phase-specific explanations for psychopathology. A pervasive pattern of parental reinforcement for dependency throughout all phases of development is more likely to be operative in the backgrounds of patients with DPD. One empirical study (Head et al. 1991) found that families of persons with DPD were characterized by low expressiveness and high control, in contrast with families in a clinical control group and a healthy control group. Another study of early family environment (Baker et al. 1996) found that the families of DPD patients were low in independence and high in control.

Insecure attachment is a hallmark of DPD, and studies of DPD patients (West et al. 1994) have found a pattern of enmeshed attachment in these patients. Many of the patients grew up with parents who communicated in one way or another that independence was fraught with danger. They may have been subtly rewarded for maintaining loyalty to their parents, who seemed to reject them in the face of any move toward independence. Interpersonal dependence also appears to have a modest genetic influence in addition to the environmental factors that contribute to the clinical picture (O'Neill and Kendler 1998); thus, a biological temperament may also be an etiological factor in the overall picture.

Bornstein (1993) stressed that dependency and passivity should not be automatically equated. The central motivation of patients with DPD is to obtain and maintain nurturant, supportive relationships. To accomplish this goal, they may engage in assertive and active behaviors that are quite adaptive. For example, DPD patients are more likely to ask for feedback on psychological tests, to solicit help when solving difficult problems in a laboratory setting, and to seek medical attention when physical symptoms occur.

A submissive stance toward others may have a myriad of meanings. Just as the avoidant patient shuns exposure as a result of multiply determined unconscious factors, the dependent patient seeks caretaking because of anxieties that lie beneath the surface. The clinician should ask each individual, "What is it about independence or separation that is frightening?" Dependent clinging often masks aggression. It may be viewed as a compromise formation in the sense that it defends against hostility that is also concomitantly expressed. As many mental health professionals know from firsthand experience, the person who is the object of the dependent patient's clinging may experience the patient's demands as hostile and tormenting.

Dependent behavior may also be a way to avoid the reactivation of past traumatic experiences. The therapist should explore with the patient any memories of past separations and their impact.

Mr. PP was a 29-year-old married postal clerk. He had a long-standing dysthymic disorder and chronically complained of insomnia, lack of energy, difficulty making decisions, and anxiety. Nevertheless, he managed to show up at his job conscientiously, even though he found it difficult to take any initiative when it was expected of him. Prior to his psychiatric hospitalization for suicidal thoughts and wishes, Mr. PP had broken down in tears in front of his supervisor when he was told he was not doing his job properly.

During the admission interview, Mr. PP expressed extreme concern about being away from his wife during the hospitalization, even though he realized that his suicidal wishes were dangerous enough to necessitate inpatient treatment. Mrs. PP explained that her husband had never liked to be away from her. He relied on her to make all decisions in the home, and he could not function very well without her. Almost immediately after being admitted, Mr. PP latched onto a female patient approximately his age and looked to her for guidance in the same way he had related to his wife. He ate all his meals with her and spent all his leisure time with her when he was not involved in treatment activities. He made no sexual overtures toward this other patient but simply reported that he felt safe in her company.

Mr. PP's history revealed a lifelong pattern of anxious dependency. He had always experienced considerable anxiety at the prospect of doing something alone or upon initiating any plan of action without consulting others. He had school phobia when he started elementary school, and his mother reported that he had cried until she would take him home. Similarly, at the age of 10, he had been sent to visit his uncle overnight and had cried so hard that his mother had to return to the uncle's house and bring him home. When he graduated from high school, all of his friends in his peer group enlisted in the service, so he followed suit. Upon discharge from the service, they went to work for the post office, so he applied along with them. Any independent action on his part seemed to reactivate the painful anxiety associated with early separations. He behaved as though convinced that he would be abandoned for any autonomous behavior.

The origins of Mr. PP's dependency and separation anxiety became clearer when his mother began to call him in the hospital. She complained about his decision to enter the hospital: "How can you justify being away from us like this? Your condition can't be that bad. What if we need you to do something and you're not available?" The patient explained that even as an adult, he had responded to his mother's call to come over to her house each week to do various menial jobs. He went on to say that his parents were virtually noncommunicative and that his mother had relied on him for conversation. Mr. PP had grown up in a household where his mother had conveyed a powerful message—namely, that she needed him as a stand-in for her emotionally estranged husband. Independence was thus regarded as an aggressive and disloyal act that would lead to the loss of his mother's love.

Psychotherapeutic Considerations

The psychotherapy of patients with DPD presents an immediate therapeutic dilemma—for these patients to overcome their problems with dependency, they must first develop dependency on their therapist. This dilemma often becomes elaborated into a specific form of resistance in which the patient sees dependency on the therapist as an end in itself rather than as a means to an end. After a period in therapy, these patients may forget the nature of the complaint that brought them to treatment, and their only purpose becomes the maintenance of their attachment to the therapist. Dreading termination, they may repeatedly remind their therapist of how awful they feel to assure continuation of the treatment. If the therapist comments on any improvement whatsoever, the patient may paradoxically worsen since the thought of improvement is equated with termination.

One rule of thumb in treating dependent patients is to remember that what they say they want is probably not what they need. They will attempt to get the therapist to tell them what to do, to allow them to continue their dependency, and to collude in the avoidance of making decisions or asserting their own wishes. The therapist must feel comfortable in frustrating these wishes and instead promoting independent thinking and action in the patient. The therapist must convey that the anxiety produced by this frustration is tolerable and also productive in that it may lead to associations about the origins of the dependency and the fears associated with it.

Another common transference development is idealization of the therapist (Perry 1995). The patient may begin to regard the therapist as all-knowing and display a wish to turn over all responsibility for important decisions to the therapist. Often patients have the fantasy that the solution to all of their problems is to become just like the therapist. This wish to bypass the difficult work of finding an authentic sense of self separate from the therapist needs to be interpreted and confronted as the therapy progresses. The patient may even attempt to undermine therapeutic goals to demonstrate that he or she cannot think or function independently of the therapist.

Time-limited dynamic psychotherapy has been successful with a number of these patients (Gunderson 1988). Knowing from the beginning of the psychotherapy that the patient-therapist relationship will end after 12, 16, or 20 sessions forces these patients to confront their deepest anxieties about loss and independence. Moreover, this approach also helps patients address powerful fantasies involving the never-ending availability of nurturing figures. When long-term, open-ended therapy reaches something of a stalemate, a modification of the time-limited technique can be utilized by setting a deadline for termination. Anxieties that may have lain dormant will be brought rapidly to the surface when the end of therapy is in sight.

A subgroup of dependent patients are simply unable or unwilling to make use of the framework of brief psychotherapy. The prospect of losing the therapist after "just getting started" creates too much anxiety. Because of lesser amounts of ego strength or greater degrees of separation anxiety, these patients need to develop a positive dependent transference to a therapist over a long time. Nevertheless, considerable therapeutic gains are possible with this supportive strategy, as documented by Wallerstein's (1986) research (discussed in Chapter 4). Some patients change as part of a "transference trade" (Wallerstein 1986, p. 690) with the therapist. They are willing to make certain alterations in their lives in return for the therapist's approval. Others may become "lifers" who can maintain change as long as they know that the therapist will always be there for them. These patients may do well even when the therapist tapers down the sessions to one every few months, provided there is no threat of termination.

Patients with DPD commonly evoke countertransference problems related to dependency conflicts in their treaters. Physicians in general, and psychiatrists in particular, may feel conflicted about their own dependency (Gabbard 1985; Gabbard and Menninger 1988; Vaillant et al. 1972). Psychotherapists must be wary of countertransference contempt or disdain toward the dependent patient. The longings of the patient may resonate with the unconscious longings of the therapist, and an empathic attunement with such dependency wishes may be acutely uncomfortable. Therapists who repudiate their patient's longings may be repudiating their own longings as well. Other countertransference difficulties include enjoyment of the patient's idealization, leading the therapist to avoid confronting the patient's lack of real change (Perry 1995). Therapists may also become overly authoritarian and directive, particularly if the patient continues in abusive relationships and does not heed the therapist's warning that the relationship is a destructive one.

Personality Disorder Not Otherwise Specified

Having completed our survey of the DSM-IV personality disorders, it is worth noting that patients generally do not present as "pure cultures" of any one personality disorder. DSM-IV has an extra category of *personality disorder not otherwise specified* to acknowledge this fact. This category can be used for personality disorders that are "mixed" and for those included in Appendix B of DSM-IV, such as passive-aggressive personality disorder.

The uniqueness of each individual is a source of continued delight and challenge for the dynamic psychiatrist. In Chapter 1 I noted that the dynamic psychiatrist is more interested in how patients differ from one another than in how they are similar. Nowhere in psychiatry is this axiom more relevant than in the treatment of personality disorders.

References

Abraham K: Contributions to the theory of the anal character (1921), in Selected Papers of Karl Abraham, M.D. London, Hogarth Press, 1942, pp 370–392

Akhtar S: Differentiating schizoid and avoidant personality disorders (letter). Am J Psychiatry 143:1061–1062, 1986

American Psychiatric Association: Diagnostic and Statistical Manual of Mental Disorders, 3rd Edition, Revised. Washington, DC, American Psychiatric Association 1994

American Psychiatric Association: Diagnostic and Statistical Manual of Mental Disorders, 4th Edition. Washington, DC, American Psychiatric Association 1994

Baer L, Jenike MA, Ricciardi JN, et al: Standardized assessment of personality disorders in obsessive-compulsive disorder. Arch Gen Psychiatry 47:826–830, 1990

Baillie AJ, Lampe LA: Avoidant personality disorder: empirical support for DSM-IV revisions. J Personal Disord 12:23–30, 1998

Baker JD, Capron EW, Azorlosa J: Family environment characteristics of persons with histrionic and dependent personality disorders. J Personal Disord 10:81–87, 1996

Barber J, Morse JQ, Krakauer ID, et al: Change in obsessive-compulsive and avoidant per-
    sonality disorders following time-limited expressive-supportive therapy. Psychother-
    apy 34:133–143, 1997
Bejerot S, Ekselius L, von Konorring L: Comorbidity between obsessive-compulsive disor-
    der (OCD) and personality disorders. Acta Psychiatr Scand 97:398–402, 1998
Bornstein RF: The Dependent Personality. New York, Guilford, 1993
Bornstein RF: Comorbidity of dependent personality disorder and other psychological dis-
    orders: an integrative review. J Personal Disord 9:286–303, 1995
Bornstein RF: Sex differences in dependent personality disorder prevalence rates. Clinical
    Psychology: Science and Practice 3:1–12, 1996
Broucek FJ: Shame and its relationship to early narcissistic developments. Int J Psychoanal
    63:369–378, 1982
Cloninger CR, Svrakic DM, Pryzbeck TR: A psychobiological model of temperament and
    character. Arch Gen Psychiatry 50:975–990, 1993
Connors ME: The renunciation of love: dismissive attachment and its treatment. Psychoan-
    alytic Psychology 14:475–493, 1997
Dahl AA: The relationship between social phobia and avoidant personality disorder: work-
    shop report 3. Int Clin Psychopharmacol 11 (suppl 3):109–112, 1996
Diaferia G, Bianchi I, Bianchi ML, et al: Relationship between obsessive-compulsive per-
    sonality disorder and obsessive-compulsive disorder. Compr Psychiatry 38:38–42,
    1997
Fenichel O: The Psychoanalytic Theory of Neurosis. New York, WW Norton, 1945
Freud S: Character and anal erotism (1908), in The Standard Edition of the Complete Psy-
    chological Works of Sigmund Freud, Vol 9. Translated and edited by Strachey J. Lon-
    don, Hogarth Press, 1959, pp 167–175
Gabbard GO: Stage fright. Int J Psychoanal 60:383–392, 1979
Gabbard GO: The exit line: heightened transference-countertransference manifestations at
    the end of the hour. J Am Psychoanal Assoc 30:579–598, 1982
Gabbard GO: Further contributions to the understanding of stage fright: narcissistic issues.
    J Am Psychoanal Assoc 31:423–441, 1983
Gabbard GO: The role of compulsiveness in the normal physician. JAMA 254:2926–2929,
    1985
Gabbard GO, Bartlett AB: Selective serotonin reuptake inhibitors in the context of an ongo-
    ing analysis. Psychoanalytic Inquiry 18:657–672, 1998
Gabbard GO, Menninger RW: The psychology of the physician, in Medical Marriages.
    Edited by Gabbard GO, Menninger RW. Washington, DC, American Psychiatric
    Press, 1988, pp 23–38
Gunderson JG: DSM-III diagnoses of personality disorders, in Current Perspectives on Per-
    sonality Disorders. Edited by Frosch JP. Washington, DC, American Psychiatric Press,
    1983, pp 20–39
Gunderson JG: Personality disorders, in The New Harvard Guide to Psychiatry. Edited by
    Nicholi AM Jr. Cambridge, MA, Belknap Press of Harvard University Press, 1988,
    pp 337–357

Head SB, Baker JD, Williamson DA: Family environment characteristics and dependent personality disorder. J Personal Disord 5:256–263, 1991

Hirschfeld RMA, Shea MT, Weise R: Dependent personality disorder: perspectives for DSM-IV. J Personal Disord 5:135–149, 1991

Horowitz MJ: Introduction to Psychodynamics: A New Synthesis. New York, Basic Books, 1988

Jones E: Anal-erotic character traits, in Papers on Psycho-Analysis, 5th Edition. Baltimore, MD, Williams & Wilkins, 1948, pp 413–437

Josephs L: Character Structure and the Organization of the Self. New York, Columbia University Press, 1992

Kagan J, Reznick JS, Snidman N: Biological bases of childhood shyness. Science 240:167–171, 1988

Kapfhammer HP, Hippius H: Special feature: pharmacotherapy in personality disorders. J Personal Disord 12:277–288, 1998

Kernberg OF: Borderline Conditions and Pathological Narcissism. New York, Jason Aronson, 1975

Krakowski AJ: Stress and the practice of medicine, II: stressors, stresses, and strains. Psychother Psychosom 38:11–23, 1982

Livesley WJ, West M: The DSM-III distinction between schizoid and avoidant personality disorders. Can J Psychiatry 31:59–62, 1986

Livesley WJ, West M, Tanney A: Historical comment on DSM-III schizoid and avoidant personality disorders. Am J Psychiatry 142:1344–1347, 1985

Loranger AW: Dependent personality disorder: age, sex, and Axis I comorbidity. J Nerv Ment Dis 184:17–21, 1996

McCullough PK, Maltsberger JT: Obsessive-compulsive personality disorder, in Treatments of Psychiatric Disorders, 2nd Edition, Vol 2. Edited by Gabbard GO. Washington, DC, American Psychiatric Press, 1995, pp 2367–2376

Meissner WW: Treatment of Patients in the Borderline Spectrum. Northvale, NJ, Jason Aronson, 1988

Menninger WC: Characterologic and symptomatic expressions related to the anal phase of psychosexual development. Psychoanal Q 12:161–193, 1943

Miliora MT: Facial disfigurement: a self-psychological perspective on the "hide-and-seek" fantasy of an avoidant personality. Bull Menninger Clin 62:378–394, 1998

Miller S: The Shame Experience. Hillsdale, NJ, Analytic Press, 1985

Munich RL: Transitory symptom formation in the analysis of an obsessional character. Psychoanal Study Child 41:515–535, 1986

Nathanson DL: A timetable for shame, in The Many Faces of Shame. Edited by Nathanson DL. New York, Guilford, 1987, pp 1–63

O'Neill FA, Kendler KS: Longitudinal study of interpersonal dependency in female twins. Br J Psychiatry 172:154–158, 1998

Perry JC: Dependent personality disorder, in Treatments of Psychiatric Disorders, 2nd Edition, Vol 2. Edited by Gabbard GO. Washington, DC, American Psychiatric Press, 1995, pp 2355–2366

Rasmussen SA, Tsuang MT: Clinical characteristics and family history in DSM-III obsessive-compulsive disorder. Am J Psychiatry 143:317–322, 1986

Reich J, Noyes R Jr: Differentiating schizoid and avoidant personality disorders (letter). Am J Psychiatry 143:1062, 1986

Rosen KV, Tallis F: Investigation into the relationship between personality traits and OCD. Behav Res Ther 33:445–450, 1995

Salzman L: The Obsessive Personality: Origins, Dynamics, and Therapy. New York, Science House, 1968

Salzman L: Treatment of the Obsessive Personality. New York, Jason Aronson, 1980

Salzman L: Psychoanalytic therapy of the obsessional patient. Current Psychiatric Therapies 22:53–59, 1983

Shapiro D: Neurotic Styles. New York, Basic Books, 1965

Skodol AE, Gallaher PE, Oldham JM: Excessive dependency and depression: is the relationship specific? J Nerv Ment Dis 184:165–171, 1996

Stein MB, Liebowitz MR, Lydiard RB, et al: Paroxetine treatment of generalized social phobia (social anxiety disorder): a randomized controlled trial. JAMA 280:708–713, 1998

Sutherland SM, Frances A: Avoidant personality disorder, in Treatments of Psychiatric Disorders, 2nd Edition, Vol 2. Edited by Gabbard GO. Washington, DC, American Psychiatric Press, 1995, pp 2345–2353

Vaillant GE, Sobowale NC, McArthur C: Some psychologic vulnerabilities of physicians. N Engl J Med 287:372–375, 1972

Wallerstein RS: Forty-Two Lives in Treatment: A Study of Psychoanalysis and Psychotherapy. New York, Guilford, 1986

West M, Rose S, Sheldon-Keller A: Assessment of patterns of insecure attachment in adults and application to dependent and schizoid personality disorders. J Personal Disord 8:249–256, 1994

Widiger TA: Generalized social phobia versus avoidant personality disorder: a commentary on three studies. J Abnorm Psychol 101:340–343, 1992

Winston A, Laikin M, Pollack J, et al: Short-term psychotherapy of personality disorders. Am J Psychiatry 151:190–194, 1994

Wurmser L: The Mask of Shame. Baltimore, MD, Johns Hopkins University Press, 1981

Index

*Page numbers printed in **boldface** type refer to tables or figures.*